BABA YAGA

Alan Dundes
General Editor

Vol. 3

PETER LANG
New York • Washington, D.C./Baltimore • Bern
Frankfurt am Main • Berlin • Brussels • Vienna • Oxford

ANDREAS JOHNS

BABA YAGA

The Ambiguous Mother and Witch of the Russian Folktale

PETER LANG
New York • Washington, D.C./Baltimore • Bern
Frankfurt am Main • Berlin • Brussels • Vienna • Oxford

Library of Congress Cataloging-in-Publication Data
Johns, Andreas.
Baba Yaga: the ambiguous mother and witch of the Russian folktale /
Andreas Johns.
p. cm. — (International folkloristics; v. 3)
Includes bibliographical references and index.
1. Baba Yaga (Legendary character). 2. Fairy tales—Russia
(Federation)—History and criticism. I. Title. II. Series.
GR75.B22J65   398.2'0947'01–dc21   2003044743
ISBN 978-0-8204-6769-6
ISSN 1528-6533

Bibliographic information published by **Die Deutsche Bibliothek**.
Die Deutsche Bibliothek lists this publication in the "Deutsche
Nationalbibliografie"; detailed bibliographic data is available
on the Internet at http://dnb.ddb.de/.

Cover design by Joni Holst

The paper in this book meets the guidelines for permanence and durability
of the Committee on Production Guidelines for Book Longevity
of the Council of Library Resources.

Printed in the United States of America

Contents

Acknowledgments

"Behind this story there is another one." It is the author's pleasant duty to thank those who have helped him in this endeavor. I would like to express my deep gratitude to Alan Dundes, who first suggested Baba Yaga as a research topic and has provided unfailing advice and encouragement throughout the ensuing journey. I owe a special debt of gratitude to Hugh McLean and to Daniel Rancour-Laferriere. I have been very fortunate in receiving helpful comments, suggestions, insights, assistance, and encouragement from Emily Albu, Ronelle Alexander, James Bailey, Julia Friedman, Jack Haney, Ellen Langer, Agnes Mihalik, Elizaveta Mnatsakanjan, Johanna Nichols, Irina Paperno, Ekaterina Porshneva, Boris Putilov, Victoria Somoff, James Taggart, Alan Timberlake, Adam Weiner, Izalii Zemtsovskii, and Viktor Zhivov. Many thanks also to the friendly and resourceful library staff at the University of California, Berkeley, and the University of Washington, Seattle. Of course, very special thanks go to my dear family: my father and mother, Karl, Alessa, Chris, and Gabriel, who have supported, encouraged, and nourished me in all senses throughout this work; it could never have been accomplished without their help. Like the heroines and heroes of the folktale, may all who have helped me live happily and prosper!

Introduction

By the cove there is a green oak;
On that oak a golden chain:
And day and night a learned cat
Paces on that chain;
When it walks to the right, it strikes up a song,
To the left—it tells a tale.

O wondrous place, where the forest goblin wanders,
and the *rusalka* sits in the branches;
Along unknown paths
Are the tracks of beasts unseen;
A hut stands there on chicken legs
Without windows, without doors...

Where Baba Yaga rides a mortar
That moves by its own power;
Where Tsar Kashchei wastes away over his gold;
There you'll find the Russian scent... there it smells of Rus'!
Aleksandr Pushkin, from "Ruslan and Liudmila" (1820)

One of the most memorable and distinctive figures in eastern European folklore is no doubt Baba Yaga, the witch of Russian and East Slavic folktales.[1] Storytellers often identify her as a witch,[2] Baba Yaga and the witch can perform the same functions in folktales, and in many ways Baba Yaga resembles the witch of East Slavic folk belief, the Russian *ved'ma,* Ukrainian *vid'ma,* and

---

[1] Bába Iagá. There are many variations on the name (see chapter 1). The Library of Congress transliteration system will be used for the Cyrillic alphabet. However, in most of the discussion, Iaga and its variant forms (Iagishna, Iagonishna) will be spelled Yaga, Yagishna, Yagonishna, etc., for greater readability. For the same reason, plural forms of Yaga (Baby Iagi, Iagishny) will be rendered in English: Baba Yagas, Yagishnas. The name will be capitalized, which is not always the case in the original texts (this point is discussed in chapter 4).
[2] For example, see Afanas'ev 114, Dobrovol'skii 14, Nikiforov 1961 no. 80, Shastina 1974: 45–46, and Zelenin Viatka 86. Specific folktale texts will be referred to by the name of the collector, compiler, or editor, and the number of the text in that collection, or by its page number, if texts are not numbered. Some collections contain more than one numbered series of tales, and in those cases the series is indicated accordingly. For example, Onchukov 2000 contains folktales from the Tavda, Shokshozero, and Samara regions, each in a separately numbered sequence; in Potanin and Adrianov 2000 there are two series of tales, one first published in 1902, the other in 1906.

Belorussian *vedz'ma*.[3] Nevertheless, the word "witch" does not describe Baba Yaga in all her complexity and richness.

The name *Baba Yaga* usually brings to mind her typical attributes: she lives in the forest, in a hut which stands or turns around on chicken or hen's legs (*izbushka na kur'ikh nozhkakh*), or goat legs and ram horns (*na koz'ikh nozhkakh, na baran'ikh rozhkakh*, in Zelenin Perm' 6) or a spindle heel (*na veretennoi piatke*). Visitors to her hut use a traditional phrase to make the hut turn around and face them: "Hut, hut! Stand with your back to the forest, your front to me" (*Izbushka, izbushka! Stan' k lesu zadom, a ko mne peredom*). When inside her hut, Baba Yaga often lies on the stove, her body stretched out from one corner of the hut to the other. Her nose has grown into the ceiling (*nos v potolok ros*), and narrators remark how large it is. Other exaggerated or grotesque features are described. Her breasts hang over a rod (*titki cherez griadku vesnut*),[4] and she rakes the coals with her nose (*nosom ugol'ia grebet*). Like some other folktale characters, she notices and comments on the "Russian scent" of her visitors (*Fu, fu, russkim dukhom pakhnet*). Baba Yaga travels in a mortar, pushing herself along with a pestle and sweeping away her tracks or traces with a broom (*v stupe edet, pestom pogoniaet, pomelom sled zametaet*). She is described by the rhyming epithet "Baba Yaga Bony Leg" (*Baba iaga kostianaia noga*). Sometimes her leg is made of other materials, such as clay (Afanas'ev 113), iron (Bandarchyk 1973 no. 52), gold (Afanas'ev 161), or even steel (Gurevich 32). Many of these traditional phrases used to describe Baba Yaga display rhyme or rhythm, which makes them easier to retain in memory and contributes to the stylistic color of the fairy tale.

Researchers have often compared Baba Yaga to similar figures from other folklore traditions, and she appears in tales which can be found in many other parts of the world. But her particular combination of traits and functions makes her unique among witches and witch-like characters in world folklore. Ol'ga Cherepanova rightfully calls her "one of the most interesting figures of Russian folklore" (1983: 100).[5] Besides her intrinsic interest, Baba Yaga is significant as a folklore figure who is truly national, such as Ivan the Fool and Koshchei the Immortal. Even today, when the Russian oral tradition appears to be dying out, virtually all Russians are familiar with her through books and animated films (Ivanitskaia 1984: 112). Baba Yaga has also made incursions into "high" culture.

---

[3] In addition to these terms, there are several other designations for witches in the East Slavic languages. Baba Yaga's relationship to the witches of East Slavic folk belief is discussed in chapter 3, and in Löwis of Menar 1912: 120, Kurotschkin 1991–92: 196, and Worobec 1995: 176.

[4] In some Russian dialects, the noun *griadka* designates "a rod for towels and other things" (Propp 1946: 61), or "a beam below the ceiling, extending from the stove to the opposite wall" (Zelenin 1914: 497).

[5] Unless otherwise indicated, all translations of texts not originally in English are the author's.

The most famous appearance of Baba Yaga in Russian literature is probably in the opening verses of Aleksandr Pushkin's narrative poem "Ruslan and Liudmila." Among other strange wonders from Russian folklore found by the sea, Pushkin describes the hut on chicken legs without windows or doors, and Baba Yaga's mortar, which moves by itself (she does not push it with a pestle). His description thus departs somewhat from the folkloric presentation. Other literary adaptations of Baba Yaga are discussed in chapter 1.

Of course Baba Yaga has attracted scholarly attention. Studies of the Russian folktale do not fail to mention her.[6] Yet this fascinating "storyland being" (Ralston 1970) still remains enigmatic. An 1891 encyclopedia entry states that "in general the question of Baba Yaga's meaning in Slavic mythology has not been sufficiently elaborated" (Andreevskii 1891 iv: 591), and Nikolai Novikov comments in 1977 (in the *Enzyklopädie des Märchens*) that in spite of the studies devoted to Baba Yaga, this figure "has nevertheless remained largely uninvestigated, especially concerning its genesis"; theories proposed so far about Baba Yaga's origin "do not go further than scholarly hypothesis and require additional and more thorough argumentation."

Perhaps the most intriguing feature that emerges when one examines a large corpus of folktales in which Baba Yaga appears is her striking ambiguity. This ambiguity calls out for explanation and cannot be ignored. Most folktale characters in European traditions (with a consistent name and set of typical characteristics) behave in a predictably unambiguous way in relation to the hero or heroine: They either help or hinder. In the *Morphology of the Folktale*, Vladimir Propp finds that the entire panoply of folktale characters (Baba Yaga, Koshchei, the dragon, Prince Ivan, the Frog Princess, Cinderella, and all others) can be defined by seven "tale roles," based on their functions (actions) in the narrative: the hero, donor, helper, villain, dispatcher, the sought-for person, and the false hero. Two very important tale roles are those of the villain, who harms or seeks to harm the protagonist, and the donor, who is helpful and gives the hero or heroine a magic agent. There are three possible relationships of character to tale role. A character can correspond exactly to a tale role; several different characters can fulfill one tale role, or a single character can take on more than one tale role.

Baba Yaga represents the last-mentioned relationship. Sometimes she acts as a donor and sometimes as a villain. When Baba Yaga appears as a series of three sisters, the protagonist occasionally receives help from one sister, while another tries to harm him or her. In a tale from Perm' province (Zelenin Perm'

---

[6] Vladimirov 1896: 164–167, Löwis of Menar 1912: 120, Speranskii 1917: 418–420, Volkov 1924: 50–53, Polívka 1932: 185–189, Wosien 1969: 133–140, Novikov 1974: 133–146, 159–180, Anikin 1977: 114–119, Kravchenko 1987: 184–204, Haney 1999: 98–101.

67), the second Baba Yaga gives the heroine magic gifts to recover her falcon husband, while the third Baba Yaga tries to prevent her from taking him and then pursues the couple. In Smirnov 130 (from Viatka province), the hero's wicked stepmother is a Yagibaba, but so is the third old woman donor who reunites the hero with his lost wife (see Appendix I: Selected Tale Texts). Two Yagishna sisters help the hero, while a third Yagishna wishes to decapitate him and his brothers (Potanin 1902 no. 36, Tomsk region). Egiboba is both donor and villain in Smirnov 141 (also from Viatka), presenting the hero with magic gifts to defeat an enemy army but turning his bride into a duck and forcing him to marry her own daughter.

Besides these ambiguities found in single narratives, there are a number of tale types (sharing a basic common recognizable plot) in which Baba Yaga appears in some versions as a donor, in others as a villain. She can also be a very hostile donor when she attempts to kill the hero but fails and relinquishes a magic object or agent. Even when she acts as a donor, her typical behavior when she greets the heroine or hero is ambiguous. At first she threatens to eat the protagonist but immediately backs down when reproached. In this book, the term "ambiguity" will describe all these manifestations. The implications of these various forms of ambiguity and the term itself are discussed in more detail in chapter 6.

According to N. M. Vedernikova, the epithet "Bony Leg" gives Baba Yaga a monstrous quality and helps to place her in a category with the hero's enemies. However, since Baba Yaga sometimes appears as a donor while maintaining the same appearance and attributes, the use of this epithet to describe her when she is a donor creates an unexpected contrast between external and internal features. This contrast gives the hero's meeting with Baba Yaga a "psychological meaning" in addition to its function in the plot, but unfortunately Vedernikova does not explore this meaning in her article (1980: 132).

This book hopes to contribute to Baba Yaga scholarship and the search for her meaning(s) by examining as many folktale texts as possible in which she appears. In previous studies, conclusions about Baba Yaga's nature have sometimes been made on the basis of only a few tale texts (or even just one), most often taken from the well-known collection of Aleksandr Afanas'ev. In fact, Baba Yaga appears in hundreds of recorded folktales, beginning in the late eighteenth century until our own time, in virtually all parts of Russia, in Ukraine, and Belarus. Obviously a large sample of tales is necessary to establish which of Baba Yaga's characteristics and attributes are most consistent and stable, which are secondary or exceptional, but might represent latent possibilities less frequently realized, and which ones might truly be distortions of the traditional image. For the present survey more than four hundred texts have been gathered. While this survey cannot be exhaustive (many folktale collections and archival recordings were unavailable), it is perhaps the most thorough to date.

Tales will be identified by tale type number according to the Aarne-Thompson tale-type index of 1964 (AT), and the 1979 East Slavic tale-type index, *Sravnitel'nyi ukazatel' siuzhetov [Comparative Index of Plots]* (SUS), compiled by Lev Barag et al. Some motifs will be identified by number according to Stith Thompson's *Motif-Index of Folk-Literature*. There are many valid criticisms of the Aarne-Thompson index and other national and local tale-type indices. The concepts of tale type and motif, and the differences between them, have not been precisely defined. The definitions of tale types are arbitrary; tale types sometimes overlap or are in some ways duplicated (for example, the same plot may be acted out by animal and human characters), and the descriptions of tale types are sometimes vague. Tale-type indices may not reflect the real fluidity and flexibility of oral tradition, where narrators freely combine and recombine episodes and motifs. Many tales recorded from oral tradition do not fit any single tale-type description very well, and this has led to unfortunate designations of such texts as "contaminations" or "defective versions."

Nevertheless, many of the AT types do reflect fairly stable narrative configurations in the European folktale repertoire (Kerbelyte 1984: 203–204). For this study, the large number of texts necessitates classification. Since our interest focuses on a character rather than any one tale type, the variability typical of folklore is not problematic. Even tale texts from less skilled performers, texts that are entirely anomalous, or texts that might arouse suspicion with regard to authenticity—all these can potentially still shed light on the nature of Baba Yaga.

Most studies of Baba Yaga are oriented toward the past and attempt to explain this folktale character in historical terms. Baba Yaga's unique features and behavior are seen as reflections of her origin or of cultural institutions or customs belonging to a distant past; the different aspects of Baba Yaga's image are attributed to different historical periods, reflecting archaic original features and later additions. Certainly Baba Yaga has an origin and a history, but in the absence of documentary evidence, these must remain a matter of speculation. What is certain about Baba Yaga is her appearance as a character in recorded folktales, and our search for her meaning(s) should begin there. Tales about Baba Yaga were in circulation for at least two hundred years, and during this documented period her image remains remarkably stable, which demonstrates the conservatism of the East Slavic folklore tradition and the culture which produced it. Based on this folkloric record, we can ask what Baba Yaga meant for the people who told and listened to tales about her.

It has become a commonplace since the Romantic period to say that a people's folklore reflects their spirit or character. Petr Bogatyrev and Roman Jakobson discuss how the creative process in folklore differs from that in literature. Folklore functions more the way language does: Any individual can invent new words, but if the great mass of speakers of the language does not accept them, they will be disregarded and forgotten. Likewise, an individual may create new tales, riddles, proverbs, or jokes, but if these creations do not pass a kind of collective censorship, they will not be retained in the folklore tradition (Bogatyrev and Jakobson 1966). Folklore inevitably provides some insight into the people who create, maintain, and transmit it, and into the social collectives who exercise this type of censorship.

Felix Oinas and Natalie Kononenko point out that the figures of Russian folk belief (the various house and nature spirits) are projections of the traditional Russian way of life. The forest spirits (*leshie*) are married and have families, while the mermaid-like *rusalka* might represent attractive but threatening aspects of female sexuality which the traditional culture wishes to deny (Oinas 1985: 87, Moyle [Kononenko] 1987: 235–236). It seems reasonable to assume that the East Slavs have also projected some aspects of their traditional life onto the popular figure of Baba Yaga, for if she did not have mass appeal, it is unlikely that she would have maintained her prominent place in this folklore tradition through the twentieth century. Like the popular and ambiguous Enfant Terrible of West African folktales, Baba Yaga probably expresses a significant cultural preoccupation (Görög et al. 1980: 241). When Russians, Ukrainians, and Belorussians tell, listen to, and enjoy stories about Baba Yaga, they are also telling us something about themselves.

A careful study of this folktale character may add to our understanding of the relationship between traditional narratives and the societies that produce them, and because of Baba Yaga's ambiguity, it can also shed light on the relationship of folktale characters to the tale roles. In this sense it is valuable in two respects; first, as an exploration of a concrete folktale character who belongs to a specific cultural and historical setting, a phenomenon that is freighted with cultural and even individual values, "lourd d'un poids humain," in the words of Marie-Louise Tenèze (1970: 42). Secondly, underlying the explicit manifestations of Baba Yaga in specific tale texts, this character's ambiguous behavior might reveal latent potential structures which are implicit in the folktale but are not expressed or activated in every folktale tradition (this kind of ambiguity does not seem to appear often in western European folktales, for example). A delineation of Baba Yaga's features and behavior in an international context reveals her as a unique Slavic variation on an Indo-European (and wider) theme; within the European context, a close examination of this character will contribute to a fuller picture of the European folktale tradition and of the differences between western and eastern Europe.

Our examination of Baba Yaga will begin with a survey of theories and interpretations that have been proposed to explain this unique character (chapter 1). Chapter 2 discusses the fairy-tale context in which Baba Yaga most often appears, her relationship to superstition and folk belief, and similar figures from other folklore traditions. For reasons that will become clear during the discussion, chapter 3 examines Baba Yaga's interactions with child protagonists, and chapters 4, 5, and 6 consider Baba Yaga as a donor, as an ambiguous figure (combining both donor and villain functions), and as a villain.

CHAPTER ONE
Interpreting Baba Yaga

Many interpretations have been put forward to account for Baba Yaga's name, image, and character. Many scholars have attempted to reconstruct her origin and historical development, while some have examined her in psychological terms. Structuralist studies of folklore have also touched on this character. A serious study of Baba Yaga necessarily begins with a review of this scholarship.

Baba Yaga's name alone has inspired a great deal of speculation. In an area as vast and as rich in folklore as Russia, Ukraine, and Belarus, it is not surprising that her name has many variant forms: *Iagaia, Iga, Ega, Iagaba, Iagabova, Egabova, Egabikha, Iagabikha, Egibaba, Iagibaba, Egibinikha, Egibikha, Egibitsa, Egibishna, Egibisna, Egiboba, Egi-boba, Ègiboba, Egibova, Iagivovna, Iaits'na-Babits'na, Iagishna, Iagisna, Iaganishna, Iaginishna, Iagaia-Babitsa, Aga Gnishna, Iagiba, Iagipitsa, Baba-Igipuvna*, and, in the Smolensk region and Ukraine, *Iuga* and *Iazia* (Novikov 1974: 133). In Belarus, *Iuga* (*Iuha*) is common as well, and the name *Iaginia* has been recorded there also (Federowski 1897: 80). Besides some of the names in the above list, other forms found in Northern Russia include *Babka Iaga, Baba-Liaga, Baushka Liaga, Oga-Bova, Iagikha, Iagishsha, Egishna, Iagibitsa, Egabovna*, as well as *Egishna, Egidichna*, and *Egibisna* to designate the daughter of Baba Yaga (Cherepanova 1983: 104–105). Another name for her daughter is *Iagarnushka* (Balashov 49).

Other forms of Baba Yaga's name are *Iagichna* (Efimenko 1878: 227), *Iaga Iagonishna* (Kozhemiakina 1973: 171–174), *Iagishnia* (Balashov 105), *Iagis'nia* (Balashov 29), *Iagabakha* (Onchukov 38), *Gigibikha* (Sen'kina 1988: 26), *Iazhenia-babisna* (ibid., 120), *Iagisna-babisna* (ibid., 122), *Iagitsna* (ibid., 123), *Gigibibikha* (Onegina 59), *Iagavaia* (Cherepanova 1983: 105), *Iagastaia* (ibid.), *Iagataia* (Mitropol'skaia 53), *Èga-baba* (Khudiakov 1964: 269–270) or *Baba-Èga* (Novikov 1961 no. 6). *Iaga-bura* (Afanas'ev 107), *Buraia-iaga* (Smirnov 250), and *Bur Iaga* (Kargin 14), include the adjective *buryi*, meaning "grayish-brown" or "grayish-red." A witch named *Ibikha* appears in a tale from the Zaonezh'e region (Onegina 27). In spite of the many regional versions of the name in Russia, "Baba Yaga" is used everywhere as well (Cherepanova 1983: 104).

The name *Indzhi-baba* is found in the Carpathian mountain region of western Ukraine (Dunaievs'ka 1987: 39). In Carpatho-Ukrainian (Rusyn) folktales recorded in eastern Slovakia, this character is called *Iezhibaba, Izhuzhbaba, Hindzhybaba, Hyndzhi-baba, Indzhibaba*, or *Ezhibaba* (Hyriak 1965–1979). An analogous figure in Czech and Slovak folktales is usually called *Ježibaba*. Czech

variations on her name are *Jedibaba* and *Jedubaba*. Jan Máchal cites a Moravian
form as *ördögbaba* (1891: 66), derived from Hungarian *ördög*, "devil, demon."
   In the East Slavic folktale, the *Baba* component can appear before or after
the forms of *Iaga* or not at all. Storytellers frequently vary the form of the name,
speaking of "Baba Yaga" and "Yaga Baba" in the same tale. *Baba* is apparently
not an essential part of the name, although more often than not it is present.
The word *baba* is found in all Slavic languages. Its primary meaning is
"grandmother, father's or mother's mother," but it has taken on the other
meanings of "(old) woman, wife," or "married woman" in all the Slavic
languages (Trubachev 1959: 72). It is derived from the Indo-European root
**b(h)āb(h)-*, from which come the English *baby*, German *Bube* ("boy"), and
Italian *babbo* ("father"). Such words may reflect the developmental character of
infant language (a consonant-vowel pattern, repeating syllables), and the way
that adults speak to infants, adjusting their speech to infants' verbal habits
(Jakobson 1971).[1]
   In Old Russian, the word *baba* could refer to a midwife, sorceress, or fortune
teller, and the standard modern Russian word for "grandmother" (*babushka*) is
derived from it. *Baba* in modern Russian is also a pejorative term for woman as
well as for an unmanly, timid, or characterless man. Like some other Slavic
kinship terms, *baba* has also been applied to concepts outside the realm of
kinship, perhaps as the result of a taboo function. In various Slavic languages
and dialects, words derived from *baba* serve as names for the butterfly, certain
kinds of mushroom, cake, pear, a (wooden) pile or block, and the pelican
(Stankiewicz 1958, Shapiro 1983). Several prominent mountaintops and stone
formations in Slovenia bear this name (*Pehtra baba, Stara baba, Velika Baba, Mala
Baba;* Kuret 1969: 225–226). In the Poles'e region of Ukraine, the plural *baby*
can refer to an autumn funeral feast, and to the Pleiades (as it does in some
Russian dialects, and in Old Russian), while *babyn poias* ("grandmother's belt") is
a name for the rainbow (Boriak 2002: 32, Tolstoi 1995: 38–39). Polish *baby*,
Czech *báby*, and Sorbian *baby* are also names for the Pleiades; the Sorbs also
refer to the Pleiades as the "seven old women" (*te sydym babki*, Schulenburg
1880: 272).[2] Given the folktale context and the character's explicit features, it

---

[1] O. Trubachev expresses skepticism regarding this "children's babble" theory (1959: 193–197).
[2] In Czech, the northeast is also the "old women's corner," the location of the "old women" or
Pleiades. In Polish, Czech, and Slovak, the Pleiades are also referred to as a hen and chicks, or
chickens. In Bulgarian, the Pleiades are a hen and chicks, the post of a threshing-floor (*stozheri*), or
Wallachians, Vlahs (*vlastsi*, Vakarelski 1969: 213). In Bulgarian folk belief, the "hen" (Pleiades)
disappears for 45 days to hatch her eggs. When she reappears on June 8, she shakes out down
feathers and vermin onto the earth, causing illness for sheep and cattle (Lettenbauer 1952: 124).
È. G. Azim-zade finds that the Slavic folk designations for the Pleiades have a primary meaning
that is agricultural or geographical; many of these terms bear the primary meanings "stack,"

seems easiest and most logical to accept this word in the name of Baba Yaga at its face value as bearing the primary Slavic meaning of "grandmother" or "old woman."

The origin and meaning of *Iaga* is far more obscure and has inspired several different interpretations among linguists. A. Preobrazhenskii tells us it is "not entirely clear" (1959: 132). The word appears in Old Church Slavonic as *jeza/jędza* ("disease, illness"). In Serbo-Croatian there is *jeza* ("horror, shudder, chill"), in Slovenian *jeza* ("anger"), in Old Czech *jězě* ("witch, legendary evil female being") and modern Czech *jezinka* ("wicked wood nymph, dryad"), in Polish *jędza* ("witch, evil woman, fury"), along with the dialectal forms *jdza*, *jędzona*, *jędzyna*, and the verb *jędzić się* ("to get angry"). There are verbs with a related meaning in dialectal Russian: *iagat'* ("yell, make a noise, rage, curse, squabble") and *egat'* ("burn fiercely, be angry, rage," Cooper 1997: 86). The etymology of *iaga* has been connected with Lithuanian *engti* ("to do something slowly, lazily") and *nuengti* ("to torture"), with Anglo-Saxon *inca* ("doubt, worry, pain"), and with Old Norse *ekki* ("pain, worry," Preobrazhenskii 1959: 133, Vasmer 1958: 479). In the nineteenth century Aleksandr Afanas'ev derived *iaga* from Proto-Slavic **oż* and Sanskrit *ahi* ("serpent, snake"). Twentieth-century scholars have further explored this etymology, attempting to demonstrate that Baba Yaga is derived from the snake (Laushkin 1970, Cherepanova 1983).

In Afanas'ev's time, I. N. Berezin proposed another etymology, deriving the name from Mongolian *eke* ("mother"). This corresponds to the word *ekä* ("elder sister, aunt") in Turkic languages. If one accepts this etymology, A. N. Kononov suggests that the familiar word *baba* was added as a gloss to explain the unfamiliar *iaga* (Kononov 1973). Michael Shapiro has proposed a proto-Samoyed derivation from words designating "god," or "god of death" (1983: 126). Václav Polák suggests that *iaga* might derive from Ostyak terms for "elder brother's wife," "uncle's wife," "stepmother," "aunt" (*ǎñege*), "mother" (*ǎŋke*), the Vogul term for "wife of an older relative" (*ǎǎñge-*), or the Hungarian "elder brother's wife" (*ángy*). Borrowed terms for "aunt" or "mother" might have been used as the result of a taboo function, in place of designations for dangerous female demonic beings, whose real names might bring harm to the person who utters them (Polák 1977: 287–288).

Iu. S. Stepanov sees Slavic *Iaga* as related to Greek *Jason*, Roman *Janus*, and the ancient Indian deities *Yama* and *Yami*. Baba Yaga was originally the female member of a couple, like the Indian Yama and Yami. This explains the *Baba* component of her name—to distinguish her from the other, male Yaga. Stepanov associates *iaga* with Baltic terms meaning "strength, force" or

---

"sheaf," "rick," or "pile" (of wheat or hay), "hill," "mound." Naming the Pleiades "the old women" would thus be a secondary derivation (Azim-zade 1980: 97–98).

"understanding, sense." This etymology associates Baba Yaga with positive, beneficent forces and suggests that the negative terms in Slavic languages which are close to *Iaga* are later associations (Stepanov 1995: 11–15). However, Stepanov's etymology is questionable.

Ute Dukova discusses terms for "sickness" or "illness" used in Western and Southwestern Bulgaria (*eʒa, enʒa, endʒa, iandʒa*), uttered in curses. While these Bulgarian nouns (and their South Slavic cognates) are abstract, the West and East Slavic cognate terms have come to designate evil women, witches, or witch-like beings. Dukova sees all these terms derived from a proto-Slavic *(j)egá* or *(j)eʒá*, meaning "female demon of illness," or "illness." In the West and East Slavic areas, the evil female being with this name left the sphere of living folk belief, became a folktale character and lost her dangerous nature. In Bulgaria, the use of the term in curses still bears witness to the dangerous nature of illness, originally conceived of as a demon (Dukova 1983: 24–27).

Based on the Slavic and other Indo-European cognates of *iaga*, Brian Cooper finds that several conclusions are possible. The name suggests "a personification of suffocating oppression," in the manner of a female spirit who weighs on or suffocates people during the night, producing nightmares. The association with illness (suggested by Old Church Slavonic *jeʒa/jedʒa*) suggests "a female demon of illness." Finally, Cooper suggests that the meanings of "rage, being enraged" lead back to a root with the meaning of "disorderedness" or "derangement," which may link Baba Yaga to "the chaos of winter storms," and suggest that she was originally "a personification of the Russian winter." In this connection, Cooper points out that the broom (*pomelo*) Baba Yaga uses to sweep away her traces is etymologically related to the snowstorm or blizzard (*metel*) (Cooper 1997: 87–88).

The linguistic interpretation of proper names presents many difficulties. In this case the etymological evidence does not seem solid enough to allow any conclusions about Baba Yaga's origin or character through her name alone, but the various Slavic lexical items just enumerated suggest illness, anxiety, negative emotions, or misfortune. Johanna Nichols finds that the name *Iaga* and its numerous variant forms, as well as the other cognate Slavic terms, display a normal range of variation for a single proto-Slavic root, with wordplay and suffixation. The root would have the form "vowel+n+g" (such as *eng*), but its original meaning is impossible to determine.[3]

In spite of its obscure origins, Baba Yaga's name is well known throughout Russia. Like the word "witch" (*ved'ma*), *iaga* was used by villagers as an unflattering designation for "old, quarrelsome and ugly women" (Afanas'ev

---

[3] Johanna Nichols, personal communication, 12 December 2002.

1869 iii: 591). The use of *iaga* as a term of reproach is documented for many provinces (Makarov 1827: 149; Cherepanova 1983: 104). Other figurative meanings of *baba iaga* include an old woman living alone, an untidy woman, or a human figure made of snow (in Russia usually called a "snow woman," *snezhnaia baba*), a female bear, and the leader in a game of *gorodki*, similar to skittles or ninepins (ibid., 104–105). In one locality a stone with a shape that could recall Baba Yaga bears her name (Sokolova 1972: 203).

Earliest Documentation and Literary Adaptations

While the name of a Novgorodian governor from the year 1200, *iaginitsa* or *iaginin*, might be derived from "Yaga" (Vladimirov 1896: 165, Novikov 1971: 5, 1974: 133), the first documentary evidence of this character dates from the eighteenth century, when she is mentioned by scholars and appears in literary tale collections inspired by the folk tradition.

Mikhail V. Lomonosov, the outstanding Russian poet, scientist, and grammarian of the eighteenth century, refers to Baba Yaga in notes to his Russian grammar (*Rossiiskaia grammatika*, 1755; notes compiled ca. 1744–1757). *Iaga baba* appears twice, among figures drawn mostly from Russian folk belief and superstition. In the second passage, Lomonosov draws up two corresponding lists, with Roman deities on one side, and Russian and Slavic figures on the other. The Slavic thunder god Perun is equated with Jupiter, the Sea King (*Tsar' morskoi*) with Neptune, and the Devil (*Chort*) with Pluto. Yaga Baba appears in a third list with no corresponding ancient Roman figure (Lomonosov 1952, vol. 7: 618, 708–709), an interesting early testament to her uniqueness.

In 1780 the author Vasilii Levshin published a collection of literary fairy tales entitled *Russian Fairy Tales* (*Russkie skazki*). One of them, "The Tale of the Noble Zaoleshanin, a Knight in the Service of Prince Vladimir," contains a colorful literary adaptation of Baba Yaga (Kostiukhin 1988: 352–484), which combines folklore and Levshin's own imagination. He presents a horrifying portrait of Baba Yaga when she kidnaps a maiden, and when the hero fights and kills her.

> Suddenly a great whirlwind arose, the trees made way on both sides, and I saw Baba Yaga, galloping in a mortar that she urged on like a horse, with an iron pestle. Her appearance was so frightening that I started trembling when I saw her. And how could one not be frightened? Imagine a very dark and thin woman seven arshins high,[4] with teeth one-and-a-half arshins long, sticking out on both sides, like a wild boar, her hands adorned with bear claws; she came up, seized me, and rushed me off with her.... The sky darkened from

---

[4] 1 arshin = 28 inches, or 71 cm.

the great number of ravens, kites, and owls that flew in; they circled over Baba Yaga's courtyard, letting out a nasty cry which must cause one to feel horror even before the witch's arrival. But she didn't give the knights time for considerations and appeared in her mortar; she intensified her blows with the pestle, driving on this carriage of hers. Her eyes were like red-hot coals, bloody foam flowed from her mouth, and her fangs made a dreadful noise when they scraped. "Oho!" she roared, jumping from her mortar and throwing aside her pestle. "I could hardly wait for you, Zvenislav! I'll eat well now; you came to take away my precious booty, and you came at the right time: I'm very hungry." (Kostiukhin 1988: 387, 390)

Levshin also accounts for Baba Yaga's origin. Wishing to concoct the most perfect essence of evil, the devil cooked twelve nasty women together in a cauldron. To capture the essence, he gathered the steam in his mouth and then spat into the cauldron without thinking. Out of this mixture came Baba Yaga, the most perfect evil (ibid., 421). This account of Baba Yaga's birth also exists as one anomalous folktale, SUS 1169*. It is impossible to say whether Levshin invented this episode or took it from oral tradition, but its appearance only once in the East Slavic tale-type index suggests that a storyteller might have been familiar with Levshin's tale.

"Baba Yaga" is the title of a 1788 comic opera by Dmitrii Petrovich Gorchakov. The villains of the opera attempt to deprive the protagonist Liubim of his inheritance, but he receives help from his beloved Prelesta and her grandmother, Baba Yaga. Baba Yaga appears with many of her traditional attributes (the hut on chicken legs, mortar and pestle, initial threat to the hero) but functions nontraditionally as a dispenser of justice and punisher of vice. At the close of the opera, Baba Yaga sings of a more harmonious future, when vices will be eradicated and reason will triumph over passion (Gorchakov 1788).

Baba Yaga appears in tale collections from the eighteenth century such as *Lekarstvo ot zadumchivosti* (*Medicine for Pensiveness*, 1786) and *Staraia pogudka* (*The Old Tune*, 1794–1795). Although these collections are obviously based on oral tales from the folk tradition, they exhibit editing and literary influences. Foreign and fanciful names completely alien to Russian folk tradition frequently appear (*Tsar' Akhridei, Tsar' Sunbul*). But along with these alien elements, we find Baba Yaga in some of the same tale types later recorded from folk narrators, and with the same typical attributes. According to Nikolai Novikov, the first authentic folktale with Baba Yaga was published by Mikhail N. Makarov in 1820 (Novikov 1974: 133–134), a version of AT 327C/F. Makarov himself declared Baba Yaga to be "some kind of Slavic deity, known to us from folktales" (Makarov 1827: 149).

Makarov also wrote a narrative poem titled "The Krivich Christian and Yaga" ("Krivich-khristiianin i Iagaia," Makarov 1827a). This poetic description of the struggle of paganism and Christianity in ancient Rus' features Baba Yaga with her hut on chicken legs, mortar and pestle, and her usual remarks about the visitor's Russian scent. The still unenlightened East Slavic Krivichi tribe worships Baba Yaga, and the sick and needy bring her their daughters in sacrifice on a certain day of the year. But rather than eating them, she sells the poor girls to other tribes. A few girls grow accustomed to her ways and stay on with her, eventually replacing her and fooling the people into believing that Baba Yaga is immortal. Baba Yaga wounds the hero and leaves him in the forest to be eaten by animals, but he survives and wanders to her hut. Baba Yaga's three "daughters" do not shoot him but hide him and give him a knife. He cuts off Baba Yaga's head while she is asleep, marries the eldest daughter, and the Krivichi learn the truth about Baba Yaga and give up their idolatrous ways.

Makarov provides notes to his tale in verse, stating that it is based on an oral tale although he has left out some indecent episodes. Concerning Baba Yaga's origin and the origin of other Russian folktales, "It is almost possible to determine decisively that *Iagaia* came to us from the south" (Makarov 1827a: 19). Makarov also speculates that the epithet "Bony Leg" (*kostianaia noga*) might be a later contribution of tale tellers who wished to create a rhyme (*nogá-iagá*). The fact that Baba Yaga identifies the smell of her visitor as a Russian scent is another sign of her foreign origin (ibid., 20).

The poet Nikolai Nekrasov composed a narrative poem titled "Baba Yaga the Bony Leg" in 1840. His fairy tale in verse takes place in pre-Christian Rus', where Baba Yaga abducts Princess Milovzora. Nekrasov includes an explanation of Baba Yaga's origin similar to that of Vasilii Levshin. The devil cooks twelve evil women together into one who will be as evil as he is. The result is Baba Yaga, who goes out into the world to do evil, occasionally returning to hell for a reward. She arrives in her mortar in a cloud of smoke and has a horrifying appearance. Wearing a toadskin cap and a snakeskin coat, she has fangs, nostril hair that hangs down to her breasts, huge ears, horns on her forehead, and holes instead of eyes. The princess's brother Bulat goes to rescue her but is unable to harm Baba Yaga, who is in love with him. Bulat rejects Baba Yaga's amorous advances, and she turns him and his sister into statues and Bulat's beloved Liubana into a tree. Finally, the warrior Spiridon arrives, kills Baba Yaga, and breaks the spell, freeing Bulat, Milovzora, and Liubana (Nekrasov 1981, vol. 1: 292–339). This entertaining early poem of Nekrasov owes much to Pushkin ("Ruslan and Liudmila") and Vasilii Levshin (Tsar'kova 1981).

There may be implicit references in Russian literature to Baba Yaga, her dwelling, and her other attributes. In the very first chapter of *Crime and*

Punishment, Fedor M. Dostoevskii describes the old pawnbroker Alena Ivanovna's neck as long and thin, "similar to a chicken's leg" (*pokhozhei na kurinuiu nogu*, Dostoevskii 1973 vi: 8). Later, in chapter 3 of part 5, when Luzhin accuses Sonia Marmeladova of theft, Katerina Ivanovna calls the unpleasant German landlady Amalia Lippewechsel a "Prussian chicken's leg in crinoline" (*prusskaia kurinaia noga v krinoline*, ibid., 303). Features of Baba Yaga can also be detected in the image of Mar'ia Timofeevna in *The Possessed* (Gourg 1988). Abram Tertz sees Baba Yaga's image (including her role as mistress of beasts and goddess of death) behind the character Korobochka in Nikolai Gogol's *Dead Souls*, and the night Chichikov spends at her house may be an echo of the folktale episode (Tertz 1975: 413–418).

Baba Yaga has inspired a 1907 poem by Ivan Bunin and may be a subtext for twentieth-century authors such as Isaak Babel' (Shcheglov 1994, Zholkovsky 1994) and Aleksandr Solzhenitsyn (Spitz 1977). A young man's search for a place to spend the night in a Russian village, a noticeable lack of old woman donor figures, and the mention of Baba Yaga and Koshchei all add humor to Viktor Pelevin's 1991 story "A Werewolf Problem in Central Russia." A famous musical tribute to Baba Yaga is Mussorgsky's *Pictures at an Exhibition*, with its movement titled "The Hut on Chicken Legs," and Aleksandr Dargomyzhskii and Anatolii Liadov both composed orchestral pieces titled "Baba Yaga."

Baba Yaga has often been represented in the visual arts. She appears in popular woodblock prints (*lubki*) from the late seventeenth and early eighteenth centuries. In a few prints, a figure identified as Baba Yaga rides a pig and goes to fight another figure called the "crocodile." The crocodile is a male figure with a human face and beard, claws, and an animal body and tail. In one print a small ship is depicted in the corner below the crocodile, leading to an interpretation of this image as a political satire. Peter the Great was called a crocodile by the Old Believers, whom he persecuted, and some scholars have held that this print satirizes Peter's relations with his foreign wife Catherine. The ship is another clue to the crocodile's identity (Peter's interest in shipbuilding), and he and his wife fight over a bottle of wine shown between them. The costume of Baba Yaga is thought to be Finnish, and Peter's wife was called *chukhonka* (a somewhat pejorative term for a Finnish woman) by the people (Baldina 1972: 91–95).

This interpretation has been challenged. Dianne Farrell considers that these prints refer to shamanic practices. Baba Yaga's chukhonka costume in fact refers not only to the Finns but more widely to other Finnic peoples. On the one hand, the identification as a Finn was meant as an insult, while on the other it suggests shamanic practices still current among Finno-Ugric peoples at the time. The crocodile represents not Peter the Great, but a sorcerer-shaman-werewolf who fights witches. The print is something of a cultural mélange and demonstrates an interest in shamanism in Russia at the time (Farrell 1993). In another print, Baba Yaga dances while a balding peasant man plays a bagpipe. According to the traditional interpretation, this may be another, somewhat happier representation of Peter's home life. Farrell comments on Baba Yaga's costume in this print, but does not offer an alternative interpretation. Neither of these two interpretations significantly changes the image of Baba Yaga familiar from folktales. Either she can be seen as a literal evil witch, treated somewhat humorously in these prints, or a figurative "witch," an unpopular foreign empress. Both literal and figurative understandings of Baba Yaga are documented in the nineteenth century and were probably present at the time these prints were made.

As for Baba Yaga's potential shamanic features, there is one anomalous tale (Khudiakov 1964: 269–270) recorded in Eastern Siberia in which Èga-Baba is said to practice the shaman's art. This tale probably reflects the direct influence of the neighboring Yakut or Evenk people (see chapter 2). Ethel Dunn discusses Baba Yaga in connection with Siberian and Russian shamanism, armless and legless doll amulets, and the use of narcotic mushrooms (1973).

Mythological Approaches

The earliest interpretations of Baba Yaga identify her as a Slavic pagan goddess. Mikhail Chulkov includes *Iagaia baba* in his dictionary of Russian superstitions (*Slovar' ruskikh sueverii* [sic], St. Petersburg 1782). "The Slavs venerated the underworld goddess by this name, representing her as a frightening figure seated in an iron mortar, with an iron pestle in her hands; they made blood sacrifice to her, thinking that she fed it to the two granddaughters they attributed to her, and that she delighted in the shedding of blood herself" (Chulkov 1782: 270). In a compilation of Russian folklore which endeavored to demonstrate the common origin of the Russians and Greeks, Matthew Guthrie equates her with the Greek Persephone (Proserpina): "*Yaga-Baba*, or *Proserpine*, was the goddess of hell or the Proserpine of the ancients, to whom blood sacrifices were offered, as to Pluto her spouse. She was represented in the form of a monster, seated in a kind of iron mortar, with a pestle of the same metal in her hand" (Guthrie 1795: 63).

The first systematic folklore theory to be applied to Baba Yaga was that of the nineteenth-century mythologists, who were influenced by the works of Jacob and Wilhelm Grimm. In Russia this school was represented by Fedor I. Buslaev, Aleksandr N. Afanas'ev, and Aleksandr A. Potebnia, among others. In their view, the striking resemblances among European folktales, like those among the Indo-European languages, indicated a common origin. Folktales are derived from ancient Indo-European myths, whose original meaning was forgotten when the Indo-European peoples dispersed. Folktales are thus merely fragments. The importance of the forgetting of original meanings was further developed in the theories of Max Müller, who explained the origin of myth through the "disease of language." This occurred when the original meaning of names and phrases referring to the ancient divinities was forgotten and stories were invented to explain such terms. This school of "solar mythology" often interpreted folk narratives as metaphorical expressions of heavenly phenomena, and Baba Yaga was identified as the embodiment of the storm cloud, also associated with death and winter.

As a comparative and solar mythologist, Aleksandr Afanas'ev interprets Baba Yaga as a personification of the storm cloud. Her mortar and mobile hut are metaphors of the storm cloud, and her staff or crutch is, like the club of Perun, the Slavic thunder god, a metaphor for lightning. Her magic objects (fire-breathing horses, seven-league boots, flying carpet, self-playing *gusli* [psaltery], self-cutting sword) represent her possession of quickly flying clouds, thunder, and lightning (Afanas'ev 1869 iii: 587–588). The legs of her hut represent lightning: Just as lightning and thunder cause the storm clouds to move quickly, so the legs cause Baba Yaga's cloud dwelling to turn (Afanas'ev 1868 ii: 531). Her breasts are equated with rain clouds (Afanas'ev 1869 iii: 593).

In a few Russian riddles Baba Yaga metaphorically represents a plough: "Baba Yaga stands, torn leg, she feeds the whole world, but is herself hungry" (*Stoit baba Iaga/rasporota noga/ves' mir kormit/sama golodna*, Sadovnikov 1959: 140, no. 1196a). In another version of the riddle, Baba Yaga does not go hungry but ruins her teeth (*Sebe tol'ko zuby portit*, Martynova 1997: 446, no. 1894). Her leg is "torn" (*rasporota*) or compared to a pitchfork (*vilami noga*, Sadovnikov 1959: 140, no. 1196b, Martynova 1997: 447, no. 1895). Afanas'ev explains Baba Yaga's identification with the plough in this riddle through an ancient conception of the thunder god who forced the cloud maidens to pull his heavenly plough and sow the earth (Afanas'ev 1865 i: 573). Afanas'ev notes the Slovak and Czech children's custom of asking Ježibaba for new iron teeth, and interprets the iron teeth of a Russian folktale witch as lightning (ibid., i: 774–775). He provides two interpretations for Baba Yaga's foiled attempt to eat a child hero (AT 327C/F): Baba Yaga represents a black cloud devouring lightning as well as death abducting human souls (Afanas'ev 1869 iii: 586). Afanas'ev derives the word *iaga* from the Sanskrit *ahi* (snake). He points out that Baba Yaga's place in Slavic tales is taken in Greek and Albanian folktales by a *lamia* (female dragon). He finds additional correspondences between Baba Yaga and snakes.

Another study of Baba Yaga in the spirit of the mythological school is that of the linguist Aleksandr A. Potebnia. Baba Yaga occupies one chapter of his book, *On the Mythical Meaning of Certain Rituals and Beliefs* (*O mificheskom znachenii nekotorykh obriadov i poverii*, 1865). The essay in this chapter contains a wealth of comparative material. Potebnia finds Baba Yaga to be identical with the Germanic figures Holda, Frau Holle, and Bertha. Holda causes snow and rain; she keeps the souls of unborn children and receives the souls of dead unbaptized children; she is associated with cloth and spinning; she is believed to reward good spinners and punish bad ones. Like Baba Yaga, she is derived from the cloud.

Potebnia establishes a connection between Baba Yaga and mice, who are the messengers of death. He finds this correspondence in Slavic and Germanic beliefs and customs concerning the loss of children's teeth. Sometimes children give their teeth to the mouse, asking for an iron tooth in exchange; in some Czech and Slovak versions of this custom, the tooth is given to Ježibaba (Potebnia 1865: 91). More evidence is found in Germanic and Slavic games of blindman's buff where the seeker's eyes are covered (Czech *slepá baba, kuca baba;* German *blindes Mäusel*), and which Potebnia interprets as a symbolic representation of death (*kuca baba*, the player whose eyes are bound) seizing children (the other players). On the basis of the name and rules of this game, Potebnia also suggests that Baba Yaga is blind, although blindness may be a way of expressing darkness or ugliness (ibid., 93–94).

Baba Yaga is associated with the crow (Serbian children ask the crow for iron teeth), and the Serbian *Gvozdenzuba* (Iron Tooth) is a folklore character who frightens children and burns the fingers of women or girls who are bad spinners. Furthermore, Czech children's songs associate the crow with childbirth, which, in turn, corresponds to Baba Yaga/Holda's role as keeper and releaser of children's souls (ibid., 98). Holda/Yaga is identified with death and with the effigies which the West Slavs carry out in procession and destroy in spring, some of whose names evoke death (Smrtnica, Smrtolenka, Mařena; cf. Czech *smrt* "death").

Potebnia also finds important correspondences between Baba Yaga and the fox. In some Czech traditions, it is the fox (rather than Ježibaba or the mouse) who takes the baby teeth and is asked for iron teeth, who brings babies, and who leaves pretzels for children at the beginning of Lent. This leads to a comparison of three groups of mainly Russian folktales. In the first, a fox kidnaps a rooster (Afanas'ev 37–39, AT 61B, Cat, Cock, and Fox Live Together). In the tales of the second group, Baba Yaga kidnaps a child who usually escapes (Afanas'ev 105–112, AT 327C/F). In the third group (also AT 327C/F), Potebnia distinguishes the child hero in these tales as being completely human (without animal siblings). The general interpretation of all these tales is that the fox and Baba Yaga (who are identical) represent the goddess Yaga-Mařena-Holda, and the act of abduction represents death. The death of Yaga is the loss of her power over the captured soul, and like the destruction of the effigies in spring, it can be understood as the death of winter and the loss of its hold on nature (ibid., 126).

Potebnia introduces many more examples from folklore to demonstrate that Baba Yaga is the death of human beings and nature, the holder of the keys to heaven (in the person of Mařena), the one who sends souls to earth and takes them back. She also oversees women's domestic work, especially spinning and weaving. Baba Yaga serves as a guardian of morality in this life, which influences the fate of the soul in the afterlife. Potebnia suggests that the kind girl's return from Baba Yaga's hut in Afanas'ev 102 and 103 (AT 480) could symbolize rebirth (ibid., 141). In tales about the abduction of the supernatural spouse, the hero must serve as a shepherd or herdsman for Baba Yaga (see chapter 5). In these tales the dragon or Koshchei, who kidnaps the hero's wife, is the cloud withholding rain, while the hero is the thunder god and corresponds to the Hindu Indra or Agni. In some tales the hero marries Baba Yaga's daughter, which represents the marriage of the rain cloud with thunder.

Potebnia concludes that Baba Yaga was originally a storm cloud. She then came to be associated with the fertility of the earth, marriage, and birth. The place beyond the clouds is also the dwellingplace of souls, so that Yaga is the giver of life and death. The seasonal qualities of the cloud (friendly in summer, inimical in winter) explain the contradictions in the image and character of Holda, Bertha, and Yaga. Compared to her Germanic counterparts, though, Baba Yaga is dominated by her severe features: "...the duality of the cloud, fertilizing the earth in summer, concealing rain in winter, was expressed in the duality of Holda's appearance and character... under the cold European sky Yaga became *winter* and devouring *death*, cast her summer image from herself and gave it to her daughters" (ibid., 197). After comparing Yaga to the Greek goddess Demeter and a few animals, Potebnia also finds a parallel with the figure of East Slavic folk belief *Paraskeva-Piatnitsa*.[5] Sunday (*Nedelia*) is the sun, and Friday (Piatnitsa and also Yaga) is the sun's mother. In some East Slavic folk songs the sun is conceived of as female, while the moon is male. Potebnia finds the source of this conception in the marriage of the sun and moon as

---

5 There appear to be three historical Orthodox saints who can be identified with this figure. In folk belief, she appears as the personification of Friday, when she prohibits women's work (spinning, weaving, washing). Her cult and beliefs about her are perhaps more popular in southeastern Europe (Romania and Bulgaria, especially) than among the East Slavs (Mesnil and Popova 1993; Chubinskii 1872: 217; Róheim 1946, 1992: 44–57). See the discussion in chapter 2.

described in the Rig-Veda and Atharva-Veda. So, on the basis of these rather tenuous connections, Baba Yaga is identified as an Indo-European goddess of death and winter, associated with clouds.[6]

Baba Yaga is explicitly associated with winter in one Russian folk song, but this very well may be a metaphor, with winter understood to be as fierce as Baba Yaga. This song was meant to ensure the arrival of spring, and addresses the sun:

Videlo li, solnyshko,	Sun, did you see
Staruiu iagu,	Old Yaga,
Babu li iagu—	Baba Yaga—
Ved'mu-zimu?	the witch winter?
Kak ona, liutaia,	That fierce one, she
Ot vesny ushla,	got away from spring,
Ot krasnoi begla,	ran away from the fair one,
V meshke stuzhu nesla,	carried cold in a sack,
Kholod na zemliu triasla,	shook out cold onto the earth,
Sama ostupilas',	stumbled and
Pod goru pokatilas'.	rolled down the hill.

(Korinfskii 1901: 146–147; Zemtsovskii 1970: 290, no. 435)

The mythological approach has been revived in the twentieth century by Evel Gasparini (1973), who interprets Baba Yaga as a lunar witch. Her revolving hut is the house of the crescent moon. Like the moon, it shifts back and forth to face east and west. In many folktales Baba Yaga is said to be stretched out, filling the hut, just as the crescent tightly occupies the dark moon face (Gasparini 1973: 639–640). The disappearance (swallowing) of the moon during its cycle accounts for Baba Yaga's cannibalism (ibid., 653). Gasparini cites folklore from around the world to support his thesis, but this lunar interpretation of Baba Yaga seems as little convincing as the earlier storm cloud hypothesis. Some natural phenomena are personified in East Slavic folklore (in folktales, *Morozko* is the personification of frost; the sun, moon, and winds appear as individual characters). There appears to be no reason why a cloud or the moon would have to be metaphorically represented by Baba Yaga, rather than directly and explicitly personified. The mythological interpretations also fail to explain why the cloud, moon, winter, or death take precisely the form of Baba Yaga and not another.

---

[6] In a study of the Russian mythological school of the nineteenth century, A. L. Toporkov finds that this chapter on Baba Yaga is the least successful in Potebnia's book (1997: 257–258).

Baba Yaga and Ritual

Another approach in the search for the historical origins of various elements of folklore is to interpret them as survivals of social customs and institutions of the past. Folktale motifs and episodes are seen to reflect totemism, animism, shamanism, exogamy, or ancient matriarchy. Like their eighteenth-century predecessors, scholars who have interpreted Baba Yaga in these terms have seen her as the later manifestation of a Slavic deity.

In his second major work, *The Historical Roots of the Magic Tale* (*Istoricheskie korni volshebnoi skazki*, Leningrad 1946), Vladimir Propp includes a discussion of Baba Yaga's historical origin which has been very influential. This work was quite a departure from the method of synchronic analysis Propp had applied in his *Morphology*. Having discovered that all Russian fairy tales have the same underlying pattern, Propp wished to explain how this structure came about. To answer this difficult question, he combined myth-ritualist and Marxist ideas. In a spirit of historical materialism, Propp interprets elements of the folktale through archaic beliefs and customs. Propp sees the source of the fairy tale morphology in rituals of initiation, practiced in societies of Africa, Oceania, and the Americas. Propp draws on a great deal of ethnographic data, frequently citing examples from Melanesia and the Pacific Northwest Coast of North America. He finds that the ritual, in which initiates underwent symbolic death and rebirth, corresponds to the hero(ine)'s journey to the other world of the fairy tale (Propp 1946: 79). The folktale arose after the ritual had lost its meaning for the community or fallen into disapproval: "As long as the ritual existed and was alive, there could be no folktales about it" (ibid., 69).

There are methodological problems with Propp's theory. Probably influenced by Lewis Morgan and Friedrich Engels, he assumes that all human societies evolve in the same manner, through a series of stages (Propp 1984: 161–172). Even if there is no direct evidence that the ancient Slavs, the ancestors of the nineteenth-century Russian peasants from whom the folktales were recorded, ever had an initiation ritual similar to those described by Propp, it is assumed that they did.[7] Propp introduces examples of initiation rituals

---

[7] For an attempt to reconstruct ancient Slavic initiation ritual, with Baba Yaga as an initiating figure, see Balushok 1993. In particular, V. G. Balushok examines Slavic legends and beliefs about werewolves, and suggests that male initiates underwent a ritual transformation into werewolves, and communicated with a totemic wolf ancestor. Besides Baba Yaga, the ancient Slavic deities Mokosh', Veles, and Perun would also have played a role in these rituals. Dmitrii Zelenin describes a ritual that marked a Russian girl's coming of age. Her mother asked her to jump from a bench down into a spread-out skirt or belt. The young woman replied, "If I want to I'll jump, if not, I won't." Most often, however, this particular act was incorporated into the wedding ritual (Zelenin 1994: 179–192). A ritual hair cutting for Russian boys (*postrigi*) took place most often between ages three and seven, and the ritual first braiding of a girl's hair might take place even

from many different societies, which must differ widely among themselves: Introducing those features of initiation rituals which bear resemblance to folktale motifs and perhaps ignoring those which do not, his conception of this ritual might be somewhat arbitrary. Another difficulty is the question of exactly how or why ritual becomes folktale. Propp supposes that narratives were told to initiates to explain the ritual they were experiencing. When the ritual died out, the narratives lost their sacred and esoteric character, became accessible to a wider number of people, and began to be transformed into secular narratives which in time became the "modern" fairy tale.[8] An important question that remains unanswered is how and why the structure of the ritual arose in the first place. Propp does not discuss the question of monogenesis (the possibility that the fairy-tale morphology arose in one place and then spread geographically) or polygenesis (that it arose in many places independently).

In spite of these difficulties, Propp's work is fascinating and has influenced much subsequent scholarship. In his exposition of the fairy tale within the framework of initiation in *The Historical Roots of the Magic Tale*, Baba Yaga as a donor is particularly important and occupies most of the third chapter, "The Mysterious Forest." Propp recognizes that Baba Yaga's image is complex and contradictory, but essentially considers her the most archaic, classical form of the donor figure. For Propp, the forest of the folktale is logically both the entrance to the land of the dead and the place where initiation took place, since initiates underwent a symbolic death, to be reborn as adult members of society.

Baba Yaga is the guardian who lives at the gateway to the land of the dead. Her hut faces toward the land of the dead and therefore the hero(ine) must make the hut turn around with a magic phrase; he or she cannot simply walk around to the other side. Sometimes initiation took the symbolic form of being swallowed by an animal (Propp 1946: 43–44). The initiation hut originally

---

later. Snejana Tempest finds that the hair-cutting ritual "served the function of completing the cultural and social construction of gender" (2001: 99). Children's gender identity was perhaps most significantly established and reinforced when they learned and took part in either men's or women's work activities (Tempest 2001, Lavrent'eva 1991). In parts of Slovakia and Eastern Moravia, adolescent boys underwent various forms of ritual hazing when they joined the socially recognized category of young unmarried men; in some rural areas of Poland, when young men began to take part in mowing and haymaking, they were hazed by older men. This induction into the recognized status of adult male worker included being "shaved" with a whetstone or a rough piece of wood (Horváthová 1989).

[8] It is hard to reconcile this conception of the origin of the fairy tale (linked to the death of ritual) with the fact that there are societies in which both initiation rituals and fairy tales coexist. The Dogon of Mali and other West African peoples practice initiation, and also tell fairy tales such as AT 480, in which the "initiatory theme" is very important (Calame-Griaule 1976, 1996; see discussion in chapter 3, and the Conclusion).

represented an animal, and in the folktale only a part of the hut (the legs) has remained zoomorphic (ibid., 51). The "Russian scent" of the hero that Baba Yaga notices is the smell of the living, which is frightening and offensive to the dead. Propp demonstrates this through a number of Native North American and African tales (ibid., 51–53).

The hero demands food from Baba Yaga before he will tell her where he is going and what he is doing in her hut. The hero's behavior is unexpected, as is Baba Yaga's reaction—she immediately complies with his request. Propp finds passages in the ancient Egyptian *Book of the Dead* in which the deceased's mouth was opened by ritual feeding, which allowed for passage onward into the spirit world. So the Russian folktale hero must eat and drink to prepare himself for passage into the other kingdom.[9] Baba Yaga lies stretched out and occupies almost the entire space of the hut and so resembles a corpse inside a coffin. Her identity as a dead person leads Propp to propose an explanation for another of her typical features, the bony leg. Baba Yaga's original form was that of an animal which underwent anthropomorphization. At a later period she possessed an animal leg, which became a bony leg because of her association with death (ibid., 57–58).

Like Potebnia, Propp supposes that Baba Yaga is blind. This is not explicitly stated in the folktales but implied by the fact that she smells the approaching hero rather than sees him. Propp considers this another indication of Baba Yaga's belonging to the other world of the dead—blindness represents her inability to see the living (the hero), just as the living are unable to see the dead (ibid., 59). Again, Propp finds parallels (symbolic blindness) in initiation rituals of Africa and Oceania.[10]

In some folktales Baba Yaga possesses exaggerated female features, such as giant breasts, even though she is an unmarried old woman. Baba Yaga is a mother without being a wife, reflecting a stage in history when humans conceived of fertility as exclusively female, without male participation. She is the mother of animals, especially forest animals. The folktales themselves do

[9] Nikolai Novikov disagrees with Propp about this formulaic episode. Novikov feels it could have arisen at a much later date, and interprets it as a realistic situation where a tired and hungry traveler does not want to be bothered by questions about where he is coming from and going, but wants to eat and rest (Novikov 1974: 178–179).

[10] Novikov criticizes this interpretation as inaccurate. In the tale cited by Propp (Afanas'ev 106), Baba Yaga arrives and does not see the hero, but this is because he is concealed, sitting behind the stove pipe (*Zhikhar' tol'ko sel za trubu na pech*). Novikov points out that if the hero knew that Baba Yaga were blind, he would not have bothered to hide. In other tales (AT 301) Baba Yaga's daughter hides the hero by transforming him into various objects (such as a pin or needle, cf. Afanas'ev 142), which would also be unnecessary if Baba Yaga were truly blind (Novikov 1974: 177–178).

not call her mother or mistress of animals, but this identity is indicated by her power over them (she summons the birds, beasts, and fish to help the hero).[11] She is the mistress of the beasts, and for the members of hunting societies, she also has power over human life and death (ibid., 62).

Propp sees the two roles—guardian of the land of the dead, mistress of animals—as historically linked. He cites a Native North American legend (reported by Franz Boas) about a dead man who is revived by wolves, turned into a wolf, and who then returns to the world of the living to teach humans the wolf dance, bearing the gift of a magic arrow. Baba Yaga can be traced back to a female totemic ancestor. Her status as ancestor explains her association with the hearth (she lies on the stove and licks up soot with her tongue), although Propp maintains that historically the hearth was the seat of male ancestral spirits. Many of her familiar attributes belong to the more conventional female sphere of the kitchen, such as her broom or pestle. Propp sees a line of development from totem animal to zoomorphic woman to goddesses such as Cybele and Artemis (ibid., 65).

The tasks that Baba Yaga sometimes sets for the hero(ine) are derived from the tests of a deceased person's knowledge of the magic words and actions

---

[11] It should be pointed out that the folktales Propp adduces to support this claim provide weak evidence. Propp cites Onchukov 3, where the donor who calls together beasts is a grandmother and "old large person" (*star-mater chelovek*) who lives in a hut on chicken legs, but who is not called Baba Yaga. Next he quotes from Afanas'ev 157, where the donor is an old woman (*starukha*) whose house is *not* the hut on chicken legs, although her second sister notices the hero's Russian bone and the hero reproaches all three sisters for asking him questions before feeding him. The next passage he cites as evidence is taken from Afanas'ev 212 (AT 465A), and here there is a significant oversight. The old woman (*starukha*) who summons the birds and beasts in this tale is not Baba Yaga, but rather the hero's mother-in-law. The hero reproaches her daughters for asking him questions before giving him food and drink, and letting him rest. However, the Baba Yaga who appears in this tale is a villain who thinks of deadly tasks, which the king then assigns to the hero. Propp is pointing out an old woman donor as an example of Baba Yaga (in itself not necessarily problematic), but at the same time ignoring the Baba Yaga in this tale who is *called* Baba Yaga.

Next Propp cites Afanas'ev 272, where Baba Yaga does call together the winds. Likewise, she possesses the keys to the sun and moon in Smirnov 304, but the "mother of the winds" Propp identifies as Baba Yaga (citing Afanas'ev 565) is an old woman (*starukha*) who lives in the forest and lacks any of the standard Yaga attributes. Propp does not cite Kovalev 9, where Baba Yaga summons fish, beasts, and birds. It is surprising that Propp does not cite the numerous Russian versions of AT 480 where Baba Yaga, as the tester of the kind and unkind girls, asks the girls to bathe her children, who are snakes, frogs, toads, and worms. The abilities of Baba Yaga and these old women donors to command animals and forces of nature recall Slavic folk beliefs about witches (see chapter 2) and prompt a consideration of the nature/culture opposition in their image. What the actual "historical roots" of these conceptions might be remains an open question.

necessary to pass over into the other world. One such task is not to fall asleep, since sleeping, like some other activities (yawning, laughing, having a scent), distinguishes the living from the dead.

Many tales begin when children go to the forest or are taken there and abandoned. Although the reason for the children's abandonment is the enmity of a wicked stepmother, it is always the father or another male, usually a relative, who takes the children to the forest. This reflects initiation practice (women were not allowed near the initiation site). Even the abduction of children by Baba Yaga has its origin in this ritual. The pledging of children to secret societies at birth is the source of another common folktale motif, relinquishing "what you do not know at home" to a forest or water spirit (in East Slavic versions of AT 313). Furthermore, Baba Yaga's cruel behavior toward the hero's companions in some tales (AT 301), in which she beats them and cuts out a strip of flesh from their backs, is explained by similar painful mutilations imposed on initiates (ibid., 74). The same is true for cutting off the hero's finger, which Buraia-Yaga asks her daughters to do in one tale (Smirnov 250). The ordeals undergone in initiation also account for this motif in The Maiden without Hands (AT 706). Propp cites the importance of fire in some initiation rituals. The purifying or revitalizing effect of fire is a conception reflected in a few folktales, but a later reinterpretation is found in tales where Baba Yaga unsuccessfully tries to push the hero into her oven (AT 327C/F).

Finally, Propp raises a fundamental question about Baba Yaga's role as initiator. Why is it that young men are initiated by a female figure? Among some Australian groups the young men were initiated not by members of their own clan, but by the clan group whose women they were allowed to marry. In some Russian tales, Yaga is a relative of the hero's wife or mother, but never of the hero himself or his father. Although Yaga's relationships to the hero's wife or mother are expressed in conventional kinship terms (mother-in-law, aunt, or sister), her true relationship is that of belonging to the same totemic clan as the hero's wife or mother. "All these materials explain the forms of the hero's kinship with Yaga, but they do not yet completely explain why Yaga is a woman. However, they show that the explanation must be sought in the matriarchal relations of the past" (ibid., 93). The folktale suggests that a woman took part in the ritual, and Propp finds instances of men dressed as women acting as initiators in New Guinea. The rise of patriarchy is the reason why women have been completely excluded from this ritual and why their role has been taken over by men.

Propp's conclusion to this chapter of his book confronts the problem of Yaga's dual nature. Both the act of abducting children and the presentation of magic objects to the hero derive from initiation. At the same time, many of her attributes and actions are associated with death. This is logical inasmuch as initiation ritual was a symbolic death. As the ritual died out, only the association with death was remembered. With the appearance of agriculture, a new religion replaced the older hunting beliefs, and the old divinities were reinterpreted as evil spirits. Yaga, the mother and mistress of the beasts, became a witch. The ritual of purification by fire was turned on its head and reversed, and the initiate (hero) thrusts the initiator (Yaga) into the fire (ibid., 95–96; AT 327C/F). Propp also mentions Baba Yaga in an essay on transformations of the magic tale, where he compares Baba Yaga to the "Mistress of the Forest" praised in a hymn from the Rig-Veda, which also mentions her forest dwelling (1976: 157–158). Propp does not claim that Baba Yaga derives from the Rig-Veda, but presents this example to show that folktales are historically derived from religion.

In spite of certain weaknesses, Propp's interpretation of Baba Yaga has been influential in subsequent scholarship, and Nikolai Novikov is one of the few Russian or Soviet scholars to criticize it. Propp's interpretation of Baba Yaga as the mistress of animals has often been repeated, as well as his view that Baba Yaga's "wicked" aspect is a later development, brought about by the rise of patriarchy (Ivanov and Toporov 1965: 176, Novikov 1974: 180). Baba Yaga's association with death has also been elaborated by other scholars. Olga Periañez-Chaverneff points out that concerns with death, mortality, and immortality in Russian fairy tales are explicitly represented by Koshchei the Immortal, and asks, "Pourquoi alors cette obstination de nombreux auteurs russes à vouloir identifier Baba-Jaga à la mort?" (1983: 192).

Eleazar Meletinskii briefly mentions Baba Yaga in his work on the Russian folktale hero, in connection with Russian versions of the tale of The Kind and the Unkind Girls (AT 480). His interpretation of folktales follows Propp, although he takes other historical factors into account (for example, customs of inheritance right) and focuses on the socially "low" hero. As for Baba Yaga, she is undoubtedly a "very ancient matriarchal mythical image, genetically connected with the image of the mistress of the forest, with the realm of the dead and more ancient totemic conceptions. It is hardly possible to determine exactly its specific nature. It is clear that at some time an ancient powerful spirit was concealed behind Baba Yaga, and that she is a generalization of demonic forces opposing the folktale hero" (Meletinskii 1958: 198).

The scholar V. N. Toporov has also examined Baba Yaga and finds that all tales about Baba Yaga are really of one type (Toporov 1963, 1987). Yaga is in fact one text, differently semanticized. Toporov sees the primary theme in the Yaga tales as that of burial and death, while he regards the themes of initiation or the seasonal cycle which might be associated with Yaga as secondary.

Toporov examines SalŠU.GI, a wise old woman in Hittite religion who receives the deceased into the land of the dead. Not much is known about her from burial texts, but she also appears in a purification ritual, making sacrifices to the sun god. Her points of resemblance to Yaga are her old age and her role in Hittite cremation practices (cf. Baba Yaga's attempts to shove children into her oven in AT 327C/F). Both the Hittite figure and Baba Yaga have their roots in a burial ritual. The two aspects of Baba Yaga's behavior have often been noted, but another deeper ambivalence (*ambivalentnost*) has escaped notice: Baba Yaga is at once both death and its cause (Toporov 1987: 20). On the one hand, Baba Yaga, cramped into her hut, resembles a corpse in its coffin; on the other, she is a mistress of ceremonies, a priestess who is prepared to sacrifice the hero and give him over to death. However, the folktale departs from the ritual in its outcome. The roles of sacrificer and sacrificial victim are reversed. This reversal is explained by the paradoxical logic of ritual, in which loss (sacrifice) becomes gain, as well as reflecting initiation. "On account of what has been said, it must be admitted that the folktale reflects not only the initiation ritual, but also— through it—*the corresponding burial ritual*, modelled at initiation" (ibid., 21). Inasmuch as Yaga is the guide to the land of the dead, there is reason to believe that she represents the first person ever to die and undergo the burial ritual, which then becomes a tradition. Although traces of different kinds of burial ritual can be found in the folktales in which Baba Yaga figures, the cremation ritual is dominant (ibid., 23). Toporov finds correspondences to Yaga in the Vedas, anchoring her (as well as the Hittite SalŠU.GI) in an ancient Indo-European tradition.

K. D. Laushkin (1970) considers Baba Yaga the Slavic goddess of death, who had an animal form before she became a folktale character. Concentrating on one of her prominent traits, the bony leg, Laushkin maintains that in fact this feature has overshadowed an older, one-legged Baba Yaga, and he cites one folktale version in which she is so addressed (Sokolov 139), and another where she jumps around on one leg (Sadovnikov 27). (She bears the epithet "one leg" in Sokolov 140 as well). Laushkin agrees with Propp that Baba Yaga originally had an animal form, and suggests that she passed through an intermediary stage of one-leggedness before acquiring the bony leg most commonly found in the recorded folktales. There are many figures of ancient Greek myth and legend who are lame, limp, or have an unusual foot or leg, and who also have some association with the snake, or exhibit a snake-like nature. According to a Belorussian legend, devils limp because they were cast down from heaven; the principal devil is called *tsmok* ("dragon"), which indicates his ophidian origin. In Onchukov 152 (AT 303), Baba Yaga turns into a snake before she dies, a "mythological atavism" which indicates her original nature. Like other one-legged divinities, Baba Yaga can be traced back to the snake, which represented or was associated with death (Laushkin 1970). Ol'ga A. Cherepanova has also presented linguistic and folkloristic evidence to argue for Baba Yaga's snake origin. Like Laushkin, she feels that Baba Yaga's one-leggedness or the bony leg in some tales probably reflect an earlier snake form. In an incantation against snake bite, recorded in the eighteenth century, a snake is called *Iaga zmeia bura* ("Yaga the brown snake"). In Ukrainian, the term *iazia* can refer both to Baba Yaga and to a legendary two-headed snake. Given that the Russian word for "snake" (*zmeia*) is perhaps a taboo term derived from the word "earth" (*zemlia*), the snake being that animal that crawls on the earth, and given that not one of the numerous Russian regional and dialect terms for "snake" can be considered older than the rest, Cherepanova suggests that this word may have been *iaga*. Baba Yaga is a transformed version of beings found in the mythologies of other peoples who are part human, part snake (Cherepanova 1983: 105–110).

Influenced by the work of archeologist Marija Gimbutas, Michael Shapiro (1983) finds that Baba Yaga is derived from two prehistoric theriomorphic prototypes—the snake and the pelican. The Slavic word *baba*, like other Slavic kinship terms, has been applied to species of plants and animals. *Baba* has come to be the indigenous term for the pelican in some Russian, Ukrainian, Bulgarian, and Upper Sorbian dialects, as opposed to the Greco-Latin borrowing *pelikan*. Shapiro then discusses the *kamennye baby* (stone women), anthropomorphic stone figures of great age found in an area extending from Russia to Mongolia. These figures often represent women and were presumably objects of worship for the ancient Slavs.

> At all events, the cult adumbrated by these anthropomorphic stelae certainly has something to do with the worship of *Baba*. What I would like to hypothesize (and then try to prove by the cumulative weight of evidence of several kinds) is the **avian nature** of that cult, reflecting the Old European veneration of the Bird Goddess, wherein the linguistic designation of a female deity may be seen as contemporaneous with or derived from the word's "pelican" meaning. (Shapiro 1983: 115)

The conception of a Bird Goddess appears to go back as far as the Paleolithic; during the Neolithic period depictions of this Goddess acquire more human features and so approach the *kamennye baby*. Shapiro finds that certain physical features of the pelican can help explain Baba Yaga's attributes. The hut on chicken legs (*izbushka na kur'ikh nozhkakh*) brings Baba Yaga into the bird realm; Shapiro suggests that the adjective *kurii* may originally have applied more broadly to all birds. Baba Yaga's bony leg could be interpreted as a bird's leg as well. Her long nose which sticks into (has grown into) the ceiling can be explained by the pelican's long neck and beak, while her tousled hair might be a reflection of the plumes on some pelican species. Although the pelican is not one of the animals associated with Baba Yaga, this could be the result of a word-taboo. The use of *baba* to designate the pelican, replacing a word existing in prehistoric Slavic, may have arisen at a time when the pelican began to be worshiped. Or a taboo may have been in effect occasionally or seasonally. Another reason for the absence of pelicans among birds which appear in Russian folklore might be the growing prominence of the evil aspect of Baba Yaga, which gradually ousted the benevolent or biaspectual Yaga. If we associate the snake with Yaga's wicked aspect, the pelican can be associated with her good aspect (which in turn connects her with the Bird and Great Goddesses). As the benevolent Baba Yaga is forced into the background, now appearing only as a relic, the pelican disappears (ibid., 124–125).

Shapiro also discusses the disputed etymologies of the word *iaga* and offers an alternative Uralic etymology. If the prehistoric Slavs had contact with the Samoyed peoples (such as the Nenets, Nganasan, and Selkup, now living in Northwestern Siberia), it is possible that they may have adopted the proto-Samoyed word *ŋga* ("god"), found in Nenets as *Nga/ŋa* ("God of Death"). An integration of the Slavic Great Goddess (Baba) with the Samoyed deity of Death (Nga) could account for Baba Yaga's hostile aspect (ibid., 126–128). If Yaga is partly derived from a Samoyed goddess, this explains why she notices the hero's particularly Russian scent.

A parallel to Yaga can also be found in the ancient Slavic pagan religion. The only known female divinity in the Kievan pantheon was Mokosh', whose name suggests an association with water or moistness (cf. Russian *mokryi*, "wet, moist"). Most of the Slavic pagan gods are known only from references in historical chronicles; their names have not left any traces in folklore. This suggests that there was a distinction between a "high," aristocratic pagan cult and a "low" popular one. In this case Mokosh' clearly belongs to the high cult, while Baba Yaga would have belonged to the low cult. Some consider that Mokosh' survived in later East Slavic popular religion as St. Paraskeva, and given the connection between Paraskeva and Baba Yaga noted by Aleksandr Potebnia, Shapiro takes the three figures to be in some way identical. He points to a ritual (*mokrida*) in which a sacrifice to Paraskeva was made by throwing some kind of woven material or thread into a well, and to representations of female figures in Russian folk embroidery which suggest a great goddess (ibid., 128–130).

Finally, Shapiro suggests that Baba Yaga may originally have been androgynous. Her daughters are called *Iagishny* (Yagishnas, daughters of Yaga), a form which is usually patronymic. A folktale ogre who seems related to Yaga is

Koshchei Bessmertnyi (Koshchei the Immortal), who invariably dies, sometimes when kicked by a horse obtained from Baba Yaga. The dyad Yaga/Koshchei is likened to the Greek pair Cybele/Attis, and so the complex history of Baba Yaga is that of the Great Goddess, who begins in theriomorphic form (the Bird and Snake Godesses), becomes anthropomorphic, and finally becomes sexually differentiated.

Maria Kravchenko (1987: 184–204) describes Baba Yaga as a "strangely ambivalent mythological figure," notes her important features, her association with the frog and horse, and comments on features Baba Yaga shares in common with the Tsar Maiden (*Tsar'-Devitsa*) in some tales. She discusses the findings of Propp, Anikin, and Novikov, their descriptions of Baba Yaga as a forest and animal goddess, totemic matriarchal ancestress, and goddess of death. She agrees with them but feels they "are to a certain extent limited and quite conservative, for there exists in the oldest cosmologies and myths a single goddess who fits all the above descriptions and many more of the features that the Baba-Yaga presents in the *skazka*" (ibid., 192), namely, the earth mother goddess. She introduces many ancient myths and legends, suggesting that certain features of Baba Yaga (her exaggerated posterior and thighs, her sedentary position inside her hut) reflect the nature of the mother goddess. Kravchenko presents a case for Afanas'ev's derivation of *iaga* having the meaning of "snake," and interprets Baba Yaga's name as "Woman-Snake," and Yaga Yagishna as perhaps "Snake of Snakes" (ibid., 203). Like the parallel figures from other folklore traditions, Baba Yaga "is the largely debased form forced upon the Earth goddess by the worshippers of the Sky gods" (ibid., 204). Kravchenko suggests that the Tsar Maiden represents the earth goddess as well, but that she has managed to retain more glory and beauty.

Joanna Hubbs also discusses Baba Yaga as an aspect of a great mother goddess, whose dual nature as genetrix and cannibal witch reflects a "fundamental paradox of nature" (Hubbs 1988: 47). Hubbs interprets the "tales of initiation" (such as AT 327C/F and 480) in psychological terms.

Richarda Becker interprets Baba Yaga as a female initiator. Her study follows Propp, but investigates the East Slavic folktale for traces of female initiation (Becker 1990). Baba Yaga is a mother goddess who initiates young women, and in the tales of female initiation her destructive aspect is emphasized. She is related to mother goddess cults dating as far back as the Paleolithic. The ambivalence of the mother goddess reflects the cyclical rebirth and death of nature. She is often associated with the moon and the earth.

Becker presumes that the original unity of the mother goddess was divided into positive and negative figures, and as a positive counterpart to Yaga she finds the *zolotaia baba* (golden old woman), an object of worship mentioned in some medieval chronicles and also by Makarov. According to Becker, other researchers have neglected the dual nature of the mother goddess and her ritual context in arguing for the later origin of Yaga's negative aspect. For Becker, the true Baba Yaga is found in the tale of The Kind and the Unkind Girls (AT 480): "Yaga appears only in tale types 480A, E and F, the other tale types contain transformations of this figure" (Becker 1990: 120). Only in this tale type is the ambiguous nature of Baba Yaga made clear, when she rewards the good girl and punishes the bad one. The cannibal ogress and child kidnapper develops when the content of the ritual has been forgotten, and so this purely negative aspect is really a distortion.

Becker also finds in Yaga a guardian of the realm of the dead, a mistress of animals, an association with natural forces, with fate (through spinning and weaving), and with the hearth and ancestors. The specifically mentioned chicken legs may indicate a fertility cult. Her animal features (such as the bony leg) are still visible and underscore her archaic character. Like other scholars, Becker sees Yaga derived etymologically and mythologically from the snake. She was probably preceded by an animal initiator, and the tales in which a wicked stepmother sends her stepdaughter to Baba Yaga represent a later development. The stepmother is a profane figure who draws attention away from the original theme of initiation (ibid., 110–151).

By investigating female initiation, Becker supplements Propp in an important way, but she gives her argument a circular character by limiting the tales she analyzes to those which suggest an initiation structure and which guarantee this conclusion. Very importantly, we can ask why *one* particular tale type, AT 480, although it is very popular and has been frequently recorded (in fact, with 48 texts, the single most popular tale type in our sample), should be the only defining one for Baba Yaga's identity, when in fact Baba Yaga appears in approximately seventy-five different tale types. Becker defines Baba Yaga as an ambivalent or ambiguous character because she both rewards and punishes in AT 480. On the other hand, in terms of imparting cultural values, we can say that Baba Yaga is being perfectly consistent—she is rewarding good qualities (the kind girl's generosity, patience, and diligence) and punishing bad ones (the unkind girl's laziness and stinginess).

Structuralist Studies

The "flesh and blood" folktale characters who fill the tale roles occupy a secondary place in most structuralist studies of the folktale. Aleksandr Nikiforov observed that "the concrete folktale characters are not a stable entity. They are infinitely changeable from one version to another. Only a character's function is constant, his dynamic role in the folktale. For example, the dragon or Yaga often appear as the hero's enemy, but they also appear as the hero's friend" (1928: 176). For Vladimir Propp, the intentions of a folktale character are unimportant. Only the real action counts. Propp uses Baba Yaga to illustrate this point (in the English translation Yaga was rendered as "witch"):

> Yaga (or any other inhabitant of the forest hut), who fights with Ivan and then runs away and so shows Ivan the way to the other world, also demands special consideration. Showing the way is a function of the helper, and therefore Yaga here plays the role of an unwilling helper (and even "directly against her will"). She begins as a hostile donor, and then becomes an unwilling helper...Yaga, abducting a boy, putting him in her oven, then robbed by the boy (her magic kerchief is seized), combines the functions of villain and (unwilling, hostile) donor. We are thus again confronted with the phenomenon that the characters' will and their intentions cannot be considered an essential characteristic in defining them. What is important is not what they want to do, not the feelings with which they are suffused, but their actions as such, evaluated and defined from the point of view of their meaning for the hero and for the sequence of events. (Propp 1969: 73–74)[12]

Not surprisingly, both Nikiforov and Propp chose Baba Yaga as an example of how folktale characters are distinct from tale roles. The problem of the tale roles and their relation to the actual characters is also addressed by Meletinskii and his colleagues (1969). Influenced by the work of Claude Lévi-Strauss, they emphasize the importance of mediation in the folktale. The mediation of the nature/culture or human/nonhuman opposition is particularly important for understanding Baba Yaga. This opposition is mediated by heroes who combine human and supernatural features (such as Ivan the Bull's or Cow's Son), by supernatural helpers, by supernatural spouses, but most importantly by the fact that the human hero is always in close contact with supernatural elements. This accounts for the appearance of ambiguous figures such as Baba Yaga or the Sea King (Meletinskii et al. 1969: 107).

Another more detailed structural study of the Russian panoply of folktale characters has been provided by Elena Novik (1975), who looks for the invariant forms of folktale characters and the mechanisms by which those forms are generated. She argues that classification by the tale roles is problematic, since the functions are defined in relation to the hero. The characters can be described as bundles of characteristic features, some constant and some changing, and one goal of analysis is to determine the rules of combination. Since people, animals, and objects in the fairy tale can themselves act, serve as a background, or simply demonstrate a feature of an acting

---

[12] For a thoughtful criticism of Propp's notion of the hostile or unwilling donor and the nature of the "gift," see Bremond and Verrier 1982: 74; the concept of hostile donor is discussed in more detail in chapter 5.

character, Novik considers only those semantic features of folktale characters which contribute to the unfolding of the folktale plot. Novik isolates four significant areas in which a character's status is defined in terms of binary oppositions—individual status, familial status, class status, and localization. Oppositions in the area of individual status include natural/supernatural, anthropomorphic/non-anthropomorphic, male/female, and young/old. Baba Yaga is supernatural, anthropomorphic, female, and old. Novik interprets her as a female counterpart to Morozko (a masculine personification of Frost) on the basis of these features, and indeed, Baba Yaga and Morozko both function as testers in Russian versions of AT 480 (Novik 1975: 223).[13] In terms of familial status, Novik finds that virtually all folktale characters (even supernatural ones) belong to some kinship group. She distinguishes two essential generations in the fairy tale—parents and children (a view shared by Bengt Holbek). Although grandparents and grandchildren do occur, they do not give rise to essential conflicts. Baba Yaga sometimes imitates the hero's mother's voice (AT 327C), while at other times she is the hero's mother-in-law. In AT 327C/F she also has her own daughters. Baba Yaga belongs to the older parent generation. In terms of class status, Baba Yaga's identity is not definable by the oppositions high/low or rich/poor, but the opposition master/servant (which is especially operative in the tsar's sphere of action) can be applied to her when she appears as the mistress of birds, animals and fish (as in Afanas'ev 212, AT 465A).[14] In terms of localization, she is a character found in the forest.

All the semantic characteristics of the folktale characters are significant in their relation to the hero and his movement. "If *Baba Yaga* acts as an abductor of children in some folktales and as a donor in others, then this completely depends on her status in relation to the hero: in the first case she is 'foreign', in the second she turns out to have 'kinship' ties to the hero (*Yaga the mother-in-law*) or is a 'borderline' character, giving the hero temporary refuge" (ibid., 245–246). Novik's insight into Baba Yaga's status (as a member of the older parent generation) and contrasting behavior (as a "foreign" character, or a relative of the hero) is interesting and worth keeping in mind as we survey the folktales in which Baba Yaga appears. A study of the relationship between characters and tale roles in a ballad repertoire has produced interesting results (Buchan 1982), and a similar consideration of the corpus of Baba Yaga tales seems worthwhile.

---

[13] However, their overall distribution in East Slavic fairy tales is not similar. Baba Yaga appears much more frequently and in many more tale types than Morozko.

[14] Here Novik has made the same oversight as Propp. In Afanas'ev 212 the old woman donor who summons animals is the hero's mother-in-law, while Baba Yaga is a villain advisor who thinks of deadly tasks the king then assigns to the hero.

Psychological Approaches

It is obvious that folktale characters such as Baba Yaga have a strong emotional content and coloring, which helps to explain their enduring popularity. For this reason it is important to consider as well those interpretations of Baba Yaga which incorporate psychology, or recognize the element of creative fantasy in folktales. Baba Yaga has caught the attention of both Freudians and Jungians.

Géza Róheim (1947) notes Baba Yaga's association with death, but identifies as most significant two of her features which are also found in some Hungarian, Romanian, Serbian, and German parallel figures: a connection with a revolving dwelling, and a peculiar nose, tooth, or foot. In psychoanalytic terms, the nose, tooth, or foot are all potential phallic symbols. Róheim finds that folktales with the revolving hut are centered on the "primal scene," the child's witnessing of parental coitus. The house (Róheim points out that Baba Yaga is almost identical with her house in that she stretches out from one corner to the other, her nose poking into the ceiling) can be read as a female symbol, and so the hut which turns about on chicken (or other animal) legs represents heterosexual coitus. Baba Yaga herself, with the distinctive leg, represents the phallic mother, or an "abbreviated image representation of the primal scene" (Róheim 1947: 83). In an analysis of the famous tale "Hansel and Gretel" (Grimm 15), Róheim adduces a Russian version of 327C from Ralston's translation, in which the villain is a witch (in other Russian versions of this tale type the villain is sometimes Baba Yaga and sometimes a witch). Róheim wishes to show that folktales are derived from dreams, and interprets this folktale as the dream of a hungry child. The cannibalistic ogress is a projective inversion of the child's own aggressive hunger: "A hungry child wants to eat its mother. In reverse, the mother is a cannibal who wants to eat the child" (Róheim 1953: 92).

Another Freudian view of Baba Yaga is provided by Olga Periañez-Chaverneff (1983). She points out the importance of folktales for children, and finds that they are centered on the mother-child relationship. The folktale gives the child a codified and ritualized way of integrating experience, especially pre-verbal experience. While a morphological analysis reveals the repetition at the heart of the folktale, an ethnopsychiatric approach can show its diversity, how it assists in the structuring of sociocultural elements by the unconscious mind. Important for Periañez-Chaverneff is the concept of the ethnic unconscious of an individual, "that part of his total unconscious which he possesses in common with the majority of the members of his culture. It is made up of everything which, in agreement with the fundamental demands of his culture, each generation learns to repress in its unconscious, and then in turn forces the next generation to repress" (Periañez-Chaverneff 1983: 186). She recognizes three types of Baba Yaga (ogress, beneficent, and versatile) and finds that the appearance of the types depends on the age of the hero. The ogress Yaga appears when the hero is a young child. These tales reflect a dominant concern with oral aggression, and the only part of Yaga's body described is her face. The customs of ritually "baking" a child among the East Slavs (see discussion in chapter 3), as well as swaddling, could contribute to the formation of aggressive fantasies directed against the mother, and Baba Yaga could serve as a culturally acceptable outlet for these hostilities. The small number of tales in which Baba Yaga is versatile, when she appears threatening but does not harm the hero, and in which the hero must pasture her herd, reflect the socialization of the young child. Tales with a beneficent Yaga always portray an adolescent hero, who is reaching adulthood and demands hospitality from her. Unfortunately, Periañez-Chaverneff does not identify these tales with type numbers (she discusses AT 327C and 302 among others), but her identification of correspondences between the age of the hero(ine) and the type of Baba Yaga she or he encounters certainly deserves closer scrutiny. It suggests another important classification of tales (child vs. adult protagonists) which might help explain the different aspects of Baba Yaga's image. Periañez-Chaverneff's short article points out a rich avenue of investigation—the relationship of the fantasy figure Baba Yaga to the mother-child relationship in traditional East Slavic culture.

The Jungian analyst Marie-Louise von Franz has also shown interest in Baba Yaga. In her work on the feminine in fairy tales, she analyzes Afanas'ev 104, "Vasilisa the Beautiful." She identifies Baba Yaga as an archaic manifestation of the Great Mother archetype who contains both good and bad (Franz 1993: 172, see discussion below). Sibylle Birkhäuser-Oeri discusses Baba Yaga and the witch in AT 327C/F (1988).

Still another psychological interpretation of Baba Yaga has been provided by Caroline Scielzo (1983). While she considers the snake origin and the association with death to be important for understanding Yaga, she considers versions of AT 480 from the Afanas'ev collection in terms of a young woman's maturation and psychic integration in which Oedipal conflict and sibling rivalry are worked out. She sees the heroine's entry into the forest as an entry into the subconscious. Scielzo also understands the tale "Vasilisa the Beautiful" as the integration of the young woman's fragmented self, in which the various female characters (the dying mother, the doll, Baba Yaga, and the old woman) represent different aspects of the heroine herself (Scielzo 1983: 174–175).

Daniel Rancour-Laferriere interprets Baba Yaga as one of a number of mother representations in his study of Russian masochism. While most of these representations are positively valued, scholars have ignored the "widespread hostile, even sadistic attitudes toward the maternal image in Russian culture" (Rancour-Laferriere 1995: 140). This hostility is based on (probably unconscious) memories of the mother's control and omnipotence in childhood. Tales like AT 327C/F, in which the hero pushes Baba Yaga into an oven, serve as an outlet for these strong negative emotions Russians feel about their mothers (ibid., 130).

Russian folklorists themselves have so far not attempted psychological interpretations of Baba Yaga. This might seem surprising in light of the Russian literary heritage, but is probably best explained by the mandatory materialist Marxist orientation demanded of humanities scholarship in the Soviet period. Nevertheless, Russian folklorists are clearly aware of the psychological dimensions of folklore. Viktor Gusev defines the folktale as a "reflection of certain essential collisions and conflicts in the sphere of social and family relations which could not be resolved in concrete historical reality, and which therefore acquired the character of fantastic fiction." This implies that the tale is a kind of wish fulfillment, resolving conflicts through fantasy (Gusev 1967: 124–125).

A study of Russian children's folklore, specifically children's own horror stories (Grechina and Osorina 1981) takes a specifically psychological approach. This short and straightforward prose genre (the horror story, *strashilka*) is of interest to us because it shows the influence of the traditional folktale. Usually a frightening event occurs when parents leave children alone at home, or misfortune is the result of breaking an interdiction. While the authors collected these tales from children between six and fifteen years of age, they found that the texts reflect the logic and cognition of very young children (ages three–five). O. N. Grechina and M. V. Osorina find that the horror story is a means for children to overcome their fears about the world outside their family circle. They discuss one particularly interesting type of horror story, about a mother or grandmother who dies and asks not to be buried, but to be put under a bed, and who turns out to be a witch (in one version the mother brings about her daughter's death, ibid., 105). The authors feel that this type of horror story might reflect traditional Slavic folk beliefs about the unburied dead, but unfortunately do not offer any speculation regarding the possible psychological meaning of this tale for the girls who tell it.

What can be drawn from these psychological/psychoanalytic interpretations of Baba Yaga is her identity as a mother figure, distorted by the fantastic imagery of the folktale. What remains to be explained are the particular fantastic attributes of Baba Yaga and her behavior in specific instances. The identification of Baba Yaga as a mother figure is a valuable insight, one which explains the importance of Baba Yaga in the folktale tradition and the emotional value she has there.

There is a qualitative difference between Freudian and Jungian approaches. For Freudian interpretation, the individual's infantile and early childhood experience accounts for the perception of the mother found in cultural projections such as the folktale. From the Jungian point of view, Baba Yaga is an emanation of the Great Mother archetype. This archetype belongs to the collective unconscious, something which all human beings share, and the individual's particular experience is not as significant. According to Erich Neumann, the child "first experiences in his mother the archetype of the Great Mother, that is, the reality of an all-powerful numinous woman, on whom he is dependent in all things, and not the objective reality of his personal mother, this particular historical woman which his mother becomes for him later when his ego and consciousness are more developed" (1955: 15).

For Marie-Louise von Franz, Baba Yaga is an aspect of the Great Mother archetype. In Christian culture, positive aspects of the Great Mother have been assimilated by the Virgin Mary, while other aspects must be sought in folklore. Baba Yaga is

...the archetypal witch in all Russian fairy tales. She is the great magician who can turn herself into a well or a paradisiacal garden in which the hero is torn to pieces "to the size of poppy seeds," or she turns into a gigantic sow that kills the hero. In our story she is not completely evil, though when she hears that the girl is a "blessed daughter" she tells her she does not want her in her house. In a hidden way, she is not thoroughly evil, and sometimes even helpful; she wonderfully portrays the Great Mother in her double aspect.

There is a Russian story of the Maiden Tsar, in which the Baba Yaga lives in a rotating little round house standing on chicken feet, and you have to say a magic word before you can enter. The Tsar's son goes in and finds her scratching among the ashes with her long nose. She combs her hair with her claws and watches the geese with her eyes, and she asks the hero, "My dear little child, are you here by your own free will or by compulsion?"

One of the great tricks of the mother complex in a man is always to implant doubt in his mind, suggesting that it might be better to do the other thing; and then the man is lamed. But the hero in the story says, "Grandmother, you should not ask such questions of a hero! Give me something to eat, and if you don't...!" Whereupon the Baba Yaga goes and cooks him a marvelous dinner and gives him good advice, and it works! So it depends on the hero's attitude. She tries to make him infantile, but when she sees he is up to her, she helps him.

So the Baba Yaga can be good or bad. Just as the male image of the Godhead has usually a dark side, like the devil, so the image of the feminine Godhead, which in female psychology would be the image of the Self, has both a light and dark side. Usually in Catholic countries the light side is personified in the Virgin Mary. She represents the light side of the Great Mother, of the man's anima, and of the woman's Self but lacks the shadow. The Baba Yaga would represent a more archaic similar figure in which the positive and negative are mixed. She is full of the powers of destruction, of desolation, and of chaos, but at the same time is a helpful figure. Viewed historically, she probably represents the surviving image of the late antique Greek Hekate, the queen of the underworld.... Russian fairy tales have been deeply influenced from the south by the late Greek civilization, and thus we have in Baba Yaga and Vasilisa really a survival of the great cosmic goddesses Hekate and Persephone. The divine rank of the Baba Yaga is clearly proved by the fact that she has three riders at her disposition—"my day," "my night," and "my sun." So she is a cosmic Godhead. (Franz 1993: 172–174)

But we are still faced with the problem of explaining Baba Yaga's uniqueness. If the objective reality of the personal mother is not significant in infancy and early childhood, and the East Slavs share the same Great Mother archetype with western Europeans, why does their folklore tradition contain this ambiguous character, a kind of mother representation not found in western Europe? Franz implies that Baba Yaga is a more archaic mother representation than those found in western Europe, such as the Virgin Mary. Why do the East Slavs possess a more archaic figure? Franz suggests a historical influence from Greece, which is questionable. Even if Baba Yaga were the result of such an influence (or any of the other historical sources that have been suggested for her), there must be a reason, specific to the East Slavic culture, for the continued survival of a more archaic figure. For this reason, it might be more helpful to look at Baba Yaga not as more or less archaic than other mother representations, but simply as qualitatively different. Perianez-Chaverneff's concept of an ethnic unconscious, particular to a specific group and derived from the culturally specific objective reality, is perhaps more suited to an investigation of Baba Yaga's unique features. Franz's specific observations about the interaction of the donor Baba Yaga with a male hero are perceptive, and may be useful in making sense of this unique donor episode.

Marxist Approaches

Most twentieth-century Russian and Soviet interpretations of Baba Yaga have been influenced, intentionally or not, by Soviet Marxist ideology. Baba Yaga is seen by most as an archaic figure and she is interpreted with reference to a cultural evolutionist scheme. Jack Zipes interpets an analogous figure, the famous witch from the Grimms' tale "Hansel and Gretel," in terms of class struggle. According to Zipes, the "witch (as parasite) could be interpreted here to symbolize the entire feudal system or the greed and brutality of the aristocracy, responsible for the difficult conditions. The killing of the witch is symbolically the realization of the hatred which the peasantry felt for the aristocracy as hoarders and oppressors" (Zipes 1979: 32).

A similar interpretation for Baba Yaga has been suggested by Nikolai Novikov, although he recognizes that her image is complex and that a satirical treatment of her as a tyrannical oppressor occurs only in certain tales. These are the tales in which a wicked stepmother sends the heroine to work for Baba Yaga or to get something from her (AT 480). Baba Yaga gives the heroine back-breaking work and threatens her with death (Novikov 1957: 49–50). Especially in regard to her own servants, Baba Yaga behaves as an exploiter (Novikov 1974: 175).

Nevertheless, the concept of Baba Yaga as a class enemy cannot account for all aspects of her character, and, in light of the larger Russian folktale repertoire, an interpretation of Baba Yaga only as an oppressor of the peasants who told tales about her is questionable. There are many Russian folktales in which the peasant narrator very clearly expresses his or her hatred for the immediate oppressors. A subgenre, referred to as the "satirical tale" (*satiricheskaia skazka*), often presents a confrontation of a clever peasant with a stupid, greedy, or lecherous landowner or priest (Sokolov 1931, 1932). Although these tales frequently involve unlikely or impossible events which exaggerate the negative qualities of the master or clergy, they express class antagonism quite openly, with no need for disguise or symbolism.

A Descriptive Approach

Perhaps the most thorough examination so far of the features and behavior of Baba Yaga as she actually appears in folktales has been carried out by Nikolai V. Novikov in his book on the figures of the East Slavic fairy tale (*Obrazy vostochnoslavianskoi volshebnoi skazki*, Leningrad 1974). Novikov's treatment is largely descriptive, but considerably more accurate than most others in encompassing a large number of tale types and versions. Novikov identifies tales with tale-type numbers and provides references for them, making his study especially useful. He treats the positive and negative aspects of Baba Yaga in two different sections of his book. In the consideration of the positive Yaga (who gives advice, magic objects, or valuable gifts), Novikov enumerates the most typical features of Baba Yaga: her dwelling and its location, the hero's arrival, the request that the hut turn around, the way she lies inside and fills her hut, smelling the "Russian scent" and potentially threatening to eat the hero, her questions about his goal, the hero's reproach and demand for hospitality, Baba Yaga's compliance, the frequent appearance of three Baba Yaga sisters, and the various magic objects or gifts she gives the hero. The role of the positive Baba Yaga is limited to the act of giving advice or an object (Propp's donor sequence). With the exception of the Baba Yaga who detains the warrior maiden in her pursuit of the hero in AT 551 (The Sons on a Quest for a

Wonderful Remedy for Their Father), the positive Baba Yaga then disappears from the tale (Novikov 1974: 133–146).

Novikov identifies no fewer than six types of negative Yaga: warrior, avenger, possessor of magic objects, evil enchantress, crafty well-wisher or evil advisor, and abductor of children (ibid., 159–175). In his survey of tales, Novikov finds that the negative Baba Yaga dominates—her positive aspect appears in only about one third of the tale texts.[15] The traditional image of Baba Yaga and her attributes is best maintained in the positive tales, while Baba Yaga takes over the roles of other folktale villains in the negative tales (ibid., 175). Novikov believes it is possible to interpret her image as a reflection of hostile forces of nature and society, although he does not state specifically which forces she represents. No other folktale character embodies so many human vices: "falsehood, envy, cunning (and with it stupidity), stinginess, cruelty, treachery and perfidy" (ibid., 176), and cannibalistic traits appear even in tales where she is the donor. The folk conception of Baba Yaga as a negative figure is reflected in the use of her name as a term of reproach and abuse.

Novikov emphasizes the need for bringing all features of Baba Yaga's character into consideration. Of the two aspects, the good Yaga is the more archaic. The benevolent Baba Yaga has her origin in a matriarchal period (she is a relative of the hero's mother, wife or bride; she guards the realm of the Tsar Maiden), while her malevolent counterpart arose during a period of struggle between matriarchy and patriarchy, which ended with the establishment of the latter.

Conclusion

After this excursion into the realm of Baba Yaga scholarship, it becomes clear that she is indeed a many-faceted figure, capable of inspiring researchers to see her as a Cloud, Moon, Death, Winter, Snake, Bird, Pelican or Earth Goddess, totemic matriarchal ancestress, female initiator, phallic mother, or archetypal image. Even the assumption of her female identity has been brought into question. All the studies discussed above raise fascinating points, but many suffer from an incomplete consideration of Baba Yaga's image and its actual diversity, as manifested in folktales.

Most studies devoted to Baba Yaga are oriented toward the past. They attempt to discover or reconstruct her origin and explain her image through this origin and subsequent history. Baba Yaga is documented in East Slavic folklore since the eighteenth century, and, given the parallel figures found in

---

[15] This conclusion is supported by the current sample. In 422 tales, Baba Yaga appears as a donor in 109 tales (26 percent), a villain in 235 tales (56 percent), and ambiguously (this includes her appearance as a very hostile donor) in 78 tales (18 percent).

other folklore traditions (especially the West Slavic Ježibaba), it seems reasonable to assume that she dates back to the medieval period, and perhaps even further back in the Slavic past (other indirect evidence for her age is presented in chapters 2 and 3). It seems possible that she *might* have her origins in Slavic religious beliefs and practices (perhaps as a figure of folk demonology, the so-called "lower mythology") which existed prior to the Slavs' conversion to Christianity. In the minds of some tale-tellers and listeners she was akin to evil spirits and witches in whose existence the East Slavs believed (discussed in chapter 2). Obviously Baba Yaga is the product of a lengthy historical development, but unfortunately this history is lost to us.

An important objection to interpretations based only on history or past customs is the fact that, during the time the folktale was recorded, it was surely to a large extent a fantasy creation recognized as fiction, and enjoyed as entertainment. Because of the important role of imagination and fantasy in fairy tales, little or nothing of them necessarily reflects an earlier reality. Fairy tales, and their motifs and imagery, certainly have a history. It is not impossible that a motif such as the ogre's heart (or Koshchei's death) in the egg (in AT 302) could derive from beliefs about a separable soul (Röhrich 1991: 66–67), or that belief in the afterlife or reincarnation accounts for the appearance in fairy tales of dead parents in human or animal form who help their children (Ivanova 1979). The "difficult tasks" that the hero or heroine must accomplish in one night have a parallel in some Slavic rituals (see chapter 3). But even if we could trace the historical origin of a motif, this is not an explanation of its meaning, or why it has entered the folktale. What seems to be important for the fairy-tale tradition is the function that a motif fulfills within the narrative—it is likely that motifs which entered the fairy tale from the "real world" were soon transformed and adapted to the poetic requirements of this narrative genre. Likewise, even if we knew when and how Baba Yaga originated, this would not necessarily have any bearing on her meaning for storytellers and audiences.

Convincing arguments about Baba Yaga cannot be made *ex nihilo*. A great deal of speculation has arisen from her name alone, when in fact the name of a folktale character might be incidental, derived from a foreign language, and might not provide any clue to the character's origin or to the meaning this character bears in its culture. Lacking the necessary documentary evidence, we cannot say with certainty that one aspect of Baba Yaga is necessarily older and therefore more authentic or genuine than another (as Propp, Novikov, Becker, and others suggest), and it seems futile to compare Baba Yaga to parallel figures from other folklore traditions in order to judge her more or less "archaic," based only on appearance and behavior. Toporov and Becker are correct in recognizing the importance of Baba Yaga's role in AT 327 and AT 480, but we cannot conclude that the Baba Yaga in either of these tales is necessarily older, or somehow a more genuine or essential Baba Yaga. Instead, Toporov's insight that Baba Yaga is a single cultural text can lead us to construct a synchronic typology of Baba Yaga, one based on objective criteria and a large sample of tale texts. Promising beginnings of such an effort have already been made by Novikov and Periañez-Chaverneff. Although contradictory, all of Baba Yaga's consistent traits form a whole entity, and are equally significant for the culture in which she circulates and which she represents. For the period of the folktale recordings, Baba Yaga is both beneficent and wicked; her ambiguity is a defining characteristic, accepted by the "folk censorship."

If Baba Yaga functions as a mother representation peculiar to the East Slavs, certain of her features in can be understood in light of the actual mother-child relationship in that culture. Baba Yaga's identity as a symbolic mother would explain her popularity and longevity, her obvious importance in East Slavic collective cultural memory, and the fact that analogous figures are found in so many other parts of the world. Novikov points out that Baba Yaga is a representation of many negative human qualities, and in fact more of these traits are found in her than in any other East Slavic folktale character. Naturally this raises a further question: Why has the East Slavic tradition chosen to represent these qualities in precisely this form and not another? A synchronic analysis, searching for potential symbolic meaning in Baba Yaga is perhaps as difficult as trying to explain her through long-forgotten archaic beliefs and customs (we are looking for meanings which the storytellers and their audiences might not have been aware of), but it might well repay our efforts.

The complexity of Baba Yaga and other folktale characters derives in part from the fact that they are, on the one hand, the products of tradition, of collective history and psychology, a collective fantasy; on the other hand, they provide material for the fantasies of individuals. It is clear that there can be no single correct interpretation or understanding of Baba Yaga. Potentially she can have a multiplicity of meanings for every individual tale-teller and listener. The performance of folklore (in this case, tales about Baba Yaga) involves a complex interaction and a form of compromise between individual (performer as well as audience) and tradition. Folklore provides a means of expression for people, but may also function as a kind of social control. Folklore is a form of expressive culture which, as J. L. Fischer states, "is characterized by the fact that its main immediate empirical effect is the expression and manipulation of the emotions of the participants" (1963: 236). The folktales in which Baba Yaga appears can express the particular worldview of a culture, serve as an outlet for taboo and therefore repressed negative emotions, reinforce a dominant ideology or norms of behavior among the culture's members, and in more subtle ways reproduce the culture's unconscious attitudes—and, of course, they are entertaining. For these reasons, an eclectic approach to understanding this complex and rich image seems necessary.

CHAPTER TWO
The Witch at Home and Abroad

Baba Yaga appears in a number of different folklore genres, but her true home is the folktale (*skazka*), and specifically that significant subgenre of folktales which lacks a precise designation, and is usually identified by its marvelous, fantastic elements. In English it is referred to as the fairy tale or wondertale, and in Russian as the "magic tale" (*volshebnaia skazka*). The Aarne-Thompson index distinguishes these fairy tales or "tales of magic" (AT 300–749) from animal tales, religious stories, romantic tales (novelle), tales about stupid ogres, and jokes and anecdotes.

Folktales are a complex creation; while they might seem naïve, straightforward, or simple at first, a closer examination reveals a rich variety of potential meanings and messages. Geneviève Calame-Griaule observes that folktales "say much more than they appear to" (1987: 8). On the surface some tales might have a didactic function, but at a deeper level, folktales address serious questions which all human societies ask themselves, without always being aware that they do so. Folktales provide an "answer" to the problems of family relationships, generational conflict, the temptation of incest, relationships between the sexes, and between individuals and the group. These answers are given in symbolic form, in the language of images (ibid., 10–11). The amazing persistence of certain folktale plots (tale types) and images (motifs) across time and space is due to the universal nature of the problems or questions addressed.

In the guise of entertaining stories, the Indo-European fairy tale reflects concerns with the human condition: life and death, sexual initiation, and old age (Belmont 1999: 211–212); the hero and heroine's journeys to and from the "other realm" are a denial of the irreversibility of real time and the inevitability of death. The passage of time is expressed in spatial terms as a journey to a symbolic "other world" or land of death. Unlike human beings, whose life journey proceeds in one direction only, the fairy tale heroine or hero can return from the other realm, reflecting the human desire to control time. This denial of time and death is the essential latent mythic content of the fairy tale.

Many authors identify the folktale essentially as fiction (Arnaudov 1969 ii: 8–9, Lüthi 1960: 79, Propp 1976: 47). Unlike myth and legend, in which storytellers and audiences believe, folktales "are not considered as dogma or history, they may or may not have happened…. Folktales may be set in any time and any place, and in this sense they are almost timeless and placeless" (Bascom 1965: 4). Humorous formulaic phrases that often begin and end East

Slavic folktales suggest that the folktale, and especially the fairy tale, is speech set apart from everyday life, and not true. One storyteller concludes by saying, "That's the whole tale, and I can't lie any more" (*Vot i skazka vsia da bol'she vrat' nel'zia*, Razumova and Sen'kina 1974 no. 69). Another narrator commented, at the end of a tale, "Well, I think this is all chatter. All of this really couldn't happen like that" (Chernyshev 63).

Statements by other East Slavic storytellers contradict this. According to V. P. Monachkova, the Frog Princess tale recorded from her in 1979 (AT 402, Leonova 17) took place "during the reign of Nikolai Nikolaevich." Another storyteller, Agaf'ia L. Zaitseva, maintained that everything could have happened in the old days. "Why would the old people lie to us? What would they have to gain by it? There were dragons, and knights, and sorcerers. And I've seen witches myself" (Tumilevich 1958: 226, Novikov 1974: 20). Storytellers might not always draw a sharp line between truth and fiction in their narratives, and Nikolai Novikov suggests that the acceptance of the folktale as fiction became more widespread toward the end of the nineteenth century (1974: 16–22). Dmitrii Zelenin also reports that tellers could not always make a clear distinction between truth and invention in the folktale, but most often believed in what they narrated. People believed in supernatural beings such as Baba Yaga, who appear in the tales together with Orthodox saints, whose existence was beyond doubt (Zelenin 1914: xlii–xliv; 1934: 232).

In arguing for the fictional status of the fairy tale, other scholars point to its distinctive structure and form, and its artistic elaboration. S. N. Azbelev finds that legends, based on fact, possess fewer artistic elements than the folktale, which requires a correct performance of its conventional form in order to have its purely aesthetic effect on the listener. For this reason the folktale is usually told only by a relatively small number of skilled narrators (Azbelev 1965). The consistent conventional structure of the folktale lets listeners know immediately that this narrative does not reproduce reality, but instead conforms to a generic category of narratives (Simonsen 1984: 58). For Aleksandr Nikiforov, folktales circulate for the purpose of entertainment; they contain unusual events and "are distinguished by a special compositional-stylistic construction" (Nikiforov 1934: 7).

R. M. Volkov made what was perhaps the first attempt at a formalistic analysis of the folktale in 1924. Aleksandr Nikiforov wrote a short article on this subject in 1926 which was published two years later, making several fundamental points which Vladimir Propp incorporated into his well-known *Morphology of the Folktale.* Propp's exposition of one basic sequence of tale actions (functions) explains the underlying stability and predictability of the Indo-European fairy tale beneath its colorful and variegated surface. Narrators and listeners are themselves probably aware of this "grammar" of fairy tales, even if they are not able to articulate it. In comparing the societal structure and worldview of the Nahuat people (Puebla, Mexico) with their traditional narratives, James Taggart observes that "I suspect that the Nahuat know a bad narrative, just as they know an ungrammatical utterance" (1977: 281).

Propp's *Morphology* has stimulated much debate. Critics have pointed out that the functions often appear in an order quite different from that presented in the *Morphology*, that certain fairy tale events are not well described by any of the functions and thus suggest a need for new functions, that the real number of functions is smaller, that Propp did not adhere strictly to the texts from the Afanas'ev collection upon which his morphology is based, and that his contention that all tale types are derived from one type (the Dragon Slayer, AT 300) is erroneous and impossible (Lévi-Strauss 1960, Pentikäinen and Apo 1978, Bremond and Verrier 1982). Propp's claim may have been overly ambitious, in that a single structural pattern cannot describe every Indo-European fairy tale (Apo 1990).[1]

Meletinskii, Segal, Novik, and Nekliudov proposed significant modifications to Propp's scheme in 1969. The folktale is derived from myth, but differs from myth in that its goal is the acquisition of individual values (the ultimate folktale value is marriage), while values acquired in the myth are collective. Two or three tests make up the tale sequence: a preliminary test (the donor sequence), a fundamental test, and sometimes a third additional test, most often involving recognition of the hero. The preliminary test shows that the hero's behavior and attitudes correspond to desirable norms; paradoxically, this preliminary test reveals his character more than the fundamental test, since the hero's feat is achieved with the help of a magic object or helper. Thus the "tale as a whole appears as a kind of three-step hierarchical compositional structure" (Meletinskii et al. 1969: 91).

The discovery of the fairy-tale morphology led Propp to search for its origin, which he ascribed to initiation ritual (1946). Many Russian and Soviet scholars have been influenced by his ideas, explaining the folktale in terms of initiation ritual, or other social institutions and customs of past ages. Iu. I. Iudin (1984) detects a ritual background not only in the fairy tale, but also in animal tales and humorous and anecdotal tales. Where initiation ritual does not exist (such as among indigenous Siberian peoples), P. A. Troiakov (1969, 1977) suggests that other rituals and customs (incantations or dramatic actions performed to ensure success in hunting, and addressed to animals, a totem animal, or the spirit masters of nature) account for the form and content of folktales. The

---

[1] A very stimulating argument for the unity of Indo-European fairy tales, including Proppian and Lévi-Straussian approaches, is presented by Francisco Vaz da Silva (2002).

humorous opening and closing phrases of the fairy tale, independent of the tale itself, might originally have had a magic function; in the closing formula, the storyteller's request for a reward for his or her performance (usually food or drink) recalls similar requests made by singers of Christmas carols (*koliadki*), songs which originally had a magic function (Gerasimova 1978: 24, 26).

Dmitrii Zelenin suggests that folktales were originally a kind of magic, told to entertain and distract forest spirits, so that hunters would be rewarded with game. In certain parts of Russia and Ukraine, telling tales or riddles is prohibited in summer, when sheep bear their young, which Zelenin interprets as the desire to keep potentially harmful spirits away from domesticated animals (Zelenin 1934: 217). The typical locale of tale performance (in the forest, while resting from woodcutting or hunting), performance time (evening or night), special status of an acknowledged teller (one was considered a sorcerer by his fellow villagers), as well as gender (in the past most tale-tellers were apparently men), all suggest that the Russian folktale in Karelia once served a ritual hunting function, now forgotten (Sen'kina 1988: 40–51). Tat'iana Sen'kina also considers that the preference for tale-telling in winter probably reflects a forgotten ritual practice (ibid., 59), although for the peasantry winter was also the season when work was less urgent and time-consuming, and when there was more leisure time for entertainment. According to a storyteller from the Tavda region, if one tells tales during the day a cow will get lost in the forest, or a magpie will poke one's eye out. Although the informant presented this information in a joking manner, the collectors find this to be an echo of prohibitions on tale-telling in the past (Blazhes and Akhaimova 1976: 78). There is certainly evidence from many parts of the world which suggests that storytelling is restricted to certain times of the day or year because of the magic effects it might have (Sartori 1930).

Eleazar Meletinskii sees the core of the fairy tale as formed by archaic motifs and episodes (such as dragon slaying, the hero's visit to other worlds, or supernatural animal spouses) which reflect an early primitive period, while the "frame" of the fairy tale depicts a social conflict, and the idealization of a socially "low" hero or heroine. The folktale arose at the end of the era of clan society, with the shift to a class society, when it replaced myth (Meletinskii 1958).

The question of the folktale's origin (among the East Slavs and elsewhere) remains open. The art of storytelling must be nearly as old as human language itself, and there is evidence for the existence of a developed oral literature in the Ancient Near East around the beginning of the second millennium B.C.E. (Jason and Kempinski 1981). Some tale types recorded in Europe in the nineteenth and twentieth centuries can be reliably dated to the early medieval period, while others may be even older. AT 313 resembles the ancient Greek legend of Jason and Medea, one written version of which (the *Argonautica* of Apollonius of Rhodes) dates back to the third century B.C.E. (Swahn 1990, Gehrts 1990); William Hansen finds that "the legend in more or less its familiar form was probably in circulation by 700 B.C., and likely long before that" (2002: 155). Hansen concludes that, as a genre, the fictional magic tale or fairy tale was probably circulating at this time, especially among the "poor and uncultured," even if it is largely absent from ancient Greek or Roman literature: "...ancient authors as a rule did not regard purely fictional narratives as meriting literary treatment, whether traditional or original" (ibid., 17). A. I. Zaitsev concludes that the magic tale or fairy tale arose during and not earlier than the first millennium B.C.E., a period which saw the appearance of new religions and changes in human consciousness, when human beings first began to see the world not simply as a given, but as an object which could be accepted, rejected, doubted, or transformed. This new perspective allowed for the development of the fairy tale, which presents an imagined world in opposition to the real one. The Indo-European fairy tale would have first arisen somewhere in the area between the eastern Mediterranean and India (Zaitsev 1984: 76–77). Bengt Holbek cautiously makes a similar suggestion, pointing out that the fairy tale, which includes an important opposition of high and low status, could only have arisen in a stratified society (1987: 603–606).

Our knowledge of the folktale's early history among the East Slavs is very limited. Given the ecclesiastical character of most writing of the Kievan period, it is not surprising that there are no recordings of the secular folktale from this time, although literary documents mention tales and storytellers. The telling of tales is condemned by church officials, such as the twelfth-century priest St. Kirill of Turov, who speaks of the punishments in the next world that await those who tell tales (*ezhe basni baiut*) and play the *gusli* (psaltery) (Propp 1984: 33–34). Petro Lintur concludes that some kind of oral narrative must have existed in the eleventh and twelfth centuries, and that the folktale acquired its present form before the thirteenth century (1994: 5).

Before the seventeenth century, Russian written records refer to an oral tale as *basn'*. The Russian word *skazka* appears to have acquired its modern meaning only in the seventeenth century. Before this time it referred to a document, announcement, statement, declaration, deposition, or testimony which had legal weight (Savchenko 1914: 2, Propp 1984: 34–35). How it came to have an opposite meaning is not clear. Propp suggests that legal documents had become so full of lies as to bring about this semantic shift. Novikov argues that the word *skazka* had its modern meaning in colloquial Russian before this time. He cites common formulaic folktale phrases in which the tale refers to itself as a skazka: *skoro skazka skazyvaetsia da ne skoro delo delaetsia* ("the tale is told quickly, but the deed is not done quickly"), and *ni v skazke skazat', ni perom opisat'* (something can be "neither told in the tale, nor described with the pen"). Novikov notes that these formulas are already present in eighteenth-century tale collections. The widespread distribution of these formulas could not have taken place within a mere century and a half, and so the formulas must have been formed considerably earlier (Novikov 1974: 7–8).

The first known recording of a Russian folktale was made in the sixteenth century by an Italian historian, who took it down from a member of a Russian diplomatic mission to Pope Clement VII (Novikov 1971: 7–10). In the seventeenth century a few Russian folktales were recorded by the Englishman Samuel Collins. True folktale collections first began to appear in the eighteenth century, although the tales were edited with a free hand and mixed genuine folklore with the collector/author's own inventions. The most famous Russian folktale collection is that of Aleksandr Nikolaevich Afanas'ev (*Narodnye russkie skazki*, 1855–1863), but many important collections were compiled later, during the second half of the nineteenth century and in the beginning of the twentieth: Sadovnikov's collection of tales from the Samara region (1884), Onchukov's collection from Arkhangelsk and Olonets provinces (1908), Dmitrii Zelenin's two collections from Perm' and Viatka provinces (1914 and 1915), the Sokolov brothers' collection from the Belozersk region (1915), and the 367 tale texts from the archives of the Russian Geographic Society published by Smirnov in 1917. Thanks to the efforts of these and many other collectors and folklorists, who often worked in difficult conditions with scant resources, we have a very rich source indeed for studying Baba Yaga and her role in the East Slavic folktale.

While the East Slavic folktale flourished primarily as entertainment for the rural peasant and artisan population, folktales were enjoyed among all social classes, including the tsar's family (Kostomarov 1992: 236–237). At one time tales were also customary at feasts and weddings. Tales were told among cooperative work groups in mines, forests, at lakes, and in shipyards, when work activities and rest periods often provided opportunities for storytelling sessions. Tradesmen such as tailors entertained their customers with folktales and cultivated them for this reason. Soldiers frequently knew tales and played an important part in their diffusion. Prisons were also a place where tales were told and learned (Zelenin 1914: xxvii–xxxii). A feature of the Siberian landscape was the presence of a large wandering population of released convicts who were taken in by peasants in exchange for work and telling tales (Azadovskii 1926: 25–35). In the Belozersk region, storytelling also occurred while peasants waited their turn at the mill, and travelling artisans, soldiers, and beggars played a part in their diffusion (Sokolov 1915: lvi). In the second half of the nineteenth century, folklorists became aware of the importance of an individual performer's skill and background. P. N. Rybnikov and A. F. Gil'ferding arranged their collections of Russian folk epic poetry (the *bylina*) by performers and included biographical and other information about them. Information about the performers of folktales began to be published in 1908, with Onchukov's collection. Nevertheless, in this survey of tales about Baba Yaga, we often know little or nothing about the men or women who told the tales.

More tales are recorded from men than women. Zelenin was not able to record tales from any women in Perm' province because it was more difficult for an outsider to gain their trust and because women were less likely to become well known as performers in their own area. Women may have been unwilling to tell tales to collectors (for the most part men), or there may have been a real difference in male and female repertoires, given the broader mobility and social network of men as opposed to women in rural nineteenth-century Russia (Nikiforov 1930: 23–35). On the other hand, many tales have been recorded from outstanding female narrators, such as Natal'ia Vinokurova (Azadovskii 1926, 1938) and Anna Korol'kova (Korol'kova 1969). The question of distinctions between men's and women's storytelling is a very complex one. Although there may be a general tendency for male narrators to prefer male-centered tales, and vice versa, men's and women's repertoires overlap. A folklorist who has examined male and female performances of AT 706, The Maiden without Hands, concludes that this tale "appeals to sensitive persons of both sexes" (Herranen 1990: 108). What might make a particular performance "feminine" is not necessarily the tale type that is narrated (although women do appear to have been the most frequent performers of AT 480, for example), but the style of a female narrator (Dégh 1995: 69).

Unfortunately, the oral folktale is a disappearing genre in Russia, Ukraine, and Belarus, and there seems little possibility of recording the tale in a context anything like that of the nineteenth- and early twentieth-century rural communities in which some of the best collections were gathered. In traditionally rich areas such as Karelia, folktales were still collected on a large scale in the 1960s and 1970s. Most of the informants were middle-aged and older women, and the traditional folktale was gradually becoming entertainment exclusively for children (Sen'kina 1988: 30). Elena Shastina noted in the 1970s that the fairy tale in Siberia was experiencing changes: While the traditional narrative structures remained, the tales expressed a different relationship between fantasy and reality, bringing many fairy tales closer to narratives about "real life" (memorates or fabulates). She observed that one accomplished storyteller seemed to become impatient with the traditional repetitions, perhaps sensing unconsciously that they reflected the lifestyle of the old Russian extended family (Shastina 1975: 105–106, 1978: 107).

What can account for the outstanding popularity and longevity of this genre? The morphology of the fairy tale may not explain its origin, but there must be some quality in this narrative structure to account for its long life in tradition and impressive geographic distribution. The fairy tale begins with a young person who leaves the parental home, undergoes various adventures and tests, and finally marries, establishing a new home of his or her own. It begins with the breakup of a family unit and ends with the formation of a new family unit (Meletinskii et al. 1969: 127). This basic movement is true of many, if not all, Indo-European fairy tales. The "realistic" initial and final situations of the fairy tale as well as the age and status of the hero(ine) suggest that the classical fairy tale pattern is in fact the story of a young person's maturation. In this sense it does resemble the initiation rituals cited by Propp. It is possible that the similarities which caused Propp to regard initiation ritual as the source of the fairy-tale structure might simply be due to the similar content and concerns of both fairy tale and ritual—in the tale a young person goes out on his or her own and ends up married (i.e., an independent adult), and in the ritual, initiates move from child to adult status.

The fact that this drama of maturation and the search for identity is the essential subject of the classical Indo-European fairy tale does much to explain its enduring popularity: every individual listener can find something of his or her own life expressed in the adventures of the fairy tale. Most people have not experienced combat with dragons, have not discovered underground kingdoms of copper, silver, and gold, and have not been forced to carry water in a sieve or to build a palace overnight, but all have experienced puberty, leaving the parental home, the development of an independent adult identity, and most people in the traditional rural cultures of Europe and Russia in the nineteenth century experienced marriage and the founding of a new household.

If storytellers and listeners find their own life experience expressed in the tale, they must in some manner identify with the folktale hero(ine). This would explain the state of "enchantment" reported in some ethnographic descriptions of folktale narration (Nikiforov 1930: 33). In the case of the Russian "satirical" tale (Iu. Sokolov 1931, 1932), it is clear that the peasant narrator and listeners identified with the clever hero who outsmarted a landlord or priest. But how can this identification take place in the fairy tale, which unfolds in a fantasy realm, where the antagonists are not figures known from daily life, but dragons, ogres, or a malevolent Baba Yaga?

One of Dmitrii Zelenin's informants was Efim'ia Mironovna Klimova, a
sixty-year-old peasant woman who apparently knew only four folktales and told
them only to her grandchildren. In her tale (Zelenin Viatka 87) the hero's name
is Mitiun'kia or Mitiun'ka, a diminutive form of Dmitrii. The hero's name was
unique to this occasion, because "usually this storyteller chooses the name of
one of her listeners. In this case my name was taken: I was the only listener"
(Zelenin 1915: 519). Although Zelenin hesitated to call this informant a genuine
tale-teller because of her limited repertoire and audience, she seems to have
been aware of the element of identification at work in her listeners' minds, and
obviously wanted her listener to identify with the boy hero and vicariously live
out his adventures with him. The same is true of the Siberian tale-teller Raisa
Egorovna Shemetova, who gives the folktale characters the names of her
listeners and addresses the listeners during her narration (Shastina 1971: 11–12).
Besides underscoring the predictability of the hero(ine)'s features, the frequency
of names such as Ivan, Fedor, Vasilii, Elena, Vasilisa, Mar'ia, Anastasiia, Anna
and their derivatives in Russian folktales might also facilitate identification with
the hero(ine), since these names are or were very common as well in daily life
(Morozova 1977: 236–238, Dorovskikh 1980: 95–97). An account of a
traditional storytelling situation by the writer Mikhail Prishvin is also revealing:

> In winter in the north the day is short: people work, get cold and return to the hut to warm
> themselves. Then they lie down next to each other and wait for sleep to come by itself.
> What is there to do in a hut on such long evenings? It seems one could die of boredom.
> But Manuilo the storyteller comes to their aid. By the light of a splinter in this forest hut he
> tells all these people dozing on the floor about some tsar, with whom the people live as
> simply as if he weren't even a tsar, but just a lucky peasant in power. Peasants bring this
> tsar grouses, give him riddles, and the tsar cleverly answers them and gives advice.
> (Prishvin 1970: 69)

The tale-teller appears to be aware of his listeners' identification and wishes
to facilitate it by creating a tsar who is not a distant figure, but one with whom
they might have dealings in their own lives. Soviet folklorists have sometimes
emphasized the triumph of the socially low hero over a high antagonist, such as
a tsar, in the fairy tale as well as the satirical tale (Sen'kina 1980), but the social
class of the folktale hero is variable. Zelenin found that it depended on the
inclination of the tale-teller. In versions collected from three different narrators
of the same district, the hero of one and the same tale is a tsar's son, a
merchant's son, and a peasant's son (Zelenin 1914: xxxi–xxxii, 525). At the
same time, the majority of folktale heroes in his Perm' collection are peasants
(ibid., xxx). Class antagonism does appear in some tales (especially the satirical
genre), and it appears that tale-tellers and their audiences tended to prefer

heroes who were like them, but nevertheless, peasant listeners were not incapable of identifying with the son of a folktale tsar or merchant. Another feature which might encourage identification is the creation of a familiar background or setting for the tale. Tale-tellers in Perm' province frequently used the nearby Ural mountains as a setting, and those in Viatka province the thick forests found there (Zelenin 1914: xx–xxiii, 1915: xv). Although Zelenin emphasizes that the uninhabited forests inspired a feeling of mystery which accounts for their use in the tales, it is also possible that this nearby location for the action would make it more immediate. A Siberian storyteller recorded in 1970 has his hero live "in that kingdom, in a small village, like our Golovskoe" (Shastina 1974: 42).

It seems that the narrator of the fairy tale has two somewhat contradictory goals. The fairy tale is set in another realm, quite apart from the one in which the listener lives. This is made clear by some traditional opening formulaic phrases (*priskazki*), concluding formulas, and by the fantastic characters or events. On the other hand, the use of listeners' names, the traditional use of common Russian names, the creation of a familiar setting, and the sometimes familiar behavior of even fantastic characters indicate that the listener might identify with the folktale hero(ine) and feel at home in the separate realm the folktale creates. All this might account for the contradictory statements by East Slavic storytellers about whether the folktales were truth or fiction. Linda Dégh points out the ambiguity of fairy tale narration, where the teller uses all his or her artistry to make the listeners believe what they know is an entertaining lie (1969: 86–87).

Baba Yaga and Folk Belief

What is Baba Yaga's status in (and outside) the "entertaining lie" of the fairy tale? Scholars disagree about whether Baba Yaga was recognized as a fictional character or believed to be real. Ethnographic and statistical surveys of East Slavic areas sometimes mention Baba Yaga together with figures in whom people believed. G. K. Zavoiko includes Baba Yaga in a survey of Russian folk belief in Vladimir province. By his own account, the image of Baba Yaga he presents is a composite one, collected from many informants:

Bába-Yagá, Babá-Yagá, Bába-liagá, Liagá-Bába, Babá-liagá, the Bony Leg, has a clay face, sharpened, gilded teeth (these last three words recorded in Orel province), and lives in the forest with her daughter Marinushka, in a marsh, in a hut on chicken legs, or a hut [*khatka*] on chicken feet, or in a little house on a spindle heel (and she also lives in a shed, in the cellar). She lies on a high bed with her nose in the ceiling, and she doesn't see the Russian scent and she doesn't hear people. She rides on a stick or in a mortar, driving it with a pestle, and she sweeps the road ahead with a broom; or she rides in a mortar, leaning on a pestle, beating with the broom (she whips herself from behind, to run faster). She is ugly and huge, her face is completely furry, sometimes mangy, her eyes are as big as eggs, and her dishevelled, matted hair always hangs loose, like a scarecrow. Her clothes are white or made of a torn white striped material, or her clothing is "like the bark of a spruce tree." She has a black cloth wound over her head, or wears a pointed *povoinik* [married woman's headdress]. She spins [wool or other material] on a beam. Human fingers float in her food. She gives children porridge with dried-up snot.

I gathered the above material about Baba-Yaga literally in little bits all over the eastern part of Vladimir province. (Zavoiko 1914: 110–111)

P. S. Efimenko describes Baba Yaga along with two figures of folk belief, the Noon Woman (*poludnitsa*) and the Rye Woman (*ržhitsa*). Yaga-Baba is "an evil female spirit who doesn't have a husband; she is tall and so corpulent that, as they say in folktales, she sits in her hut on the oven post, her feet on the benches, her breasts on the shelves, her head on a fur skin; she rides in mortars and devours people" (Efimenko 1877: 188). P. P. Chubinskii lists Baba Yaga as one of a number of "mythological beings" believed to exist: "The people imagine Baba Yaga as a one-hundred-year-old woman, terribly mean" (Ukraine, Vinnitsa district; Chubinskii 1872: 216). A survey of Belorussian folk belief lists Baba-Jaga or Jaginia (as she was called in the Volkovysk district) as a harmful spirit, along with witches. In the folk imagination, Baba Yaga, the "aunt of all witches" or "mistress of all witches," was "frightening, black, old, dishevelled, she has iron pestles instead of legs, and when she walks through the forest, she crushes it before her and clears a path for herself with those pestles" (Federowski 1897: 80).

Aleksandr Afanas'ev does not make a clear distinction between Baba Yaga's role in folktales and her appearance in superstition and belief. He reports that Baba Yaga and witches fly to their gatherings in iron mortars (Afanas'ev 1865–1869 i: 291), and that, according to a Belorussian belief, death gives the deceased to Baba Yaga. She and the witches she rules over feed on the souls of the dead in order to become as light as they are (ibid., iii: 586).

Some folktales associate Baba Yaga with the devil. In one folktale, the old woman Baba-Yaga lives next door to the protagonist and is said to have dealings with devils (Gospodarev 59). In another, Baba Yaga gets in her mortar and rushes off to the devil (Zelenin 1915 no. 97). The Baba Yaga donor who appears in a version of AT 313 (Sokolov 66) is the sister of Satan. The East Slavs clearly believed in the existence of the devil. Irina Karnaukhova found that many stories about encounters with the devil (memorates or fabulates) circulated in the Pinega region, where hardly anyone had *not* seen the devil (1928: 89). In these instances, Baba Yaga's image obviously shades into the image of a real witch.

In the Poles'e region of Belarus, certain features of "real" witches are mentioned most frequently. A witch is wounded while she is in the shape of an animal (so that she can later be identified); witches steal milk from their neighbors' cows (usually the witch gathers dew on a sheet, apron, or shirt, and then gives her own cow the dew to drink, or milk simply flows from the cloth). Memorates or fabulates also tell of people who secretly watch a witch stealing milk, imitate her actions, and then have an uninterrupted flow of milk at home. There are accounts of how difficult it is for a witch to die, and about witches' flights to their gatherings (on a broom, poker, in a mortar or sieve, Vinogradova 1992: 64). The Carpatho-Ukrainian *bosorka* or *bosorkania* also enjoys stealing milk and harming people in various ways. She can appear as a beautiful young woman, an ugly old woman, or a woman in white with long thin arms and thin legs with chicken feet (ibid., 65). In Bulgaria, witches are said to cause lunar eclipses by bringing the moon down from the sky with a magic sieve; they also turn the moon into a cow and milk it. The South Slavic witch more frequently controls the forces of nature (clouds, hail, and wind) than do her East and West Slavic counterparts (ibid., 68).

While they share stable and common features, witches in Slavic folk belief exhibit considerable regional diversity (ibid., 69–73). Baba Yaga is a witch in many senses; Baba Yaga and the witch perform the same function in certain tale types, and storytellers often refer to her as a witch, but she lacks some of the Slavic witch's typical attributes and behavior. There appear to be no folktales about Baba Yaga stealing milk from cows, for example.[2] There are only a few recorded tales about Baba Yaga's origin, while folk belief provides many explanations for how women become witches: The seventh girl born in a family becomes a *bosorka* (ibid., 65), in three generations of girls born out of wedlock, the third-generation girl becomes a witch, or a dying witch transfers her power to another woman (ibid., 62).

Linda Ivanits finds that the real witches described in folk memorates and fabulates are young or old, and their beauty or hideousness is often not mentioned, while Baba Yaga and the witches of folktales tend to be old and ugly. In the case of old witches of folk belief, "what seems to strike the popular imagination is not so much the resemblance to Baba Yaga as an unnatural longevity" (Ivanits 1989: 100). Irina Razumova cites a tale of M. Korguev (unfortunately unavailable for this survey) in which he states "there was a most frightening sorceress [*koldun'ia*], not just a sorceress, but a Baba-Yaga" (Razumova 1993: 15). His presentation implies that Baba Yaga is worse than a sorceress, or, as Razumova points out, she has a more vividly expressed demonic nature. Still, Razumova considers that "the deep genetic relationship between the witch of folk belief and demonic female folktale characters is

---

[2] In some sense Baba Yaga "steals milk" when she sucks from the breasts of a maiden in AT 519, although she may be sucking her blood as well.

indisputable" (ibid., 13): Baba Yaga existed in nineteenth-century folk belief, and her image in these beliefs was no doubt influenced by the folktale (ibid., 106). Nevertheless, Razumova recognizes an important generic difference between the folktale, where magic abilities and acts are part of the "rules of the game" and are neither frightening nor mysterious, and the memorate or fabulate, where the magic abilities of witches and sorcerers in the real world must be explained, through a pact with the devil or evil spirits, "learning" the profession, or inheriting it (ibid., 18).

Besides the witch, Baba Yaga has been associated with other figures of folk belief, such as the forest spirit (*leshii*). In the Mezen' region, at least one fabulate refers to the leshii's wife, the *leshachikha*, as Yaga-Baba (Cherepanova 1983: 104). This is not surprising, since Baba Yaga herself lives in the forest. There are also fabulates in which the forest spirits exhibit features similar to Baba Yaga, such as cannibalism (Karnaukhova 1928: 85–86).

One narrator, Natal'ia Bezrukova, identified Egibikha as one of the evil spirits inhabiting lakes or forests (Zelenin 1915: 358). Parents in one tale from Kola peninsula warn their son not to go fishing on the lake, since Yagishnia does not like losing her fish, implying that she is the guardian of the lake, something like the water spirit (*vodianoi*) of folk belief (Balashov 105). Elizaveta Ivanovna Sidorova, a tale-teller from the same region, remarks in the context of one tale (recorded in 1957) that "there used to be Yaga-Babas" (Balashov 47), and at the end of another tale, after a malevolent Yaga-Baba has been shot, "That's the kind of Yaga-Babas there used to be, they caused harm all the time. There's hardly a tale where they don't cause harm in some way!" (Balashov 49).

In the Pechora and Vologda regions, Baba Yaga was identified with the Noon Woman, *poludnitsa*, a female spirit who appeared at noon in wheat fields, guarded the harvest, and was dangerous to children (Cherepanova 1983: 104). Informants in Northern Russia reported that the Noon Woman lived in the rye fields, could tickle people to death, mow them down with a scythe, and steal children. People closed their doors and windows at noon to avoid the Noon Woman (Cherepanova 1996: 65). The essential similarity of the Noon Woman in different Slavic traditions (cf. the Sorbian Noon Woman, below) leads Èrna Pomerantseva to the conclusion that the Slavic Noon Woman ultimately derives from a single source (1978: 157). Pomerantseva notes that the Noon Woman has been less frequently documented in Russia than other spirits or figures of folk belief (like the *leshii*). Serious belief in her existence appears to have given way to the use of the Noon Woman to frighten children and keep them from trampling fields and gardens, what C. W. von Sydow called a "pedagogical fiction" (1948: 101). One informant in Siberia stated that the Noon Woman "looks like Baba Yaga" (ibid., 150). In Pechora "they say that

Baba-Yaga also ran around in the rye field, with her hair loose" (Cherepanova 1983: 104). In the Pinega region Baba Yaga was believed to abduct children and was used to frighten them (Efimenko 1877: 166). Baba Yaga and the "field grandfather" (*polevoi ded*) kept children out of fields and gardens in Poshekhon'e (Afanas'ev 1869 iii: 591–592). In connection with Baba Yaga, Afanas'ev describes the Ukrainian Iron Woman (*zalizna baba*), used to keep children from picking peas and wandering into gardens and forests. The Iron Woman also appears in Ukrainian folktales (Kalyn 1972: 195–198). Lev Barag finds that the folktale image of Baba Yaga to some extent merged with the Iron Woman of Belorussian folk belief as well. The Iron Woman was an old woman with iron breasts who caught children with an iron hook if they wandered into fields or gardens to steal vegetables. She threw them into her iron mortar to eat them. Children's belief in the Iron Woman was reinforced by fairy tales such as AT 327C, where she played the role of the folktale witch, and caught a boy in her garden or pea plants (Barag 1966: 20–21, see discussion in chapter 3).

In the Pskov region of western Russia (bordering on Estonia and Latvia), Baba Yaga appears in customs and beliefs surrounding the harvest. Baba Yaga, *Baba Gorbata* (the Hunchbacked Woman), and *Pozhinalka* (the Reaper) are female beings who are seen as mistresses of the field. The supernatural female being lives in the rye field, wears a red kerchief, and during the harvest is driven into the unharvested part of the field or into the forest. In some cases, Baba Yaga or the "Woman in the Red Kerchief" is a harmful being who harms the crop or takes away the vital force in the grains (Lobkova 2000: 27). Galina Lobkova observes a certain fluidity in these beliefs between several different supernatural beings who appear to shade into one another: the witch, the *rusalka*, Baba Yaga, the Reaper, and the female Fiery Serpent (*Ognennaia Zmeia*). Baba Yaga and the *rusalka* live in the rye field as it ripens. Baba Yaga, the *rusalka*, the Fiery Serpent and the witch can take away the vital force (*spor*) in the grain (ibid., 28).

At the end of the harvest, verbal formulas were used to "chase away the old woman" or "cut down the old woman" (*rezat' babu*). The old woman was also urged to "marry our old man" in songs that were sometimes obscene. In a few cases, it was believed that Baba Yaga "ran around" while the last stalks of rye were tied into a knot. In a few localities (Gdov district), a small patch of rye stalks remaining standing at the edge of the field were braided and decorated, and left "for Baba Yaga." As they did this, people pronounced, "Baba Yaga, you harvested our grain for us, and this is all that we've left for you," or "let her eat the ears of grain that are left over for her" (ibid., 81–82). It is very interesting that Baba Yaga appears ambiguously in these customs and beliefs, both as the owner, guardian, or mistress of the rye field, but also as a witch who might deprive people of their grain and its life-giving power, and who was driven away into the forest or another field. It seems significant that she appears in a "borderline" context between nature and culture (the cultivated field, outside the boundaries of the settled village), and in relation to nourishment (rye or other wheat, a food source).

Another supernatural figure of East Slavic folk belief who should be mentioned in this context is *Paraskeva-Piatnitsa* (Saint Friday, the name derived from Greek *paraskevi*, "Friday"). This personification of a day of the week, like the many cognate figures found in Europe, punishes women who spin or weave on her day (Róheim 1946). It has been suggested that among the East Slavs, the Christian cult of Paraskeva-Piatnitsa replaced pagan worship of the goddess Mokosh'. There are three saints named Paraskeva recognized by the Orthodox Church: Paraskeva of Rome (second century, celebrated July 26), Paraskeva of Ikonion (third and fourth centuries, October 28), and Paraskeva of Epibatas (A.D. 1023–1057, October 14). The last-mentioned Paraskeva enjoys a popular cult in Southeastern Europe that rivals even that of the Mother of God. There are many unresolved questions regarding the relationship of this saint's official hagiography to her popular cult, and to the other female personifications of days of the week found in the folklore of the Orthodox peoples (Mesnil and Popova 1993, Drettas 1995).

In Ukrainian fabulates, the Friday Woman (*Zhinka-P"iatnytsia*) appears in the hut of a woman who weaves on Friday, tears her skin off, and hangs it on the loom; she deforms the fingers of women who spin on Friday (Chubinskii 1872 i: 217). Spinning on Friday dirties Paraskeva-Piatnitsa's eyes; in Tambov province, it was thought that Mother Praskoveia would dirty the eyes of women who spun on this day (Tolstoi 1995a: 190).[3] Holy or Saint Friday (*P"iatinka sviataia*) appears as a donor in a Ukrainian version of AT 313 (Afanas'ev 223). Like Paraskeva-Piatnitsa, Baba Yaga is associated with weaving and spinning— she often asks the kind and unkind girls who come to her dwelling in AT 480 to spin for her, sometimes she is spinning herself when the protagonist arrives at her hut, and sometimes her hut stands on a spindle heel or heels. However, it is interesting that Baba Yaga has not taken on this function (overseeing spinning, and prohibiting this work on certain days) in East Slavic folk belief, and this fact seems to underscore her essential identity as a folktale character.

---

[3] Spinning on Friday is also offensive to the dead. In Voronezh province this prohibited activity would dirty the eyes of one's dead parents, or even make them blind in the other world. In the Zhitomir region, spinning and weaving on Friday harms the eyes of those in the other world, and is punished by St. Barbara. In the Gomel' region, pregnant women should not do laundry on Friday, because the steam might harm the unborn child's eyes (Tolstoi 1995a: 190, 194).

Baba Yaga's name appears in a few magic incantations, which suggests that their practitioners believed she represented a real supernatural power. Baba Yaga ignites love and passion in a spell from Novgorod province: "In the open field there is a Saracen oak and under that Saracen oak there are thrice-nine maidens. From under the Saracen oak comes Baba-Yaga and lights thrice-nine oak wood fires" (Cherepanova 1983: 104). A similar spell was recorded in the Pinega region of Arkhangel'sk province. A man who wants to make a woman love him calls on help from the devils Sava, Koldun, and Asaul. As they have served King Herod, he calls on them to gather sorrow from cities and villages and place it in the woman so that she can't live without him. The spell continues, "In the open field stands a Saracen oak, and under that Saracen oak there are thrice-nine maidens, and Yaga Baba comes out from under that Saracen oak and lights thrice-nine sazhens of oak wood."[4] As the wood burns, so too should the woman whose name is mentioned in the spell (Efimenko 1878: 142–143, no. 15).

Another incantation from Pinega, recited by a man to attract a woman, includes Egi-Baba, her daughters, and stoves:

In the open field there are 77 copper bright red-hot stoves, and on each of those 77 copper bright red-hot stoves there are 77 Egi-Babas. Those 77 Egi-Babas have 77 daughters each, and those 77 daughters have 77 walking-sticks and 77 brooms each. I, God's servant (*the man's name*) beseech and submit to these Egi-Baba daughters. "Hail to you, Egi-Baba daughters, make God's servant (*the woman's name*) fall in love with and bring her to God's servant (*man's name*), sweep [your] tracks with [your] brooms, walk with your walking-sticks,[5] strike and beat the vein under the heel, strike and beat the vein under the knee, strike and beat the spinal vein, strike and beat the crooked gnarled oak with its many branches, strike and beat the copper red-hot stoves." As ardently and hot as the copper red-hot stoves burn, may God's servant (*woman's name*) bake and burn at all times, at all hours, early in the morning, late in the evening… so that she might not be able to live without God's servant (*man's name*). (Efimenko 1878: 140, no. 4)

A charm against snakebite recorded in the eighteenth century invokes *iaga zmeia bura* [Yaga the brown snake]. The person who is casting the spell addresses the blood, telling it to clot and heal. If the bloody wound does not heal, he or she threatens: "I will send Yaga the brown snake after you. Yaga the brown snake will cover [the wound] with wool, will lock the lock with her tail,

---

[4] One sazhen = 2.13 meters.

[5] The meaning of this phrase (*klukami zakluchite*) is obscure, and this may be its only occurrence in a printed source. A dictionary of Russian dialect terms (Filin and Sorokoletov 1965) suggests two possible meanings for the noun *kluki*: "walking sticks" and "keys" (ibid., vol. 13: 312). If the seventy-seven Egi-Baba daughters have keys instead of walking sticks, the phrase might mean "lock with your keys." The meaning might even have been obscure to the man casting the spell.

and give the key to the Mother of God" (ibid., 106–107; the image of the lock
and key frequently appears at the end of East Slavic spells). In a Russian
incantation from the seventeenth century, the three devils Vezi, Puzi, and Sini
are called sons of Baba Yaga (Mansikka 1909: 13). An old woman (*staraia babka*)
in a hut on a chicken leg appears in a Belorussian spell to stop bleeding
(Eleonskaia 1994: 77). Baba Yaga is called on to calm a sleepless child in a spell
from Belarus (Vinogradova 1983; see discussion in chapter 3).

In spite of these cases in which Baba Yaga is identified as a figure of serious
folk belief, some folklorists maintain that Baba Yaga was recognized by the
people as a fictional character. In his book on Carpathian magic acts, rituals,
and beliefs, Petr Bogatyrev discusses traditional narratives about supernatural
beings, and finds that folktales (fictional narratives) may influence memorates
and fabulates (narratives about "true experiences"), but he states that

> The supernatural and fantastic figures who are the main characters of Russian folktales,
> such as Koshchei the Immortal, Zmei Gorynych, Baba Yaga, etc..., play no role in Russian
> folk demonology.
>
>   On the contrary, the common figures of the latter, the *leshii* [forest spirit], the *vodianoi*
> [water spirit], the *domovoi* [house spirit], are only rarely introduced in folktales....
>
>   In Russia the only exception is the *koldun* and *koldun'ia* [male and female witches],
> whom we meet in folktales as well as in folk beliefs. But in folktales this designation is
> applied to more than one supernatural character, for example to Baba Yaga....
>
>   By its form, conventional composition, by its traditional motifs and its various narrative
> ornaments the folktale gives the impression of a purely artistic work. From this it follows
> that supernatural beings appear there as poetic creations. For the peasant these fantastic
> and artificial figures are very clearly distinct from the supernatural beings in whose
> existence he believes....
>
>   What is the origin of the supernatural folktale characters? Are they the product of
> artistic creation or is it a matter of beings in whom past generations or other peoples
> believed? It is very difficult to determine this today. In any case, there is no reason for
> explaining all fantastic folktale motifs, as some scholars do, as survivals of certain cults.
>
>   We must not forget that the appearance of the characters of folk stories often recalls
> supernatural beings who have remained the objects of a cult....But if one of them recalls a
> figure of folk demonology, this does not necessarily mean that it was a cult object before
> becoming part of these stories. Resemblance is not a sufficient argument.
>
>   The origin of folktale characters can be different from that of the supernatural beings
> of folk demonology. They could have been purely and simply invented, like characters in
> novels. (Bogatyrev 1929: 142–144, 1971: 287–288)

Thus, there appears to be no certainty about the belief status of Baba Yaga
herself and the stories told about her, or at least there is no agreement among
scholars. She certainly resembles "real" witches, and her image shades into
those of other figures of East Slavic folk belief. However, the fact that she

appears overwhelmingly as a character in folktales suggests that her appearances in other folklore genres are secondary.

Baba Yaga's Sisters and Cousins

There are witches and ogresses in many folklore traditions who resemble Baba Yaga in one way or another. Within Europe, and especially Eastern Europe, these similarities may be due in part to a historical, "genetic" relationship, or cultural contact between different groups. Folkloric exchange has certainly taken place where East Slavic communities are in contact with Finno-Ugric and Siberian peoples. A comparison of Baba Yaga with cognate figures can help to identify what is unique about her, as well as what she shares with European, Indo-European, or other traditions, and brings her onto the international stage, where she rightfully belongs.

Baba Yaga's closest relative is found in West Slavic folklore. Slovak folktales and legends feature *Ježibaba*, who usually appears in an inimical guise, but occasionally exhibits ambiguity or goodwill. Other variations on the name are *Jenžibaba, Jendžibaba, Endžibaba, Jenžibaba,* and *Jažibaba* (Polívka 1922: 256–257). In one version of AT 313, Ježibaba also has a husband, *Ježibábel'* (Dobšinský i: 75–85). The hero flees from this couple with the help of their daughter. In another tale, Jendžibaba's husband is a bandit chief (Czambel 153). Ježibaba appears to be much less popular in Czech folktales, where the witch (*čarodějnice*) is more likely to appear as villain (Erben 1958, Kubín 1926, Sirovátka 1983, Tille 1901–1902). In Slovak tales Ježibaba is often called a witch (*striga, bosorka*), with whom she is apparently interchangeable. In printed sources her name is spelled sometimes with a lowercase letter, and sometimes with a capital, which might betray an uncertainty about whether she is an individual or a type (this is true of Baba Yaga as well; see the discussion in chapter 3). In the 1830s Ján Kollár described Ježibaba as follows:

> It is hard to determine what kind of being Jenzibaba is; she is reported in Hont, Gemer, and Liptov Counties, where she is called Jenžibaba, and Ježibaba, and is partly reported in Turiec County as well. She is also known to the Czechs, but they call her Jagababa and Jahodababa.... The Slovaks still have many tales and legends about Jenzibaba or Ježibaba; they are snotty-nosed witches with thick lips or big mouths, a nose like a pot, they frequent groves and caves, and have the most in common with hunters, because they also know how to practice magic, and they [the Ježibabas] also busy themselves with magic. Whoever goes into their grove gets so lost that he never finds his way out again. When Ježibaba disappears she causes a great wind. (Kollár 1953 i: 723)

Kollár reports a children's rhyme from Hont County, spoken when children threw their baby teeth behind the stove: "Jenzibaba, old woman, here is a bone tooth for you, give me an iron one for it" (*Jenzibaba, stará baba, tu máš zub* *kosten*ý*, daj mi *ž*a*ň *železn*ý, ibid., 1953 i: 50). He also collected legends or fabulates about this character.[6] A hunter shoots a hare near Ježibaba's cave. When she tries to pull it away from him, he threatens to shoot her with one of nine nails from a horseshoe. Ježibaba releases the hare, because only such a nail could really wound her. In another legend, a hunter wants to visit and see hell. He builds a fire under a tree at night and cooks bacon on a stick. He hears a woman in the tree complain of the cold, and invites her to join him. She takes a stick, goes to a nearby lake and catches a frog. As she cooks the frog over the fire, she pronounces a rhyming phrase (perhaps a spell) stating that her frog will turn to roasted meat, while the hunter's meat will turn into a frog. Kollár also provides a second version of the rhyme:

Mne se peče pečeňa	Meat is roasting for me
a tebe se žaba	And for you a frog
ty chceš iti do pekla,	You want to go to hell,
ja som Ježibaba.	I am Ježibaba.

This Ježibaba shows the hunter a deep hole where he will find the entrance to hell, and advises him to take a large amount of meat to feed the dragon that will carry him there. On the return trip the hunter runs out of meat and has to feed the dragon flesh from his own leg. He limps for the rest of his life (ibid., 50–51, 52).[7]

In folktales, Ježibaba's role, especially as a villain, is very similar to that of Baba Yaga, and she appears in many of the same tale types (AT 300A, 303, 313, 315, 321, 327B+531, 400, 450, 480, 513, 554). Like Baba Yaga, she possesses a herd of mares the hero must herd to receive a magic horse (AT 400+302, Dobšinský i: 183–194; combined with AT 531, Polívka ii: 326–329). She leads a fearsome army which seems capable of endlessly renewing itself (AT 300+301, Dobšinský iii: 291–308). Ježibaba is mentioned as a villain in a Slovak version of AT 402 (Gašparíková 229). She had turned the princess into a frog so that

---

[6] Carl Wilhelm von Sydow proposed the terms "memorate" and "fabulate" to designate two types of legendary narratives. The memorate is a personal experience narrative, usually concerning an encounter with a supernatural being. The fabulate, which also typically involves figures of folk belief, is not based on immediate personal experience, and often does not mention specific individuals or places. Both genres are told and accepted as true (Sydow 1948: 73–77). Russian terms for these genres are *bylichka* and *byval'shchina*.

[7] This trip to hell and back on the dragon recalls the hero's return to earth from the lower world in AT 301 on the back of a magic bird. The folktale hero runs out of meat to feed the bird, and feeds it flesh from his own leg or ankle. When they reach earth, the bird spits out his flesh and restores it to its proper place. The folktale hero is magically healed, while the protagonist of the legend (fabulate) is forced to live with the consequences, a real handicap.

no one would marry her. This contrasts with Baba Yaga's consistent role as a donor in East Slavic versions of AT 402.

After the hero has managed to steal three sought-after objects from Ježibaba, she becomes so angry that she turns into axle grease (AT 327+531, Dobšinský i: 133–147). In another version of AT 531, a Jendžibaba appears in an opening episode that recalls AT 707. In the king's absence, she writes to the king that the queen has given birth to puppies, and forges another letter in order to have the queen put in prison. Finally this Jendžibaba (also called an "old witch," *stará striga*) convinces the king to have the queen taken to the mountains and killed (Polívka ii: 332–339). Ježibaba exhibits polycephalism in a tale (AT 321, Dobšinský iii: 32–43) where three Ježibabas with seven, nine, and twelve heads attack the hero. When the hero comes to take the golden maiden from Ježibaba in a version of AT 531, Ježibaba wakes up and fights with him, turning into a twenty-four-headed monster, then a frog and a snake (Polívka ii: 340–348). Jiří Polívka mentions multiple heads and cannibalism as regular features of Ježibaba (1922: 258).[8]

In one version of AT 480, both the wicked stepmother and the threatening tester are Ježibabas. The stepmother's lazy daughter runs away from the tester Ježibaba, who pursues her in iron boots, wielding an iron rake. She rakes off the gold the girl had stolen and draws blood (Dobšinský iii: 267–276). Another tale combines AT 327B and 327C. The hero and his eleven brothers come to the house of Ježibaba, who has twelve daughters. The hero notices that Ježibaba is heating up a scythe to behead them. He takes the scythe and decapitates her daughters instead. Then he steals magic objects from Ježibaba: shoes that allow him to walk on water and a skull that causes rain when put outside. He tries to steal a talking bird and is caught. Ježibaba tells her servant to cook the hero. The hero pretends not to know how to sit on the bread spatula (baker's peel), and asks the servant to show him how. She does, and he pushes her into the oven. Ježibaba comes home, and starts cutting into the meat when she recognizes who it is. She runs after the hero, but cannot catch him (Kollár 1953: 51–52). In another very interesting tale a female heroine is confronted with tasks typical for male-centered tales (AT 531). When the king finds out that his two elder daughters have been dancing in hell (he notices that they wear out many pairs of shoes), he asks them where they have been going and why they have not been taking their youngest sister Milenka along. They tell their father that Milenka knows about Ježibaba's golden apple. Milenka retrieves the golden apple and a golden pear, but on her third attempt to retrieve the golden purse, Ježibaba catches her, and there follows an episode of

---

[8] A nine-headed Baba Yaga attacks the hero in a Russian version of AT 321 (Potanin 1906 no. 13).

AT 327C. Ježibaba tells her daughter to cook Milenka. Milenka cuts off the girl's head and puts her in the oven. When Ježibaba calls out that there will be a good feast from Milenka, the princess taunts her about eating her own daughter. Ježibaba turns to axle grease, Milenka returns home, and her sisters are killed (Polívka ii: 409). Ježibaba appears as villain in AT 303, in an episode very much like the legend-fabulate described above. The hero has been hunting in the forest and cooks meat under a tree. Ježibaba climbs down from the tree, but tells the hero she is afraid of his animals. She gives him a stick and tells him to strike his animals. When he does so, they turn to stone (ibid., 52–55).

In at least three Slovak tales Ježibaba is a donor figure, trebled as three sisters. They help the hero escape a pursuing ogre, give the hero soup and meat, let him rest, and their magic dogs help the hero (AT 315, Dobšinský iii: 433–443). Three Ježibaba sisters and their sons in lead, silver, and gold palaces direct the hero to the glass mountain, where he will find the three lemons (AT 408, Rimavský 1845: 37–52). In a version of AT 551, three Ježibabas give the hero magic gifts and tell him how to reach the princess who possesses the living and dead water (Gašparíková 555). Sometimes this donor role is taken by an "old woman" (*stará baba*) or a "wise woman" (*moudrá žena*) (Polívka 1922: 261). Most often Ježibaba appears to be a villain.

Ježibaba appears in tales which have been recorded less frequently in East Slavic areas, such as AT 408 (The Three Oranges), AT 451 (The Maiden Who Seeks Her Brothers), AT 710 (Our Lady's Child), and 327A (Hansel and Gretel). In one Slovak version of AT 545B (Puss in Boots, Dobšinský i: 416–420), the cat tricks a Ježibaba and her child by telling them an army is coming, and convinces them to hide in the oven. The cat burns them up, and his master and the princess come to live in Ježibaba's house. Ježibaba appears in a combination of AT 566 (The Three Magic Objects and the Wonderful Fruits) and AT 567 (The Magic Bird Heart). The hero has eaten a magic bird's wing. He does not realize that money appears under his pillow every morning. Ježibaba finds out about the money, confers with other witches, and gives him a potion to cough up the bird's wing. She gives the wing to her mistress, the princess, and three times removes the hero to an island in the blood-red sea. Each time a dragon brings the hero home. The hero finds magic apples that will make horns grow on the person who eats them, and apples that will take the horns away. In disguise the hero sells the horn-growing apples to the princess and Ježibaba, and forces them to confess their misdeeds. He cures them with the healing apples, marries the princess, and interestingly, also appears to forgive Ježibaba (Dobšinský ii: 11–23).

The Ježibaba villain in a version of AT 710 steals the heroine's three sons, but at the end of the tale, when the heroine is about to be burned at the stake, she appears with the children and saves the heroine. Ježibaba herself has now been released from enchantment, and goes to live with the heroine and the young king (Czambel 156). Ambiguity also appears in a version of AT 513, where a Jedžibaba tells the emperor who the culprit is who has stolen the princess. When the hero and his extraordinary companions go to retrieve her, the Moscow emperor demands that they bring him water from the Black Sea. One of the companions fetches the water, but another companion sees from far away that he is asleep on a mare's head, while a Jendžibaba is combing him and presumably keeping him asleep (Czambel 193). Ježibaba is ultimately a villain, but appears first as a victim in one version of AT 321 (Polívka iv: 179–182). The hero herds sheep for a blind Ježibaba. On three days in succession, when he blows a whistle, maidens with three, six, and nine heads appear out of the earth and ask him to pick lice from their hair. Ježibaba gives him a magic twig to decapitate the maidens, and before killing the last one, he finds out from her where Ježibaba's eyes are, and an ointment to cure her; the maidens are the ones who blinded her. The hero restores Ježibaba's eyesight, and during her absence he discovers pots full of human arms, legs, heads, and blood. He goes home and reports Ježibaba to the authorities; she is caught and killed.

The most significant differences between Ježibaba and Baba Yaga seem to be their appearances in different tale types (which probably reflects the different tale-type repertoires of central and eastern Europe), and the amount of detail provided by storytellers in their descriptions of these Slavic witches. In the East Slavic tales, Baba Yaga is usually described by formulaic phrases which are often well developed, and can form entire episodes, while in the Slovak tales there is often little or no description of Ježibaba. Comparing the Russian and Slovak folklore traditions, Petr Bogatyrev found fewer stylistic differences between the Slovak folktale and Slovak memorates and fabulates (legends about supernatural beings) than between the corresponding Russian genres. He states that the Russian folktale, of all Slavic folktales, has developed the most singular style, markedly distinguishing it from other folklore genres (Bogatyrev 1963: 20–21). It is true that in many tales Ježibaba simply appears, with little or no description: "That was the palace of a Ježibaba, whose daughter was golden Berona. When they came to the palace, Ježibaba came out to meet them, greeted them kindly and asked what they were looking for" (Dobšinský i: 266), "On the road an old woman met him, and she was a Ježibaba" (Czambel 156), "Once a Ježibaba came, who had a daughter, and who wanted to marry her to that man" (ibid., 165), and "There was not a single wise man in the whole land who could say where the princess had gone, until a Jedžibaba said that the Moscow prince had stolen her" (ibid., 193). However, in at least one tale (AT 408) we can find some description of Ježibaba, her dwelling, and her giant cannibal son, where she is a donor who first hides the hero from her son, and then feeds him:

The palace was made entirely of lead, twelve crows flew around it, and before it stood an old woman, and it was Ježibaba, leaning on a lead cudgel.

"Oh my son, wherever did you come from? No bird or flying thing has ever been heard of here, much less a person," said Ježibaba to the prince. "Run away, if your life is dear to you, for when my son comes he will eat you."

"Oh don't scare me so, old mother, no!" begged the prince. "For I have come to you for advice, could you not tell me about the glass mountain and the three lemons."

"My son, I have never heard of the glass mountain or the three lemons. But wait, I will call my servants. Perhaps they will be able to advise you."

She took out a lead whistle, blew it three times, and the twelve crows flew to her. She mumbled some incomprehensible words with them for a long time, and then turned to the prince and called out, "My son, even they have not heard of the glass mountain and the three lemons."...[Ježibaba then hides the hero behind a broom when her son arrives.]

"Fui, fui!! It smells of human flesh—I will eat it!" shouted Ježibaba's son at the door, and he struck his huge lead staff on the ground so hard that the whole palace shook, as if a hundred peals of thunder had struck it...[Ježibaba convinces her son not to eat the guest. Her son advises the hero to go on to his brother in the silver palace.]

The old Ježibaba put a large bowl on the table, and her giant son sat down. "Come and eat!" he shouted to the prince, and pounded with his lead staff.

The prince took the first noodle in his fingers, put it in his mouth, started chewing, and in his fear did not even realize that he broke two teeth—for they were lead noodles.

"Well, why aren't you eating?" Ježibaba's son asked, seeing that he wasn't eating anything. "Don't you like it?"

"Oh, they're good, I just don't feel like eating now."

"Well, if you don't feel like eating now, put some in your pocket, you can eat them on the road." So the dear prince had to fill his pocket with lead noodles, whether he wanted to or not. (Rimavský 1845: 38–41)

Because of the similarity in name (obviously derived from a common root), function, and ambiguous nature, Ježibaba and Baba Yaga must be historically related. If they developed from a common prototype, it is likely that this figure dates back to at least the medieval period, and possibly to a more distant Slavic past. An interesting question is why this figure is found only in a limited Slavic area (the East Slavic countries, Slovakia, and the Czech lands).

Carpatho-Ukrainian (Rusyn) folktales recorded in eastern Slovakia feature *Iezhibaba, Izhuzhbaba, Hindzhybaba, Hyndzhi-baba, Indzhibaba,* or *Ezhibaba* (Hyriak 1965–1979). Iezhibaba appears in some tale types that are found in East Slavic areas as well, such as AT 300A, 301, 303, 313, and 327B+531, and usually plays a similar role. But she appears in other tale types which are not as common in East Slavic tradition, such as AT 451 (The Maiden Who Seeks Her Brothers), AT 433B (King Lindorm), AT 500 (The Name of the Helper), AT 710 (Our Lady's Child), and AT 876 (The Clever Maiden and the Suitors). These tale types are probably more popular in Slovakia and have influenced the local Carpatho-Ukrainian tale tradition. The character essentially bears the Czech or Slovak name (Ježibaba) and lacks the traditional features of the East Slavic Baba Yaga (hut, mortar and pestle, formulaic phrases).

She is overwhelmingly evil, acting as a donor or ambiguously in only a few tales. A fascinatingly ambiguous Iezhibaba appears in a tale which combines AT 930 (The Prophecy) and AT 461 (Three Hairs from the Devil's Beard). Iezhibaba's negative side emerges in this tale, but not in relation to the hero. Iezhibaba first predicts to a peasant woman that her son will marry the princess. Later, the king sends the boy to the queen with a letter demanding that the boy be killed. Iezhibaba intercepts the message by putting the boy to sleep with a potion, and rewriting the letter so that the queen has the boy marry the princess. Later, when the hero is sent on a difficult task by the king, he comes to a dried-up tree which bears no fruit and to a dry well. He finds out from a supernatural donor that this is Iezhibaba's doing. The tree is barren because Iezhibaba has put a snake under its roots, and the well is dry because "there under that well there is a rock, a boulder, and under the rock is a Iezhibaba, as big as a barrel. And as long as that toad Iezhibaba stays there, there will never be water. She's arranging it so that everyone dies" (Hyriak 1979 vii: 34). Nevertheless, the donor Iezhibaba is part of the family when the hero triumphs at the end of the tale (Hyriak vii no. 2). In an anecdotal tale, two roguish heroes pasture a cow for Hindzhybaba, and then take a golden hair from her while she sleeps, so that she sleeps like a stone. Hindzhybaba tells them that she lets everyone who comes spend the night at her hut (ibid., iii no. 39).

Iezhibaba has a husband, *Iezhibabun'* (ibid., vii no. 10), in a version of AT 313. She and her husband both steal children. Iezhibaba hates the prince whom her husband has stolen, and sends him on difficult tasks. She sends the peasant girl (the child she stole herself) with poison to kill him. The girl helps the prince accomplish the tasks, and they flee when Iezhibaba wants to cook him. She sends Iezhibabun' after the children three times, but they disguise themselves. Finally, Iezhibaba goes after them herself, and finds them in the form of a duck and pond. She drinks the pond until she bursts. In a version of AT 303, one of the brothers correctly answers a question posed by the villain Hindzhybaba, who remarks that she would have eaten him otherwise. Then she gives him wine and cuts off his head. The second brother arrives, addresses Hindzhybaba as "mother" (*mamko moia*), cuts off her head, and revives his brother (ibid., iii no. 23). In one version of AT 451, Izhuzhbaba is both donor and villain. She tells the heroine about the mountain where her brothers are, and gives her a

ladder to climb it. Later, Izhuzhbaba tries to make it appear that the heroine has
killed her golden-haired son (ibid., v no. 16).

An iron-nosed woman (*zaliznonosa baba*) also appears in folktales from the
Carpathian mountain region of Western Ukraine, where there has undoubtedly
been cultural contact and exchange with Hungary (see discussion below;
Mouchketique 1991–92, Dunaievs'ka 1987: 39). Thirty old women with iron
tongues (*tryitsiat' bab zelyznymy iazykamy*) are villains who keep Golden-Haired
Ialena in a glass jar in a Ukrainian folktale from Galicia (includes elements of
AT 313H* and 302; Iavorskii 42). Another Ukrainian folktale witch is the Iron
Woman (*zalizna baba*), who owns a herd of cattle and lives in a palace on a
duck's leg in a version of AT 545B (Puss in Boots). The clever cat tricks her
into hiding in a hollow beech tree, and has soldiers shoot at the tree (Kalyn
1972: 195–198, Petnikov 1966: 114–118).[9] There are numerous Ukrainian
(Ruthenian and Hutsul) legends from the Carpathian mountain region about
Baba Jaudocha, Jeudocha, or *Dokia,* whose name is no doubt derived from
Eudoxia or Eudochia, a saint whose day is celebrated March 1, and this folklore
figure is associated with the changeable weather experienced at this time of
year. Baba Jaudocha causes snow when she shakes out her fur coats. In some
legends she takes off her fur coats and freezes to death, sometimes because she
has offended God. In other legends she and her sheep turn to stone. She
appears as the wicked stepmother in a version of AT 480, sending her
stepdaughter to find raspberries in March. The girl comes upon Christ and St.
Peter, who give her burning coals that turn to raspberries. Then Jeudocha sets
out herself, offends the month of March by declaring that she will "shit in its
mouth," and freezes to death (Kaindl 1894: 629–636). This figure (called
Dochia) also appears in Romanian folklore (see below).

Jiří Polívka mentions a Polish figure equivalent to Baba Yaga, but
unfortunately provides no further information. *Jedsi baba* and *Jendžibaba* are cited
as Polish forms of the name (Polívka 1922: 257, Novikov 1974: 133, Czambel
1906: 527). According to N. I. Tolstoi, Polish children sing that "Baba Yaga is
churning butter" when there is rain and sunshine at the same time, but
unfortunately he does not cite a source (1995: 39). The name *Baba Jaga* is found
in Polish dictionaries, which note its East Slavic origin, and while it seems that
she does not appear in many Polish folktales, it is possible that Baba Yaga and
Ježibaba entered the Polish tradition in areas where the Poles came into contact
with Belorussian, Ukrainian, and Slovak populations. The testers of the kind
and unkind girls in Polish versions of AT 480 are the Mother of God, St. Peter,

---

[9] In the Petnikov version (a Russian translation), "the [Iron] Woman's palace turned around on a
duck's leg," but this detail is missing in Kalyn 1972: 198. Other minor differences suggest that
these are two separate recordings of this tale, told by Andrii Kalyn.

an old woman, the twelve months, or the devil (Krzyżanowski 1947: 88–90), while the most common villain in versions of AT 327 appears to be the witch (*czarownica*, ibid., 35–37). In one Polish version of AT 480 (from the Opatów region), the supernatural tester is a woman who rides on a hen's foot (*pani na kurzéj stopce*, Kowerska 1896: 595–596).

In the folk belief of the Sorbs, a Slavic population in eastern Germany around Cottbus and Bautzen, the *wurlawy* or *worawy* are forest women who come out of the forest at the stroke of ten o'clock at night. They plough in the village green and make a great deal of noise. If they catch a woman still spinning at this hour, they punish her by giving her a washtub full of spindles and demanding that she spin them full of yarn in an hour. Like many other Slavic peoples, the Sorbs also have folk beliefs about a "Noon Woman" (*připołdnica*), a tall old woman with a sickle in her hand, who appears in the fields at noon. People who encounter her must be able to answer her questions for an hour, or speak about one topic, most often about flax.[10] If they fail she kills them or makes them ill. She appears most often to children and pregnant women, and replaces human children with her own (Černý 1893–1898 i: 132–153, 155–158, 1898: 28–29, Schulenburg 1880: 89–90). Mothers with newborn infants stay in bed from noon until one o'clock to avoid the threat of the Noon Woman (Schneeweis 1953: 7). Closely related to the Noon Woman is the "Sickle Woman" (*serpownica, serpašyja, serpowa baba*), who goes about the fields at all times. Children are warned that she will cut their heads off with her sickle if they wander into the wheat fields (Černý 1898: 28–29). Adolf Černý identifies the Sorbian *Wjera* or *Wjerbaba* as a figure analogous to Baba Yaga. She appears as the villain in a Sorbian version of AT 327A. *Wjerbaba* is also an insulting designation for an old woman (Černý 1893–1898 i: 223–224).

An ambiguous figure in Bulgarian folktales and songs is the *samodiva*. This figure, who resembles the East Slavic *rusalka* (a supernatural, beautiful young woman with long hair, who lives in forests and bodies of water), appears in Bulgarian folktales as a donor, as the hero's bride, and as a villain. A similar figure is the *iuda*, a shapeshifter who appears as a beautiful young shepherdess, as a witch, and sometimes in male form. Novikov finds that the *iuda* in her female form is similar to Baba Yaga in some respects. She lives in a distant forest and possesses land and trees with silver apples; she is wicked and bloodthirsty, but lets herself be fooled easily (1968: 149–152). The dragon-like, many-headed *lamia* fulfills functions in Bulgarian folktales similar to those of Baba Yaga and Koshchei the Immortal, but does not resemble them outwardly (ibid., 152–153). The villain in Bulgarian versions of AT 327A is often a blind

---

[10] Cf. motif K555.1.1, Respite from death gained by tale of the preparation of flax, and the magic preparation of "one-day" cloths (discussed in chapter 3).

ogress. In Bulgarian subtypes of AT 480, the testers of the kind and unkind girls are a vampire, an evil spirit, the devil, an old man, an old woman, the Lord, the Mother of God, the twelve months, or cats. In one frequently recorded subtype, The Golden Girl (*Zlatnoto momiche*, *480/3), the girls come to an old woman, a witch (*mag'osnitsa*), or a *samodiva*, who asks them to take care of and feed animals such as snakes or lizards (Daskalova-Perkovska et al. 1994: 126, 167–177).

The Bulgarian Forest Mother (*gorska maika*) is an old woman with protruding teeth who causes insomnia in children, and is addressed in charms to quiet the child. In some of these incantations, the Forest Mother has a child of her own, and the person reciting the charm tells her to take the crying, and to give the (human) child sleep. The name *gorska maika* also refers to a plant used to cure insomnia. In a Bulgarian lullaby, sleep is said to come from the forest. Ute Dukova points out that many South Slavic demons of illness come out of the forest, and spells and charms typically send illness back to the forest (Dukova 1985: 15–17, Zečević 1981: 20). Other female demonic figures associated with illness are *Baba Drusla* (fever), *Baba Pisanka* (measles), *Baba Sharka* (pox, measles), and *babitsi* (stomach and intestinal ailments; Dukova 1984: 5–6). In Bulgarian folklore the month of March is also female, *Baba Marta*. Customs and rituals carried out on the first of March, such as wearing or hanging out red and white tassels, might be considered offerings made to Baba Marta to placate her, and ensure warm weather (Kabakova 1994: 215). The (usually) red and white amulet or trinket, called *martenitsa*, is believed to ward off evil influences, and in some cases to keep snakes and lizards from entering homes, or to make snakes blind. "The *martenitsa* is usually worn until March ninth or twenty-fifth, because these two dates are associated with seeing storks, swallows, cuckoos, snakes and fruit trees in blossom for the first time" (Mikov 1994: 133). When the *martenitsa* is no longer worn, it is tied to a tree or placed under a stone.

In eastern Serbia, a humorous masked figure who appears at Easter is called *Baba Jega*. *Baba Korizma* is a figure of Serbian folk belief. A tall, thin woman dressed in black, she carries a stick and beats those who have broken the Easter fast. She carries away naughty children in a bag to her cave in the mountains. At Easter, parents buy their children back from her with Easter eggs. Baba Korizma may be the embodiment of the Lenten fast and carries seven sticks, representing the seven weeks of the fast. She discards one stick every week. *Baba Roga* is a similar figure who frightens small children. She is a toothless woman with a monstrous face and a horn on her head who takes away mischievous children. *Gvozdenzuba* (Iron Tooth) is also used to frighten children, especially spinners. Gvozdenzuba carries coals in a pot and burns the fingers of girls who don't spin well (Kulišić et al. 1970: 10–11, 87, Tolstoi 1995:

38). Another figure of folk belief in Serbia is the Forest Mother (*šumska majka*). She can appear as a beautiful young woman with loose hair, naked or wearing white, as an ugly old woman with conspicuous teeth, or in animal form. She appears only at night, usually at midnight. The Forest Mother can protect pregnant women and infants, but also harms them. She is invoked in charms and spells used to heal children, especially to cure insomnia and crying (Zečević 1981: 18–22, see chapter 3). *Babice* are female demonic beings who try to harm young mothers and newborn infants. They appear either as young women, or as ugly old women dressed in black (ibid., 87–93). Snowy days in March are referred to as the "old woman's days" or the "old woman's goats" or "kids" (*babini dni, babini jarci, babini kozlići*, Tolstoi 1995: 38).

An important female figure of Serbian and Croatian folk belief is the fairy *vila* (pl. *vile*). The vile appear as beautiful young women with long hair and can sometimes have donkey feet. They live in caves and on mountains and gather in meadows to dance the round dance (*kolo*), and punish those who disturb them. Vile sometimes marry mortal men and have children with them, but then run away. They can cause blindness but also restore sight. In a legend from Dalmatia, a woman goes to a pool in the evening to get water, and sees the vile dancing. They warn her not to come there again at this hour, but also help her draw water, and on the way home the woman does not feel the weight of the water she is carrying (Hovorka 1897: 300). The vile reward people who help them by giving them charcoal or leaves which later turn to gold. Vile appear in folktales and in South Slavic folk epic poetry (Zečević 1981: 39–49).

In Bosnian folk belief there is a benevolent fairy, the "duck with golden wings" (*utva zlatokrila*), whose upper body is that of a maiden, while her lower body has the form of a duck. Saint or Holy Sunday (*svetica nedelja*) suffers when people work on Sunday instead of going to church, and her body is full of wounds from needles, scissors, axes, saws, and other tools. She appears in the company of the Mother of God (Zovko 1893: 442–443).

In Slovenian folk belief *Baba Pehtra* produces rain and snow. On Twelfth Night (Epiphany) she punishes bad children and rewards good ones. She also oversees spinning and punishes women who spin on days when this work is prohibited. At dusk shepherds see her walking over the highest mountain slopes with a golden spindle, or riding a cow. In some areas she is driven out on Twelfth Night by noisy processions through the village: Young men crack whips, ring bells, bang on kettles, and let dogs run, since Pehtra cannot stand these noises. In one locality, a man dressed as Pehtra-Baba and a noisy procession run through the mountain meadows at Epiphany to keep bears from attacking the herds. Pehtra appeared at Epiphany in Fürnitz, where she was given sausages and smoked meat. In the western end of the upper Bohinj

Valley, *Pehta*, an ugly old woman, appears in the St. Nicholas day procession; in the eastern part of the valley she does not exist as a real person, but stories about her are used to frighten children. Around Bovec, *Perte* (masked young men carrying axes) frightened children (Kuret 1955: 211–212). Niko Kuret recognizes a "mythic ambivalence" in this figure; in some regions, the masked Pehtra appears as an ugly woman in fur or rags, while in others she is a bright figure dressed in white. The "dark" Pehtra also wears a mask with horns or a blackened face, while the "light" Pehtra covers her face with a white veil. There is also a clear regional division in the kind of masked procession that takes place: the Pehtra who takes part in the "chasing" or "running" custom is played by a young man, while the Pehtra who visits homes, distributes gifts, and threatens naughty children is played by an old woman. Like the light and dark Pehtras, these two kinds of masked performances are not found together in the same locale (Kuret 1969: 212, 235–236). Another female figure in Slovenian folklore who may be identical to Pehtra is *Torka* or *Torklja* (probably derived from *torek*, "Tuesday"). Torka oversees spinning and the prohibition on this and other work during the winter Ember days (in Catholic tradition, the Wednesday, Friday, and Saturday after December 13). The Slovenian *kvatre*, "Ember day," accounts for another name of this personage, *Kvatrnica* or *Kvatrna*. Children put a baby tooth in a mouse's hole, and address Torklja: "Torklja, I'm giving you a bone tooth, give me an iron one for it!" (ibid., 210, 228–232). Pehtra and Torka have much in common with the Germanic Perchta (Waschnitius 1913: 25–29). Niko Kuret concludes that Pehtra must derive from an ancient Indo-European or even Eurasian figure, while Torka is a Christianized version of this mythical being. The particular form she has taken in Slovenian folklore was determined in part by cultural contact between Germanic and Slavic tribes in the sixth century in the area of present-day Carinthia and Slovenia, and in part by older cultural traditions in this region (Illyrian, Celtic, and Roman; Kuret 1969: 220).

While Baba Yaga has been compared to other figures from South Slavic folklore, Ol'ga Cherepanova concludes that there is no truly equivalent figure in the South Slavic tradition (1983: 105). Something like Baba Yaga's ambiguity appears in a Croatian tale (a version of AT 451), where two witches appear. The first old witch (*stara coprnica*) agrees to show a lost man the way home out of the forest if he will marry her daughter, who then turns his sons into swans. The second old witch (*stara coprnica*), also called grandmother (*babica*), tells the heroine what she must do to disenchant her brothers (Neweklowsky and Gaál 1).

In the German-speaking countries, analogous figures of custom and folk belief are *Perchta* in Alpine regions (pl. *Perchten*) or *Holda* or *Holle* in Central and

Northern Germany, or some variation on these names. A related Swiss figure, associated with spinning, who has a crooked nose and long fingernails, is called *Chlungeri*. Perchta is mentioned in medieval documents. A thirteenth-century Latin tract from Oberaltaich (Bavaria) on the seven vices (*Tractatus de septem vitiis*...) mentions Domina Perchta several times: She rushes about, showing off her painted face and beautiful clothes; she looks in a mirror, is disappointed with her appearance, and demands money for new clothes from her husband; a devil sits on the long train of her extravagant dress (Rumpf 1991: 70–71). The 1411 poem of Hans Vintler, "Pluemen der tugent" ("Flowers of Virtue") denounces pagan beliefs in the woman "Precht with the iron nose" (*Precht mit der eysnern nas*) and in a 1393 poem a father warns his child about the frightful "Berhte" who appears eight days after Christmas (Waschnitius 1913: 35).

Narratives recorded about Perchta and Holle more recently are mostly legends about encounters with her (memorates or fabulates), and she appears ambiguous, sometimes kind and helpful, but often malevolent. Perchta oversees spinning (rewarding diligent spinners, punishing lazy ones or those who spin on days when spinning is prohibited), has disheveled hair, and a long or iron nose. Sometimes she has a large foot, or a goose or swan foot (Hoffmann-Krayer 1934–35: 1482). If the house has not been swept clean on Christmas Eve in parts of Styria (Austria), Perchtel cuts open the stomachs of the lazy girls and fills them with rubbish. She carries a broom, needle, and scissors for this purpose (Waschnitius 1913: 20). Sometimes she appears with the souls of dead unbaptized children. Perchta is sometimes identified as the wife of Pontius Pilate or the daughter of Herod (Rumpf 1991: 27).

In a legend from Ramsau (Styria), a woman senses she is about to give birth on the eve of Epiphany. She sends her sweetheart out to fetch a midwife. He encounters a beautiful friendly woman with a cricket chirping on her long nose. The woman asks him to carve a wooden nail for her wagon, and lets him keep the shavings, which later turn to gold. When he returns home with a midwife, a child has already been born (Waschnitius 1913: 19). In a house in Carinthia (Austria) where incense had not been burned as a precaution against Perchtl, she took a man away during the night and brought him back dead the next morning. People found foreign, unfamiliar flowers between his fingers and toes. During the night he had traveled to distant lands with her (ibid., 23).

Food is left for Perchta on certain days of the year, especially Epiphany Eve (the night of January 5–6). Often this food offering has an oracular function. If Perchta has eaten with a particular individual's spoon, he or she will enjoy good fortune in the coming year. In Alpine regions, noisy masked processions called *Perchtenlaufen* or *Perchtenjagen* (the "running" or "chasing" of the Perchten) take place in the winter season, usually between Advent and Epiphany. The participants are costumed as either "beautiful" Perchten with elaborate tall headdresses without masks, or as "ugly" Perchten with devilish masks (*schiache Perchten*), and sometimes go from house to house, receiving food in return for "blessing" the household. In the Mölltal region of Carinthia, Perchtl, wearing a frightening wooden mask and a cow bell on her back, demands either children or bacon before she will leave (*Kinder oder Speck, derweil geh' ich nicht weg!* ibid., 24). Figures like Perchta, with a similar name, are found in Slovenia (mentioned above) and the Czech lands (Feifalik 1859).

Many scholars have supposed that these processions derive from pre-Christian beliefs, and were originally intended to drive away evil spirits and promote fertility. Marianne Rumpf expresses skepticism regarding the ancient origin of Perchta, and concludes that the Perchten customs arose during the medieval period. The first appearances of this name in documents of the eleventh through twelfth centuries denote the Eve of Epiphany (*Giperchtennacht, giperahtanaht*) rather than a being. Fraw Percht and Domina Perchta appear in catechisms, commentaries on the Ten Commandments, and tracts concerning vice and superstition. This literature, most often produced in monasteries, drew on sources common to all of Christian Europe, and does not necessarily reflect local traditions. The "running" of the Perchten in winter may derive from medieval processions of beggars, especially lepers and other invalids, who might have covered their faces, or whose deformities might have inspired the later "devilish" masks or the "iron nose." Epiphany Eve was a day when pious Christians were expected to observe a meat fast, and to give alms and food, which would account for processions of beggars and lepers on this day (Rumpf 1991: 61, 174–181).

In Göttingen, Waldeck, western Thuringia, and other German localities, it snows when Frau Holle shakes out her feather bed (Waschnitius 1913: 92–93, 96, 112). She is a gray-haired old woman with long teeth who makes sure women have finished their spinning before Christmas or New Year's. Sometimes she brings gifts at this time of year. Queen Holle lives in the Kyffhäuser Mountain as housekeeper for Frederick I Barbarossa (c. 1123–1190, ibid., 107). Frau Holle is a beautiful ghostly being in a long white gown and veil, living in a mountain near Hasloch on the Main River (ibid., 81). She helps women and girls with spinning and domestic chores, but punishes the lazy. In Würzburg, Frau Hulle goes about the streets on the night before Christmas, clad in a hood and white cloak. She carries a rod and carries off bad children in a sack (ibid., 80). In Waldeck, the Hollen are dwarf-like beings who sometimes make children ill. Parents leave wool and bread in a juniper bush and tell the Hollen "you should spin and eat and forget my child" (ibid., 96). Like Baba Yaga, both Perchta and Holle frightened children (ibid., 23, 56, 78, 80, 93, 113,

128, 176). Frau Holle is the tester of the kind and unkind girls in a famous version of AT 480 in the Grimm collection (no. 24). In spite of these similarities, Sigrid Lichtenberger finds no single figure equivalent to Baba Yaga in German folktales (1986: 151).

A legendary queen with a goose foot (*la reine pédauque*) appears in France. Twelfth-century sculptures on church portals represent the Queen of Sheba with a goose foot, and legend attributes such a foot to Ragnahilde, the wife of a fifth-century Visigoth king of Toulouse. According to a sixteenth-century source, people in Toulouse swore by the distaff of the goose-footed queen, and François Rabelais mentions her in the *Quart Livre* (1548). St. Néomadie or Néomaye of Poitou is also represented with a goose foot in a few sculptures. Legend attributes a large foot to the wife of Pippin the Short, mother of Charlemagne, "Berthe au grand pied" (Maillet 1980). A legendary figure from the Jura canton of Switzerland and the adjoining Montbéliard region of France is the fairy Arie or Aunt Arie (*Tante Arie, Tantairie*). She has iron teeth and goose feet, and may appear as a giant or a snake. She performs the work of a housewife, spinning, baking bread, and washing clothes. She punishes lazy spinners and rewards diligent ones, and appears at Christmas to distribute gifts, riding a donkey. She punishes children who have been bad. She lives in a cave, guarding a chest of gold, and puts down her diamond crown when she bathes (Christinger 1965 ii: 129, Gennep 1958: 3019–3023).

Returning to eastern Europe, there appear to be a number of figures analogous to Baba Yaga in Romanian folklore:

> The Mamapadurei or mother of the forest, resides in a hut that revolves on fowl's legs, with a fence stuck full of skulls. Baba Cloanța is a tall old hag with a crooked back, long teeth like a rake. She, like the Baba Yaga of our folktale is also the mother of dragons and the owner of a tub full of souls. Baba Coaja is Queen of Witches with a long glass nose, one iron foot and brass nails. She kills unbaptized children and hides them in bushes where they rot. Baba Hârca dwells in a cave and steals the stars from the sky. (Róheim 1947: 58)

Romanian charms to calm a restless child are addressed to a Forest Mother *Muma padurii*, who is believed to kidnap lost children and turn them into trees, as well as depriving them of sleep (Agapkina and Toporkov 1990: 71). Nicolae Roşianu cites the Forest Mother, with her "hut on rooster's claws," as a donor in Romanian folktales (Roşianu 1974: 119–121). A Forest Maiden (*Fata Padurii*) appears as a villain in a Romanian version of AT 327A (Hansel and Gretel). A brother and sister get lost in the forest and come to her house made of pancakes and sausages. The Forest Maiden fattens the boy with the intention of cooking him, but at an opportune moment the children throw her in the oven (Alvarez-Pereyre 1976: 177, 254–255). In a Romanian memorate, three seductive Forest Maidens detain a shepherd in a house in the forest where he loses track of time. When he escapes and comes back to his village, he finds that he has been gone for a year and a half (Lebarbier 1996).

A "Forest Hag" appears as a vengeful cannibal ogress, the wife of an ogre the hero has killed. She sharpens her teeth on a millstone, pursues the hero, and her fight with Tuesday Night, a female donor, allows the hero and his companion to escape, in a tale containing AT 312 and some elements of AT 301 (Cartianu 1979: 143–168). "Harridan Plague" is a villain who possesses the magic horse the hero must acquire to rescue his bride from a giant (AT 552+ 554+400+302). Like Baba Yaga, she threatens the hero with beheading if he fails to retrieve her mare. Harridan Plague has claws, matted hair, a giant human head, and horse legs. Poles with skulls stuck on them (presumably those of unlucky adventurers) are attached to the roof of her dwelling (Cartianu 1979: 54–88).

Baba Cloanţa (*cloanţa*, "jaw") appears as a magic helper in a version of AT 501 (The Three Old Women Helpers). The heroine is a lazy girl. Her mother lies to the emperor, saying she is diligent, and he takes the girl into his service. The emperor's mother gives her an impossible amount of hemp to spin overnight. Baba Cloanţa appears and does the spinning for her. The emperor then decides to marry the girl, and Baba Cloanţa says she must be invited to the wedding. The girl forgets to invite her, but when Baba Cloanţa reproaches her, she calls her in to the feast. Baba Cloanţa appears, and everyone is horrified at her ugly appearance: She has a huge lip. Baba Cloanţa explains that she is ugly because she has done so much spinning and work, and so the heroine never has to work again (Alvarez-Pereyre 1976: 182–183, 260–262).

Baba Dochia is an old woman who insults the month of March when she goes out with a herd of sheep or goats. March sometimes asks February for a few days of cold with which to punish the woman and her animals. They perish from cold, or are turned to stone. Versions of this legend are found elsewhere in the Balkans, and in other Mediterranean countries (Kabakova 1994: 209–213). Baba Dochia also appears in Romanian versions of AT 480, as the wicked stepmother: When her stepdaughter succeeds in bringing back strawberries in winter (with the help of an angel, the Lord, St. Peter, or March), she thinks that spring must already have arrived, goes into the mountains herself, and dies. In a version of AT 480 from the Bukovina region, Baba Dochia is the tester. She asks the kind girl to shake out twelve pillows, which produce snow. The unkind girl shakes out a coverlet, and clouds and lightning come out of it. The kind girl receives gold, and the unkind girl is given iron clothing wiped in pitch (ibid., 214, 216). Her name probably derives from the second-century saint and martyr Eudochia, whose day is celebrated the first of March.

Saint Friday (*Sfînta Vineri*) oversees spinning and can be very cruel. In one fabulate, she appears in the evening and kills a young girl who had fallen asleep on the stove, forgotten by the other girls. "Mother Friday" has a human form, except for one chicken foot (Mesnil and Popova 1993: 755). In a version of AT 552A from Bessarabia (Moldova), St. Friday appears as a donor. She tells the father of three maidens how to steal the water of life from a witch in order to disenchant his animal sons-in-law (Karlinger 4). St. Friday is the tester in Romanian versions of AT 480 (Mesnil and Popova 1993: 758–759). St. Paraskeva (Friday) appears as a donor in a version of AT 313 from Moldova. A poor woman gives her son an icon of St. Paraskeva when he sets out into the world. The icon advises him, and he scrapes some wood shavings from its back to heal a bear, a bee, and a fish. The animals help him accomplish difficult tasks when he arrives at a dragon's house, and St. Paraskeva tells him to take what is behind the ninth door as a reward—it turns out to be the emperor's daughter (Karlinger 2). The cult of St. Paraskeva is also found among the East Slavs (see above).

Baba Yaga also bears considerable resemblance to the Iron-Nosed Woman of Hungarian folklore (*Vasorrú bába*). "The lad peeked into the house and saw an old woman sitting there. Before her was a spinning wheel. Soon he noticed that she had a huge nose that was made of iron and came down nearly as far as her knees. She was none other than the Iron-Nose Witch" (Illyés 1970: 271). The Iron-Nosed Woman or Witch often plays a role analogous to that of Baba Yaga. In AT 300A (The Fight on the Bridge), she is the mother of three dragons (or simply men, in Illyés 1970: 101–110) slain by the hero. She is the wicked midwife in a version of AT 707 (Ortutay 3). She appears as the tester of the kind and unkind girls in AT 480 (Illyés 1970: 253–256). She and her eagle husband are the villains in a version of AT 313C (Ortutay 16). The cunning cat of Puss in Boots (AT 545B) sometimes plays a trick on the Iron-Nosed Witch (Solymossy 1927: 221). She is a somewhat hostile donor in an episode of AT 554, where the hero must herd her goats for three days, but in the same tale she helps the hero in later episodes, restoring him to life and coming to live with him and his bride at the end (Illyés 1970: 269–289). This same episode, found in another tale closer to the East Slavic versions of AT 552+554+400+302, features the duplicitous Iron-Nosed Woman (who whets a sword on her tongue and threatens the hero with decapitation) as the owner of a horse the hero obtains in order to rescue his wife from a dragon (Ortutay 8). Perhaps related to the Iron-Nosed Woman are three long-nosed women, the mothers of the moon, sun, and wind, who help the heroine in a Hungarian version of AT 425 (Ortutay 2).

According to Sándor Solymossy, the Iron-Nosed Woman lives in a house that turns around on a bird's foot, although in fact this motif may be more frequently associated with dragons in Hungarian folktales. Solymossy recognizes that the Hungarian and East Slavic figures are clearly related, but he searches still further east for the source of the attribute "iron-nosed." Although Solymossy states that this feature is absent in Russia, Baba Yaga does in fact sometimes have an iron nose (Khudiakov 39, 40; Sadovnikov 4, 61).

Solymossy finds an analogous motif in the epic poetry and rituals of Ural-Altaic peoples. In some Tatar and Altai epics one finds a copper-nosed old woman (Solymossy 1927: 225–226; Radloff 1866: 45–46, 112, 116; Surazakov 1985: 44–47). Ultimately, the source of this motif can perhaps be found in ritual idols of the Mansi (Vogul) and Khant (Ostyak) peoples, which had protruding noses made of metal. The motif could have come to the Hungarians from Turk-Tatar folklore, and Solymossy also suggests that the Hungarian noun *bába* is of Turkic rather than Slavic origin. The Turkic meanings of this term, "father" or "old person," suggest that the Iron-Nosed Bába was originally a male idol, and that the term was later applied to a female figure, who became transformed into a fairy-tale witch (Solymossy 1927: 230–233). Interestingly, while iron is a constant attribute of the Hungarian folktale witch, iron could be used to destroy the witch of folk belief (*boszorkány*). This witch sometimes took the form of a horse, and if the horse were shod, traces of the iron or the iron horseshoe itself would be found at dawn on the witch's human body. The witch would die soon after (Losonczy 1986: 62). In Hungarian folk belief there is also a Tuesday Woman (*kedd asszonya*) who punishes women for washing on this day (Róheim 1946: 121).

A wicked female forest spirit who has been compared to Baba Yaga can be found in the folk belief of the Khant people, who inhabit the Irtysh river region in Western Siberia (Karjalainen 1922: 377). Yakut folktales and heroic epics have adopted Baba Yaga, and *Ëma-baba*, a figure found in Komi folktales, has adopted some features of Baba Yaga (D'iakonova 1985, Pomerantseva 1979: 35, Lashuk 1972: 283). Evenk folklore also appears to possess an analogous figure (Romanova and Myreeva 1971: 105, 209).

In a tale recorded from a Russianized population of Yukagir Chuvans in eastern Siberia, a giant woman called Yagisna appears at the house of a lazy man who never gets out of bed. His wife makes him get up, and he shoots arrows at Yagisna without effect. "By the advice of his wife the man takes aim at her buttocks. The arrow enters her anus and comes out of her mouth, killing her" (Bogoras 1902: 623). The "Yagha-Witch" appears as the wicked stepmother in a Chuvan version of AT 480 (Bogoras 1918: 142–143). In Yukagir tales showing Russian influence, a witch called Yaghishna captures a young woman, takes her clothes, and takes her place with her husband. The young woman escapes, the truth is revealed, and the husband shoots Yaghishna dead with twelve arrows (ibid., 52–54). A ten-eyed witch, Yagha, appears in a version of AT 327F. The boy hero avoids being cooked and cooks Yagha's three daughters, who have five, six, and eight eyes. He defeats the witch in combat after drinking from the well of the water of life and youth in the witch's storehouse, and causing her to drink from the water of death by mistake (ibid., 55–58). In tales recorded from a Russian creole girl in the Kolyma region, a boy outwits Yaghishna, who is chasing him and wants to kill him. He traps her in a hole (ibid., 112). Yaghishna captures a girl and tells her to look after the house in her absence. She tells the girl not to open one storehouse. The girl opens the storehouse, releases "charmed reindeer, neither living nor dead," and escapes across the river with them. When Yaghishna returns, the girl tells her that she drank the river dry to cross it. Yaghishna tries to do this, and bursts. At the end of the tale, Yaghishna tells the girl to take her head for a cup, her fingers for forks, her joints for supports, her buttocks for a mortar, her legs for a stone-scraper handle, and her backbone for a scraping-board (ibid., 112–114). The members of a hungry family kill each other until only a boy is left. Yaghishna comes, appearing in the form of a cloud of dust, cuts the boy's head off, and goes home (ibid., 114–115). Yaghishna strikes two girls with a knife, but cannot injure them. One of the girls strikes Yaghishna in the heart and kills her. Later, horses breathing fire come to seek revenge for Yaghishna's death, but cannot harm the girls (ibid., 117–118). In a tale recorded in 1895 from a Russianized Yukagir girl, the she-monster Yaghishna asks a girl if she wants to be her daughter. The girl agrees, on the condition that Yaghishna will soon die. Angered, Yaghishna slaps the girl, who turns into gravel (ibid., 122–123).

An unusual image of Baba Yaga appears in a Russian tale from Russkoe Ust'e, a remote region located along the Indigirka River in Northeastern Siberia (Shastina 1985 no. 63, a version of AT 519). The princess Marfita goes to ask for fire from Yaga-Baba, who sucks blood from the princess' breasts. The hero and his companions catch Yaga-Baba and force her to reveal where she has healing water. They fight Yaga-Baba and cut her head off, but the head continues to run, using its braids as legs. Finally they smash the head to pieces, drink all the healing water, and are healed (Shastina 1985: 403–410).

R. N. Afanas'eva sees a reflection of an archaic cult of fire in the fact that Marfita must pay for the fire with her blood. Significantly, the hero notices that Marfita is pale after Yaga has sucked her blood ("Why has your blood changed?"). Afanas'eva interprets this episode with reference to customs of Siberian peoples (Yakut and Evenk, neighbors of this Russian community) which prohibited menstruating women from touching the hearth. Yaga-Baba

does not suck Marfita's blood because she has given her fire, or as punishment
for letting the fire go out; the fire has gone out when the young woman is in
contact with demonic forces during menstruation (Afanas'eva 1986a: 146).
The motif of the head walking on its braids is clearly borrowed from the
folklore of neighboring Siberian peoples. Afanas'eva suggests that the braids
must contain Yaga-Baba's supernatural strength, which accounts for the hero's
inability to kill her simply by decapitating her. The motif of guarding the fire is
found here because of the importance of fire in this far northern region, where
traces of a cult of fire can be found among the indigenous peoples even today.
The archaic beliefs of the ancient Slavs could be "reborn" here, recalled by
analogous concepts in the folklore of the Siberian aboriginals (ibid., 154).

   Whether or not one agrees with this view of a "secondary archaization" of
Russian folktale material, the influence of Yakut or Evenk beliefs also accounts
for another unusual image of Èga-Baba in a tale recorded from a Russian native
of Russkoe Ust'e (Khudiakov 1964: 269–270). Èga-Baba is described as a
shaman (*stala shamanit' ona*) who has been called to bring a murdered man back
to life. The rogue hero distracts people's attention, takes Èga-Baba, and puts
her upside down in a tub of water she has been drinking from. She is dead, but
he manages to hide this from her children (wolves, bears, foxes, all kinds of
animals), who then think they have killed her when she falls from a horse. The
hero has the animals stick their tails into holes in the ice to bring their mother
back to life. Of course the animals freeze to death and he takes them as booty.
In this case the shamanic practices of the neighboring peoples have been
identified with Baba Yaga's witch aspect, and the animal children are perhaps
an echo of Baba Yaga's children in AT 480 (see chapter 3). The influence of the
Russian folktale tradition has even extended further east. A version of AT 402,
clearly derived from the Frog Princess tale, was recorded from a Tlingit
storyteller in Alaska (Dauenhauer 1975).

   On the western edge of Russia, the influence of the Finnish and Karelian
folklore tradition can be seen in the popularity of tale type AT 403 (The Black
and the White Bride) among the Russian population in the Karelian coastal
region. This tale is relatively infrequently recorded in other parts of Russia, but
is popular among the Karelians and in neighboring Finland (Sen'kina 1988:
115–116). Elsewhere in Russia, the villain is the nanny, but in Russian Karelian
tradition, the villain is Baba Yaga, and in most Karelian and Finnish versions of
this tale, an analogous figure, *Syöjätär*. This and a number of other tale types
exhibit the influence of Finnish and Karelian folktales on the Russian tradition
(ibid., 113–140).

   The Finnish/Karelian Syöjätär is one of two figures (the other is the *akka*,
"old woman") who sometimes correspond to Baba Yaga, and who have

probably influenced and been influenced by her (Onegina 1974). Syöjätär is as popular and well known in Karelia as Baba Yaga is in Russia. Her name is also used to describe an unpleasant woman, and as a fictional character she appears in many of the same tale types as Baba Yaga and performs the same functions. She appears as the wicked stepmother, and the hero must also herd her stallions on pain of death. Syöjätär's home is described more like a Karelian house than the typical hut of Baba Yaga.

In some tales Syöjätär is called the devil's wife, and Onegina finds an interesting correspondence between her and the image of Satan in some Russian legends: Both are believed to give rise to snakes, toads, and other unclean beings (Onegina 1974: 138). Sparrows come out of her eyes, crows from her toes, vipers from her fingernails, magpies from her hair, and ravens from her ears. Her legs become devils, her arms become snakes, and her hair turns to worms. In some tales Syöjätär sticks a finger or hand out of a tar pit and worms and mosquitoes emerge from it.[11]

Syöjätär also appears in incantations, but not in human shape. In these she is the source of evil or pain, and sometimes she is likened to a sea snake or dragon. Unlike Baba Yaga, she does not exhibit cannibalistic tendencies, and most importantly, she lacks her Russian counterpart's ambiguity: She never appears in the role of donor (Konkka 1963: 21–26). This role is taken by the akka.

The akka also resembles Baba Yaga in significant ways, and in some southern Karelian folktales she is even called Yaga. Her house is in the forest, at the seashore, or at the edge of the city, and may stand and turn on the foot of a spindle. There is a similar request made to the hut to stop turning and face the hero. The Karelian akka also expresses the intention of eating her visitor, but the hero's response is usually not to reprimand, as in the Russian tales, but to discourage the akka from eating him: "O, what good thing is there to eat in this traveler? A handful of bones, a spoon of blood, fat like slops, is that what you're going to eat?"

---

[11] Similar etiological motifs are also associated with Baba Yaga. In Karnaukhova 64 (AT 450), the villain Baba Yaga and her daughter are tied to wild horses. Parts of their bodies fall to the ground and create a rocky shore, a swamp, oven pokers, and rakes. In Zelenin Viatka 11 (AT 450), Egibisna turns into hummocks, rakes, and pokers, and a marsh with a river flowing through it. When Egabova and her daughter are thrown into a pit in Nikiforov 1961 no. 80 (AT 403), Egabova tries to fly out in the form of flies and mosquitoes. In Manzhura 1890: 24–27 (AT 300A), Baba-Yuga, harnessed to a plough, rushes to the sea, where she drinks until she bursts. Snakes, toads, lizards, tadpoles, spiders, and worms are born from her. East Slavic myths about the creation of the world by God and the devil sometimes relate how the devil created mountains and rocks by spitting out earth or sand he had gathered from the bottom of the primeval ocean (Dragomanov 1876: 15–16, 89–91).

Like her Russian counterpart, the akka is sometimes described with exaggerated or grotesque physical features: She sits on a post, her breasts are as big as milk pails, her eyes as big as salt cellars, and her legs wind around her hut three times. The akka also sometimes appears as mistress of the forest animals, and she asks the hero(ine) to fulfill various tasks also found in Russian tales: to heat the bath, to wash animals, to guard a herd of horses. Like the donor Baba Yaga, she helps the hero(ine) to recover a lost spouse or to obtain magic objects (Onegina 1974: 133–137). U. Konkka points out that the akka is often the hero's aunt, while Syöjätär's appearance as the wicked stepmother shows that the Karelian folktales have not made the stepmother completely human, but have retained her supernatural character.

Lithuanian folktales also possess an analogous figure called *ragana* or *laume-ragana*. She, however, is exclusively a villain. Donors are kind old women and men, anthropomorphic natural forces or supernatural beings (Kerbelyte 1979: 69). In his lectures on Slavic folktales given in the 1850s, Fedor Buslaev called attention to the similarity of Baba Yaga and Lauma (1861: 333–338). Witches in tales recorded from Russian storytellers in Lithuania include *Baba Ragana*, who sleeps in a mortar (Mitropol'skaia 83, AT 327B) and *ragana*, who rides in a mortar with a pestle and broom (ibid., no. 87, AT 450).

In Central Asia, analogous female figures can be found in Tadzhik folklore. Grandmother Thunder causes thunder when she shakes out her fur coat. The old woman *Odshus*, blind in one eye, is associated with cold winter weather. She causes harm and steals children. Lady Tuesday (*Bibi-Se-shanbe*) appears in folk belief and folktales. In cases of illness or infertility, Tadzhik women prepare a special meal for Bibi-Se-shanbe in which only women are allowed to participate. As part of the ritual, a bowl of flour is covered with a cloth, and after the meal, handprints or the prints of chicken feet may appear in the flour as an omen. Another important part of the ritual is the reciting of a fairy tale (AT 480+510, The Kind and the Unkind Girls, and Cinderella) where Bibi-Se-shanbe appears as the tester/donor. Bibi-Se-shanbe is also associated with spinning, and prohibits this work on certain days (Bleichsteiner 1953, Zelenin 1934: 232–233). Robert Bleichsteiner also finds general correspondences between Persian epics and legends, and motifs of Russian fairy tales with Baba Yaga (1914). In Ossetian folklore (northern Caucasus), a female donor figure who has been compared to Baba Yaga is *kulbadagus* (Guriev 1980).

An ambiguous ogress appears in Arab and North African folktales. When she acts as a donor, the hero gains her help in a curious episode which offers an interesting parallel to the typical interaction of the East Slavic folktale hero with Baba Yaga (see chapter 4). The ogress (Arab *ghouleh*, Berber *teryel*, *tsériel*) has enormous breasts and throws them over her shoulders. The hero sneaks up behind her and sucks milk from both breasts, thus becoming her adoptive or "milk son." The ogress' brothers, her son, or even the ogress herself tell the hero to do this, or he appears to know what to do already (El-Shamy 1980: 58, Mouliéras 1965 i: 17, 74, Muhawi and Kanaana 1989: 85). After the hero has succeeded in drinking the ogress' milk in a Kabyle tale, she warns him of her own cannibalistic nature: "If it weren't for the mouthful that you drank from my breast, I would eat you and the country you walk in" (Mouliéras 1965 i: 17). The Berber ogress is a deceitful and ugly old woman with long hair and big teeth, sometimes blind or one-eyed. In one locality she is said to have small bags and a pair of scissors hanging from her hair. When she sleeps, the noises of cattle and other animals she has devoured can be heard coming from her stomach (Farès 1994: 9–10). However, in a Kabyle tale (related to AT 590), the ogress befriends the hero and brings him back to life after his treacherous mother and her ogre husband have killed him (Mouliéras 1965 i: 72–87).

Other figures similar to Baba Yaga can be found in ancient Greek legend, where a monstrous female character was Empusa, who frightened children. One of her legs was copper, or an ass's leg (Tolstoi 1941). Ivan Tolstoi has also compared the hero's typical interaction with the donor Baba Yaga (his arrival at her hut) to an ancient Greek legend about Theseus. According to fragments of a poem by Callimachus (ca. 330 B.C.), Theseus spent the night in the old woman Hecale's house before he defeated the Marathonian bull the next day (Tolstoi 1941). Other analogues for Baba Yaga may be found as far away as South America (Lévi-Strauss 1969: 109–110, 1973: 273) and Melanesia (Meletinskii 1958: 20).

It is remarkable that these witch-like supernatural female beings of so many traditions (throughout Europe and even as far east as Central Asia) share so many common features: a prominent nose, leg, teeth, eye, or tongues, which may be made of metal or some unusual material, horns, loose or disheveled hair, and a bird's foot. Another persistent feature is an association with specific days of the week (Sunday, Tuesday, Friday), days or periods of the year (Christmas, Epiphany, March, Lent, Ember day), and times of the day (noon). Many are associated with winter and cold weather (snow, rain, thunder). These supernatural women sometimes embody illness and are a danger to children, but can also cure them; hostile or ambiguous behavior appears typical. They oversee and control spinning and other traditionally female tasks. They dwell far away from human communities, in the forest or in caves. At least two Slavic figures of this group (Ježibaba and Torklja) are associated with the customs surrounding the disposal of baby teeth. Other than Ježibaba, it is impossible to determine which of these figures may be "genetically" related to Baba Yaga. The presence of folktale characters with similar attributes among peoples in

Eastern Europe suggests the possibility of a common origin, or that cultural transmission and borrowing took place in the past in this region (especially between the East Slavic areas and Slovakia, Hungary, and Romania). Baba Yaga does not share all the features of the supernatural female beings described here, but it becomes clear that she is a variation on an international theme.

CHAPTER THREE
Baba Yaga and Children

The studies and observations of Nikolai Novikov, Elena Novik, and Olga Periañez-Chaverneff suggest that the type of Baba Yaga encountered in a tale depends on the age, gender, and status of the hero; it seems likely that different kinds of aggressive (or kind) behavior might be related to different kinds of protagonists. A logical first step is to organize the tales according to whether the hero(ine) is a child or an adult, male or female. Baba Yaga figures especially prominently in tales with a boy or girl protagonist, and more than one-fourth of the tales in our sample (124 of 422) concern her interaction with a child. Baba Yaga's interactions with the girl/young woman heroine of AT 480 and the boy hero of AT 327C/F in particular call for close examination, because these two tale types are the most popular tales with Baba Yaga, based on the number of recordings at our disposal. The image and behavior of Baba Yaga in these tales can provide a basis for understanding her role in other tales.

Propp (1946) and Razumova (1993) consider Baba Yaga a "type" who is represented by other characters who resemble her—witches, grandmothers, and helpful old women who sometimes live in huts on chicken legs or exhibit other features typical of Baba Yaga. For the sake of clarity, and to demarcate our subject more easily, we will only consider tales in which Baba Yaga appears and actually bears this name, or one of its many variant forms.

Baba Yaga, the Boy, and the Oven

One of the most memorable fairy tales featuring Baba Yaga is about her thwarted attempts to cook a boy in her oven (SUS 327C/F, The Boy and the Witch; AT 327C, The Devil [Witch] Carries the Hero Home in a Sack; AT 327F, The Witch and the Fisher Boy). It was reportedly one of the most popular children's folktales in northern Russia, or even the third most popular Russian folktale (Karnaukhova 1934: 402, Bakhtin and Shiriaieva 1976: 277). Its popularity may have varied by region: It was well loved in Pinega where almost everyone knew it, but unpopular in Zaonezh'e (Nikiforov 1930: 37). According to Nikolai Novikov, it was the first genuine folktale about Baba Yaga to be published.[1]

---

[1] A version of SUS 327C was published by M. N. Makarov in 1820 in "O starinnykh russkikh prazdnikakh i obychaiakh" [About Ancient Russian Holidays and Customs], *Trudy Obshchestva liubitelei rossiiskoi slovesnosti pri Moskovskom universitete* XVII, pp. 126–130. Cited in Novikov 1974: 133–134.

There are two subtypes, with different opening episodes. In SUS 327C, the hero is a young boy who lives with animal siblings (usually a cat and a sparrow) or human parents. The siblings or parents leave to go to work, often to the forest to chop wood. They warn him about Baba Yaga. Baba Yaga comes and tries to abduct the boy. The first two times the siblings or parents hear his cries or his song and rescue him, but the third time she succeeds in kidnapping him. The boy is in an apple tree or guarding the apples and Baba Yaga asks him for an apple (Smirnov 231, 250, Sokolova 1970: 32–33, Vedernikova and Samodelova 35) or offers him an apple (Afanas'ev 107, Avanesav and Biryla 1962: 290). Sometimes Baba Yaga offers the boy other kinds of food (Gorodtsov iii: 6–10). He sits on the stove behind the chimney pipe, and when Baba Yaga comes to count the spoons, he is unable to keep himself from telling her not to touch his spoon (Afanas'ev 106, Kozhemiakina 1973: 171–174, Leonova 3, Tatarintseva 1995: 20–22). Or Egibishna knocks at the window and tells the boy to look outside (Zelenin Viatka 87).

Some versions of 327F begin with a childless couple. The boy is magically born from a piece of wood, a finger (Zelenin Viatka 97), or clay (Lutovinova Index p. 18, Nikiforov 1961 no. 45). The boy asks for a boat or already has one. He goes fishing. His mother calls or sings to him from the shore and brings him food. Baba Yaga overhears this and tries to imitate the mother's voice. At first she is unsuccessful because her voice is too low or rough, but she has her voice reforged by a smith or simply tries again and finally manages to seize the boy. According to notes to Nikiforov 1961 no. 85, the narrator sung Baba Yaga's lines (her song to lure the boy to the shore) in "a low voice."

Baba Yaga may also send her daughters to catch the boy. He manages to snatch their food and get away (in Potanin 1902 no. 41 by telling the daughters' eyes to fall asleep), but finally the third daughter or Baba Yaga herself captures him. Sometimes the three daughters are said to have one, two, and three eyes (Smirnov 343). The hero may be caught because he forgets to put the third daughter's third eye to sleep (Balashov 105).[2]

After these different kidnap scenarios, both subtypes of the tale continue with the same definitive central episode. Baba Yaga carries the boy to her home and puts him away in a pantry or cellar. She tells her eldest daughter to heat the oven and roast him. In Smirnov 250 she goes off to church. The daughter calls to the boy to sit or lie down on the bread spatula (baker's peel). The boy sits down and sticks out his arms and legs and doesn't fit into the oven. He says he

---

[2] Three daughters with one, two, and three eyes are more commonly found in SUS 511 (discussed in chapter 6 below); they may have entered these versions of SUS 327F from this source. N. M. Vedernikova finds that the daughters with variable numbers of eyes are a specific feature of SUS 511, only found exceptionally elsewhere (1980a: 250).

doesn't know how and asks Baba Yaga's daughter to show him the right way. The daughter sits or lies down on the spatula and the boy shoves her into the oven. When she is roasted he takes out her meat and leaves it on a plate for Baba Yaga. Baba Yaga returns, eats the meat, and remarks how sweet the boy's meat is or how she will roll and lie around on his bones. From his corner the boy taunts her, telling her that her daughter's meat is sweet, or to roll and lie around on her daughter's bones. Baba Yaga gets angry and tells her second and then youngest daughter to roast the boy, but the same thing happens. Exceptionally, in Smirnov 40, the three girls are not Baba Yaga's daughters, but servants, and they have names (Uliashka, Matreshka, Parashka).

There are a number of variations to the end of the story. Most often Baba Yaga heats up the oven herself and tries to put the boy in, but is tricked the same way her daughters were (Afanas'ev 106, Bakhtin and Shiriaieva 54, Balashov 105, Karnaukhova 74, Nikiforov 1961 no. 70, Onchukov 38, Gorodtsov iii: 6–10, Potanin 1902 no. 41, Smirnov 40, 143, 343, Zelenin Perm' 86, Zelenin Viatka 97, 115). Sometimes Baba Yaga does not have daughters, and the oven episode occurs only once, with Baba Yaga (Tatarintseva 1995: 20–22). The boy runs home, taking her money and possessions with him.

Alternatively, the boy taunts Baba Yaga (after she eats her third daughter) and climbs to the ceiling, attic, or roof. Baba Yaga pursues him, but geese fly by and save him (Afanas'ev 107, 111). The boy knocks her down and she is killed (Smirnov 231); he has taken her iron pestle and kills her with it (Avanesav and Biryla p. 290). Or he runs away before Baba Yaga comes home (Smirnov 250, Nikiforov 1961 no. 45). The conclusion of Anastasiia Stepanovna Kozhemiakina's version departs from the norm when the hero eats Yaga Yagonishna after letting her cook in the oven. He acquires her knowledge and rides home in her mortar, with her pestle and broom (Kozhemiakina 1973: 174). The hero Zhikharka (a rooster, according to the narrator T. L. Kislitsyna) in a version from the Tomsk region also cooks and eats Yaga (Leonova 3). He puts her bones in a bag and takes them home. The bones turn to gold, and he has a feast with the cat and the sparrow. The narrator also describes how Zhikharka holds the oven door shut while Yaga squeals and squeaks inside.

In some versions the boy takes refuge in a tree. From there he taunts Baba Yaga, who starts gnawing at the tree until it is about to fall. He jumps onto another tree. Sometimes Baba Yaga has to run to the smith for a new set of iron teeth. Geese save the boy and take him home (Akimova 367, Kretov 18, Potiavin 9, Matveeva and Leonova 9, Nikiforov 1961 no. 64, Sokolova 1970: 32–33). In one version the tree then collapses on Baba Yaga (Vedernikova and Samodelova 33). Karnaukhova 74, told by a twelve-year-old girl, ends without the hero's return home. After he shoves Egibova into the oven and she roasts,

"The dogs and cats grieved and cried for their grandmother. And the forest rustled and grieved. And that's the whole tale" (Karnaukhova 1934: 159).

A few versions depart from this outline, mostly by including elements of other tale types. The heroes of Smirnov 143 are an orphan brother and sister who climb a pea plant to heaven, where they find a mill.[3] They grind peas until Egiboba comes. They hide, but she orders her hut to squeeze itself together and so finds them. Then follows the oven episode with three daughters and finally Egiboba herself. This is a rare instance in which Baba Yaga/Egiboba attempts to cook a girl:

> Finally Egiboba herself heated up the oven as hot as she could, sharpened her teeth, and seated Ivanushka and Olënushka on the bread spatula. "We don't know how, show us how, mother Egiboba!" "Like this, fu!" and she sat down herself. In an instant they shoved her into the oven and shut it tight. (Smirnov 1917: 420)

The hero of Tseitlin 10 has a number of different adventures. At one point in his journey he comes to Yaits'na-Babits'na, who tries to cook him in her oven. The hero pretends to be stupid and shoves Yaits'na-Babits'na in the oven, but this time she gets out and chases him. He throws a magic comb, brush and mirror behind him which become forest, mountain and fiery river, in which Yaits'na-Babits'na burns to death. This well-known motif (D672, Obstacle flight) occurs frequently in tales where Baba Yaga pursues the hero or heroine.

Dobrovol'skii 16 features a foolish rogue whose actions cause trouble for him and his two older brothers, who are forced to leave their village. They come to a forest hut where Baba Iga's three daughters warn them that she will eat them. The three brothers hide under the oven, but Baba Iga notices their Russian scent. Baba Iga wants to cook each of the three brothers, but each time the third brother comes out and fools Baba Iga's daughters. Finally the hero kills Baba Iga with a tobacco can. In a later episode (AT 1653, The Robbers under the Tree; AT 1653B, The Brothers in the Tree), the hero and his brothers are in a tree, and he drops Baba Iga's dead body, her mortar, pestle,

---

[3] This recalls AT 328, The Boy Steals the Giant's Treasure. However, the East Slavic tale-type index lists very few versions of SUS 328: two Belorussian versions, five Ukrainian, and only one Russian version, and these tales apparently do not include the beanstalk. Climbing a pea plant to heaven is found in East Slavic versions of AT 218*, Cock and Hen Plant Bean (SUS 218B*), and feature an old man who climbs the pea plant to heaven, and comes to a hut where goats live, and AT 1960G, The Great Tree (SUS 1960G), where the old man puts his wife in a sack and climbs up the giant pea plant. He drops the sack and his wife is killed. An anomalous tale with elements of these two types, and with Baba Yaga, is Razumova 75, discussed in chapter 6.

and broom, frightening the people below (this episode is also found in Sadovnikov 27; see chapter 6).

Onchukov 2000 Shokshozero 74 also combines AT 327C and AT 1653. The two older brothers don't want to take Ivan with them, but he hides in one of their bags. They come to the hut of Egi-Baba, who tells two daughters to cook two of the brothers. Ivan comes out and tricks the daughters, with the usual result. The third time Egi-Baba (also called Egibikha and Egibishna in this text) heats the oven herself, and Ivan pushes her in. She is cooked, and her buttocks become stuck to the oven door. In the following AT 1653 episode, the brothers are in a tree above twelve robbers who are cooking their dinner in a kettle. Ivan defecates into their kettle, and finally drops the dead body of Egibishna into the kettle. The robbers run away, frightened, and the brothers take their money and return home.

Potanin 1906 no. 4 is very similar. The third brother Ivan hides in his brother's bag. They go to steal turnips from Yaga Baba, who hears Ivan shouting (in spite of his brothers' warnings), and comes flying in her mortar. After the oven episode with the three daughters and Yaga Baba, they take her gold and silver, and Ivan takes Yaga's corpse. He urinates, defecates, and drops Yaga's dead body on the merchants who are camped under the tree. The merchants flee, and when one of them returns, Ivan cuts out his tongue.

Leonova 14 combines these two tale types (327C/F and 1653) with AT 1537 (The Corpse Killed Five Times). Ivan the Fool hides in his brother's bag. His brothers come to Baba-Yaga's house and steal from her pea plant. Ivan speaks from inside the bag, saying he wants some of the peas. Baba Yaga hears him and puts the three brothers in her cellar. Ivan cooks her three daughters in the usual way, and then Baba-Yaga returns and recognizes her third daughter's golden ring in the "meat." Ivan fools Baba-Yaga as he did her daughters, and when she starts to jump out of the oven, he hits her on the forehead with an iron bolt and kills her. In the AT 1653 episode, Ivan drops Baba-Yaga's corpse on the bandits and kills one of them. He uses the corpse to blackmail a merchant and then two others by convincing them that they have killed his "mother" (AT 1537): "What have you done! My mother is blind and deaf, and you've killed her." They give him gold and bury Baba-Yaga. When Ivan gets home he tells his brothers that his wealth came from selling Baba-Yaga's skin in the market. The brothers kill their wives, but no one wants to buy their skins, and the brothers are put in prison. These tales in which the rogue hero and his brothers steal turnips or peas from Baba Yaga's garden recall the Iron Woman of Ukrainian and Belorussian folk belief (see chapter 2, and below).

Vlasova and Zhekulina 46, collected in the Novgorod region in 1969, is an anomalous tale that includes elements of 327C/F, and a fascinating development of the theme of cannibalism. A father decides to kill his two sons and one stepson. The boys run away to the forest. They come to the hut on chicken legs, where they find Baba-Yaga at home. She warns them about the impending return of her cannibal husband (*liudoed*), and lets the two sons go. She keeps the stepson for herself, and tells her husband to spare the boy when he smells the Russian scent. The cannibal gets angry when the boy tells him that Baba-Yaga let the two other boys go. Baba-Yaga now is angry at the boy, and says she will burn him up. The cannibal husband tells Baba-Yaga he will eat her. She laughs, pointing out that he always swallows his victims whole, and that she will simply come out of his rear end. The cannibal eats her, and then catches the other two boys and eats them. Finally, he flies to the boy's house, and eats the boy's stepfather.

The hero of Onchukov 73 must be somewhat older than most of the boy heroes of this tale, since he is in the habit of visiting Yaga-Baba's three daughters, presumably to flirt with or court them. The "old woman" instructs her daughters to heat up the oven to roast Ivashko Kochevriazhko, but all three daughters are cooked instead. Yaga-Baba ends up in the oven herself, but pleads to be let out. The hero opens the oven door and catches her in a noose. She gives him a magic ring (he can have any bride he wishes), and leads him to three houses which become his as soon as he releases her. Ivashko never sees Yaga-Baba again. It is striking that Ivashko lets Yaga-Baba out of the oven; in a few other versions she pleads with the hero to be let out and reveals the location of hidden wealth, but in those cases the hero lets her roast (Nikiforov 1961 no. 85, Zelenin Viatka 97, 115).

In Akimova 367, the hero Vaniushka goes into the forest with other children and gets lost.[4] He comes upon a hut where he finds Baba-Yaga's daughter, who is happy for company. Baba-Yaga returns, and there is the familiar oven episode in which the daughter Mashka is roasted. Vaniushka climbs a tree and is rescued by geese. Once again there is an implication that the hero is flirting with Baba-Yaga's daughter and that this is the reason for Baba-Yaga's anger; the daughter is said to be approaching a marriageable age (*I goda ee takzhe podvigaiutsia k nevestam*, Akimova 1946: 244).

Baba Yaga's anger is motivated and explained differently in a version recorded in Enisei province (Zhivaia Starina 21 [1912]: 319–20). The hero, Snow Boy (*Snezhok*), is causing snow to fall, blocking the roads and making Baba Yaga angry. She sends her daughters to catch him, and only the third succeeds. The three daughters and Baba Yaga are cooked in the usual way, and Snezhok continues to make snow in the world. Here the hero is an entirely

---

[4] This opening is similar to AT 314A*, where the girl heroine and her friends lose their way in the forest and come upon Baba Yaga's hut (see discussion below).

fantastic being, not simply born of inanimate material, as are some of the heroes. It is surprising to see Baba Yaga on the side of human culture in this fairy tale, while the hero represents an aspect of nature that is inimical to human undertakings.

In three versions the oven episode is missing. After kidnapping the boy in Potiavin 9, Baba Yaga leaves to go sharpen her teeth. The hero climbs a tree and is rescued by geese, and Baba Yaga breaks her teeth while gnawing the tree. Potiavin 10 appears incomplete, since it ends abruptly after Aga Gnishna abducts Lipuniushka. Smirnov 120 contains many elements of AT 161A* (The Bear with the Wooden Leg). Egibitsa is a bear who has her tongue reforged to catch Lipuniushka, and she eats the boy immediately after abducting him. His parents cut off one of the bear's legs while she is asleep, but she comes back and eats the parents.

The villain in this folktale is not always Baba Yaga. In other versions, the villain is a witch (*ved'ma*, Afanas'ev 108, 109, 110), the witch Chuvilikha who lives in a hut on chicken legs (Afanas'ev 112), a cannibaless (*liudoedka*, Lutovinova Kemerovo 160), the wife of a cannibal ogre (*syroiydykha*, Iavorskii 22), a fox (Morokhin and Vardugin 1993: 82–83), a snake (Petnikov 1966: 52–56, Mitropol'skaia 73), or a female bear (Zhivaia Starina 12 [1912]: 289–292). E. A. Tudorovskaia believes that the witch is the original villain of this tale, and that Baba Yaga is a relatively late addition (1974: 84). Forty-seven versions of this tale with Baba Yaga as the villain were available for the present survey, while the East Slavic tale type index lists fifty-three Russian versions of this tale type, twenty-one Ukrainian, and fifteen Belorussian. Baba Yaga is likely the most frequent and popular villain.

Importantly, the fox and snake, like the witch, are both feminine in gender (*lisa*, *zmeia*). An interesting exception to this tendency is found in a Russian version of this tale recorded in Lithuania (Mitropol'skaia 74), where the hero comes to the hut of a snake (*zmeia*). Then the gender of the supernatural villain shifts. At first the narrator tells us that the hero came to a snake's den when the snake was not home, only its daughter (*Samoi zmei ne bylo—byla doch*). In the morning a masculine dragon (*zmei*) arrives and orders his daughter to cook the young man. The hero shoves the snake daughter into the oven, and climbs an oak tree. The dragon starts to cut down the oak, but birds fly by and give the hero a golden feather which allows him to fly away.

This shifting of grammatical gender in the names of supernatural characters is not unusual in Russian fairy tales. Ia. I. Gin explains these fluctuations through linguistic factors, and also by the fact that fairy-tale narrators lack a clear visual image of the amorphous supernatural beings of the "other world." Narrators do not have a very developed sense of the differences between these beings, and so they can easily be assimilated to each other, and their names become almost synonymous (Gin 1977). Nevertheless, this unusual version of 327C is an exception to what appears to be a very general tendency for the villain of this tale to be female.

For Western readers, this East Slavic fairy tale probably brings to mind the famous tale "Hansel and Gretel" (Grimm 15). In fact "Hansel and Gretel" represents a related subtype—AT 327A. Unfortunately, the Aarne-Thompson index identifies the protagonists of 327A as children, without specifying whether they are most often a brother and sister, as in the Grimm version. This does appear to be the case in French versions, where the sister is more active than her brother (Tenèze 1970: 35). 327A is also told in Morocco, where a boy and girl tell the witch that they don't know how to blow on the fire; when she shows them how, they push her in the oven (Cosquin 1910: 15–16). A popular Kabyle folktale combines various elements of 327B, 327A, and 328. The hero, a dwarf who never needs to sleep, is born miraculously when his mother eats half an apple or half a pear. At one point in the tale the ogress *(teryel)* wants to eat him, but he takes refuge in a tree or upper location. The ogress dies in a fire, or is devoured by animals (Lacoste-Dujardin 1970: 45–107). Folktales which combine elements of 327B and 327A are also found in West Africa (Paulme 1976: 242–276).

AT 327A has been recorded in western, central, and eastern Europe, but only very infrequently in East Slavic areas: the East Slavic tale type index lists only four Russian, five Ukrainian, and three Belorussian versions. In one of them (Onegina 9) a sister makes her brother fall asleep and goes to Baba Yaga's house. She sees Baba Yaga producing food from a magic millstone. The girl steals food and brings it home to her brother. The next time she intends to go, she forgets to put one of her brother's eyes to sleep, and he goes with her. This time Baba Yaga catches the two and tries to cook them. As in 327C/F, the children outsmart Baba Yaga and push her into the oven. The tale continues with an episode of SUS 715A (AT 715A, The Wonderful Cock): a greedy priest steals the magic millstone. The children's rooster demands the millstone back. The priest tries to have the rooster killed, but finally returns the stone. This particular combination of episodes appears to be unusual; it has been recorded a few times in Karelia (Onegina 1986: 200). The East Slavic folk tradition most often emphasizes a single boy's conflict with the witch in subtypes 327C/F. The definition of these subtypes in the AT index is not entirely satisfactory. Speaking of AT 327C, Stith Thompson himself admits that "This tale is so close to that of Hansel and Gretel that the two are seldom clearly differentiated" (1977: 37).

AT 327C is also very widespread in Europe, North Africa (Cosquin 1910: 67–70), and beyond. There are tales in India that appear related to 327C, in which the hero tells an ogre that he doesn't know how to walk around a cauldron of boiling oil, and then pushes the ogre in (ibid., 1–5). In Poland, 327C appears to occur less frequently than 327A, but it very much resembles the East Slavic form: a dwarf-boy born from a log or from wood avoids being cooked by a witch, climbs up a tree, and is rescued by birds or bird feathers before the witch can gnaw through the tree (Krzyżanowski 1946 ii: 35–36). The Aarne-Thompson index locates AT 327F only in Russia, Ukraine, Lithuania, and Bulgaria. The Bulgarian tale-type index does not include AT 327F; instead, there are versions of 327A, and among other subtypes, 327G, in which a boy cooks the cannibal's wife while the cannibal husband is out inviting guests (Daskalova-Perkovska et al. 1994: 126–127).

On the surface, this is a cautionary tale for children about the dangers of the outside world, with Baba Yaga as a "pedagogical fiction." Hearing the tale might also be a way for children to overcome their fears about the outside world. The importance of these concerns for children cross-culturally might account for Anglo-American and English games in which children act out episodes of being kidnapped or stolen by a witch, and rescued by a mother (Newell 1890). Storytelling among and by children is another way of dealing with fears and mastering them; this seems to be the case with Russian children's horror stories (see chapter 1), and a study of storytelling among seven- to eleven-year-old girls in the United States suggests the same (Tucker 1981). Occasional notes about informants also suggest that this tale was told mostly to children. It has been recorded from a sixty-year-old woman who told tales only to her grandchildren (Zelenin Viatka 87), from an adult who had heard the tale fifty years earlier from his nanny (ibid., no. 97), from a woman who worked as a nanny (ibid., no. 115), and from children themselves (Nikiforov 1961 nos. 45 and 64; Karnaukhova 74). The narrator of Vedernikova and Samodelova 33 said that his mother told him this tale as a child to make him behave. As Nicole Belmont (1995) points out, fairy tales typically told to children may be structurally simpler than many other tale types, but they can also be the most terrifying.

Eleven versions include a miraculous birth. The boy is born from a piece of wood (Smirnov 343) or clay, or from his mother's finger. The material from which he is made usually accounts for his name: Luton'ka (Afanas'ev 111) from *lutoshka* (dry young linden or lime sapling stripped of its bast, cf. Zelenin 1915: 446), Lipuniushka (Potiavin 10) from *lipa* (linden or lime), Glinushka (Lutovinova Index p. 18, Nikiforov 1961 no. 45) or Glinyshek (Potanin 1902 no. 41) from *glina* (clay), Ol'shanka (Nikiforov 1961 no. 85, Simina 39) and perhaps also Lishanushka (Nikiforov 1961 no. 64) from *ol'kha* (alder), and *mal'chik s pal'chik*, "the boy the size of a finger" (Zelenin Viatka 97). The boy born of a log in Vedernikova and Samodelova 33 is simply called Ivashka.

Vladimir Propp sees a historical background to the image of some folktale heroes who lie on the stove or in the ashes, or who are miraculously born on the stove (the cult of ancestors and guardian spirits, the cult of fire, and beliefs in reincarnation) and to the appearance of a child without the father's participation (myths about human origins, and ancient matriarchy) (Propp 1941: 77–84, 91–94). This motif might reflect the almost exclusive role of women in birth ritual among the East Slavs. In the tales, the mother usually instructs her husband to bring a piece of wood from the forest, and she seems to know that it will turn into a child. In one exceptional version, the father brings an alder branch from outside and puts it on the stove, but significantly without knowing why (Nikiforov 1961 no. 85). In Afanas'ev 108 both mother and father bring food to Ivashechko, but otherwise the father is largely absent from this folktale. This seems to reflect reality, in that the mother was the primary caretaker of infants and small children.

Interestingly, an evil spirit found in the Pudoga region of Olonets province was called *zhikhar'*, the name of the boy hero in Afanas'ev 106, Gorodtsov iii: 6–10, Kozhemiakina 1973: 171–174, and Smirnov 343. For the narrator of Leonova 3, the hero Zhikharka is a rooster. Afanas'ev (whose version was recorded in Perm' province) comments that the name means "dashing, bold, brave" (1984 i: 135). In Pudoga this is the name of a spirit that steals children from the cradle in their mother's absence (Dynin 1993: 82).

Another feature of the tale that identifies it as a children's tale is the presence of animal siblings in 327C, which recalls the subgenre of animal tales (*skazki o zhivotnykh*), usually told to children. One such tale, AT 61B (Cat, Cock, and Fox Live Together; Afanas'ev 37–39), is similar in its plot: The fox kidnaps the rooster, and the cat comes to the rooster's rescue. The similarity between these tales led Aleksandr Potebnia to identify Baba Yaga with the fox. The resemblance is also reflected in a version of 61B where Zhikharka (the boy's name in four versions of 327C/F) is the name of a piglet, the third of four animal siblings (Mints et al. 1957 no. 6). Like 61B, the Russian versions of 327C/F also contain short rhymed passages which the tale-teller might sing or recite in a melodic voice. In the animal tale it is the fox's enticing speech to the rooster; in 327C/F it is the mother's call to the boy, then imitated by Baba Yaga. T. G. Leonova (1998) comments on the structural and semantic relationship of these two tale types, and finds an archaic, mythological layer underlying them. Other meanings of the terms *zhikhar'*, *zhikhorka*, and *zhikharka* are "inhabitant, owner" and "house spirit, *domovoi*." Thus the conflict between the boy or rooster and the fox or Baba Yaga is also a conflict between the spirit of the home or hearth, and chthonic beings; in mythological terms it represents the order of the world and the place of human beings in it. Baba Yaga's rolling around on the (presumed) boy's bones is a symbolic representation of receiving someone else's strength or power.

The central and defining fantastic event in this tale is no doubt the oven episode. Propp interprets it in terms of cremation ritual: Baba Yaga's actions are related to both initiation and burial. While the initiation ritual (of which fire was a part) has been forgotten, death remains. What was a part of initiation is now only found in the burial ritual (cremation). This tale also reflects a historical transition from a forest religion with a female mistress and mother of beasts to an agricultural cult which transforms her into a witch. What had been a symbolic devouring becomes real. "The way of life which destroyed the ritual also destroyed its creators and carriers: the witch who burns up children is burned up herself by the tale-teller, the carrier of the epic folktale tradition" (Propp 1946: 96). Because there is no ritual (or belief) in which an initiate burns an initiator, Propp sees this as evidence for the process by which folktales arise when ritual dies out. Like Propp, Toporov interprets this tale plot as derived from Indo-European cremation ritual (1963, 1987). It is striking that Propp and other scholars go so far afield and into such a distant past to find ethnographic parallels to the oven episode in this tale, when in fact one existed in the same culture area and at same the time the tale was circulating (Toporkov 1992: 114).

A number of authors have noted the similarity of this folktale to the East Slavic ritual "baking" of children (Anikin 1977, Periañez-Chaverneff 1983, Toporkov 1992). The ritual was known by different names: *perepekanie*, *perepechen'e*, *zapekanie*, *dopekanie*. It consisted of putting an infant on a bread spatula (baker's peel) and into a warm oven, in some cases putting the child in and taking it out a number of times, with an accompanying dialogue urging the performer of the ritual to bake away the child's illness (Divil'kovskii 1914: 597, Shevchenko 1998, Toporkov 1992: 114). The ritual was supposed to cure illnesses such as atrophy and rickets (one name for them was *sobach'ia starost'*, "dog's old age"), and it was performed in the Volga region, central and southern Russia, Siberia, Ukraine, and Belarus. A similar "baking" ritual (which also includes holding the child over boiling water to cure it of the evil eye) is reported for the Banat region of Romania (Creangă 1931: 207). A description of this ritual from the Enisei region emphatically condemns it:

If the child has *sushets* (i.e. the child becomes thin) they heal it in this manner: after kneading dough in the evening, they put a stopped bottle of water into the dough and leave it there until loaves of bread are made and put in the oven in the morning. Then they tie the child to the bread spatula the bread was put on, and they hold it in the oven for several moments, over the loaves. Then they pour water over the sick child from the bottle that was left in the dough overnight. This is awful: to cook a child in the oven and then suddenly pour cold water over it! Good, but ignorant people, what are you doing?! (Krivoshapkin 1865 ii: 3)

Vladimir Anikin sees this folktale as a patriarchal distortion and reinterpretation of an originally positive ritual (based on belief in the healing properties of fire) from the earlier matriarchal period which attempted to save the child from death (1977: 119, 123–124). Belief that fire had curative powers is clear in a number of East Slavic customs which probably derive from the Slavs' pre-Christian veneration of fire (Tokarev 1957: 65–70). However, the ritual in question also incorporates the oven and baking significantly. It probably cannot be explained only in terms of beliefs about fire.

A psychoanalytic reading suggests that the oven is a female or womb symbol. Is this interpretation justified in the given cultural context? The importance of the oven in the tale might simply reflect the reality of life in a cold climate. The Russian oven was an essential feature of the home, and especially in winter, life in the peasant household was centered around the main source of heat. The traditional Russian, Ukrainian, and Belorussian oven or stove (*pech'*) sometimes occupied as much as a quarter of the entire space of the house and was built so that family members could lie down and sleep directly on top or in a sleeping structure built over it (*polati*). Beyond its many practical functions, the East Slavic oven or stove had many symbolic and ritual functions as well (Tempest 1997, Nevskaia 1999). In his study of the symbolism of the traditional East Slavic dwelling, Al'bert Baiburin finds that the cultural space of the home centered around two areas—the "beautiful corner" where the icons were placed, and the stove. He attributes primary importance to the stove. Its cooking function had not just practical but also ritual importance, transforming the raw into the cooked (Baiburin 1983: 160–168). The stove was described in anthropomorphic terms, and identified as female.

In his ethnography of the East Slavs, Dmitrii Zelenin describes magical practices used to ease a difficult childbirth. Among other things, all those present, including the mother, would remove their belts, unbutton collars, untie all knots, loosen their braids, and open locks, doors, chests, and oven doors. In especially difficult cases they might ask the priest to open the altar or iconostasis gates in the church (Zelenin 1927: 291, 1991: 320).[5] Zelenin does not interpret this data, but the symbolism implied in these actions of sympathetic or imitative magic seems obvious. Even to those who performed these acts, the symbolism of opening the oven door (and all the other objects)

---

[5] This custom appears in Anton Chekhov's 1888 short story "The Name-Day Party."

in order to open the mother's womb was probably obvious. Baiburin describes a wedding custom from Tver' province: the day after the wedding people rode around with a broom and an oven door, symbolizing the bride's loss of her virginity (1983: 166). The miraculous birth in a few versions of our folktale also supports this interpretation of the oven: The wood is placed on the stove or oven, where it becomes a child (Afanas'ev 111, Nikiforov 1961 nos. 45 and 64, Zelenin Viatka 97).[6]

A Russian proverb states that "the oven is our mother" (*Pech' nam mat' rodnaia*, Dal' 1957: 589). East Slavic, Lithuanian, and Latvian riddles suggest an isomorphism or homology between the cosmos, the human body, the house, and the oven (Nevskaia 1999: 103). The oven can be represented in riddles as an old man or an old woman, or its features may be conceived as parts of the human body (the opening as a mouth, for instance). A number of riddles depict the oven, fire, and smoke as mother, daughter, and son, respectively. These typically begin: "the mother is fat, the daughter is beautiful (or red)" (*Mat' tolsta, Doch' krasna*, Sadovnikov 1959: 43, Akimova 1946: 223, see also Nevskaia 1999: 104). Or the mother may be heavy (*gruzna*) or black (*cherna*). In one riddle the oven mother is hungry: *mat' gladukha, doch' krasnukha* (Sadovnikov 1959: 43). The line about the daughter appears to play with the double meaning of the adjective *krasna*; the person trying to guess the answer to the riddle will first understand it to mean "beautiful," since it is applied to a human being, while in fact it refers to the fire and the second meaning is most appropriate.

Baba Yaga's association with the oven, probably best established in this folktale, appears elsewhere. She appears in a riddle metaphorically describing the oven and a beam protruding from it: "Yaga stands, with horns in her forehead" (*Stoit Iaga, Vo lbu roga*) (ibid., 46). An anomalous tale that contains some elements of AT 400 (Smirnov 341) includes an episode in which Baba Yaga tells the hero: "How dare you heat my oven?" He throws her in, burns her up, and gathers her ashes in a sack (see discussion, chapter 6). In a version of AT 510, Baba Yaga breaks the oven and tells the heroine she must repair it (chapter 6). Baba Yaga cooks her own leg or falls from the oven in children's teasing rhymes (see below). In a horror story (*strashilka*) told by a ten-year-old girl, a black oven turns out to be Baba Yaga (Razumova 1995: 12). Egi-Baba's daughters appear on stoves in a North Russian love incantation (chapter 2).

The oven plays an important role in another folk narrative about a young or maturing hero, Il'ia Muromets, a hero of folk epic poetry (the *bylina*). The epic

---

[6] An association between baking and childbirth is found in West Slavic customs as well. While she was being dressed on the day of her wedding, a Sorbian bride stood in a baking tub or vat, or kneading trough. When dressed, if she jumped out with one quick movement, she would have an easy delivery (Schneeweis 1953: 28).

song of "The Healing of Il'ia Muromets" relates how he spends a long time (sometimes thirty years) on the stove as an invalid, or that he has neither hands nor legs. Pilgrims give him holy or healing water and he recovers and gains strength. V. G. Balushok interprets this epic song in ritual terms as an initiation and a second birth, and Il'ia's movement from a female to a male sphere. He does not identify the oven as specifically maternal but, citing Al'bert Baiburin, sees the oven as the female term of the male/female opposition in the context of the traditional East Slavic dwelling (Balushok 1991: 21–22). A Russian folktale hero with a happier relationship to the stove is Emelia the Fool, who rides on the oven when the king summons him to the city (AT 675, The Lazy Boy; Afanas'ev 165, 166, Zelenin Perm' 63).

Periañez-Chaverneff and Toporkov see the folktale episode of baking in 327C/F as an inversion of the East Slavic ritual, reflecting the child's wish fulfillment. It is difficult if not impossible to establish a historical or cause-and-effect relationship between ritual and folktale—questions of which is older, or which has influenced the other, if this has even been the case, cannot be answered with any certainty. However, it is possible to assume an underlying parallel symbolism in both. The ritual suggests that the oven represents the mother's womb; the same symbolism is quite clear in the ritual practices mentioned above to ease childbirth.

The suggestive name *perepekanie*, "re-baking," allows for two interpretations. The verbal prefix *pere-* can signify an excessive action or a repeated action. Toporkov finds that the most obvious level of symbolism in the ritual, realized by the practitioners themselves, was that of "baking away" an illness (an excessive action). This meaning is explicit in some dialogues which accompanied the ritual. Another level of meaning implies that the child is originally "baked" in the mother's womb, but in some cases may need to be baked again. In this case the child is likened to bread, and this is reflected in some versions of the ritual. In Kazan' province, for example, the child's face, except for its nose and mouth, was covered with dough. Toporkov finds a third level of meaning in the ritual as well, in that the oven could symbolize the world beyond the grave. For the child the ritual is then a temporary death (Toporkov 1992: 115–116).

The pliability of an infant's body is emphasized in other practices which ensured a physically well-formed child. The midwife stroked the head of a child shortly after birth, which suggests that the child's body was considered pliable like dough (Zelenin 1927: 293, 1991: 321). East Slavic ritual practice likens the oven to the womb and children to baking dough, and if the same symbolism is active (even unconsciously) in the folktale, it allows for a certain understanding of the oven episode.

In many ways Baba Yaga is a reversal or inversion of the hero's mother. The mother is good, gives birth to a boy, and feeds him; Baba Yaga is evil, wants to force the boy back into the oven (a symbolic womb), and eat him. The complementarity of the two is emphasized when Baba Yaga imitates the mother's voice. This imitation invites a consideration of Baba Yaga as a symbolic wicked mother, and of the fantastic episode in Baba Yaga's hut as a symbolic representation of the boy's relationship with his mother. The fact that the tale usually ends with the boy's return suggests that the conflicts in his relationship with his mother are resolved in the fantastic episode and so allow for a return to a harmonious situation. What appears to occur in this fairy tale is a splitting of the mother image into a good mother (the boy's mother at the beginning and end) and a bad mother (Baba Yaga).[7]

The concept of splitting maternal and paternal images into "good" and "bad" representations has been discussed in child psychology (Klein 1959: 57, 215, 249, 303), and the importance of this process for folklore has been pointed out. Otto Rank identifies two related processes, splitting and doubling. Splitting reflects the positive and negative emotions aroused by the parent figure, and allows legendary heroes to rebel against a tyrannical father, while exhibiting the culturally expected filial piety toward a good father. Doubling of mother, daughter, or sister figures allows incestuous desires to be realized safely (Rank 1922: 15–16). The practice of splitting parent figures allows children to maintain a pure image of the benevolent parent, and explains the abundance of wicked stepparents in folktales (Bettelheim 1989: 66–68). Before the cognitive-developmental stage of "object constancy," it is impossible for a child to integrate conflicting images and fantasies of a person into a single mental representation. This leads to a splitting into "good" and "bad" parental representations (Spiro 1993: 113).

Besides imitating the mother's voice, Baba Yaga's identification as a symbolic mother is suggested in three versions by the fact that she is directly addressed as "mother." In one version (Zelenin Viatka 115), the hero addresses both his mother and Egibikha with exactly the same diminutive: *mamon'kia.* He also calls Baba Yaga's daughter "sister" (*sestritsa*) (Zelenin 1915: 357–360). In another version from Viatka province (Smirnov 143), the boy and girl plead with Egiboba that they don't know how to sit on the spatula, calling her *mati*

---

[7] As a tale about a boy's conflict with his mother, the East Slavic versions of 327C/F appear to be an important exception to Alan Dundes's suggestion that "same-sex rivalry is a standard feature of all oral fairy tales. Thus young girls have to contend with wicked stepmothers and witches while young boys have to struggle with male dragons or giants" (Dundes 1989: 223). There may indeed be same-sex rivalry here between Baba Yaga and her daughters, but the main focus is clearly on the struggle between the boy hero and Baba Yaga.

Egiboba (Smirnov 1917: 420). Yaga-bura is addressed as mother (*mat*) by the hero in Afanas'ev 107. While the name "mother" could simply be an indication of Yaga's mother status in relation to her own daughters, the fact that the hero chooses to call her this can be meaningful.

The tale recorded by Dmitrii Zelenin from Natal'ia Bezrukova in Viatka province (no. 115, see Appendix I: Selected Tale Texts) suggests that Egibikha is a symbolic mother by contrasting Egibikha and the hero's mother sharply and inviting the listener or reader to compare the two. Here is how this storyteller describes the kidnapping and its immediate aftermath:

> And again that evil one came. And she had three daughters. So she came to the shore and spoke like his mother. She listened to how his mother spoke, with a fine voice: "Vaniushka, Vaniushka! Come up to the shore. There's porridge with butter for you!" So he came. She grabbed him and dragged him off to her pantry.
> She harnessed a horse herself, rode to the forest for wood, and left one daughter at home. "Heat the oven hot, really hot, so that the lower log is red hot! And cook him, that son of a bitch!" she said. Vaniushka's mother missed him, she cried, one tear streaming right after another. (Zelenin 1915: 358)

The immediate juxtaposition of Vaniushka's mother and Egibikha is striking. In one sentence Egibikha is ordering her daughter to roast the "son of a bitch," and in the next Vaniushka's mother is shedding tears for her lost son. This does not appear to be a discrepancy or a "mistake," although there may be some in this tale. In the passage quoted above, for example, the tale-teller mentions that Egibikha has three daughters before they have appeared and are necessary for the narrative development. Later she appears to forget exactly what Vaniushka has managed to carry away with him from Egibikha's house: He leaves with three pots of silver, but pours out three pots of silver *and* three pots of gold in his mother's house when he returns (ibid., 360). Nevertheless, her juxtaposition of the vicious Egibikha and the tearful mother seems intended to bring the two images together in the listener's mind.

The symmetry of this tale (and the juxtaposition of the two spheres of action) is expressed very clearly in Avanesav and Biryla 1962: 290 (see Appendix I: Selected Tale Texts). At the beginning of the tale the boy Hryshka climbs an apple tree; at the end of the tale he climbs a tree and is given feathers by geese to fly home. The second tree-climbing and the rescue by geese are unnecessary, because Hryshka has already killed Baba-Yaga. The narrator appears to have wanted this symmetry, even if it meant adding an episode without logical motivation. As in Natal'ia Bezrukova's version, there is a close juxtaposition of Baba-Yaga and the boy's parents, and in this case, of their respective dwellings: "Hryshka stretched out his hand to take an apple, and Baba-Yaga grabbed him and carried him off to her hut. The old man and woman came out of their hut and called for Hryshka, but he was gone" (ibid., 290).

In several versions of this tale there are obscenities expressing hostility between mother and child: The boy calls Baba Yaga a bitch (*suka*) or a whore (*kurva, bliad'* in Zelenin Viatka 97), and she calls him a son of a bitch (*sukin syn*), a Tatar (*tatarin* in Nikiforov 1961 no. 85), and a red dog (*ryzhii pes, krasnyi pes* in Zelenin Viatka 115). While for educated Russians it would probably be unthinkable to address one's mother with these terms, Ol'ga Semenova-Tian-Shanskaia reports that peasant children learned abusive terms at a very early age, before they could even form complete phrases, and that boys could commonly be heard to call their mothers "bitch" (*suka*) if they were refused something. Rather than discouraging children from using swear words, the family in fact encouraged it and even the mother herself was amused by it (Semenova-Tian-Shanskaia 1914: 18–19). This feature in the folktale could either be a realistic one, or it might serve as an outlet for the listener's unconscious hostility toward the mother.

A striking example of hostility toward a child in traditional Russian culture is found in the lullaby (*kolybel'naia pesnia*). While most lullabies express affection for the child, a small number express a wish for the child's death. Typically they state this wish, and describe the burial, the funeral feast, or the grave site. They may have reflected the difficult conditions of Russian peasant life, the burden a child posed to its mother or nanny, the belief that a sick child was the child of an evil spirit taking the real child's place, or the desire to rid oneself of an illegitimate child (Martynova 1975: 152–155). They may have been intended to fool evil spirits and prevent them from harming the child (Eremina 1992). While Antonina Martynova maintains these lullabies were sung in a "mechanical" way, through the force of tradition, it seems possible as well that these lullabies might function as a culturally accepted outlet for a mother's hostile feelings toward a child.

Nikolai Novikov considers 327C/F rather "realistic," compared to other tale types in which Baba Yaga appears. Baba Yaga does not live in another world, but close by. In Afanas'ev 109, the witch lives in the neighboring village and knows Ivan'ka's parents. In a children's book version of this tale, the Russian illustrator and author explains Baba Yaga to North American readers in the following manner: "She is so familiar to Russian children that she's almost a member of the family—like an elderly aunt who is either mean or nice, depending on her mood" (Arnold 1993: no pagination).

This remark supports identification of Baba Yaga as a mother figure, but raises other questions. Psychoanalytic interpretation usually sees the abundance of kings and queens, helpful old men and women, and ogres and witches in folktales as symbolic fathers and mothers. However, just as the styles of mothering and fathering vary from culture to culture, so, too, we should expect to find qualitatively different father and mother images in the folk narratives of different cultures. For example, Stanley Kurtz (1992) has found that a pattern of multiple mothering in Hindu India is reflected in a multiplicity of goddess figures whose identities converge and are essentially one. If Baba Yaga is a mother figure, her image must in some way reflect the mother's role and the style of mothering that prevailed in the communities in which these tales circulated.

Psychoanalysis places great emphasis on the mother-child dyad and its relation to the Oedipus complex. While this emphasis on an exclusive relationship of two individuals reflects the child's situation in the nuclear family of modern Western Europe and North America, such exclusivity might not have been the case for most Russian peasant and rural children. The structure of the family in rural Russia varied, and it was likely to change through the life cycle of the individual and the family. It ranged from small, nuclear families of married couples with children to the so-called *bol'shaia sem'ia* (extended family), the joint family consisting of several related couples under the rule of a family patriarch (*bol'shak*). In this situation it is likely that many infants and young children had caretakers other than their biological mother (grandmothers, aunts, sisters, cousins). The phenomenon of multiple mothering, or a diffusion of maternal responsibilities, has been observed in Russia in the second half of the twentieth century, with persons other than the child's natural mother, even complete strangers, taking on a mothering role (Bronfenbrenner 1972: 10–11).

This consideration of who in fact mothered the rural child should inform a consideration of Baba Yaga as a mother figure. Certainly the biological mother was the primary caretaker of infants, and children distinguished their natural mother from other family members who might take on their mother's role at times. Still, if Baba Yaga is a mother figure, she is probably a reflection not of one individual biological mother but of a number of people, of anyone who might have mothered the child, or more broadly, of a style of mothering typical for this culture.

Multiple mothering might account for the uncertainty about whether Baba Yaga is an individual or a type, as well as her frequent appearance in trebled form, as three sisters. Because of the lack of articles in Russian, Ukrainian, and Belorussian, it is not always clear whether Baba Yaga is a proper, individual name or a generic one ("Baba Yaga," "a Baba Yaga," or "the Baba Yaga"). This is reflected in folktale collections, where the name is sometimes capitalized and sometimes not. One storyteller from Viatka province identifies Egibikha as an evil spirit, one of a breed that "lives in lakes and forests" (Zelenin 1915: 358), and Abram Novopol'tsev, a tale-teller from the Samara region, has one of his characters married a second time to one "of the Yaga Babas" (*iz Iagikh Bab*, Sadovnikov 1884: 11), suggesting that she is only one of many. In tales with three Baba Yaga sisters, the hero progresses usually from the youngest to the oldest Baba Yaga. Of course, trebling is a common device in Indo-European folklore, and the trebling of Baba Yaga is by itself hardly surprising or unusual.[8] Russian versions of the dragon slayer tale (AT 300) are usually animated by successive battles with three dragons, each with an increasing number of heads. Interestingly, this splitting into three almost identical figures never occurs with the anthropomorphic male ogre Koshchei, and rarely with old men donor figures (an exception is Parilov 6, AT 530, where the hero comes to three grandfathers in huts that turn around). Perhaps this is an echo of the Russian rural patriarchal joint family, with its single all-powerful and sometimes tyrannical male head, and its multiple mothers.

Returning to the main adventure found in this tale, the oven episode, what meaning(s) can be found in it? What meaning(s) would be most relevant to those who listened to this tale? Periañez-Chaverneff argues that the ritual itself could serve as a channel for a mother's aggressive feelings toward a child (perhaps resentful feelings toward a child not born healthy enough), while the tale represents the wish fulfillment of a child who has been subjected to this ritual (1983: 189–190). Toporkov agrees with the conception of this tale as a reversal of the ritual. Róheim feels that this tale originates in the dream of a hungry child, in which the desire to devour the mother is projected onto the mother (1953). The presence of two versions in which the child does in fact eat Baba Yaga (Kozhemiakina 1973: 171–174, Leonova 3) is evidence for this argument, or at least that the desire of the child to eat the mother figure is a potential, latent meaning in this tale.

Periañez-Chaverneff finds that this tale lacks a physical description of Baba Yaga's house or body, concentrating on her mouth and teeth instead. This general infantile focus on the mouth is aggravated in the East Slavic context by the traditional practice of swaddling, which leaves the infant unable to move and allows it to express anger only through biting (Periañez-Chaverneff 1983: 189–190; for other discussions of swaddling in East Slavic culture, see Benedict 1949; Gorer and Rickman 1949; Gorer 1949; Mead 1954; Rancour-Laferriere 1995: 116–121).

Whether or not the practice of swaddling has had any influence on the image of Baba Yaga in this tale, Periañez-Chaverneff's assertion about the image itself is largely correct. For the most part, the tales mention only those features of Baba Yaga's hut which are essential to the story (the oven, the place where she

---

[8] Cf. Axel Olrik's epic law of threefold repetition (1999: 89–90).

puts the boy, or where he finds her wealth). A number of versions mention
Baba Yaga's tongue or teeth, but they do not provide much description of Baba
Yaga or her dwelling. Her mortar and pestle appear in a few versions (Afanas'ev
106, 107, Avanesav and Biryla 1962: 290, Dobrovol'skii 16, Kozhemiakina
1973: 171, Zelenin Viatka 97), and the Bony Leg epithet in only one, where
Baba Yaga also smells the hero's Russian scent (Dobrovol'skii 16). The hut on
chicken legs appears in Vedernikova and Samodelova 33. Zelenin Perm' 86 is
different from all the other versions in that it contains the hut on chicken legs,
and the hero's name is Ivan the Fool. The appearance of the hut and this name
(in a tale with a male hero) are both typical features of tales with adult heroes.
Another version with an unusual degree of detail is Zelenin Viatka 97. After
Baba Yaga eats her daughter, she lies down. She hears the boy's taunts but has
eaten so much she cannot move. Baba Yaga falls asleep and snores, and the
whole hut shakes when she farts.

Two important factors have been neglected in previous discussions of this
tale. First, there is variation in the apparent age of the hero: The subtype 327C
is clearly about a very young child left at home, while in 327F the boy must be
older, since he goes off to fish on his own for most of the day. The implication
that the hero is flirting with Baba Yaga's daughter(s) in Akimova 367 and
Onchukov 73 suggests that the hero is approaching puberty or is already an
adolescent. The oven episode and Baba Yaga's desire to eat the hero are felt by
at least some tale-tellers to apply to a boy who is no longer an infant, who may
be approaching puberty or even beyond it. The oven episode appears in Tseitlin
10, where the hero has other "adult" adventures and marries. It is also
interesting that the older hero of Onchukov 73 is the only one able to trust
Baba Yaga enough to release her, suggesting that she does not represent as
great a threat to him as to younger heroes. In a few versions the boy marries at
the end of the tale (Onchukov 73, Smirnov 143, Zelenin Viatka 97), but the
narrator appends this information in a single sentence, and it does not give rise
to new episodes. It seems to be an afterthought which fits the tale but is not
essential.

The second, and perhaps more important, point is that the hero is always a
boy. With the exception of the brother and sister in Smirnov 143 and Onegina
9 (SUS 327A), Baba Yaga never attempts to cook a girl in this tale, although she
unwittingly eats her own daughters. An oven episode with a heroine occurs in
Afanas'ev 114, embedded in a tale which combines a number of types (SUS
313E, 327A, 313H*, discussed in chapter 6). There the villain is Baba Yaga, but
Baba Yaga's daughter helps the heroine.[9] In Zelenin Viatka 11, also a
composite tale with a heroine and an oven episode (SUS 450, 218B*, 327A, see

[9] The Slovak Ježibaba tries to cook a heroine in a 327C episode (Polívka ii: 409).

chapter 6), the villain is a male goat. Besides her own daughters, Baba Yaga shows herself capable of eating girls in SUS 333B and C*, and in some versions of AT 480 Baba Yaga reveals the desire to cook or eat the heroine, but these tales lack the oven episode (see discussion below). The majority of storytellers, the weight of the tale tradition, and the tastes of audiences as well indicate that the oven episode is an adventure suitable for boys but not for girls. Why is this adventure gender-specific?

On the surface, Baba Yaga's actions threaten to bring about the hero's death when she eats him. If the oven symbolizes a womb (based on evidence from other folklore genres), then both of Baba Yaga's intentions are in a sense equivalent: forcing the hero into her body. Entry into the mouth is explicit, while entry into the womb is symbolic and implicit. On this deeper level, Baba Yaga threatens a boy with being forced back into the mother's womb.

This popular folktale probably expresses a dominant concern of traditional East Slavic culture. The creation of a "bad mother" must express the fear that a mother in some way presents a danger for her son, expressed by Baba Yaga's desire to force the son back into the mother's body (oven). This might represent the temptation of incest, the mother's desire for her son, or the son's projection of his own desire onto the mother. It can also be seen as the mother's desire to prevent the boy from moving out into the world. The mother or mothers symbolized by Baba Yaga wish to hinder the boy's development, to keep him in the womb, which might result not in a literal death, but in a failure to grow and mature (a metaphorical death).

Some psychologists have described the anxiety about unsuccessful separation from the mother as "symbiosis anxiety." Both male and female infants develop their first sense of identity in a state of being merged with their mother, a protofemininity. Symbiosis anxiety is significant for the male child, who must develop a core gender identity different from his mother's, while the female child must separate from her mother, but is not forced to form a different gender identity. Male symbiosis anxiety is expressed in defensive negative attitudes about femininity and women: fear, envy, and disparaging of qualities and attributes perceived as feminine, and, especially, fear of finding these qualities in oneself (Stoller 1985: 181–183). Whether or not symbiosis anxiety exists in nature, these manifest expressions do exist in many cultures. The East Slavic versions of 327C/F hint at the danger (or anxiety about the danger) a mother presents if she is too attached to a male child, or if he is too attached to her.

If this tale dramatizes the danger of too great an attachment between mother and son, and the temptation of incest, then who is to blame? In most versions, the initiative for the kidnapping comes from Baba Yaga. But in a few versions there is an implication that the hero himself brings on this adventure. In Potanin 1906 no. 4 and Leonova 14, Baba Yaga's attention is aroused when she hears the hero shouting or speaking—a reversal of what often happens in 327F (Baba Yaga's voice lures the boy to the shore). In both these versions, and in Onchukov 2000 Shokshozero 74, the hero hides in his brother's bag. While there is a practical motivation for this (Ivan hides in the bag because his older brothers don't want him to go with them), it is possible to see this as another symbolic womb. It suggests that this hero, who wants to put himself inside a bag, is still infantile and immature. He shouts or speaks and alerts Baba Yaga to his presence (unlike the very young boy in 327C who cries out when Baba Yaga counts or touches his spoon, this hero is old enough to know better)—in this case, it is the boy who seems too attached, and who wants the kidnapping to occur.

Symbiosis anxiety and the temptation of incest are overcome in the tale. The boy escapes and presumably will go on to mature into a young man. Baba Yaga does not succeed in cooking or eating him. What do we make of her daughters' fate? The daughters might appear to function merely as extensions of Baba Yaga and her will, but the most gruesome moment in the tale is probably when Baba Yaga eats their cooked flesh, a female version of the "feast of Atreus."[10] If we ignore Baba Yaga's expressed indignation when she finds out whose meat she has eaten, she reveals herself essentially as a bad mother who eats her daughters and wishes to eat her symbolic son. Her curses and indignation might in fact be nothing more than a "moralizing façade" (Calame-Griaule 1987: 115–117) covering up her own desire to get rid of her daughters as sexual rivals (in Akimova 367 and Onchukov 73, the hero appears to be flirting with Baba Yaga's daughters, which might provoke Baba Yaga's jealousy), or, in eating them, to appropriate their youthful fertility and femininity. Baba Yaga is also a consumer of young women in AT 519, when she sucks milk or blood from a maiden's breasts (see chapter 5). Baba Yaga's behavior is unnatural not only because it is cannibalistic, but also because she attempts to prevent the normal succession or cycle of the generations. Her wish to devour children can be seen as incestuous desire, as jealousy, as the selfish wish to keep the younger generation from growing up and taking her place, or as the wish to usurp that place herself.

The cooking of the girls in this tale might reflect the lower value of female children in a patriarchal society, or it might also be a way for the hero to escape the danger of incestuous desire for his sisters (in Zelenin Viatka 115 the hero addresses Baba Yaga's daughter as *sestritsa*). In analyzing French versions of AT

---

[10] Atreus, the father of Agamemnon and Menelaos, tricked his brother Thyestes into eating the flesh of his own children; motif G61, Relative's flesh eaten unwittingly.

327 in which a girl and boy confront an ogre or devil couple, Marie-Louise Tenèze suggests that the ogre or devil's wife is a passive villain and might represent a latent benevolent capacity (in some versions, she lies to her husband about the smell of human flesh he notices). This involves the transformation of the opposition active/passive into the opposition evil/good. In many East Slavic versions of AT 327C/F, Baba Yaga and her daughters all behave in almost exactly the same way, which discourages such an interpretation. The acts of Baba Yaga's daughter in other tale types, such as 327B (see below), where she occasionally helps the hero or heroine to escape or overcome her mother, might support Tenèze's conception.

Camille Lacoste-Dujardin has analyzed a Kabyle folktale which includes many elements of the European AT 327 tales (1970: 45–107). She interprets the figure of the ogress (*teryel*) as an image of negative femininity, as well as the dangers of hostile nature (ibid., 326–327). The ogress is opposed to the hero in many respects (she is a giant woman, he is a dwarf; she has a devouring appetite, he displays self-control; she is a noisy sleeper, he doesn't need to sleep; she is one-eyed or blind, he is perceptive; she is stupid, he is intelligent). The tale involves several themes, of which the oppositions nature/culture and sterility/fertility are perhaps the most important. In East Slavic versions of 327C/F, the elements of nature and culture appear to be in a more complex relationship. Like the Kabyle hero Mqideš, the East Slavic hero is born miraculously (from a piece of wood), enabling him to mediate the realms of nature and culture. However, it is impossible to place Baba Yaga entirely on the side of nature. While the Kabyle ogress eats her victims raw (and her fire cannot therefore be considered a cultural fire), in the East Slavic tales, the mediating instruments of culture (the smithy, the oven) and cultivated nature (the apple, pea, or turnips) facilitate the kidnapping and cannibalism, while elements of wild nature (the tree, birds) save the boy from being eaten. Perhaps we can see Baba Yaga's actions as an abuse of the instruments of culture to satisfy desires that are beyond nature. The themes of fertility and sterility are hinted at by two food items which mediate between the hero and Baba Yaga— the apple and the pea. Both are associated with fertility in folktales: A childless woman eats an apple (Smirnov 305, Zelenin Viatka 108) or a pea (Afanas'ev 133, 134) and becomes pregnant. The fertility symbolism of the apple is discussed below, with AT 480.

The East Slavic versions of AT 327C/F are very rich in potential meanings. If this tale has to do mostly with separation from the mother(s), then perhaps the range in the hero's age reflects a cultural anxiety about male children and their ability to form a masculine identity, not only as infants and small children, but even into puberty. While separation issues are also important for girls, the absence of female heroines in this tale and the small number of tales in which a heroine experiences the oven episode suggest that separation from the mother(s) was perceived differently for female than for male children. For the traditional culture in which this tale circulated, it seems that the achievement of an independent adult female identity did not require the kind of rupture expressed in the symbolic language of the oven episode.

The Boy and His Brothers at Baba Yaga's House

SUS 327B, The Boy the Size of a Finger at the Witch's House (AT 327B, The Dwarf and the Giant) is somewhere between being a pure "children's" tale and an adult tale. Although the tale lacks a final wedding, the hero and his brothers are old enough to marry. Many versions also continue with AT 531 (Ferdinand the True and Ferdinand the False), which is an adult "quest" tale.

In some versions the hero and his brothers are born from eggs (Afanas'ev 105, Bandarchyk 1971 no. 154, Chubinskii 1878 no. 8, Sokolova 1970: 36–40). The hero, usually the unpromising youngest son, obtains horses for himself and his brothers. In Khudiakov 103, someone is stealing their father's millet. Only the third fool son is able to catch the thief, the horse Sivka-Burka. Likewise, the hero of Afanas'ev 105 catches a marvelous mare that has been stealing hay and obtains forty-one stallions for himself and his brothers.

The hero and his brothers set out. They come to Baba Yaga (sometimes the third of three sisters), who has just as many daughters as there are brothers. Baba Yaga's home is also surrounded by the same number of empty stakes or poles, presumably for the brothers' heads. In Bandarchyk 1971 no. 154 the Baba Yuga sisters live in huts that turn on chicken legs. Preparations are made for a wedding. The hero's horse warns him and his brothers to exchange clothes or trade places with Baba Yaga's daughters that night (Afanas'ev 105, Bandarchyk 1971 no. 154, Khudiakov 103, and Potanin 1902 no. 36). Baba Yaga's youngest daughter Mar'ia Yaginishna tells the hero to have his brothers exchange caps with her sisters (Novikov 1971, no. 43).

Baba Yaga mistakenly decapitates her own daughters. The hero and his brothers flee, and Baba Yaga chases after them. The hero throws magic objects in her path which become obstacles (D672, Obstacle flight), and finally he throws a magic kerchief over the sea which becomes a bridge. After crossing he removes the bridge and Baba Yaga cannot follow them or she drinks up more than half the sea and bursts (Afanas'ev 105, Novikov 1971 no. 43, Potanin 1902 no. 36).

Bandarchyk 1973 no. 9 is a long, elaborate tale including an episode which bears resemblance to 327B. The hero and his extraordinary companions come to the house of Baba Yaga Zhaleznaia naga (Baba Yaga Iron Leg), surrounded by an iron fence. Inside, her twelve daughters tell them that their mother has gone beyond the sea for wedding preparations. When Baba Yaga arrives, she sees the hero's horse and expresses her intention to take his head off and put it on the fence. She has her daughters heat an iron bath for the hero and his companions, but the companions (one of whom is *Maroz*, Frost) manage to foil Baba Yaga's plan and cool down the bath. The hero rides to the bath with Baba Yaga in her mortar, and finally threatens to behead her if she does not provide food and drink. After feasting, he kills her, puts her head on the fence, and marries her daughter.

Gorodtsov i: 275–294 includes an episode of 327B. The hero comes and works as a groom in another realm. He goes with the other eleven grooms to Yaga Yaginichna, and they each go to spend the night with one of her twelve daughters. The youngest daughter Marfa Yaginichna warns the hero about her mother's plans and decides she will let her mother kill her. The two exchange clothing, and that night, after killing the eleven grooms, Yaga decapitates her daughter. She sucks her blood and falls asleep. The hero then cuts her head off. He returns to the tsar, who is not terribly upset that his eleven grooms have been killed, but sends the hero on quests for a maiden, ring, and dress (AT 531). The first quest is instigated after the hero picks up a golden braid, even though his horse warns him not to do so. Yaga had cut the braid from Elena the Fair in a fight.

Two versions differ from all the others. In Potanin 1902 no. 36 the hero Ivan and his brothers come to three Yagishna sisters, the first two being donors. The first Yagishna sends them onward, the second Yagishna gives Ivan a magic towel to cross the fiery river, while the main adventure occurs at the third Yagishna's (the villain's) house. Likewise, in Sokolova 1970: 36–40, the first Baba Yaga Bony Leg is a donor who gives the hero a magic horse. The main adventure with the decapitation of Baba Yaga's daughters occurs at the house of the second Baba Yaga Bony Leg. These two texts are the only tales with a boy protagonist where Baba Yaga exhibits some ambiguity (in this case, donor sisters and a villain sister)—in all other tales with boy heroes, she is purely a villain.

The miraculous birth sequence found in this tale is characteristic of some children's tales, but the fact that the hero and his brothers are ready for marriage, that they sleep with Baba Yaga's daughters, and that Baba Yaga behaves as a castrator all imply genital sexuality. The hero of this tale is already on the threshold of adulthood, and this is probably why some tale-tellers append AT 531, an "adult" tale which ends in marriage. The hero serves a tsar in another realm, and must obtain magic objects and a maiden for the tsar. In Bandarchyk 1971 no. 154, Chubinskii 1878 no. 8, Potanin 1902 no. 36, and

Sokolova 1970: 36–40, he obtains the objects from Baba Yaga. These 531 episodes are discussed in chapter 5.

What is striking about our survey of tales with boy heroes is Baba Yaga's almost exclusive identity as a villain. There are no tale types with boy heroes in which Baba Yaga is a donor, and only two tale texts where she appears ambiguously (Potanin 1902 no. 36, Sokolova 1970: 36–40). It is interesting that this ambiguity (in the form of a kind, donor Baba Yaga who helps the hero before he comes to her villain sister) is found in a tale type which is not purely a children's tale, but borders on adult male "quest" tales. This suggests that Baba Yaga is essentially a villain for the boy protagonist, which is not true for tales with girl heroines.

Baba Yaga and the Kind and the Unkind Girls

A girl's path to maturity and womanhood is symbolically expressed in a folktale cycle which is well represented in East Slavic tradition, the tale of The Kind and the Unkind Girls (AT 480). The significant stable elements in this tale type are a wicked stepmother, a supernatural figure who tests the kind stepdaughter and the unkind stepmother's daughter, the rewarding of the kind girl, and the punishment of the unkind one. Because of this essential conflict, Russian scholarship generally refers to the various subtypes of AT 480 as the tale of the "stepmother and stepdaughter" (*machekha i padcheritsa*).

The description of the subtypes of AT 480 in the Aarne-Thompson index does not correspond to some national and local tale repertoires, and the problem of these subtypes has been solved differently in different national tale-type indices (Kerbelyte 1984: 226). The East Slavic tale-type index identifies several distinct subtypes, and Baba Yaga appears in at least five of them: SUS 480A* (a sister or sisters try to rescue their kidnapped brother), 480* (the girl drops a spindle down a well, performs tasks en route to a witch's house, where she serves the witch), 480*B (the stepdaughter is abandoned in the forest, where a supernatural figure tests her), 480*C (the girl plays hide-and-seek or blindman's buff with a bear, and a mouse helps her), and 480B* (the stepdaughter is sent to Baba Yaga's house for fire, and a magic doll or the members of Baba Yaga's household help her accomplish tasks or escape) (Barag et al. 1979: 140–142).

In 480A*, Baba Yaga is purely a villain, a cannibal kidnapper, behaving much as she does in SUS 327C/F. In 480*, she is a tester who sometimes exhibits hostility toward the kind girl, and in one version she is the wicked stepmother. She is both tester and wicked stepmother in 480*B. The same split occurs in 480*C, where she is either the stepmother, or plays blindman's buff with the girls. She is a very threatening, hostile tester in 480B*.

In SUS 480A* Baba Yaga's behavior recalls the 327C/F cycle. Parents leave their children alone at home. While the sisters play, leaving the younger brother alone, Baba Yaga, the swan-geese (*gusi-lebedi*), or an eagle kidnap him. The older sister goes to look for him. She encounters three donor figures who ask her to perform various tasks: An oven asks for wood, a milk river with custard banks asks the girl to eat from it, an apple tree asks her to shake the apples from it or eat an apple, a barn or a haystack asks her to sweep and rake, a fire asks her to put a log on it. The girl refuses to do any of these favors, but arrives at Baba Yaga's hut on chicken legs and finds her brother. Baba Yaga asks her to pick the lice from her hair. She does so and Baba Yaga falls asleep or she pricks Baba Yaga's head with a knife and incapacitates her. Once Baba Yaga is asleep, the girls in Khudiakov 12 and 13 seal her eyes shut with tar.

Then the girl flees with her brother, but the donors refuse to hide her and Baba Yaga snatches her brother back. The same thing happens to the second sister, but the youngest sister fulfills the donor figures' requests. She gets her brother from Baba Yaga and the donors help her hide on the way home. In Afanas'ev 113, the single sister fulfills the requests on the return journey, while fleeing from the swan-geese. Kargin 23 is unusual in that the hero is a boy who rescues his sister. He encounters the oven, apple tree, and river with custard banks. A bear helps him grease the gates of Baba Yaga's dwelling so that they don't make noise when he goes in to rescue his sister. When the children get home, their mother scolds the boy.

The episode of the unsuccessful retrieval attempt by an unkind sister can be absent (Kargin 24, Lutovinova 45, 46), the heroine may carry out all the requests made to her along the way (Kargin 24), or the sister may succeed in retrieving her brother even though she does not do what the oven, apple tree, and river ask, but does give porridge to a mouse in Baba Yaga's house (Lutovinova 46).

One Belorussian tale includes an episode which somewhat resembles SUS 480A*, as well as the magic flight, SUS 313H* (Bandarchyk 1978 no. 24). An orphan brother and sister come to Baba Yuga Iron Leg's hut on chicken legs. Baba Yuga has the girl weave and the boy chop wood while her cat guards them. The children give the cat meat. In return, the cat gives them a ball and a kerchief, and takes the girl's place. The cat deceives Baba Yuga for a while, but then she discovers the children's absence and chases them in her mortar, with a poker and a broom. The children follow the ball to a fiery sea and use the kerchief to make a bridge. When the bridge is removed, Baba Yuga cannot follow them.

Some versions describe what Baba Yaga and the boy are doing, including the hut with its traditional formulaic phrases. The heroine comes to a hut on chicken legs, where her brother is playing with golden apples on the porch, while Baba Yaga is spinning (Lutovinova 45). The heroine of Lutovinova 46 addresses Baba Yaga with words that recall the typical donor sequence: "I walked through the marsh and got my dress wet. I want to warm myself" (Lutovinova 1993: 104). The unsuccessful sister of Lutovinova 47 comes to the hut turning on a chicken foot and a spindle heel, and tells it to stand still, with its eyes to the forest and its gate toward her (*Ostoisia, izbushetska, k lesu glazami, k mene vorotami*). Inside the hut, Egibova is sifting wheat with a hook, while the girl's brother sits on a bench, drinking goat's milk. In Khudiakov 13, the girls come to a hut on chicken legs and spindle heels and tell the hut to turn around. They enter, pray to God, and bow to the four corners. Baba Yaga in Afanas'ev 113 has a sinewy face (*morda zhilinaia*) and a clay leg. She lies on a bench, her head at the wall, her feet touching the ceiling, her teeth on a shelf (Khudiakov 13). In Lutovinova 48 and Karnaukhova 87, Egibova flies by in a wooden mortar with a broom to kidnap the boy, and is seen scratching her head at the window, while the boy sits on the oven, eating iron biscuits.

While this tale opens with a boy's kidnapping, the focus is on the girl's actions and the test of her kindness. Baba Yaga is unambiguously evil. In the light of 327C/F, the kidnapping of a small boy implies that Baba Yaga intends to eat him. Baba Yaga in Lutovinova 46 tells the girl to sit and spin, while "I'll go heat the oven and cook Ivan." Her threatening character emerges most clearly when she is chasing the girl and her brother.

In SUS 480* Baba Yaga tests the kind and unkind girls, exhibiting both kindness and hostility. A wicked stepmother sends her stepdaughter out to spin. In one version (Onchukov 2000 Shokshozero 4) Egi-Baba is the wicked stepmother, while the tester is an old woman. In spite of a warning, the girl drops a spindle, distaff, skein, thimble, or thread and goes down a well, jumps into a river, goes down to the cellar, or walks along the river to retrieve the lost object.

In most versions, the girl passes by people, animals, or objects who ask her to do something. She sweeps and rakes for the herdsmen or helps them tend their animals, drinks from a brook, ties a ribbon to a birch tree, pulls hairs from horses' tails, removes a splinter from a dog's paw, milks a cow, combs a horse's mane, or eats an apple from a tree or a pie from an oven.

The heroine comes to Baba Yaga's hut, where Baba Yaga asks her to carry water in a sieve, heat the bath, and bathe her and her children (human sons or animals: mice, rats, worms, insects, frogs, toads, snakes, or lizards). A bird instructs the girl to rub clay on the sieve, which allows her to bring water for the bath. The heroine fulfills the other tasks Baba Yaga gives her. Baba Yaga rewards her and sends her home, while the donor figures may reward her on the way home as well. In Mitropol'skaia 77, the two girls are given a choice of three chests: red, blue, and white. The stepmother envies the heroine and sends her own daughter, who refuses to do as the donor figures ask. She carries out Baba Yaga's instructions poorly or not at all, is rude to the bird, or injures Baba Yaga's children. Baba Yaga gives her a bad gift (Potiavin 8), no gift at all (Lutovinova 40), or punishes her in some way: When the girl returns home to her mother, she opens the bag or chest and fire bursts out from it and burns her to death (Onchukov 2000 Shokshozero 4), burns her and her wicked mother to death (Lutovinova 39, Khudiakov 101, Mitropol'skaia 77), or the house catches on fire (Erlenvein 9). Baba Yaga pours tar over the girl and chases her in her mortar, the girl gets home barely alive, and her mother dies of shock (Lutovinova 41). Baba Yaga eats the girl (Lutovinova 42), or "breaks" the girl and leaves her bones on the riverbank (Morokhin and Vardugin 1993: 121–123). In one exceptional version, the girl has been given coals and burns down Egibova's hut with them, forcing Egibova to run away. The girl simply returns home without the lost thread (Nikiforov 1961 no. 63).

Several versions include the hut on chicken legs, the phrases used to enter, and a grotesque description of Baba Yaga, who lies stretched out across the hut and smells the Russian scent (Khudiakov 101, Lutovinova 39, 40, 41). Baba Yaga Bony Leg in Lutovinova 42 lives in the cellar, and her question to the heroine ("'is the sun high in the sky?"') is unique. In a version from the Volga region, the heroine dives into the river and comes to the hut on chicken legs (Morokhin and Vardugin 1993: 121–123). In this underwater realm, a fish advises the girl how to carry water in a sieve to wash Baba-Yaga's children. In Razumova and Sen'kina 1974 no. 69, the heroine's arrival at the hut and the sight of Baba Yaga Bony Leg are almost entirely formulaic:

> So she went on. She walked, walked, and walked, and there stood a hut on chicken legs. She said, "Hut, hut, turn your eyes to the forest, your gate to me, so I can go in and out." The hut turned its eyes to the forest, and its gate toward her. She went in. She went in, and there sat Baba-Yaga, Bony Leg, her breasts hanging over a rod, she was raking the coals with her nose, sweeping the stove with her tongue. Ugh, how frightening. Well, the girl got scared. She said, "Fu, fu, fu, I haven't been to Rus', I didn't smell the Russian scent, and now the Russian scent has come into the hut. Go, you maiden, go, you pretty one, heat up the bath, bathe my children, I have seven children, seven sons." (Razumova and Sen'kina 1974: 321, see Appendix I: Selected Tale Texts)

In Lutovinova 39, Baba Yaga is quite surprised that the kind girl is able to carry water in a sieve (*Vot ei divo vzialo, Iagu-to Babu*), which might imply hostility. Lutovinova 40 hints that Baba Yaga wanted to harm or keep the girl from returning home: After the girl has accomplished the washing, "there was nothing [she] could do, Baba Yaga let her go home with the skein" (Lutovinova 1993: 93).

Vlasova and Zhekulina 50 is an unusual tale which combines some elements of 314A* (discussed below) with 480*. Two boys and two girls go to the forest for berries. They get lost and come to the hut on chicken legs, where Baba-Yaga sits in the cellar. She says she will eat them, but they offer to do work for her. She tells them to heat the bath, and gives them a sieve. A bird tells the girls how to stop up the sieve with clay, and the children wash the frogs, snakes, and mice, who are Baba-Yaga's children. Baba-Yaga gives them chests which contain wealth. A boy in the village envies their gifts and goes to Baba-Yaga's hut. He harms the children, gets a chest from Baba-Yaga, and impatiently opens it before he gets home. Fire comes out of the chest and burns him to death. The presence of boys is unusual, as well as the opening episode.

In SUS 480*B, Baba Yaga appears as the tester of the girls in some versions (Afanas'ev 102, Lutovinova 43, 51, 81, Matveeva and Leonova Prilozhenie 2, pp. 304–305, Shastina 1971 no. 28, Vedernikova and Samodelova 44), but appears as the wicked stepmother in others (Onchukov 108, Simina 21, 22, Zelenin Perm' 77). The wicked stepmother has the heroine driven out or abandoned in the forest; the heroine is polite to or performs tasks for the supernatural figure; the heroine's father brings her home, where her stepmother is disappointed that she is not dead (the stepmother kicks the dog who announces the heroine's triumphant return). After the stepmother's daughter fails, the father brings her bones home.

When Baba Yaga is a tester, the heroine comes to her hut, or Baba Yaga appears. The heroine spins, cleans, or heats the bath, sometimes with the help of animals, and is rewarded. The stepmother in Lutovinova 43 sends the heroine to work outside the home. She comes to Baba Yaga, who seems rather hostile: After the girl has managed to carry water in a sieve, she is surprised, but resolves to "catch" the girl. When she is unable to do so, she gives the girl earrings and a bracelet and lets her go home. When the heroine in Vedernikova and Samodelova 44 arrives at the hut on chicken legs, Baba Yaga is feeding animals cabbage soup and porridge. The girl greets Baba Yaga politely, and Baba Yaga gives her a small amount of porridge. Although she is hungry herself, the girl gives her porridge to animals who ask for it. The animals reward her with a trunk of gifts and new clothing. The same animals tear the unkind stepsister to bits.

In Lutovinova 51, the wicked stepmother has the heroine's father leave her in the forest to freeze to death. Baba Yaga rides by in her mortar, warms her with a current of warm air, and tells her to get in the mortar. The girl goes with

Baba Yaga and serves her for two years. Baba Yaga rewards her with food and clothes and sends her home, whereas she freezes the stepsisters.

In Lutovinova 81, the kind heroine is tested by *Moroz* (Frost), a series of tree and animal donors, and by an old woman (*babka*), who takes her in for a year. The old woman lives in a hut on chicken legs. When the unkind girl comes, the hut is facing the forest, but she walks in without uttering any phrase. When the old woman tells her to go, she is referred to as Yaga Baba. Yaga Baba gives her a chest. The unkind girl sets off, does not receive the rewards the kind girl had, and Moroz freezes her. Snakes crawl out of the chest and entwine her. It is interesting that this storyteller reserved the name Yaga Baba for the tester when she punishes the unkind girl.

Afanas'ev 102 is somewhat unusual. The heroine's father takes her to the forest. They come to the hut on chicken legs. The father pronounces a phrase to make the hut turn and goes in with his daughter. He bows to Baba Yaga Bony Leg and tells her he has brought his daughter to serve her. Mice help the heroine perform the tasks, but the stepmother's daughter throws rocks at them, cannot perform the tasks, and Baba Yaga "breaks" her and puts her bones in a basket. L. V. Belova adds unusual details to her version of this tale (Matveeva and Leonova Prilozhenie 2, pp. 304–305, see Appendix I: Selected Tale Texts). When the kind girl arrives, she tells Baba Yaga that she has no mother. Baba Yaga threatens to eat the kind girl if she does not manage to do a large amount of spinning in one night. Mice help the girl, and then Baba Yaga is happy that she has accomplished the task (*Vot Baba Iaga obradovalasia...*). Baba Yaga herself takes the kind girl home (and the bones of the unkind girl) in her sleigh.

In other versions of this subtype, the father's new wife is Baba Yaga or her daughter (Zelenin Perm' 77, Onchukov 108). Sometimes Yagabova threatens to eat the man and his horse if he does not marry her (Simina 21, 22). Baba Yaga orders her husband to take his daughter to the forest and abandon her there. The girl is tested by Frost (Moroz or Morozko). This masculine element comes and usually asks if the heroine is cold. The heroine answers him politely: She says she is not cold even though she is freezing. Morozko gives her warm clothing and money. Later, Baba Yaga's daughter is rude to him and he freezes her to death (Zelenin Perm' 77, Onchukov 108, Simina 22). In Simina 21, the heroine offers food to anyone in the forest. Two-, four- and five-headed creatures (*tsiudo*) come. She carries them over the threshold and is magically fed and clothed by climbing in and out of their ears. When Yagabova's daughter goes to the forest, she doesn't offer food or carry the creatures over the threshold. She climbs in and out of their ears, becomes ugly, and dies.

This subtype provides a basis for comparing Baba Yaga and Morozko (as Elena Novik has done). The narrator of Lutovinova 51 has given Morozko's attribute to Baba Yaga, and even made her more powerful: Baba Yaga has the power to warm or freeze the heroine, while Morozko can only freeze, and usually provides warm clothing to reward the kind girl.

Baba Yaga's ambiguous nature as a tester is well expressed in Shastina 1971 no. 28. Baba Yaga arrives, frightens the heroine in the forest, and tells her: "Don't be afraid of me, girl. Heat up the bath for me. Here's a sieve, get water with it. And if you don't heat the bath, I'll eat you" (Shastina 1971: 143).

The motif of freezing is a particularly striking one. While it certainly is based on the reality of the cold Russian climate, it is hard not to see the kind girl's behavior as a cultural script or symbolic representation of female endurance in unpleasant situations. The expectation that a young woman should be docile and not complain in the face of unpleasantness might be particularly relevant to a young woman in traditional East Slavic culture who was soon to marry and move to her husband's household. There, in her new married life, the "frost" she might encounter could be verbal and physical abuse, unwanted sexual advances, and longer work hours than those of other household members. The demands placed on young women not to complain, not to appear dissatisfied, to say they feel "warm" even when they are "freezing" are certainly found in many cultures.

In SUS 480*C, Baba Yaga is the wicked stepmother, or, in one version, a rather threatening tester (Lutovinova 25). The wicked stepmother orders her husband to take his daughter to a forest hut, or she orders the heroine to go there. The heroine manages to cook dinner, even though her stepmother had given her only sand and ash, and she feeds a mouse.

An old man appears out of the forest (Smirnov 42); an old, big man comes, eats, and then wants to sleep with the heroine (Lutovinova 29, Onchukov 2000 Shokshozero 30); a monster comes who says he will eat the heroine (Balashov 29); or Baba Yaga comes to play blindman's buff (Lutovinova 25). The mouse turns the girl into a needle and hides her, or the mouse wears a bell or keys and runs around the hut, deceiving Baba Yaga or the old, big man. This may happen three times. The threatening tester departs and leaves sacks or chests of gold or money. The father brings the heroine home and takes the stepmother's daughter to the hut. The stepmother's daughter does not feed the mouse or even kills it. The old man comes and crushes her, or sleeps with her and tears her apart, eats her, Baba Yaga devours her, or the monster eats her. The father brings back her bones.

Balashov 29 includes an appended episode which emphasizes the evil character of the stepmother Yagis'nia: She tries to trick the heroine into stepping into a pit of tar, but is pushed in herself and burned to death. The narrator does not immediately identify the wicked stepmother as Baba Yaga.

Only after the kind girl returns home with her gifts does she say that "Yaga-Baba was horrified" (Balashov 1970: 98). After that point she refers to her as both Yaga-Baba and Yagis'nia.

In SUS 480B*, Baba Yaga is a hostile tester, and there is no episode with an unkind, unsuccessful girl. Because of the divergences among the versions discussed here, SUS 480B* is probably the most problematic subtype. The wicked stepmother sends the heroine to Baba Yaga for fire, a needle and thread, or a sieve. In Lutovinova 59 and Afanas'ev 103, Baba Yaga is the stepmother's sister, and the heroine first visits her own aunt, who advises her on what to do at Baba Yaga's house. In Lutovinova 59, the heroine's mother, not a stepmother, sends her, and there is no outward indication of any hostile intention on her part.

The heroine comes to Baba Yaga's house, where she must work or be eaten. A doll given her by her dying mother performs the tasks for her (Afanas'ev 104), or the heroine gives gifts to the members of Baba Yaga's household, who help her escape. She gives the servant girl a kerchief, bread to the cat and dogs, ties a ribbon around the branches of the birch tree, or oils the gate. The household members may also give her magic gifts which keep Baba Yaga from catching her: A magic comb becomes a forest, and a magic towel becomes a river (D672, Obstacle flight). Baba Yaga pursues the heroine but cannot catch her. She is angry at her household, but they reproach her for her stinginess and praise the girl's generosity.

When the heroine comes home and her father finds out about her adventures, he gets angry at his wife and shoots her (Afanas'ev 103), or drives her away (Lutovinova 57). Or when she returns her parents praise her (Lutovinova 59). In Afanas'ev 104 the heroine returns home with the fire (in a skull), which burns the stepmother and her daughters to death. In a further episode, the heroine goes to live with an old woman, spins a fine cloth which comes to the tsar's attention, and marries the tsar. Her father returns, and she never parts with her doll.

Afanas'ev 104, "Vasilisa Prekrasnaia" ("Vasilisa the Beautiful"), is one of the most famous tales from the Afanas'ev collection, and has frequently been commented upon (Becker 1990: 152–166, Eleonskaia 1994: 51–61, Franz 1993: 160–177, Scielzo 1983: 171–175). Elena Eleonskaia uses its title to refer to all folktales about a stepmother-stepdaughter conflict. Nevertheless, it must be pointed out that "Vasilisa the Beautiful" is not a typical representative of East Slavic oral versions of AT 480. It clearly exhibits literary style and editing, and differs significantly from the other versions discussed here in style, in its greater length, and in a number of details. Eleonskaia describes "Vasilisa the Beautiful" as the most artistic version of this tale type, and this artistic quality is probably due to its editor or compiler (Eleonskaia 1994: 56). One motif which has caught the attention of many authors is that of Baba Yaga's three horsemen. On her way to Baba Yaga's hut, Vasilisa sees three riders: When a white rider on a white horse gallops past her, it begins to get light; then she sees a red rider on a red horse, and the sun begins to rise; finally, when she reaches the hut, a black rider on a black horse rides up to the gate and disappears, and night falls. Baba Yaga explains to Vasilisa that the three riders are her clear day, her fair sun, and her dark night. Marie-Louise von Franz concludes that the three horsemen indicate Baba Yaga's divine rank (1993: 173).

This motif does not occur in any other version of AT 480 with Baba Yaga. Instead, it is found in a few versions of SUS 333B, The Cannibaless. In spite of its title in the East Slavic tale-type index, the tale features a cannibal godfather or godmother.[11] In one version of this tale, the heroine goes to visit her godmother, who is Yaga-Yaginishna (Smirnov 151). The heroine encounters men on white and black horses who warn her that she will be eaten. She comes to Yaga-Yaginishna's house and finds the gate locked with a human leg, a bucket of blood stands in the courtyard, small children are lying about on the porch, the doors are locked with a human hand and finger, and a head is lying on the floor inside. The heroine asks Yaga-Yaginishna the meaning of all she has seen. The riders on the horses are Yaga's white heaven and black earth, the children are her pigs, and the head is her broom. Then Yaga-Yaginishna gets angry and eats the heroine. These gruesome details recall "Vasilisa the Beautiful."

In other versions of the tale, the villain is an old man or ogre (Smirnov 73, 294) or the heroine's mother, whom the heroine visits after her wedding (Smirnov 102). These short tales suggest that the compiler of the Afanas'ev tale may have drawn on versions of SUS 333B. The confrontation with a male ogre suggests anxiety about male sexuality, as in Smirnov 73, where the girl notices breasts in the oven, the ogre's lunch. He invites her to eat with him. She eats reluctantly, but he with great gusto. When he finishes the cooked breasts, he starts to eat the heroine's breasts, and finally eats her alive.

"Vasilisa the Beautiful" is also the only version of AT 480 with such a detailed description of Baba Yaga's hut. While the use of human body parts for locks and bolts may have been taken from oral versions of SUS 333B, the lighted skulls, and the skull the heroine takes home with her, are probably inspired by male-centered tales, such as AT 327B, or the 552+554+400+302

---

[11] This tale is a subtype of AT 333, Little Red Riding Hood, which is well known in western Europe, but does not appear to be common in East Slavic folklore. The 1979 East Slavic tale-type index lists only one Belorussian version (SUS 333A).

"herding mares" cycle (see chapter 5), in which the hero is threatened with beheading—one empty pole awaits his head outside Baba Yaga's dwelling.

In "Vasilisa the Beautiful" ghostly hands appear and perform tasks for Baba Yaga. This motif does not appear in any other version of AT 480, and is perhaps the editor's invention. Franz interprets the hands as the secret of complete destruction or death (1993: 174), but they cannot be considered a typical attribute of Baba Yaga. Likewise, she and other scholars point to the importance of Vasilisa's doll, a feature missing from other Russian versions of 480, although the heroine may have a doll answer for her in tales where she flees from her father or brother (AT 313).

Two tale texts remain which are difficult to assign to any of the above subtypes. Lutovinova 50 combines elements of 480*B and *C: The heroine is taken to the forest by her father, where Baba Yaga appears and tells her to cook porridge. The heroine feeds a cat, and Baba Yaga rewards her with wealth and sends her home. The stepmother's daughter goes to the forest but refuses to cook and must play blindman's buff with Baba Yaga. She is killed and ground up in Baba Yaga's mortar. Lutovinova 78 begins like 480B*, in that the heroine is sent to Yaga-Baba for a sieve. Then, as in 480*, a bird tells the heroine how to carry water in a sieve for the bath. The heroine washes Yaga-Baba's children (frogs and snakes), and Yaga-Baba gives her an apple tree, which she plants under a window at home. The stepmother's daughter is also sent to Yaga-Baba, but fulfills the tasks badly and returns home empty-handed. When a young man passes by and wants an apple, the tree lifts its branches and refuses to let the stepmother's daughter pick an apple, but gives an apple to the heroine, who marries the young man.

AT 480 is a very widespread folktale. Warren Roberts has made an impressive historic-geographic study of this tale, compiling and comparing versions from Europe, Asia, Oceania, Africa, and the Americas. There are Polish, Czech, Slovak, and South Slavic versions in Roberts's survey, and thirty-two Russian versions, although he includes Ukrainian, Belorussian, and even Georgian versions among them (Roberts 1994: 13–70). Many of the motifs found in the East Slavic subtypes of AT 480 are widely distributed elsewhere and none appear to be uniquely Russian or East Slavic.[12]

---

[12] Carrying water in a sieve is found in Scandinavian and Finnish versions; the mouse as helper is found in Scandinavia, Germany, Estonia, Latvia, and Hungary; playing blindman's buff with an ogre or bear is found in Germany, Finland, Hungary, Estonia, and Latvia; the witch has animal children in Sweden, Finland, and Romania; and the heroine must wash animals in Finland and Romania, as well as in some New World Spanish and African-American versions.

AT 480 is obviously a female-centered tale. Not only is the heroine female, but in Russia the tale was apparently told mostly by women. Out of eighty-seven versions in Lutovinova's collection, only twelve were told by men. On the surface, the didactic message of the tale is obvious. Traits considered good in a young woman are rewarded, while "bad" ones are punished. Diligence and compliance with requests stand out as desired qualities, which in fact were those required of women in traditional Russian culture and those sought for in a prospective bride. There is no doubt that the East Slavic versions of this tale concern a young woman at puberty. The "bad girl" is essentially the negative mirror image of the heroine, and sets off the heroine's qualities. The relationship of the two episodes (one precipitates the other) and the fact that the unkind girl has learned nothing from the kind girl's experience also demonstrate the seemingly paradoxical simultaneous coherence and disjunction of the fairy tale (Tenèze 1970: 61), or the particular nature of the miraculous in fairy tales, where a positive hero or heroine (unlike the false hero) acts "unreasonably," without motivation or understanding of cause-and-effect relationships (Somoff 2002: 286–287).

Ernest Jones's observations on the image of the witch are particularly apt in the context of this folktale: "The Witch idea is an exteriorization of a woman's unconscious thoughts about herself and her mother, and this is one of the reasons why Witches were for the most part either very old and ugly or very young and beautiful" (1951: 232). Based on western European versions of AT 480, Gail Kligman has interpreted this tale as having to do with "a young girl's ambivalent feelings about her mother and herself. These feelings are aroused when the young woman enters the stage of puberty. Not only is her attitude towards her mother contradictory, but she experiences the same doubts about her own role as a maturing young woman" (Kligman 1973: 48). The contrasting episodes of kindness and unkindness reflect a young woman's own love and hate, for herself and her mother. The old woman or witch tester of AT 480 is a good mother who is not a sexual rival for the heroine (e.g., Baba Yaga has children, but no husband). The witch's frightening appearance or attributes make her sexually undesirable.

The heroine's adventures symbolize her adjustment to her proper role, and to menstruation and masturbation (symbolized by spinning). At the same time, behind the kind acts of the "good" girl, there is concealed aggression toward the mother, whom the heroine holds responsible for her situation in life (ibid., 54). The oven (womb), apples (breasts), and cows (weaning) are associated with the mother.[13] The act of taking bread out of the oven can be seen as an

---

[13] Apples are explicitly linked with fertility in some Russian folktales, when a childless woman eats an apple and becomes pregnant (Smirnov 305, Zelenin Viatka 108). Apples symbolize female

expression of hostility toward a sibling, and the heroine's acts also express her own hostility toward menstruation. Many traditional cultures consider menstruating women unclean and dangerous and therefore prohibit them from carrying out various activities. So while the heroine's actions toward the donor figures encountered en route to Baba Yaga's dwelling are helpful and kind on the surface, "they are really unthinkable things for her to do at this particular time" (ibid., 59).[14] At the witch's house, the heroine's tasks usually involve cleaning. In reaction to "dirt" (the recurring menstrual cycle and sexual urges), the heroine continually cleans. She accomplishes the tasks given her, accepts her role, and masters and represses her hostility and anxiety. She emerges from the witch's house ready for marriage.

The "bad" actions of the stepmother's daughter express sibling rivalry, but also allow the heroine's own latent hostility to be acted out. The stepsister does what the heroine would like to do; she "violates" the mother by not carrying out the tasks. At the same time, the stepsister's punishment fulfills an important fantasy related to sibling rivalry for the mother's love: "Since she is seen as the favored daughter, the heroine fantasizes that the step-sister does something unforgivable to the mother so that she will lose favor and, as a consequence, illustrate the good girl's worth" (ibid., 65–66).

Stephen Jones (1986) finds that the two halves of the narrative correspond to the rite of passage pattern identified by Arnold van Gennep: separation, initiation, and return. The initiatory pattern is appropriate, since AT 480

---

fertility in some Slavic customs. On her wedding day, a Sorbian bride leaves apples behind the altar in church in order to ensure that she will have children. Or the bride drops an apple there and the further the apple rolls, the longer she will live; the lighter the apple falls, the easier her first birth will be (Schneeweis 1953: 37). A wedding tree was made by the bride's maids of honor in Poland. Although the tree was made from fir, blackthorn, or other branches, it was called the "apple tree" (*jabłoneczka*); apples, cakes, candies, cigarettes, and other small gifts were hung from the branches. The tree was placed near the bride, the groom ritually bought the tree, and the objects hanging from the branches were distributed to the wedding guests (Dekowski 1970). In parts of Bulgaria, the bride's female friends make a wedding tree by decorating a pine or fir branch. The tree is topped by a gilded apple or other fruit (Vakarelski 1969: 291). In parts of Serbia, a man who courts a woman gives her father a monetary gift, and gives her an apple with coins stuck in it. The gift to the woman may be only coins, but it is still called the "apple" (*jabuka*). In Slavonia, a bride carries an apple in her bosom on her wedding day to ensure children (Krauss 1885: 275–276, 396).

[14] Traditional Slavic culture, like many traditional cultures, considers menstruation dangerous and restricts the activities of menstruating women (Agapkina 2000). According to informants from Sudogda, Vladimir region, menstruating women should not look at infants or small children (danger of the evil eye), go to church (they might grow a beard), light a candle in front of the house icon, eat communion bread brought from church, drink holy or blessed water, plant seeds (nothing will grow), pickle cabbage, bake bread, or cut bread (Kargin 1999: 178–180).

represents an unmarried girl's maturation and preparation for life as a mature woman in society. Her quest is a metaphor for her search for a new identity. The pattern of unsuccessful repetition (the unkind girl episode) has a didactic purpose, presenting an exaggerated caricature of undesirable behavior. It also functions to reassure the maturing girl about an underlying morality in the world. Sibling rivalry is important in explaining the opening of the tale, and the need for approval from a parent figure explains why the heroine performs tasks for an old woman in so many versions of AT 480. The heroine is not old enough to establish a home of her own, but old enough to begin learning adult responsibilities.

Dropping or losing a spindle or other object may symbolize anxiety about fulfilling an adult role; the water container, bowl, bucket, or sieve may represent female sexuality and express the girl's awareness of and curiosity about her own development. The girl may be curious about male sexuality as well, but is mostly concerned with her own. A number of motifs (searching for berries or fruit in winter, falling down a well) express existential anxiety: the desire to find the regenerative element in nature, and to understand where life comes from. The motif of being left in a forest hut or other secluded place expresses the girl's fears about eventual abandonment by her parents and her future life away from them. This motif again suggests that the heroine is not yet ready for adult life, but is being prepared for it (Jones 1986: 155–156).

Geneviève Calame-Griaule has studied this tale type among the Dogon of Mali (1976, 1987: 177–206) and in Upper Volta (1975). Even in this very different cultural context, the Dogon tale is remarkably similar to European versions. At the instigation of the stepmother, the kind girl puts powder made of baobab leaves on her father's plate, a kind of symbolic incest. Her stepmother does not allow her to use water from inside or near the house to clean the plate, but sends her to a distant pond. On the way, the girl meets shepherds, whom she greets politely. Then she meets an old woman who gives her advice. Nommo, an androgynous supernatural being whose feminine aspect is expressed in this instance, takes her to the bottom of the pond and asks her to guard eggs while she goes away. Nommo's children are hatched from the eggs. Nommo rewards the girl when she goes home; the girl knocks on the door of a granary and returns home without looking back. When she arrives home, she sees that cows, goats, and sheep have followed her. The unkind girl is rude to everyone, and breaks Nommo's eggs. She is rewarded with a thin horse and a plate of excrement. Calame-Griaule suggests that the inversions and reversals typical of the supernatural realm (for example, in one version from Upper Volta the heroine must cook a meal in vessels that are upside-down) symbolically represent a return to the mother's womb, and the inverted position of the fetus (1975: 3–4, 1976: 40).

In their interactions with the mother/stepmother and the old woman, the girls mention three kinds of containers for the baobab powder: a white calabash, a "good" calabash, and a broken calabash. For the Dogon, these three kinds of calabash refer to three stages in a woman's life: the preadolescent virgin girl, the married and fertile woman, and the old woman. Calame-Griaule interprets this tale as the girl's journey to and arrival at the status of fertile adult woman. In order to accomplish this journey and gain her fertility, the girl must overcome her incestuous wishes for her father and her rivalry with her mother and women of the older generation. There is some ambiguity in the figure of the stepmother. Although her actions are hostile on the surface, in fact she provides the impetus for the girl's journey, a necessary quest for adult female identity.

This study is particularly interesting because it comes from a society which practices an initiation ritual for young people. Both folktale and ritual coexist (cf. Propp's conception that the fairy tale arises when ritual dies out). While the folktale bears resemblance to the ritual (there is a shared theme and shared symbolism), the tale appears to exist independently of the ritual. In some cases, the events of the fairy tale are a reversal of what might take place during initiation, as when the kind girl washes the back of the old woman tester (Calame-Griaule 2002: 159–160). Calame-Griaule concludes that "the initiatory journey of our tale corresponds less to real rites (even though certain elements are easily recognizable) than to the quest for fertility which characterizes the Dogon woman from her youngest childhood" (1976: 38, 1987: 194). In another instance, a Dogon version of AT 480 may prepare young girls psychologically for the physical ordeal of initiation. In this tale spirits remove a goiter from the kind girl while she sleeps, and attach this "extra goiter" to the unkind girl. Calame-Griaule interprets the goiter as a symbol of the clitoris, the tale demonstrating the necessity of the painful ritual of excision (1993: 106–107). The simplicity of the tale (the lack of difficult tests, the painless loss of the goiter) indicates that it is directed at very young girls, and it addresses not just the ritual of initiation, but Dogon concepts of adult femininity. The studies of Kligman, Jones, and Calame-Griaule are only a few of many interpretations that have been proposed for AT 480.[15]

---

[15] For an interpretation of AT 480 in the spirit of the solar mythological school, with the kind and unkind girls as sun and moon, see Drewermann and Neuhaus 1982. Dagmar Burkhart (1982) interprets a Bulgarian version of AT 480 in terms of a matriarchal past (the unkind girl resents the inheritance right of the youngest daughter) and proposes a distinctive female structural model for this tale.

In many European and East Slavic versions, the girls drop a spindle into a well. The well is a logical entry point into the other world, and it has a similar function in some East Slavic rituals, which invites us to examine ritual (and other forms of folklore) for symbolic parallels to the typical motifs in East Slavic versions of AT 480. There are many East Slavic magic practices to bring about rain in time of drought. One such ritual involves making an offering by scattering poppy seeds in a well, churning the water with sticks, and calling on a certain Macarius to come out of the water and shed tears on the earth (*Makarko, synochok, da vul'ez' iz vody, rozl'ei s'l'ozy po s'v'etui z'emli*, Tolstoi and Tolstaia 1981: 91). This ritual was recorded in the Poles'e region of Belarus in 1974, but may be very old, since medieval documents mention the Slavic pagan cult of rivers and springs, and offerings made to them. Another part of this ritual was the spinning or weaving of a towel. Women had to accomplish this outdoors, and finish it in one day. The towel was brought to the well (ibid., 91–92, 93). The ritual demand that the women of the community finish this work in a day recalls the "difficult tasks" of the fairy tale (such as spinning a large amount of wool in one night in AT 480).[16]

---

[16] Other rituals in which a towel, cloth, or shirt must be spun and woven in one day or night have been recorded among the East and South Slavs, to cause rain, to prevent disease, and to protect men who went to war In a village in Pirin Macedonia, three widows wove a cloth in one night to keep cholera or plague out of the village. During a cholera epidemic in 1892, the women in a Catholic Belorussian village (in a region now in Lithuania) spun and wove a cloth in one night. Before dawn, the cloth was spread and fastened across a road which led out of the village in order to keep cholera from entering. According to an informant from a village of the Poles'e region, women carried out this ritual in 1943, weaving a cloth in one night "so that the men of the village would return home from the war." During the Second World War in a village in the Chernigov region, twelve widows took flax and performed all the tasks needed to make a towel from it within twenty-four hours. The remaining men made a cross and set it up at a crossroads. The towel was hung on the cross, and a religious service was performed to bring the war to an end (Tolstoi 1994: 150, 155, 264, Zelenin 1994: 194–195). Historical documents of the late fourteenth–sixteenth centuries record that a number of wooden churches were built in one day to bring an end to epidemics in the Moscow and Novgorod lands (Zelenin 1994: 193–213). Dmitrii Zelenin explains the magic properties of the "one-day" cloths or churches through their newness and purity, which make them immune to the influence of evil spirits. Nikita Tolstoi considers the compression of time to be a significant feature of this kind of magic (1994: 159). The magic practice of spinning and weaving a shirt from hemp in one night is also reported in Romania. The "plague shirt" was made to prevent the spread of plague, cholera, typhus, or influenza. There are Romanian legends or fabulates about a girl or young woman who is caught alone with an evil spirit or ghost. She falls asleep while the other girls notice that the young men who have come to visit them while they are spinning have some supernatural feature, such as hooves or goose feet. After the other girls leave, the heroine of the legend spins and recounts the "torture of the hemp," the whole process of planting, cultivating, harvesting, and processing hemp to make a shirt. When she finishes her story, dawn breaks and the ghost disappears. In Romanian versions

In some versions, Macarius is addressed as someone who has drowned (ibid., 91, 94). This suggests a connection to the "unquiet" dead (those who have died an unnatural or untimely death, or who had dealings with evil spirits during their lifetime). The use of the name Makarka might have to do with its resemblance to the word for poppy (*mak*) (Tolstaia 1997: 109). Among the East Slavs, the unquiet dead were sometimes held responsible for drought (and other natural calamities), and the bodies of those suspected of causing drought were sometimes exhumed and removed from graveyards (Zelenin 1995: 99–109). The Tolstois disagree with Dmitrii Zelenin about the folk conception of drowned people. In some parts of Poles'e (Belarus), the drowned may have been regarded as holy, rather than dangerous or evil (Tolstoi and Tolstaia 1981: 96–97).[17] To cause rain in the Zhitomir district (Ukraine), nine women poured holy water on a hanged man's grave, through a sieve (Tolstaia 1997: 107; see the discussion of the sieve below).

Another significant element of this rain-making ritual is scattering or sprinkling poppy seeds into a well, although other items may replace the poppy seeds. In Poles'e, poppy seeds also have a magical protective function: They are scattered in the home to keep away the spirits of the dead, and in animal sheds to protect cattle from evil spirits. Poppy seeds were strewn on the grave of a person who had committed suicide with the words, "you'll come [back to visit] when you've counted all the poppy seeds" (ibid., 92–93), a measure obviously meant to keep the dead spirit too busy to come back and disturb the living. In the Voronezh region, poppy seeds were placed in a bride's stocking to ensure her fertility (Zelenin 1994: 206). Tat'iana Bernshtam analyzes a large corpus of East Slavic folk songs which express the maturation of young women at puberty through the image of sowing or planting various seeds, including the poppy, flax, hemp, and millet. One song describes the process of planting, growing, and harvesting poppies, and its refrain ("Are the poppies ripe?" *Pospel li mak?*) is an apparent metaphor for the timely "ripening" of a young woman. Other songs concern sowing or planting the seeds in an inappropriate place; in one song the girl sows poppy seeds near a tree stump, and a bird comes and

---

of AT 511A, the hero prematurely opens the gift of a magic horn, and herds of animals scatter. A dragon appears and gathers the animals in exchange for the hero's life "the moment he would love life the most." The dragon appears on the day of the hero's wedding to claim him, but the wedding bread jumps from the table in front of the dragon and tells of its "torture," from tilling the soil to baking, and the dragon is driven away (Ispas 1985: 402, 406, 409–410; cf. motifs K555.1.1, Respite from death gained by tale of the preparation of flax, and K555.1.2, Respite from death gained by tale of the preparation of bread, and the Sorbian beliefs about the Noon Woman in chapter 2).

[17] The spirits of drowned people are called on to divert hail storms in Bosnia (Lilek 1896: 439) and Serbia (Tolstoi and Tolstaia 1981a: 74–80).

pecks them away (Bernshtam 1991: 246–247). These songs address both a young woman's physical maturity, and her behavior during this period of life (especially in regard to the opposite sex). There are also Russian and Ukrainian folk games involving a dialogue about the planting and harvesting of poppies which do not reference a girl's development (a chorus stands in a circle asking questions, and a player or players in the center, a boy and a girl, or two girls, answer them) (Tolstoi 1994: 144–145).

There are also folk songs in which the maturation of a young woman is linked to spinning and being a diligent spinner. While this theme in folk songs reflects real skills that were expected of young women, there is also no doubt a symbolic dimension. In one cycle of songs (also a dance or game), one singer (or player) represents Sleepiness (*Drëma*). She dozes rather than spins, and fails to wake up when others inform her that various in-laws have arrived. Sleepiness only wakes up and begins to spin when her father or sweetheart arrives (Bernshtam 1986: 28). Tat'iana Bernshtam finds a general symbolism of sexual maturity in these songs. Spinning is associated with success in love and marriage, and a diligent spinner is one who is ready for marriage. Bernshtam cites songs in which young women who sleep rather than spin (because they are lazy) end up married to old men. Young women who have the misfortune to be married to old men stop spinning; young married women who become "sleepy" or stop spinning lose their attractiveness (ibid., 31–32). All these patterns suggest fertility or sexual symbolism in the act of spinning.[18]

The task of washing frogs and snakes, a frequent motif in AT 480, also calls to mind East Slavic magic rain-making practices. In Poles'e, killing and burying a frog or toad was one way to cause rain; another was to kill a snake or frog and hang it on a tree, fence, or gate. The practice of killing frogs to cause rain is also found in Bulgaria (Tolstoi and Tolstaia 1978: 112, 114, Tolstaia 1986). In Slovakia, hanging a snake on a cloth over a stream or brook causes rain (Holuby 1898: 61). In Belarus and in the Carpathian mountain region of

---

[18] This coincides with Kligman's interpretation of spinning in AT 480 (see above), and with that of Frank Alvarez-Pereyre, regarding Romanian versions of AT 501 (The Three Old Women Helpers, see chapter 2). This tale concerns the extremes of spinning too much (Baba Cloanţa) and not spinning at all (the heroine). In the case of Baba Cloanţa, too much spinning (sexual activity) has made her hideous (Alvarez-Pereyre 1976: 105–106). In a discussion of ancient Roman divinities who oversee childbirth, Nicole Belmont finds symbolic equivalences between the act of spinning, Indo-European conceptions of women who spin the thread of destiny (such as the three Fates), and a successful birth (1971: 175–177). Geneviève Calame-Griaule cites a French wedding day custom: On the way to the church, the bride found a distaff in her path and was supposed to spin a little bit (1976: 56). Besides asking the girls to spin for her in AT 480, Baba Yaga is sometimes spinning herself when the protagonist arrives at her hut, and her hut sometimes stands on a spindle heel or heels.

Ukraine, a stick that has been used to separate a frog and a snake can drive away a storm (Sudnik and Tsiv'ian 1982, Kaindl 1894: 625).[19] In one of the Carpatho-Ukrainian (Rusyn) tales discussed in chapter 2, Iezhibaba takes the form of a toad that sits beneath a well and withholds life-giving water. The association of frogs, toads, and snakes with bodies of water, fertility, fecundity, and regenerative power is probably found in many cultures. It is also a very ancient symbolic association. In the Sumerian epic of Gilgamesh (third millennium B.C.), the hero Gilgamesh, distraught by the death of his friend Enkidu, travels to the edge of the world and receives a plant that can restore lost youth. On his return journey, he stops to rest by a well. While he is bathing, a serpent comes out of the well, steals the plant, sloughs its skin, and disappears, depriving Gilgamesh (and humankind) of eternal youth.[20]

---

[19] In Romania, this same stick can drive away storm clouds, but also separate a man and a woman (Sudnik and Tsiv'ian 1982: 138–139); in Slovakia, carrying such a stick concealed on one's person guarantees that one will win a court case (Holuby 1898: 61); and Friedrich Krauss reports the South Slavic belief that touching a woman in childbirth with this stick will ease her pains (1885: 540). The combat of a snake and a frog appears in two tales (Nos. 99 and 105) of the *Gesta Romanorum*. In both tales a man helps the snake and kills the frog or toad; the snake rewards and heals the man.

[20] A few examples from other Slavic contexts are worth mentioning. Frogs are used in Sorbian love magic. A woman catches a tree frog and touches a man with it to make him fall in love with her. A man places a frog on an ant hill and returns a few hours later. He takes the frog's "hand" and presses it into the desired woman's hand at the first opportunity. Frog bones are sewn into the clothing of a man and woman to make them fall out of love (Schneeweis 1953: 17). Sorbian children are told that storks bring babies, but in at least one local tradition, babies are in the Spree river near a mill. Frogs pull them out between the roots of trees, and the midwife catches them in a net (ibid., 3). If a Slovak girl dreams of a snake crawling or swimming upstream, a man will soon come to court her (Holuby 1898: 59). In Bosnia, if frogs are found in the home, they are left undisturbed, for fear that the cows will lose their milk. Throwing a frog in the neighbor's milk will make the neighbor's cow lose milk and transfer it to one's own cow. Old women forbid others to speak about frogs in the presence of children, and children should not open their mouths in front of frogs, lest the frogs count their teeth (Lilek 1896: 441). Around L'vov (Galicia), people avoided talking about frogs around children because it might give them pimples on the roof of their mouth (Stecki et al. 1896: 137). Snakes are of course feared, and there are incantations and other magic defenses against snakes and snakebite, such as a Croatian charm dating from the fourteenth century (Putanec 1962). At the same time, there is evidence of a snake cult in Slavic folklore. The belief in a guardian spirit of the home who may take the form of a snake exists among the South and West Slavs, and in Belarus. In Bulgaria, every house, building, and plot of land possesses such a spirit (Arnaudov 1967: 129, Dukova 1985: 41–44). To harm such a snake would bring misfortune on the household. In one account from Slovakia, a woman killed a snake that had been drinking milk from her cow; the cow stopped giving milk and became sickly and thin (Holuby 1898: 60). In the village of Orman (near Skopje, in Macedonia), people gather at the "Snake Hill" (*Zmijarnik*) on March 22 and await the emergence of the snakes, who are not dangerous on this day. Clothes are placed on the ground so that the snakes will crawl over them,

One of the other typical tasks assigned in AT 480 is to carry water in a sieve. The Russian proverbial expression or folk metaphor, "carrying water in a sieve" (*nosit' vodu reshetom*) designates a useless, pointless activity, a waste of time. It recalls the ancient Greek conception of this activity as a punishment for unjust souls in Hades' realm, and a Roman legend in which a Vestal Virgin proves that she has not broken her vow of chastity by carrying water in a sieve (Hansen 2002: 69–75). In other East Slavic contexts, the phrase bears other meanings. In Ukrainian and Belorussian songs, girls and boys tease each other: "As much water as there is in a sieve/That's how much truth there is in girls (boys)." According to a Belorussian belief, speaking through a sieve will reveal if the speaker is telling the truth (Agapkina and Toporkov 1986: 82–83). This associates the sieve with the truth/falsehood opposition, an opposition related to the opposition of the kind and unkind girls in AT 480. Besides being an absurd or nonsensical activity, carrying water in a sieve in the other world represents a reversal of the order of "this" world, as Calame-Griaule suggests for West African versions (when the heroine must cook in upside-down pots). At the same time, this motif has been "rationalized" in East Slavic versions of AT 480, since the heroine stops up the holes in the sieve with clay.

In the East Slavic ritual context, offerings of poppy seeds to wells and actions with frogs and snakes are linked to the return of rain and fertility to the soil. It is not surprising, then, that the kind and unkind girls, who are becoming women, and thus fertile, are asked to bathe these animals. Besides the implicit symbolism of the tales (snakes, frogs/the water element/fertility), the rituals and folk songs supply other related concepts, concerned with the idea of fertility (of nature and women) and apotropaic power. The symbols found in the three genres are summarized in the following table.

---

and these clothes then bring the wearer health or fertility (in the case of a childless woman). In the same region, snakeskin has the power to help one obtain a desired man or woman as spouse (Spirovska 1971, Filipović 1954: 366–367). It is possible that the ancient Slavs looked upon these animals as embodiments of deceased ancestors or a local guardian spirit (*genius loci*). According to Russian informants (Vladimir province), frogs are the soldiers of Pharaoh's army drowned in the Red Sea, or people who drowned in the Biblical Flood, or people who have been cursed. Therefore it is a sin to strike a frog (Zavoiko 1914: 102–103). The symbolism of the frog and snake in Slavic folklore is too vast a topic to be taken up here. The snake displays both male and female symbolism, an association with the earth and bodies of water; there are beliefs in a king of snakes, and customs and beliefs associating the snake with the seasonal cycle (Gura 1997: 277–358). The frog shares many of these characteristics in Slavic folk belief; it has female associations, is used in love magic, is associated with rain and bodies of water, can appear as a guardian spirit of the household, but can also harm people (ibid., 380–391). Both animals have an ambiguous status and are accorded supernatural power, and in some contexts both are associated with fertility.

Folktale (AT 480) (Young women)	Ritual (Rain-making)	Folk song
well (entrance to other world)	well (point of contact with other world)	
water (bath)	water (rain)	
water carried in sieve	water poured through sieve	
frogs, snakes bathed	frogs, snakes killed	
	poppy seeds	poppy seeds
supernatural tester rewards heroine	"unquiet" dead man rewards ritual practitioners	
diligent spinner ready for marriage	diligent spinning causes rain	diligent spinner happily married
lazy spinner left empty-handed or dead	(implied failure to spin = lack of rain)	"lazy" sleeping spinner married to old man

This comparison of folktale, ritual, and folk song does not mean to imply any historical or cause-and-effect relationship between these three genres, but the correspondences between them suggest a common symbolism underlying all three (as appears to be the case with the oven in AT 327 and in ritual). Some of these symbolic relationships (water, snakes, frogs, fertility) are probably very widespread, while others (poppy seeds) may be "local," oicotypical, perhaps limited to the East Slavs. Needless to say, all these symbols are complex and probably polyvalent, bearing other meanings in other contexts.

In discussing an alternative typology of AT 480, Bronislava Kerbelyte defines one important constitutive element (what she terms an "elementary plot") of AT 480 as: "The protagonist takes care of the antipode as one of his/her own, like kin." She finds this to be the real reason for the kind girl's success. The unkind girl fails, not so much because she is quarrelsome or lazy, but because she is alienated by the tester, or disgusted by the tester's outward appearance (Kerbelyte 1984: 229). Kerbelyte does not discuss any symbolic implications of this insight, but it seems relevant to consider it in the context of the maturing young woman's ambivalent feelings about her mother and herself. Kerbelyte's observation might also apply to the common task of handling and bathing frogs or snakes. When the kind girl accomplishes this task, she shows she is not afraid of something strange, alien, or "foreign" (involving the oppositions of own/foreign, human/nonhuman). The strange and foreign element could be male sexuality and the male body (which suggests a symbolic and thematic link between AT 480 and the numerous tales about animal spouses), in which case the heroine shows she is not squeamish about contact with men's bodies. On the other hand, for young women (and men) at puberty, their own changing bodies can also seem strange or foreign. Another potential symbolic meaning of this episode in AT 480 is that the kind girl has learned to accept or has adjusted to her own adult female body.

Other versions of AT 480 appear to look forward to the heroine's married life and express her anxiety or uneasiness about male sexuality. The versions of 480*C, in particular, hint at sexual relations with men, and portray them in a threatening fashion. This is quite explicit in Lutovinova 29, where the male tester wants to sleep with the heroine and tears apart the stepsister. In the same tale the mouse helps the heroine sew her dowry. Frost (Morozko) might also represent the future husband in 480*B, and the action of freezing could reflect fear of unknown male sexuality, or fear of a future husband's abusive behavior, which a girl or young woman listening to the tale might well have witnessed at home (Semenova-Tian-Shanskaia 1914: 5–6). In the role of supernatural tester, Baba Yaga fulfills the same function in East Slavic versions of AT 480 as Frost; the two are allomotifs (Dundes 1980). Vladimir Propp cites Russian versions of AT 480 as an example of the importance of functions in fairy tales. The function of testing in this tale is what matters, while the question of who carries out the testing function (Baba Yaga, Morozko, a bear, a forest spirit, a mare's head) is of secondary interest (Propp 1969: 24). Nevertheless, Baba Yaga and Frost's actions and images (distinctively female or male) in these tales probably had distinct meanings and resonances for the audience, especially for young women who heard the tale.

Evidence for Baba Yaga's potential identity as a mother-in-law in the 480 cycle is provided by another tale type, AT 428, in which the heroine is also subjected to a number of tests by her wicked mother-in-law (see chapter 5). In particular, she is sent to Baba Yaga's hut in an episode that very much recalls SUS 480B*. The presence of this tale in the traditional repertoire suggests that Baba Yaga in AT 480, depending on the teller or listener, could represent the mother-in-law as well as the mother, or perhaps a condensation of both.

In some versions the heroine returns to her father, who gets rid of the stepmother. This is easy to understand as the girl's wish fulfillment: She is able to have her father to herself by removing the only obstacle, the mother. In order to make this kind of fantasy acceptable, the mother is represented as a wicked stepmother, a stranger who has interrupted the familial harmony that prevailed before the beginning of the tale.

Feminist folklore criticism suggests that folktales are the product of a patriarchal society and reflect a male point of view, even in the case of a (step)mother-(step)daughter conflict. The wicked (step)mother can represent men's hostility to women, as well as fear of them. The witch or (step)mother's hatred for her (step)daughter also expresses a woman's disappointment at giving birth to a daughter rather than a son, her self-hatred in patriarchal society, which places greater value on male than female life (Meyer zur Capellen 1980: 104–106). It is impossible to say who "created" the tale of The Kind and the Unkind Girls. In Russia it appears to have been told mostly by women, but women might certainly contribute to their own oppression in a patriarchal society. There is no doubt that one of the tale's multiple messages encourages young women to be docile and compliant, even as it celebrates the kind girl's triumph over difficult circumstances.

AT 480 and AT 327C/F have a common narrative structure: There is a sojourn in the fantastic realm, a confrontation with a supernatural figure, and the hero(ine) returns home, where conflicts have now been resolved. In one tale (Razumova and Sen'kina 1974 no. 69), the narrator contrasts the comfortable feather bed the kind girl sleeps in at Baba Yaga's hut to the bad treatment she had received from her stepmother (see Appendix I: Selected Tale Texts), giving this tale a symmetry and juxtaposition of opposing realms like those of AT 327C/F. However, this simple structural reversal

| AT 327C/F—male hero | leaves kind mother | comes to wicked Baba Yaga |
| AT 480—female heroine | leaves wicked stepmother | comes to kind Baba Yaga |

describes only a few of the East Slavic versions of AT 480. Compared to the Baba Yaga who tries to cook the boy in her oven, the Baba Yaga in AT 480 is more complex and far less uniform. In AT 327C/F, Baba Yaga is unambiguously always the villain, while in AT 480, the heroine leaves a bad mother (the wicked stepmother or, in twenty-five of forty-eight versions, Baba Yaga) to confront a Baba Yaga or other tester/donor who (at least initially) may be just as hostile. Baba Yaga is the ambiguous tester in twenty-three of the forty-eight versions.

Unlike the splitting between the good mother and Baba Yaga in AT 327C/F, the splitting in AT 480 occurs within Baba Yaga's image, if we consider all her manifestations in the different versions of AT 480 as parts of a collective image. Another important qualitative difference is that many versions of AT 480 include elements of the formulaic sequence typical for tales where Baba Yaga is a donor (the arrival at the hut, the phrases spoken to make the hut turn around, the dialogue with Baba Yaga), while these elements are infrequent and exceptional in AT 327C/F.

Other Tales with Girl Heroines

SUS 314A*, The Bull Savior, could reflect a very real part of a village girl's life. A girl, who may be made from a clump of snow or a mushroom, goes to the forest with other girls. They get lost and end up at Baba Yaga's hut. The hut may be described with its traditional features and the girls may request that it face them. In Sadovnikov 20 the heroine gets lost alone and Yaga Baba kidnaps her. Baba Yaga gives the heroine and her friends food. Because the heroine is the only one who eats or doesn't eat, she must stay with Baba Yaga. In Sokolova 1970: 47–48, Yaga-bura gives the girls pancakes. The two other girls hide some of the pancakes in their sleeves, while the heroine Snegurushka does not hide any. When they get ready to leave, Yaga-bura demands her pancakes back. Because Snegurushka has no pancakes, she must stay.

Then the heroine is forced to rock Baba Yaga's child, to rock Baba Yaga, or to delouse Egi-Baba with a horse's hoof. In Kargin 15 she must heat the oven, clean the house, cook porridge, and rock Baba Yaga to sleep. In Sadovnikov 20 the heroine sings an unflattering lullaby to Yaga Baba's baby boy (calling him mangy), and Yaga Baba calls her a whore (*bliad*). The heroine tries unsuccessfully to escape on an animal's back (rooster, ram, sheep), or an animal (hare, wolf) encourages her to run, and finally a bull saves her. The bull defecates all over Baba Yaga as she is chasing them (Kargin 15, Morokhin and Vardugin 1993: 185–186, Sadovnikov 20, Vedernikova and Samodelova 28, version 2). The calf savior in another version (Lutovinova Kemerovo 159) kicks up swamp dirt with its hooves and spatters Baba-Yaga. In Ivanitskii 635, the girl's father comes out with a gun and shoots Egi-Baba.

A wolf tries unsuccessfully to rescue the girl in Kargin 14. They are chased by Bur Yaga, who summons her mortar and utters the words "Mother Mortar, go further than four versts!" (*Stupushka-matushka, shagai shire versty po chetyre!*)[21] Bur Yaga catches the girl, and then a bear comes and tells her to bake pies that he will take to her grandparents. The girl hides in the basket and the bear brings her home (see Appendix I: Selected Tale Texts). In Smirnov 238 the villain is a "frightening old woman" (*strashnaia starukha*), but the collector or editor gave the tale the title "Baba-Yaga." The villain of Vedernikova and Samodelova 28, version 1, is an old man who has many of Baba Yaga's features (a house on chicken legs and spindle's heels; he pursues the girl in a mortar, with pestle and broom). The events of this tale, while fantastic, could quite naturally express a girl's feeling about having to look after younger siblings as a kind of terrible servitude, imposed by her mother in daily life and by Baba Yaga in the tale.

Baba Yaga appears in one version of AT 451A (The Sister Seeking Her Nine Brothers). The heroine's father builds her a carriage so she can go to visit her nine brothers, and she sings a song to make the carriage go. She comes to the hut on chicken legs, and Yaga-Baba exchanges clothing with her. Yaga-Baba sings in a bass voice, and is unable to make the carriage move. The heroine sings, the carriage rolls, they come to the girl's brothers, and Yaga-Baba usurps

---

[21] The rhythm and assonance of the phrase suggest incantatory power. A unit of measure used in pre-Revolutionary Russia, a verst is equivalent to about two-thirds of a mile, or 1.06 km.

her place. Locked in the stable, the heroine sings, and one brother hears her. The truth is revealed, and Yaga-Baba is tied to a horse's tail and torn to pieces (Giliarova and Frumkin 14). Yaga-Baba's villainy in this tale recalls her role in many tales about adult women, when she or her daughter usurps the heroine's rightful place (see chapters 5 and 6).

Baba Yaga makes another appearance in a tale from the Tomsk region. A girl has managed to escape from robbers who wanted to cook her. On her way home, she sees Baba-Yaga grinding people in her mortar. Baba-Yaga bares her teeth and says she will grind up the girl. The girl throws a magic ball that becomes a forest and mountains. Baba-Yaga digs up the mountains and breaks through the forest. The girl waves a magic kerchief which turns into rivers that Baba-Yaga cannot cross (Potanin 1906 no. 20, AT 313H*, motif D672, Obstacle flight).

Baba Yaga appears as a cannibal devourer of girls in an anomalous tale, recorded only once, in the Nizhnii Novgorod region in 1914 (SUS 333C*, Baba-Yaga, Devourer of Children, Potiavin 12). Parents leave with their seven sons and tell their daughters to invite grandmother to spend the night. One of the daughters mistakenly invites Baba Yaga, who says she will not come unless the girl cuts off one of the dog's legs. Baba Yaga does not come until the girl has cut off two of the dog's legs and its head. Then she comes and eats all seven daughters.

Although it is an animal tale, AT 123, The Wolf and the Kids, features Baba Yaga as a cannibal eater of animal children. A goat or sheep mother goes out and leaves her children at home. She warns the children about Egibisna or Egibovna, and the children recognize that the latter is not their mother from her rough voice. In Zelenin Viatka 113, Egibisna has her tongue reforged twice until she fools the kids, gets in, and eats them. In Karnaukhova 85, the lambs fall asleep and cannot open the door when their mother returns. Egibovna eats the mother and then her children. This tale clearly resembles 327C/F with animal actors. This tale prominently portrays Baba Yaga's cannibalistic aggression, but also treats children's fears of the outside world and gives expression to fear of abandonment by their mother.

Baba Yaga appears as part of the background in another tale involving a girl heroine, AT 163, The Singing Wolf. A one-eyed wolf comes to a man's house and demands his granddaughter Arinushka (Novgorod-Severskii: 61–65). The wolf eats seven sheep, a foal, and a dog, and then seizes Arinushka. The wolf carries her off and comes to a hut on chicken legs. He threatens Baba Yaga and forces her out of her hut, but she does not resist him, because she "knew that a wolf's luck does not last long" (ibid., 64). The wolf goes hunting, and when he comes home to Baba Yaga's hut, the girl scratches his back and sings him a lullaby. The wolf thinks that Arinushka loves him and falls asleep. She spins thread from his fur, fashions a rope from the thread, and ties the wolf up while he is sleeping. Then she runs home. Compared to the voracious wolf in this tale, Baba Yaga and her hut appear closer to human culture and much less threatening.

Baba Yaga has a different relationship to the wolf in an anomalous tale from the Sudogda area (Vladimir region). A girl defecates into her boots, and goes to the river to wash them. Angry at the girl for dirtying the water, a crayfish pulls at the girl's skirt. She calls for a "guard," and Baba Yaga comes, "shaggy and dirty" (*kosmata, chumaza*). When Baba Yaga scolds the crayfish, the crayfish grabs her also. Baba Yaga calls a wolf for help, and promises him a sheep in exchange for taking her home. The wolf rescues Baba Yaga, takes one of her sheep, and the tale continues with his hunting adventures (Kargin 33).

Baba Yaga in Other Genres of Children's Folklore

Besides folktales, there are other folklore genres involving children in which Baba Yaga appears. A charm used to calm crying children at night was recorded in the Gomel' region of Belarus in 1975: An adult carried the child out of the house at midnight and called out three times: "Forest grandfathers and grandmothers, oho! Baba-Yaga, uhu, uhu, uhu! Take the crying and take it off to the forest, and bring my Katia sleep!" (*Lesovye dedy i baby, ogo! Baba-Iaga, ugu, ugu, ugu! Berite kriksy i nesite v les, a moei Kate nochnitsy prinesite!*) Charms addressed to the "forest woman" (*lesnaia baba*) were recorded in the adjoining Zhitomir region of Ukraine (Vinogradova 1983: 101–102). A charm recorded in the Pinega River region of northern Russia addresses Mother Midnight (*Matenka polunotsenka*), and gives her Baba Yaga's attributes. She is told: "Don't play with my child, play with your pestle and mortar, and broomstick" (Astakhova 1928: 58). A cognate charm from Arkhangel'sk province addresses the Midnight Woman, and even gives her a first and middle name. "In the name of the Father and the Son and the Holy Spirit. Midnight Woman [*Polunoshnitsa*] Anna Ivanovna, don't walk around at night, don't wake up God's servant (*child's name*)! Here is work for you: play with the pestle and mortar by day, and with the tie-beam by night, for ever and ever, Amen" (Efimenko 1878: 199, no. 8). When this spell was recited, the child's feet were made to touch the tie-beam in the ceiling three times.

A confession manual for priests composed by the Cistercian monk Rudolph in the thirteenth century, *Summa de confessionis discretione*, describes magic practices and beliefs of Upper Silesia, around Katowice and the Opole region. Rudolph's nationality is not known, but the practices he describes are probably those of the West Slavic population of that time and place. Because the manuscript (dated 1235–1250) was composed before the founding of the monastery where it was kept (Rudy Raciborskie, founded in 1255, near Katowice), and because Rudolph and the other monks who first inhabited this monastery came from Jędrzejów in the Małopolska region, it is possible that Rudolph collected some of his material in areas further east (Karwot 1955: 7–18). The manuscript describes a magic practice and an incantation addressing a forest woman that appears very similar if not identical to later recorded Slavic spells:

> Standing behind the door at evening, holding a child in their embrace they call the forest woman, the one we call Fauna, that Fauna's child might cry and theirs be silent, and they perform many other utterly mad remedies for children to make them quiet or studious [*Retro ostium stantes vespere puerum in sinu gestantes vocant mulierem silvestrem, quod faunam dicimus ut puer fauni ploret, suus taceat, et multas alias faciunt medicinas pueris insania plenas, ut uel quieti uel literati fiant*].[22] (Agapkina and Toporkov 1990: 68–69, Budziszewska 1982: 411, Karwot 1955: 23, Vinogradova 1983: 101)

Analogous charms addressed to the Forest Mother, often strikingly similar to the charm described by Rudolph, are found among the South Slavs and in Romania (see chapter 2). In the Boljevac region of eastern Serbia, a mother takes her child out to the threshold at dusk and looks for the first house where a light appears and says, "O forest mother, until now my child cried for your child, but from now on let your child cry for mine!" (*O šumina mati, do sad plaka moje dete za tvojim detetom, a od sad neka plače tvoje dete za mojim!*, Grbić 1909: 124). South and East Slavic charms to quiet a child also address the sun, moon, the dawn or dusk, morning stars, trees, or the Mother of God (Divil'kovskii 1914: 596–597, Mansikka 1909a: 37–44). It is not surprising that Baba Yaga would appear in some versions of this incantation, given that she is a supernatural mother figure who lives in the forest. Her appearance in this context makes her functionally equivalent to the South Slavic Forest Mother, and to Mother Midnight of the Russian spell. The apparent antiquity of this Slavic incantation and the supernatural forest woman might also serve as an indirect indication of Baba Yaga's age.[23]

Baba Yaga's role as a "pedagogical fiction" has already been mentioned. P. S. Efimenko reports that Baba Yaga was used to frighten children in Arkhangelsk province. Children were told that Baba Yaga would seize and eat them, that

---

[22] The author wishes to thank Emily Albu for this English translation, and for the translation on page 210, fn. 9.
[23] V. J. Mansikka concludes that the Mother of God is the central figure in these spells, and that other figures (such as the Forest Mother) are later substitutes (1909a: 38). The opposite evolution seems just as likely; pre-Christian mother figures might have been replaced by the Mother of God.

"there she is, right here behind the door" (Efimenko 1877: 166). It seems that children very much believed in the existence of these figures. Peasant children were perhaps more fearful than city children because of the stories "about werewolves, witches, house and forest spirits which the adults themselves believe"; parents consoled their frightened and crying children by telling them "I won't give you away" (Semenova-Tian-Shanskaia 1914: 27). It seems quite possible that children believed in the existence of Baba Yaga as well, and certainly stories about her as a cannibalistic ogress and abductor of children must have made a great impression on their imaginations.

Finally, there are children's rhymes (performed by children themselves) in which Baba Yaga becomes the object of hostility. Some of these short verses are addressed to natural phenomena (the sun, rain, rainbow, insects, animals) or to steamships and airplanes. The rhymes addressed to the rain sometimes include the wish that it not rain on us (the speaker), but on Baba Yaga: "Rain-rain, pour, pour/don't pour on me/but on Baba Yaga/pour a whole bucket" (*dozhdik-dozhdik, lei, lei/na menia ne nalei/a na Babu Iagu/lei po tselomu vedru*, Loiter 1991: 92–93, no. 253). Other versions contain slight variations (ibid., 93–94, nos. 254, 256, 263).

A few other rhymes describe a humorous accident that befalls Baba Yaga: "Baba Yaga, Bony Leg/heated the oven, cooked her leg/And when she went out into the garden/she frightened everyone" (*Baba Iaga, kostianaia noga,/pechku topila, nogu svarila./A kak vyshla v ogorod,/raspugala ves' narod*, ibid., 127, no. 482). Another version has Baba Yaga fall from the oven, break her leg, and frighten a hare (ibid., 127, no. 484). A similar teasing rhyme, perhaps used to taunt a mean old woman, states: "Baba Yaga, Bony Leg/with a hooked nose/with a head like a stump/with an ass like a box" (*Baba iaga/kostianaia noga/nos kriuchkom/golova suchkom/zhopa iashchichkom*, Weiss 1999). Efimenko also reports a humorous nursery rhyme (*peregudka* or *pribautka*) in which Baba Yaga the Torn Leg sleeps, farts, and spins like a wheel; her buttons pop off and her clothes tear (*Baba iaga/porotaia noga/ona spit, perdit/kolesom vertit/lish' pugovitsy rvutsia/prorekhi derutsia*, Efimenko 1877: 166). In a children's humorous song, Grandmother Yaga leads a unit of soldiers. She wears a kerchief and carries a bottle of cognac instead of a rifle, runs into a tree, and grows horns. "That's how brave Grandmother Yaga is!" teases the song (Belousov 1998: 458–459). In another song, Baba Yaga sleeps in a chicken coop (ibid., 463).

Conclusion
A number of interesting points emerge from this consideration of Baba Yaga in children's tales. Given the typology of Baba Yaga and the protagonist we began with, there are potentially six categories of children's tales, based on the

encounter of two types of protagonist (boy, girl) with three types of Baba Yaga (donor, ambiguous, villain). In fact, only four of the six possible categories are present, and one of these four (an ambiguous Baba Yaga confronts a boy hero in 327B) is represented only by two texts. For the boy hero, there are no tale types in which Baba Yaga is a donor, and in only in the two versions of 327B (usually combined with AT 531, an adult tale ending with the hero's wedding) is she ambiguous—otherwise, she is always a villain. For the boy hero, Baba Yaga is essentially a villain. For the girl heroine, Baba Yaga is never purely a donor, appears ambiguously in one major tale type (AT 480), and is a villain in all others.

It appears to be no coincidence that two tale types emerge as particularly popular (based on the number of recorded versions) among not only the children's tales (a total of 124 texts) but in our entire corpus—AT 480 (forty-eight versions) and 327C/F (forty-seven versions). Otherwise, there are eleven versions of 314A*, nine versions of 327B, two versions of 123, and only one version each of 163, 313H*, 327A, 333B, 333C*, and 451A. No doubt these numbers would change if a greater sample of tale texts were available, but it seems likely that the relative proportions of recorded versions (and thus some indication of the relative popularity of these tales) would not change significantly.

The two most popular tales (327C/F and 480) represent different scripts for the mother-son and mother-daughter relationships, focusing on the most essential "moment" of the boy's or girl's development. Snejana Tempest points out that the sexual identity of an infant in Russian rural peasant communities in the nineteenth century was stabilized in the first days of life through "strongly sex-typed rituals," while gender identity developed more gradually, through participation in gender-specific chores and work activities (2001: 96–97). It seems likely that these two popular folktales were, among other things, another form of gender acculturation. East Slavic traditional culture appears to advocate or consider necessary a boy's break from his mother, who represents a danger to the development of an adult male identity (the temptation of incest, or of maintaining an infantile relationship to the mother). For the girl at the onset of puberty, it is not as easy to construct an entirely evil mother figure apart from oneself. In some tales Baba Yaga is the wicked stepmother, well known in European and East Slavic folklore, a negative mother figure in relation to whom negative emotions can be expressed. But Baba Yaga also appears ambiguously as the tester, sometimes kind and sometimes hostile. The fact that Baba Yaga is almost exclusively a villain in tales with boy heroes, but does act ambiguously in relation to a girl heroine (in AT 480), suggests that a girl might have a more differentiated or changing view of her mother than a boy, or that for a girl, whose separation from her mother proceeds differently, it is more difficult to see and construct the mother entirely as an evil Other. Both these folktales obviously occupy an important place in East Slavic oral tradition. In spite of the harmful or evil actions of the stepmother or Baba Yaga in relation to the hero or heroine, it seems that in a hidden way she is performing a necessary function in the East Slavic folk imagination. Geneviève Calame-Griaule suggests that the stepmother may ultimately be doing the folktale heroine a favor by pushing her out on the quest for adult femininity. The same could be said about Baba Yaga or the stepmother for both these tales. Both AT 480 and 327C/F are adventures that girls and boys in traditional East Slavic culture are supposed to experience.

In both tales this important moment is dramatized by a sojourn in the "other world" of the fairy tale, and a conflict or confrontation with Baba Yaga, who has a human appearance, yet is not entirely human either. While there is no evidence that this journey to Baba Yaga's hut reflects any customs of the past, it may reflect East Slavic folk attitudes about the period of puberty. Tat'iana Bernshtam finds that young people at the age of puberty were seen to be closer to the "cosmobiological" than to the social world (1991: 252), in other words, closer to nature than to culture. The places where young women and men of this age group gathered for socializing, games, or working together tended to be on the periphery of the village. Fall and winter gatherings were held in a hut on the edge of the village, usually the home of a widow, an unmarried adult, or someone else whose status was not fully that of a "normal" adult member of society. In northern Russia, there was a belief that letting young people use one's home for their gatherings might attract evil spirits. The "wild" and immature nature of this period of life required the isolation of these young people during their leisure and amusement. To apply the terms James Taggart uses in discussing Nahuat narratives, young people at the time of puberty were perceived as being closer to the "things of the forest" than to the "things of the center."

Another difference between the male and female children's tales is found in the features of Baba Yaga. Perianez-Chaverneff's assertion about the focus on Baba Yaga's face and mouth in the children's tales is largely correct for the male-centered tales. Only in a few exceptional cases do the boy's tales include the traditional descriptions of Baba Yaga's hut, the formulaic phrase used to make it turn, and any description of her body. (Some description of her dwelling is found in AT 327B, but this tale presents Baba Yaga in a different light because it borders on the "adult" tales, and most versions continue with another tale episode ending with a wedding). In the female tales, on the other hand, the traditional descriptions can be found in many instances (in 314A* and in many versions of 480). This particular pattern of distribution suggests that the presence of the hut and associated formulaic phrases has a different meaning for a male hero than for a female heroine. The episode may be a marked and significant category for the male-centered tales, while it is unmarked in tales about a female protagonist. This becomes clearer when Baba Yaga's donor role in adult tales is taken into account. The picture of Baba Yaga's kindness and hostility changes in her relation to adult heroes and heroines.

CHAPTER FOUR

The Hut on Chicken Legs

As a donor, Baba Yaga helps the hero or heroine in the quest for a magic object or a spouse. Baba Yaga's behavior and attributes as a donor are presented in a typical and well-known donor sequence: the protagonist's arrival at the hut on chicken legs, the phrases to make the hut turn around and face the protagonist, the description of Baba Yaga's cramped position inside the hut and other grotesque details, her remark about the Russian scent and her declared cannibalistic intentions, the protagonist's demand for hospitality and Baba Yaga's compliance.

Baba Yaga appears as a donor in tales with male and female protagonists, but if we look first at tale types where she is exclusively a donor, we find that all of them, with the exception of one anomalous text (a version of AT 451), are male-centered. Baba Yaga reunites the hero with a lost wife or mitigates the tension or distance between the spouses. In these male-centered tales, this tension is often caused by a wife who is supernatural and threatening in some way.

The Quest for the Firebird, the Water and Apples of Youth, and the Tsar Maiden

Baba Yaga appears in a few versions of SUS 550, The Prince and the Gray Wolf (AT 550, Search for the Golden Bird). Golden apples disappear at night from the tsar's garden. His two older sons try to guard the tree but fall asleep. Only the youngest, Ivan, stays awake and manages to get a feather from the culprit, the firebird (*zhar-ptitsa*). The three set off to find the firebird, and at a crossroads the hero chooses a difficult road. In Khudiakov 113 the hero comes to three Baba-Yaga sisters who give him magic objects and instructions. With these objects he is able to obtain the firebird.

More commonly, and in four other versions of the tale (Gurevich 24, Mints et al. 1957 no. 18, Nikiforov 1961 no. 98, Sorokovikov 8), the hero meets a gray wolf who kills or eats his horse. In spite of this initial hostile action, the wolf becomes the hero's helper and takes him to the firebird. The hero ignores the wolf's warnings, sets off alarms, and is sent on other quests by tsars of other realms. The wolf helps the hero obtain the firebird, a golden-maned horse, and a maiden.

Ivan returns to the fork in the road. His brothers kill him and take the bird, horse, and maiden, but the ogre Koshchei comes and seizes the objects and kills the brothers (Gurevich 24, Nikiforov 1961 no. 98, Sorokovikov 8). At this point storytellers add another tale type to the narrative—AT 302, The Ogre's (Devil's) Heart in the Egg. The wolf forces a raven to fetch the living and dead water, revives the hero, and advises him to go to Baba Yaga, who is his *kuma* (either a co-godparent, the godmother of his child, or the mother of his godchild). The hero comes to the hut on chicken legs. Baba Yaga advises him on where to find Koshchei's death (nested in a series of animals and objects) and gives him the magic horse Sivka-Burka.

The hero obtains Koshchei's death egg, comes to Koshchei's realm, kills Koshchei by crushing the egg, takes the maiden, and returns home, where he marries her. In Nikiforov 1961 no. 98, the hero and princess Yaguta stop and visit Yagaia Baba on the way home. Khudiakov 113 does not include the AT 302 episode, but continues as AT 300, the Dragon Slayer tale. The hero's brothers throw him in a pit, after which he goes to another kingdom, kills a dragon, and marries the princess. He returns home, the truth is revealed, and his brothers are punished.

The development of this tale in East Slavic oral tradition is closely tied to its appearance in print in 1786 in a collection of literary fairy tales, *Dedushkiny progulki* (*Grandfather's Strolls*). Baba Yaga does not appear in the 1786 tale. The poets N. M. Iazykov (1836) and V. A. Zhukovskii (1845) both composed versions of this tale in verse. In a number of different prose and verse redactions, the tale was frequently printed as a popular woodblock print (*lubok*); between the 1850's and 1918, more than 150 lubok editions appeared (Korepova 1999: 69–74). AT 550 is found in the *Thousand and One Nights* and is widespread in Europe, Asia, and Africa (Thompson 1977: 107). While this tale type may have some roots in East Slavic tradition, the oral versions all display the influence of the lubok, and K. E. Korepova concludes that in this case, the printed fairy tale essentially introduced this tale type into oral tradition (1999: 67–111). The literary origin of the tale would account for the fact that the names of most characters are not Russian or not typical for the Russian folktale (Arkhipat, Dalmat, Dalma, Raflet, Germid, Ekuta, Yaguta) and the unusual presence of a wolf donor (ibid., 70).

The theme of sibling rivalry is quite explicit. Most of the tale-tellers include episodes in which the maiden is lost and recovered. Usually it is from Koshchei, an anthropomorphic ogre. If we regard this ogre as a father figure, there has been a splitting of the father into a benign explicit father figure at the beginning, and a threatening and malevolent disguised father figure in Koshchei. The other objects of the hero's quest might be symbols of emergent sexuality. The only mother figure present is the donor Baba Yaga.

Baba Yaga's appearances in AT 302 present a certain complexity, because this tale type is typically combined with other types (for example, with AT 402, discussed below). In these two cases she is a donor, but in an exceptional tale with a Yaga-Yagishna villain, the hero kills her by crushing her death egg (Matveeva and Leonova 1, see chapter 5). Baba Yaga acts as a hostile donor in a cycle of tales where the hero must graze her herd of mares (see chapter 5). By obtaining a magic horse from Baba Yaga, the hero is able to overcome Koshchei in another type of AT 302 episode. Given this complexity, and the apparent stability of these distinct tale type combinations in East Slavic tradition, it seems most logical to consider them separately.

Baba Yaga plays an important role in SUS 551, The Apples of Youth (AT 551, The Sons on a Quest for a Wonderful Remedy for Their Father). One version of this tale includes an appended episode of SUS 321 where Baba Yaga is a villain and hostile donor, making her appearance in the tale ambiguous overall (Balashov 43, see chapter 5).

A tsar sends his sons to search for the water or apples of youth, or water that will cure blindness. The two elder sons avoid taking the road that promises death and fail to reach their destination or are detained and imprisoned by deceitful maidens. The third son sets out, takes the most dangerous road, and arrives at Baba Yaga's hut. She gives him a horse or advice and he goes on to her second and third sisters. The third Baba Yaga instructs him. The sought-after objects are to be found in the garden of the Tsar Maiden (*Tsar'-Devitsa*), or under her pillow. The hero comes to her kingdom and jumps the city walls. He obtains the sought-after object, but cannot resist kissing the Tsar Maiden, in spite of Baba Yaga's warning not to do so. On his way out the horse brushes against strings fixed to the city or garden wall and sets off an alarm. The Tsar Maiden sets out in pursuit of the hero.

The hero returns the way he came. The three Baba Yaga sisters change his horse and delay the Tsar Maiden when she passes by. They lie to the Tsar Maiden or employ various tricks to make the hero seem more threatening than he really is. When the hero reaches his own realm, she sees him and threatens to return for him. The hero meets his brothers. They find out that he has the healing water or apples and dispose of him, killing him or throwing him into a pit. The hero is revived or manages to find his way out of the underground realm. The Tsar Maiden's tents appear in the tsar's meadows and she demands that the "guilty one" be sent to her. The two elder brothers are sent, but her sons beat or otherwise humiliate them. The hero appears and goes to the Tsar Maiden, who wishes to marry him. They are married, and the hero receives the tsardom, or he moves to the Tsar Maiden's realm to live there with her.

Onchukov 8 also adds a dragon-slaying episode (AT 300) in which the hero saves a tsar's daughter in the underground kingdom from dragons. However, he does not marry her but returns to earth on the Magovei bird. Then, the Tsar

Maiden arrives in his father's realm and the tale ends like most versions of 551. A similar episode appears in Smirnov 1. Additional episodes are also found in Razumova and Sen'kina 1974 no. 35. The hero follows an old dwarf villain under the earth (as in AT 301), comes to three maidens who are captives of Koshchei, and kills Koshchei. His brothers pull up the maidens but leave him underground. With the help of an old woman, he returns home on a bird, lives with an old man, and ultimately brings about the wedding of the maidens and his brothers. At that moment the warrior maiden arrives, and the tale ends in the usual manner.

As in AT 550, there is sibling rivalry, and perhaps disguised father-son conflict: The tsar sends his sons away for the apples or water of youth, suggesting a desire to remove them, or envy of their youth and beauty. However, the quest for the magic objects in this tale is overshadowed by the hero's encounter with the powerful Tsar Maiden. Curiously, although she has become pregnant and given birth, the Tsar Maiden is referred to as a maiden throughout the tale. This probably reflects the poetics and conventions of the folktale, where the names of characters are fixed and unchanging.

Some Russian scholars have interpreted the Tsar Maiden as a survival of ancient matriarchy, and Maria Kravchenko feels she is historically related to Baba Yaga (Novikov 1974: 180; Kravchenko 1987: 204). While it is impossible to verify her origin, it seems possible to suggest that, in this male-centered tale, she serves as a representation of men's fears about women. There may be a hint of this in the symbolic castration (blindness) at the beginning of some of the versions (Onchukov 8, Kozhemiakina 1973: 99–104), although the narrator of Onchukov 8 was himself blind and may have been projecting his own situation into the tale. In oedipal terms, the tsar's action of dispatching his sons might express his own perception of his sons as a sexual threat and the desire to remove them. If so, this is masked in the tale: The hero and his brothers always express the desire to go out into the world. This tale appears to deal less with oedipal issues than with the hero's (a young man's) anxieties about women, female sexuality, and impending married life.

The danger women pose to men is particularly clear in those versions where the hero's brothers come to a house where a maiden or maidens beckon them into bed, but then open a trap door under the bed and imprison them (Afanas'ev 174, Onchukov 8, Sokolov 139). The narrator of Onchukov 8 elaborates the episode in which the hero rescues his brothers and the other trapped men, and punishes the maidens, threatening to behead them.

The hero's own adventure with the Tsar Maiden ends more happily, but only after she has failed to catch him. The threat of death (and symbolic castration) is emphasized in one version when the third Baba Yaga sister warns the hero that stakes with the heads of knights (*bogatyri*) surround the Tsar Maiden's palace and that one empty stake awaits his head (Balashov 43, Razumova and Sen'kina 1974 no. 35, Smirnov 1), and when the hero tells the second Baba Yaga sister that he would have cut off her head if she had not fed him (Smirnov 1).

While the Tsar Maiden is ostensibly angry because the hero has taken the magic water or apples without her permission, many versions of the tale indicate that the hero has come into her bedroom and had sexual relations with her. Even when this fact is not suggested, it becomes obvious in the final episode because the Tsar Maiden has given birth to the hero's children. The hero's relations with the Tsar Maiden are stated most clearly in Onchukov 8, where Ivan-tsarevich "thought of making love with her" (*Ivanu-tsarevichu pridumalos' s ei liubov' tvorit'*, Onchukov 1908: 39). In other versions this moment is suggested more obliquely: The hero "gazed at the maiden's beauty..." (*na devich'iu krasotu pozarilsia...*, Afanas'ev 172), "crushed the maiden's beauty" (*smial on devich'iu krasu*, Afanas'ev 173), "kissed the maiden and joked with her a little" (*potseloval devitsu i poshutil s nei negorazdo*, Afanas'ev 174), and "sweetly kissed her" (*sladko potseloval ee*, Afanas'ev 178). Other tale-tellers emphasize that the hero's action was wrong: He "committed his crime" (*sdelal prestuplenie svoe*, Razumova and Sen'kina 1974 no. 35), "did wrong" (*sdelal khudo*, Smirnov 1), or "committed a sin with her" (*grèkh pamew z ëi*, Bandarchyk 1973 no. 65). In a Siberian version, "He couldn't resist, kissed the tsar maiden, she woke up, looked at him, he stayed with her. After a while he left with the living water and the berries of youth" (Kozhemiakina 1973: 101–102). In most versions, however, the Tsar Maiden does not wake up until the hero is leaving and sets off the alarm, as unrealistic as this might seem.

In Kargin 26, Baba Yaga Bony Leg warns the hero that if he looks at the maiden, his horse will not be able to clear the wall. Of course he "gazed at her maidenly beauty" (*na dev'iu krasotu pozarilsia*), and his horse tells him that he won't be able to jump over the wall, because "you sinned with the maiden tsarevna-princess" (*ty s devoi tsarevnoi-korolevnoi sogreshil*). In some versions the hero's horse complains that the hero has become too heavy. This could be attributed to the weight of the objects the hero has retrieved, while a symbolic reading of this episode might suggest the weight of sin,[1] or perhaps a fantasy of male pregnancy. An intriguing variation on this episode is found in Gorodtsov ii: 415–431. Baba Yaga does not appear as a donor in this version; instead, she

---

[1] Some Estonian, Lithuanian, and Irish legends portray the devil as extraordinarily heavy, perhaps reflecting a conception of the heavy weight of sin. A man offers a stranger a ride and notices how hard his horse is having to pull the sledge or cart, and realizes that the stranger is the devil (Valk 2001: 33–34). Cf. motif G303.3.5.3, Devil becomes heavier and heavier.

fights the hero later in an anomalous episode (see chapter 6). After the hero has arrived at the palace of Marfa Kantsybarovna and obtained the living and dead water and the berries of youth, he cannot restrain himself and commits "fornication" with her (*sovershil s neiu blud*, Gorodtsov 2000 ii: 419). The hero's horse then refuses to carry him, saying that Ivan is now "unclean" (*nechist*, ibid.), and makes him bathe in three wells before he can ride away. Of course, the hero is unclean because he has committed a crime or a sin: He has raped Marfa Kantsybarovna in her sleep. On the other hand, the idea of impurity and cleansing is also associated in many traditional cultures (including traditional East Slavic culture) with menstruation (see chapter 3). Perhaps these episodes of AT 551 express men's envy of female procreative ability in a disguised, symbolic fashion.

The Tsar Maiden's transformation at the end of the tale is at first somewhat surprising for a reader unfamiliar with the East Slavic tradition. It occurs without any outward motivation. In the version from the 1787 collection of Petr Timofeev, the Tsar Maiden wishes to marry the hero because of his cleverness (Novikov 1971 no. 29) or bravery (Afanas'ev 563). It seems that the eighteenth-century editor felt the need to explain and motivate this change in the Tsar Maiden's attitude toward the hero. Il'ia Semenov, a teller from whom the Sokolov brothers recorded this tale, doubles the "forgiveness" episode. In his version (Sokolov 139), the warrior maiden Sineglazka (Blue-Eye) catches up with the hero, even though the three Baba Yaga sisters detain her. He falls on his knees and asks for forgiveness. She decides that "the sword doesn't cut off a submissive head" (*pokornoi golovy mech ne sechet*, Sokolov 1908: 252). Sineglazka accepts the hero as a spouse a second time at the end.

Another curious motif appears at the end of the tale, when the hero is sent to the Tsar Maiden. He disguises himself to look ridiculous (Onchukov 8), is drunk (Kozhemiakina 1973: 99–104), or comes with drunk companions and tears the fine carpet the Tsar Maiden has laid out, while the hero's brothers avoid even stepping on it (Sokolov 139). It seems that the hero wants to abase himself, somewhat masochistically, before the Tsar Maiden. Or his behavior might express aggression indirectly, and his remaining anxiety about marriage, about his own ability to fulfill the role of husband expected of him.

Given the real power men had over women in traditional patriarchal Russian society, this tale cannot reflect real relations between men and women, but must function as a fantasy, and the surprising sudden transformation in the Tsar Maiden's attitude from a hostile to a benign one suggests that this tale is a male fantasy about women. On the other hand, while women in traditional societies may not have power or influence in public life, they may have a great deal of influence in the family, and dominate the sexual and emotional realm.

Another female figure appears in the versions with additional episodes where the hero kills dragons (Onchukov 8, Smirnov 1) or Koshchei (Razumova and Sen'kina 1974 no. 35). This appears to be another instance of splitting: The threatening Tsar Maiden who pursues the hero is offset by the tsar's daughter or the maidens saved by the hero in another kingdom. It is likely that both the Tsar Maiden and the women in these additional episodes are representations of the same person: They are the only female figures of the hero's age in this tale, and the women in the additional episodes are then forgotten, disappearing from the tale. The hero says he must first go home for the parental blessing and does not marry the rescued maiden, which may seem inconsistent. The narrator of Smirnov 1 resolves this by having the hero's younger brother marry the tsarevna from the other kingdom. In psychological terms, though, this "disappearance" or "forgetting" about the woman or women he has rescued in the additional episode makes perfect sense, since she represents the positive side of the hero's perception of his bride-to-be, the Tsar Maiden.

One function of this tale, in any of its versions, might be to reassure male listeners about marriage, and to give expression to their anxieties about it. The transformation of the female figure from hostile Tsar Maiden to an accepting Tsar Maiden (in the versions with a dragon or Koshchei episode, this transformation passes through an intermediate positive representation of a caring tsarevna) shows the way a man's perception of married life might change, and suggests that his anxieties can be overcome.

Baba Yaga's role as a donor in this tale is striking as the only nonthreatening female character in most versions. In this instance Kligman's interpretation of the witch's role as a sexually nonthreatening woman is particularly apt. Not surprisingly, the tale-teller Vokuev also emphasizes grotesque features of Baba Yaga and her hut (Onchukov 8). The hut on chicken legs stands in fresh manure (*na syrom goveshki*). Baba Yaga bears epithets referring not only to her bony leg, but also to her "sinewy, wiry" buttocks and "soaped" vagina (*zhopa zhilena, manda mylena*). In Baba Yaga these features evoke disgust or revulsion, but in an attractive young woman these are precisely features which might be sexually appealing and therefore dangerous for a young man, while they render Baba Yaga sexually harmless.

On the basis of these external features, Baba Yaga is an inversion of the other female characters in the tale. The Tsar Maiden and the maidens who trap the hero's brothers are young, beautiful, and sexually appealing, while Baba Yaga is old, ugly, and presumably asexual. At the same time, she is the only female character in the tale (before the end when the Tsar Maiden expresses her wish to marry the hero) who is nonthreatening, with the exception of versions which include the dragon-slaying or Koshchei episode. The important function of the Baba Yaga sisters is to guide the hero to the Tsar Maiden, to warn him about her, and to save him by detaining her while she pursues him. Sometimes the Baba Yaga sisters are the Tsar Maiden's aunts, appropriate for the role of mediator between her and the hero. The location of their dwellings is also logically between the realms of the hero and the Tsar Maiden.

The Hero Searches for His Lost Wife

Baba Yaga appears as a donor in SUS 400, A Man Searches for His Vanished or Abducted Wife. East Slavic tradition also combines this tale with SUS 329, Elena the Wise (AT 329, Hiding from the Devil; AT 400, The Man on a Quest for His Lost Wife). The East Slavic index distinguishes two subtypes of AT 400. Baba Yaga appears ambiguously in the second subtype, SUS 400/2, The Tsar Maiden (discussed in chapter 5). The two subtypes are distinct enough to warrant treating them as separate tales.

The hero of SUS 329+400 goes to live and study with an old man. The hero sees three maidens in the twelfth room and manages to get the key from the old man while he is asleep. The maidens ask him to give them dresses made from semiprecious stones (*samotsvetnoe plat'e*). As soon as they put on the dresses, they fly away. The hero tells the old man what has happened. The old man retrieves his three daughters and the hero marries the youngest, after the old man warns him that the older two are too dangerous for him, and tells him never to give his wife the magic dress.

The hero forgets the old man's warning and gives his wife the dress. She flies away. The hero sets out to search for her and comes to three Baba Yaga sisters, who give him magic objects, usually animal bones. The third Baba Yaga directs him onward. The hero arrives at his wife's dwelling. He must win at playing hide-and-seek with her three times. He uses the animal bones to summon animals (raven, pike, firebird, falcon, eagle) who hide him, but each time his wife finds him. A servant girl advises him to hide behind his wife's magic mirror. He does so and she cannot find him. She tells him to come out of hiding and agrees to marry him. They return to the hero's kingdom.

The servant girl and the Baba Yaga donors might serve to mitigate a man's anxiety about marriage, embodied by the powerful supernatural spouse. In most versions, the Baba Yagas are aunts of the supernatural wife, or the hero's wife has at least dined at their houses (Nikiforov 1961 no. 86). Mark Azadovskii feels that the hero's interaction with Baba Yaga in Zelenin Perm' 1 has been changed by the tale-teller Antip Lomtev, who leaves out descriptions of Baba Yaga and constructs a "realistic" dialogue between her and the hero (Azadovskii 1960: 52). Nevertheless, their interaction contains many of the traditional elements (see discussion below).

Three Baba Yaga sisters direct the hero toward his vanished spouse in four versions of SUS 400/1 which are not combined with AT 329. In Smirnov 35, the hero obtains the tsar's daughter with a magic ring. She finds the ring and disappears. The hero comes to three Baba Yaga sisters. His wife comes to the home of the third Baba Yaga and picks lice from her hair while the hero eavesdrops. Then the hero goes and sells the three magic objects he has obtained from the Baba-Yagas to their nieces, who allow him a night with his wife in return. On the third night he manages to wake her and they return home. The episode of "buying three nights" in order to recover a spouse is more commonly developed in tales about female heroines who search for their husbands (AT 425, 430, and 432; see chapter 5).

In Zelenin Perm' 20 the hero Ivan marries Elena, a priest's daughter. She scorns him on their wedding night and disappears. Ivan sets off to look for her. He comes to a Yaga Yagishna, who warns him he will lose his head. A second Yaga Yagishna tells him that Elena is with her nephew Khark Kharkovich Solon Solonych, and warns him against going: Only one empty fence post remains outside Khark's house, awaiting his head. Ivan goes there and is twice hidden by Khark's wife. Then, Ivan kidnaps a princess for Khark Kharkovich, who gives him a whip in return. Ivan beats his wife and she disappears again. The hero passes by the two Yaga Yagishnas and returns home, where he finds Elena.

In Potanin 1906 no. 15, the hero Prince Ivan sets out to find the maiden "Rúsa-Rusá, Black Braid, the sister of thirty brothers, granddaughter of forty grandmothers, daughter of three mothers" that his father sang about in a lullaby when Ivan was a child. He comes to three Baba Yaga sisters, each in a hut that turns on a chicken leg. The third Baba Yaga warns him that Rúsa-Rusá's palace is surrounded by an iron fence, that its stakes hold the heads of her unsuccessful suitors, and that one stake remains empty, but she also tells him that he can see Rúsa-Rusá if he goes to church. Three times the hero defeats Rúsa-Rusá's brothers, and then follows her to her palace, where her forty grandmothers attack him "like hornets." He seizes one grandmother by the legs and uses her as a weapon to swing at the others, a maneuver that recalls the folk epic (bylina) hero Il'ia Muromets and his combat with the Tatar army. When the three mothers bring him a chest, he opens it and finds Rúsa-Rusá. They marry and set out for his kingdom. While Ivan sleeps, the ogre Koshchei the Immortal kidnaps Rúsa-Rusá, and the tale continues with an episode of AT 302.

Baba Yaga is both donor and villain in Gorodtsov ii: 150–173. The tale begins with an episode of AT 301. The hero and his brother defeat Baba Yaga's army, and he decapitates her in her underground home (see chapter 5). He takes Baba Yaga's daughter Marfa Yaganichna to his brother, who marries her. He overhears Marfa speaking of the beauty Rusa Kosa ("light brown braid"), and sets out to find her. He comes to three Baba Yaga donors in huts on a chicken leg. They send him on toward the Distant Kingdom (*Dalekoe gosudarstvo*), where Rusa Kosa is about to marry Koshchel' the Immortal. A witch (*koldun'ia*), a friend of the three Baba Yaga sisters, brings the hero to Rusa Kosa. The tale continues with episodes of AT 302 and 516.

Baba Yaga helps the hero in two rather anomalous versions of SUS 401, The Enchanted Princess (AT 401, The Princess Transformed into a Deer). She directs the hero on his way to find a widow tsarevna (Nikiforov 1936 no. 4). The hero accomplishes tasks previously set by her deceased husband and marries her. They are separated, and after various adventures, the hero returns home with his wife.

Baba Yaga is instrumental in reuniting the hero with his wife in Afanas'ev 272. The hero comes to a castle where an enchanted bear is transformed into a beautiful princess. They marry, and the hero then wants to return home. On the way, he is deceived by evil spirits (*nechistye*) and put to sleep. His wife finds him, curses, and he is carried off by the wind. The hero wakes up in the middle of the sea and comes to an island where he tricks some devils out of a magic flying carpet, magic boots, and an invisibility cap (AT 518, Devils Fight Over Magic Objects). He flies on the carpet and comes to three Baba Yagas to find out where his wife is. The third Baba Yaga lives on the edge of the world and calls the winds together. Only the south wind knows where the princess is and takes the hero to her. Many suitors are seeking his wife's hand, but he arrives in time to recover her.

SUS 402 (AT 402, The Mouse [Cat, Frog, etc.] as Bride), is a very popular fairy tale in East Slavic tradition. This charming narrative is most often referred to in Russia as the tale of the Frog Princess or Frog Tsarevna (*Tsarevna Liagushka*) and is combined with AT 400.

The tsar or king instructs his sons to shoot arrows; they will find their brides wherever the arrows land. In Gorodtsov ii: 25–30, the sons throw magic sticks. The elder two sons marry daughters of the socially prominent, but the youngest shoots his arrow into a swamp, where it is caught by a frog. Everyone laughs at him, but at night the frog becomes a beautiful maiden. In Burtsev 1895: 265–286, Karnaukhova 65, and Kovalev 12 he marries not a frog but an old woman.

The tsar sets tasks for his three daughters-in-law: They must sew shirts, weave carpets or linen, and bake bread or pies in one night. The frog tsarevna outdoes her sisters-in-law, who send a servant girl to spy on her, but cannot imitate her success. Sometimes the frog calls forth supernatural help (Afanas'ev 269, 570, Gorodtsov ii: 25–30, Karnaukhova 65, Kovalev 12,

Rudchenko/Löwis of Menar 1921 no. 5). The tsar has a feast prepared. The frog tsarevna pours some of her wine in her sleeve, and some of her food in the other sleeve. When she dances, she swings her sleeves and creates lakes, a river, geese, swans, or a forest. Her sisters-in-law try to imitate her, but only spatter the guests, tsarina, and tsar.

The hero wants his wife to remain in the form of a beautiful maiden and burns the frog skin, or throws her ring into the sea (Karnaukhova 65). She disappears, sometimes reproaching the hero for not waiting until she could have remained with him in human form. In Rudchenko/Löwis of Menar 1921 no. 5, she turns into a cuckoo and flies away.

The hero goes to search for her. He comes to three Baba Yaga sisters, and the tale has a number of different concluding episodes. His wife comes to visit the first two, but the hero fails to seize her when she turns into a frog, toad, and snake. At the third Baba Yaga's hut, he manages to hold on to her. His wife turns into an arrow, the hero breaks the arrow in two, and she recovers her human form (Afanas'ev 570, Novikov 1971 no. 37). The hero fails to hold his wife in dragon form at the huts of the two Baba Yagas, but an old man feeds him and has him sleep for many months, and then the hero proceeds across the sea to the castle of an evil sorcerer whom he kills in combat. He releases the sorcerer's prisoners and finds his wife (Karnaukhova 65). Baba Yaga directs him to an island. Animals help him reach the island and a glass palace in the middle of a thick forest, where he finds his wife (Rudchenko/Löwis of Menar 1921 no. 5). The third Baba Yaga sister in Gorodtsov ii: 25–30 tells Prince Ivan to await twelve swans, who turn into maidens. He steals the clothes of his wife, and makes her promise to remain with him. She persuades him to return her clothes, and tells him to seek her at her father's house. She disappears, and the hero wonders whether she has lied to him. He returns to Baba Yaga, who reassures him, and tells him to go to his father-in-law. He finds his wife there, and they marry again. In Leonova 17, the hero comes to the hut on chicken legs and strikes Baba Yaga with a magic twig. She "turned into a woman" (*ona v zhenshchinu oborotilas*) and shows Ivan the way to find Elena. The tale ends with a very concentrated episode of retrieving Elena from Koshchei and killing a dragon. The tale-teller's (V. P. Monachkova, a seventy-five-year-old woman recorded in 1979) remark about Baba Yaga is very interesting; it implies that Baba Yaga is either not human, or not a woman.

Several versions continue with an episode of AT 302 (The Ogre's [Devil's] Heart in the Egg), or include motifs that recall this tale type. The Baba Yagas show the hero the way to the dragon, who holds his wife captive. The hero has his wife find out where the dragon's death egg is (Shastina 1971 no. 26). Baba Yaga tells the hero where Koshchei's death egg is. With animals' help he obtains the egg and breaks the needle inside it. Koshchei dies and the hero retrieves Vasilisa (Afanas'ev 269). The hero helps animals and giants, who accomplish tasks set by Koshchei, and an old man (Grandfather Kunai, the fiancé of the third Baba Yaga) tells him how to obtain a horse and retrieve his wife (Kovalev 12). Baba Yaga tells the hero the location of Koshchei's death egg, and animal helpers retrieve the egg for him. When he breaks open the egg, there is a needle inside. When he breaks the needle, Koshchei dies (Vedernikova and Samodelova 37). Baba Yaga tells the hero where to find an egg with a needle in it. He obtains the egg, breaks the needle, and his wife appears (Bakhtin and Shiriaeva 72). This last version very artfully combines the "death egg" motif of Koshchei, and the motif of the transformed wife.

Zelenin Perm' 28 differs significantly from all these versions. The hero Ipat wants to marry, crosses a swamp in a boat, and comes to the hut of Yaga Baba. She sends him on to her friend, who is even more frightening than she (the hero sees through the window that she is chewing on a live cat). Yaga Baba's friend takes Ipat to his frog bride. The frog gives him gifts for his family, and he returns home. Then they set off to fetch the bride, who appears as a beautiful maiden. The bride bakes pies by the following morning, but on the way to go visiting, the frog falls through a hole in the carriage and disappears. Zelenin attributes this unusual ending to the humorous tone of this narrator.

The added episodes in Karnaukhova 65 and the replacement of the frog by an old woman reflect the influence of the folk woodblock print (*lubok*) tradition. The first *lubok* version was Timofeev's, of 1787 (reprinted in Novikov 1971 as no. 37), which was reproduced throughout the nineteenth century and influenced the 1856 version of F. M. Isaev. Isaev changed the frog to an old woman, added episodes with an old man donor, crossing the sea, and arriving at the palace of a sorcerer Karachun, where the hero rescues his wife (Korepova 1987). Isaev's tale influenced an 1895 version by Ivan Ivin, under the pseudonym Kassirov (Korepova 1984: 7–10, 1999: 111–130). These literary renditions probably account for the version recorded by Karnaukhova. The version in Burtsev's collection is also taken from a *lubok*.

Propp sees in the Frog Tsarevna's dance a ritual dance of the totemistic era, and in the Tsarevna herself an early form of the folktale princess whom he traces in other tale types (1976: 200–201). Vladimir Anikin considers the contrast between external appearance and internal qualities an important theme of this tale. The hero is ashamed of his frog bride, even after she has shown herself more skilled than his sisters-in-law. He appreciates her only when she has revealed her human beauty, and then he rushes to burn her frog skin so that she will retain this form. The hero still values external beauty over internal qualities, and therefore the frog princess disappears. Certain additional episodes (the hero's combat with Koshchei, for example) are superfluous and represent a contamination of the original tale. The versions in which the frog calls on supernatural help to accomplish the tsar's tasks are also a deformation of the tale's true meaning, since the frog princess in these instances fails to show her own intrinsic qualities. The hero proves his love for his wife when he must hold on to her even as she turns into a frog, toad, and snake. The tale ends happily when outward circumstances (the princess's appearance in human form) reflect inner qualities. The tale causes the listener to ponder true human values. Baba Yaga's role in the tale is secondary: She is there only to show the hero how to free his wife from her enchantment (Anikin 1966).

Specific fantastic motifs are reflections of social customs of the past (the tale's preference for the third son, who in ancient times inherited nothing) and totemism (the hero's marriage to a frog). The tale hints at a relationship between Baba Yaga and the frog. Because she is now related to the hero, it is natural for Baba Yaga, a protector spirit, to help him (ibid., 37–38). The later folklore tradition has given these mythological conceptions a new meaning.

The poetics of folklore and the folktale genre in particular explain certain features of Baba Yaga and her behavior. Contrast is important in this tale (the status of the hero and his frog bride, her abilities, and the failure of her sisters-in-law), and the use of contrast as a device accounts for the change in Baba Yaga's tone toward the hero: first threatening, then benign. Contrast also is the reason for the extremes of beauty and ugliness, the latter embodied in Baba Yaga's enormous nose (ibid., 42–43).

For Evgenii Neelov, the Frog Tsarevna represents the beneficent aspect of the forces of nature, and their creative principle which is responsible for the beauty of the world. This meaning is implied in some versions where a tablecloth made by the Frog Tsarevna includes seas, forests, moon, stars, and ships, and where her loaf of bread is ornamented by cities. The meaning is stated clearly in her dance at the banquet, where she creates lakes and birds, and "before the eyes of the tsar's stunned guests, and the stunned listeners of the folktale, the world is created anew in the dance" (Neelov 1989: 46). The beauty of nature, symbolized by the Frog Tsarevna, can only be made manifest through human activity (represented by the hero's marriage to the frog), otherwise the destructive, death-dealing forces of nature will have the upper hand (represented by Koshchei, who in some versions is said to be responsible for Vasilisa's transformation into a frog). In the person of the hero, Neelov sees an evolution from a "common sense" view of the world (when he bemoans the fact that he must marry a frog) to one reflecting the fairy tale's values.

According to Dmitrii Zelenin, storytellers of Perm' and Viatka province tended to identify fantastic figures such as Baba Yaga and the Frog Tsarevna with the neighboring Finno-Ugric and other non-Slavic peoples, such as the Mari (Cheremis), Khant (Ostyak), and Mansi (Vogul). The tale of the frog princess might reflect actual intermarriage among the Russians and Mari (Zelenin 1914: xxiii, 533, 576). AT 402 is usually considered a male-centered tale, but in these East Slavic versions, the Frog Tsarevna becomes an active heroine when she accomplishes the difficult tasks assigned by her father-in-law, making this a tale with two protagonists.

Episodic, Humorous, and Anomalous Appearances

In SUS 552A, The Animal Brothers-in-Law (AT 552, The Girls Who Married Animals), the hero's sisters are taken away by animals. He wants to visit them and comes to the hut of Baba Yaga, who directs him onward (Novikov 1971 no. 24, Onchukov 167). The hero may acquire magic objects from three Baba Yaga sisters (Gurevich 32, Sorokovikov 5). Then, the tales proceed differently, but Baba Yaga does not appear again.

Sadovnikov 4 is a complex tale which combines several different tale types (including SUS 554, The Grateful Animals) and reflects the talent of the gifted narrator Abram Novopol'tsev. Yagaia Baba appears in one episode only, directing the hero onward in his search for Mar'ia-krasa.

Akimova 394 is a humorous tale (SUS 564, The Miraculous Gifts; AT 564, The Magic Providing Purse and "Out, Boy, out of the Sack!"). An old man is sent by his wife to get flour. The wind blows the flour away on the way home, and the man goes to complain to the wind. He comes to Baba-Yaga's hut. The wind is her son, and she has him give the man a bag with two magic servants. The servants feed the man and his wife, and she has him invite the landlord. The landlord takes the bag. The man goes to complain, again comes to Baba-Yaga, and this time the wind gives him a bag with two Cossacks who come out and beat him. At home the man has the Cossacks beat his wife. Then they invite the landlord again, and the Cossacks beat him until he gives back the first bag. The hero of this tale is something of a hen-pecked husband. His wife calls him a fool, and later he does not want to go complain to the landlord, but "the old woman forced" him. Although Baba-Yaga tells him what to do, just as his wife does, she helps him get even with his wife and the landlord.

Baba Yaga appears very briefly as an unusual donor in Matveeva and Leonova 22, a version of AT 560 (The Magic Ring). Betrayed by his wife, the hero has lost his magic ring and been returned to his former poverty. His cat and dog go and retrieve the ring, but drop it in the sea on the way home. They capture a sea devil, who then threatens all the water spirits and orders them to find the ring. Baba Yaga, in the form of a frog, has caught the ring and presents it to the devil, who returns it to the cat and dog.

Baba Yaga appears as a donor with many typical traditional features in a literary fairy tale from the 1786 collection *Dedushkiny progulki* (*Grandfather's Strolls*). In an episode influenced by oral versions of AT 302, the princess sends the hero to the realm of Koshchei the Immortal to obtain the self-playing gusli (psaltery). He comes to the hut of Yaga-baba, who gives him instructions (Korepova and Belikova 13).

Nikiforov 1936 no. 11 includes elements of different tale types, and is therefore difficult to classify. In one episode, a king from another realm demands that the hero obtain Koshchei and Solovei (Nightingale the Robber, more commonly a villain in the Russian folk epic). The hero comes to three Baba Yaga sisters who give him instructions.

Lutovinova provides a summary of an anomalous tale from the Kemerovo region. The firebird steals peas from a childless couple, and then rewards them with a daughter. In spite of a warning, they let their daughter out, and the firebird kidnaps her. Baba Yaga gives the father a ball that leads him to the firebird's realm. The firebird assigns him impossible tasks which a mouse helps him accomplish, and he flees with his daughter (Lutovinova Index p. 12 no. 6).

Baba Yaga appears as donor in one exceptional version of AT 451, The Raven Brothers (Kovalev 28), a tale found in western Europe, but infrequently recorded in Russia, Ukraine, or Belarus. Ivan Kovalev learned this tale during his captivity in Germany in World War I. A wicked stepmother turns her stepsons to swans, and drives away her stepdaughter. The heroine comes to the hut of Baba Yaga Bony Leg, who advises her how to find and then disenchant her brothers, by remaining silent for three years. During this time a tsarevich finds and marries her. She is accused of witchcraft and is about to be hanged when the three years elapse, her brothers return and are disenchanted, and the heroine can speak again. Of the few recorded Russian versions of this tale, some are clearly derived from the Grimm collection (Kovalev 1941: 333). This anomalous tale is also the only example in our survey of a tale type in which Baba Yaga acts purely as a donor in regard to a female heroine.

Baba Yaga's Specific Features as a Donor

Baba Yaga's interactions with the hero or heroine who arrives at her hut form a curious episode, but her behavior is not so surprising if we consider her overall ambiguity. The hero or heroine typically arrives at the hut on chicken legs after long travels, usually without being shown the way. Nikolai Novikov finds that about half the tales do not specify the hut's location. Otherwise, the hut is often in the forest, in a forest clearing, near a forest, in the taiga

(Krasnozhenova 19), or in a marsh (Novikov 1974: 136–137). Most often, the hut stands on chicken legs (*na kur'ikh nozhkakh*), but it may stand on one chicken leg (*na kur'ei nozhke*), on a rooster's shin (*na petush'ei goliashke*) on roosters' heads (*na petush'ikh golovkakh*), on a ram's horns (*na baran'ikh rozhkakh*), on a dog's shin (*na sobach'ei goleshke*), on chicken's "paws" (*na kur'inykh lapkakh*), or on spindle heels (*na veretennykh piatkakh*). In Gromov 3, the hero comes to a hut without windows or doors (*khatka stoit, bez okon, bez dverei*). This description of the hut is not common, but recalls the hut in Aleksandr Pushkin's opening to "Ruslan and Liudmila." One wonders if this narrator was influenced by Pushkin's poem.[2]

Often the hut turns around on its unusual base and the protagonist must pronounce a formulaic phrase to make the hut stop. The hero or heroine usually knows exactly what to say, without being told or prompted. This formulaic phrase varies, but generally the hut is first addressed directly (as if to get its attention), and told to stand or turn with its back to the forest, its front facing the speaker: *Izbushka, izbushka! Stan' (Obratis', Vstan') k lesu zadom, ko mne peredom* (Khudiakov 39, Afanas'ev 102, 172, 224, 235, 310, Zelenin Viatka 118, Zelenin Perm' 67). Sometimes the visitor states that he or she intends to spend only one night, or to eat bread and salt. In some tales the hut is told to stand the "old way," or the "old way, the way mother put you": *Stan' po staromu, kak mat' postavila* (Afanas'ev 204, Zelenin Perm' 1, 20, 28, Krasnozhenova 19). It is not clear from the context who the mother in question is, whether the speaker's mother, or the "mother" of the hut, Baba Yaga.

When the visitor enters the hut, Baba Yaga is usually at home. Less frequently Baba Yaga arrives a moment later (Zelenin Perm' 1). She either sits or lies sprawled out inside the hut. Her head lies in one corner, her feet in another (Khudiakov 101). At this point storytellers often mention grotesque features of Baba Yaga's body. Some of the grotesqueness comes from the fact that the body parts are mentioned separately and seem far apart from each other (in different parts of the hut), implying that Baba Yaga is either enormous or terribly misshapen. She has a bony leg (*kostianaia noga*), her large nose is stuck (literally has grown) into the ceiling (*nos v potolok ros*), she steams her feet in *kvas* (a fermented rye or barley beverage) and her nose hangs on a hook (Tumilevich 21), she has a clay face and stops up the oven with her breasts (Karnaukhova 14), her breasts hang over a rod, and she rakes the coals with her nose and sweeps the oven with her tongue (Razumova and Sen'kina 1974 no. 69). The features in the last-mentioned tale even cause the narrator to remark: "Ugh,

---

[2] In any case, this attribute or phrase might ultimately derive from folklore. Russian riddles metaphorically describe certain fruits (the watermelon and the apple) as "without windows, without doors" (*bez okoshek, bez dverei*); see Sadovnikov 1959: 110, nos. 835, 844.

how frightening" (*Oi, kakaia strashnaia*). The mention of her buttocks and vagina (Onchukov 8) has already been noted.

Baba Yaga immediately notices the guest's presence and traditionally first makes a remark about his or her Russian smell, also set in traditional formulaic phrases: "Fu, fu! It smells of the Russian scent" (*Fu, fu, russkim dukhom pakhnet*). Baba Yaga often adds that the Russian scent has never been heard of or seen in those parts (*slykhom ne slykhat', vidom ne vidat'*).[3] Novikov finds that this first part of the phrase ("it smells of the Russian scent") is the most stable, while the second part may vary widely (the scent has been neither heard of nor seen, has come to the courtyard of its own will, rolls into her mouth). Some versions speak of the Russian bone (*russkaia kost'*), and only a few versions combine the Russian scent and bone (Smirnov 279, Sokolov 139, Novikov 1974: 140). These formulaic phrases about the Russian scent are frequent in Russian tales, but rarely appear in Ukrainian or Belorussian tales. After this first response to the protagonist's arrival, Baba Yaga states directly that she will eat the visitor, or somehow implies that she intends to eat her guest. When reproached, she backs down immediately and complies with requests for food and lodging:

> In the middle of that valley he saw a hut on chicken legs turning around by itself; he rode up to this hut and said: "Hut, hut, stand with your back to the forest, facing me." After these words the hut stopped, and Prince Ivan got off his horse and tied it up, and entered that hut and saw Baba Yaga sitting in it, asking him in an angry voice: "Until now the Russian scent has been neither heard of nor seen, and now the Russian scent appears to the eyes. Have you come of your own will or not?" Prince Ivan answered that he came twice as much of his own will as not. Then he told her where he was going. (Literary fairy tale from the 1787 collection *Russkie skazki* [*Russian Fairy Tales*] of Petr Timofeev. Novikov 1971 no. 29)

> She walked, walked, and walked, wore out her boots, broke her twig, and swallowed the bread. She walked up to a hut, and the hut stood on chicken legs and turned around. "Hut, hut! Stand with your back to the forest, facing me." The hut turned. So she went into the hut, and there Baba-Yaga was turning around from one corner to the other: she was wiping the floor with one lip, and closing up the chimney with her nose (she had a nose as big as the Perevitskii bridge!). "Fu, fu, fu," she said, "it used to be that the Russian scent was neither heard of nor seen, and now the Russian scent sits down in a spoon and rolls into my mouth. Fair maiden, are you attempting a deed or flying from a deed?" (Zholchino village, Ryazan' province. Probably recorded in the late 1850s. Khudiakov 39)

---

[3] A certain ambiguity arises in this traditional phrase because of the secondary meanings of some terms. *Slykh* can refer to the sense of smell as well as hearing, thus, *slykhom ne slykhat'* might mean "not smelled with the scent" as well as "not heard with the hearing." Given Baba Yaga's frequent statement about smelling the Russian scent (*russkii dukh*), this might be a valid understanding of this phrase in some contexts. Besides the meaning of "scent" or "smell," the noun *dukh* can also mean "spirit" or "breath."

He came to a hut. The hut stood, turning on a chicken shin. He said, "Hut, hut! Stand with your front facing me, and your back to the forest!" The hut stood still. He went in—Yagaia Baba was lying there, her legs stretched from corner to corner, her iron nose was sticking into the ceiling, her breasts were hanging over rods, and her little children were suckling. He went in and prayed to God, and bowed to Yagaia Baba. Yagaia Baba said to him, "What is this here? Formerly the Russian scent was neither heard of nor seen, and now the Russian scent appears to my mouth and comes right at my eyes! Ba! ba! ba! Prince Ivan! Are you flying from a deed, or are you attempting a deed?" "Ekh, grandmother, I'm not flying from a deed, but rather attempting one." "Where are you going?" "I'm looking for Mar'ia Erid'evna." (Abram Novopol'tsev, 1820–1885. Samara region. Published 1884. Sadovnikov 61)

He rode, rode, and rode for a day or two and rode to where a hut stood on chicken legs, with one window, on fresh manure, and turned around. Prince Ivan said: "Hut, stand with your eyes to the forest and your gate toward me." The hut stopped. Out of the hut jumped Baba-Yaga bony leg, wiry buttocks, soaped vagina. "Oh greetings, Prince Ivan," she said, "the raven never brought the Russian bone our way, to our place, but Prince Ivan has arrived." She took Prince Ivan's horse, put it where there were oats and hay, so it could eat either one, and led him into the hut. Then she farted, shook the table, farted, poured out cabbage soup, shook her buttocks and brought pancakes, fed him, gave him something to drink and put him to bed, and asked him for his news. "Prince Ivan, where have you set out to go, of your own will or against it?" (Anisim Fedorovich Vokuev, blind, age seventy. Ueg village, near Ust'tsyl'ma, Arkhangel'sk province. Recorded 1900–1908. Onchukov 8)

He came to the sea, and a hut on a chicken leg stood by the sea, and didn't turn around. "Hut, hut, stand the old way, the way mother put you: your back to the forest, your front toward me!" The hut stood the old way, the way mother put it: its back to the forest, its front toward him. He opened the door, went into the hut, and there stood Yagishna. "Fu, fu, the Russian bone has been neither heard of nor seen, and now it has come into the courtyard. I'll gobble and eat it up!" "Quiet, you old whore, eat yourself!" "Where are you going, where are you wandering?" "First give me something to drink, and feed me, and then ask for my news." The old woman set the table and fed the fine young fellow. She put his head on her knees and picked lice from his hair, and asked his news. "Grandmother, I've been given to One-Eyed Erakhta, and I don't know where he lives and how to get there." "Keep going, by this same sea there stands a hut where my second sister lives." (A forty-five-year-old man. Barnaul district, Tomsk province. Recorded in 1905. Potanin 1906 no. 38)

The tale is told quickly, but much time goes by, and Ivan rode through thick forests and hadn't seen a living soul in many days when he finally came to a forest clearing and there saw a hut standing on a chicken leg, on a dog's paw, facing the forest, with its back to him.

"Hut, stand the old way, hut, stand the way you used to, with your back to the forest, your front to me."

The hut turned around and Prince Ivan went in. Prince Ivan went in and saw old Baba Yaga lying on a bench, her head sticking in one corner, her feet in another. Baba Yaga caught sight of Prince Ivan and bellowed in an angry voice,

"Fu-fu-fu! It smells of the Russian scent! Russian scent, Russian bone, no one called it, no one invited it. It came to the house on its own, it called on its own. Why have you come here, why have you called?"
Prince Ivan answered her, "Don't roar, old witch! First give me something to drink and eat, put me to bed, and then ask for my news."
The old woman jumped to her feet, sat Prince Ivan down at the table, brought pies and different drinks. She gave Prince Ivan things to drink and eat and put him to bed. Prince Ivan slept well after his travels, and when he woke up, he told the old woman, "Listen, grandmother! I am Prince Ivan, I'm going to the Distant Kingdom to obtain Rusa Kosa. I want to marry her." (Luka Leont'evich Zaiakin. Artamonova village, Tyumen' region, Siberia. Recorded on 15 December 1906. Gorodtsov ii: 150–173)

He came and there stood a hut turning on a chicken's shin. "Well, hut, stand the old way, the way mother put you! With your back to the forest, your front toward me!" He went into this hut, took off his shoes and clothes, lay down on the oven and lay there the way he would at home. From nowhere came Yaga Yagishna: she ran, and the forest rattled. She came into the hut and opened her mouth wide—she wanted to eat Vania, that Yaga Yagishna. Vaniushka said: "What are you doing, you old bitch? Do old women in other villages do this? You should heat the bath, give me a steam bath and a bath and ask: where have you been living?" The old woman came to her senses: she heated the bath, gave him a steam bath and fed him. "Where have you been living?" (Antip Dem'ianovich Lomtev, age sixty-five, illiterate. Ekaterinburg region, Perm' province. Recorded in 1908. Zelenin Perm' 1)

So he rode up to the tower, the tower stood there, a hut on a chicken leg, on a dog's shin. "This hut—[turn your] back to the forest, front to me!" This hut turned its back to the forest, its front toward him. He went into that little house and there sat the old woman Baba-Yaga, many years old. She was tossing a silk tow, and throwing the threads over a beam. "Ah," she said, "I haven't seen the Russian scent, and the Russian bone has come to me by itself. And I will roast this man, I won't let him out into the wide world again." "Oh you grandmother Yaga, you One Leg, without having caught a bird you're plucking at it; and without having recognized a fine young fellow you're abusing him. You should jump up now, fart, pull out the post[4] and shake the sieve and bring meat pies, give me something to drink, give the fine young fellow, the traveller, something to eat, and prepare a bed for the night; I would lie down to rest, and you would sit at the head of the bed, you would ask and I would answer: whose son are you and from where do you come, dear man? What is your name?" Then the old woman took care of everything, fed him as she should and sat down at the head of the bed and asked questions, and he answered. "Whose son are you, dear man, and from where, and what is your name. From what land, from what horde do you come, the son of which father and which mother?" "Well grandmother, I am from such-and-such a kingdom, from a distant realm, I am the tsar's

---

[4] This phrase (*stolp otdernula*) might be a "mistake" or "distortion" of "pull out the table" (*stol otdernula*). Cf. Gorodtsov ii: 355–384, a version of AT 300A, where the hero comes to the underground realm and is given food and drink by the daughter of the old man villain. At first he reproaches her for asking questions, and then "the girl pulled out the table" (*devushka otdernula stol*, ibid., 363).

son Prince Ivan. I rode beyond thrice-nine lands and thrice-nine lakes, to a distant realm to the maiden Sineglazka [Blue-Eye] for the living water, the water of youth, I am an ambassador of my father." "Well, my dear child! She is a strong warrior, she is my niece, my brother's daughter; you can't be sure you'll get what you are after, dear." So in the morning he got up very early, and washed himself clean. He bowed in all four directions and thanked her for the night's lodging. "You don't have to thank me, Prince Ivan! Everyone is entitled to a night's lodging, whether on foot, on a horse, naked or wealthy. All people." (Il'ia Semenov, age fifty-nine, a talented narrator who also knew songs and incantations. Konechnaia village, Kirillovsk district. Recorded in 1909. Sokolov 139)

He saw a hut standing on chicken legs, on a rooster's head. And he said, "Hut, stand still, my dove, stand still! With your eyes to the forest, your gate to me, so I can go in and out."
He went into the hut and saw Baba Yaga sitting there.
"Fu, fu! It smells of the Russian scent. Are you travelling far, well-wisher?"
"Grandmother," he said, "why are you asking when you haven't given me anything to drink or eat. If you gave me something to drink and eat and put me to bed, then I would tell you." The old woman fed him and asked again. (Fedor Vasil'evich Ogarkov, age eighty-four. Onega district, Arkhangel'sk province. Recorded in the summer of 1912. Smirnov 1)

The prince threw the ball—the ball rolled—the thread stretched out, the ball went on, the thread grew longer, the prince followed the ball; for a long time he went through the thick taiga, ahead he could see a meadow; he came to the meadow, and there stood a hut on chicken legs. The prince said, "Hut, hut, turn your back to the taiga, your front toward me, stand the old way, the way mother put you."
The hut turned, the prince went in, and there Baba-Yaga lay from one corner to the other.
"Fu-fu, the Russian scent itself has come to the courtyard, like a ram onto the table. Where are you going, Prince?"
"And you, first give me something to drink, to eat, put me to bed, and then ask."
So she gave him something to drink, to eat, and put him to bed. In the morning he got up, and she asked him—where was he going, and why? (G. D. Kuznetsov, age forty-one. Krasnoyarsk, Siberia. Recorded in 1927. Krasnozhenova 19)

He went through the thick forest and finally came to an open clearing. A hut on chicken legs was standing there, turning around, and Prince Ivan said,
"Hut, turn your back to the forest, and your front toward me."
The hut turned and he went in. When Prince Ivan went into the hut, he saw Baba-Yaga Bony Leg with a tin eye, she was riding around in a mortar, urging it on with a pestle and sweeping her tracks away with a broom. The old woman began to grumble and snort,
"Fu, fu, fu! Such a bone has not been seen or heard of here, and now this bone has come into the courtyard itself."
Prince Ivan started to prevail upon the old woman. "Don't be angry with me, grandmother, the gray wolf sent me to you."
"Yes, I know the gray wolf," the old woman said, "he is my *kum*."[5]

The wolf is the godfather of her child, or she is the godmother of his child, or they are both ⎯odparents of the same child.

The old woman farted, pulled up the table, squatted down, got some bread from under the table and sat Prince Ivan down to drink tea. (Egor Ivanovich Sorokovikov, hunter, age seventy. Malyi Khobok village, Tunka aimak, Irkut river valley, Buryat Autonomous S. S. R., Siberia. Recorded in 1938. Sorokovikov 8)

She reached the forest and saw a hut standing on chicken legs with its back to the forest, its front facing her. She swung the door of the hut open and saw Baba-Yaga sitting there, steaming her feet in kvas, and her nose was hanging on a hook. And Baba-Yaga asked, "What are you doing, girl, flying from a deed or attempting a deed?"

"No, grandmother, first feed me, give me something to drink, and then ask about all my grief." (Tat'iana Ivanovna Kapustina, born 1849. Don Cossack community in Georgia and Krasnodar region. Recorded in the 1930s or 1940s. Tumilevich 21)

She walked through open fields, thick forests, and meadows soft as velvet. She saw a hut on chicken heels, on dog paws, turning around. She said, "Hut, hut, stand with your back to the forest, your front facing me. Let me go inside you and eat bread and salt."

The hut turned. Mar'iushka went in. There was Baba-Yaga. Her feet were on the threshold, her lips on the roof-pillar, her arms stretched from corner to corner, her nose in the ceiling.

"T'fu, t'fu, it smells of the Russian scent."

She saw her.

"Why did you come here, beautiful girl, are you attempting a deed or flying from a deed?"

"Grandmother, I'm looking for Fenist the Bright Falcon." (Anna Nikolaevna Korol'kova, born 1892. Voronezh. Recorded 1955–1957. Korol'kova 1969: 155–156)

And suddenly he saw—there stood a hut on a chicken's leg, on a rooster's head.

"Hut, hut, turn your eyes to the forest, your gate to me!"

The hut turned its eyes to the forest, and its gate to him. He went into the hut, and there sat an old woman: her nose was on the oven, her eyes on a shelf above it, she was dragging pots around with her lips, and raking the oven with her tongue:

"Fu, fu," she said, "the Russian scent, it smells of the Russian scent, I haven't smelled it for a long time. A good piece of meat has come to me," she said.

"No," he said, "grandmother, don't enjoy your piece [of meat]. First give a tired traveller something to drink and eat, bathe him, and then treat yourself."

The grandmother started to bustle about, heated the bath and cooked a meal. He bathed and steamed himself, ate his fill and fell into bed. When he woke up, she started asking him and inquiring:

"Whose son are you, and where do you come from?" (Avdot'ia Anisimovna Moshnikova, age sixty-eight, who reputedly could tell tales for three days in succession without repeating herself. Lesnoi village, Kola peninsula. Recorded in January 1963. Balashov 7)

Suddenly he got there, in the open field stood a hut on chicken legs, on a spindle's heels, it stood and turned around. He said, "Hut, hut, stand in place, let me, a fine young fellow, go in and out."

Well, that hut stood in place, he went into the hut, in the hut sat Baba-Yaga, Bony Leg, she was heating the oven, sewing a silk carpet with her hands, stirring up coals in the oven with her nose, and sweeping the floor with her tongue. And she said to herself, "Fu, fu, fu, I haven't been to Russia, I didn't take in the Russian scent, and now the Russian scent has come into my hut"—she slapped herself on one cheek and straightened out the other one. "Oh what a fool I am," she said, "I ask a hungry guest for news, I have to give him something to eat, to drink, and put him to bed, and then ask for news."

So she fed him, gave him something to drink and put him to bed and sat at his head, and then started to ask, "Where are you going, fine young fellow," she said, "where are you headed?" (Petr Iakovlevich Nikonov, age fifty-one. Sukhoi Navolok village, Belomorsk district, Karelian coastal region. Recorded in 1968. Razumova and Sen'kina 1974 no. 35)

She came to the forest and saw a hut standing on a chicken leg. She said, "Hut, hut, turn your back to the forest, your front to me." The hut turned around and the girl went in and saw Baba Yaga Bony Leg lying on the oven, on the ninth brick, with her nose in the ceiling. The girl bowed. Baba Yaga fed her, gave her something to drink, and gave her a golden apple and a silver dish. (Tat'iana Afanas'evna Groshikova, born 1925. Moshok village, Sudogda district, Vladimir region. Recorded in 1996. Kargin 21)

This episode is found in many tales where the donor is *not* Baba Yaga, but a grandmother (*babushka*) or old woman (*starushka*) with some of the same attributes: the hut on chicken legs, the visitor's request to the hut and its owner, or the remark about the Russian scent.[6] The donor may be an old mother (*stara mat' rozhena*, Azadovskii 1947 no. 6), a large old woman (*stara-matera zhenshchina*, ibid., 7), a terrible, frightening woman (*uzhasnaia, strashnaia baba*, Aslamov 9), an old frightening woman (*staraia strashnaia baba*, Zelenin Viatka 117), simply a woman (*baba*, Chubinskii 1878 no. 68, who lives in a hut on a chicken and a goose foot), or a large old person (*star-mater chelovek*, Onchukov 3). In a Belorussian version of AT 480, the hostile tester of the kind and unkind girls is a witch (*vedz'ma*) who lives in a hut on a chicken's foot (Bandarchyk 1978 no. 53). An old woman (*staraia babka*) in a hut on a chicken leg is also found in a Belorussian charm to stop bleeding (Eleonskaia 1994: 77).

In other tales, a hut on chicken legs may stand alone (Chernyshev 44, Khudiakov 1964: 277), or its inhabitants may be an old man (*ded*, in Parilov 6, 7, Zelenin Viatka 22, Chubinskii 1878 no. 126; *starichok*, in Vasilenok 1958: 51–53 where he is an ambiguous donor; *staryi starik*, in Khudiakov 1), a bear (Chernyshev 26, Kitainik 9, Simina 17), a maiden or maidens (Azadovskii 1947 no. 9, Karnaukhova 124, Chubinskii 1878 nos. 5, 53, Petnikov 1966: 198–206), a maiden and a dragon (Chubinskii 1878 no. 74), twelve robbers (Zelenin

---

[6] Cf. Afanas'ev 175, 176, Aslamov 2, Azbelev 52, 66, Bakhtin and Shiriaeva 8, Balashov 1, 27, 131, Chernyshev 35, Karnaukhova 46, Khudiakov 46, 49, 95, Korguev 1938: 59–84, 135–166, Matveeva 1981 nos. 15, 21, 36, 37, Matveeva and Leonova 5, 12, Novikov 1961 nos. 20, 83, 85, Onchukov 2000 Tavda 30, Onegina 48, 76, Razumova and Sen'kina 1974 no. 12, Razumova and Sen'kina 1982 nos. 2, 10, 21, Shastina 1971 no. 22, Shastina 1985 nos. 1, 16, Sidel'nikov 5, and Zelenin Viatka 74, 117.

Viatka 34), the heroine's wolf brothers (Bandarchyk 1978 no. 22), or simply the owners (*khoziaeva*, in Razumova and Sen'kina 1982 no. 37). Beautiful maidens live in stone houses that the hero causes to turn with a formulaic phrase (Dobrovol'skii 17, 1891: 503–504). The kind and unkind girls in another Belorussian version of AT 480 are left in a hut standing on a chicken's leg; the testing figure, a bear, asks them to prepare him a bed with an iron mortar for a pillow (Bandarchyk 1978, no. 46). In a tale from the Smolensk region, a hostile old man lives cramped inside a hut on chicken legs, in a grotesque position, like Baba Yaga: He sits on a partition, his nose is on a hook, and his legs are on beams (Dobrovol'skii 11, 1891: 467).

Meletinskii and his colleagues feel that Baba Yaga became associated with a forest hut later than figures such as the forest spirit (*leshii*) or the bear (1971: 76). Presumably Baba Yaga is a later kind of "forest demon" because of her anthropomorphic and therefore less archaic form. Whether or not she is the original owner, Baba Yaga is probably the most frequent and popular inhabitant of the forest hut in East Slavic fairy tales.

Baba Yaga is not the only character in this folktale tradition who notices the hero(ine)'s Russian scent. The dragon and hero's animal or supernatural brothers-in-law also pronounce this formulaic phrase. Still, speaking of traditional formulaic phrases, Irina Razumova feels that "cases when a formula marks two different situations are rare and apparently are a later transfer of the formula from one situation to another. On the whole the formula is a signifier of definite folktale situations, and traditionally a presence of more than one meaning is not characteristic of it" (Razumova 1991: 80–81). In particular, Razumova has in mind the fact that this formula is used by both the donor Baba Yaga and by the villain dragon. But given Baba Yaga's ambiguous nature, it is not surprising to find that the formulaic phrases or motifs associated with her might also exhibit a certain elasticity and be applied to villains as well as donors.

Razumova finds that this episode is one of the most purely formulaic episodes in the Russian fairy tale, consisting of almost nothing but traditional formulaic phrases (Razumova 1991: 81–82). She explains the relatively great number of formulas associated with Baba Yaga and with the magic horse Sivko-Burko by the fact that they are derived from archaic conceptions and belong to the "other world" of the folktale. Novikov finds the visitor's response to Baba Yaga's threat to be a note of realism, since it reflects how a weary traveler might feel.

Many scholars have interpreted the hut on chicken legs as a survival of archaic or ancient customs. Elena Eleonskaia believes that its unusual mobility is a vague echo of the nomadic life of past ages. The chicken legs and spindle heels that the hut rests on reflect the light construction of nomad dwellings (Eleonskaia 1994: 58). Boris Rybakov believes that the hut derives from an ancient Slavic burial practice of placing the ashes of the dead in small hut-shaped structures which sometimes stood on short poles (1987: 89–92). Between the sixth and thirteenth centuries this practice gave way to interment in a burial mound (*kurgan*), while the hut (*domovina*) lived on as Baba Yaga's hut on chicken legs (ibid., 110). Valerii Sanarov suggests that this folktale hut on chicken legs might inspire some modern narratives about UFOs: "the flying saucer often revolves about its axis and has three-legged landing gear (i.e., a three-clawed hen's foot)" (1981: 165).

Vladimir Propp interprets Baba Yaga's hut as the border post separating the land of the living and the dead. The protagonist cannot simply enter the hut from the other side, but must use the appropriate magic formula to make the hut turn around. In ancient Scandinavia, doors were never built on the north side of houses, considered the unlucky side, and the dwelling of death in the Edda has a door on the north side. The peculiar attributes of Baba Yaga's hut are explained as remnants of the initiation hut, which among some peoples has the form of an animal. In the later folktale, the animal form has been retained only in the hut's legs (Propp 1946: 46–51).

Razumova agrees with Propp, but points out that the image of the hut on chicken legs, as a product of creative fantasy, cannot be explained by reference to archeological data alone (1991: 66). Richarda Becker finds the hut's former association with the mother goddess in the hero or heroine's occasional command to the hut to stand "the way mother placed you." The chicken legs derive from a fertility cult and Becker presents examples of chicken sacrifice in East Slavic custom (1990: 72–75, 121–122).

According to Nicolae Roșianu, Propp's interpretation is supported by the existence of a similar "hut on rooster claws," home of the Forest Mother, a donor in Romanian folktales (1974: 119–121). Dwellings that rotate on animals' feet are also found in Hungarian folktales, where dragons live in a copper castle that turns on webbed feet (Illyés 1970: 26), a copper castle turning on a magpie's leg, a silver castle turning on a silver crow's leg, and a golden castle spinning around on a golden duck's leg (ibid., 144–172). In Ukrainian-language tales from eastern Slovakia, the hero finds kidnapped princesses in castles that turn on goose, duck, and chicken feet (Hyriak vi no. 31), the ogre Loktyboroda lives in a hut on a duck's foot (ibid., i: 46–65), and the hero and his bride come to a foreign kingdom and find a house turning on an egg (ibid., iii no. 36). The Slovak ogre Iron Monk lives in a palace that shakes on a chicken foot, as the magic horse points out to the hero (*Vidíš, ako trasie sa tam na kuracej nohe; to je Železného Mníchov zámok!*, Dobšinský iii: 305).

Sándor Solymossy finds that the motif of the turning castle or dwelling on an animal foot, and most often on a goose or duck foot, is typical for all of Hungary. The motif is most commonly found in AT 301 (The Three Stolen Princesses) as the underground dwelling of dragons. Solymossy feels that this form of the motif is the original one, from which it spread to other tale types. There are a few intriguing motifs in western European medieval literature that resemble this folktale dwelling: Turning castles appear in a twelfth-century French epic poem ("La demoiselle à la mule," or "La mule sans frein" of Paien de Maisière), in a prose romance of the same period ("Perceval le Gallois"), and in a thirteenth-century German epic, "Diu Crône" of Heinrích von dem Türlin. A turning castle also figures in some Grail romances (Rhys 1966: 116, 300–303, 325; MacCulloch 1911: 368). These appear to be isolated instances which have left no trace in the folklore of western Europe, and the distribution of this motif in folklore is limited to eastern Europe and western Asia. A Vogul (Mansi) folktale features monstrous supernatural beings who live beyond this world, in a revolving dwelling. Solymossy concludes that the motif of the revolving dwelling derives from ancient Ural-Altaic religion, from shamanistic conceptions of a cosmic tree that connects heaven, earth, and the underworld, and serves as an axis around which the heavens revolve. The Hungarian form of the dragon's castle is closer to the older, mythological conception than Baba Yaga's hut on chicken legs, whereas the East Slavic motif is "paler," probably due to the influence of Christianity (Solymossy 1984).

In his analysis of eastern European versions of AT 300A, Géza Róheim compares Baba Yaga's hut to its Hungarian analogues and finds that "the connection between the revolving castle and a female being of the Baba Yaga type should be regarded as one of the fundamental elements of the whole complex" and that "this female being has something peculiar about her nose, teeth or foot and is closely connected with anxiety and the fear of annihilation" (1947: 58–59). The revolving castle motif as found in various tales represents the primal scene, where "the parents as persons are absent, [and] we have part objects (leg and castle) and the representation of coitus as lasting for an eternity" (ibid., 66).

Róheim interprets the revolving castle in the context of a tale (AT 300A) in which Baba Yaga appears most often as a villain; in fact, the revolving hut on chicken legs appears in only a few Russian versions of this tale. Nevertheless, Baba Yaga is so firmly associated with this hut in the folk tradition that any mention of her (even in a tale where the hut does not appear) is likely to bring this dwelling to mind. Róheim's interpretation of Baba Yaga as a phallic mother has a bearing on her role as antagonist and can explain her popular attributes (the bony leg, pestle, broom, large nose) and the attributes of analogous figures from other traditions (iron nose, iron teeth, bird's foot). Although Koshchei and Baba Yaga can be considered father and mother figures, they rarely if ever meet;[7] instead, their meeting is symbolized by the perpetually turning hut on chicken legs. Róheim discusses the hut as a source of anxiety, but anxiety might flow more from Baba Yaga's own hostile words and stance than from the hut itself.

Olga Periañez-Chaverneff explains Baba Yaga's cramped position inside the hut as another reflection of infantile experience. The child who was swaddled and constrained and who has now become a young adult, free to move about, puts Baba Yaga in her place, keeping her immobile in her hut (Periañez-Chaverneff 1983: 190–192). Of course, this image also suggests the child in the womb, and an interpretation of Baba Yaga's hut as a mobile womb with legs.

The uncanny, weird, and frightening nature of the hut must derive to some extent from its combination of opposing elements—a house, a solid creation of human material culture which is meant to be stable, has a will of its own and moves around on chicken legs. It combines stability and instability, animate and inanimate, nature and culture. The occasional mention of the hut's eyes by the protagonist ("turn your eyes to the forest"), while it can be understood as a metaphor for windows, also suggests animacy (human or animal) and that the hut is watching him or her. If we accept the possibility of latent sexual or gender symbolism, it combines male and female symbols. In this it may be an extension of Baba Yaga herself, who combines explicit female features with implicit male ones (see the conclusion). Demonic beings with bird or animal feet are very widespread (cf. the western European Perchta and Tante Arie), and the Carpatho-Ukrainian witch of folk belief (*bosorka* or *bosorkania*) sometimes appears with chicken feet (Vinogradova 1992: 65), as does the Romanian Mother Friday (Mesnil and Popova 1993: 755). Thus, it is not at all surprising that the dwelling of a demonic or supernatural being might acquire this characteristic. It is possible that these unique dwellings on birds' feet in eastern European folklore are entirely the product of creative fantasy or imagination (as Petr Bogatyrev suggests for folktale characters), rather than a reflection of some historical reality.

The chicken feet of Baba Yaga's hut call to mind the role of hens and chickens in some East Slavic healing rituals. According to Russian folk beliefs, a pregnant woman was supposed to avoid going to the chicken coop, or wherever the hens and chickens slept. If she went there, her child might have the "chicken" or "hen illness" (*kurinaia bolezn'*, *krik*, *kurinaia slepota*, *kurinyi kriak*, Trushkina 1998: 121). The illness was manifested when a child constantly

---

[7] This does happen in Serzhputovskii 1911, no. 72, where Baba Yaga and Koshchei are portrayed as a couple (see chapter 6).

cried. One way of healing it was to take the child to the chicken coop in the evening or early morning, and to ask the chicken coop to return sleep to the child, or to give the child a "human life" instead of a "chicken life" (*Ty kurinyi boleznia, ty rebenku daesh' kurinyi zhizn', i dai emu ne kurinyi zhizn', a chelovecheskoi*, ibid., 122). Other means of healing the "hen illness" were to wash the child with holy water, to pull the child through a cleft made in a tree (which suggests symbolic rebirth), or to have the hens or chickens peck up grains of wheat from on top of the sleeping child (ibid., 122–125). There may be no direct relationship between these magic practices and the chicken legs of Baba Yaga's hut, but the chicken's associations (positive or negative) with pregnancy and small children suggest that Baba Yaga also bears a relationship to this domain. Dmitrii Zelenin describes a ritual performed in Viatka province in cases of difficult childbirth, illness, or other misfortune. This was a ritual meal in which only women were allowed to take part. The main dish was a chicken, a hen which had already hatched three broods of chicks, which accounted for one of the common names for the ritual, *troetsypliatnitsa* (*troe tsypliat*, "three chicks"). Zelenin concludes that the hen has an ambiguous status in Russian folklore, linked to evil spirits, but also representing fertility (1994: 105–150).

The grotesque features of Baba Yaga, and especially the mention of her genitals and buttocks by some male tale-tellers, recalls Kligman's and Jones's view that the image of an ugly witch presents a sexually nonthreatening female. Perianez-Chaverneff interprets the physical description of Baba Yaga as a realistic reflection of peasant life. Peasant women were worn out with work and childbearing and became elderly by age forty. The practice of swaddling accounts for the isolated mention of parts of Baba Yaga's body. Russian peasant children, rendered immobile, were late to realize the body as an entire entity (Perianez-Chaverneff 1983: 193). The mention of grotesque bodily features might also serve as an outlet for aggression, and when performed by male tale-tellers, it might express a certain degree of misogyny, and fear as well as fascination in regard to the female body. Like the refusal to be eaten and the demand for hospitality, the denigration of Baba Yaga's body by male tellers and listeners might also emphasize their separation from the mother.

An interesting problem concerns the different distribution of the donor sequence (with its description of Baba Yaga's body) in male and female tales. For the male, the female body as an Other becomes especially significant with the development of genital sexuality; for the female child, the mother's body, and the female body in general, is not as alien. Perhaps for this reason Baba Yaga's hut and the mention of her grotesque features are absent from most tales with a boy protagonist, while they are present in tales with a girl heroine, and present in tales with adult heroes and heroines. This different distribution certainly suggests that the hut on chicken legs has a different meaning for male and female protagonists.

Periañez-Chaverneff has suggested that Baba Yaga as a donor represents a mother representation from a later stage of development than the cannibal ogress. She discusses two aspects of Baba Yaga the donor, a "versatile" Baba Yaga and a "benevolent" one. The versatile Baba Yaga appears threatening, but provides the wished-for object if her tasks are accomplished (the ambiguous donor in 480 and 552+554+400+302). In these tales her dwelling is surrounded by a fence of human bones.[8] The third type of Baba Yaga discussed by Periañez-Chaverneff, the benevolent one, is the typical donor.

The changing nature of these three images reflects the individual's development from infancy through adolescence to young adulthood. In the tales of the second type, the hero(ine) is subjected to tests which reflect the adolescent's mastery of accepted norms of behavior. In the third class of tales, the protagonist has mastered social norms: He or she knows how to address the hut and how to demand Baba Yaga's respect. The hero or heroine behaves appropriately: aggressively if a man, deferentially if a woman. The fear of the mother reflected in the "infantile" tales has been overcome. Marie-Louise von Franz also sees the hero in this episode as overcoming a mother complex: "One of the great tricks of the mother complex in a man is always to implant doubt in his mind, suggesting that it might be better to do the other thing; and then the man is lamed…. So it depends on the hero's attitude. She tries to make him infantile, but when she sees he is up to her, she helps him" (1993: 173).

Baba Yaga's initial threat to eat the hero or heroine recalls her role as cannibal ogress in tale type 327C/F. This "reference" is especially evident in Sokolov 139 (excerpt presented above), where the Baba-Yaga in question says she will roast the hero. The reproach made to Baba Yaga, a situation in which a child reproaches a mother, might represent wish fulfillment on the child's part: The omnipotent mother of infancy and early childhood is put in her place. The hero's (and less frequently, heroine's) assertive or aggressive stance, his or her refusal to be eaten, is also a way of maintaining the boundary between the self and the mother, a declaration that one has ended the infantile relationship to her. It is interesting to compare this East Slavic folktale episode with a cognate sequence in Arab and North African tales. There the hero overcomes the dangerous nature of the ogress (Arab *ghouleh*, or Berber *teryel*) by sucking milk from her breasts and thus establishing a kinship bond with her. He becomes her adoptive son and she then loves and helps him. There is aggression by the

---

[8] This is true for the second tale type, where the hero herds Baba Yaga's mares (see chapter 5). The fearsome fence or gate is not found in the 480 cycle, except for Afanas'ev 104, "Vasilisa the Beautiful," a tale which is atypical in many respects, and shows literary influence.

hero against this fantastic mother figure (he sneaks up behind her when she has slung her breasts over her shoulders), but in order to accomplish his goal, the hero needs to put himself in an infantile situation.

Periañez-Chaverneff interprets the night spent in Baba Yaga's hut as a kind of test after which the hero(ine) is capable of fulfilling the role of a sexually mature adult in society. In tales about the adventures of a young adult for whom emergent sexuality is an important concern, it should not be surprising to find sexual symbolism. Some folktales discussed in this chapter represent sexual experience rather directly (the episode of the hero and the Tsar Maiden in AT 551).

The presence of powerful women such as the Tsar Maiden in male-centered tales does not seem to reflect the reality of women's status in traditional culture, and so may represent a male fantasy to some extent (although women would certainly enjoy hearing a tale with a powerful female character). At the same time, it would be incorrect to say that women had no power whatsoever: Women played an important part in marriage arrangements and might in fact control them (Semenova Tian-Shanskaia 1993: 70–73). Baba Yaga emerges in these tales as a mediator, not only between the ordinary and supernatural worlds, but between spouses. Her role appears to serve the functioning of traditional culture in tales which successfully bring the two spouses together and reassure young people about their impending married life. In the tales about the Tsar Maiden in particular, Baba Yaga appears to assuage men's fear of women, allowing for reconciliation and harmony. This role of mediator probably accounts for Baba Yaga's frequent appearance as a relative of the hero's spouse: Presumably, she could appeal to the threatening bride or wife. For the male-centered tale, Baba Yaga can become a donor after the temptation of incest, the threat of merging and loss of identity are overcome (as in the 327C/F cycle).

Even Baba Yaga's role as donor is tinged with hostility. In the traditional donor sequence, there is an echo of the cannibal ogress, although not all tale-tellers retain the expression of cannibalistic intentions at this point. Baba Yaga's combination of hostile and benign behavior seems more than just an artistic device to create contrast, as Anikin suggests. If we recognize Baba Yaga's cannibalistic wish in the donor sequence as an echo of the cannibal ogress found in the children's tales, then Periañez-Chaverneff's interpretation of Baba Yaga in terms of a changing relationship with the mother can explain the ambiguity of this traditional formulaic episode.

CHAPTER FIVE
The Ambiguous Baba Yaga

This chapter examines a large number of tale types in which Baba Yaga is an ambiguous character, appearing as a donor in some versions, and as a villain in others. In a few texts, she appears in both roles in the same tale, as one individual, or as sisters: One sister is a donor, while another sister is a villain. This chapter also includes tales where Baba Yaga's behavior is extremely hostile and immediately identifies her as a villain or opponent of the hero; later, when the hero forces her to relinquish some magic object or agent (often healing water to restore her victims to life) she becomes a "hostile donor." Baba Yaga behaves ambiguously in a large number of tale types, and it is possible, given more texts than were available for this study, that more tale types would fall into this category, rather than being purely "donor" or "villain" types.

The Dragon Mother

Folktales about dragon slayers are widespread in Europe, and AT 300 (The Dragon Slayer) is popular in Russia as well. Baba Yaga appears ambiguously in two other types of dragon slayer tales, which are geographically more restricted: SUS 300A, The Battle on Guelder-Rose [*Kalina*] Bridge (AT 300A, The Fight on the Bridge) and SUS 300A*, The Dragon Slayer Returns the Heavenly Bodies Stolen by the Dragon.[1] Besides the East Slavic regions, these two subtypes are found among the West Slavs, in Hungary, Romania, the Baltic countries, Estonia, Finland, and among some other Caucasian, Finno-Ugric (Mansi, Mari, Mordvin), and Turkic peoples (Tatar, Chuvash, Bashkir). There is one reported German version (Barag 1981: 160). Based on this geographic distribution and a comparison of the specific features of the tales as found among these different peoples, Lev Barag (1981) concludes that these subtypes are of East Slavic origin. Only a few versions have been recorded in Poland, and they unmistakably show Ukrainian, Belorussian, and perhaps Russian influence (Kapełuś 1963: 67–69). The distribution of this tale type partially corresponds to the geographic distribution of Baba Yaga and her closest Eastern European relatives, which suggests a distinct Eastern European tradition area.

The tale often begins with the hero's birth: He and his brothers are born when the tsarina, a servant woman, and an animal (a cow, cat, dog, or bull) eat

---

[1] The East Slavic tale type index also lists a third subtype, SUS 300A**, The Dragon Slayer Obtains the Dragon's Magic Horse, represented by only two Russian and four Ukrainian versions.

of a magic fish. Like heroes of Russian folk epic poetry, the three brothers grow quickly, not by days but by hours. The animal's son is strongest and becomes the leader of the three. In SUS 300A*, the hero is sent to retrieve the sun, moon, and stars that have disappeared from the sky (Zelenin Perm' 9). Light has disappeared from the kingdom (Vedernikova and Samodelova 21), or the tsar asks for the keys to the sun and moon (Smirnov 304).

After acquiring horses, the three brothers come to a hut by a bridge, or build their own hut. One of the other two sons is supposed to stand guard at night, but he falls asleep and the hero takes his place. On three successive nights, dragons with an increasing number of heads (three, six, nine, twelve) appear on the bridge and the hero slays them. The dragon-slaying episode is often well developed. At this point there is often an interesting moment in the tale: as the dragon approaches, his horse stumbles. The dragon reproaches his horse for stumbling, and reveals that he knows the hero's name. The dragon may admit that there is only one man in the world he fears, namely the hero (Gorodtsov ii: 355–384, Onchukov 27, Zelenin Perm' 9), but states that he will crush him on the palm of his hand nevertheless. The dragon belittles the hero in one way or another, stating that the hero has not even been born yet (Afanas'ev 137), that he is still young (Gorodtsov ii: 355–384, Zelenin Perm' 9), or that it would be impossible for him to reach the dragon's realm: even the raven would not bring his bones here (Smirnov 304). In Afanas'ev 136, the dragon asks if the hero is coming to wed his (the dragon's) sisters or daughters, implying that there is a possibility of establishing kinship relations with the hero. Referring to this tale and the encounter at the bridge with the dragon, Vladimir Propp calls attention to this special connection: "The dragon somehow knows of the hero's existence. Not just that, but he knows that he will perish at the hand of precisely this hero... There is some kind of connection between the hero and the dragon which began somewhere outside the story. This connection began before the story begins" (1946: 202, 1996: 221).[2] Propp also observes a link

---

[2] Propp interprets dragon slaying as a transformation of initiation ritual, in which initiates were symbolically swallowed. Presumably this interesting moment in the fairy tale reflects the "knowledge" or recognition the initiator has of the initiated. The perfect match of the dragon with the only hero who can slay him might reflect the nature of the European fairy tale, where all objects and situations fit together perfectly (Lüthi 1960: 31–32). If the dragon is a disguised father figure, the confrontation of the two might reflect the inevitability of father-son or father-in-law/son-in-law conflict. The magic fish and the dragon both represent the father, who is removed in an oedipal scheme underlying many fairy tales, "a sacrificial pattern of rejuvenation through bloodshed" (Vaz da Silva 2002: 163–168). Heroes in Portuguese versions of AT 303 (who are also born when their human mother eats a magic fish) slay dragons and thus overcome an obstacle that keeps them from marrying a maiden, but "the beast which needs the periodic sacrifice of a maiden can be related to the periodicity of women's blood" (Cardigos 1996: 66). The woman's

between Baba Yaga and the dragon. Both are guardians, and the hero and his brothers often find a hut near the bridge that resembles Baba Yaga's hut. "Yaga guards the periphery, and the dragon guards the very heart of the thrice-tenth kingdom" (Propp 1946: 200, 1996: 219).

The dragons blow and clear a combat field many miles wide before each fight. On the third night the hero is not able to kill the dragon as easily as on the first two nights, and the dragon begins to pound him into the ground. The hero asks for permission to rest three times and throws both his boots and his hat at the hut until it collapses and finally his brothers awaken and release his horse. Or he may only release the horse, who comes and helps him kill the dragon.

The hero turns into a fly (or a dove, in Khudiakov 6) and flies to the dragons' home. There he overhears the dragons' wives and the dragon mother Baba Yaga planning his doom. The hero in a Siberian version (Potanin 1902 no. 34) turns into a cat and climbs into the hut where Baba-Yaga is telling her daughters how to kill him and his brothers. She recognizes his disguise and says, "Oh, Russian people have left a Russian cat. We'll dine and catch it." The plan of Baba Yaga and her daughters is usually that one daughter will cause heat and disguise herself as a well, the second will disguise herself as an enticing apple tree, the third as an enticing bed. The hero sets off with his brothers and keeps them from succumbing to these dangers: He slashes the well, tree, and bed with his sword and blood flows from them. Then he and his brothers part ways.

Baba Yaga pursues the hero in the form of a giant pig, with her mouth gaping open from heaven to earth. He saves himself by running into a smithy. The smiths trick Baba Yaga by promising her the hero if she sticks her tongue into the smithy. They seize the tongue with red-hot tongs and then beat her to death or beat her until she turns into a horse. In Afanas'ev 136, Khudiakov 6, and Potanin 1902 no. 34, Baba Yaga has eaten the hero's two brothers and spits them out when the smiths beat her. After the hero defeats the dragons in Manzhura 1890: 24–27 he buys bags of salty cakes and salt. Baba-Yuga pursues him, her mouth open from heaven to earth. He throws the bags into her mouth, and she has to rush off to drink and quench her thirst. He escapes to a smithy, where he finds God's smith, Kuz'ma-Dem'ian.[3] The smiths pound

---

periodic flow of menstrual blood is what keeps her under the "dragon's power." While slaying a dragon usually leads the hero to marriage in AT 300, in these East Slavic versions of AT 300A the hero does not inevitably marry, and if he does, this occurs at the end of another episode (AT 513).

[3] This name appears to be a conflation of the saints Cosmas and Damian, whose day is celebrated November 1. Their association with the smithy might derive from the chance assonance of the name Kuz'ma and *kuznia* (smithy). This folktale episode also exists in the form of East Slavic

Baba-Yuga's tongue and harness her to a plough. She pulls the plough far and wide and comes to the sea, where she drinks until she bursts. Snakes, toads, lizards, tadpoles, spiders, and worms are born from her body. The hero of Potanin 1902 no. 34 sees a cloud in the distance which is Baba-Yaga. He throws salt, flour, and bran loaves into Baba-Yaga's mouth, and so delays her as she runs back to wash out her throat in a lake.

The tale ends in a number of different ways. In Vedernikova and Samodelova 21 the smiths pound Baba-Yaga's tongue and turn her into a horse. Later, the hero breaks interdictions, starts to dance, the horse disappears, and the story ends. Khudiakov 6 ends when Baba-Yaga spits out the hero's two brothers. Smirnov 150 presents interesting variations. On the three nights the hero kills a dragon and a giant cat. He puts on the cat skin and comes to a turning hut on a chicken shin in the forest. He enters the hut with a typical formulaic phrase and finds Yaga-Yaginishna Ovdot'ia Kuzminishna inside. She quickly perceives the disguise, and the hero kicks and knocks over the hut. On the third night Yaga-Yaginishna tells the hero to meet her on the bridge for a fight. The hero and his brothers hide under the bridge while Yaga-Yaginishna comes and talks to herself about how her daughter will be disguised as traps for the hero. The hero fights with her and gets tired. He asks for time to rest, Yaga-Yaginishna falls asleep, and he cuts her into little pieces. On the way home the hero keeps his brothers from stopping at the tempting apple tree, well, and bed. At home they tell their father about the adventures, and he dies of fright or shock (*so strastei*). The three then divide the kingdom among themselves.

The other versions continue with an episode of AT 519, The Strong Woman as Bride (Afanas'ev 136, Gorodtsov ii: 355–384) or AT 513, The Extraordinary Companions (Afanas'ev 137, Bandarchyk 1973 no. 4, Onchukov 27, Potanin 1902 no. 34, Smirnov 304, Zelenin Perm' 9).

In Gorodtsov ii: 355–384, it is the three Baba Yaga mothers of the three dragons slain by the hero who disguise themselves as a well, a bed, and finally a giant cat. The cat pursues them to the smithy of Kozma-Dem'ian, sticks its tongue inside, and dies when the smith pinches its tongue with red-hot tongs. The tale continues with an episode of AT 519 (see discussion below). In

---

legends about sacred smiths who defeat a winged serpent and hitch it to a plough. The serpent ploughs "snake ramparts" which still exist, or drinks up a river. Cosmas and Damian also appear as smiths in East Slavic magic incantations (Barag 1981: 171–173, Ivanits 1989: 32–33). Vera Sokolova considers the legend to be a combination of two mythological images: "In the south of Russia the *Zmejevy Valy* or Serpent Swells are often pointed out: the hero, after having vanquished the serpent, harnessed it to a plow and made these furrows. Here the image of the fighter of the serpent has merged with that of the mythical cultural hero who taught the people how to cultivate the earth" (1976: 58–59). In Ukrainian versions of AT 300A the helpful smiths are the saints Boris and Gleb, and in a Polish version, St. Peter (Kapełuś 1963: 68–69).

Afanas'ev 136 the hero and his brothers come to another kingdom where the hero subdues a murderous princess for his brother Prince Ivan (AT 519).

When the tale continues with AT 513, the hero meets an old man or other villain and must obtain a bride for him from a distant realm. In Smirnov 304 the third dragon tells the hero that the keys to the sun and moon are under the front corner of Baba Yaga's hut. The hero obtains the keys, kills Baba Yaga's white cat, puts on its skin, and overhears the murderous plans of Baba Yaga and her daughters-in-law. After Baba Yaga is turned into a mare at the smithy, the hero is sent to obtain Elena the Marvelous. The hero returns home with her and the tsar wants to hang him (his two companions claim that they obtained the keys to the sun and moon). The hero asks to ride his mare one last time. He turns her back into Baba Yaga and frightens everyone. The truth is revealed, the hero marries the tsar's daughter, and the treacherous companions are killed.

Baba Yaga is both donor and villain in Zelenin Perm' 9. The hero Iuvashka stops at the huts (standing "on goat horns, on ram legs") of three Yaga Yagishna (presumably) sisters who warn him about the dragons. The hero kills the dragons and retrieves the sun, moon, and stars. When he returns, the first two Yagas create heat and try to trap him by disguising themselves as a garden with a well. The third Yaga turns into a storm. Each time, the hero overhears the plans of the Yaga Yagishna (the second one is telling her daughter about them), and then thanks the "old bitch" for her previous hospitality. After the smith has turned the third Yaga Yagishna into a mare, he warns the hero about her son and daughter, who will try to entrap him. The hero ignores the daughter, who is disguised as an old woman. But he responds to the son, Oleshka korotin'ka nozhka (Oleshka the Short Leg), who takes away his horse and the heavenly bodies. In order to get them back, the hero must obtain the daughter of another Yaga Yagishna for Oleshka. In taverns the hero gathers four extraordinary companions who are able to accomplish the tasks set by Yaga Yagishna. Yaga Yagishna's daughter wishes to marry the hero, and so he kills Oleshka by having him fall into a pit. The two return to the hero's home and the heavenly bodies are restored.

Baba-Yaga appears as donor in Afanas'ev 137. The three brothers first come to a hut on chicken legs and ram horns and enter with the traditional phrase. Baba-Yaga Bony Leg warns Ivan Bykovich and his companions about the dangerous dragons. The mother-in-law of the dragons is an old witch (*staraia ved'ma*). Disguised as a beggar, she fools the hero and brings him to her husband. He lies on an iron bed, and his eyes are closed by heavy black eyelashes and brows; twelve knights raise his heavy eyelids with iron pitchforks. For killing his children, he orders the hero to obtain the golden-haired tsarina.

The witch drowns herself out of anger. In the AT 513 episode the hero obtains the tsarina, returns, and fools the old man into falling into a pit.

In a Belorussian version (Bandarchyk 1973 no. 4) Baba Yuga is a donor. After the hero has disposed of the three dragon wives, he searches for their mother and comes to the hut of Baba Yuga. She bakes three loaves of bread for him and instructs him to feed them to the dragon mother. The dragon mother attacks the hero three times. Each time, she announces that she will eat the hero, but he says she must eat what he offers her first (*Nu, shto zh, paesh upiarod maiu khleb-sol', a tady esh i miane!*). The hero throws a loaf of bread in the dragon's mouth, and the dragon has to run to a lake to drink, which she has drunk dry by the third time. The hero runs for shelter to a smithy, where the smiths pound the dragon mother into a horse. In the AT 513 episode, the dragons' father forces the hero to obtain a bride, and then challenges the hero to walk on a stake over a pit, but falls in himself. After Baba-Yuga's death in Manzhura 1890: 24–27 the hero obtains an iron horse. He breaks an interdiction by laughing at a man with snot dripping from his nose into the sea. He gets his horse back when he brings a princess to the snot-nosed man, but he himself does not marry. In Potanin 1902 no. 34 Baba-Yaga releases the hero's two brothers and simply goes home. In the AT 513 episode, the one-eyed demon Erakhta steals the hero's iron horse. The hero accomplishes tasks with the help of his companions and marries Erakhta's daughter. In Onchukov 27 Egabikha is turned into a mare. The hero loses a race and the old man sends him to obtain a bride, but the hero marries her himself. When he returns he fools the old man into walking on a stick over a pit of hot coals.

Unfortunately, we know little about the tellers of any of these tales. Onchukov 27 and Zelenin Perm' 9 were recorded from men, and one suspects that most of the tellers of this male-centered tale were men. The tale features father-son rivalry (particularly in Smirnov 150, with its oedipal wish fulfillment at the end, when the sons remove the father and take his place, without having to kill him) and castration anxiety (the three dragon wives as traps meant to tempt the hero and his brothers). The presence of an unusual leg also distinguishes a few versions and may have a phallic meaning: Yaga's son Oleshka has a short leg at least in name (Zelenin Perm' 9), and one of the helpers encountered by the hero in Onchukov 27 is an old woman with both feet in one shoe (*dve nogi v odnom laptiu*).

In spite of the hero's adult task (slaying the dragons) and the threat of female sexuality (the dragon wives disguised as tempting objects, especially the bed), the third, last and most terrible danger is the dragon mother/giant sow/Baba Yaga with her enormous mouth. (In Smirnov 150, the hero's fight with Yaga Yaginishna on the bridge is very similar to his combat with the dragons in this tale cycle: He asks for time to rest and uses it to deceive her. For this narrator, Baba Yaga is as formidable an opponent as the dragons). This third danger is the only one that the hero is unable to eliminate on his own. He receives some help in slaying the third dragon, but in this third adventure it is the smith or smiths who destroy the power of the dragon mother, and often they are not ordinary smiths, but legendary or even mythological (semi-divine) figures, the saint(s) Cosmas-Damian. The hero is forced to take cover from the devouring dragon mother/Baba Yaga, who recalls the cannibalistic Baba Yaga from the SUS 327C/F cycle. Cannibalism, oral aggression, and the oven are important in the Bandarchyk version, where Baba Yuga helps the hero by baking bread. The hero's reproach to the dragon mother, to eat the food he offers before she eats him, recalls the reproach addressed to Baba Yaga in the canonical donor sequence.

Of course, Baba Yaga is not the dragon mother in every version of AT 300A, only in the versions examined here. Lev Barag suggests that Baba Yaga entered the tale along with motifs and images from various other East Slavic folktales, but even if Baba Yaga were not the mother of the dragons in the earliest, original versions of the tale, her frequent appearance should establish that she is an appropriate candidate for this role. The hero's confrontation with Baba Yaga and his rescue by smiths is transformed in a humorous way in one tale (Manzhura 1890: 123–124, see chapter 6). Baba Yaga has tricked the hero into removing his clothes; he gets them back with the help of a smith when they catch Baba Yaga with tongs and a hammer. According to Géza Róheim, the loss of the heavenly bodies in SUS 300A* suggests that the hero may have witnessed something "in the dark," not meant to be seen, which in fact occurs later in the tale when the hero overhears the murderous plans of the dragons' wives and mother. What the hero has witnessed is the primal scene, and in the tale the hero must overcome the anxiety associated with this scene as well as castration anxiety in order to marry. Overcoming this anxiety is represented by combat: "The antagonists he has to fight with are derived from the primal scene as the trauma of infancy" (Róheim 1947: 70).

This East Slavic tale is rich and dense, treating several anxieties and conflicts which figure significantly in the formation of an adult male identity. It contains father-son or father-in-law/son-in-law conflict, anxiety about the sexuality of a future wife, and perhaps most significantly, mother-son or mother-in-law/son-in-law conflict. It is certainly interesting that the hero does not inevitably marry at the end of the tale. While he may help his brother Prince Ivan subdue his powerful wife in an episode of AT 519 (Afanas'ev 136, Gorodtsov ii: 355–384), the hero himself marries in only six of the twelve versions examined here, and this happens not immediately as a result of slaying the dragons, but at the end the AT 513 episode (Afanas'ev 137, Bandarchyk 1973 no. 4, Onchukov 27, Potanin 1902 no. 34, Smirnov 304, Zelenin Perm' 9). Lev Barag concludes that the most stable and probably original elements of the tale are the departure of the hero and his brothers, the combat at the bridge, and foiling the schemes of the dragons' wives. The episode at the smithy, taken from legend, probably entered the tale at an early point. The miraculous birth from eating a magic fish may have entered the tale from AT 303, and the AT 513 episode is also a later addition. This complex folktale is a distinct Eastern European form of the Dragon Slayer tale, and it is interesting to consider it (especially its possibly original core, as identified by Barag) as a kind of "commentary" on the more widespread AT 300. Instead of unmasking a false hero and winning a princess, the hero contends with two more dangerous opponents, both female (the dragon wives and mother). The tale dramatizes the dangers of marriage for a man, who overcomes these dangers and proves his manhood or adult status, like the hero of AT 300, but often does not marry. In at least one tale (Smirnov 150) the hero and his brothers return and inherit the kingdom, surely the sign of arrival at adult status and responsibility, but without marrying. This is a curious ending for the tale, in the context of both the fairy tale genre and life in traditional East Slavic culture.

The Three Underground Kingdoms

In some versions of SUS 301A, B The Three Underground Kingdoms (AT 301, The Three Stolen Princesses), Baba Yaga appears as a donor. The hero sets off to rescue a maiden (Kretov 42) or find his mother (Karnaukhova 14). He is lowered into an underground realm. In Karnaukhova 14, the hero goes first to a grandmother and to two Baba Yagas who give him magic gifts and direct him to a mountain, which he climbs. The hero comes to three realms of copper, silver, and gold. He retrieves three maidens there, kills three dragons (Kretov 42) or the Whirlwind (Karnaukhova 14). The hero or the maidens collect the wealth of the underground realms in an egg. On his return the hero's brothers or companions pull up the maidens, but leave the hero underground. The hero comes upon donor figures who transport him back to earth or give him a bird which carries him back (two men who appear out of his spear in Karnaukhova 14, two old men and Yaga-Baba in Afanas'ev 128, Baba Yaga in Kretov 42 and Kovalev 8).

The hero returns and marries one of the maidens. Karnaukhova 14, Kitainik 7, and Kovalev 8 include a recognition episode: Only the hero is able to produce items from the underground realm, and the false hero is exposed. In Karnaukhova 14 the hero is recognized by the silver tsarevna as he sweeps the golden bridge. He appears to want recognition while he is in this low status.

The silver tsarevna says: "My groom is not the one who sits with me, but the one who sweeps the bridge" (Karnaukhova 1934: 32). This motif of the low hero being recognized by a high-status spouse is similar to the hero's self-abasement before the Tsar Maiden in some versions of AT 551. Here, as well, it might express a man's lack of confidence or self-esteem, anxiety about his ability to fulfill the role of husband, or hostility toward his future wife. The eggs found in some versions might indicate the expectation that the hero's marriage will produce children.

Karnaukhova's version, where the hero rescues his mother (cf. Afanas'ev 129 and 130 as well) can be seen as an oedipal fantasy lived out, but sublimated by the end of the tale, when the hero marries the princess from the silver kingdom. He appears to be content with the "second best" of the three possibilities.

Khudiakov 81 has been assigned to this tale type but departs from it markedly. Three Baba-Yagas point the hero onward in his search for his two sisters, carried away by whirlwinds. The Tsar Maiden releases a dragon, who kills the whirlwinds. She, the hero, and his sisters return home. In Kitainik 7, when the hero is lowered into the earth, he comes upon Yagishna, who points him toward the copper kingdom. Then there follows an episode of AT 321, where three Yagishnas attack the hero, making Yagishna's appearance ambiguous in this same tale (see the discussion of AT 321 below).

Baba Yaga's role as a donor is very straightforward: either to show the hero the way to the three kingdoms, or to help him return home again. When Baba Yaga appears as a villain, the tale is rather different. These versions often begin with the hero's birth from a human mother and a bear father (recalling SUS 650A, AT 650A, Strong John). He displays great strength and in fact disrupts life in the village. He is forced to leave and acquires two or three extraordinary companions, who are usually named for their abilities to pull up trees (*Dubynia*; *dub*, "oak"), move mountains (*Gorynia*; *gora*, "mountain"), or dam a river with a moustache (*Usynia*; *usy*, "moustache").

They find a forest hut and settle in it. In some versions this is a hut that turns on chicken legs (Afanas'ev 141, Burtsev 1895: 215–223, Dobrovol'skii 6, Novikov 1971 no. 47). One day they go hunting and leave one of the companions at home. Baba Yaga comes and beats the companion, who does not tell the others about what has happened. The same thing happens to the other companions, but the hero beats Baba Yaga and follows her to an opening in the earth. He has his companions lower him into the ground. In other versions of this tale type, the villain may be an old man (Nikiforov 1961 no. 109) or an ogre the size of a fingernail with a long beard (Onchukov 241).

In Afanas'ev 141, Baba-Yaga with wiry buttocks (*zhopa zhilenaia*), accompanied by a dog, comes to demand food, and cuts a strip of flesh from the companions' backs. She demands food as well in Afanas'ev 142, and drags the companions around by their hair. In Novikov's version (taken from the eighteenth-century tale collection *Staraia pogudka* [The Old Tune]), Baba Yaga comes in an iron mortar and pestle, sweeping away her traces with her tongue. She eats all the food the companion has prepared and beats him half-dead. The Baba-Yaga of Balashov 55, who arrives in her mortar with a broom and shovel, is not truly aggressive. She forcefully tells the companion what to do: to greet her, carry her inside, and carry her outside when she leaves. She blows and spits on the oven and produces food, which she shares with the companion, all actions which resemble those of a willing donor. This Baba-Yaga also addresses her mortar with the rhyming phrase "Go, mortar, go three versts!" (*Stupa-stupai, po tri versty shagai!*) which might be a magic incantation. When the hero Ivan refuses to do as she asks, she becomes frightened and runs away. Baba-Yagaba in Onchukov 34 makes the companions lift her over the threshold and onto a bench before fighting them. Ivan refuses to lift her, saying: "Your buttocks are fat, sit down yourself" (*zhopa u tia tolstaia, sama posed'*, Onchukov 1908: 96). He kills her and throws her body outside. The Onchukov version also includes an earlier episode where the hero encounters an old woman donor in a hut turning on chicken legs.

The hero then comes upon three underground realms and three maidens. Sometimes the maidens are Baba Yaga's daughters, and one of them tells the hero how to fool Baba Yaga in combat. In the Onchukov version, the hero and his companions simply find an opening in the earth, and the maiden in the underground realm may have no association with Baba Yaga. Baba Yaga's daughter in Afanas'ev 142 turns the hero into a pin to hide him when her mother comes home, but Baba Yaga notices the Russian scent. The hero switches vessels with "weak" and "strong" drink, and Baba Yaga drinks the weak water (or wine) by mistake, while the hero drinks the strong water and is able to overcome her (Afanas'ev 142, Dobrovol'skii 6, Gorodtsov ii: 186–203, Novikov 1971 no. 47), or the hero only strikes her once with a sword, because a second stroke would have brought Baba Yaga back to life (Afanas'ev 141). Afanas'ev 141 also contains what may be an echo of the 327C/F cycle: The hero offers Baba Yaga a golden apple in order to snatch the sword from under her pillow. In Dobrovol'skii 6, Baba Yaga sleeps atop Mt. Zion (*na Siian'skei gare*). The hero in Gorodtsov ii: 186–203 encounters Baba Yaga after his brothers have betrayed him and taken the princesses. He comes to a hut, where an old woman warns him that Baba Yaga will soon arrive and tells him to drink the strong water, and exchange the barrels of strong and weak water. Baba Yaga drinks the weak water and the hero kills her and beats her into the ground. He finds out that the old woman is a princess who was captured by Baba Yaga in her youth. She does not go with the hero but decides to stay in the underground realm. The hero of Matveeva 1980 no. 13 beats Baba Yaga so badly when she appears in the hut that she forgets her broom there; after slaying a dragon in the underground realm, he finds Baba Yaga by a river, washing her mortar. She tries to fly away, but because the mortar is wet, it cannot fly. He drowns Baba Yaga and destroys her mortar.

Other than Balashov 55 (in which the companions do not betray the hero and he does not marry the maiden), the villain versions of AT 301 end in the same manner as the donor versions discussed above, with the companions' treachery, the hero's return to earth, and his revenge. The teller of Dobrovol'skii 6 has avoided the issue of treachery: After the hero kills Baba Yaga, he takes her cap. The frightened companions see the cap, think they are lifting Baba Yaga out of the ground, and let him fall back. The hero in Gorodtsov ii: 186–203 forgives his treacherous brothers at the end.

This tale type is problematic if we examine Baba Yaga's behavior separately. The hero's sojourn in the underground kingdoms of copper, silver, and gold unites the various versions considered here, and has given the tale its title in East Slavic tradition, "The Three Underground Kingdoms" (*Tri podzemnykh tsarstva*, Barag et al. 1979: 106). It is a popular tale, and judging by the versions at our disposal, Baba Yaga appears in perhaps only twelve of some 148 indexed versions. If Baba Yaga is not the only or most typical donor or villain encountered in this tale, it is not as surprising that her behavior has not become as fixed as in other tale types, although her behavior as villain is more consistent than as a donor. The differences between the donor and villain tales also suggest that the folk tradition may distinguish these tales, even though scholars choose to classify them both as the same type.

The fact that Baba Yaga (or the defeated ogre) shows the hero the way into the underground realm causes Propp to define her as an unwilling donor, but this definition has been questioned by Claude Bremond (Bremond and Verrier 1982: 74, see the conclusion of this chapter). While Baba Yaga's aggression in this tale cycle consists of beating the hero's companions or cutting flesh from their backs, the cannibalistic/oral element is still present, when she demands food from the companion and eats everything he has prepared.

Baba Yaga as a Warrior

A few tales contain an episode which features a particularly fearsome manifestation of Baba Yaga, as a warrior at the head of an army. Because the hero pursues Baba Yaga underground, the tales with this episode are frequently classified or identified as SUS 301 (The Three Underground Kingdoms), although they lack many other elements of that tale. The consistent elements are the hero's companion, a warrior Baba Yaga with a large army, an underground realm where smiths and seamstresses produce soldiers for her, and a deception which weakens Baba Yaga and allows the hero to kill her. These tales usually include other episodes in which Baba Yaga does not appear.

In Afanas'ev 161, the hero encounters Belyi Polianin (the White Field-Dweller), who has been fighting Baba-Yaga Golden Leg (*zolotaia noga*) for thirty years and wants to marry her daughter. The two trample thousands of soldiers in Baba-Yaga's army. She flees and disappears under the ground. Polianin lowers Ivan into the earth, where he decapitates tailors and shoemakers who are fashioning Baba-Yaga's soldiers. He comes to a maiden, her daughter, who leads him to where Baba-Yaga is asleep. He cuts Baba-Yaga's head off, but avoids striking her another time when the rolling head urges him to do so.

The hero of Manzhura 1890: 14–18 also meets a companion named Bylyi Polianyn. He chases Baba-Yaga three times, but each time she gets home, and the cast-iron gates of her dwelling close behind her. A voice tells the hero to ambush Baba-Yaga, and he waits for her to come out. Then he cuts down the gates, and they fall down and crush her. This tale lacks an army or an underground episode.

In Bandarchyk 1973 no. 12, the hero and his companion fight Baba Yuga three times. The third time the hero shoots a stone arrow into her mouth, and she disappears underground. There the hero kills the smiths and seamstresses who are producing soldiers, and engages in hand-to-hand combat with Baba Yuga. A maiden in Baba Yuga's hut shows the hero where the vessels of strong and weak wine are. They move the wine barrels so that Baba Yuga drinks the weak wine by mistake. Twice Baba Yuga asks to rest from fighting, and the hero pounds her to dust in the third round.

Kovalev 3 is an anomalous tale containing this episode. The hero (son of the Eagle) finds the smiths and embroidering maidens in a forest, not underground. They tell him which pots contain the strong and weak beer; he drinks the strong beer and switches the pots to overcome Baba Yaga. Baba Yaga then fights the warrior woman Olenka, because she wants the Eagle to marry her own niece rather than Olenka. The hero encounters his Eagle father and marries Olenka, but Baba Yaga does not appear again in the tale. In Kovalev's tale, Baba Yaga flies on a broom and uses it to strike the hero, knocking him into the ground.

Prince Ivan, the hero of Potanin 1906 no. 13, follows the advice of an old woman and marries a maiden who is washing clothes. At night she disappears and tells him that only Tarkh Tarkhovich can possess her. The old woman then tells him how to obtain a magic horse in the tsar's garden, and he sets off. He comes to the tower dwellings of Yagaia-Babitsa, who warns him about Tarkh Tarkhovich, and then Yaga-Babitsa, who warns him about Tarkh Tarkhovich's mother. The third dwelling is Tarkh Tarkhovich's, where the mother of Tarkh Tarkhovich hides the hero at first. Prince Ivan tames a wild horse and shows that he is stronger than Tarkh Tarkhovich. They go together to the open field and fight the army of Baba-Yaga, which first appears as a cloud. In the battle the hero inadvertently kills Tarkh Tarkhovich (he revives him in a later episode). The hero follows Baba-Yaga underground, where peasants are hammering, children are playing with a ball, and maidens are weaving, all of them making an army for Baba-Yaga with these activities. He tricks them by telling them that he will show them how this is done in Rus': He has them stand in a row and beheads them. Then he comes to the enormous house of Baba-Yaga and her daughter. He fights and kills them, and burns them and their house. To gain strength, the hero drinks some "strong" water which he has brought along himself. This tale also includes an episode of AT 321 (see below). In Gorodtsov ii: 150–173, an old woman sorceress tells Prince Fedor to marry Marfa Yaganichna, the daughter of Baba Yaga, in the Distant Kingdom. Later his brother Ivan is born. Ivan finds him in the field, where he has been fighting Baba Yaga for many years. The two brothers defeat Baba Yaga's army and Ivan follows Baba Yaga underground. He decapitates two maidens, who are embroidering and producing soldiers, and then cuts off the head of Baba Yaga, who is lying in a cradle, while nannies and nurses are rocking her and singing to her. This strange infantile feature of Baba Yaga is also found in several versions of AT 314A* (see chapter 3), and seems especially strange at this moment, immediately after Baba Yaga has appeared as a fierce warrior. This tale continues with an episode of AT 400 (chapter 4) with three Baba Yaga donors, making it an ambiguous tale overall.

Shastina 1985 no. 54 (a version of 552A+554+400+302, the "herding mares" cycle, see discussion below) includes the same episode. The hero goes to fight Yaga-Baba, who has been fighting against Belomonet for three years. The hero chases Yaga-Baba, who rides in an iron mortar, and follows her underground. There, he kills her smiths, and then Yaga-Baba herself. Later he comes to a yurt where Yaga-Baba lives, and where he herds stallions and obtains a magic foal. Azadovskii 1947 no. 8, where Yaga-Baba already appears as a villain in AT 519 (The Strong Woman as Bride), also includes this episode: Yaga-Baba's army looks like a cloud on the horizon, maidens and smiths are fashioning it underground, and Yaga-Baba drinks the dead water by mistake. In a literary fairy tale published in 1787, the hero falls into a pit where a smith is creating soldiers with each blow of his hammer. The hero slays Baba Yaga (Chernyshev 1934: 590).

Baba Yaga Gouges Out Men's Eyes

Baba Yaga is a fearsome opponent who gouges out eyes and the owner of a field in the underground realm in SUS 321, The Youth Serves as Shepherd for the Blind Old Man and Woman (AT 321, Eyes Recovered from Witch). This tale type frequently appears as an episode added to other tales, such as AT 301 (see above) and AT 551 (chapter 4). Baba Yaga is essentially a villain, but she is forced to heal the injury she has caused, in this case to provide healing water or restore the eyes of the man she has blinded.

In AT 301, the hero's companions abandon him in the underground realm. He comes to an old man who has been blinded by Baba Yaga and asks for work. The man has him graze his cattle, but warns him not to let the cattle wander into Baba Yaga's field (Matveeva and Leonova 1, Nikiforov 1961 no. 109, Onchukov 241). The hero ignores the warning, and Baba Yaga, her daughters, or her sons come to kill him. In the Onchukov version, the two daughters and Baba Yaga come riding on a shovel, a broom, and an oven fork; each threatens to strike the hero's testicles with this instrument (*Ia tebia ukhvatishshom-to, po mudishsham-to!* Onchukov 1908: 513). The hero decapitates Baba Yaga's daughters, jumps on Baba Yaga, rides home on her, ties her up, beats her with iron switches, and forces her to tell him where she has the old man's eyes. After he restores the old man's eyes, he beats her to death (Onchukov 241). Or he kills Baba Yaga by striking her with her own mortar (Nikiforov 1961 no. 109). In Shastina 1974: 42–52, the hero comes to the witch Baba Yaga herself and offers to herd her cattle if she will give him a horse in return. While the hero sleeps, the horses get into a wheat field, and Baba Yaga sends her daughter there in a mortar. She hits him with a pestle. He kills her and the other two daughters, as well as their witch mother. He takes one of the horses, who carries him back to the upper world.

Kitainik 7, discussed above, features Baba Yaga as a donor in AT 301, and a villain in its AT 321 episode. The hero herds the old man's cattle in the forbidden field, and on three successive days three Yagishnas come to drink tea and then fight with him. He cuts their heads off and makes the heads into cups which he gives to the old man. In Balashov 43 the hero of AT 551 herds animals in Yaga-Baba's pasture. Her three daughters and then Yaga-Baba herself appear, but the hero tears their heads off. He forces Yaga-Baba to show him the source of the living water and give the old man's eyes back. Then the old man summons a giant bird, which takes the hero back to earth.

In Potanin 1906 no. 13, two donors (Yagaia and Yaga-Babitsa) give the hero instructions, and he fights against Baba-Yaga and her army (AT 301, discussed above). He has accidentally killed his companion Tarkh Tarkhovich, and Tarkh Tarkhovich's mother uses magic to make the hero fall back into the underground realm. There he comes to Mt. Zion (*na Siianskuiu goru*) and a palace with a blind knight (*bogatyr*). Baba-Yaga has blinded the knight for driving his cows into her wheat field. The hero takes out the cows again, and Baba-Yaga sees him through her spyglass (*Baba-Iaga v podzornuiu trubu gliadit*). He hides behind a tree, and when Baba-Yaga passes by, he cuts off her nine heads. Then he returns and heals the knight. This exceptional instance of polycephalism, usually attributed to dragons, suggests a relationship between Baba-Yaga and the dragon.[4]

After the hero has killed Yaga-Yagishna's three sons, Matveeva and Leonova 1 continues with an unusual episode of AT 302 (The Ogre's [Devil's] Heart in the Egg). In this version the hero searches for Yaga-Yagishna's (rather than Koshchei's) death. The hero tries to kill her with his sword, but only blunts the sword. Yaga-Yagishna then causes a terrible storm, and the hero saves a nest of baby eagles. The parent eagle returns and tells the hero Svetovik to kill Yaga-Yagishna by finding her death in an egg, in a duck, in a hare, in a chest that is under an oak tree on Buian island. With animal helpers, the hero gets the egg and breaks it open. Gray smoke comes out of the egg, and before she dies, Yaga-Yagishna tells the hero how to summon the magic horse Sivka-burka. The death egg, nested in other objects, is usually only associated with Koshchei, and its application to Yaga-Yagishna in this tale appears to be an exceptional instance in the East Slavic folktale tradition.

Baba Yaga's role in versions of AT 302 presents a certain complexity, because it is most often combined with other tale types. Baba Yaga helps the hero defeat Koshchei in an AT 302 episode in several versions of AT 550, in one version of SUS 400/2, and in AT 402, after the hero's frog wife has been abducted by Koshchei or a dragon. In an anomalous tale (Nikiforov 1936 no. 11) she helps the hero obtain Koshchei, but this particular tale lacks other features of AT 302. In the "herding mares" cycle, discussed below, the hero receives a horse from her that defeats Koshchei, but otherwise she is extremely hostile. In the light of these different tales, it seems most logical to consider Baba Yaga's role in AT 302 to be an ambiguous one. The motif of the "death egg" is transformed in an interesting way in some versions of SUS 400/2, where it contains the heart, love, or sorrow of the maiden (see below).

---

[4] In a Slovak version of AT 321 (Dobšinský iii: 32–43) three Ježibabas with seven, nine, and twelve heads attack the hero.

Baba Yaga Turns Men to Stone

SUS 303, The Two Brothers (AT 303, The Twins or Blood-Brothers), is a rather elaborate folktale, with two or three brothers as protagonists and a dragon-slaying episode. In several versions Baba Yaga is a hostile donor when she is forced to show the hero the location of the living water with which he can revive his brother.

In Onchukov 4, a princess who has been kept in confinement is taken outside, and drinks twice from a well. Two sons are born, Ivan and Fedor, and are given the patronymic middle name Vodovich, "Son of Water." Fedor sets out on the road of death and arrives at the hut of a kindly old woman, a grandmother who lives "behind the courtyard" (*babushka-zadvorenka*).[5] She tells him of three princesses who are to be eaten by dragons. He slays the dragons and marries the youngest princess. One day a golden bird lures him to Yaga-Baba's hut. Yaga-Baba jumps out, strikes him with a pestle, and turns him into a stone.

His brother Ivan returns from the other road, where he had been making merry with fair maidens (*krasnye devichi*). He comes to the city where people think he is Fedor. He sees the same golden bird. Yaga-Baba jumps out of the hut, but Ivan curses her and turns her into a stone. Then, he forces a raven to fetch the living water and uses it to revive Fedor. Fedor returns to his wife and kingdom, and Ivan returns home to his mother.

Onchukov 152 is quite elaborate, containing many elements of other tale types. Three brothers set out down three different roads. An old man in a hut remarks on the eldest brother's Russian scent and warns him about a sorceress (*volshebnitsa*) who lives in the forest with Baba Yaga. Then the old man turns the eldest brother and his animals to stone. Baba Yaga comes riding in her mortar, strikes the old man with a pestle, and puts the stones on top of him.

The second brother comes to a city and stays in a hut with a kind old woman. She informs him that the princess is about to be given to a serpent. He saves the princess from the serpent with his bird that can cause sleep. He marries the princess, but some time later a snake jumps into her mouth. She dies and the second brother leaves. He finds his enchanted eldest brother, and while he is looking at the strangely shaped stones, Baba Yaga comes in her mortar and strikes him and his horse, turning them to stone as well.

The third brother meets a companion. They come to a house where the companion gnaws through its iron wall. They release an old man who had been

---

[5] The "behind-the-courtyard" grandmother (*babushka zadvorenka*) is a frequent female donor in East Slavic fairytales. Her epithet implies that she lives behind the courtyard or yards, behind homes or homesteads, and places her at the edge or beyond the edge of a settled town or village.

chained inside for forty years, lured there by the sorceress. They flee, but a storm forces them to spend the night in a forest still within the sorceress's realm. The sorceress attacks them astride a serpent. The companion kills her and they burn her and take two bottles from her, but the serpent gets away. The old man goes to look for the eldest brother.

The third brother and his companion arrive at the hut of the old woman, who tells them that the princess is about to be buried, but that someone must guard her coffin for three nights. Following his companion's advice, the third brother is able to disenchant the princess and remove the snake from her (cf. AT 507C, The Serpent Maiden, and AT 307, The Princess in the Shroud). They then go down the eldest brother's road, and with the water from the sorceress's bottle, they revive the two elder brothers and the first old man. Baba Yaga arrives in her mortar and attacks them, but the companion splashes water on her. She turns into a snake and a frog; the frog bursts and turns into a stone. The companion puts the stone into the bottle and departs. The first and third brothers return home, and the second brother returns to his wife. When he returns home, the youngest brother realizes that his helpful companion was a dead man whose debt and burial expenses he had paid (cf. motifs E341, The grateful dead, H972, Tasks accomplished with help of grateful dead, and tale type AT 506, The Rescued Princess).

Baba Yaga appears in this tale along with another female villain. Although the sorceress is not described in detail, she is presumably an attractive younger woman (she was able to lure the second old man into the house). The only woman in the tale who is not dangerous is the old woman in the hut encountered by the second and third brothers. The male heroes and the abundance of dangerous women suggest that this tale is a male fantasy, and Baba Yaga may be symbolically rendering men impotent when she turns them to stone.

The two brothers of the version from Manzhura's collection (1890: 30–33) are born after their mother eats peas that roll by. The first brother slays two dragons in another kingdom, saves two princesses, and marries the older one. He goes into a forbidden chamber, and through a window there he sees the sea, and across the sea a stone shore, with stone people, animals, trees, and birds. An old man tells him that Baba Yaga lives there, and turns everyone who comes there to stone. The brother crosses the sea, and asks Baba Yaga why everything there is stone. She tells him to wait, that she first must wash her spoons. He turns to stone. A sack left as a sign to the second brother falls over. The second brother comes to the same kingdom and then to the stone realm. He does not let Baba Yaga deceive him, but painfully twists her braid and forces her to take him to the living and healing water. He revives his brother, his animals kill Baba Yaga, and they return to the kingdom, where the second brother marries the second princess.

In Erlenvein 3, the two heroes are born from a magic fish eaten by the tsar's granddaughter and a maid. They ask the tsar for permission to go to the forbidden meadow, but the tsar warns them that Baba Yaga lives there. Ivan the Maid's Son goes to the meadow, is overcome by sleep, and lies down:

> Baba Yaga Bony Leg came in an iron mortar, driving it with an iron pestle. "What vermin has come to my meadow?" She walked up, tore some hairs from her head, and told Ivan the Maid's Son, "Tie three knots and blow on them." He tied them, blew, and he and his horse turned to stone. She put them in her mortar and ground them. She ground them into fine little pieces, put them in a sack, and put the sack under some stones. (Erlenvein 1863: 9)

Ivan the Tsar's Son is not fooled by Baba Yaga when he arrives at the meadow. When Baba Yaga tells him to blow on the knots, he pretends not to know how, and tells her to show him, much like the hero of AT 327C/F. Baba Yaga turns to stone, and even as Ivan the Tsar's Son grinds her in the mortar, he finds out from her where his brother is, and where to obtain the living and dead water to revive him. At the end of this episode, he revives Ivan the Maid's Son, and Baba Yaga is left lying in the mortar. Whether she is dead or alive is not entirely certain.

An unmarried priest's daughter drinks magic water from a well and gives birth to the two brothers in Pomerantseva 30. In this tale Yaga the witch (*iaga-koldun'ia*) induces the first brother to tie up his animals with a belt she gives him. The animals turn to stone, and she chews and tears Ivan to pieces, salts him, and buries him in a basket. The second brother Mikhail forces the old woman to give him magic water to revive Ivan's animals, and the blood of a witch-magpie then revives Ivan. The old woman is cut to pieces and buried. In Gorodtsov ii: 308–323, a secluded tsarevna drinks sea water and has two sons. After slaying dragons and marrying a princess, the first brother Ivan goes hunting and sees a golden-horned goat, who is in fact Baba Yaga, and the mother of the dragons he has killed. She turns him and his animals to stone with a whip. The second brother Eruslan hides and catches Baba Yaga, gets the whip from her, and revives his brother. He tears Baba Yaga in two and throws the two halves in opposite directions so that they will not grow together again.

The two versions from Dobrovol'skii's collection (nos. 13 and 14) are not quite as elaborate. The first brothers are warned not to go riding or hunting in a certain place. Of course they do, and there they encounter Baba Yaga. In Dobrovol'skii 13 the sorceress (*valshebnitsa*) Baba Yaga lives twelve versts beyond the city and has a giant iron tooth (*u ëi bal'shoi-prebal'shoi adin zialeznyi zub*) as well as the conventional mortar, pestle, and broom. She cuts the first brother in half, and the second brother forces her to deliver the living and dead water. His animals tear her to pieces and she is burned on a fire.

In Dobrovol'skii 14, the witch Baba-Iga Bony Leg who is dark and whose eyes are like coals (*sama ina byla smugyl', a glaza u iae, kak vugyl'*) turns the first two brothers to stone. The third brother and his animals force her to breathe life back into them, and then they burn her on the fire. The tale includes another episode. The teller adds that Baba-Iga lived by the sea, and her child, the Sea Monster (*Marskaia Chudovishcha*), threatens the three brothers and the realm. The animals help kill the Sea Monster, the first brother becomes tsar in the realm, while his two brothers rule in Asia and America.

The two brothers in Iavorskii 31b have eaten a magic bird, and gold coins appear under their pillow every morning. After other adventures, the elder brother comes to a city, where he slays the dragon and marries the princess. He sees a light on a mountain, and his wife does not tell him what it is. He goes there and finds an old hut with corpses around it. Inside the hut he finds Baba-Yazia. She strikes him and his animals with a twig and turns them to stone. The younger brother comes to his rescue and has his animals attack Baba-Yazia before she can enchant him. He forces her to take him to the living water, and she first takes him to the dead water, which makes his staff burst into flames. He revives his brother, and their animals tear Baba-Yazia to pieces.

Baba Yaga Sucks a Maiden's Breasts

SUS 519, The Blind and the Legless Men (AT 519, The Strong Woman as Bride), is sometimes combined with other tale types (AT 300, 303, 518, 671) or exists as a tale independently. Baba Yaga appears in episodes of AT 300A and 519 in Gorodtsov ii: 355–384. As in AT 303, Baba Yaga is forced to relinquish healing water.

A prince is helped by an extraordinary companion. The prince seeks the hand of a formidable maiden, who demands that he accomplish certain feats of strength (shooting a giant pistol and taming a giant horse in Sokolov 143, presenting a riddle that the maiden cannot solve in Afanas'ev 198). The companion carries out the tasks for the prince. On their wedding night she places her hands and feet on the prince, weighing him down and nearly killing him. The prince slips out and his companion takes his place. The companion subdues the maiden, sometimes beating her with copper, tin, and silver switches (Shastina 1985 no. 63, Sokolov 143). When the maiden finds out that she has been subdued not by her husband but by his companion, she has the companion's legs cut off at the knee and forces her husband to herd cows. In Matveeva and Leonova 21, the companion has knocked three princesses from their horses. At the wedding feast they get him drunk and cut off his legs in revenge.

The companion meets a blind man (sometimes also a man without arms) and they live together. In some versions, the other men are already living with a maiden; in others, the legless man and his new friends kidnap a maiden to come and live with them as their sister. While they hunt during the day, Baba Yaga comes and sucks milk or blood (Shastina 1985 no. 63) from the maiden's breasts. In Gorodtsov ii: 355–384, Baba Yaga sucks her "juices and maidenly blood." One day they ambush Baba Yaga and force her to take them to the location of the living or healing water. She tries to deceive them and takes them to the dead or fiery water, but the prince's companion first throws a twig or a bird into the water to test it. They continue to beat Baba Yaga until she takes them to the living water. They are healed and they throw Baba Yaga into the fiery water (Afanas'ev 198), bury her under the corner of her house (Zelenin Perm' 7), shove her under the roots of a tree (Sokolov 143), cut her to pieces (Shastina 1985 no. 63), or cut her up, burn her, and scatter her ashes in the wind (Matveeva and Leonova 21). After the hero and his brother are healed with the living and dead water in Gorodtsov ii: 355–384 they thank God, and there is no mention of what happens to Baba Yaga.

The companion returns to the realm where the prince is still a cowherd. He disciplines the prince's wife and order is restored (Afanas'ev 198, Sokolov 143). In some tales her evil doings are explained by enchantment, from which she is now released (Balashov 54). In Afanas'ev 199 she is shot.

The encounter with Baba Yaga is unusual in Afanas'ev 199. Nikita Koltoma and his blinded brother come to her hut in the forest. They eat all her food and Nikita finds a whistle which makes his brother, the hut, and everything inside it dance. Then Baba Yaga returns home and they force her to take them to the healing and living water. She does not try to deceive them. After they are healed, they thank her and release her.

Shastina 1985 no. 63 and Azbelev 6, recorded from the same narrator, present an unusual image of Yaga-Baba (her severed head runs away on its braids and does not die until it is cut to pieces), reflecting the influence of Siberian indigenous folklore, in which parts of the body function as independent beings (Afanas'eva 1986a, Shastina 1985: 38; see the discussion on regional variation in Baba Yaga's image in chapter 2).

In Razumova and Sen'kina 1982 no. 1, the hero climbs on Baba-Yaga's back and forces her to take him to the living water. Although she has been thrown into the dead water, the Yaga-Baba of Azadovskii 1947 no. 8 reappears later as a villain with an underground army (301 episode, see discussion above). Baba Yuga sucks blood from the maiden's heart with a pipe in Bandarchyk 1973 no.

52. The hero and his companion start to grind her in a mortar before she shows them the healing water. They leave her hair stuck in a cleft of a tree, but she disappears. When they come to her house, her daughter helps them kill her, and the formerly armless man marries Yuga's daughter.

Scholars have noted the resemblance of this folktale to episodes from the Nibelungenlied, in which Siegfried, wearing a magic cloak of invisibility, wins Brunhild and then subdues her for Gunther. Stith Thompson believes that the tale "seems to have developed in Russia, from which a few versions have spread to countries immediately adjacent" (Thompson 1977: 113), while Löwis of Menar felt that an earlier version of the Germanic epic had reached Russia around the end of the twelfth century and been adopted by peasant tale-tellers about four hundred years later (Löwis of Menar 1923: 103–107). C. W. von Sydow argues for the East Slavic origin of the "strong woman as bride" in the Nibelungenlied: "The Russian folk-tale attracted a German minstrel, who heard it in Russia, and on account of certain associations worked it into the Brynhild poem instead of an earlier motive of perhaps the same content as the Scandinavian Brynhild episode" (1948: 54, 1999: 148). The theme of a blind and lame man helping each other is found in the medieval *Gesta Romanorum* (Tale 71), and in a parable of Kirill of Turov (twelfth century).

Baba Yaga is not the only villain who comes to suck the maiden's breasts. In other versions of the tale, the culprit is a witch, a dragon, an evil spirit, or a dwarf with a long beard (Löwis of Menar 1923: 37–43). In sucking milk or blood from the young woman, Baba Yaga apparently wishes to appropriate her youthful fertility and femininity. Baba Yaga's presence is not surprising in this tale, which is male-centered and focuses on men's fear of women and the dangers of the wedding night. Of the versions for which information is available about informants, only one was told by a woman (Balashov 54), while eight were told by men. The tale abounds with castration symbolism (blinded, legless, and armless men) and features a frightening woman (similar to the Tsar Maiden) who nearly kills her husband on the wedding night. Baba Yaga's role is overwhelmingly hostile. For the maiden in the forest hut she is entirely a villain, while for the hero and his companions she acts as a villain and a hostile donor.

The Hero Rescues His Sister and Brothers

In SUS 312D, Katigoroshek (AT 312D, Brother Saves His Sister and Brothers from the Dragon), the tsar's daughter is kidnapped by Voron Voronovich (Raven Son of Raven). The elder two sons set out to rescue her. They come to one or three Baba-Yagas, who send them on their way. At Voron's dwelling their sister hides them. Voron smells the Russian scent, offers them more food than they can eat, forces them into an overheated bath where they roast to death, or kills them with iron switches or a spear.

The youngest brother receives a magic switch and bottle from the Baba-Yagas. He drinks from the bottle first and is able to outeat Voron, and kills him with the switch. A raven is sent for living and dead water, the two elder brothers are revived, and they return home (Balashov 7). The youngest brother offers Voron food and a bath first, and Voron burns to death. He gives Voron's house to Baba Yaga and returns home with his sister (Smirnov 279). Ivan Perekati-Goroshek, born after his mother eats a pea, goes to look for his elder siblings in Matveeva 1980 no. 7. He comes to three Baba Yaga donors, slays dragons, and finds his sister, who is married to the Wind (*Veter*). He forces the Wind to revive his brother, and then they kill the Wind.

In Zelenin Perm' 27, the third brother encounters Yaga Baba, not on the way to Voron's house, but after killing him. He demands to know where the living water is and seizes Yaga Baba by her braids, threatening to kill her if she lies or does not produce the water. He revives his brothers and they return home with their sister.

Herding Baba Yaga's Mares

In a tale which combines several different tale types (SUS 552A, 554, 400/1, and 302/2—AT 552, The Girls Who Married Animals, AT 554, The Grateful Animals, AT 400, The Man on a Quest for his Lost Wife, AT 302, The Ogre's Heart in the Egg), the hero acquires a supernatural and powerful spouse, and confronts an ogre and Baba Yaga, who appears as a very hostile donor. The hero faces death if he does not successfully guard Baba Yaga's herd of mares.

The hero's three sisters are married to animals or natural forces. He goes to visit them, and eventually comes to the realm of a woman warrior whom he defeats and marries (Azadovskii 1938 no. 30), who throws him in prison and whom he then overcomes with magic objects traded for three nights with her (Zelenin Viatka 86), or who simply agrees to marry him (Afanas'ev 159, Novikov 1971 no. 30). On his way to his sisters the hero encounters a defeated army and finds out that Mar'ia Morevna has vanquished it. He meets her and they marry (Afanas'ev 159). Marfa-tsarevna agrees to marry the hero after his sword defeats her army and he outweighs her on a scale (Gorodtsov i: 205–226).

The hero's new wife goes off to war and forbids him to open one room. He does and a monster (Koshchei or a dragon) imprisoned there asks him for a drink of water. He complies with the request and inadvertently releases the monster, who seizes Mar'ia. Matveeva 1984 no. 39 begins with episodes resembling AT 315 (The Faithless Sister) and AT 532 (I Don't Know). The hero's mother plots with her lover to have the hero killed. She offers him poisoned food and then feigns illness and asks to eat his horse's heart. The hero rides away on his magic horse and comes to another kingdom. He covers himself with soot and works in the tsar's garden. He slays three dragons, reveals himself, and marries the tsar's youngest daughter. The tsar makes him his heir, leaves, and forbids him to open one cellar. The hero does and releases Koshchei, who kidnaps his wife.

In some versions the hero now visits his sisters and brothers-in-law, receives gifts from them, and leaves them tokens which will bleed if he dies (Afanas'ev 159, Azadovskii 1938 no. 30, Novikov 1971 no. 30). The hero makes three attempts to rescue his wife, but each time Koshchei catches up with him. The last time the hero is killed by the ogre. The animal brothers-in-law (or animal helpers) come and revive the hero with living and dead water. The hero returns to his wife and finds out that a horse faster than Koshchei's can be obtained from Baba Yaga.

The hero then sets off and acquires three animal helpers. Usually he is hungry and intends to kill and eat an animal or its child, but the animal pleads with him and promises to be helpful to the hero. Then he goes on to Baba Yaga's dwelling. Baba Yaga tells him he can have the horse of his choice, but he must guard her herd of mares for three days and keep them from running away. If he fails he will die. Each day the mares (who are Baba Yaga's transformed daughters) run away, but each time the hero's animal helpers drive them back. The hero takes the worst-looking foal (which is in fact a magic horse) from Baba Yaga's stable. Sometimes Baba Yaga chases him, but without success. With his new horse he is able to outrun Koshchei and rescue his wife. In many versions his horse convinces Koshchei's horse to throw the ogre down to his death. (The East Slavic index recognizes this as a distinct subtype—SUS 302/2, Koshchei's Death from His Horse). In some versions the hero obtains an egg containing the ogre's death or soul and smashes the egg (Azadovskii 1938 no. 30, Gorodtsov i: 205–226, Matveeva 1984 no. 39, Vasilenok 1958: 115–122, Zelenin Perm' 6).

Two Belorussian versions begin differently. In Bandarchyk 1973 no. 71, the hero throws a stick and hits Baba Yuga on the leg. She tells him about the distant maiden in the White Field. The hero sets out, coming to three old men donors in huts on chicken legs who call together birds, beasts, and clouds to find out where the White Field is. The hero finds the maiden there, and she forbids one room to him. In Bandarchyk 1978 no. 6, the hero leaves home as an infant and is raised by a forest spirit who later tells him how to obtain a dove maiden, but warns him not to accept vodka from her after they marry. He drinks the vodka and she flies away to the glass mountains. He goes back to the forest spirit and the spirit's two brothers to find the glass mountains. After he finds his wife there, the tale proceeds more or less as above. In both of these tales Baba Yuga beats her daughter-mares with iron switches, and tries to deceive the hero when it is time for him to choose a horse.

Some versions of this tale include typical donor attributes of Baba Yaga: the conventional dialogue, the grotesque description of Ega's body, the hero's reproach and demand for hospitality, and Ega's compliance (Azadovskii 1938 no. 30), the turning hut on chicken legs and the accompanying traditional phrases (Zelenin Perm' 6), and Baba Yaga's feeding the hero (Afanas'ev 159, Azadovskii 1938 no. 30, Shastina 1985 no. 54, Zelenin Viatka 86). Nevertheless, Baba Yaga is a highly unwilling and hostile donor in this tale. The hero is threatened with beheading. When he arrives he sees twelve stakes (or some other number) around Baba Yaga's house. Human heads are on eleven of them, while only one remains empty (Afanas'ev 159, Azadovskii 1938 no. 30, Matveeva 1984 no. 39, Zelenin Viatka 86). Baba Yaga reproaches the mares for allowing themselves to be rounded up. In Zelenin Viatka 86 she calls her herd of cows "whores," and in Azadvoskii 1938 no. 30 she beats them with three copper, iron, and tin switches and reproaches them: "You know, your mother hasn't eaten Russian meat for a long time! You couldn't run away from him!" In Shastina 1985 no. 54 she calls them "bitches" and "whores" who want to "sleep with Prince Ivan." After the hero has left with Ega's horse in Azadovskii's version, the horse tricks her by coming back. Ega has her daughters put a fine saddle on it and sits down to drink tea and admire it. At that moment the horse runs away again and Ega-Egishna chases Prince Ivan in her mortar. In some versions the hero in fact steals the foal, and when Baba Yaga notices this, she chases the hero in her iron mortar. She falls into a fiery river and dies (Afanas'ev 159) or is left on the other side (Novikov 1971 no. 30). After the hero takes the foal as payment, it returns twice at night to its mother for milk, and buries the hero to hide him from Yaga Yaginichna, who comes and tries to kill him (Gorodtsov i: 205–226).

In the *Morphology of the Folktale*, Vladimir Propp coded this episode (the hero's service at Baba Yaga's hut, as found in Afanas'ev 159) as a donor sequence, with the functions no. 12 (the donor tests the hero), 13 (the hero withstands a test), and 14 (the agent is seized). Afanas'ev 159 (like the other "herding mares" tales) is a complex formation. Propp also identifies the immediately preceding episode, when the hero spares animals and acquires them as helpers, as a donor sequence. Thus, there are two donor sequences, one immediately after the other. Without stretching Propp's scheme too much, one might also code the "herding mares" episode with the functions "difficult task" and "resolution," which in fact the difficult task posed by Baba Yaga very much resembles. Not surprisingly, Claude Lévi-Strauss suggested that these two sets of functions (as well as the "struggle" and "victory" functions) might be transformations of each other (1960: 139–140, 142). Propp's definition of Baba Yaga as a hostile donor in this case still seems justified, since the hero has acquired a magic agent (the horse) with which he will rescue his wife from the ogre.

The daughters of Yaga Yaganishna appear as ambiguous donors in Onchukov 2000 Tavda 57, a version of AT 566 (The Three Magic Objects and the Wonderful Fruits). Thirteen soldiers who have run away from the army come to the hut on chicken legs. At night Yaga Yaganishna's thirteen daughters come, and ten of them seduce ten of the soldiers, who vanish. The three soldiers who resist their temptations are rewarded the next morning with magic objects: a sack that produces gold, a stick that produces soldiers, and an invisibility cloak. One of the soldiers then encounters a deceitful woman who gets the objects, but he regains them by selling her berries which cause her to grow horns. Although he has berries that can remove the horns, as soon as he has retrieved the objects, he leaves her with horns. The thirteen Yaga Yaganishna daughters, the night spent at her house, and the threat of female sexuality in this tale all recall AT 327B.

The Hero Deceived and Sent on Deadly Errands

In SUS 465A, The Beautiful Wife (AT 465A, The Quest for the Unknown) a king or tsar desires the hero's beautiful supernatural wife, and sends the hero on a series of deadly errands, including "I know not where" to obtain "I know not what" (which usually turns out to be an invisible magic servant). In Afanas'ev 212 Baba-Yaga is a villain who suggests the difficult tasks to the king's commander. Baba Yaga in Kovalev 9 is a donor who summons fish, beasts, and birds to help the hero find "I know not what." In Mitropol'skaia 36, the hero marries a bird maiden who attracts the tsar's attention when she sews a magnificent carpet decorated with cities, groves, fields, rivers, and the heavenly bodies (this recalls the carpets sewn or woven by the Frog Princess in AT 402). When her husband is faced with the third task, she consults her magic books but finds no answer. She goes to the middle of the sea, summons fish and birds, but they have no advice. The next morning she sends the hero to Baba Yaga, who is her mother, and the hero's mother-in-law. Baba Yaga sends him on to her two sisters. The third Baba Yaga sister takes the hero to an enchanted frog, who carries him over a fiery river to a realm where he obtains the supernatural servant Naum. In the end the tsar is killed, and the hero takes his place. SUS 465B is essentially the same tale. The three donors in Karnaukhova

7 are the wife's aunts: first an old woman in a forest hut, and then Baba Yaga (it is not clear whether these are two Baba Yaga sisters or the same person).

An unusual donor sequence is found in a literary tale, somewhat resembling 465A, from a popular woodblock print (*lubok*) collection of about 1820 (Novikov 1961 no. 5). Baba-Yaga jumps on the hero to devour him alive, but he ties her to a post and beats her with a club. She pleads for mercy and agrees to obtain the princess Dariia. Rushing home with Dariia in her mortar, she throws a brush and a kerchief behind her, which become a forest and a river to block her pursuers (D672, Obstacle flight). Finally, the hero subdues the soldiers chasing Baba-Yaga. He takes Dariia and Baba-Yaga goes home. Nikolai Novikov notes this curious role reversal, when Baba-Yaga obtains the princess herself, rather than advising the hero. Usually Baba-Yaga is the pursuer rather than the one pursued, and magic objects are thrown in her path (Novikov 1961: 349–350).

Deadly tasks are also an important element of SUS 315, The Beasts' Milk (AT 315, The Faithless Sister), where the hero is usually deceived by his sister. In Afanas'ev 204 two Baba Yagas warn the hero that his sister will harm him, and they give him magic objects. He and his sister cross a river and then a dragon appears to the sister as a handsome man. She gets the magic towel from her brother (Baba Yaga had warned him not to let her see it) and lets the dragon cross the river. She pretends to be sick and asks for wolf, bear, and lion milk, and then for flour dust from a mill in the thrice-tenth kingdom, behind twelve locked doors which only open once a year. The hero's animals are caught behind the doors. The dragon prepares to eat the hero upon his return, but the hero asks to take a bath first. Meanwhile, his animals gnaw their way through the doors, arrive, and tear the dragon to pieces. The hero's sister is not deceitful in Afanas'ev 201, but simply abducted by a dragon in the form of a handsome man. The hero comes to Baba Yaga's hut and she instructs him. With his animal helpers the hero kills the dragon and releases his sister.

In Matveeva and Leonova 9 the dragon instructs the hero's sister to send her brother for wolf, bear, and lion milk, and then to Baba Yaga for flour. All the animals and Baba Yaga give him warnings, and Baba Yaga tells him not to stay at the mill too long. He waits too long there, and his animal companions stay behind. They get out of the mill in time to help him kill the dragon. Baba-Yagishna appears as a donor in Potanin 1906 no. 29. She tells the hero where to look for his sister, who has disappeared, and gives him a magic kerchief to cross the sea. Later, his sister uses this kerchief to allow her demon lover Idolishche to come to her. As in other versions, the hero's animals kill the demon, and the hero goes on to slay dragons in another realm (AT 300). The hero's sister has saved her lover's tooth, and uses it to kill her brother. His animals revive him and his sister is shot on a gate. The hero Ivanushko of Simina 18 contends with a wicked stepmother and her demon lover. While the hero's dog goes for medicine beyond nine iron doors (the stepmother says her teeth ache), the demon prepares to eat Ivanushko, who asks to bathe and cool off first. His dog arrives in time to kill the demon. Then Ivanushko marries. His stepmother, now identified as Yagabova, shoves her dead lover's iron tooth into his mouth. Ivanushko dies, but his dog brings him home, where the tooth falls out of his mouth and he comes back to life. The tale ends with no mention of punishment for the wicked Yagabova. In spite of the wedding episode, it seems close to the children's tales because of the principal conflict between the hero and a mother figure, and the threat of being eaten.

In Kulish II: 48–57, the hero is deceived by his mother and her lover, Solovei the Robber (Nightingale the Robber, a villain taken from the Russian folk epic). His mother feigns illness and sends him first for cherries from Baba Yaga. The hero is welcomed by Baba Yaga's daughters, who give him food, but he must fight Baba Yaga. They pound each other into the ground, but the hero wins the encounter and gets the cherries. Finally, his mother tricks him and Solovei cuts him to pieces. At his request they put his remains into a sack and let his horse carry it away. Baba Yaga finds the horse and revives the hero with living and healing water, but Solovei had kept the hero's eyes, so he remains blind. This tale, which also resembles AT 590, The Prince and the Arm Bands, is interesting in its juxtaposition of a wicked real mother with a first hostile, but ultimately kind, Baba Yaga (the opposite of AT 327C/F).

In SUS 318, The Unfaithful Wife (AT 318, The Faithless Wife), the hero's wife betrays him when she finds out about his magic shirt or other object. In Sokolov 55 she goes off to her lover. The hero comes to two Baba-Yagas and a grandmother, who sells him as a horse to the lover. The lover kills the horse, but a maid buries one piece which grows into an apple tree. The lover cuts the tree down, but the maid throws one piece of it into the sea. As a duck the hero lures the lover into the sea, recovers his magic objects, and has him killed. He kills his unfaithful wife and marries the maid who had helped him.

In Sokolov 140, the hero saves a snake-maiden from a fire and is rewarded with a magic shirt. He marries a princess, who takes the shirt and has him killed. His horse carries his remains back to the maiden, who goes to Baba Yaga for living water. Baba Yaga twice tries to deceive the maiden, but the third time shows her the true source of the living water. Then there are disguise and transformation episodes similar to Sokolov 55, ending with revenge on the wife and her lover.

SUS 531, The Little Humpbacked Horse (AT 531, Ferdinand the True and
Ferdinand the False), is often added as a continuing episode to AT 327B, and in
some versions, Baba Yaga appears again in this second part of the tale. After
the hero of Bandarchyk 1971 no. 154 has foiled Baba Yuga's plot to decapitate
him and his brothers, he goes to serve the ruler of another realm. He must
obtain the self-cutting sword and the self-playing gusli (psaltery) from Baba
Yuga. When he flees from Baba Yuga, she chases him on a goat, urging the
goat on with an iron pestle. He fights with her for three hours, kills the goat,
and she has to walk home. The last time, when he fights with Baba Yuga for a
day and a half, he kills her third goat, and she cries out that he has "offended
her forever" (*aharchyw miane navek*). The hero in Chubinskii 1878 no. 8 comes to
a tsar who is Baba Yaga's brother. He must obtain objects from Baba Yaga,
who catches him during his third raid and locks him behind twelve iron doors,
from where his horse releases him. In Potanin 1902 no. 36 the hero's brothers
are jealous of him when he becomes the tsar's confidant. At their instigation,
the hero is sent to fetch the golden cupola from Yagishna's palace and her self-
playing gusli. The hero Karpik and his brothers in Sokolova 1970: 36–40 go to
work in the tsar's stables. The brothers are not happy that Karpik, the youngest,
is giving them orders. The brothers tell the tsar that Karpik wants to get the
self-playing gusli. In the earlier 327B episode, the hero had encountered the
first Baba-Yaga sister, who was a donor and gave him his magic horse; the
horse is also Baba-Yaga's brother. The hero's horse helps him steal the gusli
from Baba-Yaga (the second sister, a villain). Karpik ignores his horse's
warning not to touch the strings of the gusli and alerts Baba-Yaga. She
discovers the hero and recognizes him as the killer of her twenty-one daughters.
He distracts her by telling her that his horse (her brother) is dying, and then
rushes off. With the horse's help he then obtains the Sea Tsarina (*tsaritsa
morskaia*) and her mares, gets rid of the tsar and marries the tsarina, but Baba-
Yaga does not appear again in the tale.

In a version of AT 531 which is not attached to AT 327B, three Baba Yaga
sisters with one, two, and three eyes appear as donors (Matveeva 1984 no. 33).
The three-eyed and youngest Baba Yaga sister, whom the hero visits last, tells
him how to capture the Tsar Maiden. The Tsar Maiden demands that the old
tsar become young. He must jump in three cauldrons: one with cold water, one
with boiling water, and one with boiling milk. The hero is forced to jump in the
cauldrons first, and his horse helps him to survive and emerge handsome. The
tsar tries to do the same but perishes. The Tsar Maiden marries the hero and he
becomes ruler. Nikolai Novikov lists another version of this tale type with a
donor Baba Yaga, unavailable for this survey.

A Tale Derived from Folk Epic and Two Anomalous Tales

Afanas'ev 310 (SUS 650C*, "Il'ia Muromets"; AT 650A, Strong John) is made up of episodes from oral epic poetry (the bylina). (Folktale and bylina elements are also combined in a few bylina texts which feature Baba Yaga; see chapter 6). The hero Il'ia sets out to slay a twelve-headed dragon who torments the princess of a neighboring land. On the way there, Il'ia comes to two huts with Baba-Yaga sisters, who are at first quite hostile. The first tries to decapitate him with a scythe, the second with a sabre. Yet they back down when Il'ia reproaches them.

Manzhura 1890: 51–52 includes a Baba-Yaga donor and villain, and is not easily classified. Baba-Yaga tells the hero how he can win the princess (he hides in her room). The hero promises to obtain red boots for Baba-Yaga. A villain, Ivan Nasmishko, arrives on the scene and claims to have spent the night with the princess. The hero challenges him to produce her ring. Ivan Nasmishko goes to Baba-Yaga, who puts the princess to sleep and obtains the ring in exchange for red boots (the hero had forgotten his promise). Fooled by his wife's apparent infidelity, the hero casts her out. Eventually, she becomes sexton in a church. When the tsar dies, people see that her candle begins to burn by itself, and she is made tsar. She has the hero released from prison, while Ivan Nasmishko and Baba-Yaga are tied to a horse's tail and dragged to death in a field.

Kovalev 11 includes some elements of AT 707. The youngest daughter of a merchant marries a king. Her jealous sisters intercept letters, discard her child, and have her walled up in a stone pillar. The boy child is raised by a poor gardener and grows up with the gardener's daughter. Later, he comes to a castle in a forest and falls in love with a maiden, the daughter of Yaga Yaginishna. In order to marry her, he must build a fine house and obtain three singing leaves. On this quest he breaks an interdiction and turns to stone. The gardener's daughter rescues him and he marries Yaga's daughter. The singing leaves reveal the truth about his mother, and the boy goes to revive her. Ivan Kovalev's treatment of Yaga Yaginishna is not typical: She lives in a castle (*zamok*), and although at first inimical to the hero, does not exhibit any cannibalistic intentions. She seems concerned that the hero may not be a good match for her daughter, but she even gives him money to build the fine house. Ivan Kovalev displays a fair amount of psychological realism in the hero's encounter with Yaga Yaginishna.

> The king's son also pleased the beautiful young woman, but she said, "Well, but what will my mother, Yaga Yaginishna, say about this."
>
> And an hour had not gone by when Yaga Yaginishna flew into the castle and got so angry at the king's son that the poor young man didn't know what to do. But the daughter

reproached her mother, saying, "Mother, is it really forbidden for any young men to come visit me here in our castle? After all, I get bored here alone, and I've taken a real liking to him." When Yaga Yaginishna calmed down she asked him, "Who are you, and where do you come from?"... "I'll let you marry her, but you must plant three singing leaves in your garden, because I've heard that they grow somewhere, they sing and play very well, and no one has ever found such music." "And where are they?" the king's son asked her. "I have no way of knowing. You have to find them yourself." (Kovalev 1941: 92)

The Hero Searches for His Lost Wife

Baba Yaga appears ambiguously in SUS 400/2, The Tsar Maiden (AT 400, The Man on a Quest for His Lost Wife), another subtype of the tale about a man in search of his lost supernatural wife (see chapter 4 for the discussion of SUS 400/1). The hero is put to sleep, usually with a needle, when his supernatural wife comes to visit him. Two versions conclude with AT 302, when the hero kills an ogre by crushing his death egg, and three include an interesting variation on this motif, where the egg is associated with the supernatural wife.

In Zhivaia Starina 21 [1912]: 365–386, Prince Ivan and the Cat's Son are born when their mothers eat a magic fish. The Cat's Son is jealous when Ivan wins the supernatural maiden, and seeks the help of a Yaga-Baba, who gives him the sleep-inducing needle. The hero is aided by animal brothers-in-law, and retrieves his betrothed from Kashshei by finding Kashshei's death egg. The tsarevna of a distant realm in Sadovnikov 61 agrees to marry the hero and says he must stay awake until she arrives. A servant girl pricks the hero's head with a needle when the tsarevna arrives so that he falls asleep. The hero wakes up and sets out to find the tsarevna. He comes to two huts on chicken shins, and the elder Yagaia Baba tells him that the tsarevna has been married to Kot Bezsmertnyi (Immortal Cat, derived no doubt from Koshchei the Immortal). As with Koshchei, the hero finally manages to kill Kot by obtaining his death egg and crushing it.

A wicked stepmother in Afanas'ev 232 tries to prevent the hero from meeting his betrothed. The narrator explicitly states that the stepmother is in love with her stepson. She has a servant put Ivan to sleep when the Tsar Maiden comes to meet him. The hero sets out and comes to the huts of two Baba-Yagas, who direct him on to their *younger* sister. The second Baba Yaga warns him that her younger sister will want to eat him and that he must blow on three horns there. The hero blows on three horns while the youngest Baba Yaga goes to sharpen her teeth, and birds come flying in from all directions. The firebird carries him away in time and leaves him at the seashore. This episode heightens Baba Yaga's ambiguity even as a donor, and is reminiscent of the cannibal ogress Baba Yaga found in SUS 327C/F. The hero then comes to a hut by the sea where an old woman (*staraia starukha*) lives. She tells him that the Tsar Maiden no longer loves him. Her daughter lives with the Tsar Maiden, and at the old woman's request she finds out where the Tsar Maiden's love (*liubov*) is hidden. The hero must obtain an egg which is inside a duck, inside a hare, inside a chest, on an oak in the sea. After the hero obtains the egg, the old woman cooks it and serves it to the Tsar Maiden, who comes to celebrate her saint's name day. The Tsar Maiden eats the egg and loves the hero again. They return to his kingdom and are married.

In Smirnov 130, the stepmother (a Yagibaba) has her son put the hero to sleep when he meets his bride for a second and third time. The hero comes to three huts with old women. The third is a Yagibaba and also his wife's godmother. The hero hides when his wife comes to visit this Yagibaba. Questioned by Yagibaba, she says she will love him again if he obtains her heart (*serdcho*), which is nested inside an egg, a duck, and a mare's head, all inside an oak. The hero obtains the egg and Yagibaba serves it to his wife, who regains her love for him. Yagibaba brings the hero out from hiding. The two return to his realm, and the wicked stepmother is shot (see Appendix I: Selected Tale Texts).

Balashov 57 also has a Yaga-Baba as wicked stepmother. While hunting, the hero spares a duck who turns out to be Marfa-tsarevna. Yaga-Baba's son puts the hero to sleep with a needle when Marfa returns. The hero goes off and stops at three huts on chicken legs where old women donors tell him they are Marfa's aunts. Directed by them, the hero is able to obtain the egg inside a duck which contains Marfa's sorrow (*toska*). Marfa comes to visit the third aunt, eats the duck, and "remembers" the hero, who then goes to live with her.

The hero in Novikov 1961 no. 6 angers his father when he declares he has found a woman more beautiful than his mother, namely the Tsar Maiden. First the tsar orders his son killed, but then lets him depart with the Tsar Maiden. The hero falls asleep (this time quite naturally, it seems) and the Tsar Maiden cannot wake him. She leaves him a warning against staying with Baba-Èga. Then the hero sets off and stays the night with Baba-Èga. He refuses to say where he is going, but his servant reveals the secret (Baba-Èga promises the servant her second daughter in return). At Baba-Èga's instigation, the servant puts the hero to sleep with a needle. He sleeps through a visit by the Tsar Maiden, who leaves him another message. The hero kills his servant in front of Baba-Èga's house. After acquiring a lion helper, the hero arrives in the Tsar Maiden's realm just as she is to be married. He works for the palace cook, bakes a pie which depicts his adventures, and is recognized by the Tsar Maiden, who marries him. This final episode is striking. It is a masculine version of AT 313C, The Forgotten Fiancée, but it may be the invention of a literate editor, since this tale is taken from a collection of literary fairy tales, *Skazki moego dedushki* (*My Grandfather's Tales*, 1820). The motif of the ogre's heart (or in Koshchei's case, death) in the egg has been explained as the remnant of beliefs about a separable soul. Clearly, the egg contains Koshchei's life force, but the egg containing the spouse's heart, love, or sorrow suggests that the egg might also represent deep-seated emotions. (Bengt Holbek has suggested that the ogre's heart in the egg represents the oedipal attachment between father and daughter, which the hero must overcome; 1987: 425–426, 508). The association of the magic egg with the maiden's heart, love, or sorrow appears to be a secondary development of this motif in East Slavic tradition, and in fact it may be unique to the East Slavic tradition. Baba Yaga's donor role in these tales is that of mediator between the hero and his supernatural wife, as in AT 551.

Running from the Ogre

In SUS 313 A, B, C, The Magic Flight (AT 313, The Girl as Helper in the Hero's Flight), the hero confronts an ogre, and Baba Yaga is most often a donor. The East Slavic versions of this tale are complex, and include three protagonists: the hero's father, the hero, and his supernatural wife (the heroine). There is one version of this tale which only mentions Baba Yaga's name, where a person is said to be as stingy as Baba Yaga (Matveeva 1981 no. 17).

The tale sometimes begins when an eagle is wounded in a dispute with other animals (SUS 222B*, AT 222, War of Birds and Quadrupeds). A man comes and three times intends to kill the eagle, who asks to be spared. Then, the eagle carries the man up in the air on its back three times, and drops him. The eagle catches him before he falls to the ground, as a lesson to the man: The man learns what the eagle felt when faced with death. Later, the eagle takes the man to his three sisters. The first two refuse to give the man the gift the eagle tells him to ask for. The third sister gives the man a basket, chest, or box. He is told not to open the box until he comes home (AT 537, The Marvelous Eagle Gives the Hero a Box). He opens it prematurely and a palace, city, army, or herd of cattle comes out. The man cannot get these objects back inside the box, and an old man with a long beard (Sokolov 66), a man from the sea (Afanas'ev 219), the Tsar Water-Spirit Grandfather with an iron nose (*Tsar'-Vodianoi dedushka*, Kovalev 10), the Sea Tsar (*Morskoi tsar'*, Morokhin and Vardugin 1993: 77–80), or a heathen tsar (*Tsar' Nekreshchenyi lob*, Afanas'ev 224) offers to do so in exchange for "what you do not know at home" (*chego doma ne znaesh'*).

In other versions the man (a merchant or tsar) is traveling abroad and stoops to drink from a river or lake. Satan (*sotana*, Zelenin Viatka 118), the devil (*chert*, Simina 11), the Water Tsar (*vodianoi tsar'*, Smirnov 281), the Sea Tsar Tokman

Tokmanych, who is tall as a fingernail, with a beard a cubit long (*Sam s nokot',
boroda s lokot', Tokman Tokmanych morskoi tsar'*, Zelenin Perm' 55), or a dragon
(*Chudo-Iudo Bezzakonnyi*, Afanas'ev 225) grabs him by the beard and forces him
to relinquish what he does not know at home, or otherwise deceives him into
giving it up. In one version a tsar has been at war in a foreign land for twelve
years. A magician (*volshebnik*) offers to end the war in exchange for "what has
been found at your house without you" (*chto bez tebia doma nashlos'*, Gromov 3).

The man returns home to find that his wife has given birth to a son. After a
time the son (the hero) leaves. When Baba Yaga is a donor, the son sets out and
comes to Baba Yaga, or two or three Baba Yaga sisters, who may give him gifts,
but most importantly give him instructions (Afanas'ev 219, 224, 225,
Bagizbaeva 20, Chernyshev 63, Erlenvein 6, Gromov 3, Kovalev 10, Morokhin
and Vardugin 1993: 77–80, Potanin 1906 no. 38, Simina 11, Smirnov 281,
Sokolov 66, Zelenin Perm' 55, Zelenin Perm' p. 293, Zelenin Viatka 118).
Bagizbaeva 20 includes a very unusual interaction between the young man and
Baba Yaga, told by a male narrator, K. I. Sasin:

> He walked and walked and wandered up to Baba Yaga's house. Baba Yaga saw him and
> said "I will eat you." The youth answered, "Grandmother, let me clean up your house, I'll
> make your supper and put you to bed." Said and done. Baba Yaga liked the youth and told
> him, "Because you take such good care of things, you can ask me for anything you want."
> (Bagizbaeva 1991: 378)

The hero comes to a lake or the sea. Birds fly down, become maidens, and
bathe. He steals the clothes of one of the maidens. The others fly away, and the
last maiden promises to marry the hero (cf. motifs D361.1, Swan Maiden,
K1335, Seduction [or wooing] by stealing clothes of bathing girl, and tale type
AT 465, The Man Persecuted Because of His Beautiful Wife). Baba Yaga's role
is expanded in Smirnov 281, where she becomes a mediator between the hero
and the supernatural maiden. After the hero has stolen the duck maiden's shirt,
he returns to Baba Yaga's house and hides behind her oven. Baba Yaga makes
the maiden promise to marry the one who returns her shirt.

The hero comes to the dwelling of an ogre, who is also the maiden's father.
The ogre sets impossible tasks for him under pain of death, usually to be
accomplished overnight: He must clear a forest, plough, plant and harvest
wheat, and grind flour for a pie; tame a wild horse; build a flying ship, a self-
driving carriage, a church, a garden, or a crystal bridge; fashion a rope from
sand; recognize the heroine from among her (often twelve) identically dressed
sisters. On the way to church to marry the sorcerer's daughter, apple trees must
blossom; on the way home, the apples must ripen (Bagizbaeva 20).

The maiden (the heroine) accomplishes the tasks and tells the hero how to recognize her. They marry and decide to flee. The heroine spits into the corners of their room, and when the ogre sends for them, her spit answers. When their absence is finally made known, the ogre's servants pursue them. The heroine disguises herself and the hero in various forms: shepherd and sheep, priest and church, well with water and a ladle, lake with a duck or fish, garden and cabbage, or the sky with moon and stars. In some tales the ogre himself carries out the third pursuit and bursts when he tries to drink up the lake. In some versions the heroine throws magic objects (comb, brush, towel), which turn into a forest, mountain, and fiery river to block the pursuers (D672, Obstacle flight).

They return to the hero's home. In many versions the heroine tells him not to kiss a certain family member, but he forgets this interdiction and does so (AT 313C, The Forgotten Fiancée). In Krasnozhenova 19, the heroine tells him not to kiss the newborn sister "he does not yet know." He forgets about his wife, and his family finds a bride for him. On the wedding day the heroine appears and bakes a pie, which is brought to the wedding table. Doves fly out of the pie and remind the hero of the heroine. They are reunited. In most versions a dove or doves serve to remind the hero of his wife. In Afanas'ev 225 the heroine drops blood into the pie to make doves fly out of it. The heroine Alena in Chernyshev 63 uses doves to make the hero remember her, but also causes fires to go out on the day of his wedding. The heroine of Krasnozhenova 19 foils the attempts of a captain, a colonel, and a general to spend the night with her; they bring the hero to see her, and he remembers.[6]

In Krasnozhenova 19, Baba Yaga is both donor and villain. The hero comes to two huts on chicken legs, and then to the brother of the two Baba-Yaga sisters. Later, when he flees with his wife from Koshchei, they are chased by a Baba-Yaga riding a broom.

Yagaia Baba and her husband Tsar Doroda are villains in Sadovnikov 1, which begins with AT 300A. After slaying a dragon, the hero Ivashka Belaia Rubashka Gor'kii P'ianitsa (Ivashka White Shirt Bitter Drunkard) is chased by a giant cat (the dragon's mother) and takes refuge in a smithy. The smiths seize the cat and pound it into a horse, and tell the hero to greet all those he meets. He fails to greet a maiden with snot running from her nose, and she reproaches him. He apologizes and she warns him about Tsar Doroda. The hero then encounters Tsar Doroda and loses a race with him, even though one of the tsar's legs is shorter than the other. He comes home with Doroda and is given tasks typical for AT 313: He must recognize Doroda's one daughter from a

[6] This tale appears in English translation in Haney 2001: 121–133, no. 175.

previous marriage from among twelve identical daughters, recognize her chamber, and build a church and then a bridge overnight. Doroda's daughter helps him and they are married. Each time he assigns a task, Doroda consults with his second wife, Yagaia Baba. She recognizes that her stepdaughter, whom she calls a whore, has accomplished the tasks. She then goes twice to the newlyweds and demands a meal. They cook a ram and a bull for her, which she completely devours. The hero's wife disguises him as a needle and a coal, which Yagaia Baba almost discovers. Then they decide to flee and are pursued three times. First, Yagaia Baba sends her daughter who returns empty-handed when she cannot cross a forest the hero's wife has created. The second time, she sends her husband Doroda, who is fooled by their disguise as a church (the hero) and sexton (his wife). The third time, Yagaia Baba comes after them herself in her iron mortar and recognizes them as two ducks swimming in a milk lake with custard banks. They kiss each other to annoy her, and she begins drinking the lake and eating the banks until she bursts.

An interesting variation in the episode of the difficult tasks appears in Potanin 1906 no. 38, recorded in Siberia. The second task assigned to the hero by the one-eyed devil Erakhta is to plant and harvest flax and weave a napkin overnight. Rather than accomplishing this by magic, the maiden (in this tale she is not identified as the ogre's daughter) responds with a clever counterdemand: She pulls three twigs from a broom and tells the messenger that the ogre should make a plough, harrow, and loom from the twigs for them. This response recalls folktale heroines who have clever answers for riddles, as in AT 875 (The Clever Peasant Girl). It also recalls the beautiful legend of the Saints Peter and Fevroniia of Murom, who were canonized in 1547. The literary legend, which owes a great deal to folklore, was composed in the 1540s–1550s by the Moscow priest Ermolai-Erazm, who might have intended it as a parable about the moral testing and growth of a human being (Demkova 1997, Haney 1979). A dragon or serpent takes the appearance of Prince Paul and seduces his wife. She manages to find out from the dragon that he can only be killed by the hand of Peter, Paul's brother.[7] Peter slays the dragon and its blood spatters him, covering him with wounds and making him ill. Only the peasant woman Fevroniia is able to heal his wounds. When she first appears in the legend, she speaks to the prince's messenger in riddles. As a reward for healing the prince, she wants to marry him. He tries to avoid marrying her, and requests that she weave a shirt, pants, and towel from a bundle of linen while he is taking a bath. She responds by sending him a small block of wood and asking him to make a loom from this block.

---

[7] This recalls the moment in AT 302 when the hero's wife, now the captive of Koshchei the Immortal, manages to find out from him the secret of where his death is located.

Five versions of this tale with Baba Yaga depart significantly from the typical outline of AT 313 by including elements of other tale types, often to the point where classification is difficult or impossible. In Balashov 95, a tsar's son and daughter leave before the devil comes for them. Three Baba-Yagas give them stones and paper, which become mountains and a fiery river which the devil cannot cross (Obstacle flight). The sister finds the devil handsome and then ferries him across (this recalls AT 315). Animals save the hero's life, kill the devil, help the hero rescue a princess, and revive her after the sister kills her on her wedding night.

Mints and Savushkina 11 partially recalls AT 707, The Three Golden Sons. An envious midwife puts the hero to sea. Another midwife later sends him on dangerous tasks, finally telling him to marry one of Koshchei's daughters. He is directed onward by Baba Yaga, and then Elena, the wisest daughter of Koshchei, tells him how to recognize her among her sisters. They escape from Koshchei and return to the hero's father, who recognizes his children. The woman who told this tale gave the third disguise-transformation an interesting twist: Elena disguises herself as a priest, while the hero is disguised as the priest's wife.

Zelenin Viatka 13 begins with a mouse and sparrow's quarrel and the eagle kept for three years. The eagle and its keeper fly to three Egibobas. The first two are the eagle's sisters, while the third is the eagle's mother. The eagle itself turns into a beautiful Egibisna, and the hero stays to live there. Eventually, the hero wanders into a prohibited field and remembers his home. He is then carried against his will to an ogre (Idol Poganoi), who demands that he obtain a foreign princess for him. With the aid of companions with magic abilities (AT 513) the hero obtains the princess, who tricks the ogre into a fiery pit and marries the hero.

Cattle appear when the hero breaks an interdiction and opens a magic book in Bandarchyk 1973 no. 23. The magician who gave him the book appears as a wolf and threatens to eat him, but spares him when he promises never to marry. When the hero finally does marry, the magician appears and chases him. The hero flees and takes refuge with three Baba Yaga sisters. The third sister gives him a kerchief which becomes a bridge. The hero crosses the sea, but his pursuer falls in and drowns.

Nikiforov 1936 no. 6 is a complex tale beginning with a man who must give his son and daughter to the devil. The hero's sister is deceitful and tries to kill him (as in AT 315), and the tale includes a dragon-slaying episode. Most interesting for us are the two Baba-Yagabova sisters. The first is an unwilling donor. She and the hero fight to see who will eat whom; she loses and feeds the hero and his companions. She later gives him a flying carpet, while the second Yagabova directs him to the next kingdom.

AT 313 is a very complex tale, containing many episodes and variations. James Taggart has provided an insightful analysis of this tale type as told in rural Spain. In that context the episode with the ogre and his tasks could be understood as the difficulties a young man faced in approaching his future father-in-law and proving himself worthy as a husband (Taggart 1990: 165–199). In the Russian context this interpretation has to be modified, since young people in rural communities for most of the nineteenth century were not free to choose their marriage partner. Marriages were arranged by the parents, who took the initiative in beginning negotiations.

Besides conflict with a father-in-law, in the Russian context the episode with the ogre-father might also represent a man's conflict with his own father. The father-son relationship might be particularly difficult if a man remained in his father's household after marriage. A man still remained under the firm authority of his father and reportedly would not even dare to purchase a small gift for his wife without his father's permission (Kosven 1963: 74). One remarkable form of despotism on the part of the household head was a form of incest known as *snokhachestvo* (from *snokha*, "daughter-in-law"). Household heads had sexual relations with their sons' wives, sometimes sending their married sons to work outside the community or having them marry before they were sent away for military service. The daughter-in-law was powerless to resist her father-in-law's advances, and in some cases she might even react favorably toward them, since this situation would improve her standing in the extended family. This practice appears to have been fairly widespread. In the central Volga region in the nineteenth century, there were on average one to two families in medium-sized villages where this occurred (Busygin et al. 1973: 101–102). While *snokhachestvo* may not have been the norm, it certainly illustrates the despotic and unlimited power of a family head to dispose of the lives of family members. Despotism and abuses of power of various kinds by the family head, which must have been commonly experienced, would give special meaning to the figure of a sadistic folktale ogre or father figure who seizes the heroine and tries to have the hero killed.

Some degree of father-son conflict might also be present in the first part of the tale, when the hero's father also confronts an evil father figure, the supernatural being (always male) who tricks him into giving away his child. Castration imagery is explicit in some versions (Afanas'ev 224, 225, Krasnozhenova 19, Sokolov 66) when the impossible tasks assigned to the hero must be accomplished overnight, under threat of being beheaded, or when the hero sees the heads of unfortunate previous visitors outside the ogre's palace.

The accomplishment of difficult tasks in one night has a parallel in some East and South Slavic rituals, which might be based on a magical conception of "compressed time" (see chapter 3).

The episode in which the hero forgets about the heroine by kissing one of his family is not difficult to interpret from the point of view of a young woman entering her husband's extended family household: She must compete with her mother-in-law and other in-laws for his affection and loyalty, and it might indeed often have seemed to a young bride that her husband had "forgotten" her. Discussing a French version of AT 313, Michèle Simonsen notes that this fairy tale shows women in a particularly "prestigious light," while the young man does not show himself to be very capable. Nevertheless, she concludes that it is a male-centered tale, with a meaning for a young man that "the problem of one's relation to one's father and to work requires recourse to femininity and to the supernatural; but both femininity and the supernatural, fascinating as they may be, must be controlled in the end" (Simonsen 1985: 36). Isabel Cardigos disagrees with this view, and finds that this tale is in fact a "marriage" of female- and male-centered tale types (1996: 163).

Although the young man in AT 313 is usually considered the hero or protagonist of this fairy tale, and although he is married in his own realm at the end of the tale (whereas his spouse has given up her realm), the East Slavic versions are complex and in fact present three potential heroes at different points in the narrative: the father in the first episode, who gives away what he does not know at home and is reminded of his mortality by the eagle; the young man; and the ogre's daughter, who is very powerful but forgotten by her fiancé. The East Slavic form of this tale appears to be a dialogue not just between men and women, but also between generations; both the father and the son confront the ogre. The hero comes from this world and his conflict with his father (or father-in-law, or a condensation of the two) is played out in the other world, with the antagonist represented by a supernatural ogre. The heroine is herself a supernatural being, but by the end of the tale has entered the human world of the hero. In most of the versions here she does not use magic to awaken the hero's memory. Her conflict involves the hero's family, and is not symbolically disguised. This tale is particularly rich, and allows for listeners to identify with three different characters and situations: the father and his anxieties about paternity, or his feeling of being distant and removed from the birth of a child (the motif of "not knowing"); his irrevocable mistake of opening the chest too soon and thereby giving his son to the supernatural being; the young man and his struggle against the ogre-father, and his fears about accomplishing his life tasks; and the young woman, who must somehow regain the affection she has lost. The theme of memory and forgetting is important, and not only to the heroine. The father forgets about his wife and home during his sojourn with the eagle. In Krasnozhenova 19 the eagle reminds him of his home; in Zelenin Viatka 13 the hero remembers his home when he wanders into a prohibited field while seemingly married to the eagle Egibisna. Both the father and the son "forget," and in Krasnozhenova 19 both of them do "not know" something at home: the father his son, and the son his sister. In each case the loss of memory (and "not knowing") is also the loss of an affective bond.

Female power is conspicuous in this tale. The heroine or her helpers accomplish the difficult tasks set for the hero. In Sokolov 66, Mar'ia puts Ivan to sleep by sticking a pin in his head (usually this action is performed by villains), telling him that the task will be completed by the next morning. Besides the usual proverb that "the morning is wiser than the evening," she also states that the "mare is bolder than the gelding: [she] draws a cart and bears foals" (*utro vechera mudreniae, kobyla merina udaliae: vozku vozit i zherebiat nosit,* Sokolov 1915: 123). According to M. M. Larina, the female narrator of Gromov 3, the magician father was particularly angry at his daughter because she was "wiser" than he, that is to say, had greater magic power (*rasserdilsia na dochku, chto ona mudrei ego,* Gromov 1952: 262). There is only scant information about informants, but the tale was apparently recorded from women about as often as from men.

A Woman Searches for Her Lost Husband

Tales where an adult female heroine encounters Baba Yaga often concern the heroine's separation from her fiancé or spouse. As a donor Baba Yaga helps the heroine find and regain her husband; as a villain, she tries to separate or estrange the two.

SUS 425A, Amor and Psyche, and 425C, The Scarlet Flower (AT 425, The Search for the Lost Husband), is a very widespread tale, often referred to as the Tale of Cupid and Psyche, after the famous literary version of Apuleius from the second century A.D. Oral versions have been recorded throughout Europe, in the Near East, and in parts of Asia and Africa, as well as in the New World (Swahn 1955). This tale concerns a woman's loss and recovery of her husband. In the Russian versions of interest to us, Baba Yaga emerges in a particularly ambiguous light. She is a donor (Khudiakov 40, Matveeva and Leonova 15, Razumova 78, Razumova and Sen'kina 1974 no. 67) and a villain (Balashov 33, 59, Onchukov 178, Onchukov 2000 Shokshozero 69, Onegina 59, Razumova and Sen'kina 1982 no. 21). In Balashov 88 she is both donor and villain.

There are several different opening episodes. The heroine's brother promises to find her a husband, and a carriage or sled comes for her (Onegina 59,

Razumova and Sen'kina 1982 no. 21). Her father is forced to give her to a supernatural spouse (Balashov 88, Onchukov 178, Razumova 78). The spouse comes to her after her parents die (Balashov 59). In Razumova and Sen'kina 1974 no. 67 an old man catches a crayfish, who wants to marry the tsar's daughter and manages to accomplish overnight the tasks the tsar sets for him. The heroine in Balashov 33 picks a louse from her father's hair. The louse grows to be very large, and the heroine's father offers her in marriage to any man who can guess where the louse skin comes from. A young man enchanted as a bear guesses and marries the heroine. At night he turns into a man. In Onchukov 2000 Shokshozero 69 the third son Ivan changes his skin to appear handsome, and the tsar's daughter chooses to marry him.

The heroine breaks an interdiction and her supernatural husband disappears. She is told that she may light a match to look at the mysterious night visitor, but she must be careful not to burn any hairs (copper, silver, or gold) on his head. Or she must not tell her family that the golden head or the crayfish is in fact a young man. She lights a match and inadvertently burns a few of the spouse's hairs or tells her family that her spouse in fact becomes a man at night. The heroine burns her husband's bear skin (Balashov 33), or hides his skin (Onchukov 2000 Shokshozero 69). The supernatural spouse disappears. The heroine goes to a smithy to get three iron staves, three pairs of iron shoes, three iron hats, or other iron objects. She comes to three huts on chicken legs where three female donors live, either grandmothers (*babushki*), old women (*starukhi*), or Baba Yaga sisters. The donors give her golden objects (distaff, spindle, reel).

The heroine comes to the place where her spouse is. Following the donor's instructions, she trades the three golden objects (or her own embroidery, Balashov 33) for three successive nights with her spouse. On the third night she manages to wake her spouse and he recognizes her. They dispose of the villain and return home. In Balashov 33, 59, and Onegina 59, Baba Yaga pursues the couple, and they throw objects behind them which become various obstacles and finally a fiery river which Baba Yaga cannot cross or in which she is burned (D672, Obstacle flight).

The differences between the versions of this tale are of particular interest because of Baba Yaga's changing role of donor and villain. The villains in some tales are Baba Yaga (Balashov 33 and 59), Yagivovna (Onchukov 178), Egi-Baba's daughter and the niece of the three old women donors (Onchukov 2000 Shokshozero 69), Gigibibikha (Onegina 59), and Yagi-Baba (Razumova and Sen'kina 1982 no. 21). In Razumova and Sen'kina 1974 no. 67 the donors are three Yaga-Baba sisters, while the villain is the sister of Rak Rakovich (Crayfish Son of Crayfish), the heroine's supernatural spouse. In Matveeva and Leonova 15, the donors are three Yaga Yagishnia sisters, but her rival is the third Yaga

Yagishnia's daughter, with whom Prince Ivan has already had a child. Similarly, in Razumova 78, the heroine encounters a series of donors: an old woman, Baba-Yaga, her sister Babushka-Yaga, and their third sister, simply called Babushka ("grandmother"). Prince Ivan is about to marry the third sister's daughter.

Balashov 88 is the most striking example of ambiguity. The heroine is aided by three Baba Yaga sisters, while another Baba Yaga has taken control of her spouse, Prince Ivan. It is interesting to observe how the narrator of this version (the sixty-two-year-old Marina D'iachkova) names the villain and donors. The donors in the three huts on a chicken leg and a rooster's head are called 1. *baba-iaga kostianaia noga* (Baba-Yaga Bony Leg), *starukha, starushka* (old woman); 2. *baba-iaga kostianaia noga, starukha*; 3. *starushka, baba-iaga tret'ia* (the third Baba-Yaga), *babushka* (grandmother). The first time the villain is mentioned, she is called *baba-iaga*, the second time *iaga-baba*, the third and fourth times *iagisnia*, and and the following twelve times *iagishnia*. After the appearance of the villain, the third Baba Yaga donor becomes a grandmother "behind the courtyard" (*babushka-zadvorenka*). The "Bony Leg" epithet is reserved for the donors, and as soon as the villain appears on the scene, the remaining donor changes her name. Likewise, the name of the villain changes to the distinct forms *iagisnia* and *iagishnia*. While these changes in name are meant to clarify the distinction between the villain and the donor Baba Yaga sisters, they also reveal how close the two are, or that they share the same essence. In the name changes of the villain, who begins as Baba Yaga (potentially like her donor sisters) and finishes as Yagishnia (the villain), a shifting between a potential donor and a villain takes place "before our eyes."

In several versions the villain is Baba Yaga, while the villain of Razumova and Sen'kina 1974 no. 67 is the heroine's sister-in-law, the sister of her husband Rak Rakovich (Crayfish Son of Crayfish). This suggests that Baba Yaga the villain in this context might represent a member of the husband's family who is a rival for the husband's affection. In traditional Russian peasant culture, a young woman usually moved to her husband's household, and the principal female rival she faced was likely to be her mother-in-law.

The East Slavic tale-type index lists Khudiakov 40 under type 425C, although it departs from its general outline. The opening episode recalls AT 559, The Princess Who Would Not Laugh. Only a jumping dog is able make the heroine laugh (all the suitors had failed), so she must marry it. At night the dog becomes a man, but the heroine's father burns the dog skin and puts knives on the window sill (as in AT 432, see below). The husband must leave, he hurts himself on the knives, and the heroine must seek him after three years. The heroine comes to three huts on chicken legs. Baba Yaga sisters live in the first and third huts, while the second is inhabited by a kind woman. They give the heroine gifts, and she comes upon maidens who have been trying without success to wash the blood from a shirt for three years. The heroine immediately succeeds in washing the blood away, and her husband (who has remarried and has a boy child) recognizes her when he hears about this feat.[8] They do not let others know their secret. The boy wants to play with the brush, plate, and ball, and so the heroine obtains the right to stand at the foot of her husband's bed for two nights. She tells him she has been searching for three years, and after the second night he leaves his second wife and returns with her. In this case the poetics of the folktale are stronger than the demands of logic or "realism." Even though her husband has recognized her, she still performs the difficult task and trades her objects.

Our one example of SUS 430, The Donkey Husband (AT 430, The Ass; Kozhemiakina 1973: 105–110), presents donor and villain Yaga figures in the same tale, which resembles AT 425. In this version the tsar's third daughter dreams of a goat and so must marry one. When she is invited to parties by her sisters, she goes alone, but a young man appears later. One evening she slaps him and comes home to find that he is in fact her husband and must now depart for the thrice-ninth kingdom. She sets out to find him and comes to three Yaga Yagonishna sisters, who give her golden objects. They tell her that Ivan is living with their sister. The heroine trades the golden objects for three nights with Ivan, and on the third night she combs his hair, dislodging the pin that kept him asleep. Ivan sets Yaga Yagonishna on the gate and shoots her.

SUS 432, Finist the Bright Falcon (AT 432, The Prince as Bird), tells of the heroine's search for her lost husband, the "bright falcon." A man goes to the fair and asks his three daughters what he should bring for them. The two elder daughters ask for clothes, but the youngest asks for the feather of Fenist (Finist, Fefelist, Feni, Fifilisno) the Bright Falcon. The father brings her the feather or obtains it from a donor. Some versions introduce an element of SUS 425C when the heroine asks her father for a scarlet flower (Kabashnikaw 1989 no. 99, Kovalev 13).[9] Fenist flies to visit the youngest daughter at night. In

---

[8] This recognition motif (only the heroine is able to wash blood from a shirt) also occurs in Hungarian versions of AT 425 (Dégh 1995: 140), where the heroine drops blood on her husband's shirt and places a curse on the stain. The narrator of Khudiakov 40 does not include any such explanation, but this image is certainly suggestive of menstruation, and perhaps the magic power of female blood.

[9] The scarlet flower requested by the heroine recalls words or phrases used in Slavic folk tradition to designate menstruation; in many cases these include some form of the terms "flower," "blossoming," or "red." The flower as a symbol of menstruation dates back at least to the medieval period; it appears in the thirteenth-century confession manual of the Cistercian monk Rudolph, described in chapter 3. Rudolph describes and discredits a magic practice used by

some versions the feather also supplies her with magnificent clothes which she wears to mass, where her sisters recognize her only the third time (Afanas'ev 235, Mints et al. 1957 no. 21, Zelenin Perm' 67, Zelenin Viatka 74). The sisters eavesdrop on her meeting with Fenist and put knives, swords, or needles in the window. The next time Fenist flies in he injures himself and flies away, telling the heroine she must search for him in a distant realm.

The heroine has a smith forge iron shoes, staves, caps, and wafers for her and sets off. She comes to three Baba Yaga sisters, who give her golden and silver objects (distaff, spindle, reel, comb, apples, bracelets, ring, dish and egg, a golden hammer and diamond nails, a magic horse) and instructions (Afanas'ev 235, Kabashnikaw 1989 no. 99, Kargin 21, Khudiakov 39, Korol'kova 1969: 152–166, Kovalev 13, Mints et al. 1957 no. 21, Novikov 1971 no. 44, Vedernikova and Samodelova 42). She comes to the place where Fenist is. He has married or is about to marry another woman.

On three days in succession the heroine goes to a place where Fenist's new wife or her servants will see her. She displays one of her golden and silver objects. Fenist's wife wants to buy it, but the heroine will exchange it only for a night with Fenist. His wife agrees to the bargain. The heroine tries to wake Fenist but cannot, because his wife has had him drink wine or has pricked him with a magic needle which keeps him from waking. On the third night she manages to wake him and they return home. In some versions Fenist has the treacherous second wife killed (Afanas'ev 235, Khudiakov 39, Tumilevich 21), and sometimes he calls together advisers who tell him to take the wife who bought him, not the one who sold him (Afanas'ev 235, Korol'kova 1969: 152–166, Khudiakov 39, Novikov 1971 no. 44). In two versions (Kabashnikaw 1989 no. 99, Vedernikova and Samodelova 42) the heroine's burning tear falls on Finis or Finist and wakes him up.

Korol'kova's version departs from the above outline in that she repeats the search episode a second time, while Kovalev adds a unique episode. In his version the heroine arrives at the hut of the third Baba Yaga and must herd her stallions for three days successfully before receiving the golden objects. No doubt Kovalev was influenced by the male-centered tales in which the hero herds Baba-Yaga's mares, discussed above.

Egibisna appears as the villain in one version (Zelenin Viatka 74) where the donors are three grandmothers and Fifilisno is about to marry Egibisna's

---

(presumably Slavic) women in Upper Silesia to avoid pregnancy: "They toss what they call their flower onto the elder tree, saying, 'You carry for me, and I will blossom for you.' Nevertheless the tree blossoms, and she gives birth to a child in pain" [*Quiddam, quod florem suum vocant, in arborem sambuci mittunt dicentes: Porta tu pro me, ego floream pro te. Non tamen minus arbor floret et ipsa parit puerum cum dolore*] (Agapkina 2000: 152, 177, Karwot 1955: 27).

daughter. Explicit ambiguity is found in Tumilevich 21, where the donors are two Baba-Yaga sisters and their elder sister Proskunchikha, while Feni the Falcon has married a Baba-Yaga. In Zelenin Perm' 67 the first Baba-Yaga tells the heroine that the Bright Falcon is to marry another Baba-Yaga's granddaughter. The second Baba-Yaga gives her a golden distaff, silver spindle, golden pails, and a jug. The third Baba-Yaga wants to buy the golden objects. The heroine obtains three nights with the Falcon and wakes him the third night. The two flee from Baba-Yaga, blocking her way by throwing a brush behind them which becomes a forest, and a flint which becomes a fiery river in which Baba-Yaga drowns (D672, Obstacle flight; see Appendix I: Selected Tale Texts).

The name Fenist and its various forms derive from *feniks* (phoenix), the legendary bird known in Rus' by the thirteenth century. The name most likely entered folklore from a written source (Kolesov 1979, Korepova 1982: 8). V. V. Kolesov believes that the name of the phoenix was added to the falcon in this tale in order to enhance it. Over time, the falcon as it appeared in folklore came to represent any brave handsome young man, not necessarily a prince. For this particular tale the image of the heroine's marvelous spouse needed to be made more glorious, and so the name of phoenix was added to it (Kolesov 1979: 68–69). K. E. Korepova finds that the name has merely a decorative function, lacking content. In spite of this sign of literary influence and the existence of literary versions of this tale type (in Western European medieval literature), the East Slavic versions largely reflect oral tradition. Out of seventeen recorded oral versions, four are perhaps in part derived from a written source which has not survived (Korepova 1982).

The falcon appears in Russian wedding songs, where it represents young married and unmarried men, usually the groom or his retinue. In the Central Volga region, when the groom and his family came to see the bride after the initial negotiations, the matchmaker might address the bride's parents with the words "look at our bright falcon, show us your swan!" (*nashego iasnogo sokola posmotrite, vashu lebëdushku pokazhite!*, Zorin 1981: 75). In other wedding lyrics the falcon comes flying from far away, arrives unexpectedly, and carries away a female bird by force. The epithet "bright falcon" is also found in oral epic poetry (bylina), and in certain Christmas songs from the Gomel' region (Bernshtam 1982: 30–31).

Baba Yaga also appears in a few less common female-centered tales. She appears in four versions of SUS 884B*, "Vasilisa the Priest's Daughter," (AT 884B*, Girl Dressed as Man Deceives the King): Afanas'ev 316, Chudinskii 30, Novikov 1971 no. 50, and Smirnov 260. This tale should be discussed together with SUS 428, "The Girl in the Witch's Service" (AT 428, The Wolf), represented in our survey by Khudiakov 20, Onchukov 2000 Shokshozero 51, and Zelenin Viatka 27. These two types are sometimes combined (as in Balashov 52, Khudiakov 19, Matveeva and Leonova 13, Sadovnikov 16, and Sokolova 1970: 54–55). Baba Yaga's role in this complex of tales is overwhelmingly hostile, but in one version she helps the heroine (Novikov 1971 no. 50). Many of these tales suggest an identification of Baba Yaga as a wicked mother-in-law. There are not many recorded East Slavic versions of these tale types, and J. Swahn believes that they came to Russia from the Balkans (1955: 270–271).

The heroine of AT 884B* disguises herself as a man and foils various tests intended to determine her true sex.[10] Usually she dresses as a man in order to take her father's place in the army. In most versions, she lives with another soldier whose mother suspects that she is a woman, and tests her sex. The heroine disdains "feminine" objects offered to her (an embroidery frame, pearls, silks) and expresses interest in weapons or horses. In what is often the final test, she is invited to bathe in the bathhouse with the young man. She manages to finish bathing and leave before he arrives (in Khudiakov 19 she sends him to get soap). Another test involves a flower placed over her bed, hay or grass placed under the bed, or a broom placed next to it. If the heroine is a woman, the flower will wilt, the hay turn black, the grass or broom will turn yellow. The heroine usually evades this test by moving the flower, grass, or hay.[11] In Afanas'ev 316, the tsar turns for advice to a "behind-the-courtyard" grandmother who is also a Yaga, *babushka-zadvorenka-iaginishna*. She devises three tests, which fail to reveal that the heroine is a woman. In Smirnov 260, the heroine's father is called to serve Yaga-Baba. The heroine goes in male disguise to take his place. Yaga-Baba notices that she is female and decides to test her by hanging flowers over her bed. The heroine, who sleeps next to Yaga-Baba's son, cleverly exchanges her faded flower with the still fresh flower which hangs over the son, leaving Yaga-Baba confused. The heroine reveals her sex to the son after she has crossed a river on the boundary of Yaga-Baba's

---

[10] The failed tests of a disguised woman's sex are also found in the Russian folk epic about Stavr Godinovich. This motif may be related to European medieval legends about women disguised as men who entered monasteries, about the legendary ninth-century Pope Joan, whose sex was revealed when she gave birth during a procession in public, to folk songs from Western and Eastern Europe about a young woman who serves in the army in place of her father, who is noticed by and marries the king, and to AT 514, The Shift of Sex, although this tale type is apparently not part of the East Slavic repertoire (Krzyżanowski 1963).

[11] This motif recalls Slavic folk beliefs about menstruation. According to Ukrainian beliefs, a menstruating woman might cause trees to dry up or gardens to become infertile. An informant from Poles'e stated that trees would dry up if a menstruating woman walked under them or climbed them. (Agapkina 2000: 171–173).

territory. This tale-teller describes Yaga-Baba as a "solicitous mother" (*zabotlivaia mat'*).

The heroine of an eighteenth-century literary tale undergoes tests and also remains undetected (Novikov 1971 no. 50). She obtains a peace treaty from a prince who had declared war on her father. When the prince wishes to marry her, she goes to Yaga-Baba, who gives her a doll to take her place on the wedding night. The prince reproaches her for trickery and cuts the doll's head off. He regrets what he has done, but when he returns the heroine has come back to bed. They then live happily together. In Chudinskii 30, Baba Yaga unsuccessfully tests the heroine's sex, but then succeeds in bringing her back and marrying her to her son. Baba Yaga tries to kill her but fails. The heroine throws a birch log outside and declares that she "will live well with her husband" when a grove grows from the log. A grove suddenly grows and the tale ends happily; curiously, the narrator does not say anything more about Baba Yaga. In the different versions of this tale, the tests of the heroine's sex generally move from tests of her personal tastes and interests (she exhibits traditionally masculine rather than feminine ones) to a final and more difficult test that involves the exposure of her female body (in the bathhouse, and perhaps the symbolic expression of menstruation in the wilting flower, hay, or grass). While the tale was no doubt amusing for some listeners, it also concerns the serious question of female identity.

The tales combining this type with type 428 include the heroine's marriage. In Sadovnikov 16 the heroine goes to the army and lives with Yagaia Baba and her son Ivan Agich (or Yagich). He fails to realize she is a woman, but after she has returned home he comes in disguise and sells doves to her. The doves carry her back to Ivan Yagich and she marries him. The heroine in Balashov 52 has collected a debt from a prince and outwitted his mother, remaining undetected as a woman. She returns home and asks for a bed with four doves. The doves carry her back to the prince and she marries him. A bed with geese and swans carries the heroine back to Yaginishna's house in Matveeva and Leonova 13. In Khudiakov 19, the heroine comes home from military service, and a soldier with whom she served comes in the form of a cat and carries her away.

The tales then continue with type 428: After the heroine's wedding her evil mother-in-law makes the heroine milk cows which are in fact bears, shear sheep which are actually wolves, obtain clay from beyond the sea (Zelenin Viatka 27), or feed geese and chickens which are snakes (Sadovnikov 16). Or the heroine must shear bears and milk wolves (Khudiakov 20). The heroine receives instructions from her husband, grandmother (Zelenin Viatka 27), a servant girl (Matveeva and Leonova 13), or an old man (Smirnov 141) and is not killed by the animals.

The mother-in-law then sends the heroine to Baba Yaga for a loom reed. Baba Yaga is the mother-in-law's sister in Khudiakov 19 and 20; in Sadovnikov 16 the mother-in-law is a Yagaia Baba, as is her sister; and Yaga-Baba is called "aunt" in Balashov 52. The heroine receives instructions about how to pacify the members of Baba Yaga's household. She gives them gifts and receives help, including magic gifts (comb, towel), which then impede Baba Yaga (the Obstacle flight motif, D672). This part of the tale is almost identical to some versions of 480B*, and suggests that the wicked Baba Yaga of type 480 could represent a woman's mother-in-law as well as her negative emotions about her own mother. Egi-boba in Zelenin Viatka 27 is particularly vicious, sharpening her teeth to eat the heroine, then boiling tar to kill her, and finally chasing her on a broom. She complains that her mare daughters don't weave, complains about being called to work as a midwife, and eats her own daughters by mistake. V. I. Chernyshev describes a literary version of this tale from a 1794 collection in which the heroine has married Baba Yaga's son. Baba Yaga allows the marriage, but then turns against her daughter-in-law, sending her to milk bears and shear wolves. The heroine is sent to another Baba Yaga for a loom reed. When she returns, her mother-in-law Baba Yaga experiences a change of heart and "from that time on began to love her." Chernyshev attributes this edifying conclusion to the literate editor, rather than the folk tradition (1934: 596, 605).

Onchukov 2000 Shokshozero 51 begins with an episode recalling AT 510B: The heroine runs away from her father, who wishes to marry her. He chases her to a river, and then throws his testicles at her, which grow onto her neck. Later her mother-in-law sends her to Egi-Baba, who addresses the heroine as "niece," and gives her human meat to eat. After fleeing Egi-Baba, she returns at the moment her husband is going to marry another woman. She is brought to work in the kitchen, and her father's testicles jump down from her into a boiling kettle. When she carries a pot of soup into the dining room, her husband recognizes her and they are reunited. In Sokolova 1970: 54–55 an old woman tests the heroine's sex. The heroine Mar'ia returns to her father, and the old woman sends doves to bring her back to marry her son Buian Buianych. Mar'ia refuses to address the old woman as "mother," and says she will do so only when her ring becomes overgrown with grass. The old woman wants to send the heroine to Buryaga, but Mar'ia refuses. Finally, Mar'ia notices that grass has grown on her ring, she calls the old woman "mother," and the conflict is resolved.[12]

---

[12] This miraculous event (grass grows on the heroine's ring), and the similar event in Chudinskii 30 (a grove grows out of a cut log), both recall an episode from the legend of Saints Peter and Fevroniia (see the discussion of AT 313). In a later episode of the legend, the boyars of Murom

Baba Yaga appears in three versions of SUS 709, The Magic Mirror (AT 709, Snow-White). A sister and her brothers live in the forest. The brothers hunt and kill a wild goat, who is in fact Baba Yaga's daughter. Baba Yaga twice tries to kill the young woman by selling her a strangling necklace and a poison apple, but her brothers and then a prince revive her (Khlanta 1989: 138–144). AT 709 is not as popular in Russia as in Europe; this version was recorded from a Ukrainian-speaking (Rusyn) narrator in eastern Slovakia, who calls the villain "Baba Yaga" rather than using a Slovak-influenced name (see chapter 2). In other East Slavic versions of this tale, the villain is usually a wicked stepmother (Novikov 1974: 165–166). Egi-Baba is a wicked stepmother in Onchukov 2000 Shokshozero 29. The heroine is driven out and comes to a hut with dwarves. The dwarves warn the heroine not to look out the window when they leave, but Egi-Baba finds out from her magic mirror where the heroine is. She comes by twice, first putting a poison necklace on the heroine, and then a poison dress. The first time, the dwarves remove the necklace, and the heroine is revived. The second time, they do not think of removing the dress, and the heroine dies, an exceptional tragic ending.

Baba Iga appears as donor in a version from Kursk province (Löwis of Menar 1921 no. 23). The wicked stepmother has the heroine taken to the forest to be killed. Three Baba Iga sisters take her in and give her a ball, a hammer, and chicken bones. The heroine follows the ball to a crystal mountain and hammers in the chicken bones into the side of the mountain. She climbs up the mountain to a crystal palace, where twelve falcon brothers adopt her. The wicked stepmother sends a witch with three deadly gifts, and the last time her father revives her. The heroine returns home, and the stepmother and witch are killed.

The Wedding in Folktale and Traditional Life

The conflicts of the fairy tale usually develop from a primary traditional concern—the acquisition of a spouse, which serves as the typical ending (the wedding, function thirty-one in Propp's morphology). As Meletinskii points out, the difficult tasks of the fairy tale are for the most part directly related to

---

dislike Fevroniia because of her common origin and manage to drive Peter and Fevroniia away. While they are camped at a spot outside the city, servants cut some branches to make a cooking spit. Fevroniia blesses the branches, saying that they will grow into trees by morning. In the morning the branches have grown into trees, and a messenger comes from Murom, asking Prince Peter to return. In both folktale and legend, there is a wise or clever heroine, miraculous growth of trees or plants, and the resolution of a conflict. Natal'ia Demkova finds it significant that this third "miracle" performed by Fevroniia in the legend, which brings about the social acceptance of her marriage to Prince Peter and his restoration to power, occurs in a liminal place, on the bank of a river, between two worlds (1997: 84).

the search for a marital partner, and many folktale motifs bear resemblance to actual wedding customs. For Meletinskii, the importance of the wedding as a culmination of the fairy tale distinguishes it from the myth. In myths, marriage is a means of acquiring cultural goods, and occurs in the beginning or middle, but not at the end (Meletinskii 1974: 61–66).

What relation did these folktales, with their obligatory outcome, have to the lives of their listeners? Just as in the folktale, a wedding was an essential part of the traditional life cycle, in fact one of its most important events. All young adult members of the community were expected to marry. By present-day standards, Russian peasants in the late nineteenth and early twentieth century married young. In the central Volga region, men tended to marry beginning at age eighteen, women at sixteen, and a majority of both men and women were married by age twenty-five (Zorin 1981: 36–38). Given a certain degree of regional variation, this age range for marriage was typical for Russia as a whole. Certainly, not only physical maturity, but economic and social factors strongly influenced traditional marriage patterns: Families might be eager to marry a son early (before age twenty) in order to benefit from the daughter-in-law's free labor. After the establishment of universal mandatory military service in 1874, men might marry after serving, between ages twenty-two and twenty-five (Bernshtam 1988: 47–51).

Strong pressure was exerted on all young adults to marry, and very few remained unmarried. There were special designations for unmarried adults, who were regarded with scorn, or at least ambivalence (Zorin 1981: 29). Unmarried women were believed to possess magical power and were called on for certain ritual occasions, yet from the traditional point of view they had not carried out their female destiny and so were regarded with a certain disapproval (Bernshtam 1988: 75–76). A mock wedding was sometimes part of the funeral of an unmarried woman, or she was buried in wedding clothes, presumably so that she might complete the normal life cycle before being buried (Sokolova 1978: 156).

The meaning and implications of marriage were of course different for women and men. There was certainly anxiety involved for both, but probably more for the woman. A man's position in his community was improved, particularly since the husband-wife labor unit (*tiaglo*) acquired the right to farmland. For a woman, the typical patrilocal residence pattern meant that she had to move to the home of her in-laws, who might be hostile and abuse her. The obvious anxiety involved in this move is expressed by the remarkable sadness of some traditional wedding lyrics, particularly the bride's laments. Laments were also performed at funerals and when young men were recruited into the army, and similarities in ritual and the poetic imagery in songs have been noted between wedding and funeral (Sokolova 1978). It is difficult to say how much the wedding laments expressed the demands of tradition, or to what degree they might reflect the bride's true feelings. The presence and persistence of the lament in the ritual suggest that it had some real meaning for many who performed it.

The traditional Russian wedding ritual was elaborate, and might last from a week to a month. In spite of considerable local variation, A. V. Gura divides it into five essential phases: initial negotiations and agreement of the two sides, preparations for the wedding, acts immediately preceding the wedding, the wedding itself, and acts marking the completed wedding. This structure appears to be very old, predating the introduction of Christianity, which inserted the church wedding into the pagan ritual without greatly changing it (Gura 1978). The following description is a very general one.

The wedding cycle began when the groom's family looked for a suitable bride and sent a matchmaker to negotiate with the woman's family. The matchmaker(s) might be the groom's godparents, or another close relative (uncle, aunt, married brother or sister). There was also a class of professional matchmakers found in provincial cities and large villages, women who were respected and paid for this service. In the Central Volga region the matchmaking process (*svatovstvo*) was dominated by women (Zorin 1981: 68).

The woman's parents sometimes went to inspect the prospective groom's household (*smotrenie dvorov*). The groom and his family then returned the visit to inspect the bride (*smotriny*). If both families agreed to the match and the young people themselves did not refuse, they met again to discuss financial arrangements and the details of the wedding (*sgovor*). As a sign of agreement, the fathers shook hands (the handfast, *rukobitie*), the pair exchanged rings, and there followed a feast and drinking (*zapoi*) (ibid., 74–84).

At this point the pair publicly became bride and groom. The bride remained at home and began to prepare gifts for the groom and his family, helped by female friends of her own age. During this period before the wedding (in some areas called *devichnik* or *devishnik*; in other regions this term referred only to the bride's evening party the day before the wedding), the bride was expected to perform laments and display grief. The groom came to visit her, but only exceptionally did the bride call on the groom. Instead, he was visited by her friends (ibid., 88–89). On the last day of this period the bride took leave of her home and village. She went to the bath with her friends, and held a party with them in the evening. She lamented the loss of her "beauty" or "freedom" (*krasota, volia*). In the laments the bride's "beauty" or "freedom" might be a girl, an animal, or a bird, or might take concrete form as the young woman's single braid, headdress, or ribbon (Kolpakova 1973: 259–260). At the same time the groom might hold a party of his own (*mal'chishnik*).

On the wedding day the groom and his retinue came to the bride's house. At a number of points along the way their path was blocked. Each time the passage or place had to be "bought" by the groom or one of his company. A significant moment was when the bride loosened her braid; this was a clear symbol of the end of maiden status. The couple left for the church, and after the ceremony the bride's hair was woven into two braids and covered, symbolizing her new status as a married woman. In some villages of the central Volga region, the bride was met by her mother-in-law wearing a fur coat turned inside out. This ritual action may have been an effort to inspire fear and obedience in the bride, but Nikolai Zorin feels that it originally had an opposite meaning. In order to gain more power in her new home, a bride might try to step on the threshold or enter the hut before her husband (ibid., 98–114).

After a feast at the groom's house, the newlyweds were led to the wedding bed, which was set in a special place (such as the stable or cowshed) and might have objects placed in it to guarantee children. The bride took off her husband's shoes, a ritual that is mentioned in the medieval Primary Chronicle. Depending on the locality, the newlyweds were left alone for a night or only a few hours. Then they were "wakened" and the bride's bloodied shirt was displayed to the wedding guests, followed by more celebration and revelry. If the bride was "spoiled," her parents and godparents might be given beer in a sieve or have harnesses or torn shirts placed on them. The groom might beat his bride in front of the guests, and her parents were chased out or simply left (ibid., 114–118). In Tula province a bride who had already lost her virginity was given a three-legged stool (Bernshtam 1988: 111, fn. 269).

On the day after the wedding the bride and groom were given a ritual bath, and then they rode around the village and invited relatives to another feast. At these feasts the newlyweds received gifts, usually money, from relatives. Other ritual actions included the bride's first trip to the local well, where she left an offering of bread or a coin. The end of the festivities was marked by serving a special pirog (pie). The length of the wedding celebrations depended on the wealth of the families involved (Zorin 1981: 118–128).

In Russian patriarchal peasant culture, the wedding was not as much an attachment of two individuals as an agreement and alliance between two families. The groom's family was most interested in acquiring a hard-working member who would not create trouble for her in-laws. Traditionally, the son's own wishes may have been taken into consideration, but the choice of a bride remained with his parents, who were advised in the matter by other relatives (Zorin 1981: 67–68). Later in the nineteenth century, there appears to have been a gradual loosening of patriarchal authority, caused in part by the emancipation of 1861, the appearance of new forms of outside income (work in factories or cities), and the end of self-contained village life. If a young couple had already had sexual relations, their parents might be coerced into allowing them to marry. Sexual relations between two people already betrothed were reported to be almost customary among peasants in Ryazan' province by the turn of the century (Semenova Tian-Shanskaia 1914: 38). Nevertheless, the head of the household still exerted great authority over the choice of marriage partners in many regions, and there was still pressure on young women to remain virgins until marriage (Engel 1990).

The Supernatural Spouse

Many of the tales about young women and men protagonists involve the search for a spouse who has been lost or the winning of a spouse from the other world. The spouse is an animal or a supernatural being, and narrators frequently describe the search in a similar fashion. For example, the motif of wearing out iron shoes, staves, hats or bread during the search is found in many of these tales (it is a widespread international motif, cf. motif H1125, Task: traveling till iron shoes are worn out) and shows that narrators recognize a thematic relationship among these tales.

These tale types are widespread and have an obvious appeal. In the context of traditional East Slavic culture the appeal of tales about courtship and marriage is obvious. However, there is a lack of correspondence between these tales and the reality of traditional life. In the tales the hero or heroine may or may not choose the spouse (the heroine of AT 432 requests the feather of Finist the Bright Falcon, while the hero of AT 402 is compelled to marry the Frog Tsarevna), while in the traditional culture the final decision often rested with the parents and families of the young woman and man. Perhaps the feature of free choice found in the tale functioned as a kind of wish fulfillment or compensation.

K. E. Korepova derives the motif of marriage with an animal spouse from totemism. The animal wife reflects matriarchal traditions, while the tales with an animal husband come from a later period of patriarchy. She suggests that the original form of these tales involved a man's voluntary marriage with an animal spouse who gave him success in hunting. Under patriarchy there developed the motif of forced marriage: The hero compels the animal-woman to marry him by stealing her animal feathers or skin. Finally, when totemistic beliefs disappear, the motif of the secret marriage and the persecution of the animal spouse by the other members of the hero(ine)'s family appears. The tales of the heroine who marries an animal groom also arise at this time (Korepova 1978: 9).

Tat'iana Bernshtam suggests more cautiously that totemistic beliefs might account for the origin of bird imagery so frequent in East Slavic wedding songs, perhaps related to the tale of Finist the Bright Falcon (1982: 32). In the wedding cycle the animal symbolism is made quite explicit through the device of parallelism. One wedding song describes how the wind carries a white swan into a flock of ducks and geese, who peck at the swan. Then the swan is identified: "the white swan, the beautiful maiden" (*bela lebed', krasna devitsa*); the maiden laments that she cannot please her mother-in-law, and tells her in-laws not to scold her. She has not come to them of her own free will, but a fine young man has brought her there on his horse (Kolpakova 1973: 138–139).

While in the wedding songs the animal figures are explicitly symbolic (representing bride, groom, and other players of the wedding ceremony), in the folktale the spouse exists concretely as an animal, and this gives the tale its fantastic or humorous nature. The tales literally concern a distance between the newly married couple. A certain analogy might be found in the wedding ceremony, where the groom's party goes to fetch the bride from her house and bring her to the groom. For the groom there is an element of departure and search in the ceremony, while for the bride the journey proceeds in one direction only. There is a certain parallel in the traditional East Slavic life cycle for the quest in tales where a man searches for his wife, but less so for the heroine-centered tales (such as AT 432). If there is symbolic meaning in this motif, it might concern another kind of distance between husband and wife.

The idea that the search for the spouse overcomes an emotional distance is suggested in the tales themselves. This is especially true in SUS 400/2, where Baba Yaga finds out from the young woman where her heart, love, or sorrow is to be found. In this and other tale types (AT 425A and C) the lost husband or wife "remembers" the other spouse and the feeling of affection is awakened. The supernatural bride in AT 313 is also forgotten by her husband in the final episode of some versions. It seems likely that affection or attachment might not immediately arise in a marriage if the choice of a marriage partner was traditionally the prerogative of the parents. Under these circumstances, when the newlywed couple might not even know each other, it is not surprising that familiarity and affection could only develop later, if at all. With its fantastic, exaggerated language, the fairy tale seems to give expression to the "difficult task" of trying to win someone's affection, and the optimistic hope that it can be accomplished.

Baba Yaga's role of bringing the spouses together makes sense in light of the important role of older women in the traditional wedding ceremony.

Matchmaking appears to have been largely a female domain. Nikolai Zorin also reports a custom found in the Sviiazhskii district of the Central Volga region, where an unattractive old woman led the prospective bride out to be seen by the young man's family, apparently in order to make the young woman seem more beautiful. In other regions the woman's godmother, aunt, or another married female relative might bring her out (Zorin 1981: 75–76). In many tales Baba Yaga is the aunt of the supernatural female spouse.

Other correspondences between wedding ritual and folktale can be pointed out. For example, the bride's female friends, while visiting the groom before the wedding day, might request to be carried over the threshold (ibid., 91). This is found as a motif in some tales; however, the request is made by the villain Baba Yaga (some versions of AT 301) or by the tester of the kind and unkind girls (AT 480).

Baba Yaga's function as donor ultimately leads the hero(ine) to find or be reunited with his or her spouse. The distance between the two is expressed in the fantastic language of the fairy tale: The spouse disappears beyond thrice-nine lands. If the fantastic distance in the tale expresses an emotional distance between wife and husband in traditional East Slavic culture, then perhaps the telling of these tales was a manner of mediating this distance, and mitigating anxieties on the part of young women and men about their impending married life.

These tales might also reflect the differing perceptions men and women have of each other. The messages implied in them seem to be different for men than for women, although both have anxieties about the other. Both heroes and heroines have to adjust to a partner who is somehow different and "strange." This may be foreshadowed in AT 480 when the kind and unkind girls must wash Baba Yaga's children, who are frogs and snakes, and expressed at the end of AT 402, when the hero must succeed in holding on to his wife, who takes the form of a frog, toad, and snake (this also occurs in AT 511+409 and AT 405, see chapter 6). The male hero confronts the Tsar Maiden or a maiden with magical abilities whom he must outsmart; alternatively, she is an unattractive frog, and as one hero complains when he has to marry her, "the frog is not my equal" (Afanas'ev 269). In AT 425 the heroine may be forced into what appears as a less-than-ideal marriage with a crayfish or bear, but in other versions of 425, the husband comes in the dark and remains mysterious and capable of idealization. In the AT 432 cycle, the Bright Falcon is without a doubt a highly idealized, positive figure. The male-centered tales express anxiety through the image of a powerful woman (perhaps embodying men's own fear of women and their insecurity about their male identity) and through an animal spouse (an undesirable marriage partner). While the male-centered tales progress from this anxiety through its mediation (sometimes by the donor Baba Yaga) to an adjustment to the married state (the hero finds his wife and is reconciled with her), the female-centered tales often present an idealized spouse at the beginning, and if the heroine's further adventures express anxiety, it is not caused by the spouse, but by a female rival or rivals. It is interesting that East Slavic patriarchal peasant culture, in which marriages were arranged largely for economic reasons, still produced these rich fantasies about affection between spouses.

Conclusion

This survey of tale types in which Baba Yaga appears as both villain and donor, or as a hostile donor, demonstrates the objective existence of Baba Yaga's ambiguity. It is not something created or imagined by an outside observer, or based on a subjective impression. It is possible to compare the tale types examined in this chapter by how many versions demonstrate donor, villain, or ambiguous roles in each case, summarized in the tables below.

Male Hero	Donor Baba Yaga	Villain Baba Yaga	Ambiguous Baba Yaga	Total
300A and 300A*	2	9	1	12
301	6	9	0	15
301 (Baba Yaga's army)	0	5	1	6
303	0	2	7	9
312D	3	0	1	4
313	20	1	2	23
315	4	1	1	6
318	1	0	1	2
321	0	0	5	5
400/2	1	3	2	6
465	3	1	1	5
519	0	0	11	11
531 (+327B)	1	0	3	4
566	0	0	1	1
650A	0	0	1	1
"Herding mares"	0	0	12	12
Manzhura 1890: 51–52, and Kovalev 11	0	0	2	2

Female Heroine	Donor Baba Yaga	Villain Baba Yaga	Ambiguous Baba Yaga	Total
425	4	6	1	11
430	0	0	1	1
432	9	1	2	12
709	1	2	0	3
884B*+428	1	11	0	12

Does the term "ambiguity" adequately describe this shifting of tale roles in different versions of one tale type? In fact, we have used the term "ambiguity" to describe several distinct phenomena: 1) the behavior of one and the same Baba Yaga in a single tale text, who acts at one moment willingly as a donor, and at another, as a villain (Manzhura 1890: 51–52, Zelenin Perm' 9); 2) the contrasting behaviors in one tale text of one Baba Yaga who acts as a donor, and another who (although almost identical or very similar to the first Baba Yaga) acts as a villain (Balashov 43 and 88, Kitainik 7, Kozhemiakina 1973: 105–110, Krasnozhenova 19, Potanin 1902 no. 36, Potanin 1906 no. 13, Smirnov 130 and 141, Tumilevich 21, Zelenin Perm' 67); 3) in different versions of one tale type, the contrasting behaviors of a donor Baba Yaga in one version, and a villain Baba Yaga in another;[13] 4) the behavior of a single Baba Yaga who tries to harm or even kill the hero(ine), but then provides him or her with help or a magic object unwillingly (a "hostile donor," as in the "herding mares" cycle); 5) in tales where Baba Yaga is a donor, the typical narrative sequence of the protagonist's arrival at the hut on chicken legs, Baba Yaga's threat to eat the hero(ine), and her immediate compliance with his or her requests. It seems no coincidence that all these various forms of ambiguous behavior cluster around the figure of Baba Yaga.

In her perceptive essay on the nature of the fairy tale, Marie-Louise Tenèze examines the problem of the hostile donor. She cites examples of French and Turkish fairy tales with villains who at one moment act as donors. Very importantly, she points out that this shifting does not exhibit any ambiguity—at successive moments of the narrative, one and the same character is given two roles which are diametrically opposed. Tenèze relates this opposition of tale roles (donor/villain) to other such oppositions (hero/false hero, active hero/passive hero, active villain/passive villain). She illustrates the concept of active and passive heroes and villains with French versions of AT 327, where a

---

[13] A contextual factor involved in this particular type of ambiguity and its manifestations is the presence, in the minds of storytellers and audiences, of memories of previous performances. Their familiarity with the tales, and their exposure to different narrators, might bring together in their minds instances of Baba Yaga as donor and villain in the same tale type.

brother and sister come to the devil's house. The sister Jeannette represents the active aspect of the hero, while the brother Jean is passive; likewise, the devil is the active villain, while his wife is passive. Tenèze suggests that the active/passive opposition can become transformed into the villain/donor opposition (1970: 37–38).

Tenèze is correct in her assessment of this behavior, at each separate moment, as beyond any ambiguity ("hors de toute ambiguïté," ibid., 38), and it might be more accurate to describe it as an oscillation between opposing tale roles. Tenèze applies these observations to an understanding of the underlying structures of the fairy tale. The relationships between these several oppositions in the area of tale roles suggest that a fundamental feature of the fairy tale is a dynamic relationship between opposing, contrary terms. The shifting between villain and donor tale roles by one character is a demonstration of this underlying dynamism.

Tenèze's observations imply that this dynamic shifting (which a reader might first perceive as inconsistency or lack of skill on the part of a narrator) is in fact part of the underlying structure of the Indo-European fairy tale, in the field of tale roles and their relationships, and that such a shifting is a latent potential in any fairy tale. This leads to another question, and back to the issue of cultural specificity. Why does this dynamism surface in some fairy tales but not in others, in relation to some characters but not others? Why does this dynamic shifting occur so frequently with the character of Baba Yaga in East Slavic fairy tales, while it is apparently much less common in western Europe? In this regard, Baba Yaga is a valuable "piece of the puzzle" for scholars of the Indo-European fairy tale, in that she represents both a specific surface manifestation of the fairy tale in a given cultural and historical context (Saussure's *parole*), while at the same time manifesting latent structural possibilities of the tale roles in general (*langue*). In connection with the frequent activation of this dynamic shifting or oscillation in the case of Baba Yaga, it is interesting to recall Ia. I. Gin's observations about the frequent shifting in the grammatical gender of supernatural beings in East Slavic fairy tales, and the shifting of names (from Baba Yaga to Yagishnia) by the storyteller Marina D'iachkova (Balashov 88).

The "hostile donor" is a problematic concept or category. Claude Bremond and Jean Verrier point out difficulties in Propp's identification of two characters in Afanas'ev 139 (AT 301) as hostile donors. In both cases, they find that there is not really a transfer of a magic agent. Defeated by the hero, the White Field-Dweller (Belyi Polianin) puts himself at the hero's disposal; beaten by the hero, the old man in a mortar with a pestle escapes (his beard was stuck in the cleft of a log) and unwittingly shows the hero and his brothers the way to the underground kingdom. In the first case, Propp has misidentified this episode, which is better described by the functions: villainy (the White Field-Dweller captures the hero's brothers), struggle, and victory. In the second, the "information" provided by the villain old man is better described as a connective incident between two sequences (moves). According to their view, Propp has applied the term "hostile donor" outside of a true donor sequence, and without the bestowal of a real "gift." Following this line of reasoning, one could call the dragon villain a hostile donor, because it gives the hero the opportunity to display his heroism and obtain a princess (Bremond and Verrier 1982: 71–74). Bremond and Verrier correctly warn against identifying folktale characters as hostile donors too quickly or eagerly, and Propp might have done this in some cases, but Baba Yaga's role in the "herding mares" cycle of tales seems to justify the "hostile donor" concept. In this tale she does, of course, very much resemble a villain who sets a "difficult task" for the hero, yet the result is the receipt of a magic agent. Perhaps we can best understand Baba Yaga in this and other tales examined in this chapter if we consider her to be in a state of dynamic tension between villain and donor roles. If this is the case, Baba Yaga's behavior is a good demonstration of the underlying dynamism that Marie-Louise Tenèze observes in the fairy tale.

CHAPTER SIX
The Evil Witch

In contrast to the remarkably consistent donor sequence, Baba Yaga exhibits a number of different kinds of villainy. This might be due to the greater appeal of evil to the human imagination, but Nikolai Novikov finds that Baba Yaga's image in these "villain" tales is paler and exhibits fewer of the traditional features; in some cases she may have replaced other folktale villains and adopted their attributes (1974: 175).

Baba Yaga as a False Mother

Baba Yaga is a wicked stepmother or false mother in two versions of SUS 516, The Faithful Servant (AT 516, Faithful John), which have different beginnings. In Karnaukhova 141 the hero's two elder brothers go to search for brides, and come to the dwelling of Baba-Yaga, where they find a dove maiden. There is an interesting reversal in the description of Baba-Yaga's dwelling in these two encounters. The first brother comes to an old hut (*vetkha izbushka*) with a luxurious interior of velvet and gold. The second brother comes to a golden palace, but inside there is a poor room covered with bast matting (*khuda komnata rogozhei kryta*). Yaga-Baba gives them food and drink which quickly incapacitates them, picks them up on the palm of one hand, and throws them in the cellar. Prince Ivan acquires a special horse and goes to find his brothers. He comes to Baba-Yaga's hut, where she sits in a dark chamber (*v temnoi gornitse*). The hero takes off his cap and bows, and there is another curious reversal, this time of the dialogue typical for the donor sequence:

> "Where," he said, "Yaga-Baba, are my brothers?"
> "In my house you drink, eat, and then ask about things."
> "I'm not a guest in your house, I came to ask for an answer." (Karnaukhova 1934: 281)

Then Baba-Yaga sets a table of food before the hero, but he throws it out of the window. When she sees she cannot trick him, she takes two snakes from a bag and attacks him. Prince Ivan cuts the heads off the snakes, demands the truth from Baba-Yaga, and cuts her head off. He rescues his brothers and the dove maidens. In Balashov 40 Prince Ivan helps his brothers overcome an enormous army, but they abandon him in a hole in the earth. He acquires a servant and a wife in the underground realm, and prepares to return home by sea.

Then, in both tales, on the way back to the hero's realm, birds come and warn the hero's servant about impending dangers. In Karnaukhova 141 a second Yaga-Baba has ravaged the land, gouged out the hero's parents' eyes, thrown them in a dungeon, and disguised herself as the hero's mother. In Balashov 40, the hero's mother has died and his father has married a Yaga-Baba. The stepmother or false mother plans to kill the hero with dangerous gifts (vodka, a silk shirt, a silver spoon, wine, a horse, a carriage). The birds in Balashov 40 also warn that whoever tells the hero about this will turn to stone.

The servant asks for the dangerous gifts and destroys them. At night Yaga-Baba attacks the servant with snakes. He cuts the snakes' heads off and Yaga-Baba cries out that the servant has raped her. The hero gets angry, but his servant reveals to him that this Yaga-Baba is not his mother. As he is warning the hero, Yaga-Baba turns the servant to stone. The hero rescues his family, restores their eyes, and kills Baba-Yaga (Karnaukhova 141). In Balashov 40 the stepmother Yaga-Baba is not killed; the teller does not mention her again. In both versions the hero revives his servant with his own son's blood. Either his son does not die or he is brought back to life.

Baba Yaga as Polyphemus, Competitor, and Evil Advisor
SUS 1137, The Blinded One-Eyed Giant (AT 1137, The Ogre Blinded), is a folktale related to the episode of the one-eyed cyclops Polyphemus in the *Odyssey*. In Kretov 25 and Kabashnikaw 1989 no. 212, a man goes to find out what grief and misfortune are (like the hero of AT 326, who goes to find out what fear is). The hero of Kretov 25 comes to Baba Yaga's hut. She throws an axe at him that cuts off his hand. He manages to escape by cutting open a sheep and hiding in its skin, and now knows what grief and misfortune are. The hero of Kabashnikaw 1989 no. 212 puts out Baba Yaga's one eye. The hero of Nikiforov 1961 no. 92 comes to Baba-Yaga's hut and enters with a traditional formulaic phrase. Baba-Yaga comes home and asks him to forge her a second eye, since she is one-eyed. He burns her one eye, takes her fur coat, and disguises himself as a ram. She unwittingly lets him out.

Baba Yaga makes a brief appearance in another version of this tale (Gorodtsov i: 163–175). The hero has come to an island and the dwelling of the One-Eyed Knight (*Krivoi Bogatyr*). The knight had lost one eye in a fight with Baba Yaga. The hero deceives the knight and pours molten lead and tin into his one good eye. He escapes, and comes upon a lion who is fighting with Baba Yaga. Baba Yaga offers him gold, but the lion offers to take him home. He kills Baba Yaga and the lion carries him home. In other Russian versions of this tale, the villain is a tall, thin one-eyed woman (Afanas'ev 302), a cannibalistic one-eyed woman (Nikiforov 1961 no. 75), a giant (Afanas'ev 572), a one-eyed knight

(Nikiforov 1961 no. 127, Onchukov 160, Sadovnikov 2), or a one-eyed old man (Smirnov 217).

Bandarchyk 1973 no. 6 includes an episode of SUS 513A, The Six Marvelous Companions (AT 513, The Extraordinary Companions). In the first part of this tale the hero fights Kashchei's three sons, and releases the sun, moon, and stars (SUS 300 A*, see chapter 5). Kashchei's two daughters and his wife, a serpent (*zmiaia*), fail to kill the hero. In the 513A episode, the hero is sent twice by Kashchei to obtain brides, and must retrieve beautifying water from another kingdom. The hero's companion quickly outruns Babulia Yaga Kastsianaia Naga, who has been sent for the same water. On the way back, Baba Yaga knocks him to the ground and puts him to sleep (she puts a magpie on his head). The hero calls out in his heroic voice (*bagatyrskim golasam*) and wakes up the runner, who overtakes Baba Yaga again and seizes the water.

Kretov 30 is related to SUS 532, Neznaika (AT 532, I Don't Know). The hero works for the tsar of another realm. The tsar's second wife, a wicked stepmother, goes to Baba Yaga to ask how she can be rid of her stepchildren. Baba Yaga first tells her to kill them with magic belts, and then gives her poisoned strawberry jam. The hero's horse warns him about these evil plans, and he disposes of the dangerous objects. Finally, Baba Yaga tells the stepmother that she must feign illness and ask for the horse's heart as medicine. The tsar orders the horse killed, but the hero asks for one last ride. He and his horse fly to another kingdom. Novikov also lists an unavailable version of this tale type with a donor Baba Yaga, which would make this an "ambiguous" tale type.

Baba Yaga as Koshchei's Partner

Baba Yaga freezes a princess and turns knights to stone in one anomalous tale: SUS 410**, The Knight Liberates from Enchantment, Serzhputovskii 1911 no. 72. It is related to another tale type in East Slavic tradition, AT 410*, The Petrified Kingdom, where the hero releases a realm from an enchanted sleep by overcoming evil spirits in a castle for three nights in a row. The closest related tale type in Europe is probably AT 410, Sleeping Beauty.

In this Belorussian tale, the hero comes to another realm, where Baba Yaga (in her mortar, wielding pestle and broom) kidnaps the princess. The prince and his companions go to her rescue, but Kashchei breathes on them and turns them to stone. The hero then sets out for the mountain inside which the princess and her brother are trapped, but he falls asleep in the forest. He has taken the princess's horse, who goes in to find her. Kashchei hears the horse, gets in the mortar with Baba Yaga, and kills the horse with the pestle.

Eventually, the hero comes to the mountain and fights Kashchei. He breaks the mortar and pestle and almost cuts Baba Yaga's throat. Kashchei takes Baba Yaga in his arms and they flee. The hero has the sun on his forehead and finds his way inside the mountain in spite of the darkness Kashchei creates. He finds the stone prince and his companions (here the narrator changes his account and says that Baba Yaga was the one who had turned him to stone), and the princess, whom Baba Yaga has frozen. With his sun and the living water he has acquired, the hero revives them. On his way home the hero fights with Kashchei again, subdues him, and makes him promise to stay in the marsh. This tale is interesting because Kashchei and Baba Yaga appear together as a couple, and it is the one case where a "married" Baba Yaga does not appear to dominate (or "wear the pants") in the relationship. It is also an exception to the general rule (noted by Géza Róheim) that Baba Yaga and Koshchei do not appear simultaneously. (Koshchei and Baba Yaga are said to be brother and sister in Krasnozhenova 19, a version of AT 313).

Koshchei the Immortal (*Koshchei Bessmertnyi*) is a well-known villain figure in East Slavic fairy tales, but he appears in far fewer tales than Baba Yaga.[1] He is most often associated with one tale type, AT 302, although it is frequently combined with other episodes and types. In a distinct subtype of AT 302 (SUS 302/2), the hero overcomes Koshchei not by finding his death egg and crushing it, but by obtaining a horse that is faster than Koshchei's horse. There is delightful hyperbole in the storytellers' expressions of how much faster Koshchei's horse is: The horse tells Koshchei not to worry, because they can drink, eat, and bake pies for three days and nights and still catch up with Ivan and his wife Anastasiia (Khudiakov 22). Koshchei is sometimes the ogre in AT 313. In one version of SUS 300A* cited above, he is the father of the dragons. His most consistent and typical attribute is his death, hidden inside an egg (cf. motifs E710, External soul, and E711.1, Soul in egg). The egg is further nested in a series of objects and animals, which vary from one tale to another, but often the egg is inside a duck, inside a hare, in a chest, buried under an oak tree, on Buian Island on the ocean-sea. The formulaic rhyming phrase that frequently begins the series, "on the sea, on the ocean, on Buian Island..." (*na more, na okeane, na ostrove na Buiane*) is interesting because it also occurs in East

---

[1] As with Baba Yaga, Koshchei's name has many variant forms: Kashchei, Koshshei, Koshchai (Razumova and Sen'kina 1982 no. 2), Kashshei (Zhivaia Starina 21: 365–386), Kovshei (Balashov 145), Kosh (Afanas'ev 156), Kashch (Bandarchyk 1978 no. 6), Kashel', Kashel (Sorokovikov 3), Kostei, Kostsei, (Karnaukhova 42), Kashshui (Sokolov 59), Kozel, Koz'olok, Korachun, Korchun bessmërtnyi (Gospodarev 8), Kot Bezsmertnyi (Sadovnikov 61), and Kostii bezdushnyi (Chubinskii 1878 no. 64). As a character in the bylina, he sometimes appears with the name Koshcheiushko, Koshcheg, Koshcherishcho, Koshchui, and Koshel'.

Slavic incantations. It seems that one genre has influenced the other; a practitioner of spells might also be a folktale narrator, or a tale-teller might be familiar with incantations. Irina Razumova concludes that this correspondence between folktale and incantation is not due to borrowing, but derives from the same archaic view of the magic power of words (1991: 90–94). Elena Eleonskaia supposes that the folktale has influenced the incantation, but that both genres have deep roots in the same mentality and worldview (1994: 77–78, 103). In what is perhaps a unique feature of the East Slavic folktale tradition, the nested egg also contains the Tsar Maiden's love in some versions of SUS 400/2. The death egg is associated with Baba Yaga in a version of AT 321 (Matveeva and Leonova 1) (see the discussion of these two tale types in chapter 5). In one anomalous tale the hero finds a princess inside a duck inside a series of objects who helps him capture Koshchei (Nikiforov 1936 no. 11).

Koshchei casts everyone in his and the hero's realm into a state of enchanted sleep; when the self-playing psaltery (*gusli*) begins to play, everyone wakes up (Mints et al. 1957 no. 18). Everyone in Koshchei's realm has been turned to stone, and the hero revives them by playing the gusli (Korguev 1944: 31–49). An enchanted princess tells the hero to capture Koshchei by playing the gusli and putting him to sleep (Nikiforov 1936 no. 11). Koshchei's dwelling is surrounded by a fence or wall of stakes, with human heads impaled on them, and one empty stake for the hero's head (Krasnozhenova 19, Mints and Savushkina 11). Sometimes Koshchei smells the Russian scent of the intruding hero. In one tale Koshchei has tusks or fangs, like a hog (Mints et al. 1957 no. 18), and in another, his eyelids are so heavy that other people must lift them (Bandarchyk 1973 no. 6). Koshchei rides a three-legged horse (Khudiakov 22), a seven-legged horse (Razumova and Sen'kina 1974 no. 1), or a three-legged goat (Potiavin 6). He is served by an evil spirit who takes the form of a dove (Khudiakov 22), and in Razumova and Sen'kina 1974 no. 35 his captive maidens weave armies for him. In a few tales Koshchei possesses magic objects the hero is sent to obtain, such as a magic coat that is cold in summer and hot in winter (Onchukov 107), or a magic ring that helps the hero reach the Sea King and obtain the unknown (AT 465A, Sokolov 59).

Koshchei is consistently the male hero's rival for a woman, most often the hero's fiancée or wife, sometimes his mother. He corresponds to Baba Yaga in her role of usurper: Baba Yaga or her daughter appropriate the heroine's husband, while he appropriates the hero's wife. In a few tales the hero is not married, and finds captive maidens when he arrives at Koshchei's dwelling, or he is helped by Koshchei's own daughters (Karnaukhova 42, Onchukov 107, Razumova and Sen'kina 1974 no. 35). In a version of AT 560 (Sorokovikov 3) the hero's wife betrays him with Koshel-Tsar' Bessmertnyi, who has her find out where her husband has obtained his magic powers. This is an interesting reversal in that the hero, rather than Koshchei, has a secret to reveal. In a version of AT 532 (Sokolov 144) the hero battles against a foreign army and Koshshui to keep his wife, the princess. In an exceptional text, a version of AT 502 (Afanas'ev 124, variant 3), Koshchei is a donor who helps the hero accomplish feats, win a princess, and defeat the servant who had usurped his place. Other villains (a dragon, an old man sorcerer, a demon) occasionally take Koshchei's place in East Slavic versions of AT 302.

Koshchei appears as the antagonist in the Russian folk epic (bylina) about Ivan Godinovich. Ivan Godinovich fights with Koshchei over the woman Mar'ia or Nastas'ia. At a critical moment in the battle Koshchei tells the woman to help him. If she marries Koshchei she will enjoy a high status, but if she marries Ivan, she will be a servant, a peasant, or a washerwoman. She helps Koshchei subdue Ivan and tie him up. Doves or a raven prophesy that Koshchei will not have Mar'ia as a wife, refer to her in unflattering terms, or imitate the couple's lovemaking. Koshchei shoots an arrow at the birds, but it flies back and kills him. Mar'ia unties Ivan, and he cuts her to pieces in return for her treachery. In the folk epic and the tales, there is obviously an element of sexual rivalry between the hero and Koshchei. In one tale (Onchukov 107) there is strong antipathy both toward a hostile grandfather who sends the hero out on deadly tasks, and toward Koshchei, who appears to be the grandfather's alter ego. The hero kills Koshchei and crushes his grandfather to death. There is probably a reference to male sexuality when the narrator specifies that Koshchei's death is not in a single egg, but inside eggs, plural, which suggests the vernacular and somewhat obscene expression for testicles. The same use of the plural by a seventy-four-year-old woman might well have been meant humorously (Balashov 24).

Besides the implication that he is a negative father figure (and in some sense a companion to Baba Yaga; see the discussion of AT 313 in chapter 5), the folktales and folk epic suggest that seduction, deceit, infidelity, secrecy, and betrayal are important themes associated with Koshchei. Koshchei deceives the hero after the hero has released him from captivity, and later the hero's spouse or fiancée deceives Koshchei when she finds out the location of his death. East Slavic narrators enjoy developing this latter episode, when the hero's wife uses her feminine charm to undo Koshchei by convincing him that she loves him. Sometimes he lies down, putting his head on her lap, and she asks her questions while picking lice from his hair. Koshchei often lies to her about his death's location, usually twice. He tells her his death is in a broom, in a cow's or ram's horns, or some other object. She then gilds or decorates the object, and Koshchei laughs at her, sometimes quoting unflattering proverbs about women's long hair and short intelligence. Then he seals his own fate by revealing where his death is.

These two thematic areas (the negative father, seduction and deceit) are beautifully interwoven in a tale narrated by the talented Siberian storyteller Natal'ia Vinokurova (Azadovskii 1938 no. 1). The Eagle Prince seduces Kashshei's wife (Kashsheikha) and Kashshei beheads him. Kashsheikha gives birth secretly and manages to remove her son. The son Vasilii grows up, comes to Kashshei's city and finds out about his origins. He disguises himself as a woman and plays a violin outside Kashshei's palace. Pleased by the music, Kashshei dances and calls for the musician. Vasilii gains access to Kashshei's palace and leaves notes to his mother, instructing her to find out where Kashshei's death is. Vasilii obtains the egg, kills Kashshei, and then uses the same egg to revive his death father. This close juxtaposition of Vasilii's father and Kashshei (the egg kills one and revives the other) suggests that the paternal image has been split into a good and bad father.

Of the different etymologies proposed for Koshchei's name, Nikolai Novikov finds most convincing the Old Russian *koshchii*, "youth, boy" or "captive, slave, servant," because of Koshchei's initial appearance as a captive in many fairy tales (1966: 173, 1974: 218). "Koshchei" appears as a personal name in a Novgorodian birch bark document from the early fifteenth century; the name Koshchei was also known in the Moscow lands at this time (Artsikhovskii and Borkovskii 1963: 64–65). The questions of death and immortality, or the concern with the inevitability of death, are of course expressed by Koshchei's most frequent epithet. The epithet "immortal" or "deathless" (*bessmertnyi*) seems paradoxical because Koshchei invariably dies, but it may refer to the fact that he is "without" his death (Russian *bez*, "without"; *smert'*, "death") inasmuch as he does not possess it; it lies somewhere outside his body. Tsar Kashchei appears in one Russian riddle as a metaphor for an earthenware pot: It drank, it ate, it fed many people, and now it has died and lies by the fence (Martynova 1997: 459, no. 1969). Nikolai Novikov describes a lubok (popular woodcut print) with a text that represents Koshchei as a miser, endlessly hoarding money, assisted by a devil (1966: 150–151), and Koshchei appears as a miser in Pushkin's prologue to "Ruslan and Liudmila," but this conception of Koshchei does not appear to be derived from his image in folktales. Ogres in other Eastern European folktale traditions who are close to Koshchei (their force or strength is secretly located in a series of nested animals or objects) are the Hungarian Lead-Headed Friend or Lead-Headed Monk, the Slovak Iron Monk, and the Serbian Baš-Čelik (in Turkish, "Head of Steel").

The Heroine Comes into Conflict with Her Brother

SUS 313E*, The Sister Sank into the Earth (AT 313E*, Girl Flees from Brother Who Wants to Marry Her) is a tale which explicitly concerns brother-sister incest. In spite of the concluding wedding, some of its features recall the children's tales with a villain Baba Yaga. Parents die, and their son wishes to marry his sister. He is told he must find a wife like his sister (Karnaukhova 70), a witch causes a ring to fit only his sister (Afanas'ev 114), or he simply cannot find a woman more beautiful than his sister (Onchukov 71). His sister evades him with the help of dolls, who sing and cause her to sink into the earth (Karnaukhova 70).

The heroine comes to another world and arrives at a hut turning on chicken legs. There, a maiden is embroidering or weaving human hair. The maiden warns her that Baba-Yaga will soon return and eat her. The maiden turns the heroine into a needle or hides her. Baba-Yaga comes home and smells the Russian scent, but she cannot find any flesh to eat and goes to sleep (Karnaukhova 70). The third time Baba-Yaga returns home, she catches the heroine and wants to cook her. Just like the boy hero of SUS 327C/F, the heroine sticks one leg out so that she won't fit in the oven. Baba-Yaga demonstrates, and the two girls shove her in and seal the oven door. Nevertheless, Baba-Yaga manages to get out (Afanas'ev 114). The maiden prepares a thick oat flour porridge to stop up the seven throats of Baba-Yaga's son (*u nei byl syn o semi gorlakh*). Eventually, he licks up all the porridge and can cry out with all seven throats that the girls have left. Baba-Yaga hears him and rides home (Onchukov 71).

The heroine and the maiden flee and are chased by Baba-Yaga in her mortar. They throw three objects (brush, steel, flint, comb, scissors, or cloth) which become obstacles (mountain, forest, fiery river). Baba-Yaga is held back or destroyed by the last obstacle (D672, Obstacle flight). They return to the heroine's home and the maiden from Baba-Yaga's hut marries the heroine's brother. In Onchukov 71 the heroine agrees to marry the maiden's brother, who had also wanted to marry his own sister.

The conclusion of this tale resolves the problem of the brother's desire to marry his sister by providing a substitute—the maiden from Baba-Yaga's dwelling. Her identity is variously explained in these tales. In Onchukov 71 she appears very strikingly as the heroine's alter ego: At the end of the tale we find out that she had gone under the ground for the same reason the heroine did. In Karnaukhova 70 the maiden and the heroine are almost identical in appearance: The heroine's brother at the end of the tale cannot tell which one of them is his sister. In Afanas'ev 114 the maiden is Baba-Yaga's daughter.

Afanas'ev 114 presents one of the few instances in which Baba-Yaga attempts to cook a girl. Unfortunately, the only information provided about this rather anomalous tale text is that it was recorded in Kursk province. This version also emphasizes Baba-Yaga's cannibalistic tendencies. When Baba-Yaga comes home and smells the Russian scent, her daughter makes up the excuse that some people passed by and drank water. Baba-Yaga reproaches her for not keeping them there, but her daughter says that the passersby were old and not the right thing "for your teeth" (*ne po tvoim zubam*). The presence of this episode suggests that this tale is closer in spirit to the children's tales, in spite of the concluding wedding.

Onchukov 44 begins with episodes from SUS 780 (AT 780, The Singing Bone): The heroine goes to the forest with her elder sister to gather berries. Because the heroine finds a golden stone and will receive a new dress, her envious elder sister kills her. Although dead, the heroine sings to her family about her murder. She asks her brother to open the gates for her so that the wolves won't eat her. He agrees to do this only if she calls him her husband. She refuses, but when her second brother demands the same thing, she agrees. She goes behind the oven and makes two dolls, who sing about this shameful event (a brother calling a sister his wife), and the heroine sinks through the earth. She comes to a hut on a chicken's leg with a grandmother. The heroine sees a large cloud approaching and the old woman tells her it is Yagabikha. The two hide under a needle and then the heroine keeps running. At the next hut there is an old man. When the cloud approaches again, they hide under a piece of flint and then run together. Yagabikha pursues them through a mountain (she runs back for shovel and axe) and over a river, but the heroine and the old man cut the piece of canvas they had crossed the river on, and Yagabikha falls into the river and drowns. They come to the tsar's house and ask for shelter. The text ends there because the narrator could not remember the rest of the story.

Baba Yaga as Usurper

Baba Yaga or her daughter take the heroine's place in a group of tale types which is perhaps the most typical and representative for Baba Yaga as a villain opposing the heroine. The first type in this group is SUS 403, The Substituted Wife (AT 403, The Black and the White Bride). The tale opens in a number of different ways. If the tsar's wife bears a daughter, she is to hang a distaff from the palace wall. She does so, but the witch Egabova finds out and replaces the distaff with a gun and arrow. The tsar sees the gun and does not return home. His daughter grows up and wants to see him (Nikiforov 1961 no. 80). Three sons go to work in Petersburg, and their parents hire Egibikha as a servant

(Onchukov 218). The heroine produces gold or rubies when she laughs, pearls when she cries, and her footprints are golden and silver. In spite of her warning, her brother boasts of her at a prince's banquet, and the prince wishes to summon her (Razumova and Sen'kina 1974 no. 20, Simina 45).

The heroine is going to visit her brothers (Onchukov 218), her father (Nikiforov 1961 no. 80), or the tsar or prince she is to marry (Simina 45, Smirnov 32). Baba Yaga accompanies her, in one case threatening to drown the heroine if she is not allowed to go along (Simina 45). She turns the heroine into a pike and throws her into the sea (Simina 45, Smirnov 32). She or her daughter take the heroine's clothing and take her place (Nikiforov 1961 no. 80, Onchukov 218). In Razumova and Sen'kina 1974 no. 20, the heroine and her brother are on a ship going to the prince's realm and pass by an island. Baba Yaga forces them to take her along by threatening them with deafness, with blindness, and with capsizing the ship. She then turns the heroine into a swan.

Baba Yaga or her daughter takes the heroine's place. The heroine is forced to herd the tsar's cows (Nikiforov 1961 no. 80) or her brothers treat her like a servant (Onchukov 218). The tsar or prince is disappointed with his bride and throws the heroine's brother in prison (Razumova and Sen'kina 1974 no. 20, Simina 45). In animal form the heroine appears, casts off her animal skin, and laments. Her lament is heard by her brother, by guards, or by brewers who are brewing beer for the wedding.

The heroine's parents find out the truth from a newly born son (Onchukov 218), or the tsar or prince hears from his servants (Nikiforov 1961 no. 80). Baba Yaga and her daughter are killed by being driven into a hole which may be filled with fire or burning tar (Nikiforov 1961 no. 80, Razumova and Sen'kina 1974 no. 20, Simina 45) or they are shot on a gate (Smirnov 32, Onchukov 218).

Razumova and Sen'kina 1982 no. 40 combines this tale type with SUS 409 (AT 409, The Girl in the Form of a Wolf). A man's wife dies. His daughter (the heroine) tells him to set a trap for birds, and he finds Yagibikha and her three daughters in the trap. She threatens to eat him if he does not marry her. Prince Ivan hears of the heroine's beauty and comes to ask for her hand. Yagibikha puts one of her own daughters in her place and shoves the heroine under a trough. A dog reveals the truth, and the prince finds the heroine and leaves Yagibikha's daughter under a bridge.

The heroine and the prince have a boy. A messenger bears the news to the heroine's father and is intercepted by Yagibikha. She finds her daughter under the bridge and puts her in the heroine's place, turning the heroine into a deer. But the boy will not suck the false mother's breast. The prince goes to a kindly grandmother, who tells him what has happened. The heroine comes to nurse her child and casts off her deerskin. The second day the prince seizes her. She changes into several different animals and finally a spindle. He breaks the spindle and she regains her original form. Yagibikha and her daughter are tied to stallions and torn apart.

Smirnov 141 combines this type with SUS 428 (AT 428, The Wolf). The hero finds a magic horse with the help of an old woman donor. The hero comes to the hut on chicken legs, where Egiboba feeds him and gives him gifts, displaying a certain measure of ambiguity, but she does this because she wants him to marry her own daughter. The hero comes to another kingdom, defeats an enemy army, and wishes to marry Princess Mar'ia. Egiboba finds out, flies by in her mortar, and turns Mar'ia into a duck. Then Egiboba forces the hero to marry her daughter, threatening to eat him otherwise. An old man donor catches the duck and restores Mar'ia to her human form, although she is mute. Egiboba's daughter has Mar'ia milk bears, shear wolves, and clean fish. Mar'ia finds her wedding ring in a fish and regains the gift of speech. She tells the hero about Egiboba's villainy. He has Egiboba and her daughter shot on the city gate.

There is one example in this corpus of SUS 533, The Substituted Princess (AT 533, The Speaking Horsehead, Razumova and Sen'kina 1974 no. 59). This tale bears close resemblance to AT 403, The Black and the White Bride. Seven sons say they will go to live in the forest if their mother bears another son. Their mother bears a daughter and hangs a distaff outside as a signal. Yaga-Baba takes the distaff and puts a gun in its place. The sons stay in the forest, and when the heroine has grown up her mother sends her to visit them. Three times she is stopped by Yaga-Baba, and each time her dog warns her not to say where she is going. Yaga-Baba is angry and breaks all the dog's legs (one leg at each encounter), and finally the heroine tells her where she is going. Yaga-Baba goes along and suggests that they go swimming. Yaga-Baba gets out of the water first and takes the heroine's dress, and then her place when they arrive at her brothers' house. The heroine is sent out to herd the horses and given a stone and a splinter of wood to eat. Each day she laments to her parents, and on the second and third days her brothers hear the lament. They bring her into the house, feed her, and shoot Yaga-Baba at the gate. This could be considered a children's tale, since it concerns a sister and her brothers, and there is no final wedding. It is very similar to AT 451A (Giliarova and Frumkin 14, see chapter 3).

SUS 405, Jorinde and Joringel (same title in the Aarne-Thompson index), appears to be very infrequent in Russia. The East Slavic tale-type index lists only three versions, one of which (Balashov 49) features Baba Yaga as the villain. The heroes are an orphan brother and his sister, who produces pearls when she laughs and gold when she cries. The sister is about to marry Agar Agarovich, but on the wedding day Yaga-Baba comes, asks for her possessions, and finally strikes her with a whip. The heroine is turned into a bird, and Yaga-Baba puts her own daughter Yagarnushka in her place. Agar Agarovich marries Yagarnushka but realizes something is amiss when she fails to produce pearls and gold. He throws the hero into prison. The heroine comes to visit her brother, casts off three skins, and regains her human form. She laughs and cries and leaves pearls and gold in her brother's cell. The guards notice this and report it to Agar Agarovich. He comes and watches for three nights. On the third night he burns the skins and holds on to the heroine. Yaga-Baba is shot "on seven gates."

The unusual heroine of Onchukov 278 (somewhat resembling SUS 407, The Flower-Girl, AT 407, The Girl as Flower) is plagued by a talking boil or abscess (*kila borbotukha*) that repeats everything she says. Eventually, her husband leaves her because of the talking abscess and marries a Yaga-Baba. At their wedding the heroine releases the abscess into the beer she is cooking and reproaches Yaga-Baba for her remarks. The heroine's husband returns to her and gets rid of Yaga-Baba. The heroine's release of the boil into the beer suggests contagion (cf. Onchukov 2000 Shokshozero 51, a version of AT 428, in chapter 5), and the dialect word *kila* can also refer to male genitalia, as it does in the Onchukov tale, which implies a subtext of disease, perhaps venereal disease.

In SUS 450, Brother and Sister (AT 450, Little Brother and Little Sister), the heroine and her brother pass by a series of animal footprints with water in them. Her brother is thirsty and wants to drink, but she warns him not to. The last time, he ignores her advice and turns into a goat. The two come to a place (often they live with a kind old woman) where the heroine meets a prince who marries her. She and her brother go to live with him. In the prince's absence Baba Yaga lures the heroine outside, either to bathe or go swimming. She ties a rope with a stone to the heroine and pushes her into the water. Then she puts her daughter in the heroine's place. In Tseitlin 11, Yaits'na-Babits'na takes the heroine's place herself.

The false heroine urges the prince to kill the goat. She may say she is pregnant and must have goat meat (Tseitlin 11). The prince starts to carry out her wish, but three times the goat asks for another day of life. He goes to the sea and calls to his sister, who is unable to leave the sea because of the rope that holds her down. The third time, the prince sees what is happening. He rescues the heroine and kills Baba Yaga and her daughter.

Although the episodes of Baba Yaga's villainy and her punishment are fairly uniform in all versions of this tale, there is significant variation in the preceding episodes. A wicked stepmother has the heroine and her brother abandoned in the forest in Balashov 155. Other beginnings recall SUS 313A (AT 313, The Girl as Helper in the Hero's Flight): A merchant's ships are becalmed at sea or a tsar wants to drink from a well and the water spirit (*vodianoi*) forces him to relinquish what he does not know at home (Karnaukhova 64, Onchukov 128, Onegina 19). When he arrives he finds that a daughter has been born. She flees with a goat who hides her from envoys of the water spirit's wedding party. Later, they are pursued by the same envoys, and the heroine throws magic objects behind her, which become obstacles (Onchukov 128, Karnaukhova 64; D672, Obstacle flight). They come to another city or realm and live with an old woman. The heroine weaves and sells carpets and is noticed by a wealthy merchant, who marries her (Onchukov 128). They come to a house in a meadow. Hunters knock on the door, and the heroine refuses to let them in, but finally one comes in. He is a king and marries her (Karnaukhova 64). In Onegina 19 Prince Ivan comes to the old woman's house looking for a bride.

Onegina 27 begins with the witch Ibikha pursuing the heroine and her beloved he-goat. The heroine throws magic objects behind her to block Ibikha's path, but the witch later finds out that she has married. The grandmother who has taken in the heroine warns her about Ibikha, but the heroine opens the door for her. Ibikha throws the heroine in the river and takes her place. The husband is surprised when his false wife wants the goat killed; he hears the goat speaking with the heroine in the river, finds out the truth from the grandmother, rescues the heroine and kills Ibikha.

The accomplished tale-teller Abram Novopol'tsev (Sadovnikov 65) combines this tale with SUS 511 (AT 511, One-Eye, Two-Eyes, Three-Eyes). A wicked stepmother makes the heroine and her brother tend cattle. The stepmother wonders how the heroine manages to weave and spin at the same time, and when she finds out that a bull has been doing this work for her, she has her husband kill the bull. The heroine buries the bull's intestines, and an apple tree grows which allows only the heroine to pick its apples. A passing landlord wants an apple and so notices the heroine. He marries her, and when they leave, the apple tree jumps onto the back of their carriage.

Unfortunately, one of the heroine's new neighbors is Yagaia Baba, who is angry that the landlord has not married one of her own daughters. She leaves goat lard in the bathhouse. Later, the heroine forgets her ring in the bathhouse and when her brother goes to fetch it he ignores her warning, licks up some of the lard, and turns into a goat. Yagaia Baba's daughters lure the heroine outside to go swimming with them, and their mother binds the heroine to a stone and throws her in the river. Time passes and the landlord decides to marry one of Yagaia Baba's daughters, who urges him to kill the goat. The goat pleads for its life and reveals the heroine's location to the landlord. Yagaia Baba and her daughter are shot on the gate, and their meat is thrown to the dogs.

Three versions of the tale contain elements which bring them close to children's tales (chapter 3). Smirnov 43 and Zelenin Viatka 11 begin with a pea plant that grows up to the sky (SUS 218B*, AT 218*, Cock and Hen Plant Bean), and the latter tale includes an oven episode (SUS 327C/F). An orphan brother and sister drop a pea, and a pea plant grows to heaven. In Smirnov 43 the heroine climbs the stalk and finds a mill which grinds food. She brings some home, and then her brother wants to go along. They go together and the miller catches them. The heroine warns her brother several times not to drink water, but finally he does and turns into a goat. They live with the miller. He goes out hunting and tells her not to go anywhere. Yaga-Baba comes, lures her outside, and ties her to a bush by the river. Yaga-Baba replaces the heroine with her own daughter, and the tale continues as outlined above. Strictly speaking, this is a children's tale, because the heroine does not marry the miller, who addresses her as "girl" (*devushka*).

In Zelenin Viatka 11, the heroine climbs up the pea stalk and finds a hut that turns on chicken legs. She enters with the traditional formulaic phrase and finds a goat (a male goat, *kozel*). The goat is stretched out inside the hut. The heroine finds millstones which produce food and manages to get away while the goat calls out, summoning various body parts (legs, arms, head, eyes, beard) to come. The second time she goes to the hut, her brother comes along and the goat catches them. The goat puts the children in the cellar and first asks for fingers and toes from them. Then, the goat decides to cook the girl, but is fooled and cooked himself (SUS 327C/F). In spite of her warnings, the heroine's brother licks up some of the juice from the cooked goat and turns into a goat.

The heroine grows up and is married to the merchant Ivan. One day he loses a glove. Egi-boba finds the glove and uses it to gain entry into the house. Egi-boba puts her own daughter in the heroine's place, ties a stone to the heroine, puts snakes on her breasts, and throws her in the river. Ivan recognizes that something is wrong because his wife no longer has gold and silver legs, but rather one leg of excrement, the other of manure (*odna noga govenna, drugaia nazëm"na*).

Simina 34 introduces elements of SUS 123 (AT 123, The Wolf and the Kids) and SUS 327 into the tale. A sheep mother with presumably human children leaves for the day and warns her children about Yagabova. She tells them to lie to Yagabova about which road she has taken. Twice the children recognize that Yagabova is not their mother and she is fooled. The third time Yagabova has a smith sharpen her tongue and manages to fool one child. He lets her in and she eats him and his sheep mother when she returns. The two other children hide in the cellar. After Yagabova leaves they come out, the brother drinks from a sheep's hoofprint in spite of his sister's warning and turns into a lamb. The come to the home of the peasant son Ivan, who marries the sister, and the tale proceeds as outlined above, with Yagabova as the villain who replaces the heroine with her own daughter. V. I. Chernyshev briefly mentions a literary version of AT 450 from an eighteenth-century collection in which Baba Yaga turns the heroine Alena into a lynx (1934: 597, 604).

SUS 510A, Zolushka (Cinderella), is a very widespread tale type, but appears to be less popular among the East Slavs than it is in western Europe. In Razumova and Sen'kina 1974 no. 21 the heroine and her mother are searching for a lost black sheep. An "aunt" they meet on the way says she knows where the sheep is and leads away the mother. She then turns the mother into a black sheep and takes her place. The heroine's grandmother tells her that this woman is not her mother, but a Yagishna, and that she will have the black sheep killed. The heroine runs to her sheep mother with the news, and her mother tells her not to eat her meat, but to bury her bones under the window. The heroine does this, and flowers grow where the bones are buried. According to notes to an unpublished version of Cinderella, after the heroine marries the prince, an envious Baba Yaga rubs magic pitch on the ceiling of the bathhouse and kills the heroine (Balashov 1970: 428).

There is a general proclamation that Prince Ivan is searching for a bride. The false mother Baba-Yaga takes her own daughter to the feast, breaks the oven, and tells the heroine she must repair it. The heroine's grandmother tells her to take flowers from her mother's grave to restore the oven and make herself beautiful, and tells her where in the forest she can find a carriage to take her to the prince's feast. The heroine goes there three times (Baba-Yaga mixes sour milk with water which the heroine must separate, then cuts the head of a sheep which must be restored to life). The prince spreads tar on the threshold and door handle and so keeps the heroine's shoe and ring. He comes to the heroine's house three times. Baba-Yaga presents her own daughter and even chops at her foot, which still will not fit the shoe. The heroine marries the prince, Baba-Yaga demands to know the grandmother's secret, and she kills all the sheep in anger.

In SUS 511, The Miraculous Cow (AT 511, One-Eye, Two-Eyes, Three-Eyes), Baba Yaga is a wicked stepmother who persecutes the heroine. Sometimes this tale is combined with SUS 409 (AT 409, The Girl in the Form of a Wolf), where Baba Yaga tries to replace the heroine with her own daughter.

The heroine's mother dies and her father marries Baba Yaga. Before she dies, the mother tells the heroine that a certain cow will take care of her, or she blesses the cow. Baba Yaga has three daughters of her own: a one-eyed, a two-eyed, and a three-eyed girl. Baba Yaga treats the heroine badly. She gives her work to do, sends her to herd the cows, and gives her no food or clothes. The cow magically provides the heroine with food and clothing. The stepmother wonders how this is possible and sends her daughters to watch the heroine. Baba Yaga's three daughters go out with the heroine, who picks lice from their hair and puts their eyes to sleep. She forgets to put the third daughter's third eye to sleep, and so Baba Yaga finds out about the cow. Baba Yaga orders her husband to kill the cow. The cow tells the heroine to bury its intestines, bones, blood, horns, or hooves, or the heroine simply knows to do this. An apple tree, a garden with apple trees, a bush with berries, or a garden with singing birds grows on the spot. Prince Ivan, a merchant, or another man hears about the tree or passes by and wants an apple. The tree will only allow the heroine to pick apples from it, and the man marries the heroine.

In Balashov 130, the stepmother's daughters go into the garden, where birds peck all their eyes out, except for the third daughter's third eye. Simina 42 begins somewhat differently. Yagabova's two daughters go with the heroine to the forest to gather berries. Yagabova's daughters are rude to an old man, but the heroine politely answers his question and he gives her a magic piece of bark which can produce food. The heroine uses it to summon a cow as well. The three-eyed daughter finds out about the cow, and events proceed as in the other versions. Razumova and Sen'kina 1974 no. 71 has an unusual tragic ending: The man who weds the heroine is overly talkative. She tells him about the magic tree, and he tells her stepmother, who tears out the tree and so kills the heroine. The storyteller ended her tale with the remark: "Poor thing, she died because of that fellow" (Razumova and Sen'kina 1974: 332).

Four versions of the tale continue with SUS 409. Baba Yaga turns the heroine into a goose or a lynx after she contrives to get into the heroine's home and lures her outside, or during her return visit with a newly born son. Baba Yaga replaces the heroine with her own daughter. The heroine returns to nurse her child and casts off her animal skin. Her husband finds out from a servant and comes to watch. He burns the animal skin and seizes the heroine, who turns into a lizard, reptiles, and finally a spindle. He breaks the spindle in half and the heroine regains her human form (as in AT 402). He throws out Egibisna (Zelenin Viatka 14), shoots Yagishna's daughter at the gate (Afanas'ev 101), or says he will live with the one who first climbs the gate. Yagichna gets on the gate first and he shoots her (Efimenko 1878: 227). Smirnov 41 mentions no punishment for Yaga-Baba.

The final tale of this category is SUS 736B*, The Princess's Fortune (AT 736, Luck and Wealth), Ozarovskaia 27. The tsar is told that one day his daughter will be whipped in the marketplace. He does not let her out until one day, when she boards a ship and arrives on another shore. She climbs a tree by a well and Ega-Baba's daughter comes to fetch water. She thinks the heroine's reflection in the water is her own, and reproaches her mother for calling her ugly (*nekrasishsha*). Ega-Baba comes and finds the heroine, who goes with her to live and work. One day the tsar of that realm wants a cap sewn with pearls. Ega-Baba tells the tsar her own daughter will complete the work, but has the heroine sew the cap. While the heroine is sewing, a raven flies down and carries away the last pearl. The tsar is angry, Ega-Baba blames the heroine, and she is whipped in the marketplace.

A childless couple takes pity on her and she goes to live with them. On their name days, they call out to their Fortune (*talan*) to come and eat. The Fortunes of the man and woman are gracious maidens who leave silver and gold in gratitude. On the third day the heroine calls her own Fortune, who comes in rags, devours the food, and leaves nothing in return. The heroine pursues her Fortune, who gives her three rag bundles. The first is empty, but the other two contain a golden hook and loop. Soon the tsar declares that he needs just such a hook and loop for a caftan, and the heroine's are the only ones to be found in the realm. The heroine marries the tsar, and while walking in the garden with him, the raven returns the pearl. She tells the tsar what happened, and Ega-Baba is shot at the gate.

The Maiden without Hands and the Marvelous Children

In these tales, Baba Yaga disrupts the heroine's relations with her father, brother, or husband, and causes her to be driven away from home. In SUS 706, The Maiden without Hands (same number and title in the Aarne-Thompson index), the heroine's brother or widowed father marries Egibikha, Yaits'na-Babits'na, or Yaga-Baba's daughter. The new wife kills animals, breaks dishes, cuts down a tree, and finally kills her own child. She accuses the heroine. The heroine's brother or father takes her to the forest and cuts off her hands. Prince Ivan finds her, takes her home with him, and marries her. After some time he leaves and she bears a child. A messenger with a letter is sent to Ivan. The messenger stops and spends the night at Egibikha's house. Egibikha forges the letter to say that the heroine has given birth to a being which is half-animal, half-human. Ivan writes back, and his letter is intercepted as well. Egibikha instructs his parents to drive away the heroine.

The heroine leaves and comes to a river or well. She stoops to drink and her child falls in the water. A voice tells her to reach for him. In Potanin 1906 no. 1

it is the voice of the Lord, and is repeated three times. She reaches for the child and her hands grow back. She comes to her brother's or father's house, where she is not recognized. Ivan arrives and asks her to tell a tale. She tells her own story. He recognizes the heroine, and Yaga-Baba is shot on seven gates. In Tseitlin 12, Yaits'na-Babits'na crawls behind the oven, eats mercuric chloride, and dies.

Balashov 134 differs from the other three versions in its structure. In the beginning the heroine (who is already without hands) begs at Prince Ivan's window. The third time he marries her. He leaves to go study and the letter episode is trebled. The heroine gives birth to a marvelous son with the sun on his forehead (similar to the children of AT 707, see below). The worker sent with the letter is detained by Yaga-Baba, who forges the letters and writes that the child is only half-human, and half-dog, half-mouse, or half-cat. When the child falls into the river, an old man with a white beard tells the heroine to reach for her child, and she then goes to live with him. The boy stands next to his father in church and invites him to their house for the feast day. The boy tells him the beginning of the story, and then the heroine comes out from behind the oven. Prince Ivan recognizes his wife, and when they return home, Ivan's mother dies. Yaga-Baba is not punished or even mentioned again. The tale-teller does not seem quite sure what Ivan's mother died of: "She saw her daughter-in-law and grandson, was either frightened or overjoyed and fell down, and died right then from fright. She experienced all this, felt pity, and then died" (Balashov 1970: 375). That Prince Ivan's mother dies from fright suggests that she is the one guilty of causing the heroine's misfortunes and that she fears punishment. Although the narrator was somewhat confused about why Ivan's mother dies, it seems likely that she unconsciously identified the Yaga-Baba who intercepted the letters with Prince Ivan's mother.

Explicitly this tale develops out of a young woman's conflict with her stepmother (Tseitlin 12) or sister-in-law (Balashov 47, Nikiforov 1961 no. 39, Potanin 1906 no. 1). In Balashov 134 Yaga-Baba may be a symbolic equivalent for the heroine's mother-in-law. Any of these conflicts could be found in the lives of young women in the traditional culture (the stepmother could be a disguised mother). SUS 706 is clearly related to SUS 707 by the appearance of a "marvelous child" in one version, and by the defining motif that the heroine's arms are cut off up to the elbow. In SUS 707 the marvelous children sometimes have arms that are gold up to the elbow, and legs that are silver up to the knee.

SUS 707, The Marvelous Children (AT 707, The Three Golden Sons), is a popular tale in East Slavic tradition, and inspired Aleksandr Pushkin's fairy tale in verse "Skazka o tsare Saltane" ("The Tale of Tsar Saltan"). Some features of Pushkin's popular literary fairy tale have in turn been accepted in oral tradition

(Onegina 1986: 212–213). Generally, Baba Yaga plays the part of a wicked midwife in this tale.[2] In the versions available for the present survey, Baba Yaga is consistently a villain. Novikov reports one exceptional version of SUS 707 where Baba Yaga appears as donor and helps in the prince's search for his young wife (see Appendix II: Index of Tales). Perhaps this version is similar to Bandarchyk 1978 no. 65, discussed below.

The tsar's son overhears three sisters, who each say what she would do if he were to marry her. The eldest would weave enough cloth for the whole world, the second sister would brew enough beer for the whole world (Balashov 46), but the third sister says she would give birth to three (or nine) marvelous sons. The tsar's son marries the youngest sister. In Potanin 1902 no. 5, Baba-Yaga's daughter says she will spin enough linen for the army, while the heroine, a peasant's daughter, will give birth to marvelous children. While her husband is away, the heroine gives birth to marvelous sons who may have the sun on their foreheads, the moon on the back of their heads, stars or pearls on the sides of their heads, arms which are golden up to the elbow, and legs silver up to the knee (*vo lbu krasnoe solntse, na zatylke svetel mesiats, po lokot' ruki v zolote, po koleno nogi v serebre*, Kitainik 10).[3]

Sent to fetch a midwife, the servant (in some versions the husband) encounters Baba Yaga, who offers her services or threatens harm if she is not hired. Baba Yaga steals the marvelous children and replaces them with animals (dogs, cats, pigs). The third time the heroine gives birth, she hides one of the sons (in her braid, in her sleeve). After the third birth the heroine's husband does not forgive her and puts her in a barrel and casts her into the sea. Inside the barrel her son grows quickly and expresses his wishes: that the barrel may be washed ashore, that it might open, that they might find food, that a palace might appear for them. Each time the heroine answers: "from your mouth to God's ears" (*iz tvoikh ust da Bogu v ushi*) and the wish is granted (Balashov 46).

Three times sailors or wandering beggars stop at the previously deserted island and visit the heroine and her son. They then go to the tsarevich's realm and report to him what they have seen. In the meantime he has married Baba Yaga or her daughter. He may express the wish to visit the island, but his new wife keeps him from going. When the sailors tell of the wonders there, Baba Yaga boasts that she possesses greater things: a bull with a bathhouse on its tail, a lake in its middle, and a church on its head, a crystal lake with custard banks

---

[2] Her activities as a midwife are hinted at in Zelenin Viatka 27, AT 428, when the villain Egi-boba complains that she is being called five times a day to help with births.

[3] This motif is found in at least one Russian incantation, in which the person being healed is said to have the sun on his forehead, the moon on the back of his head, and stars in the locks of his hair (Maikov 1994: 84, no. 214).

and silver spoons from which one can eat as much as one pleases (Razumova and Sen'kina 1974 no. 11), gates that sing (Potanin 1902 no. 53), a horse both stallion and mare with a silver tail, and a singing cat which causes grass to wither (Karnaukhova 69). Finally, she boasts of the marvelous sons. In some versions there is no boasting; the traveling merchants simply tell the heroine's husband about the island, where the heroine and her son live with a cat that tells tales when it climbs up a tree stump and sings songs when it climbs down (this recalls Pushkin's cat in the prologue to "Ruslan and Liudmila"), and a hog that defecates wheat (Potanin 1902 no. 35).

Each time the heroine's son has taken the form of an insect and gone with the sailors. He overhears and reports Baba Yaga's boasting. Either he wishes for and is granted the wonders Baba Yaga boasts of, or he steals them from Baba Yaga. After the third round of boasting the heroine prepares bread with milk from her own breasts. Her son takes it to the other sons. They recognize their mother's milk and he brings them back to the heroine.

Finally, the tsarevich (in some versions he has become tsar at this point) goes to the island and recognizes his wife and children. He returns with them or stays to live with them on the island. Baba Yaga or her daughter is shot by the sons (Razumova and Sen'kina 1974 no. 11), shot at the gate (Karnaukhova 69, Smirnov 37, Tseitlin 9), tied to a stallion that is let loose in a field (Onegina 57), tricked into walking over and falling into a fiery pit (Simina 8), beheaded (Khudiakov 84), or simply killed (Simina 37). In Smirnov 131 Yagi-Baba runs around the hut shooting a gun, realizing that she will be killed. Yaga Yaganishna's daughter is shot on the gate, but her mother does not know what has happened in Potanin 1902 no. 59. When she comes to visit she sees parts of her daughter's body lying on the ground. She thinks the dismembered arms are rakes for raking hay, and that the skull she sees is a cup.[4] Finally, she sees her daughter's face, realizes what has happened, howls, and runs home. The heroine's third son in Potanin 1906 no. 41 flies in the form of a falcon and kills Yagishna, who has turned into a hawk. In Afanas'ev 284 Baba-Yaga simply has nothing more to boast of and is left to sit and be silent (*sidit da molchit*), while the teller of Balashov 46 does not mention the fate of Yaga-Baba at the end of her tale.

Bandarchyk 1978 no. 65 has an unusual opening. The tsar's son overhears Baba Yaga's two daughters and her stepdaughter. Baba Yaga hides her stepdaughter by presenting her in a group of thirty maidens who look alike, but

---

[4] This recalls Smirnov 151 (SUS 333B), where the heroine goes to visit her godmother Yaga-Yaginishna, and finds a human hand and finger being used to lock the door and a human head used as a broom. Human body parts are used for locks and bolts in Afanas'ev 104, "Vasilisa the Beautiful" (SUS 480B*).

Baba Yaga's stepdaughter lets the hero know how to recognize her and he marries her. After the heroine is put to sea, the tsar's son marries one of Baba Yaga's own daughters. While the abandoned heroine and one of her sons build a new city, Baba Yaga's daughter boasts of a series of wonders found in her mother's, Baba Yaga's, realm. The heroine's son kills Baba Yaga (smoke issues from her nostrils, flames from her mouth, and sparks from her ears) and Baba Yaga's daughter kills herself when she hears the news.

Kitainik 10 was recorded in a mining region of the Ural mountains. The villain Yaga-Yagishna is the owner of a mine and sends the heroine's marvelous sons there to work. After arriving on the other shore, the one son the heroine has hidden in her sleeve encounters a hunchbacked old man who tries to kill him three times. Each time his dog saves him from the old man, who is Yaga-Yagishna's brother (this episode bears some resemblance to SUS 563, AT 563, The Table, the Ass, and the Stick). With his dog's help and using the magic axe he has obtained from the old man, the son then releases his brothers and a thousand captive workers from Yaga's mine. They come to the palace, where the tsar's son is about to marry Yaga-Yagishna's daughter. Yaga-Yagishna and her daughter turn to snakes and are crushed by the workers' cast-iron boots.

Kitainik 10 and other versions (Khudiakov 84, Onegina 57, Smirnov 37, 131, Tseitlin 9) do not contain the boasting sequence. Khudiakov 84 is a combination of SUS 531 (AT 531; Ferdinand the True and Ferdinand the False; the hero Vaniusha finds a shining feather and presents it to the tsar, who sends him on other errands) and SUS 707. The bride Vaniusha has acquired for the tsar becomes the heroine of the SUS 707 episode, which makes up less than a third of the tale text.

In versions other than those we have considered here, the villains are the heroine's jealous sisters (Afanas'ev 283, 285–289, Onchukov 5). The tale appears to concern a young woman's changing status after she bears children in her new home. Presumably, her status among her in-laws would improve after she had become a mother. The villains in the tale might represent a woman's sisters-in-law and her mother-in-law. Besides their punishment, the heroine's "recognition" by the tsar's son might reflect the greater respect or consideration a man would show his wife after she had borne children, or the woman's hope that this might happen. Significantly, the children in the tale are male. Ol'ga Semenova Tian-Shanskaia reports that peasant fathers were pleased with a first-born son, but were entirely indifferent to daughters. In the case of a first-born daughter, a man's companions even had the right to beat him. A peasant mother-in-law's remarks to a daughter-in-law who bore children every year, disapprovingly referring to the children as puppies, are perhaps relevant to our understanding of this tale (Semenova Tian-Shanskaia 1914: 7–8).

At the same time, the tale celebrates a woman's unique ability to create life. This tale, told mostly by women (Karnaukhova 69 is an exception), appears to place procreation and creation side by side. There is a literal birth at the beginning of the tale, and then a symbolic birth (the barrel floating at sea which opens up on land). The theme of creation continues when the heroine's son wishes for food, for a palace, or for various wonders, and the wished-for object simply appears *ex nihilo* (presumably granted by God).

The marvelous characteristics of the children might serve as a symbolic expression of how a mother could feel about her children. From a mother's point of view, every birth is miraculous, and all children are marvelous. Perhaps the false reports to her husband about animal children or children who are half-human, half-animal, represent an expecting mother's anxiety about the healthy outcome of the birth; perhaps also they could represent the unenthusiastic response to the birth of a daughter in a traditional patriarchal setting.

The final tale type of this category is SUS 708, The Monster Prince (AT 708, The Wonder Child). Only two versions of this tale type are listed in the East Slavic index. The heroine is opposed by a wicked stepmother (in Balashov 136, a Yaga-Baba). While the father is away, Yaga-Baba writes him letters, reporting that the heroine is consorting with men, and finally that she is pregnant. Yaga-Baba makes her pregnant by giving her the ashes of animal skins to drink. She puts the heroine in a box and abandons her in the forest. The heroine gives birth to a magic son Pestreiushko, who cannot be harmed by bullets, and sends him to obtain food from a tsar. They go to live with the tsar, and in a curious episode, Pestreiushko compels the tsar to marry his mother. He transports the tsar to another realm, where the tsar fails to guess which one of three maidens is his. Pestreiushko threatens to leave the tsar in this other realm if he does not promise to marry Pestreiushko's mother. Then the heroine sets tasks for the tsar (such as sewing a dress without a needle or scissors), but the tale-teller neglects to mention whether or not the tsar accomplishes them. The heroine marries the tsar and they remove Pestreiushko's skin. He appears as a handsome young man and rules after the tsar. The fact that the heroine sets tasks for the tsar, and replaces him with her son, suggests that this tale, which resembles AT 707 and was told by a woman, is a female fantasy. Yaga-Baba's actions might represent an unwanted pregnancy, the foolish and ineffectual tsar might reflect a woman's feeling about an irresponsible partner (father of her child), and the strange nature of the boy (the narrator does not provide any details, but the fact that he is transformed by removing his skin at the end of the tale suggests a monstrous or unattractive appearance) might reflect the status of an illegitimate child.

Humorous, Satirical, and Anomalous Tales

Besides male-centered tales and female-centered tales, there is a third group of Baba Yaga's villain tales which are distinguished by their relative brevity, and their anecdotal and often humorous quality. They are all male-centered.

The hero and his animal companions brew beer in a lake or sweeten the lake with honey in SUS 176**, Man, Wolf, Bear, and Others (AT 176**, Man and Animals Brew Beer). Baba Yaga comes at night to drink, and water from the lake begins to disappear. Each animal in turn guards the lake, but Baba Yaga comes riding in her mortar and beats them with her pestle. When it is the hero's turn to guard the lake, he beats her until she is barely alive (Smirnov 247). In Zelenin Perm' 62, when the hero plays the violin, Yaga-Baba dances and wants to learn to play it (AT 1159, The Ogre Wants to Learn to Play). The hero tricks her into sticking her fingers into a cleft and kills her. In Potanin 1906 no. 24 hay disappears from a peasant's field. Only the third son Ivan catches the culprit, Baba Yaga. He beats her and tricks her into putting her hand in a cleft in a tree. Baba Yaga stays there until winter, when the hay is sold.

Baba Yaga steals magic objects from the hero in SUS 563, The Miraculous Gifts (AT 563, The Table, the Ass, and the Stick). In Khudiakov 8, a bird gives the hero Ivanushka the Fool a magic food-providing tablecloth and a gold-producing horse. He inadvertently tells Baba-Yaga about the gifts, which she replaces with ordinary ones. The third time the gift is a pair of pincers, which the hero uses to punish Baba-Yaga and retrieve his tablecloth and horse.

A bird with an iron nose and a wooden tail gives the hero of Balashov 96 a magic pot that produces rice porridge, a magic tablecloth, and a dog that can either sift flour or attack viciously. The dog attacks Yagishnia (she does exactly what the man told her not to do: pronounce the words that cause the dog to attack) and she relinquishes the magic tablecloth. At home the man's wife makes the same mistake by doing what she is told not to do.

In Mitropol'skaia 53, the seventh fool son discovers a bird stealing peas from his father's field. The bird gives him a magic horse, a carpet, and a sack with magic servants. Yagataia Baba steals the horse and replaces it with an ordinary one of her own, and the hero fails to impress his father's guests, who have heard of this marvel. The hero compels Yagataia Baba to return the horse, and summons the magic servants, who beat her. A second time guests come to his father's house, and the magic horse stamps its hooves and produces coins and precious stones. The guests rush to gather them up, and the hero summons the magic servants, who beat the guests.

Baba Yaga causes marital strife in SUS 1353, The Woman Worse Than the Devil (AT 1353, The Old Woman as Trouble Maker; Gospodarev 59). A devil is unable to make a married couple quarrel. Baba-Yaga lives nearby and offers to help if he will give her a pair of red boots. She tells both husband and wife that the other is unfaithful, and tells the wife to get three hairs from her husband's head. When the wife does this, the suspicious husband beats her. The devil is overjoyed but hands the red boots to Baba-Yaga on a pole, afraid to come too close to her.

Sidel'nikov 19 is an anomalous, class-conscious tale, the only one of its type in the East Slavic index (SUS 1353B*, Yaga's Advice). The devil wants to put a horse's collar on the peasant. He creates a merchant, a landlord, and a priest. The peasant refuses to do what they ask, and they all complain to the devil, who goes to Yaga-Baba for advice. The landlord sits on an egg (laid by a demonic bird), and the tsar is hatched. The peasant defeats the tsar's army. The devil goes to Yaga a second time. She forges a nail and tells the devil to pound it into the peasant's head while he is praying, enter the peasant's ear, and steal his heart. When the devil does so they are able to place the collar on him and ride on his back to plough and sow.

Baba Yaga becomes the hero's victim in SUS 1653 A, B, C, The Fool, His Brothers, and the Robbers. Sadovnikov 27 consists of numerous episodes in which the hero, the third fool brother, tricks his brothers and other people (SUS 1535, The Expensive Hide, AT 1535, The Rich and the Poor Peasant). In one episode, the roguish hero and his brothers are camped in the forest. Yagaia-Baba appears, hopping around them on one leg. The hero warns her not to fall in their cooking pot, but she does and he tears out her leg. Later, he and his brothers are sitting in a tree while a band of robbers is sitting below. The hero drops Yagaia-Baba's leg into their porridge and splatters the eyes of the robbers, who run away. This episode in the tree (AT 1653, The Robbers under the Tree; AT 1653B, The Brothers in the Tree) is combined with SUS 327C/F in some tales (Dobrovol'skii 16, Leonova 14, Onchukov 2000 Shokshozero 74, Potanin 1906 no. 4; discussed in chapter 3 with 327C/F).

A devil gathers the twelve most wicked women, cooks them together in a pot, and one, Baba-Yaga, jumps out in SUS 1169*, Where Baba-Yaga Comes From (Serebrennikov 19, see Appendix II: Index of Tales). This oral tale is nearly identical to an episode from Vasilii Levshin's 1780 tale about the knight Zaoleshanin, which suggests either that Levshin's tale entered oral tradition, or that Levshin was influenced by the oral tradition of his time.

Baba Yaga does not appear, but is referred to in SUS 1164, The Nasty Wife in the Hole (AT 1164, The Evil Woman Thrown into the Pit; Khudiakov 24). The hero's nagging wife falls into a river. But instead of his wife, he pulls out a devil, who begs him not to be put back in the water, because "a Baba-Yaga has come to us, and she's making life impossible!" (*k nam baba-iaga prishla, nam zhit'ia ot nee ne stalo*, Khudiakov 1964: 100). The devil helps the man make money by haunting the houses of the wealthy, and finally the house of the tsar, who, like the others, pays the hero money to "drive out" the evil spirit. The last time, he calls forth the devil and threatens him with Baba-Yaga. The devil promptly runs away and jumps back into the river. The quick-thinking hero receives half the kingdom. In other versions, it is simply a mean woman who torments the devils. Baba Yaga's name in this version probably reflects its use to describe quarrelsome women (Cherepanova 1983: 104).

Baba Yaga is also indirectly present in a version of SUS 1053A, The Big Rope (identical title in the Aarne-Thompson index). In Zelenin Viatka 42 a Gypsy outsmarts a dragon several times. The dragon tells him to go butcher one of Egi-Boba's forty bulls. The Gypsy ties all forty tails together, and says he intends to sling all the bulls over his shoulder. The credulous dragon is terribly frightened.

Five anomalous texts remain difficult to classify. The first consists of several episodes in which a roguish hero tricks a dead man's family, Èga-Baba, and her animals (Khudiakov 1964: 269–270, see chapter 2). Èga-Baba is a shaman, and the tale, recorded in eastern Siberia, has been influenced by the beliefs and customs of Siberian peoples (the Yakut and Evenk). Strictly speaking, Èga-Baba is a villain in this tale, since she opposes the hero, but his behavior can hardly be described as praiseworthy.

The second text (Smirnov 341) also consists of several episodes and elements of many different tale types (Novikov relates it to SUS 400 [1974: 162, fn. 12]). After fleeing from a monster (*chudovishche*), the hero comes to an iron trap door, and beneath it finds an oven. He heats up the oven, and Baba Yaga comes and declares: "How dare you heat my oven?" The hero kills her, burns her in the oven, and throws her ashes in a bag. In the following episodes the hero obtains maidens for the monster and himself.

A tale recorded from a twelve-year-old boy resembles AT 218* (Cock and Hen Plant Bean) and AT 1960G (The Great Tree). A tree grows in the hut of an old couple, and despite the man's efforts, grows into the sky. The old man climbs the tree and comes to a hut made of pancakes. He goes inside, hears someone coming, and hides behind the oven. Yazhenia arrives and notices the Russian scent. The old man comes out, Yazhenia gives him pancakes, and takes him with her, implying that he will become her "old man" or husband (Razumova 75). Told by a child, this tale resembles the children's tales.

One version of AT 551 recorded in Siberia includes an anomalous episode in which the hero fights Baba Yaga (Gorodtsov ii: 415–431). After the hero has obtained the living and dead water and the berries of youth from Marfa Kantsybarovna, he goes down the road that promises death for his horse. A "behind-the-courtyard" grandmother warns him that Baba Yaga Yaginichna has kidnapped Princess Marfa. Baba Yaga Yaginichna arrives in her mortar, attacking the hero with fire. She asks for a reprieve and scatters pearls on the ground so that the hero slips. The hero then asks to rest, but Baba Yaga Yaginichna refuses. Her daughter reproaches her, and she then grants the hero time to rest. He scatters soot and ashes which keep him from slipping on the ground, overcomes and kills Baba Yaga Yaginichna, and tears her in two pieces.

Baba Yaga appears as a villain in a humorous text from Ukraine (Manzhura 1890: 123–124), which might appear as a prologue to a fairy tale, or could stand on its own as a "tall tale." Among other adventures, the hero comes to a hut on a chicken leg and sees Baba Yaga Bony Leg and her pretty daughter. He asks Baba Yaga if he can spend the night with her daughter. Baba Yaga agrees, if he will jump out of the hut, naked and astride a poker. The hero immediately complies, and the "whore" Baba Yaga (*a vona skurva baba*) locks him out. Eventually, the hero enlists the help of a smith. They manage to catch Baba Yaga with tongs and a hammer, and she returns the hero's clothing and belongings. Baba Yaga has shamed and emasculated this hero by making him appear naked in public, and forcing him to take on a woman's role (riding a poker is a typical activity of female witches). The smith helper recalls AT 300A.

In the introduction to another tale, the storyteller comments on the vastness of Siberia, and relates that Baba-Yaga tried to measure it with her walking stick, but went home, since she could measure neither its length nor its breadth (*Baba-Iaga merila kliukoi, da vorotilas' domoi: ni dliny, ni shiriny*, Novgorod-Severskii: 28–29). Baba Yaga is only mentioned in another tale from Siberia (Novgorod-Severskii: 81–90), which bears some resemblance to AT 550. The hero sets out to obtain a feather from the firebird. An old man donor warns him about Baba-Yaga, who eats frogs and spreads scurvy. The hero then comes to a hut on a chicken leg and a dog's shin, but it is empty. At dawn a flock of firebirds arrives, and one bird flies into the hut. The hero manages to grasp one of its feathers.

The Villain Baba Yaga in a Folk Epic Song

Baba Yaga appears in three epic songs recorded by A. F. Gil'ferding at Kenozero in the Onega region of Northern Russia in 1871, and in two more songs recorded in the same region by Iurii and Boris Sokolov from 1926 to 1928. These are five versions of the bylina "Dobrynia and Alesha" (Gil'ferding 1951 nos. 228, 290, 292; Sokolov and Chicherov 1948 nos. 239, 242). In Gil'ferding's no. 228, sung by Petr Voinov, Dobrynia is sent from Kiev to combat an unnamed fool who has asked for an opponent. Dobrynia first takes leave of his mother, then his wife, telling her to wait for nine years before remarrying. He warns her about the dishonest Alesha Popovich. Dobrynia rides off and decides to bathe in the Puchai river. The "whore Yaga Baba" (*kurva Iaga baba*) comes flying and wants to devour him naked. Dobrynia asks to get dressed first, and then fights with Yaga Baba for six years. Alesha sees him fighting, goes to Kiev, reports that he is dead, and forces Dobrynia's wife to marry him. In the meantime Dobrynia's uncle Il'ia Muromets informs Dobrynia of what has happened, and Dobrynia asks for help in killing Yaga Baba:

Govoril Il'ia da takovo slovo:	Il'ia then said:
—Da ai ty Dobryniushka Mikit'evich!	"O you Dobryniushka Mikit'evich!
Ne chest' ne slava molodetskaia.	It is no honor or glory
Dvum bogatyriam bit'sia s ódnoi baboiu.	For two knights to fight one woman.
A bei-ko ty babu po bab'emu,	Strike the woman in the woman's way,
Po tit'kam bei da i pód guzno.	On her breasts and buttocks."
Da spomnil on starye ukhvatochki,	He remembered his old ways,
A stal bit' po tit'kam da i pód guzno,	Struck her on her breasts and buttocks
Ubil on kurvu Iagu babu.	He killed the whore Yaga Baba.

(Gil'ferding 1951, vol. 3, no. 228, pp. 222–223)

Dobrynia returns just in time for the wedding feast, disguised as a minstrel. His wife recognizes him and reveals his identity before Prince Vladimir and all the guests. Dobrynia beats Alesha, who retires to a monastery. In no. 290, sung by Andrei Gusev, Dobrynia is sent to fight the knight Yaga Baba (*s bogatyrem bit'sia s Iagoi baboi*). Dobrynia does not bathe in the river. He has fought Yaga Baba for nine years when Il'ia arrives, who tells him to strike her breasts and kick her buttocks (*A bei babu po titkam, pinai pod guzno*). He kills her, cuts her to pieces, and scatters the pieces in the field. No. 292, performed by Andrei Gusev's son, Kharlam Gusev, is very much the same. Yaga Baba is called "knight" (*bogatyr*) and "female warrior" (*polianitsa*). In the two versions recorded by the Sokolov brothers, Dobrynya is sent out to fight Yaga-Baba. In no. 239 Il'ia gives him similar advice; the text of no. 242 is incomplete and breaks off before the arrival of Yaga-Baba.

Baba-Yaga's appearance is unusual and makes these five songs exceptional in the folk epic song tradition. She appears to have taken the place of the dragon, Dobrynia's usual opponent. While the songs are exceptional, they confirm and repeat certain folktale patterns. The structure of Dobrynia's adventure is very much reminiscent of SUS 327C/F: Dobrynia has a realistic good mother, toward whom he is respectful, and in a fantastic episode he kills Yaga Baba. Of course, the bylina is more complex: Dobrynia is already an adult and married, but his mother is still a significant figure in his life. Interestingly, there is no father, but Il'ia (as his uncle) appears as a belated father figure who teaches him how to deal with women—roughly. Once Dobrynia has shown that he is a man, he is able to put Alesha in his place. In no. 228 Alesha goes to a monastery, thus relegated to a nonsexual role. Women are disparaged in the figure of the "whore" Yaga Baba, who is defeated when her breasts and buttocks are beaten.

A prose tale clearly based on bylina elements is found in Gorodtsov i: 22–36. The knight Alesha Popovich goes to fight Baba Gorynka because he wishes to marry her daughter, the beauty Yaga Yaginichna. Alesha cannot overcome Baba Gorynka, and Il'ia Muromets advises him to strike her breasts and and kick her under her buttocks, because "all of Baba Gorynka's strength is there." Alesha kills Baba Gorynka and marries Yaga Yaginichna, but she does not love him and gives him a threatening warning.

Conclusion

Perhaps Nikolai Novikov is correct in considering the villain Baba Yaga "paler" than the donor. Her image as villain seems less unified, although she appears more frequently as a villain than as a donor.[5] Some features of the donor sequence may appear when she is a hostile donor, or even a villain. Perhaps the most common attributes of Baba Yaga as a villain are the mortar and pestle. The traditional formulaic phrase describing them states that Baba Yaga rides in her mortar, pushes or urges it along with her pestle and sweeps her tracks or traces away with a broom (*sela na stupu, tolkachom pogoniaet, pomelom sled zametaet*, Afanas'ev 103; *edet v stupe, pestom ponuzhat, a pomelom sledy zametat*, Afanas'ev 106; *vo ves' dukh na zheleznoi stupe skachet, pestom pogoniaet, pomelom sled zametaet*, Afanas'ev 159; *Ona siala v stupu, pogoniat pestom*, Azadovskii 1938 no. 30; *Baba-Iaga, kastsianaia naga na stupe edze, tawkachom paganiae da pamialom sled zametae*, Serzphutovskii 1911 no. 72). She may steer with the pestle (*A sama baba-iaga ezhdit na zheleznoi stupe i zheleznym pestom pravit*, Shastina 1985 no. 54). Baba Yaga may also ride on an oven fork (*Vyekhala baba-iaga sama na ukhvate*, Onchukov 241), on a goat (*uziala kazla, sela viarkhom, stala zhaleznym tawkachom paganiats'*, Bandarchyk 1971 no. 154), on a shovel (Onchukov 241), or on a broom (Onchukov 241, Kovalev 3). These attributes are usually brought into play when Baba Yaga is pursuing someone or abducting someone, as in the obstacle flight episode (motif D672), which occurs in many tales. In what appears to be an exceptional case, two Baba Yaga sisters (donors in this version of AT 551) help the hero by lending him their mortar, poker, and broom: He rides in the

---

[5] In this corpus of 422 tales, based on the criteria used in this study and Baba Yaga's behavior in individual tale texts (not tale types), Baba Yaga appears as a villain in 235 tales (56 percent of the total), as a donor in 109 tales (26 percent), and ambiguously in 78 tales (18 percent). The ambiguous category includes tales where Baba Yaga is a hostile donor, close in nature to the villain category.

mortar to the next sister's house (Bandarchyk 1973 no. 65). A rather benign Baba Yaga arrives in her mortar in a version of SUS 480*B (Lutovinova 51). A. L. Toporkov observes that these attributes, in particular the pestle, are shared in East Slavic folk belief by the witch, *rusalka,* and Iron Woman (who haunted wheat fields and kidnapped children), and that there were rituals to prevent cattle disease in which women went naked, rode on brooms, carried oven forks and pokers, let down their hair, and called out obscenities (Toporkov 1989: 127). Toporkov believes that the pestle was the original attribute, and that the mortar appeared later (ibid., 130). The mortar and pestle were also used in some healing rituals for children's illnesses (atrophy, rickets), called the "dog's old age" (*sobach'ia starost*). Children were placed in the mortar, ritually "ground," and some words were pronounced (Shevchenko 1998: 118). A humorous account of where babies come from in the Gomel' region (Belarus) is that they fall from heaven into a mortar. In the Minsk region, a parodic ritual of grinding water in a mortar was carried out when the groom's retinue left to fetch the bride. In the Ukrainian Poles'e region, the mortar and pestle were dressed in female and male clothing on the occasion of a wedding. East Slavic folk tradition appears to treat the mortar as a female symbol (Toporkov 1995).

In two tales Baba Yaga addresses her mortar with a rhyming phrase that suggests a spell or incantation: "Mother Mortar, go further than four versts!" (*Stupushka-matushka, shagai poshire versty po chetyre!* Kargin 14, AT 314A*), "Go, mortar, go three versts!" (*Stupa-stupai, po tri versty shagai!* Balashov 55, AT 301). E. N. Ivanitskaia emphasizes that the mortar is something like Baba Yaga's horse, and that representations of Baba Yaga in animated films, which show her flying in the mortar, are inaccurate and do not reflect the folk tradition. If Baba Yaga's mortar could fly, she would not fall into the fiery river the hero or heroine creates between them (Ivanitskaia 1984). The location of Baba Yaga's dwelling is not as fixed in the villain tales as it is when she is a donor. She may live in a forest hut, but also by the sea (Dobrovol'skii 14), in the underground realm (AT 301, 321), in the sky (Smirnov 143, a version of 327C/F), on Mt. Zion (Dobrovol'skii 6), or in the protagonist's household (AT 706, 707). In Bandarchyk 1978 no. 65 (AT 707), Baba Yaga has adopted the features of the magic horse of East Slavic fairy tales: Smoke comes out of her nostrils, flames from her mouth, and sparks from her ears (Barag 1969: 184).

Just as Baba Yaga's donor role (with some of its attributes) is taken by kind old women or grandmothers, Baba Yaga is not the exclusive villain in the tale types examined here. The villain may be simply a mean or frightening old woman. Baba Yaga's villain roles in the ambiguous and villain tales are quite varied, and can be seen as more than the six roles Nikolai Novikov enumerates (warrior, avenger, possessor of magic objects, evil enchantress, crafty well-wisher or evil advisor, and abductor of children). They are difficult to categorize neatly, because they frequently combine. Baba Yaga is an evil advisor, giving advice to a villain (SUS 465A, 532, 884B*, 1353B*); she provides a villain with a magic object (a sleep-inducing needle in 400/2); sells deadly objects to the heroine (709); she is a wicked stepmother (315, 400/2, 480), a false mother (510A, 516), a deceitful guardian of living (or healing) and dead water (303, 318, 519); she rivals the hero in a race for beautifying water (513A, only one tale); she is a murderous dragon mother and giant sow with a mouth reaching from heaven to earth (300A); she is a fierce physical combatant, apparent ruler of an underground realm, overcome when strong and weak drink are switched (301); she is the owner of a field in the underground realm, who gouges out an old man's eyes, and combats the hero (321); she gouges out eyes (516); she is leader of an underground army (301-like episodes); she pursues the protagonist in many tales (313H*); she keeps lovers apart (400/2); she keeps the heroine's husband under enchantment (425, 430, 432); she possesses objects the protagonist must obtain (428, 480, 531); she tricks the hero out of magic objects (563); she kidnaps children (327, 480) or a princess (410**); she is a cannibal ogress (313E*, 327, 480); she turns men to stone (303, 410**, 516); she freezes a princess (410**); she sucks a maiden's breasts (519); she is a one-eyed ogress (1137); she or her daughter takes the heroine's rightful place (403, 405, 407, 409, 450, 510A, 511, 533, 736B*); she drives the heroine away (706, 707, 708); she steals beer (176**); and she causes marital strife (1353).

Conclusion

This study of Baba Yaga has brought her complex nature into focus, as manifested in single tales, in different versions of the same tale type, and in tales where Baba Yaga's basic donor function is cloaked in hostility. Her malevolent aspect is the dominant one, but neither is she entirely evil. Nikolai Novikov finds that Baba Yaga's traditional attributes are most fully represented in the donor tales, while she could have taken on the villain roles of other characters as a later development, which might explain why her donor image is more unified and predictable than her various manifestations as a villain. On the other hand, her villain roles are more frequent in numbers of recorded tales (in 235 tales, 56 percent or almost two-thirds of the tales in this corpus), so that both aspects are outstanding: the donor in its unity and well-developed traditional formulaic phrases and episode, and the villain in its sheer numbers and variety. Even if Baba Yaga had been entirely good or evil at an earlier point in her history, for the folk tradition recorded in the nineteenth and twentieth centuries, she was essentially ambiguous.

Following V. N. Toporov, this survey has approached Baba Yaga as a single cultural "text," and accepted her contradictory, ambiguous image and behavior as an essential part of her persona, developed over generations by talented narrators. Baba Yaga's ambiguity has been explained as the result of a historical shift from matriarchy to patriarchy, the wicked Baba Yaga being a later patriarchal reinterpretation (Ivanov and Toporov 1965: 176, Novikov 1974: 180, Propp 1946: 62, 64, 93, 96), or as a reflection of the respect and fear that the all-powerful, prophetic old woman inspired (Novikov, 1974: 180), or through the poetics of the folktale, as a device of contrast (Anikin 1966: 42). Marie-Louise von Franz and Erich Neumann see ambivalence as an archaic characteristic. Ambiguity might be a characteristic of some other Russian or East Slavic folklore characters as well. The dragon, virtually always a villain, appears in one tale (Afanas'ev 128) as a donor who shows the hero the opening to the three underground kingdoms, and Prince Vladimir's ambiguity in the Russian folk epic (bylina) has been noted (Putilov 1988: 52–53).[1] Figures of folk belief (such as the forest spirit, *leshii*) are commonly ambiguous, but in the habitually "black and white" world of the folktale, and compared to other East

---

[1] Other folktale dragons who may appear as donors as well as villains are the Romanian *zmeu* (Niculescu 1991: 335) and the Bulgarian *zmei* (Dukova 1970: 246). In one Slovak tale, the dragon carries the hero home after Ježibaba has abandoned him three times on an island (Dobšinský ii: 11–23).

Slavic folktale characters, Baba Yaga's frequent ambiguity is nevertheless unusual.

Female figures of European folk belief who most resemble Baba Yaga are distinguished by a frightening appearance, an unusual nose, leg, foot, or tooth, an association with mothers and children, with days or periods of the week or year, with winter and cold weather, and with spinning, weaving, or other traditionally female tasks. Many authors have pointed out the ambiguity or dual aspect, the "mythic ambivalence" of these female figures (Kuret 1969: 212). The Forest Mother of southeastern Europe causes insomnia and crying in children, but can also cure them. Frau Holle causes snow and cold weather, while Baba Dochia dies from the cold. Perchta causes one man's death (after he travels with her during the night), but ensures the healthy delivery of a baby in another legend. The Perchten of Alpine custom are "beautiful" or "ugly," while the Slovenian Pehtra is "light" or "dark." Paraskeva-Piatnitsa (Saint Friday) cruelly punishes women who spin on Friday (in belief and legends), but appears as a donor in folktales. For the historian, the wide geographic distribution of these figures is an argument for their antiquity and possible common origin; for the psychologist, the persistence of certain themes in connection with these figures reflects the need of many societies to create maternal representations. Baba Yaga resembles the female supernatural figures associated with days of the week and spinning, but among the East Slavs this legendary role in folk belief is represented by Paraskeva-Piatnitsa, not Baba Yaga. Baba Yaga is associated with winter at least once (in a Russian folk song), and with the harvest season (in the Pskov region), but otherwise is not commonly attached to a specific time period. Traditional cultures (the Slavs among them) surround menstruation with taboos and restrictions; perhaps the periodicity of menstruation accounts for why so many figures of traditional folk belief who are associated with cyclic time, with days, seasons, or times of the day (cf. the Noon Woman and Mother Midnight), are female. Traditional cultures associate maternity with warmth and nourishment; an inversion of this maternity might account for the frequent association of these female figures with winter, a cold and infertile season. For the most part Baba Yaga lacks an association with a time or season, perhaps because she is essentially a character in folktales, a genre which treats time differently than legend or myth (cf. William Bascom's observation that the folktale is almost "timeless and placeless"). Thus Baba Yaga emerges as a unique figure, but a comparison with other witch-like characters in European folklore shows that her image is a Slavic variation on an Indo-European (and wider) theme. She appears most frequently as a folktale character, which suggests that her occasional appearances in other folklore genres (riddles, incantations, songs, popular woodcut prints, children's rhymes, harvest customs, folk epic poetry, legendary narratives) represent a secondary development. Previous studies of this character make it clear that she is a complex formation, a product of history and psychology, tradition and creative imagination. Unfortunately, Baba Yaga's history is lost to us: her age, origin, development, and what her original meaning(s) might have been remain open questions. Witches or monstrous female beings with an unusual nose, tooth, leg, or foot, and a dwelling which turns on animal legs or feet, are found in adjoining regions of eastern Europe (Hungary, Slovakia, Romania), which indicates the possibility of a common origin, cultural exchange, and a long history of parallel development, or that similar cultural and historical circumstances gave rise to these images. The geographic distribution of AT 300A also suggests a distinct eastern European tradition area, and it is interesting to find that Baba Yaga's ambiguity is shared by Ježibaba, the Hungarian Vasorrú bába, and perhaps the analogous Romanian figures.

The first reliable written records concerning Baba Yaga date from the eighteenth century. Given the conservative nature of the East Slavic folklore tradition and the presence of the obviously related Ježibaba among the West Slavs, it seems possible to assume that Baba Yaga dates back to the medieval period, and perhaps even further back in the Slavic past. Baba Yaga appears in an incantation to quiet a sleepless crying child, like the Forest Mother addressed in cognate East and South Slavic spells, and the Forest Woman in a Slavic incantation of the thirteenth century (Agapkina and Toporkov 1990: 68–69, Karwot 1955: 11, 23, Vinogradova 1983: 101–102). It is also likely that Baba Yaga is as old as the Germanic Perchta, who is already documented in the late fourteenth century (Waschnitius 1913: 61). Many authors have argued for the great antiquity of Baba Yaga and figures like her. Niko Kuret sees the Slovenian Pehtra as a manifestation of a female midwinter spirit with ancient Indo-European or even Eurasian roots (1969: 220). More cautiously, Marianne Rumpf (1991) argues for the medieval origin of Perchta, and Géza Róheim expresses the view that much of European folklore was diffused during the Middle Ages; the female personifications of the days of the week, based on the calendar, are not pre-Christian (1946: 122). Nevertheless, it is always possible that older beliefs and conceptions might become transformed and survive in new guises, as have many European pagan customs and beliefs, in Christianized form.

In an early period Baba Yaga or her prototype might have had some cult status, or been conceived as a figure of the "lower mythology," a demon of illness or some other negative manifestation of nature. Some narrators treat her like a figure of folk belief, and scholars disagree about whether "the folk" believed in her existence or not. Statements made by East Slavic narrators themselves on this matter contradict each other. Baba Yaga shares the ambiguity and frequent malevolence of the East Slavic place and nature spirits. However, Petr Bogatyrev's call for caution in identifying folktale characters with the figures of folk belief is justified, as well as his emphasis on the role of invention, of creative fantasy in folktales. (The striking and memorable image of the dwelling on a bird's foot in eastern European folktales might not have any concrete "historical roots," but might be the invention of a creative storyteller who transferred the bird foot of a demonic being onto its dwelling). If Baba Yaga had a cult status in the past, certainly by the time of the recorded folktales she had become largely a figure of folk imagination. Her behavior is frightening in many tales, but there are also short anecdotal and humorous tales which bring her down to earth, to a world much closer to the listener's, and make her seem more like an exaggerated unpleasant woman than a demonic being. Nikolai Novikov suggests that these humorous tales are a late development. Perhaps Ute Dukova is correct in supposing that Baba Yaga and Ježibaba derive from a proto-Slavic term for "illness" or "female demon of illness"; while the term retained something of its original meaning among the South Slavs, it became applied to a folktale character in West and East Slavic areas (1983: 24–27). There is no doubt that Baba Yaga's image is the result of a long history.

Pille Kippar identifies a transitional cultural zone in eastern Europe which runs through Finland, Estonia, Latvia, Lithuania, Belarus, Ukraine, and south to Turkey. The tale-type repertoires of these countries include tales known in western Europe, and tales found to the east (e.g., in Russia), while the eastern and western repertoires are distinct. A brief comparison of East Slavic and Slovak repertoires (e.g., the tale types in which Ježibaba and Baba Yaga appear, see Appendix II: Index of Tales) supports this conclusion. Kippar also finds stylistic differences between East and West, which can be observed in the Estonian and Baltic traditions. Western tales are characterized by concreteness, exactitude, and objectivity, while eastern tales display emotionality, resourcefulness, and improvisation, and have a greater tendency to "contamination," i.e., a freer combination of different tale types and episodes in forming new narratives (Kippar 1996). In comparing German and Russian folktales, August von Löwis of Menar concludes that Russian tales display fantastic elements, hyperbole, suspense, and formulaic style to a greater degree, while German tales are characterized by more realistic representation. He also finds that the names of folktale characters are more colorful and expressive in the East than in the West, and that in this regard, Ukrainian and Belorussian tales occupy a middle position between the German and Russian traditions

(Löwis of Menar 1912: 129, 134). Comparing Slovak and Russian folktales, Petr Bogatyrev observes that the Russian folktale has developed a more distinct generic identity; the difference between the folktale and legendary narratives about supernatural beings (memorates and fabulates) is more strongly felt in the Russian than in the Slovak tradition (1963: 20–21). It has also been suggested that the fantastic, magic, and marvelous elements in folktales increase as one moves across Europe from West to East; the western tales are more "rational" (Tenèze 1970: 52–53). If this observation is correct, is it a question of differences in national character or temperament, or differences of historical development? Have the traditions of eastern Europe, where industrialization and urbanization occurred later, maintained an "earlier" state of the folktale? Probably all these factors contribute to differences in the folktale traditions of Europe. Future folktale studies, especially of eastern European traditions, should help in clarifying this problem. Baba Yaga's frequent ambiguity, the fact that she so frequently occupies a place of dynamic tension between villain and donor roles, might be an "eastern" trait within Europe.

A study of Baba Yaga is necessarily a study of folktales, and must take into account the important contributions made by Vladimir Propp. Propp identifies an initiatory pattern in the fairy tale, and sees the donor Baba Yaga and her hut as a reflection of an initiation practices. The fairy tale would have had its origin in initiation ritual; when ritual died out, narratives with a ritual structure began to circulate. Studies of West African folktales have shown that both initiation rituals and fairy tales with initiatory themes coexist in the same societies and traditions. The relationships between ritual and narrative are probably more complex than Propp supposed. There may be no direct historical or cause-and-effect relationship between ritual and folktale, but the two can share a certain symbolism. The dialogue that takes place in West African folktales between the baobab tree and animals (the tree rewards the hare and punishes the hyena) may resemble the sequence of questions and answers found in initiation rituals, where the initiated progressively receives "gifts" of esoteric knowledge, and the violent, antisocial, and even suicidal actions of the Enfant Terrible in a popular folktale cycle might make sense in light of initiation; the Enfant Terrible shows that he has esoteric knowledge which places him above social values and conventions (Calame-Griaule 1987: 148–149, Görög et al. 1980: 247–249). West African folktales with an initiatory structure appear to have an important didactic function which is related to initiation, but also more generally to young people's maturation and adjustment to an adult identity. The folktale has not replaced the ritual, but complements it, exists independently of it, and appears to fulfill a different function in society than the ritual does. The initiation ritual occurs once in an individual's lifetime, while one listens to tales throughout one's life. Perhaps this is because the folktale addresses not just the significant changes at puberty, but the question of identity, which remains important at all stages of life. There is no doubt an intriguing resemblance between the Indo-European fairy tale structure and the pattern of rites of passage. But might this resemblance derive not from any historical influence of one upon the other, but rather from a shared symbolic framework that represents the essential changes in human life as a journey? The origin of a phenomenon does not necessarily explain its meaning; even if there were solid historical evidence that the fairy tale structure derived from initiation (or other) ritual, we would still have to account for the meaning the fairy tale has and had for narrators and audiences over many centuries. The historical origin of the Indo-European fairy tale morphology remains obscure, but its treatment of essential themes relevant to any narrator or listener might account for its spectacular longevity and persistence in oral tradition.

The fantastic, supernatural elements of the fairy tale are its most difficult aspect to explain. Numerous authors have interpreted these elements in one way or another as a symbolic language. Their studies suggest that this symbolism expresses essential conflicts and tensions found in all human societies, in the family, between generations, between men and women, between individuals and groups. This narrative form is both fantastic and familiar, a marvelous fiction about listeners' real lives, both a lie and the truth at the same time. The journey of the fairy tale appears to follow a heroine or hero through the necessary adventures that lead to an adult identity, and the rich language of its images touches on very personal themes. In their own ways, listeners identify with the father who loses his child to a supernatural ogre, the young mother who is slandered but rejoices in her marvelous children, the child abandoned in the forest. The traditional folktale is a house with many doors, expressing a consistent optimism about the life journey and presenting this in a polished work of verbal art. At the same time, the issues raised or questions asked by the fairy tale are common enough and articulated in a commonly shared cultural framework so that its symbolism passes the test of group approval or acceptance necessary for survival in oral tradition. The interaction between received tradition and individual narrators and audiences results in a two-sided negotiation. Traditional narratives like the fairy tale both express and manipulate their listeners' emotions and might also be one way for a group to control the experiences of its members (Fischer 1963: 236, Honko 1964: 18). Michèle Simonsen sees the fairy tale as a compromise formation between personal gratification and moral imperatives: "Stories fulfill both the need to understand life as it is and to dream of life as it ought to be" (1998: 213).

In the rich images of the East Slavic folktale, there is good evidence for Baba Yaga's identity as a mother or a mothering figure, albeit often as a representation of negative maternity. Baba Yaga appears as a wicked stepmother in AT 480, SUS 400/2, and AT 315. She imitates the hero's mother's voice in AT 327C/F in order to kidnap him. She disguises herself as the hero's mother in Karnaukhova 141. In Balashov 134, Prince Ivan's mother dies at the end of the story (of fright, shock, or excessive emotion), while Yaga-Baba, who has committed the villainy, simply disappears, with no mention of punishment. The tale-teller herself did not seem to know why, but this outcome certainly suggests that Yaga-Baba is an alter ego for Prince Ivan's mother. Baba Yaga is associated with pregnancy and motherhood when she works as a midwife in Zelenin Viatka 27, and as a wicked midwife in many versions of AT 707. She causes an unwanted pregnancy in Balashov 136 (AT 708). Baba Yaga sucks a maiden's breasts in AT 519, which may be seen as an inversion of motherhood. Baba Yaga's oven as a womb symbol in AT 327C/F has been discussed, and her hut is associated with a mother when the protagonist tells it to stand "the way mother placed you." Baba Yaga addresses her mortar as "mother" (*Stupushka-matushka*) in Kargin 14. The rogue hero of Leonova 14 uses the corpse of Baba Yaga to blackmail people, convincing them that they have killed his "mother." Baba Yaga is obviously a mother herself in those instances when she has children of her own: human daughters in AT 327C/F; human sons in Smirnov 260 and Sadovnikov 16; monstrous daughters with one, two, and three eyes in AT 511; a monstrous son with seven throats (and presumably seven heads) in Onchukov 71; dragons in AT 300A; a sea monster in Dobrovol'skii 14; and frogs, mice, insects, and reptiles in AT 480. The kind girl in one version of AT 480 explains to Baba Yaga that she has no mother (Matveeva and Leonova Prilozhenie 2). Baba Yaga is addressed in a Belorussian incantation to quiet a sleepless child, and she fulfills the same function as the Forest Mother and Mother Midnight in South Slavic and Russian cognate versions of this spell. It also seems significant that the two most frequently recorded tale types with Baba Yaga appear to be AT 327C/F and AT 480, which concern the boy's or girl's adjustment to his/her gender role and relationship to the mother. It is important to emphasize that this docs not imply a static symbolism, whereby one could simply replace "Baba Yaga" with "mother" on each occasion. The folktale is a dynamic, living phenomenon. Its meanings are generated actively by its audiences in an interaction of the individual with tradition.

Of course, there are many mother representations in East Slavic culture besides Baba Yaga. The earth is identified in folklore by the epithet "mother moist earth" (*mat' syra zemlia*), Russia is called a mother (*Matushka Rus'*), as is the

Volga river (*Volga matushka*). The cult of Mary has an important place in the Orthodox Church, which refers to her most often as the "Mother of God" (*Bogoroditsa, Bogomater'*, Hubbs 1988: 87–123). Russian autobiography and pseudoautobiography also express the importance of mothers in Russian culture in their idealized portraits of mothers (Wachtel 1990, Stoliarov 1986: 33). Lev Tolstoy contributes significantly to this tendency in his *Childhood*, and has his character Platon Karataev speak of the importance of mothers in *War and Peace*. In an interview, the "village prose" writer Valentin Rasputin expressed his regret at the loss of traditional Russian values with the following words:

> You understand, even if we have buried our mother, we constantly remember her, and besides mental memory there's also cellular memory. In our cells we remember that our mother bore us, that we are all beholden to our mother, beholden to our parents, that in life we suffer a fearful loss because we have buried our mother, and we must remember that the same fate awaits us. The same is true of peasant Russia, of old Russia. We buried her, and we cannot return to the former ancient peasant countryside. (Rich 1995: 50)

The multiplicity of positive mother representations in Russian folklore and literature suggest that the early mother-infant bond is strong and that the desire to reproduce it resurfaces in adult life in other forms. However, in a culture where the child's primary and most intense relationship is with the mother or mothering figure(s), it seems inevitable that this relationship will exhibit some ambivalence. The early mother-infant relationship is seductive, but might threaten the independence of the child's self.

Baba Yaga is close to the negative end of the spectrum of maternal images, which suggests that she is a focus and an acceptable outlet for negative emotions experienced toward the mother(s) in East Slavic culture. It is striking how often aggression is acted out or expressed against Baba Yaga in folk tales and the other genres in which she appears (e.g., the children's rhymes which tell the rain to rain on Baba Yaga, in which Baba Yaga breaks her leg, and the folk song in which Baba Yaga, identified as winter, stumbles and rolls down the hill).

As stated earlier, there are twelve potential categories of tales in this corpus, based on the encounter of four different kinds of protagonists (boy, girl, young man, young woman) with three different kinds of Baba Yaga (donor, ambiguous, villain), represented in the table below. But in fact, only ten of these potential groups are represented in the tale material available for this survey, and this number could be reduced to eight, since the "boy/ambiguous Baba Yaga" and "adult heroine/donor Baba Yaga" categories are only tenuously present. A larger survey of tales might uncover more "ambiguous" versions, and move more tale types into the "ambiguous" category.

	Donor Baba Yaga	Ambiguous Baba Yaga	Villain Baba Yaga
Boy Hero		327B	327A, 327C/F, (123, related animal tale)
Girl Heroine		480	313H*, 314A*, 327A, 333B, 333C*, 451A
Adult Hero	329+400, 400/1, 401, 402, 550, 551, 552A, 554, 560, 564	300A, 300A*, 301, 301 (Baba Yaga's army), 302, 303, 312D, 313, 315, 318, 321, 400/2, 465, 519, 531, 566, 650A, 552+554+400+302 ("herding mares" cycle)	176**, 410*, 513, 516, 532, 563, 1053, 1137, 1164, 1353, 1653
Adult Heroine	451	425, 428, 430, 432, 709, 884B*	313E*, 403, 405, 407, 450, 510, 511, 533, 706, 707, 708, 736

In the children's tales, Baba Yaga is a villain in almost every male-centered tale. There are no tale types with boy heroes where Baba Yaga is purely a donor. In AT 327B she is a villain in all but two tale texts, where donor and villain Baba Yagas appear. The most popular tale type in this category is SUS 327C/F, which plays out the dangers of maternal seduction and the temptation of incest, and allows listeners to vent hostile feelings toward the mother by laughing at Baba Yaga when she is cooked. In tales with a girl heroine, Baba Yaga is also never purely a donor, and often a villain. In the most popular tale type (AT 480) she is ambiguous, appearing sometimes as the wicked stepmother, sometimes as a hostile tester who would like to kill the girl, and sometimes as a relatively kind tester. While Baba Yaga is overwhelmingly a negative mothering figure in the children's tales, this important exception (AT 480) suggests that for the girl, who is more likely to feel her identity as being continuous with her mother, the creation of an entirely negative mother figure is not as easily possible as for the boy, whose gender differs from his mother's and raises different issues.

The picture of Baba Yaga's hostility, benevolence, and ambiguity changes when we examine the adult tales. There are a number of male-centered tale types (such as AT 550 and 551) where Baba Yaga is exclusively a donor. In the tale about the hero's search for the apples of youth or healing water (AT 551), the hero confronts the threatening Tsar Maiden, and Baba Yaga appears as the only nonthreatening female figure. She seems to assuage a man's anxiety about his sexual and gender role, as she mediates between the Tsar Maiden and the hero. She keeps the Tsar Maiden from capturing him, she is the Tsar Maiden's aunt, and her dwelling is located between the realms of the hero and the Tsar Maiden. In AT 301 she mediates between the lower (supernatural) world and the upper (human) world when she provides the hero with a bird to return home. As a donor in AT 313, Baba Yaga's mediating position is expressed by the fact that she helps the hero but is a relative of the villain: she is the daughter of the Sea Tsar (Simina 11), the sister of Koshchei (Krasnozhenova 19), or the sister of the dragon Chudo-Iudo (Afanas'ev 225). In Sokolov 66 she is the sister of Satan, although he is not the villain in this tale. Baba Yaga's hostile stance typical of the villain tales threatens male identity (she decapitates, gouges out eyes, and turns men to stone, all of which could be seen as symbolic castration or control over the man's sexuality).

There are almost no female-centered adult tales where Baba Yaga is exclusively a donor. Only one tale text represents this category (AT 451), a tale learned by Ivan Kovalev while in Germany. It seems to be an exception underscoring Baba Yaga's essentially ambiguous or villainous nature for the adult female heroine. In the ambiguous group, the tales mostly concern the search for a lost spouse, and Baba Yaga's function is that of a mediator who reunites the spouses or keeps them apart. In her donor role she most often provides the heroine with magic objects or advice which enable her to recover her lost husband. In the female-centered villain tales, Baba Yaga most often is a usurper, ousting the heroine and putting herself or her daughter in the heroine's place. While this could be interpreted in oedipal terms, with the mother as the daughter's rival for the father's affection, the circumstances of East Slavic peasant culture suggest that these tales refer to a later stage in a woman's life. Given a young woman's normal life experience, this villainy might express the woman's postmarital experience in her husband's household, where her claim on her husband's affections (if in fact affection existed at all between husband and wife) might be strained by the presence of his mother, sisters, and other female relatives. The tales in which Baba Yaga causes the heroine to be driven away also concern lack or loss of an affective bond between a woman and her husband or brother.

Overall, a different pattern emerges for the male and female protagonists of East Slavic folktales in which they confront Baba Yaga. For the boy, Baba Yaga is essentially a villain, but for the young adult male, while still a villain, she can also be purely a donor. For the girl, Baba Yaga is essentially ambiguous, and appears to remain so for the young adult female, without a shift to a more positive aspect. This certainly suggests different perceptions of the mother or mothering figures by women and men.

If certain of Baba Yaga's attributes have a latent sexual meaning (her iron pestle, broom, occasional iron nose, bony leg, hut on chicken legs), then we might expect these attributes to be differently distributed in tales with male heroes than in those with female heroines. In fact there is a qualitative difference in the distribution of these attributes. The significance of the oven episode in AT 327C/F and its usual absence in female-centered tales has already been discussed. The donor sequence (the arrival at Baba Yaga's hut, the phrases spoken to make the hut turn around, the greeting and Baba Yaga's response) is found in male adult tales, in female adult tales, and in female children's tales. It is largely absent in male children's tales. It is a matter of speculation whether or not the hut and the associated attributes have a subconscious meaning related to sex or gender, but their different distribution in male and female-centered tales certainly suggests that they have different meanings for female and male protagonists.

We might expect the body of Baba Yaga to arouse less anxiety in the female-centered tales; for the female heroine, the female body (even if Baba Yaga is grotesque) is less foreign than for a male hero. Besides making her sexually unappealing, the grotesqueness of Baba Yaga might function as a distancing device, allowing both male and female listeners to differentiate themselves from the maternal image. However, for the male hero, Baba Yaga's body does not appear until the "adult" tales. This might reflect the new awareness and importance of the female body for boys at puberty.

In both child and adult tales Baba Yaga often displays oral aggression. Most obviously, she threatens or attempts to eat the protagonist, or prepares for this by sharpening her teeth (AT 327C/F). The theme of eating, feeding, food, or cannibalism is important throughout a large number of the Baba Yaga tales. Boy or girl protagonists escape being eaten by Baba Yaga, and even in adult tales the threat of cannibalism is part of the donor sequence. In AT 314A*, a group of girls comes to Baba Yaga's hut. The heroine is the only one who either eats or does not eat the food Baba Yaga offers them, and therefore must stay with Baba Yaga. Baba Yaga feeds from a maiden when she sucks her breasts in AT 519. Food and the oven are important in Bandarchyk 1973 no. 4 (AT 300A), when Baba Yaga the donor bakes bread that the hero force-feeds the dragon. In another version of the same tale type, the hero escapes from the monstrous devouring mouth of Baba-Yuga by feeding her salty cakes and salt (Manzhura 1890: 24–27). As a bad mother, Baba Yaga gives kidnapped children inedible food (iron bread).

While Baba Yaga's grotesque features make her sexually unappealing and
therefore nonthreatening to men as well as women, some of her traditional
attributes are obviously masculine, either explicitly or implicitly. Baba Yaga
displays a male attribute when she speaks in a bass voice, in Zelenin Viatka 14
(narrated by the male tale-teller Grigorii Verkhorubov) and in Giliarova and
Frumkin 14, or in a rough voice that fails to fool the boy hero of AT 327F, and
which forces Baba Yaga to have her voice reforged. The narrator of Nikiforov
1961 no. 85 sung Baba Yaga's lines (her song to lure the boy to the shore) in "a
low voice." In a number of tales related to AT 301 discussed in chapter 5, Baba
Yaga is the fearsome leader of an entire army. Baba Yaga's daughters are called
iagishny, her daughter is Marfa Yaginichna (Gorodtsov i: 275–294, AT 327B),
and in two tales, the son of Baba Yaga is called *Agich* or *Iagich*, "son of Yaga"
(Sadovnikov 16, Balashov 57). Of course, Baba Yaga is very often herself called
Yaga Yagishna, "Yaga the daughter of Yaga." In a culture where everyone has a
patronymic middle name, this is a rare instance of a matronymic, a name
derived from one's mother, and it apparently could only arise in the fantasy
world of folklore.[2] When Ježibaba has a husband, his name is also clearly
derived from hers (*Ježibábel*). Baba Yaga frequently has children but no
husband (in Zelenin Perm' 27 her married status might be suggested by the
mention of her two braids), and when she does have a husband, she is often
domineering.

Implicitly, Baba Yaga typically possesses many masculine or phallic
attributes. Baba Yaga wields a pestle and broom when she travels (*pestom
pogoniaet, pomelom sled zametaet*). She has a bony leg or a leg made of some other
unusual material, and is occasionally one-legged (Sokolov 139, 140, Sadovnikov
27). In one tale she has a steel leg and a golden eye (Gurevich 32). She has a
large nose that sticks into the ceiling (an iron nose, like her Hungarian
counterpart, in Khudiakov 39, 40, and Sadovnikov 4, 61). The narrator of
Dobrovol'skii 13 gives her a giant iron tooth (cf. the baby teeth customs
associated with Ježibaba and Torklja). Baba Yaga wields an iron hook in
Karnaukhova 74 and Lutovinova 47. When the villain Baba Yaga is dragged to
death by horses, parts of her body turn into rakes and pokers (Nikiforov 1961

[2] Other folktale heroes are Ivan Suchich ("son of a female dog," Novikov 1974: 56–67, Potanin
1902 no. 34), Marko Suchchenko (Manzhura 1890: 24–27), and Suchkin syn (Bandarchyk 1973
no. 4). These heroes' names are most often distinct from the insulting designation "son of a
bitch" (*sukin syn*), although a few heroes do have this name, such as Sukin Syn Paramokha
(Nikiforov 1961 no. 66) and Vasilii Sukin syn (Sokolov 37). Other male folktale characters who
either bear matronymic middle names or are otherwise identified by their mothers appear in AT
300A: Ivan the Maid's Son, called Ivan Devich (Erlenvein 3) or Ivan devkin syn (Afanas'ev 136),
Ivan the Cow's Son, Ivan korovii syn (Afanas'ev 136), and Ivan the Cat's Son, Ivan Koshkin
(Khudiakov 6).

no. 80, Zelenin Viatka 11). In riddles she is metaphorically likened to a plough or an oven with beams protruding from it. Yaga-Baba attacks the hero and his servant with snakes in Karnaukhova 141. Her appearance as a one-eyed ogress in AT 1137 can also be interpreted in phallic terms. (In this context it is interesting to recall that women who spin on Friday dirty the eyes of Paraskeva-Piatnitsa; Tolstoi 1995a: 190).

Some psychologists have interpreted fantasies about "phallic women" as an expression of male castration anxiety. As frightening as the fantasies about phallic women might be in themselves (Baba Yaga, the Medusa, and others), they deny women's genital difference and the more frightening possibility that a man might lose his penis (Chodorow 1978: 107, Freud 1968, Rancour-Laferriere 1985: 185–191, Spiro 1993: 118). Fantasies about phallic women are especially significant for men who have an insufficient sense of self separate from the mother (Chodorow, citing Greenacre, 1978: 107), and might tend to appear in cultures where male children are exclusively taken care of by women. The hostile Baba Yaga is an object for hostile emotions, but unconsciously, the phallic attributes of Baba Yaga might ease anxieties about male identity for male listeners. Readers who are not inclined to see the above-mentioned attributes as masculine or phallic symbols would nevertheless agree that Baba Yaga is behaving in a masculine way when she speaks in a bass voice. If it is correct to see so much sexual symbolism in these folktales, why is it present? The heroine or hero's search for identity necessarily involves grappling with the mysteries of masculinity and femininity. As so many scholars of this genre have shown, the folktale (and the Indo-European fairy tale in particular) is fond of strong contrasts and extremes. It is not surprising that the fairy tale would represent these important categories of human identity in terms of what is most masculine about a man and most feminine about a woman.

Baba Yaga's masculine features also make her into a cautionary figure, a negative example of what a woman should not be (dominant, aggressive, assertive, masculine). Obviously, Baba Yaga's behavior as a villain is deviant, and a threat to social order and harmony. She represents a reversal or inversion of the cultural expectations of motherhood when she wants to cook or eat a child instead of feeding a child, or offers a child food only in order to kidnap him (AT 327C/F). The iron bread she offers to the kidnapped boy in AT 480 (Karnaukhova 87, Lutovinova 48) and 327F (Nikiforov 1964 no. 64) is inedible, as is the food containing snot or human fingers (in G. K. Zavoiko's description, see chapter 2). In some tales, she transgresses the mother's role and the appropriate roles of the two generations by wanting a heroine to mother her in some way: She sucks a maiden's breasts in AT 519, or forces the heroine to sing her a lullaby or rock her to sleep in AT 314A*. In one version of AT

301, immediately after appearing to the hero as a fierce warrior and the leader of an army, Baba Yaga is lying in a cradle, and nannies and nurses are rocking her and singing lullabies to her (Gorodtsov ii: 150–173). Her actions in AT 519 might also represent her wish to "suck the youth" or youthful femininity from the maiden, and usurp her place in the natural cycle of the generations. This is a striking and powerful image of negative maternity, of a bad mother who wants to eat her children (in AT 327 and AT 519), either because of an excessive attachment (incestuous wishes) or its opposite (envy and jealousy in relation to a female child). Baba Yaga's wish to appropriate the young woman's fertility (and her attempts to reduce others to a state of symbolic sterility or death, by turning them to stone) suggest that she herself is sterile; yet in other tales she has an abundance of children (often animals or monstrous beings) and provides nourishment for the protagonist. Baba Yaga's image in terms of the opposition fertility/sterility (as in so many other ways) is contradictory. Some of Baba Yaga's unpleasant aspects no doubt reflect a culturally based misogyny as well. Not surprisingly, the masculine features of Baba Yaga are most prominent in male-centered tales. The phallic and oral aspects of Baba Yaga appear combined in the riddle that compares her to a plough: Baba Yaga is a plough that feeds the world but goes hungry herself (Sadovnikov 1959: 140). The fact that Baba Yaga is made to go hungry is perhaps another expression of aggression against her.

Another result of her masculine features is to make Baba Yaga sexually ambiguous, combining implicit male with explicit female features. The narrator of Leonova 17 says that Baba Yaga turned into a woman (*ona v zhenshchinu oborotilas*) when the hero struck her with a magic twig, leading one to wonder what she was before this moment. Her possession of both pestle and mortar, which are sometimes explicitly identified as male and female in East Slavic customs (Toporkov 1995), suggests androgyny. No doubt, this contributes to her supernatural and uncanny nature; it might also make her better suited to her role as mediator, not only between the supernatural and human worlds, as Eleazar Meletinskii and others point out, but also (and this is perhaps more immediately significant for the folktale listeners) between male and female. She mediates both positively (bringing the spouses together) or negatively (separating them). She has a significant role in AT 884B*, where the heroine's sex is brought into question and tested, and where a larger question of feminine identity is raised. She or her daughters bring men and women together in love incantations. The hut on chicken legs, as an extension of Baba Yaga, also combines opposing features: animate and inanimate, nature and culture, symbolic male and female.

Besides her characteristic masculine features and oral aggression, another important aspect of Baba Yaga is the insistence that she is an Other. Most obviously, she is never the protagonist of any folktale; the tale concerns a protagonist's encounter with her. Two exceptional tales (both are versions of AT 327C) begin with the phrase "once upon a time there lived Baba Yaga" (*zhila byla baba-iaga*, Zhivaia Starina 21 [1912]: 319; *zhila byla Iaga-baba*, Onchukov 73). These two tales are unique in other ways as well, but nevertheless, Baba Yaga is not the heroine of either tale. The usual location of her dwelling (in the forest on the way to another realm, in the underground realm, in the sky, in a river), her remark about the hero or heroine's Russian scent, and her occasional statement that she has never been to Rus' or Russia all suggest that she is an Other. In two versions of 327C (Afanas'ev 106, Gorodtsov iii: 6–10) she tells her daughter to roast the boy while she goes off to Rus', implying that she lives somewhere other than Russia. This "foreignness" is what has inspired scholars to search for her origin outside the East Slavic area, and the reason some storytellers might have identified her with neighboring non-Slavic peoples (Zelenin 1914: xxiii, 533, 576). Her frequent kinship with animals and other supernatural beings (dragons, ogres, the Sea Tsar) has already been mentioned.

Baba Yaga's foreignness can be seen as a distancing or masking device. Baba Yaga's "non-Russian" characteristics might in fact allow the Russians to vent negative emotions safely on a fantastic figure who will not consciously be recognized as the mother. If Baba Yaga's image also reflects anxiety surrounding separation issues, this "foreignness" is another way of emphasizing the ego boundary, of stating emphatically that the mother is separate and different from the self.

Many authors have pointed out that Baba Yaga is a liminal, borderline character, mediating between human and supernatural, human and nonhuman. The present survey suggests that she also mediates the oppositions of male/female, own/foreign, Self/Other, and, of course, nature and culture.[3] Her associations with nature are obvious. Her dwelling, which combines natural and cultural components, is very often located in the forest. Baba Yaga is functionally equivalent to the Forest Mother in Slavic incantations to quiet a sleepless child. The forest itself mourns for her in one version of AT 327C, after the hero kills her (Karnaukhova 74). In the harvest customs from the Pskov region discussed in chapter 2, Baba Yaga occupies the rye field, an area between nature and culture, and appears ambiguously as both the "owner" of the field, and as a demonic being who threatens to deprive the grains of their

---

[3] In this Baba Yaga resembles the devil in European folk tradition, who also represents both culture and nature in different contexts (Wolf-Knuts 1992).

life-giving power. Baba Yaga's association with spinning (she spins herself, she asks the heroine to spin, her hut stands on a spindle heel) also places her between nature and culture, in that spinning is an activity that turns raw natural material (wool or plant fiber) into a cultural artifact.

In some tale types such as AT 327C/F, animals (the female bear, snake, and fox) and Baba Yaga are allomotifs, occupying the same villain role. In one tale (Smirnov 120) the cannibalistic villain is the bear Egibitsa. The eagle's sisters and mother are Egibobas in Zelenin Viatka 13 (AT 313). In numerous versions of AT 480 Baba Yaga has children who are frogs, toads, snakes, or other animals. She drinks sea water until she bursts and gives rise to snakes, toads, lizards, tadpoles, spiders, and worms (Manzhura 1890: 24–27, AT 300A). Iezhibaba is herself a toad in a Carpatho-Ukrainian tale (Hyriak vii no. 2). In Onchukov 152 (AT 303) Baba Yaga turns into a snake, a frog, and then a stone. In one incantation, Yaga is a brown snake (*Iaga zmeia bura*, Cherepanova 1983: 106–107). There may be a symbolic parallel between Baba Yaga and snakes when she sucks the maiden's breasts in AT 519; in Slavic folk belief, snakes drink milk from cows, and witches steal their milk. In Kitainik 10 Yaga-Yagishna and her daughter turn into snakes before they are killed. Baba Yaga has dragon sons in AT 300A (she is equivalent to the dragon mother in other versions of this tale) and turns into a giant sow. In Russian and Slovak versions of AT 321, Baba Yaga (Potanin 1906 no. 13) has nine heads, and three Ježibabas (Dobšinský iii: 32–43) have seven, nine, and twelve heads. In a Slovak version of AT 531, Ježibaba turns into a twenty-four-headed monster, then a toad and a snake (Polívka ii: 340–348). The presence of multiple heads is most typical of dragons and suggests a dragon-like nature. In a few versions of the Russian folk epic "Dobrynia and Alesha," Baba Yaga has taken the place of the dragon, Dobrynia's traditional opponent at the Puchai River.

In some tales Baba Yaga, or a figure resembling her, summons animals or natural elements to aid the hero. Baba Yaga pursues her victims in the form of a cloud in Onchukov 44. Baba Yaga is identified with winter in one Russian folk song (Korinfskii 1901: 146–147). She can produce both cold and warm air in Lutovinova 51 (AT 480). Ježibaba possesses a skull that causes rain (Kollár 1953: 51–52). Baba Yaga eats frogs and is the cause of illness, specifically scurvy (Novgorod-Severskii: 81–90; cf. the Bulgarian dialect terms for illness, such as *iandza*). Her wish to devour humans places her clearly in the nonhuman, supernatural world, or might be seen as an exaggerated and unbridled form of a natural urge (hunger). In one tale she shows herself to be less dangerous and closer to human culture than the wolf villain (Novgorod-Severskii: 61–65). In some versions of AT 550, she is the wolf's *kuma*, and he her *kum*: she is the godmother of his child, or he is the godfather of her child, or they both are godparents of the same child. Her kinship relations with other animals and supernatural beings have been mentioned. Baba Yaga's position as a mediator between nature and culture is logically related to her role as a maternal representation, inasmuch as the mothering role involves moving infant children from a "wild" natural state to a cultural human state.

Baba Yaga's manifold associations with nature have led many authors to interpret her as a metaphorical embodiment of natural forces, as a nature goddess, or a female totemic ancestor. In this context, Baba Yaga's ambiguity logically reflects the human relationship to nature, which is fundamentally ambivalent. Nevertheless, Baba Yaga's close association with nature does not completely account for her image. It seems more accurate to describe this aspect of Baba Yaga as a secondary component of her image, often combined with her role in fairy tales as an ambiguous or negative maternal representation. It should also be pointed out that in East Slavic folklore, the ambivalent human relationship to nature is more directly expressed through beliefs and narratives about place and nature spirits—the forest spirit (*leshii*), water spirit (*vodianoi*), and field spirit (*polevoi*), among others. Legendary narratives (memorates and fabulates) about these spirits circulated at the same time and in the same places as the folktales about Baba Yaga, which suggests that her image and persona fulfilled other functions or needs for narrators and audiences than did those of the nature spirits.

Baba Yaga's relation to the hero and heroine suggest a concern with separation and individuation issues, which have their roots in the infant's first symbiosis with its mother. This seems to be the reason for the persistence of oral aggression and the concern with food in Baba Yaga's image (her threat to eat the protagonist even in the donor sequence, for instance). It seems possible that her function, compared to the more benevolent mother images produced by East Slavic culture, is to express anxieties and tensions which have their roots in this early period, and which concern separation and the establishment of ego boundaries. The hostility felt toward the mother and her embodiment in Baba Yaga is perhaps more significant for the male child, since masculine identity might be more difficult to arrive at, and therefore surrounded by greater insecurity. The girl was surrounded by other girls and women who provided her with models for learning her gender role; for boys, male gender models were probably not as easily available. A study of gender role socialization in late twentieth-century Russia suggests that this remains true (Kerig et al. 1993). The recollection of the overwhelming maternal presence in childhood could account for hostility to the mother image later in life, and for men, hostility to women in general. In folktales this is found in the denigrating references to Baba Yaga's body, especially her breasts and vagina. Russian men's jokes expressing a high degree of hostility to women, recorded during the last decades of the Soviet period, and in the post-Soviet period, suggest the same (Draitser 1999: 102). The complexity of the folktale, with its multiple meanings and messages, is reflected in the fact that it can allow the expression of hostility toward a negative maternal representation while reinforcing cultural expectations of gender for men and women—and no doubt interaction with the mothering figures is an important part of forming this gender identity. This seems especially true of the East Slavic versions of AT 480 and AT 327C/F, which, like other folktales and other genres of folklore, probably contributed to children's and young people's sense of their gender identity. Snejana Tempest (2001) finds that the sex of children in Russian peasant culture was immediately fixed by rituals in the first days of life, while gender identity was arrived at later, notably through participation in gender-specific work activities. Obviously, folklore also played a part in this process, although the specific importance of folktales in reinforcing gender identity might not have been obvious to the narrators and listeners.

If we identify as typical and significant features Baba Yaga's oral aggression (or an emphasis on food, whether in a benevolent or hostile context) and her masculine or phallic features in male-centered tales, then these features suggest that separation issues are significant in determining Baba Yaga's image. She appears most frequently in tale types that symbolically represent a child's development and the mother-child relationship (AT 314A*, 327, 480). In AT 519 she is a hostile donor for the male hero, but her interaction as a villain with the maiden acts out a generational, mother-daughter conflict. In adult tales, she most often appears as a mediator between men and women, either positive or negative (AT 301, 313, 402, 425, 432, 450, 551, 707, the "herding mares" cycle).[4] Although Baba Yaga is overwhelmingly a villain in East Slavic folktales and functions as a focus for a variety of negative emotions felt toward the maternal image, her ambiguity shows that she cannot be constructed entirely as an evil Other. This suggests that issues of separation from the mother and individuation are important in the fantasy life of the East Slavic folktale tellers and listeners, probably more so than in traditions which lack such an ambiguous figure. Further research on the characters of different folktale traditions, especially those of eastern Europe, will no doubt help elucidate the question of ambiguity in folktales, the complex historical, cultural, and psychological factors that bring about this ambiguity, and clarify the

---

[4] In this corpus, out of 422 tale texts, the most "popular" tale types in numbers of versions are AT 480 (48 versions), AT 327C/F (47), AT 313 (23), AT 707 (18), AT 301 (15), AT 551 (15), AT 402 (13), the "herding mares" cycle (12), AT 432 (12), AT 450 (12), AT 314A* (11), AT 425 (11), and AT 519 (11). All other tale types are represented by fewer than ten versions.

relationship of folktale characters to tale roles. Besides revealing Baba Yaga's dynamic shifting between donor and villain roles, this excursion into the rich domain of East Slavic folktales has also shown that some of these traditional narratives are a kind of dialogue (between men and women, or between the generations), rather than being centered on one hero or heroine.

A beautiful inheritance from the past, a cultural treasure, the folktale is a complex, many-sided phenomenon. Its multiple aspects and potential meanings seem inexhaustible. The same is true of its characters: Reborn every time a tale is told or read, they are never finished or complete. As a unique creation of human imagination and verbal art, Baba Yaga defies any single or simple definition or interpretation, and no final, definitive word can ever be said about her. Cramped in her hut on chicken legs like a child in the womb, or a corpse in a coffin, her image seems an apt expression of the eternal contradictions inherent in the human condition: life and death, male and female, nature and culture. In that wonderful and unique "forest of symbols," the Indo-European fairy tale, she occupies a special place. It is the author's hope that these pages have contributed to a better understanding and appreciation of this truly marvelous East Slavic folktale character.

APPENDIX I
Selected Tale Texts

"Baba Yaga." AT 327C. Recorded in Rechitsa, Brest region, western Belarus. Probably collected in the early 1950s. Avanesav and Biryla 1962 no. 554.

There was an old man and woman. They had a son, Hryshka. Once Hryshka went into the garden. He climbed up an apple tree and started picking apples.

Baba-Yaga rode along the road in a mortar; she drove the mortar with a pestle, and swept away her tracks with a broom. She saw Hryshka, stopped, and said to him, "Hryshka, why are you picking sour apples? Here, come have a sweet red apple."

Hryshka stretched out his hand to take an apple, and Baba-Yaga grabbed him and carried him off to her hut. The old man and woman came out of their hut and called for Hryshka, but he was gone. They cried.

Baba-Yaga had a daughter, Don'ka-hol'on'ka. Baba-Yaga told her to heat up the oven and cook Hryshka. Don'ka-hol'on'ka heated up the oven, took the bread spatula [baker's peel], and said to Hryshka, "Lie down on the spatula." No matter how he lay down, it was always wrong. Then he told Don'ka-hol'on'ka to show him how to lie down properly. When she lay down on the spatula, Hryshka shoved her into the oven. When Don'ka was cooked, he took her out, put her on the table, and took the iron pestle and climbed up on the oven. Baba-Yaga came and ate. When she had eaten her fill, she threw the bones on the ground and jumped up and down on them. Jumping, she said, "I'm jumping, jumping on Hryshka's bones."

And Hryshka said to her from the oven, "Jump, jump on your daughter's bones."

Baba-Yaga looked up at the oven, saw Hryshka and rushed at him. Hryshka struck her with the iron pestle and killed her, and went outside and climbed up a tall tree.

Geese flew by, and he asked them, "Geese, [my] doves, throw me each a feather, and I'll fly with you to my father's place." The geese threw him feathers. He covered himself with feathers and flew with them to his hut. The old man and woman were very happy, they summoned guests, and drank and made merry for a long time.

"Igrashen'ka." AT 327F. Told by K. S. Buidova, age seventy-four, Spirovo village, Boksitogorsk district, Leningrad (St. Petersburg) region. Recorded in 1971 by Rita Buidova. Bakhtin and Shiriaeva 1976 no. 54.

Once there lived an old man and a woman. They had a son, Igrashka. The man died, and Igrashka started going fishing.

Once he went early to the river to fish. He caught some fish and heard his mother calling out: "Igrashen'ka, my child! Mother has come, she's brought porridge and a pancake."

And Igrashka answered, "Closer, closer, little boat! Mother is coming, she's bringing porridge and a pancake." The boat sailed up to the bank. Igrashka ate his fill and gave his mother the fish. And he went to catch more fish.

Baba-Yaga heard this conversation. As soon as the mother had left, Baba-Yaga was right there. She said in a rough voice: "Igrashen'ka, my child! Mother is coming, she's bringing porridge and a pancake."

And Igrashka said: "Closer, closer, little boat! Mother is coming, she's bringing porridge and a pancake."

Igrashka sailed up, and Baba-Yaga grabbed him—and carried him home to her place. She brought him and said: "Go get wood! Heat up the oven!"

Igrashka brought wood. He heated up the oven. And Baba-Yaga said: "Lie down on the bread spatula!" Igrashka stood on the spatula. He didn't fit in the oven. He sat down—and didn't fit in the oven. And he said: "Well show me, how do you do it?"

Baba-Yaga lay down, and Igrashka shoved her into the oven and ran home.

Baba-Yaga burned up, and Igrashka and his mother lived [happily ever after].

"About Lishanushka." AT 327F. Told by Anna Timofeevna Danilova, age twelve, Sura village, Pinega region. Recorded in 1927 by Aleksandr I. Nikiforov. Nikiforov 1961 no. 64.

Once there lived an old man and an old woman. They had no one, no one. They cut a piece of wood from a tree and put it on the oven. And the piece of wood began to speak:

"Grandmother, I want to eat!"

She took him down and put him on the bench. He ate his fill. There was a big, big puddle under the window, and a river there flowed far away.

"Well," he said, "Grandfather, make me a boat and an oar."

He made him a boat and an oar, and he went off to sail and [the water] carried him far, far away. And Egibova got him, that boy Lishanushka. She got him and put him in her cellar. She gave him an iron loaf of bread to eat. She had three daughters. So she told the girls to heat up the oven and told them to burn him up in the oven and told them to roast him. The youngest girl started to heat it, heated up the oven, called him, and said, "Lishanushka, sit on the bread spatula!"

"Sit on it yourself, teach me how!" he said. The girl sat down, and he pushed her into the oven. And she roasted there in the oven. He took her out again and cut up the meat into pieces on a plate, and put it on the window sill. And he crawled back into the cellar.

Egibova came in and started to eat. "Lishanka's meat is tasty and sweet!" And he said, "Eat and roll around, it's your daughter's meat!" She started cursing. "You've burned up my girl!"

The next time she ordered the elder daughter to heat up the oven. To heat it up good and hot. So the girl came and said, "Lishanushka, Lishanushka, sit on the bread spatula!"

And she sat on the spatula. And he shoved her into the oven. He took her out of the oven again, she was roasted through and through, and he cut her into pieces and put her on a plate. Yagibova came and started eating.

"Lishanka's meat is tasty and sweet!"

And he said, "Eat and roll around, it's your daughter's meat!"

Well, she started cursing him again, she swore, and started heating the oven herself, wanting to burn him up. So she said, "Sit on the shovel, Lishanushka, like a pike, like a pike!"

And he said, "Lie down yourself, teach me [how to do it] like a pike!"

He started to shove Egibova; Egibova stuck out her arms and stuck out her legs and couldn't fit into the oven. And he ran away quickly. He locked the hut; and for a long time she couldn't get out of the hut.

Geese were flying by. He said to the geese, "Geese, geese, carry me away to my grandfather and grandmother!"

And those geese didn't take him. He climbed up a high fir tree. Egibova came out, saw him, and started biting the tree, gnawing it. The tree started falling, but just then geese flew by. He said, "Geese, geese, carry me away!"

And they carried him away. And at the old woman's place in the cellar he had taken a basket of money. He gave it to his grandmother and grandfather.

They lived [happily ever after]; they live and chew bread.

"Ivashko and the Witch." AT 327F. "Natal'ia Ivanovna Bezrukova, née Strel'nikova, forty-five, a native of Vilkovy (Il'kino) village, Rozhdestvenskii subdistrict, Urzhum district; illiterate. She married into the neighboring village Lavrukhiny, Nolin district. She was soon widowed and works as a household servant for priests. Now she lives in Otarakh village, Urzhum district, where I recorded folktales from her.

N. I. Bezrukova heard her tales in early youth at social and work gatherings. Now she remembers few of them and poorly, although she used to tell them when she worked as a children's nanny. I only recorded two folktales from her: She couldn't remember any more. In everyday life N. I. Bezrukova has a lively tongue and is eloquent in her own way. Besides folktales she knows incantations and is known as a healer among the local peasant population" (Zelenin 1915: 357).

In the introduction to this volume of folktales Zelenin states that the realistic details in the beginning and end of this tale (the signs of the woman's poverty, the hero's dull-wittedness, the boat-building) are Bezrukova's own contribution to this tale. Recorded by Dmitrii Zelenin in autumn 1908 in Viatka province. Zelenin 1915 no. 115.

Once there lived an old woman. The old woman had a son, Vaniushka. They were very poor, and their hut was even falling apart. She said, "You have to go to the forest to cut down logs for the room." "Well, mother, I'll go," he said when he got up in the morning. "Well, my child, go with God! Do what you can!"

He was probably a half-wit. So he went to the forest and cut down a log. He tore the bark off this log and made a boat. [This was] at a river. He pulled the boat into the river and made oars. And he sailed around in this boat.

His mother was waiting for her Vaniushka to come home, and couldn't wait. So she baked some bread and set off. "If he went away, then he can come home too," she said. She baked bread and took it to him to eat. She came to the woods and found a piece of cut wood. "What is this, my son isn't here," she said. "And why is the bark torn from this fir?" she said. "And the splinters look like they had been cut?" So then she went down to the shore. "Maybe he thought of [doing] something else?" she said.

She came to the shore. "Vaniushka," she said, "Vaniushka, child! Come to the shore! There's porridge with butter here for you, child!" He said, "I hear mother's voice!" He came up and ate up the porridge. So his mother went home.

Then that Egibikha came (one of those evil spirits who live in lakes and forests) and spoke. She came to the shore and said "Vaniushka, Vaniushka! Come to the shore: There's porridge with butter for you!" And he answered, "I can hear that it's not mother's voice!" "Oh you red dog," she said, "you red dog!" Then she left.

After she left, his mother came back again with porridge. "Vaniushka, Vaniushka! Come to the shore: There's porridge with butter for you!" And she called him to come home, but he wouldn't go.

And again that evil one came. And she had three daughters. So she came to the shore and spoke like his mother. She listened to how his mother spoke, with a fine voice: "Vaniushka, Vaniushka! Come to the shore. There's porridge with butter for you!" So he came. She grabbed him and dragged him off to her pantry.

She harnessed a horse herself, rode to the forest for wood, and left one daughter at home. "Heat the oven hot, really hot, so that the lower log is red hot! And cook him, that son of a bitch!" she said. Vaniushka's mother missed him, she cried, one tear streaming right after another.

That daughter of Egibikha shouted, "Vaniushka! Come here, onto this bread spatula!" He came out. "Lie down on the spatula," she said. He sat on the spatula and stretched out his arms and legs; he wouldn't fit into the oven. "Sister, I don't know how!" he said. "What do you mean you don't know how! The way cats sleep, the way dogs sleep, lie down like that!" "But I don't know how! You lie down and teach me how!" he said. She lay down, he didn't hesitate, shoved her into the oven, fastened the oven door shut, and she was roasted. Then he took [her] out and cut [her] up and put [her] on the middle *polati* [sleeping shelf above the oven].

Then that Egibikha came home. (And he returned to where he was before, and didn't say anything.) She took that meat down, to eat it. She ate her fill and started to roll around. She rolled around and said, "I'm rolling around, I'm lying around on Vaniushka's bones!" (In the pantry) he answered her; he said, "Roll around, you whore, lie around, you whore, on your daughter's bones!" "Oh, am I imagining this, or am I seeing things?" she said. "Oh you red dog," she said, "You red dog! You've cooked my daughter!"

Well, the same thing happened again. Three of them in that family: He cooked all three daughters, and then got to that very one herself. Then she herself stayed home.

And she heated the oven up herself good and hot and shouted, "Vaniushka! Come here, onto this bread spatula!" "All right, all right, mother, I'm coming!" he said. He came out. "Lie down on the spatula," she said. She wanted to put him in that oven, but he held out his arms and legs firmly. "Mother, I don't know how!" "What do you mean you don't know how, you son of a bitch! The way cats sleep, the way dogs sleep, lie down like that!" "But mother, I don't know how! Teach me!"

When she lay down on the spatula, he shoved her in there, and shut [the oven door]. She cried out, "Vaniushka, let me go! Child, let me out! You can have three pots of silver, a golden carriage, a pair of black horses, and a golden harness! All this will be yours!" "Oh you old bitch, you've fallen for it! Everything will be mine anyway!" he said. So he left her in the oven.

He ran, got the carriage, dragged the three pots of silver from the cellar, put everything together in the carriage. He led the horses out of the stable, put on their collars, harnessed them, and set off.

He came home to his mother. She was very worried that he was not alive, and had cried a great deal. And her hut was in really bad shape, even the wood corner-pieces had fallen off. So he rode up to his house, and there wasn't even a gate, nothing—nothing to harness [the horses] to. Well, [sitting] on those horses, on the pair, he asked the old woman if he could spend the night. "Well, grandmother, will you let me stay the night?" he said. "Oh child, I have no place to take the horses and nothing to tie them to and nothing to feed you with!" she said. "Grandmother, we'll tie them there behind the garden. Please, let me stay!" he said. "Well child, unharness them and tie them up!" she said. He unharnessed them and tied them up.

He took the pot with silver first and dragged it into the room. He brought it into the room, prayed to God, and poured it out on the floor. This grandmother said, "Oh you child, you child! I had a son, Vaniushka, just like [you]!" "Well, mother, I'm that very one!" he said. "My dear child, wherever did you come from?" she said.

Then he brought everything in—he dragged in three pots of silver, poured them out on the floor, and dragged in three pots of gold, poured them out on the floor, another pile. She said, "Oh Vaniushka, my child, my dear one! Wherever did you get so much money?" "Well, mother, I almost died for this money!" he said.

Well, then, with that money he built such a house, merciful God! He painted the ceilings and everything.... And I was there at their place and drank tea. And finished it all.

No title. AT 314*. Recorded in 1996 from Galina Petrovna Shumilova, born 1932. Gonobilovo village, Sudogda area, Vladimir region. Kargin 1999 no. 14.

Once there lived an old man and woman, and they had a little girl, Niuron'ka. The girl went into the forest with the other children, got lost, and ended up at Bur Yaga's place. She walked up to the hut. "Hut, hut, turn your front to me, stand with your back to the forest." She walked in, and there was Bur Yaga.

"Oh, what a pretty girl has come!"

She gave her something to drink, to eat, and lay down in the mortar.

"Rock me." She rocked her. Yaga fell asleep. She went outside and cried, because she wouldn't let her go home.

A wolf came by. "Niuron'ka, why are you crying?" "Well this is what happened. I lived with grandfather and grandmother, I went into the forest, got lost, and Bur Yaga won't let me go home." "Sit down on my back, I'll carry you away from here!" She sat down, and they took off.

Then Bur Yaga woke up and said, "Mother Mortar, go further than four versts!" She caught up with them. She took the girl. All right.

A bear came by. "Niuron'ka, why are you crying?" "Well this is what happened." "Let me take you away from here." She said no. "Well, you know what we'll do? Bake some pies, I'll take them to your grandmother and grandfather and tell them where you are."

All right, she baked the pies, rocked Bur Yaga to sleep, climbed into the basket, and covered herself with the pies. The bear was carrying them and he said, "This basket is heavy! I'll sit on a tree stump and eat a pie!" She answered him, "Don't sit on the stump, don't eat the pie. I sit high and see far!" "So small, and yet she sees so far. I have to keep carrying it."

So he walked, walked, and walked on. "No, I'll sit on a tree stump and eat a pie." "Don't sit on the stump, don't eat the pie. I sit high and see far!"

He came to the grandmother and grandfather. "Here are gifts your granddaughter sent you, she baked pies."

Then dogs attacked the bear. He ran away to the forest, and the grandmother started looking at the pies, and she was sitting there, in the basket. The bear had brought her home.

For you a pot of porridge, and for me a sack of money.

For you a hoof, and for me a trough of money.

"About the Daughters." AT 480/SUS 480*. Recorded in 1981 in Ust'-Kobyrza, Novokuznetsk district, Kemerovo region, Siberia. No information provided about the performer. Lutovinova 1993 no. 40.

Once there lived an old man and an old woman. The old man had a daughter, and the old woman had a daughter. The woman had spun some wool, and she sent her daughter and the old man's daughter to rinse it in the river. The old man's daughter dropped the skein. The old woman beat her and said, "Go and find the skein."

So she set off. She walked and walked and met a man who was herding piglets. She asked him, "Did a skein of wool float by here?"

"Help me round up my pigs, and I'll tell you, and on the way back I'll give you a piglet."

She helped him round up the piglets. She went on. She saw people herding cows. She asked the cowherd about the skein. He said, "I saw it float by. Help me round up the cows, and on your way back I'll give you a calf."

She helped him round up the cows. She went on. She saw people herding horses. She asked the horseherd about the skein. The horseherd said, "I saw a skein float by. Help me round up the horses, and on your way back I'll give you a foal."

She walked and walked and saw a hut standing on chicken legs. She said, "Hut, hut, turn your back to the forest, your front facing me."

The hut turned around, the girl went in, and there Baba Yaga was sitting on the oven, her nose stuck in the ceiling, her hair lying on the floor. Terribly, terribly frightening. The girl asked her,

"Did a skein of wool float by here?"

"I have the skein, I caught it," Yaga answered.

Then she said, "Bring me water in a sieve, heat up the bath, and bathe all my children!"

The girl thought, "How will I bring water in a sieve?"

A bird came flying and said, "Mud and clay, mud and clay."

The girl understood. She stopped up the sieve with mud and clay, brought water, and heated the bath. She bathed Baba Yaga herself. Then her children ran up, and her children were snakes, lizards, and frogs.

She bathed them all. So there was nothing Baba Yaga could do about it; she let her go home with the skein. The girl went home, and on the way the herdsmen gave her a foal, a calf, and a piglet.

She came home, and her stepmother saw what she had brought. She made her own daughter drop a skein and go after it. And her daughter did that: She dropped a skein in the water, went after it, but didn't help anyone on the way; she was too lazy. And she came home empty-handed.

"Stepmother and Stepdaughter." AT 480/SUS 480*. Told by Anastasiia Grigor'evna Sotnikova, age sixty-nine. Recorded in 1968 in Niukhcha village, White Sea region of the Karelian coast. The kind girl sells the animals she receives, since this narrator finds that money is more useful to a household. Razumova and Sen'kina 1974 no. 69.

There once lived an old man and an old woman. They had a very pretty daughter. Well, a terrible thing happened, the mother died, the young little girl was left. Well, the father had to get married. He got married to a woman who also had a daughter. And that girl was ugly and foul-mouthed. Well, the mother's daughter was fair, clean, and neat. Well, she [the stepmother] didn't love the old man's daughter, and that was that.

"All right, I'm going to send [your] daughter to spin where there is a mound of ice, next to the hole in the ice. Let her spin there. Whatever you do, don't drop the spindle."

So she span and sat there, and all at once her spindle fell into the hole in the ice. She said, "Pike, pike, give me the spindle, and if not, I'll go down there myself."

The pike wagged its tail, but didn't give her the spindle. So the girl had to go down after the spindle. She went down there, and the spindle was rolling along a road, and the girl walked, walked, and walked after the spindle. She walked, walked, and walked. Herdsmen were grazing horses, and she called to them, "Herdsmen, herdsmen, who is your master?"

They answered, "We are the herdsmen of Voron Voronovich, Grokhot Grokhotovich [Raven Son of Raven, Thundering Son of Thundering]. Girl, girl, sweep for us, rake for us, we'll give you a mare and a foal. The girl swept and raked, and went on.

"Girl, take the mare and the foal."

"I'll come back and get them."

She walked, walked, and walked again. Cowherds were pasturing cows. She asked again, "Herdsmen, herdsmen, who is your master?

They answered, "We are the herdsmen of Voron Voronovich, Grokhot Grokhotovich. Girl, girl, sweep for us and rake for us. We'll give you a cow and a calf." The girl swept and raked, and went on.

"Girl, take the cow and the calf."

"I'll come back and get them." So she went on. She walked, walked, and walked again. Shepherds were pasturing sheep. And the spindle kept on rolling ahead of her. So, the shepherds were there, pasturing their sheep. She called out again, "Herdsmen, herdsmen, who is your master?"

They told her, "We are the herdsmen of Voron Voronovich, Grokhot Grokhotovich. Girl, girl, sweep for us, rake for us, we'll give you a sheep and a lamb." The girl swept and raked, and went on.

"Girl, take the sheep."

"I'll come back and get it." So she went on. She walked, walked, and walked, and there stood a hut on chicken legs. She said, "Hut, hut, turn your eyes to the forest, your gate to me, so I can go in and out."

The hut turned its eyes to the forest, and its gate toward her. She went in. She went in, and there sat Baba-Yaga, Bony Leg, her breasts hanging over a rod, she was raking the coals with her nose, sweeping the stove with her tongue. Ugh, how frightening. Well, the girl got scared.

She said, "Fu, fu, fu, I haven't been to Rus', I didn't smell the Russian scent, and now the Russian scent has come into the hut. Go, you maiden, go, you pretty one, heat up the bath, bathe my children. I have seven children, seven sons."

The girl didn't know what to do. She had come there, so she had to do it. Well, she gave her something to eat and drink and said, "So go heat the bath, and bathe my children."

The girl went. She gave her a sieve. "Carry water in the sieve, but don't get the sieve wet." Well, that's no easy matter, how can you carry water in a sieve? Try it yourself, go carry water in a sieve. Well, she set off. She went outside, and a bird flew by.

"Girl, girl, rub the sieve with clay."

So the girl rubbed clay on the sieve and fetched water, and heated up the bath. She heated the bath and said, "All right, let's go have a bath with your children."

She carried the first child to the bath and washed him. He came and told his mother, "Oh, Mama, I've never had a bath like the one she gave me." The second one came. "Oh, Mama, how well she bathed me." The third one came. "Mama, she gave me such a bath, I don't know how she did it. You couldn't do better." The fourth one came, and again, "Oh, how well that girl washed me." Well, and so on. The fifth one came, "Mama, she bathed me well." The sixth one came. "Oh, I've never had a bath like the one I had today." The seventh one came, "This girl has hands as soft as down feathers, she bathed me like down feathers."

Well, then the girl came. She came there.... Well, the old woman Baba-Yaga was glad, she was ready to do anything for her, and she gave her something to eat and drink.

"Well, I'll give you your reward!"

And she put her to bed...in a feather bed, with a feather pillow, and covered her with a feather blanket.

"In the morning you'll go home, I'll give you your reward."

So the girl fell into bed, and how happy she was after what she had endured from her stepmother. She had a bad life with her stepmother. In the morning she got up, and again gave her something to eat and drink. As a reward she filled a bag full for her and said, "Don't untie the bag until you get all the way home."

Those were her instructions to the girl.

So the girl set off. She thanked her and showed her out, and she set off on the road. She walked, walked, and walked, and the shepherds said, "Girl, take the sheep and lamb."

The girl took them and sold them. Again she walked, walked, and walked, and the cowherds said, "Girl, take the cow and calf." The girl took them and sold them. After all, she got money for them. Again she walked, walked, and walked, and the herdsmen who were tending horses said, "Girl, take the mare and foal." She took them and sold them.

Then she came to the hole in the ice. Her poor father was walking around it, waiting for her. Well, that's where she fell in. The spindle fell in the hole, and he was walking around there, keeping watch and looking for her. Then after he came there, he'd been walking around for a week or more, the spindle surfaced, and a string was tied to it. So the father grabbed the string and pulled. He pulled her out and was overjoyed. How couldn't he be, his daughter had appeared.

He came home, they opened the bag, and the bag was full of gold. In the hut the bag opened wide, and everything shone. The stepmother came.

"Oh, you went around thieving and wh..."

Well, she cursed.

"My daughter will go, she will bring back more."

She had her own daughter.

Well, her father couldn't be happier. What do you think, he was beside himself with joy.

"My daughter will go, she'll bring a hundred times more. The father said, "Send your daughter."

So she sent her own daughter to the mound of ice to spin. She gave her a blanket to sit on, and told her on purpose, "Now matter what you do, don't drop the spindle."

So her daughter went to where the mound of ice was. She sat and spun, the spindle didn't fall down, and she was bawling. Then she threw it, and the spindle fell. The spindle her mother gave her. So she went down, and that pike [appeared].

"Pike, give me the spindle, and if you don't give it to me, I'll go down there myself."

The pike turned its tail, didn't give her the spindle, and she went down herself. So she set off. She went down the road, and the spindle rolled. She walked along. The herdsmen were grazing their animals, and she didn't say anything. They saw her and called out, "Girl, sweep for us, rake for us, we'll give you a mare and a foal." They thought it was the same girl.

"Go to the devil [lit. *leshii*, forest spirit], I didn't come here for you."

They beat her and threw sticks at her. Well, she just walked by. Again, she walked and walked, and the cowherds were grazing their cows. They thought the same girl was walking by.

"Girl, girl, sweep for us, rake for us. We'll give you a cow and a calf."

"Go to the devil, I didn't come here for you. I'd be happy to take the cow and calf..."

So she went on. Again she walked, walked, and walked, and again there were the shepherds. They called out again,

"Girl, girl, sweep for us, rake for us. We'll give you a sheep and a lamb."

"Go to the devil. I don't need your sheep or lambs."

They beat her, shoved her, and threw [something at her]. Well, what then? She left. She walked, walked, and walked, and there stood the hut on chicken legs. She said, "Hut, hut, turn your eyes to the forest, your gate to me, so I can go in and out."

The hut turned its eyes to the forest, its gate to her, and she went in. She went in, and there sat Baba-Yaga, Bony Leg, her breasts hanging over a rod, she was raking the coals with her nose, sweeping the stove with her tongue, frightening, unpleasant. She got scared. And she said,

"Go, go, girl, go, go fair one, heat up the bath, and bathe my children."

And she said, "All right, I'll bathe them."

She gave her a sieve.

"There you are, bring water in this sieve and don't get the sieve wet."

How can you fetch water in a sieve? Well, then the bird ran by, and called out again, "Girl, girl, rub clay on it, rub clay."

"Die! Get lost! I don't need your help."

Well, she already had rubbed it with clay herself. She rubbed it, brought water, heated the bath. She didn't clean or sweep up the bathhouse. They went to the bath, she took the first son. The first one came. "Oh, Mama, she gave me a bad bath, oh how bad."

The second one came. "Mama, she bathed me badly, very badly."

The third one came. "Mama, she almost tore my legs off."

The fourth said, "Mama, she almost tore my legs off, and my arms off."

The fifth one came, with the same bad news. The sixth came, and the seventh said, "She almost tore my head off."

Well, the old woman got very angry, in a bad temper, and then came and gave her something to eat. But she only gave bread and water to a girl like that. She was fed according to how she had worked. She put her to bed, on a sheet, and covered her with a sheet. She didn't give her a pillow. Her work was bad, so she didn't get anything. She said, "Lie here until morning, and when you go home tomorrow, I'll give you a reward."

Well, this poor girl slept on a fine feather bed at her mother's house, and here she slept on the bare ground, with only a sheet. She lay there and thought, "This is bad." In the morning she got up, she gave her a bag and filled it.

"See that you don't touch the bag, don't open it until you get home."

She loaded it with coal, bricks, and pieces of clay. That was her pay. Well, as her work had been, so was her reward.

"And don't open it until you get home!"

Well, this poor girl walked along, carrying the bag, and the spindle rolled ahead of her. Of course, her mother had already run to the hole in the ice...

"My daughter will come home soon with gold." She cursed at the old man, "You fools, when my daughter comes, she'll bring more."

Well, she [the old woman's daughter] walked and walked.... The shepherds beat her, kicked her, and shouted at her, she barely got past them.... She kept on walking, walking, and walking, the cowherds kicked and shoved her, then the horseherds, the poor girl walked along barely alive. And she wasn't allowed to open the bag. She came to the hole in the ice, and then her mother ran up.

"Praise the Lord, the spindle floated up."

She came and pulled, and the rope snapped. She brought it and shouted at the old man, "Run, bring something sturdier."

She brought a second rope, and it broke, and then the old man brought a third rope. Well, then with the third rope they brought [the girl and the things] up. When they brought [it] home, they opened [the bag], and inside there were clay, stones, and bricks. The mother cursed and swore.

"You fool, what were you thinking? What [the hell] did you bring? What's the matter with you?"

Well, they parted ways with the old man and his girl, the stepdaughter.

And with their gold, the old man and his daughter are living happily and prospering. That's the whole tale and I can't lie any more.

"The Stepdaughter." AT 480/SUS 480*B. Told by L. V. Belova, age sixty. Recorded in 1975 in Kirensk, Irkutsk region, Siberia. Matveeva and Leonova 1993, Prilozhenie no. 2, pp. 304–305.

An old man lived with an old woman. Well, they had a daughter and no other children. Well, suddenly the old woman fell ill and died. Well what then? They went on with their life, and the child was still small. He found himself another old woman. And she had a daughter too. Well, she became a stepdaughter.

She loved her own daughter very much, but plagued the poor girl in all sorts of ways. Well, she plagued her and once said to the old man, "Old man, here's a task for you. Get your daughter, put her on a horse, take her to the forest, so no one sees her [around here any more], otherwise I won't live with you."

Well, all right. There was nothing the old man could do, he didn't want to live alone, so he went, harnessed the horse, and took her to the forest. He drove her and cried, and the girl didn't know anything, the girl was fifteen years old.

Well, all right. He brought her and put her down in the taiga, in a ravine. She got up and followed her eyes [lit. "went where her eyes looked," the Russian equivalent of "following one's nose"]. The girl walked and walked, and saw a hut standing on chicken legs, on ram horns. She said to the hut, "Hut, hut! Turn your front to me, your back to the forest."

The hut turned, and the girl went in. The girl saw Baba Yaga lying there, her feet on the ceiling, her breasts on a rod. She said, "Hello, girl, how did you get here?"

She said, "Grandmother, [she] sent me here."

"Well, all right."

"I don't have a mother."

All right.

"Well, dear, I'll give you two tasks now. One task is to heat up the bath for me. And the second task is to spin a bag of wool in one night."

All right. She gave her a sieve to carry water in. She piled up wood, heated the bath, and...[had to] bring water in a sieve. The girl sat and wailed and wailed. Well, what? She dipped the sieve, but it held no water. She sat there, and a swallow flew by. "Why are you crying, girl?" "My dear bird, why do you ask, help me, rub clay on this sieve and I'll bring water."

The swallow rubbed clay on the sieve very quickly. She dried it and brought enough water for the bath. Baba Yaga bathed and went home. Good.... She gave her dinner. Well, all right, she went off to sleep, and dragged over a bag of wool for her. "Here, you have to spin this overnight, otherwise I'll eat you."

Well, all right. The girl was sitting there with the distaff and the spindle. So now she was sitting there, she spun and spun, spun and spun, and hadn't spun half the sack yet. And the night would soon be over. She wanted to eat something. So she decided to cook some porridge. She cooked the porridge and was going to eat. She looked and saw a mouse that ran up to her and said, "Girl, girl, give me some porridge on a spoon, I'll help you with the spinning."

She put some porridge on the spoon for the mouse. And again. Ten mice came running, and she fed them all porridge. And they set to spinning, and she spun. They spun all the wool and wound it into balls by morning. The girl lay down and slept. She slept, and the wool was all spun. And Baba Yaga was happy and rewarded her, she dressed her in beautiful clothes, and harnessed a horse to a beautiful sleigh and took her home.

The old woman was making pancakes, preparing a funeral feast for her. The dog was sitting there and said, "Bow wow wow! They're bringing the old man's daughter in gold and silver.... They're bringing the old man's daughter in gold and silver."

All right. So what did the old woman do now? She beat the dog, kept making pancakes and preparing for the funeral feast anyway. And suddenly the [old man's] daughter arrived, looking splendid, well dressed, beautiful. And how many coins she brought!

She looked her all over: "O, Lord! What a daughter has returned!"

Well, then a week, perhaps two weeks went by, and she told the old man, "Take my daughter where you took yours."

Well, he got her together, loaded her things and took her off. The same thing happened again. He took her to the same ravine, dropped her off there. She walked and walked down the same path and came to that same old woman.

So Baba Yaga gave her the same task, to fetch water in a sieve. She didn't heat the bath for her, she didn't spin the wool, and she beat all the mice. And she ate that girl up. She gathered up the bare bones onto the sleigh and took them away. The old woman was preparing to meet her. And the dog said, "Bow wow wow! They're bringing the bare bones of the old woman's daughter!"

That was what the dog said. Then she beat the dog, cursed at it, she didn't understand at all. The dog repeated, "Bow wow! They're bringing bare bones!"

The gate opened, Baba Yaga threw out the sack with the bones, and the old woman fainted, and was gone.

And that's the end of the tale, and a cucumber for Marfushka.

"About the Girl Masha." AT 480/SUS 480*C. Recorded in 1939 from E. A. Vasil'eva, Novinki village, Kondopoga region, Karelia. Lutovinova 1993 no. 25.

Once there lived a father and mother, and they had a girl, Masha. The mother died, and Masha was left with just her father. Her father married another woman. The stepmother didn't like Masha and gave birth to her own daughter, Natasha. Both girls were already growing up. The stepmother said to the old man, "Take Masha out to the cabin in the forest; she doesn't do enough spinning for me here."

The father prepared to take Masha out to the forest, and the stepmother loaded a lot of tow. The father took Masha there and left her alone in the forest hut. Masha went into the cabin and sat down to spin. Then she wanted to eat a little. Masha cooked porridge, and suddenly a little mouse came out from under the stove.

"Masha, give me some of your porridge." Masha fed that mouse porridge. She sat down to spin again until it grew dark. Suddenly, Masha saw Baba Yaga Bony Leg riding in a mortar. She was riding in a mortar, driving it with a pestle, and sweeping with a broom. Baba Yaga threw down her mortar in the entrance hall and came in to where Masha was.

"Fu, fu, it smells of the Russian scent here. Why did you come here, Masha?" "Well, grandmother, mother ordered me to spin a bit." "Well, let's play blindman's buff! Here's a kerchief, tie it over my eyes."

Masha tied the kerchief over her eyes. The old woman shoved a little bell in her hand, and the mouse ran up and said to Masha, "Give me the bell, and go hide behind the stove." The mouse grabbed the bell and ran all over the cabin, and ran between [Baba Yaga's] feet and hands. She couldn't catch [it] at all. The mean old woman got angry and started throwing whatever she found—logs and sticks, but she didn't hit the mouse.

"All right, girl, untie the kerchief." The girl untied her kerchief, gave her back her bell, and with that the old woman left. The girl rested a bit, heated the stove again, cooked porridge, and the mouse ran out. The mouse didn't have to ask for any porridge, and the girl gave it almost half of what there was. After breakfast she sat down to spin and spun until evening. It grew dark, and the girl saw a harmful old woman riding along, sitting backwards on a horse. She urged it on with a pestle, and swept with a broom. When she came to the little hut, she knocked and walked in.

"Fu, fu, it smells of the Russian scent! Why are you here in this little hut in the forest, Masha; let's play blindman's buff! Here's a kerchief, tie it over my eyes. Here's a little bell, run around the room with it." And from behind the stove the mouse grabbed the little bell from Masha and ran around the whole room. The old woman tried to catch the mouse, and the mouse ran over her arms and legs, but she couldn't catch it. The old woman got angry and threw wood and sticks at it, but couldn't hit it.

"Well, girl, untie the kerchief!" The girl untied the kerchief, gave her back the little bell, and with that the old woman went home. The girl rested a bit, heated the stove again, cooked porridge, and fed the mouse as much as it wanted. The girl sat down to spin until evening. She saw Baba Yaga riding on a broom. She was driving it with a pestle, and sweeping with a broom. She came, knocked, and walked into the little forest hut.

"Fu, fu, fu, the Russian scent has come into the hut, why are you here, Masha?" "My mother sent me to spin here." "Well, let's play blindman's buff! Here's a kerchief, tie it over my eyes. Take this little bell and run around the room." And the mouse took the bell from behind the stove and ran around the hut. And no matter where she went, she didn't catch the mouse, and she got angry, and threw whatever came to hand.

"Well, girl, untie the kerchief." The girl went up to her, untied the kerchief, and handed her the little bell, and the old woman left. The girl rested and heated the stove, and sat down at the window to spin, and looked out the window. The old woman was riding in a mortar and carrying a large sack, and the old woman threw the sack in the corridor and left. Masha saw the other old woman carrying a sack on the horse. She threw it in the corridor and left. Again Masha saw the old woman riding on the broom and carrying a sack. She came, threw it in the corridor, and left. Masha went into the corridor, and the sacks were full of gold money.

The stepmother told her husband, "Go and get Masha's bones. She's probably been dead a long time now." The old man went to the forest hut for his Masha. Masha saw her father riding on a sled. Masha loaded the three sacks of gold on the sled and sat down on it. The old man drove his Masha home, and the dog barked, "Masha's coming, and gold is rattling on the sled."

The wicked stepmother hit the dog with a poker. "Those are probably Masha's bones that are rattling." The dog repeated, "Bow, wow, Masha's coming here wealthy!"

The old man came and brought the three bags of gold into the hut, and the mean old woman grew very envious. "Old man, take my daughter Natasha there, and my Natasha will come back twice as wealthy."

She gave Natasha good groats, and very little wool to spin. The old man brought Natasha to the forest. Natasha stayed in the forest. She came to the forest cabin, cooked porridge, and the mouse said from under the stove, "Girl, give me some porridge!"

She kicked the mouse. "I want porridge myself; I won't give you one spoon!" And she lay down to sleep on the stove until evening. She woke up when Yaga Baba knocked [at the door].

"Fu, fu, fu, it smells of the Russian scent here! Why have you come here again?" "I came here for gold!" "Well, tie this kerchief over my eyes, and here's a little bell, run around the hut." Natasha tied the kerchief over the old woman's eyes and ran around the hut herself. Natasha hadn't managed to run around the hut more than two or three times when Baba Yaga caught her. She tormented her until Natasha was barely alive. Baba Yaga left the hut, and Natasha lay down to sleep and slept for a long time. She got up, heated the stove, cooked porridge, and the mouse said from under the stove, "Girl, give me some porridge!" The girl kicked the mouse. "I'm tired, I want porridge myself."

Evening came, and the girl didn't notice when Baba Yaga Bony Leg rode up. She knocked and walked in the door. "Fu, fu, fu, the Russian scent has come into the hut! Why are you here, girl?" "My mother sent me here for gold." "Here's a kerchief, tie the kerchief, we'll play blindman's buff, I'll give you a little bell, run around the hut."

The girl tied the kerchief over her eyes, and ran around the hut herself. She hadn't managed to run around two or three times when the old woman caught Natasha. She tormented her until she was barely alive. The old woman said, "Untie the kerchief!" The girl was barely able to untie the kerchief from her eyes and lay down on the floor, and the old woman left. The girl rested, heated the stove, and cooked porridge, and the mouse said from behind the stove, "Girl, give me some porridge!" She threw the mouse so that it flew up to [the top of] the stove.

The girl lay down to sleep and didn't see when Baba Yaga rode up again. She knocked, walked into the hut, and said, "Fu, fu, fu, it smells of the Russian scent here, why have you come here, girl?" "My mother sent me here for gold."

"Here, tie this kerchief over my eyes, take this bell, and run around the cabin." The girl tied the kerchief over her eyes and started running. She hadn't managed to run around more than twice when the old woman caught her and started tormenting her. And then she started biting her and ate her all up, and threw her bones into the corners.

The old woman told her old man, "Go and get my Natasha. She probably has twice as much gold." The old man came to the forest cabin, and there were no sacks in the corridor. The old man went into the hut, and was surprised that Natasha wasn't there, and that the floor was covered with blood, and that Natasha's bones were lying in the corners. The old man gathered the bones in a sack and went home. The dog said to the mean old woman, "Bow, wow, Natasha's bones are rattling in a sack!"

The mean old woman threw a log at the dog and broke its leg, but the dog repeated, "Bow, wow, Natasha's bones are rattling in a sack!"

The old man came up to the house; the mean old woman came out and wailed so that the whole village could hear it, about how he had only brought Natasha's bones, and then they buried her.

I was at the funeral feast and drank beer, but it didn't go in my mouth.

"The Tale of Dun'ka-Durka and the Bright Falcon." AT 432. Recorded by a pupil from Solikamsk district, Perm' province. Manuscript acquired by the Russian Academy of Sciences in 1898. Zelenin 1914 no. 67.

Once there lived an old man and an old woman. They had three daughters, two clever daughters, and the third was Dun'ka-Durka [Dun'ka the Fool]. Their mother died. They lived with their father. When their father went to the city, the two clever daughters asked for new things: one for a ribbon, the other for a kerchief, and Dun'ka-Durka asked him to buy her the Bright Falcon. In the city the father found a feather from the Bright Falcon and brought it for Dun'ka-Durka.

Each of the three daughters had her own hut. Once Dun'ka-Durka was having dinner in her hut. The Bright Falcon flew into her hut, gave her a beautiful dress, and flew away.

Once there was a holiday. The two clever sisters dressed up and went to mass. Dun'ka-Durka also asked to go to church. Her sisters told her, "Dirty girl, you aren't fit to go anywhere! Sit on the stove and shovel the soot!"

When the sisters had left to go to mass, Dun'ka-Durka put on the beautiful dress the Bright Falcon had given her and went to mass. All the people in church feasted their eyes on Dun'ka-Durka. Her sisters also looked at her. When everyone returned from mass, Dun'ka-Durka was already at home.

The sisters came and told Dun'ka-Durka whom they had seen in church, and what she was wearing. "It wasn't me that you saw, my sisters?" Dun'ka-Durka asked. Her sisters said, "You! How could a girl like you ever be beautiful!" In the evening the Bright Falcon flew to her and gave her another dress, better than the last.

The next day the sisters got ready to go to mass again. Once again Dun'ka-Durka asked to go to mass with them. Again her sisters told her, "Dirty girl, you aren't fit to go anywhere! Sit on the stove and shovel the soot!" "At least give me a comb, to comb my hair," Dun'ka-Durka asked. Her sisters threw a comb right at her head.

When the sisters had left for mass, Dun'ka-Durka put on the dress that was even more beautiful than the last one and went to mass. Everyone looked at her again, and they asked, "Where do you come from, you beauty? From what city?" Dun'ka-Durka said, "I'm from the city where they hit you in the head with a comb."

The sisters came home from mass and told Dun'ka-Durka whom they had seen and what she was wearing. "It wasn't me that you saw, my sisters?" Dun'ka-Durka asked. Her sisters said, "You! How could a girl like you ever be beautiful!" In the evening the Bright Falcon flew to her and gave her another dress, better than the last ones.

On the third day the sisters got ready to go to mass again, and again Dun'ka-Durka asked to go to mass with her sisters. Her sisters told her, "Dirty girl, you aren't fit to go anywhere! Sit on the stove and shovel the soot!" "At least give me soap to wash with," Dun'ka-Durka said. Her sisters threw the soap right at her head.

When the sisters had left for mass, Dun'ka-Durka dressed even better than before and went to mass. Everyone looked at her and asked, "Where do you come from, you beauty? From what city?" Dun'ka-Durka said, "I'm from the city where they hit you in the head with soap."

The sisters found out that the Bright Falcon was visiting Dun'ka-Durka, and they put knives on the window sill. When the Bright Falcon flew in and sat in the window, he cut himself.

He thought it was Dun'ka-Durka who had cut him, and from that time on he stopped coming to see her.

When Dun'ka-Durka came home from mass and saw blood on the window sill, she knew they had cut him. She set off to look for the Bright Falcon.

She walked and walked and came to a hut on chicken legs. Dun'ka-Durka said, "Hut, hut, stand with your back to the forest, your front facing me." The hut stood with its back to the forest, with its front facing Dun'ka-Durka. Dun'ka-Durka went into the hut, and Baba-Yaga was sitting on a beam, one leg on a shelf, the other on the beam.

Baba-Yaga said, "Fu-fu, I smell the Russian scent! A fair maiden has arrived. I'll eat her." Dun'ka-Durka said, "No, you won't eat me! First give me something to drink, something to eat, put me to bed, and then ask where and what family I come from." Baba-Yaga gave her something to drink, something to eat, and put Dun'ka-Durka to bed.

Dun'ka-Durka slept and then said where she was going. Baba-Yaga said, "The Bright Falcon is already engaged to the granddaughter of [another] Baba-Yaga. She's terribly wicked and will eat you." Dun'ka-Durka said, "I'm not afraid of her." And she went on.

She walked and walked and again came to a hut. The hut also stood on chicken legs and turned around. Dun'ka-Durka said, "Hut, hut, stand with your back to the forest, your front facing me." The hut stood with its back to the forest, with its front facing Dun'ka-Durka. Dun'ka-Durka went into the hut and saw Baba-Yaga sitting with one leg on a shelf, the other on a beam.

Baba-Yaga said, "Fu-fu, I smell the Russian scent! A fair maiden has arrived. I'll eat her." Dun'ka-Durka said, "No, you won't eat me! First give me something to drink, something to eat, put me to bed, and then ask where and what family I come from." Baba-Yaga gave Dun'ka-Durka something to drink, something to eat, and put her to bed.

Dun'ka-Durka slept and then said where she was going. Baba-Yaga said, "The Bright Falcon has married the granddaughter of [another] Baba-Yaga. She'll eat you." "I'm not afraid of her."

Baba-Yaga said, "I'll give you a golden distaff, a silver spindle, golden pails, and a golden jug. Go to the Bright Falcon and spin with the golden distaff."

Dun'ka-Durka went to the Bright Falcon, walked into the hut and started to spin. Baba-Yaga smelled her and said, "Fu, fu, the Russian scent has wafted in!" and saw Dun'ka-Durka spinning with the golden distaff. Baba-Yaga said, "Sell me your golden distaff!" Dun'ka-Durka said, "My distaff is not for sale, but [to trade] for a night with the Bright Falcon." Baba-Yaga said, "Go ahead, you can have two nights if you like."

Dun'ka-Durka went to the Bright Falcon and tried again and again to rouse him, but couldn't wake him up. Baba-Yaga had put him into a [state of enchanted] sleep.

Dun'ka-Durka went to Baba-Yaga again [the donor]. She came and said, "I couldn't wake up the Bright Falcon. She put him to sleep [with a spell]." Baba-Yaga said, "Take the golden pails, sit there, and rattle them. Baba-Yaga will hear this and come running, and want to buy the pails from you. Don't sell them, but say that you will trade them for something."

Dun'ka-Durka went back to Baba-Yaga and rattled the pails. Baba-Yaga ran up and said, "Sell me those pails!" Dun'ka-Durka said, "My pails are not for sale, but [to trade] for a night with the Bright Falcon." Baba-Yaga said, "Go ahead, you can have two nights if you like."

Dun'ka-Durka went to the Bright Falcon and tried again and again to rouse him, but couldn't wake him up, and went back again.

Dun'ka-Durka told Baba-Yaga, "I tried again and again to rouse him, but I couldn't wake him up." Baba-Yaga said, "Take this golden jug. Go and pour water from one horn into another."

Dun'ka-Durka went and poured water from one horn into another. Baba-Yaga ran up and said, "Sell me that jug." Dun'ka-Durka said, "My jug is not for sale, but [to trade] for a night with the Bright Falcon." Baba-Yaga said, "Go ahead, you can have two nights if you like."

Dun'ka-Durka went, she roused and roused the Bright Falcon, and was barely able to wake him up.

Dun'ka-Durka said, "Will you come with me?" The Bright Falcon said, "She'll catch us and eat us." Dun'ka-Durka said, "I have a brush and a flintstone." They took off. They had gone far when they heard Baba-Yaga coming. They threw the brush, and it turned into a thick forest. Baba-Yaga couldn't get through it, and she went back home to get axes. They chopped down the forest and she started after them again.

They heard her again, and threw the flint. It turned into a fiery river. Baba-Yaga saw it and said, "At least throw me a kerchief!" They asked her, "Will you eat us?" Baba-Yaga said, "No, I won't eat you." They threw her the kerchief. Baba-Yaga stepped on the kerchief and drowned.

They lived happily and prospered.

"Stepmother and Stepson." AT400 (SUS 400/2), and AT 302. Kaliamova village, Orlov district, Viatka province, 1882. Smirnov 1917 no. 130. The motif of pins or needles is treated unusually in this tale. Most often the villain, or his or her agent, sticks pins or needles into the hero's head to make him sleep when the maiden arrives. In this tale the hero sticks pins into his head himself, and they have no effect on him. At first there is no explanation for this. Before her second and third visits the maiden herself instructs the hero to do so, but she gives no reason. The maiden's active role (when she tries in vain to wake up the hero) and her own account of the events, related to Yagibaba when she visits her, make this tale into something of a dialogue between Prince Ivan and the maiden, rather than a tale centered on one protagonist only.

Once there lived a tsar, and he had a son. His stepmother didn't give him clothes or find a bride for him. So he got ready and set off down the road. And he met God. God said, "Why are you sad, young man?" He said, "My stepmother wrongs me, she doesn't give me any clothes or find a wife for me. Why shouldn't I be sad?" God said, "Just leave her, never mind about that, but instead do this: Take a basket of wheat, go out to the cleared forest land, and sow it. When the wheat grows, three martens will come running; but they aren't three martens, they are three maidens. Catch one by the tail, break the tail, and throw it back and forward. That will be your maiden; marry her."

All right. Prince Ivan went, took the basket of wheat, and sowed it. Then three martens came running, but they weren't three martens, they were three maidens. He caught one of them by the tail, broke it, and threw it back and forward, and it turned into a maiden. She said to Prince Ivan, "You've caught me, but not completely." "What do you mean, I haven't caught you completely?" "Well," she said, "None of my wealth is here. I live alone, like a gentlewoman, beyond three seas, beyond three fields, and beyond three forests." She asked him, "Let me go to get my wealth, Prince Ivan. I'll bring it to you on ships." For she was very wealthy. "But you'll deceive me." "No, why would I deceive you, I'll bring you my wealth. Just let me go, and make sure to wait for me by the river." Prince Ivan let her go and went home.

In the morning he got up, washed, got dressed, combed his hair, and went to the river. The stepmother Yagibaba had a son who was ten years old. Yagibaba the stepmother told him, "Take my son with you for a walk." "Let's go," he said. All right, they set off. He stuck three pins in his head and set off. They were sitting by the river. Yagibaba's boy put the young man to sleep: His mother had taught him these tricks. The fiancé fell asleep. Then his fiancée arrived with three ships and all her wealth. She saw her fiancé sleeping, senseless. She tried to wake him up, in tears, "You're probably angry at me. I only brought three ships, but I'll bring six ships of wealth." She told the stepmother's son, "When he wakes up, tell him not to be angry, to stick six pins in his head. I will come with six ships. Will he truly not wake? Maybe he will wake up. Tell him that."

She left. Then he woke up and said, "Was my fiancée here?" "She was." "You scoundrel, you son of a bitch! Why didn't you wake me up?" "No matter how much [we] tried to rouse you, you just kept sleeping. What the devil made you sleep so soundly?" So they went home. In the morning he got himself ready as he should, combed his hair, stuck six pins [in his head], and went to the river. The stepmother Yagibaba told her son, "See that you don't hesitate; don't leave his side." She drove him out without any feeling. So he went along with him. Prince Ivan asked him, "Young man, why are you tagging along?" "Well, my mother told me to." "Well, then, come along and sit. There's plenty of room."

So they arrived and sat down. Half an hour later the young man put Prince Ivan to sleep. He fell asleep. And then the maiden sailed up. She saw that he was already sleeping. She tried to rouse him, "Get up, my dove, you've been sleeping long enough!" Lord have mercy, how she tried to wake him up. She tried and tried, but couldn't wake him up. So she left, said goodbye, and kissed him, "Farewell, don't be angry. I'll go and bring even more, if you're not satisfied with this." She told the youth, "Tell him that tomorrow I'll come with nine ships, and bring even more wealth. Let him stick nine pins into his head." Well, she left.

Then he woke up and asked, "Was my fiancée here?" "She was." "Why didn't you wake me up?" "I tried to wake you, and she tried to wake you, but what could we do? You were sleeping like a dead man."

Now he understood and saw that something foul was going on. He said, "For Christ's sake, don't come with me." He went off and didn't take him along. Yagibaba said to him, "Take him along, you can't refuse, otherwise he'll cut your throat or mine." Well, there was nothing to be done about it, and he took him along. They came to the river, and again the youth put him to sleep. He fell asleep again. The maiden came with nine ships, and he was sleeping again. She started to try to rouse him. She tried, tried, and tried, but he didn't feel anything, no matter what you did to him. She shook him, sat him down on his behind, and said, "For God's sake, take pity on me. I didn't bring my wealth from nearby, but from beyond three seas." No, he just kept sleeping. She stepped away and said, "Now let him look for me beyond three seas, beyond three lands, beyond three rivers. If he wants to [look for me], let him forge three copper hats, three iron spears, and then set out. When he blunts the spears and wears out the hats, then he'll find me."

He woke up, and the youth told him everything that had happened. So he went to a smith and had three iron spears and three copper hats made, and set off down the road. He crossed a sea, and a country. He wore out the hat and wore down one of the spears. Then he came to a hut where there was an old woman. The old woman asked, "Young man, where have you set out to go?" Prince Ivan said, "Well, grandmother, I wanted to get married, but God has not brought us together. I don't know what to do now." The grandmother said, "Go on, Prince Ivan. My sister lives there. Go see her. She has her [i.e., Prince Ivan's fiancée] over as a guest. If you tell her, she'll have your fiancée over. Then you'll see her. So go now."

So he set off. He walked and walked, crossed a sea, a country, and a river. He wore out a hat, and wore down a spear. He saw a hut standing there, with an old woman in it. He asked her, "Do I still have far to go to reach my fiancée? After all, she visits you sometimes." "No, Prince Ivan, I don't know. Go on, my elder sister lives there. She has her over to visit. Ask her: Where is my fiancée? She'll tell you; she'll have her over to visit. Hide and listen to what your fiancée says. Then you'll find out if her heart still pines for you or not." All right, he went on.

He walked and walked. He crossed a sea, a country, and a river. He wore out a hat, broke a spear, and came to a hut. He saw an old woman sitting inside. He asked her, "Grandmother, do you know where I can find my fiancée?" "I know, she is my goddaughter." "Have her come visit you, I'd just like to look at her, [to find out] if she still loves me." So Yagibaba sent for her, told her to come visit. She put Prince Ivan in the cellar. She said, "Sit here for now, and when she comes, listen to what she says. Then you'll find out your fate." Prince Ivan sat down there and listened.

His fiancée arrived. Yagibaba sat her down at the table, and offered her everything. [They talked about] this and that, and then Yagibaba asked her, "Goddaughter, you were going to get married, but you didn't." "How do you know about that?" she asked. "I know about it," she said, "and I know your fiancé." "No, you couldn't know him," she said. "He's far away, he stayed beyond three seas, beyond three lands, and beyond three rivers. How could you know him?" "Oh, I know him," is what Yagibaba said. The fiancée said, "I married him, and came with three ships of dowry. He didn't accept it, he got angry; I hadn't brought enough. So I went again, and brought six ships, and again he didn't accept me. I brought nine ships, and he didn't accept it either. He just kept sleeping; it was all too little for him. And I had brought [these ships] from far away—Lord preserve me! My heart has turned away from him." And she didn't feel any regrets about him either. "If I see him, I'll eat him," she said. "It would be better for him not to come here."

In the cellar Prince Ivan listened. The matter was not going well, so he didn't come out, and just sat there. Yagibaba asked her goddaughter, "Tell me, my goddaughter, what could turn your heart to him, so that you love him again?" Her goddaughter answered, "On the sea there is an oak, on the oak a mare's head, in the head a duck, in the duck an egg, and in that egg is my heart. If he gets it, I will love him again, but if not, he shouldn't bother waiting." She said that and didn't sit still any more, jumped up, and left.

The grandmother let him out of the cellar and said, "Now go and look for that oak, go due east." Prince Ivan set off. He came to a city and saw people beating a servant, Vasilii, with red-hot twigs, demanding thirty rubles of debts, thirty rubles of taxes. Prince Ivan asked them, "Why are you doing this?" "We're beating thirty rubles in debt out of the servant Vasilii." So he took some money from his purse and gave it to them. "Here, take this, and let him go." So he bought him free. Fine. They let Vasilii go.

They set off together. They walked and walked and saw a wolf. "Let's shoot it. It'll make a good meal." "No, Prince Ivan, wait; he'll be useful to you." Prince Ivan listened to him, didn't shoot the wolf, and let him go. A kite flew by. Prince Ivan said, "Well, there's our meal, let's shoot him." Once again Vasilii restrained him, and said, "Wait, don't hurt him, he might help you when you need him." They went on. They saw a fish lying on the sand, squirming. Prince Ivan said, "Well, God sent us a meal." "No, wait, Prince Ivan, perhaps the fish will be of help. Let's put it back in the sea; that will be better." All right, they let it go. So then they went on. They saw an oak tree standing in the middle of the sea, looking at the sun, covered with a cloud. Vasilii said, "That's the oak. How can we get there?" They set to building a bridge. They built and built, they brought logs and tied them with branches, but it was still a long way to the oak. They kept adding on to the bridge, but no, it was still far away. They chopped wood and chopped. They came to the oak. Then Vasilii the servant took out a little knife and said, "This is a knife blessed by Tikhon the priest." When he cut with the knife, the shavings flew. And then a horse's head flew out of the oak tree. Immediately the wolf ran up and shook the head with all its might. A duck fell out of the head. Then the kite came flying, pecked at the duck, tugged at it and broke it open. An egg fell out from under the duck, it rolled and rolled and fell into the sea. Then the fish rushed up and pulled the egg out of the water. It grabbed the egg and brought it out onto the shore.

Prince Ivan grasped and took the egg, and said, "Thank you, fish. I wanted to make a meal of you, and now you've done me a good turn, so return to live in the sea."

So then they set off to grandmother Yagibaba. Prince Ivan told her, "Well, we got the egg, so what should we do now?" She put them in the cellar and put a basket of eggs on the table, and in front she put the egg that contained the heart. Then she sent for the fiancée. Well, she came. The grandmother sat her at the table and treated her to everything. The fiancée ate her heart, peeled the egg and ate it. She ate it and suddenly became troubled. She sat there and was so pensive! The grandmother asked her, "Why are you so sad? Why don't you eat more?" "Well, I'm unhappy now." "Well, what is it that is making you unhappy?" "Well, I miss my young man." "Don't worry about it," she said, "I'll get your fiancé." "Really?" she asked. "Yes, I'll get him," she said. "I'll give you several thousand in money, if you just get him." "I'll get him, my goddaughter, I'll get him." "But how will you get him? Right now he remains beyond three seas, three lands, and three rivers. How far I sailed, and how long.... How will you get him?" "In faith, I'll get him," she said. "Get him, please get him," she said. "If that's what you want, give me your hand that you won't harm him in any way." "I won't do anything to him, I swear on my Nicholas cross."

Well, all right. The grandmother opened the cellar and said to them, "Come out, the young bride really wants to see you." They came out. The bride said to Prince Ivan, "Oh, my soul, where did you come from?" He said, "I came for you. I crossed three seas, three lands, and three rivers, and now I've found you." "And I, your bride, how much I wore myself out. I came to see you three times." Well, all right. "Should I bring you much wealth?" "I don't need anything," he said, "as long as you are with me, that's fine." "No," she said, "I'll gather twelve ships for you." She went and brought twelve ships. Prince Ivan said to her, "Let's go home." So they set off.

They took Vasilii with them, since he had done so much to help him. And Yagibaba stayed at home: "I can't go anywhere with you, what, and break my [old] bones?" So they set out. When the stepmother saw them coming, she started to shove and butt [horns like a goat or cow]. Then they shot her. And so Prince Ivan lived with his bride.

APPENDIX II
Index of Tales

Baba Yaga appears in the following tale types. They are listed by their number as found in the 1979 East Slavic tale-type index (SUS, compiled by Barag et al.), and according to the Aarne-Thompson index (AT). Following each tale type, the texts used in this study are cited by collection. For the sake of simplicity, only the episodes containing Baba Yaga have been taken into consideration in classifying these texts.

Children's Tales

123 (AT 123, The Wolf and the Kids): Karnaukhova 85, Zelenin Viatka 113.

163 (AT 163, The Singing Wolf): Novgorod-Severskii (no date): 61–65.

313H* (AT 313H*, The Girl Escapes from a Witch): Potanin 1906 no. 20.

314A* (AT 314A*, The Bullock-Savior): Akimova 362, Ivanitskii 635 (this same tale appears in Burtsev 1895: 119–121), Kargin 14, 15, Khudiakov 79, Lutovinova Kemerovo 159, Morokhin and Vardugin 1993: 185–186, Sadovnikov 20, Smirnov 238, Sokolova 1970: 47–48, Vedernikova and Samodelova 28.

327A (AT 327A, Hansel and Gretel): Onegina 9.

327B (AT 327B, The Dwarf and the Giant): Afanas'ev 105, Bandarchyk 1971 no. 154 (+AT 531), Bandarchyk 1973 no. 9, Chubinskii 1878 no. 8 (+AT 531), Gorodtsov i: 275–294, Khudiakov 103, Novikov 1971 no. 43, Potanin 1902 no. 36 (+AT 531; reprinted in Matveeva and Leonova 17), Sokolova 1970: 36–40 (+AT 531). Bandarchyk's 1971 text is taken from E. Romanov, *Belorusskii sbornik*, vyp. VI, no. 31, pp. 286–297. Mogilev 1901; a Russian translation can be found in Vasilenok 1958: 94–109. Bandarchyk 1973 no. 9 is also from Romanov, vyp. VI: no. 29, pp. 262–276.

327C (AT 327C, The Devil [Witch] Carries the Hero Home in a Sack): Afanas'ev 106, 107, Akimova 367, Avanesav and Biryla 1962: 290, Chernyshev 59, Gorodtsov iii: 6–10, Kozhemiakina 1973: 171–174, Leonova 3, Lutovinova Index p. 18, Onchukov 73, Smirnov 143, 231, 250, Sokolova 1970: 32–33, Tatarintseva 1995: 20–22, Vedernikova and Samodelova 35, Zelenin Viatka 87, Zhivaia Starina 21 (1912): 319–320.

327F (AT 327F, The Witch and the Fisher Boy): Afanas'ev 111, Bakhtin and Shiriaeva 54, Balashov 105, Karnaukhova 74, Kretov 18, Lutovinova Index p. 18, Matveeva and Leonova 9, Nikiforov 1961 nos. 45, 64, 70, 85, Onchukov 38, Potanin 1902 no. 41, Potiavin 9, 10, Simina 39, Smirnov 40,

120, 343, Vedernikova and Samodelova 33, Zelenin Perm' 86, Zelenin Viatka 97, 115.

327C/F, combined with other tales: Dobrovol'skii 16 (+AT 1653), Leonova 14 (+AT 1653 and AT 1537), Onchukov 2000 Shokshozero 74 (+AT 1653), Potanin 1906 no. 4 (+AT 1653), Tseitlin 10, Vlasova and Zhekulina 46.

333B (AT 333B, The Cannibal Godfather [Godmother]): Smirnov 151.

333C*: Potiavin 12.

451 (AT 451A, The Sister Seeking Her Nine Brothers; not listed in the East Slavic tale-type index): Giliarova and Frumkin 14.

AT 480, The Kind and the Unkind Girls

480*: Erlenvein 9, Khudiakov 101, Lutovinova 39, 40, 41, 42, Lutovinova Index p. 23, Mitropol'skaia 77, Morokhin and Vardugin 1993: 121–123, Nikiforov 1961 no. 63, Onchukov 2000 Shokshozero 4, Potiavin 8, Razumova and Sen'kina 1974 no. 69, Vlasova and Zhekulina 50.

480A*: Afanas'ev 113, Bandarchyk 1978 no. 24 (includes an episode resembling 480A*, as well as the magic flight episode, 313H*), Kargin 23, 24, Karnaukhova 87, Khudiakov 12, 13, Lutovinova 45, 46, 47, 48, Novikov 1971 no. 46.

480B*: Afanas'ev 103, 104, Lutovinova 57, 59. The East Slavic tale-type index recognizes only Afanas'ev 104 as a true version of 480B*. It classifies Afanas'ev 103 as 480A*, even though the heroine in this version has no brother.

480*B: Afanas'ev 102, Lutovinova 43, 51, 81, Matveeva and Leonova Prilozhenie 2 (pp. 304–305), Onchukov 108, Shastina 1971 no. 28, Simina 21, 22, Vedernikova and Samodelova 44, Zelenin Perm' 77.

480*C: Balashov 29, Lutovinova 25, 29, Onchukov 2000 Shokshozero 30, Smirnov 42.

Versions of 480 difficult to classify in the above subtypes: Lutovinova 50, 78.

Anomalous tales, difficult to classify: Kargin 33.

Baba Yaga as Donor

AT 329, Hiding from the Devil

AT 400, The Man on a Quest for His Lost Wife

329+400/1: Nikiforov 1961 no. 86, Shastina 1975: 114–122, Zelenin Perm' 1, Zelenin Perm' pp. 303–304.

400/1: Gorodtsov ii: 150–173 (+AT 301, where Baba Yaga is a villain with an army, making her appearance in this tale ambiguous overall), Potanin 1906 no. 15, Smirnov 35, Zelenin Perm' 20.

401 (AT 401, The Princess Transformed into a Deer): Afanas'ev 272, Nikiforov 1936 no. 4.

402 (AT 402, The Mouse [Cat, Frog, etc.] as Bride): Afanas'ev 269 (+AT 302), Afanas'ev 570, Bakhtin and Shiriaeva 72, Burtsev 1895: 265–286, Gorodtsov ii: 25–30, Karnaukhova 65, Kovalev 12 (+AT 302), Leonova 17, Löwis of Menar 1921 no. 5 (this text is a German translation from Rudchenko, *Narodnye iuzhnorusskie skazki* II, Kiev 1870, no. 28, p. 99; a Russian translation can be found in Petnikov 1966: 88–95), Novikov 1971 no. 37 (also reprinted in Korepova and Belikova 26), Shastina 1971 no. 26 (+AT 302), Vedernikova and Samodelova 37 (+AT 302), Zelenin Perm' 28. An old woman donor with some of Baba Yaga's attributes appears in Afanas'ev 267 and 268.

451 (AT 451, The Maiden who Seeks Her Brothers): Kovalev 28.

550 (AT 550, Search for the Golden Bird): Gurevich 24, Khudiakov 113, Mints et al. 1957 no. 18, Nikiforov 1961 no. 98, Sorokovikov 8. This tale often continues with an episode of AT 302 (The Ogre's [Devil's] Heart in the Egg), where Baba Yaga tells the hero how to find Koshchei's death. In an exceptional version of AT 302 attached to AT 321, the hero kills her by finding her death egg (Matveeva and Leonova 1).

551 (AT 551, The Sons on a Quest for a Wonderful Remedy for Their Father): Afanas'ev 172, 173, 174, 178, 563, Bandarchyk 1973 no. 65, Kargin 26, Kozhemiakina 1973: 99–104, Novikov 1971 no. 26 (also reprinted in Korepova and Belikova 5), Novikov 1971 no. 29 (also reprinted in Korepova and Belikova 18), Onchukov 8, Razumova and Sen'kina 1974 no. 35, Smirnov 1, Sokolov 139, Zelenin Viatka 47.

552A (AT 552, The Girls Who Married Animals): Gurevich 32, Novikov 1971 no. 24 (an eighteenth-century literary version also found in Korepova and Belikova 3 and Afanas'ev 562), Onchukov 167, Sorokovikov 5.

554 (AT 554, The Grateful Animals): Sadovnikov 4.

560 (AT 560, The Magic Ring): Matveeva and Leonova 22

564 (AT 564, The Magic Providing Purse and "Out, Boy, out of the Sack!"): Akimova 394.

Donor tales difficult to classify: Korepova and Belikova 13, Lutovinova Index p. 12 no. 6, Nikiforov 1936 no. 11.

Baba Yaga as Donor and Villain (Ambiguous Tales and Tale Types)

300A (AT 300A, The Fight on the Bridge): Afanas'ev 136, 137, Bandarchyk 1973 no. 4, Gorodtsov ii: 355–384 (+ AT 519), Khudiakov 6, Manzhura 1890: 24–27, Onchukov 27, Potanin 1902 no. 34 (also reprinted in Matveeva 1979 no. 8), Smirnov 150.

300A* (not listed in the Aarne-Thompson index): Smirnov 304 (also reprinted in Matveeva 1979 no. 29), Vedernikova and Samodelova 21, Zelenin Perm' 9.

301 (AT 301, The Three Stolen Princesses, AT 301A, Quest for a Vanished Princess, AT 301B, The Strong Man and His Companions): Afanas'ev 128, 141, 142, Balashov 55, Burtsev 1895: 215–223, Dobrovol'skii 6, Gorodtsov ii: 186–203, Karnaukhova 14, Khudiakov 81, Kitainik 7, Kovalev 8, Kretov 42, Matveeva 1980 no. 13, Novikov 1971 no. 47 (reprinted in Medvedev 5, and Vedernikova and Samodelova 156), Onchukov 34.

(Baba Yaga's underground army, contains some elements of **301**): Afanas'ev 161, Bandarchyk 1973 no. 12, Gorodtsov ii: 150–173 (+AT 400, where Baba Yaga is a donor), Kovalev 3, Manzhura 1890: 14–18, Potanin 1906 no. 13 (also includes an episode of AT 321). Azadovskii 1947 no. 8 is a complex tale which includes Baba Yaga as a villain in AT 519, and then an encounter with her army. Shastina 1985 no. 54 belongs to the "herding mares" cycle, AT 552A+554+650B*+400, but also includes the hero's combat with Baba Yaga and her underground army.

302 (AT 302, The Ogre's [Devil's] Heart in the Egg): Most often, Baba Yaga is a donor who helps the hero find Koshchei's death egg, in versions attached to AT 402 and 550 (see above). In a version attached to AT 321 where she is the villain (see below), the hero kills her by finding and breaking her death egg (Matveeva and Leonova 1). The hero obtains a horse from Baba Yaga in the "herding mares" cycle, which includes SUS 302/2 (552A+554+400+302, see below), and this tale type is also attached to SUS 400/2 (see below).

303 (AT 303, The Twins or Blood-Brothers): Dobrovol'skii 13, 14, Erlenvein 3, Gorodtsov ii: 308–323, Iavorskii 31b, Manzhura 1890: 30–33, Onchukov 4, 152, Pomerantseva 30.

312D (AT 312D, Brother Saves His Sister and Brothers from the Dragon): Balashov 7, Matveeva 1980 no. 7, Smirnov 279, Zelenin Perm' 27.

313A, B, C (AT 313, The Girl as Helper in the Hero's Flight): Afanas'ev 219, 224, 225, Bagizbaeva 20, Balashov 95, Bandarchyk 1973 no. 23, Chernyshev 63, Erlenvein 6, Gromov 3, Kovalev 10 (reprinted in Morokhin and Vardugin 1993: 87–102), Krasnozhenova 19, Mints and Savushkina 11, Morokhin and Vardugin 1993: 77–80, Nikiforov 1936 no. 6, Potanin 1906 no. 38 (reprinted in Matveeva 1981 no. 14), Sadovnikov 1, Simina 11, Smirnov 281, Sokolov 66, Zelenin Perm' 55 and p. 293, Zelenin Viatka 13, 118. Baba Yaga's name is mentioned in Matveeva 1981 no. 17.

315 (AT 315, The Faithless Sister): Afanas'ev 201, 204, Kulish II: 48–57, Matveeva and Leonova 3, Potanin 1906 no. 29 (also reprinted in Matveeva 1980 no. 36), Simina 18 (Simina classifies this tale as AT 502).

318 (AT 318, The Faithless Wife): Sokolov 55, 140.

321 (AT 321, Eyes Recovered from Witch): Balashov 43, Kitainik 7, Matveeva and Leonova 1 (also reprinted in Matveeva 1979 no. 2), Nikiforov 1961 no. 109, Onchukov 241, Potanin 1906 no. 13 (also belongs to the AT 301 cycle about Baba Yaga's underground army), Shastina 1974: 42–52.

AT 400, The Man on a Quest for His Lost Wife

400/2: Afanas'ev 232, Balashov 57, Novikov 1961 no. 6, Sadovnikov 61, Smirnov 130, Zhivaia Starina 21 (1912): 365–386. The Sadovnikov and Zhivaia Starina versions are combined with AT 302, The Ogre's (Devil's) Heart in the Egg.

425 (AT 425, The Search for the Lost Husband): Balashov 33, 59, 88, Khudiakov 40, Matveeva and Leonova 15, Onchukov 178, Onchukov 2000 Shokshozero 69, Onegina 59, Razumova 78, Razumova and Sen'kina 1974 no. 67, Razumova and Sen'kina 1982 no.. 21. The riddle concerning the louse's skin in Balashov 33 resembles a similar riddle in SUS 621; the 1979 East Slavic tale-type index assigns Balashov 33 to this tale type, but the rest of the tale clearly belongs to the SUS 425 cycle.

430 (AT 430, The Ass): Kozhemiakina 1973: 105–110.

432 (AT 432, The Prince as Bird): Afanas'ev 235, Kabashnikaw 99, Kargin 21, Khudiakov 39, Korol'kova 1969: 152–166, Kovalev 13, Mints et al. 1957 no. 21, Novikov 1971 no. 44, Tumilevich 21, Vedernikova and Samodelova 42, Zelenin Perm' 67, Zelenin Viatka 74.

465A (AT 465A, The Quest for the Unknown): , Afanas'ev 212, Kovalev 9 (reprinted in Morokhin and Vardugin 1993: 111–120), Mitropol'skaia 36, Novikov 1961 no. 5.

465B (AT 465B, The Quest for the Living Harp): Karnaukhova 7.

519 (AT 519, The Strong Woman as Bride): Afanas'ev 198, 199, Azadovskii 1947 no. 8, Azbelev 6, Balashov 54, Bandarchyk 1973 no. 52, Gorodtsov ii: 355–384 (+ AT 300A), Matveeva and Leonova 21, Razumova and Sen'kina 1982 no. 1, Shastina 1985 no. 63, Sokolov 143, Zelenin Perm' 7.

531 (AT 531, Ferdinand the True and Ferdinand the False): Bandarchyk 1971 no. 154, Chubinskii 1878 no. 8, Potanin 1902 no. 36 (reprinted in Matveeva and Leonova 17). (All these tales begin as SUS 327B). Matveeva 1984 no. 33.

552A+554+400+302 (The Hero Herds Mares for Baba Yaga—AT 552A, Three Animals as Brothers-in-Law; AT 554, The Grateful Animals; AT 400, The Man on a Quest for His Lost Wife, AT 302, The Ogre's [Devil's] Heart in the Egg): Afanas'ev 159, Azadovskii 1938 no. 30, Bandarchyk 1973 no. 71, Bandarchyk 1978 no. 6, Erlenvein 31, Gorodtsov i: 205–226, Matveeva 1984 no. 39, Novikov 1971 no. 30 (also reprinted in Korepova and Belikova 19), Shastina 1985 no. 54 (this text includes the hero's combat with Baba Yaga's underground army [related to AT 301] and is also found in Azbelev 1986, no.

31), Vasilenok 1958: 115–122 (This text is a Russian translation from E. Romanov, *Belorusskii sbornik*, T. I, vyp. III, Vitebsk 1887), Zelenin Perm' 6, Zelenin Viatka 86.

566 (AT 566, The Three Magic Objects and the Wonderful Fruits): Onchukov 2000 Tavda 57.

650C* (AT 650A, Strong John): Afanas'ev 310.

709 (AT 709, Snow-White): Khlanta 1989: 138–144, Löwis of Menar 1921 no. 23 (the text in Löwis of Menar is a German translation from *Kurskii sbornik* IV, no. 3, pp. 87–92, Kursk, 1903), Onchukov 2000 Shokshozero 29.

884B* (AT 884B*, Girl Dressed as Man Deceives the King): Afanas'ev 316, Chudinskii 30, Novikov 1971 no. 50, Smirnov 260.

428 (AT 428, The Wolf): Khudiakov 20, Onchukov 2000 Shokshozero 51, Zelenin Viatka 27.

884B* and 428: Balashov 52, Khudiakov 19, Matveeva and Leonova 13, Sadovnikov 16, Sokolova 1970: 54–55.

Ambiguous tales difficult to classify: Kovalev 11, Manzhura 1890: 51–52.

Baba Yaga as Villain

176** and 1159 (AT 176**, Man and Animals Brew Beer, AT 1159, The Ogre Wants to Learn to Play): Potanin 1906 no. 24, Smirnov 247, Zelenin Perm' 62.

218B* and 1960G (AT 218*, Cock and Hen Plant Bean; AT 1960G, The Great Tree): Razumova 75.

313E* (AT 313E*, Girl Flees from Brother Who Wants to Marry Her): Afanas'ev 114, Karnaukhova 70, Onchukov 44, 71.

403 (AT 403, The Black and the White Bride): Nikiforov 1961 no. 80, Onchukov 218, Razumova and Sen'kina 1974 no. 20, Razumova and Sen'kina 1982 no. 40, Simina 45, Smirnov 32, 141 (some ambiguity in 141).

405 (AT 405, Jorinde and Joringel): Balashov 49.

407 (AT 407, The Girl as Flower): Onchukov 278.

409 (AT 409, The Girl in the Form of a Wolf): See SUS 511.

410** (AT 410, Sleeping Beauty; AT 410*, The Petrified Kingdom): Serzhputovskii 1911 no. 72 (reprinted in Serzhputovskii 1965: 146–164).

450 (AT 450, Little Brother and Little Sister): Balashov 155, Karnaukhova 64, Lutovinova Index p. 21, p. 22, Onchukov 128, Onegina 19, 27, Sadovnikov 65, Simina 34, Smirnov 43, Tseitlin 11, Zelenin Viatka 11.

510A (AT 510, Cinderella): Razumova and Sen'kina 1974 no. 21.

511 (AT 511, One-Eye, Two-Eyes, Three-Eyes): Balashov 130, Razumova and Sen'kina 1974 no. 71, Simina 42.

511 + 409 (AT 409, The Girl in the Form of a Wolf): Afanas'ev 101, Efimenko 1878 p. 227 no. 3, Smirnov 41, Zelenin Viatka 14.

513A (AT 513, The Extraordinary Companions): Bandarchyk 1973 no. 6. A Russian translation of this tale is found in Vasilenok 1958: 162–173.

516 (AT 516, Faithful John): Balashov 40, Karnaukhova 141.

532 (AT 532, I Don't Know): Kretov 30.

533 (AT 533, The Speaking Horsehead): Razumova and Sen'kina 1974 no. 59.

563 (AT 563, The Table, the Ass, and the Stick): Balashov 96, Khudiakov 8, Mitropol'skaia 53.

706 (AT 706, The Maiden without Hands): Balashov 47, 134, Nikiforov 1961 no. 39, Potanin 1906 no. 1, Tseitlin 12.

707 (AT 707, The Three Golden Sons): Afanas'ev 284, Balashov 46, Karnaukhova 69, Khudiakov 84, Kitainik 10, Onegina 57, Potanin 1902 nos. 5, 35, 53, 59, Potanin 1906 no. 41, Razumova and Sen'kina 1974 no. 11, Simina 8, 37, Smirnov 37, 131, Tseitlin 9.

708 (AT 708, The Wonder-Child): Balashov 136.

736B* (AT 736, Luck and Wealth): Ozarovskaia 27.

1053A (AT 1053A, The Big Rope): Zelenin Viatka 42.

1137 (AT 1137, The Ogre Blinded): Gorodtsov i: 163–175, Kabashnikaw 212, Kretov 25, Nikiforov 1961 no. 92.

1164 (AT 1164, The Evil Woman Thrown into the Pit): Khudiakov 24.

1353 (AT 1353, The Old Woman as Troublemaker): Gospodarev 59.

1353B*: Sidel'nikov 19.

1653 (AT 1653, The Robbers under the Tree; AT 1653B, The Brothers in the Tree): Dobrovol'skii 16 (attached to AT 327C/F), Onchukov 2000 Shokshozero 74 (attached to AT 327C/F), Sadovnikov 27 (as one episode of AT 1535, The Rich and the Poor Peasant).

Tale texts with an inimical Baba Yaga, difficult to classify: Gorodtsov i: 22–36, Gorodtsov ii: 415–431 (a version of AT 551 including an anomalous combat episode with Baba Yaga), Khudiakov Prilozhenie no. 8, Manzhura 1890: 123–124, Smirnov 341. A hostile Baba Yaga is only mentioned in Novgorod-Severskii: 81–90, which bears some resemblance to AT 550. Baba Yaga appears in the introduction to a tale where she tries to measure the length and breadth of Siberia, but fails (Novgorod-Severskii: 28–29).

A tale listed with only one version in the East Slavic tale type index is SUS **1169*** (Serebrennikov 19, unfortunately unavailable for the current survey). V. N. Serebrennikov, *Metkoe slovo. Pesni. Skazki. Dorevoliutsionnyi fol'klor Prikam'ia.* Perm' 1964. In this tale a devil gathers the twelve most wicked women, cooks them together in a pot, and one, Baba-Yaga, jumps out (Barag et al. 1979: 270). Novikov mentions a tale with an inimical Baba Yaga which was not available, and which lacks type assignment: No. 23 in N. I. Rozhdestvenskaia, *Skazy i skazki Belomor'ia i Pinezh'ia*. Arkhangelsk 1941. Novikov also discusses versions of a few tale types in which Baba Yaga appears as a donor, and which were unavailable for the present survey. An exceptional version of AT 707 (The Three Golden Sons) where Baba Yaga appears as donor and helps in the prince's search for his young wife is 1b in A. S. Mashkin, "Materialy po ètnografii Kurskoi gubernii. Prigotovil k pechati V. I. Rezanov. Ch. III. Sborniki A. S. Mashkina." *Kurskii sbornik* vyp. IV, 1903. The same collection contains a version of AT 709 (Snow-White), with Baba Yaga as a donor (Mashkin 3). Baba Yaga likewise appears as donor in a version of AT 531 (Ferdinand the True and Ferdinand the False), in *Skazki Kupriianikhi* no. 1 (ed. Novikova, Ossovetskii, and Plotnikov, Voronezh, 1937), and in a version of AT 532 (I Don't Know) (E. R. Romanov, *Belorusskii sbornik* T. 1, Vyp. III, no. 43; Vitebsk, 1887).

West Slavic Tales
These tales featuring Ježibaba are from the collections of Dobšinský, Czambel, Rimavský, the Carpatho-Ukrainian (Rusyn) tales from the Hyriak collection, Jiří Polívka's extensive catalogue of Slovak folktales, *Súpis slovenských rozprávok* (Polívka), Ján Kollár's *Národnie spievanky*, and the catalogue of Slovak folk prose compiled by Viera Gašparíková.

Ježibaba as Donor
AT 313 (The Girl as Helper in the Hero's Flight) + 315 (The Faithless Sister): Dobšinský iii: 433–443 (Three Ježibabas feed the hero, and her dog warns him of the approach of the ogre Zelezník).
AT 408 (The Three Oranges): Rimavský 1975: 37–52 (discussed in chapter 2).
AT 551 (The Sons on a Quest for a Wonderful Remedy for their Father): Gašparíková 555 (Three Ježibabas give the hero magic objects).

Ježibaba as Donor and Villain: Ambiguous Tales
AT 321 (Eyes Recovered from Witch): Dobšinský iii: 32–43, Polívka iv: 179–182 (there is some ambiguity in this tale, since Ježibaba first appears as a blinded victim who aids the hero in overcoming the villain many-headed maidens, but she is then revealed to be a cannibalistic witch).
AT 365 (The Dead Bridegroom Carries Off his Bride [Lenore]): Gašparíková 382.
AT 400 (The Man on a Quest for His Lost Wife) + 302 (The Ogre's [Devil's] Heart in the Egg): Dobšinský i: 183–194.

AT 451 (The Maiden Who Seeks Her Brothers): Dobšinský iii: 89–101 (Ježibaba is a villain), Hyriak v no. 16 (Izhuzhbaba appears ambiguously in this tale; she first helps the heroine, and then tries to have her killed).

AT 461 (Three Hairs from the Devil's Beard): Gašparíková 95.

AT 480 (The Kind and the Unkind Girls): Dobšinský iii: 267–276, Gašparíková 411, 428, 557, Polívka iii: 322, 323, 324.

AT 502 (The Wild Man) + 554 (The Grateful Animals): Dobšinský ii: 325–333.

AT 513 (The Extraordinary Companions): Czambel 193 (A Jedžibaba advises that emperor that the Moscow prince has stolen his daughter; another Jendžibaba keeps one of the hero's companions from accomplishing his task by making him sleep).

AT 531 (Ferdinand the True and Ferdinand the False): Gašparíková 75, 255 (the hero herds mares for Ježibaba, making her a hostile donor in this tale), Gašparíková 170 (Ježibaba sets tasks for the hero), Polívka ii: 326–329 (includes herding mares for Ježibaba), Polívka ii: 332–339 (Ježibaba appears in an opening episode that recalls AT 707), Polívka ii: 340–348, 348–349.

AT 710 (Our Lady's Child): Czambel 156 (Ježibaba pays for a poor man to baptize his daughter, and then comes for the daughter when she turns twelve. The girl breaks an interdiction and Ježibaba sends her back into the world mute. She marries a king and Ježibaba steals her children. When the heroine is about to be executed, Ježibaba, who has been released from an enchantment, returns with the children. Ježibaba goes to live with the family), Hyriak v no. 17 (In the king's absence the heroine's three children are taken away by a woman in black. The cook Izhuzhbaba claims that the heroine has eaten the children).

AT 930 (The Prophecy) + AT 461 (Three Hairs from the Devil's Beard): Hyriak vii no. 2 (discussed in chapter 2).

Ježibaba as Villain

AT 300 (The Dragon Slayer): Dobšinský iii: 291–308 (the hero helps a king defeat Ježibaba and her army).

AT 300A (The Fight on the Bridge): Dobšinský ii: 199–209, Gašparíková 105, 230, Hyriak i: 46–65 (Hyndzhi-baba is the dragons' mother-in-law), Hyriak ii no. 63.

AT 301 (The Three Stolen Princesses): Hyriak vi no. 31.

AT 303 (The Twins or Blood-Brothers): Dobšinský ii: 411–418, Hyriak iii no. 23, Kollár 1953: 52–55.

AT 313 (The Girl as Helper in the Hero's Flight): Dobšinský i: 75–85, Gašparíková 529, Hyriak vii no. 10, Hyriak vii no. 14 (+AT 400; the hero releases princesses and a city from enchantment. Iezhibaba had wanted a princess to marry her son).

AT 315 (The Faithless Sister): Czambel 153.

AT 326 (The Youth Who Wanted to Learn What Fear Is): Gašparíková 303.

AT 327A (Hansel and Gretel): Dobšinský iii: 251–258.

AT 327B (The Dwarf and the Giant): Gašparíková 544.

AT 327B (The Dwarf and the Giant) + AT 531 (Ferdinand the True and Ferdinand the False): Dobšinský i: 133–147, Gašparíková 215, 333, 485, Hyriak iii no. 5 (Hyndzhibaba mistakenly decapitates her twelve daughters. The hero steals self-playing gusli and a magic flower from her), Hyriak vi no. 21, Hyriak vii no. 4.

AT 327B (The Dwarf and the Giant) + AT 327C (The Devil [Witch] Carries the Hero Home in a Sack): Kollár 1953: 51–52.

AT 327C + AT 531 (Ferdinand the True and Ferdinand the False): Polívka ii: 409 (a female heroine).

AT 400 (The Man on a Quest for His Lost Wife): Gašparíková 448.

AT 400 (The Man on a Quest for His Lost Wife, but resembles SUS 400/2): Dobšinský i: 263–270, Dobšinský iii: 147–158, Gašparíková 507.

AT 402 (The Mouse [Cat, Frog, etc.] as Bride): Gašparíková 229, 447 (a Ježibaba has turned a princess into an animal).

AT 425 (The Search for the Lost Husband): Gašparíková 313, 515.

AT 425 (The Search for the Lost Husband) + AT 433B (King Lindorm): Hyriak vii no. 1 (The heroine's snake husband disappears when his skin is burned. After a long search in iron boots she comes to the place where Iezhibaba has him under enchantment. She gives golden objects to Iezhibaba's cook, is allowed to stand at his threshold for three nights. On the third night, he awakens, the snakes around him disappear, and they return home with the cook).

AT 450 (Little Brother and Little Sister): Czambel 151, 165, Dobšinský i: 195–203, Hyriak v no. 9 (Izhuzhbaba cuts off the heroine's hands and replaces her with her own daughter).

AT 500 (The Name of the Helper): Hyriak vii no. 17 (Iezhibaba is wicked stepmother who forces the heroine to spin flax; a dwarf whose name the heroine must find out comes and spins gold).

AT 545B (Puss in Boots): Dobšinský i: 416–420.

AT 554 (The Grateful Animals): Hyriak iii no. 36 (The hero spares animals while hunting. Hyndzhibaba offers to be the hero's servant, but kidnaps his wife and cuts off his head. The animals obtain a healing ointment from Hyndzhibaba and restore the hero).

AT 566 (The Three Magic Objects and the Wonderful Fruits) + 567 (The Magic Bird Heart): Dobšinský ii: 11–23 (discussed in chapter 2).
AT 707 (The Three Golden Sons): Gašparíková 565.
AT 709 (Snow-White): Hyriak vii no. 9.
AT 876? (The Clever Maiden and the Suitors): Hyriak iii no. 22 (Hyndzhibaba is a cook for a band of robbers).
Difficult to classify: Gašparíková 287, 579, Hyriak iii no. 39 (two heroes come to the hut of Hyndzhibaba, tend her cow, and take a golden hair from her to keep her in a deep sleep while they rob her).

Bibliography

Abbreviations

AN SSSR	Akademiia Nauk SSSR
FFC	*Folklore Fellows Communications*
IJSLP	*International Journal of Slavic Linguistics and Poetics*
JAF	*Journal of American Folklore*
LGU	Leningradskii Gosudarstvennyi Universitet
RAN	Rossiiskaia Akademiia Nauk
SEEFA	Slavic and East European Folklore Association
Zapiski IRGO	*Zapiski imperatorskogo russkogo geograficheskogo obshchestva po otdeleniiu ètnografii*

Folktale Collections

Afanas'ev, A. N. 1984–1985. *Narodnye russkie skazki*. 3 vols. Moscow: Nauka.

Akimova, T. M. 1946. *Fol'klor Saratovskoi oblasti. Kniga pervaia*. Saratov: Ogiz.

Arnold, Katya. 1993. *Baba Yaga*. New York: North-South Books.

———1994. *Baba Yaga & the Little Girl*. New York: North-South Books.

Aslamov, Dmitrii. 1991. *Skazki Dmitriia Aslamova*. Ed. E. I. Shastina. Irkutsk: Vostochno-sibirskoe knizhnoe izdatel'stvo.

Avanesav, R. I., and M. V. Biryla. 1962. *Khrèstamatyia pa belaruskai dyialektalohii*. Minsk: Vydavetstva AN BSSR.

Azadovskii, M. K. 1932. *Russkaia skazka. Izbrannye mastera*. 2 vols. Leningrad: Academia.

———1938. *Verkhnelenskie skazki*. Irkutsk: Ogiz.

———1947. *Russkie skazki v Karelii (Starye zapisi)*. Petrozavodsk: Gosudarstvennoe izdatel'stvo Karelo-Finskoi SSR.

Azbelev, S. N., and N. A. Meshcherskii. 1986. *Fol'klor Russkogo Ust'ia*. Leningrad: Nauka.

Bagizbaeva, Maiia M. 1991. *Russkii fol'klor Vostochnogo Kazakhstana*. Alma-Ata: Rauan.

Bakhtin, Vladimir, and Pelageia Shiriaeva. 1976. *Skazki leningradskoi oblasti*. Leningrad: Lenizdat.

Balashov, D. M. 1970. *Skazki Terskogo berega Belogo moria*. Leningrad: Nauka.

Bandarchyk, V. K. 1971. *Kazki pra zhyvël i charadzeinyia kazki*. Minsk: Navuka i tèkhnika.

———1973. *Charadzeinyia kazki. Chastka I*. Minsk: Navuka i tèkhnika.

————1978. *Charadzeinyia kazki. Chastka II*. Minsk: Navuka i tèkhnika.

Burtsev, Aleksandr. 1895. *Derevenskie skazki krest'ian Vologodskoi gubernii*. St. Petersburg.

Cartianu, Ana, trans. 1979. *Romanian Folk Tales*. Bucharest: Minerva.

Chernyshev, V. I. 1950. *Skazki i legendy pushkinskikh mest*. Moscow and Leningrad: AN SSSR.

Chubinskii, P. P. 1872 and 1877. *Trudy ètnografichesko-statisticheskoi èkspeditsii v Zapadno-russkii krai. Tom I*. St. Petersburg: IRGO.

————1878. *Trudy ètnografichesko-statisticheskoi èkspeditsii v Zapadno-russkii krai. Tom II*. St. Petersburg: IRGO.

Chudinskii, E. A. 1864. *Russkie narodnye skazki, pribautki, i pobasenki*. Moscow.

Czambel, Samo. 1906. *Slovenská reč a jej miesto v rodine slovanských jazykov*. Turčiansky Sv. Martin.

Dobrovol'skii, V. N. 1891. *Smolenskii ètnograficheskii sbornik. Chast' I*. Zapiski IRGO 20. St. Petersburg.

Dobšinský, Pavol. 1958. *Prostonárodné slovenské povesti*. 3 vols. Bratislava: Slovenské vydavateľstvo krásnej literatúry.

Dragomanov, Mikhail. 1876. *Malorusskie narodnye predaniia i rasskazy*. Kiev: Iugo-Zapadnyi Otdel IRGO.

Efimenko, P. S. 1877. *Materialy po ètnografii russkogo naseleniia Arkhangel'skoi gubernii. Chast' I. Opisanie vneshnego i vnutrennego byta*. Trudy Ètnograficheskogo Otdela Imp. Obshchestva liubitelei estestvoznaniia, antropologii i ètnografii pri Moskovskom universitete, kniga 5, vypusk 1. Moscow.

————1878. *Materialy po ètnografii russkogo naseleniia Arkhangel'skoi gubernii. Chast' 2. Narodnaia slovesnost'*. Trudy Ètnograficheskogo Otdela Imp. Obshchestva liubitelei estestvoznaniia, antropologii i etnografii pri Moskovskom universitete, kniga 5, vypusk 2. Moscow.

Erben, Karel J. 1958. *České pohádky*. Prague: Státní nakladatelství krásné literatury, hudby a umění.

Èrlenvein, A. A. 1863. *Narodnye skazki, sobrannye sel'skimi uchiteliami*. Moscow: F. B. Miller.

Gašparíková, Viera. 1991–1992. *Katalóg slovenskej ľudovej prózy. Catalogue of Slovak Folk Prose*. 2 vols. Bratislava: Národopisný ústav, Slovak Academy of Sciences.

Giliarova, N. N., and A. K. Frumkin. 1994. *Riazanskii ètnograficheskii vestnik. Detskii fol'klor Riazanskoi oblasti. Riazanskaia glinianaia igrushka. Narodnye muzykal'nye instrumenty Rossii*. Ryazan': Riazanskii oblastnoi tsentr narodnogo tvorchestva.

Gorodtsov, Petr Alekseevich. 2000. *Byli i nebylitsy Tavdinskogo kraia v trekh tomakh*. 3 vols. Tyumen': Izdatel'stvo Iu. Mandriki.

Gospodarev, F. P. 1941. *Skazki Filippa Pavlovicha Gospodareva.* Ed. N. V. Novikov. Petrozavodsk: Gosizdat K-F SSR.

Grimm, Jacob and Wilhelm. 1978. *Kinder- und Hausmärchen.* Munich: Winkler Verlag.

Gromov, P. T. 1952. *Narodnoe tvorchestvo Dona. Kniga 1.* Rostov na Donu: Rostovskoe oblastnoe knigoizdatel'stvo.

Gurevich, A. V., and L. E. Èliasov. 1939. *Staryi fol'klor Pribaikal'ia.* Ulan-Ude: Gosudarstvennoe Buriat-Mongol'skoe izdatel'stvo.

Hyriak, Mikhailo. 1965–1979. *Ukrains'ki narodni kazky Skhidnoi Slovachchyny.* 7 vols. Bratislava: Slovenské pedagogické nakladatel'stvo.

Iavorskii, Iu. A. 1915. *Pamiatniki galitsko-russkoi narodnoi slovesnosti. I. Legendy. II.Skazki. III. Rasskazy i anekdoty.* Zapiski IRGO 37, vyp. 1. Kiev.

Illyés, Gyula. 1964. *Once upon a Time: Forty Hungarian Folk-Tales.* Budapest: Corvina.

Ivanitskii, Nikolai A. 1960. *Pesni, skazki, poslovitsy, pogovorki i zagadki, sobrannye N. A. Ivanitskim v vologodskoi gubernii.* Ed. N. V. Novikov. Vologda: Vologodskoe knizhnoe izdatel'stvo.

Kabashnikaw, K. P., and G. A. Bartashèvich. 1989. *Kazki w suchasnykh zapisakh.* Minsk: Navuka i tèkhnika.

Kalyn, Andrii. 1972. *Dvanadtsiat' brativ. Zakarpats'ki kazky Andriia Kalyna.* Uzhgorod: Karpaty.

Kapitsa, O. I. 1930. *Russkie narodnye skazki.* Moscow and Leningrad: Gosudarstvennoe izdatel'stvo.

Kargin, A. S. 1999. *Fol'klor Sudogodskogo kraia.* Moscow: Gosudarstvennyi respublikanskii tsentr russkogo fol'klora.

Karlinger, Felix. 1982. *Rumänische Märchen ausserhalb Rumäniens.* Kassel: Erich Röth-Verlag.

Karnaukhova, I. V. 1934. *Skazki i predaniia severnogo kraia.* Moscow and Leningrad: Academia.

Khlanta, Ivan V. 1989. *Kazky Karpat.* Uzhgorod: Karpaty.

Khudiakov, I. A. 1964. *Velikorusskie skazki v zapisiakh I. A. Khudiakova.* Moscow and Leningrad: Nauka.

Kitainik, M. G. 1949. *Ural'skii fol'klor.* Sverdlovsk: Sverdlovskoe Oblastnoe Gosudarstvennoe Izdatel'stvo.

Kollár, Ján. 1953. *Národnie spievanky.* 2 vols. Bratislava: Slovenské vydavatel'stvo krásnej literatúry. First published 1834–35.

Konkka, U. S. 1963. *Karel'skie narodnye skazki.* Moscow and Leningrad: Izdatel'stvo AN SSSR.

Korepova, K. E., and L. G. Belikova. 2001. *Lekarstvo ot zadumchivosti. Russkaia skazka v izdaniiakh 80-kh godov 18 veka.* St. Petersburg: Tropa Troianova.

Korguev, M. M. 1938. *Belomorskie skazki.* Ed. A. N. Nechaev. Leningrad: Sovetskii pisatel'.

———1944. *Skazki M. M. Korgueva.* Petrozavodsk: Gosudarstvennoe Izdatel'stvo Karelo-Finskoi SSR.

Korol'kova, A. N. 1969. *Russkie narodnye skazki. Skazki rasskazany voronezhskoi skazochnitsei A. N. Korol'kovoi.* Ed. È. V. Pomerantseva. Moscow: Nauka.

Kovalev, Ivan Fedorovich. 1941. *Skazki I. F. Kovaleva.* Ed. È. Gofman and S. Mints. Letopisi Gosudarstvennogo Literaturnogo Muzeia 11. Moscow: Gosudarstvennyi Literaturnyi Muzei.

Kozhemiakina, A. S. 1973. *Sibirskie skazki.* Ed. I. S. Korovkin. Novosibirsk: Zapadno-sibirskoe knizhnoe izdatel'stvo.

Krasnozhenova, M. V. 1937. *Skazki Krasnoiarskogo kraia.* Leningrad: Khudozhestvennaia literatura.

Kretov, A. I. 1977. *Narodnye skazki voronezhskoi oblasti.* Voronezh: Izdatel'stvo Voronezhskogo universiteta.

Kubín, Josef Štefan. 1926. "Lidové povídky z českého Podkrkonoší." *Rozpravy České akademie věd a umění* III: 62.

Kulish, Panteleimon. 1994. *Zapiski o Iuzhnoi Rusi.* 2 vols. Kiev: Dnipro. First published St. Petersburg, 1856–1857.

Leonova, T. G. 1982. *Fol'klor Zapadnoi Sibiri. Skazki.* Omsk: Omskii pedagogicheskii institut im. A. M. Gor'kogo.

Löwis of Menar, August von. 1921. *Russische Volksmärchen.* Jena: Eugen Diederichs.

Lutovinova, Elena I. 1993. *Russkie narodnye skazki o machekhe i padcheritse.* Novosibirsk: Nauka.

Lutovinova Index = 1997. *Volshebnye skazki Kemerovskoi oblasti: Ukazatel' siuzhetov.* Kemerovo: Kuzbassvuzizdat.

Lutovinova Kemerovo = 1997. *Fol'klor Kemerovskoi oblasti.* Kemerovo: Kuzbassvuzizdat.

Manzhura, I. I. 1890. *Skazki, poslovitsy i t. p., zapisannye v Ekaterinoslavskoi i Khar'kovskoi gub.* Sbornik Khar'kovskogo istoriko-filologicheskogo obshchestva, tom II, vyp. 2. Khar'kov.

Matveeva, R. P. 1979. *Russkie narodnye skazki Sibiri o bogatyriakh.* Novosibirsk: Nauka.

———1980. *Russkie geroicheskie skazki Sibiri.* Novosibirsk: Nauka.

———1981. *Russkie volshebnye skazki Sibiri.* Novosibirsk: Nauka.

———1984. *Russkie narodnye skazki Sibiri o chudesnom kone.* Novosibirsk: Nauka.

Matveeva, R. P., and T. G. Leonova. 1993. *Russkie skazki Sibiri i Dal'nego Vostoka: volshebnye i o zhivotnykh.* Novosibirsk: Nauka.

Medvedev, Iu. M. 1985. *Boi na kalinovom mostu. Russkie geroicheskie skazki.* Leningrad: Lenizdat.

Mints, S. I., and N. I. Savushkina. 1955. *Skazki i pesni Vologodskoi oblasti.* Vologda: Oblastnaia knizhnaia redaktsiia.

Mints, S. I., N. S. Polishchuk, and È. V. Pomerantseva. 1957. *Russkoe narodnoe tvorchestvo v Bashkirii.* Ufa: Bashkirskoe Knizhnoe Izdatel'stvo.

Mitropol'skaia, N. K. 1975. *Russkii fol'klor v Litve.* Vilnius: Vilnius State University.

Morokhin, V. N., and V. I. Vardugin. 1993. *Volzhskie skazki.* Saratov: Nadezhda.

Neweklowsky, Gerhard, and Károly Gaál. 1987. *Totenklage und Erzählkultur in Stinatz im südlichen Burgenland.* Wiener Slawistischer Almanach, Sonderband 19. Vienna: Gesellschaft zur Förderung slawistischer Studien.

Nikiforov, A. I. 1936. "Pobeditel' zmeia. (Iz severno-russkikh skazok). 15 skazok novoi zapisi A. I. Nikiforova." *Sovetskii fol'klor. Sbornik statei i materialov* 4–5: 143–242. Moscow and Leningrad: AN SSSR.

———1961. *Severnorusskie skazki v zapisiakh A. I. Nikiforova.* Ed. V. Ia. Propp. Moscow and Leningrad: AN SSSR.

Novgorod-Severskii, Ivan. No date. *Skazki sibirskie. Legendy o Bozhiei materi. Skazki Mikheicha.* Paris: Russisches Wissenschaftliches Institut.

Novikov, N. V. 1961. *Russkie skazki v zapisiakh i publikatsiiakh pervoi poloviny XIX veka.* Moscow and Leningrad: AN SSSR.

———1971. *Russkie skazki v rannikh zapisiakh i publikatsiiakh (XVI–XVIII veka).* Leningrad: Nauka.

Onchukov, Nikolai E. 1908. *Severnye skazki.* Zapiski IRGO 33. St. Petersburg.

Onchukov 2000 = 2000. *Neizdannye skazki iz sobraniia N. E. Onchukova (tavdinskie, shokshozerskie i samarskie skazki).* Ed. V. I. Zhekulina and V. I. Eremina. St. Petersburg: Aleteiia.

Onegina, Nina F. 1986. *Skazki Zaonezh'ia.* Petrozavodsk: Kareliia.

Ortutay, Gyula. 1962. *Hungarian Folk Tales.* Budapest: Corvina.

Ozarovskaia, Ol'ga È. 2000. *Piatirechie.* St. Petersburg: Tropa Troianova.

Parilov, I. G. 1948. *Russkii fol'klor Naryma.* Novosibirsk: Ogiz-Novosibgiz.

Petnikov, Grigorii N. 1966. *Ukrainskie skazki i legendy.* Simferopol': Krym.

Polívka, Jiří. 1923–1931. *Súpis slovenských rozprávok.* 5 vols. Turčiansky Sv. Martin: Matica slovenská.

Pomerantseva, È. 1957. *Russkie narodnye skazki.* Moscow: Izadatel'stvo Moskovskogo universiteta.

Potanin, Grigorii N., and A. V. Adrianov. 2000. *Russkie skazki i pesni v Sibiri. Zapiski Krasnoiarskogo podotdela Vostochno-Sibirskogo otdela Imperatorskogo*

Russkogo Geograficheskogo Obshchestva po ètnografii 1902 i 1906 gg. St. Petersburg: Tropa Troianova.

Potiavin, V. 1960. *Narodnaia poèziia Gor'kovskoi oblasti. Vypusk pervyi.* Gor'kiy: Gor'kovskii gosudarstvennyi universitet.

Razumova, A. P., and T. I. Sen'kina. 1974. *Russkie narodnye skazki Karel'skogo Pomor'ia.* Petrozavodsk: Kareliia.

————1982. *Russkie narodnye skazki Pudozhskogo kraia.* Petrozavodsk: Kareliia.

Razumova, Irina A. 1995. *Deti-skazochniki.* Petrozavodsk: Karel'skii nauchnyi tsentr RAN.

Rimavský, Janko [Rimauski, Ján Francisci]. 1845. *Slovenskje povesti.* Levoča. Reprinted 1975, Martin: Matica Slovenská.

Sadovnikov, D. N. 1884. *Skazki i predaniia samarskogo kraia.* Zapiski IRGO 12. St. Petersburg.

Serzhputovskii, Aleksandr K. 1911. *Skazki i rasskazy belorussov-poleshukov. (Materialy k izucheniiu tvorchestva belorussov i ikh govora).* St. Petersburg: Imp. Akademiia Nauk, Otdelenie Russkogo iazyka i slovesnosti.

————1965. *Kazki i apaviadanni Belaruskaha Palessia.* Minsk: Belarus'.

Shastina, Elena I. 1971. *Skazki lenskikh beregov.* Irkutsk: Vostochno-Sibirskoe knizhnoe izdatel'stvo.

————1974. *Skazki Prilen'ia.* Irkutsk: Irkutskii Gosudarstvennyi Pedagogicheskii Institut.

————1975. *Skazki i skazochniki Leny-reki.* Irkutsk: Vostochno-Sibirskoe knizhnoe izdatel'stvo.

————1985. *Russkie skazki Vostochnoi Sibiri.* Irkutsk: Vostochno-Sibirskoe knizhnoe izdatel'stvo.

Sidel'nikov, V. M., and V. Iu. Krupianskaia. 1937. *Volzhskii fol'klor.* Moscow: Sovetskii pisatel'.

Simina, Galina Ia. 1975. *Pinezhskie skazki.* Arkhangel'sk: Severo-zapadnoe knizhnoe izdatel'stvo.

Sirovátka, Oldřich, and Marta Šrámková. 1983. *Moravské národní pohádky a pověsti ze sbírek J. S. Menšíka, J. Pleskáče, K. Orla, J. Soukopa a V. Švédy.* Prague: Odeon.

Smirnov, A. M. 1917. *Sbornik velikorusskikh skazok arkhiva Russkogo geograficheskogo obshchestva.* Zapiski IRGO 44. Petrograd.

Sokolov, Boris and Iurii. 1915. *Skazki i pesni Belozerskogo kraia.* Moscow and Petrograd: Otdelenie Russkogo Iazyka i Slovesnosti Imperatorskoi Akademii Nauk.

Sokolov, Iurii. 1931. *Pop i muzhik.* Moscow and Leningrad: Academia.

————1932. *Barin i muzhik.* Moscow and Leningrad: Academia.

Sokolov, Iurii, and V. Chicherov. 1948. *Onezhskie byliny.* Letopisi, kn. 13. Moscow: Gosudarstvennyi literaturnyi muzei.

Sokolova, V. K. 1970. *Skazki zemli Riazanskoi.* Ryazan'.

Sorokovikov, Egor I. 1940. *Skazki Magaia (E. I. Sorokovikova).* Leningrad: Khudozhestvennaia literatura.

Tatarintseva, M. P. 1995. *Skazki, pesni, zagadki. Russkii fol'klor v Tuve.* Kyzyl: Tuvinskii nauchno-issledovatel'skii institut iazyka, literatury i istorii.

Tèffi, N. A. 1932. *Baba-Iaga.* Paris: YMCA Press.

Tille, Václav. 1901–1902. "Povídky sebrané na Valašsku r. 1888." *Narodopisný sborník českoslovanský* 7: 45–133, 8: 35–108.

Tseitlin, G. 1911. "Pomorskie narodnye skazki." *Izvestiia Arkhangel'skogo obshchestva izucheniia Russkogo Severa* 1911 (2): 77–92 and (3): 180–200.

Tumilevich, Fedor V. 1958. *Russkie narodnye skazki kazakov-nekrasovtsev.* Rostov na Donu: Rostovskoe knizhnoe izdatel'stvo.

Vasilenok, S. I., K. P. Kabashnikov, and S. I. Prokof'ev. 1958. *Belorusskie narodnye skazki.* Moscow: Gosudarstvennoe Izdatel'stvo Khudozhestvennoi Literatury.

Vedernikova, N. M., and E. A. Samodelova. 1998. *Fol'klornye sokrovishcha moskovskoi zemli. Skazki i neskazochnaia proza.* Moscow: Nasledie.

Vlasova, M. N., and V. I. Zhekulina. 2001. *Traditsionnyi fol'klor Novgorodskoi oblasti. Skazki. Legendy. Predaniia. Bylichki. Zagovory (po zapisiam 1963–1999 g.).* St. Petersburg: Aleteiia.

Zelenin Perm' = Zelenin, Dmitrii. 1914. *Velikorusskie skazki Permskoi gubernii.* Zapiski IRGO 41. Petrograd.

Zelenin Viatka = 1915. *Velikorusskie skazki Viatskoi gubernii.* Zapiski IRGO 42. Petrograd.

Zhivaia Starina 21 (1912): 221–388. Petrograd: Otdelenie Etnografii IRGO.

General Bibliography

Aarne, Antti, and Stith Thompson. 1964. *The Types of the Folktale: A Classification and Bibliography.* FFC 184. Helsinki: Academia Scientiarum Fennica.

Adon'eva, Svetlana B. 2000. *Skazochnyi tekst i traditsionnaia kul'tura.* St. Petersburg: Izdatel'stvo Sankt-Peterburgskogo universiteta.

Afanas'ev, A. N. 1865, 1868, 1869. *Poèticheskie vozzreniia slavian na prirodu. Opyt sravnitel'nogo izucheniia slavianskikh predanii i verovanii, v sviazi s mificheskimi skazaniiami drugikh rodstvennykh narodov.* 3 vols. Moscow. Slavistic Printings and Reprintings, The Hague and Paris: Mouton, 1969–1970.

Afanas'eva, R. N. 1986. "Obraz Baby-iagi v skazke Russkogo Ust'ia. (K kharakteristike otritsatel'nogo personazha odnoi skazki russkikh starozhilov severo-vostoka Sibiri)." In *Problemy nravstvenno-psikhologicheskogo soderzhaniia v literature i fol'klore Sibiri.* Ed. E. I. Shastina. Irkutsk: Irkutskii gosudarstvennyi pedagogicheskii institut. 142–157.

Agapkina, Tatjana. 2000. "Slovenski obredi i verovanja o menstruaciji." In *Erotsko u folkloru Slovena.* Ed. Dejan Ajdačić. Belgrade: Stubovi kulture. 147–193.

Agapkina, T. A., and A. L. Toporkov. 1986. "K probleme ètnograficheskogo konteksta kalendarnykh pesen." In *Slavianskii i balkanskii fol'klor. Dukhovnaia kul'tura Poles'ia na obshcheslavianskom fone.* Ed. N. I. Tolstoi. Moscow: Nauka. 76–88.

———1990. "K rekonstruktsii praslavianskikh zagovorov." In *Fol'klor i ètnografiia. Problemy rekonstruktsii faktov traditsionnoi kul'tury.* Ed. B. Putilov. Leningrad: Nauka. 67–75.

Alvarez-Pereyre, Frank. 1976. *Contes et tradition orale en Roumanie. (La fonction pédagogique du conte populaire en Roumanie).* Paris: Société d'Études Linguistiques et Anthropologiques de France.

Andreev, N. P. 1929. *Ukazatel' skazochnykh siuzhetov po sisteme Aarne.* Leningrad: Gosudarstvennoe Russkoe Geograficheskoe Obshchestvo.

Andreevskii, I. E, ed. 1890–1907. *Èntsiklopedicheskii slovar'.* St. Petersburg: Brockhaus, Efron.

Anikin, Vladimir P. 1966. "Volshebnaia skazka 'Tsarevna-liagushka'." In *Fol'klor kak iskusstvo slova.* Ed. N. I. Kravtsov. Moscow: Izdatel'stvo Moskovskogo universiteta. 19–49.

———1977. *Russkaia narodnaia skazka. Posobie dlia uchitelei.* Moscow: Prosveshchenie.

Apo, Satu. 1990. "The Variability and Narrative Structures of Magic Tales: from universal models to describing the differences between tales." In *D'un conte... à l'autre: la variabilité dans la littérature orale.* Ed. Veronika Görög-Karady. Paris: Centre National de la Recherche Scientifique. 487–502.

Arnaudov, Mikhail. 1967. "Der Familienschutzgeist im Volksglauben der Bulgaren." *Zeitschrift für Balkanologie* 5 (2): 129–137.

———1968–1969. *Ochertsi po bŭlgarskiia folklor.* 2 vols. Sofia: Bŭlgarski pisatel.

Artsikhovskii, A. V., and V. I. Borkovskii. 1963. *Novgorodskie gramoty na bereste (Iz raskopok 1956–57 goda).* Moscow: AN SSSR.

Ashliman, D. L. 1987. *A Guide to Folktales in the English Language. Based on the Aarne-Thompson Classification System.* New York: Greenwood Press.

Astakhova, A. M. 1928. "Zagovornoe iskusstvo na reke Pinege." In *Krest'ianskoe iskusstvo SSSR. II. Iskusstvo Severa.* Ed. Ia. A. Nazarenko. Leningrad: Academia. 33–76.

———1966. "Improvizatsiia v russkom fol'klore (ee formy i granitsy v raznykh zhanrakh)." *Russkii fol'klor* 10: 63–79.

Azadovskii, Mark. 1926. *Eine sibirische Märchenerzählerin*. FFC 68. Helsinki: Academia Scientiarum Fennica.

———1960. *Stat'i o literature i fol'klore*. Moscow and Leningrad: Gosudarstvennoe izdatel'stvo khudozhestvennoi literatury.

Azbelev, S. N. 1965. "Otnoshenie predaniia, legendy i skazki k deistvitel'nosti (s tochki zreniia razgranicheniia zhanrov)." In *Slavianskii fol'klor i istoricheskaia deistvitel'nost'*. Ed. Astakhova et al. Moscow: Nauka. 5–25.

Azim-zade, È. G. 1980. "K sopostavitel'nomu analizu slavianskikh i tiurkskikh nazvanii sozvezdii." *Sovetskoe Slavianovedenie* 1980 (1): 96–103.

Baiburin, Al'bert K. 1983. *Zhilishche v obriadakh i predstavleniiakh vostochnykh slavian*. Leningrad: Nauka.

———1991. "Obriadovye formy polovoi identifikatsii detei." In *Ètnicheskie stereotipy muzhskogo i zhenskogo povedeniia*. Ed. A. K. Baiburin and I. S. Kon. 257–265.

———ed. 1992. *Fol'klor i ètnograficheskaia deistvitel'nost'*. St. Petersburg: Nauka.

Baldina, Ol'ga. 1972. *Russkie narodnye kartinki*. Moscow: Molodaia gvardiia.

Balushok, V. G. 1991. "Istselenie Il'i Muromtsa: drevnerusskii ritual v byline." *Sovetskaia Ètnografiia* 1991 (5): 20–27.

———1993. "Initsiatsii drevnikh slavian (popytka rekonstruktsii)." *Ètnograficheskoe Obozrenie* 1993 (4): 57–66.

Balzer, Marjorie M, ed. 1992. *Russian Traditional Culture: Religion, Gender, and Customary Law*. Armonk, New York and London: M. E. Sharpe.

Barag, Lev G. 1964. "O traditsionnoi stilisticheskoi forme belorusskikh skazok i ee izmeneniiakh." In *O traditsiiakh i novatorstve v literature i ustnom narodnom tvorchestve*. Ed. L. G. Barag. Ufa: Bashkirskii gosudarstvennyi universitet. 201–232.

———1966. "Skazochnaia fantastika i narodnye verovaniia (Po materialam belorusskogo fol'klora)." *Sovetskaia Ètnografiia* 1966 (5): 15–27.

———1969. *Belaruskaia kazka*. Minsk: Vyshèishaia shkola.

———1971. "Siuzhety i motivy belorusskikh volshebnykh skazok (Sistematicheskii ukazatel')." In *Slavianskii i balkanskii fol'klor*. Ed. I. M. Sheptunov. Moscow: Nauka. 182–235.

———1972. "Traditsionnoe i novoe v khudozhestvennoi leksike volshebnoi belorusskoi skazki." In *O traditsiiakh i novatorstve v literature i ustnom narodnom tvorchestve*. Vypusk II. Ed. P. A. Karabanov. Ufa: Bashkirskii gosudarstvennyi universitet. 25–42.

———1981. "Siuzhet o zmeeborstve na mostu v skazkakh vostochnoslavianskikh narodov." In *Slavianskii i balkanskii fol'klor. Obriad. Tekst*. Ed. N. I. Tolstoi et al. Moscow: Nauka. 160–188.

Barag, L. G., I. P. Berezovskii, K. P. Kabashnikov, and N. V. Novikov. 1979. *Sravnitel'nyi ukazatel' siuzhetov. Vostochnoslavianskaia skazka.* Leningrad: Nauka.

Barker, Adele M. 1986. *The Mother Syndrome in the Russian Folk Imagination.* Columbus: Slavica.

Bascom, William. 1954. "Four Functions of Folklore." *JAF* 67: 333–349.

———1957. "The Myth-Ritual Theory." *JAF* 70: 103–114.

———1965. "The Forms of Folklore: Prose Narratives." *JAF* 78: 3–20.

Becker, Richarda. 1990. *Die weibliche Initiation im ostslawischen Zaubermärchen. Ein Beitrag zur Funktion und Symbolik des weiblichen Aspektes im Märchen unter besonderer Berücksichtigung der Figur der Baba-Jaga.* Veröffentlichungen der Abteilung für Slavische Sprachen und Literaturen des Osteuropa-Instituts (Slavisches Seminar) an der freien Universität Berlin, Band 71. Wiesbaden: Otto Harrassowitz.

Belmont, Nicole. 1971. *Les signes de la naissance. Étude des représentations symboliques associées aux naissances singulières.* Brionne: Gérard Monfort.

———1995. "*Pouçot:* Conception Orale, Naissance Anale. Une Lecture Psychanalytique du Conte Type 700." *Estudos de Literatura Oral* 1995 (1): 45–57.

———1999. *Poétique du conte. Essai sur le conte de tradition orale.* Paris: Gallimard.

Belousov, A. F. 1998. *Russkii shkol'nyi fol'klor. Ot "vyzyvanii" Pikovoi damy do semeinykh rasskazov.* Moscow: Ladomir, AST.

Benedict, Ruth. 1949. "Child Rearing in Certain European Countries." *American Journal of Orthopsychiatry* 19: 342–350.

Bernshtam, Tat'iana A. 1982. "Ornitomorfnaia simvolika u vostochnykh slavian." *Sovetskaia Ètnografiia* 1982 (1): 22–34.

———1986. "K rekonstruktsii nekotorykh russkikh perekhodnykh obriadov sovershennoletiia." *Sovetskaia Ètnografiia* 1986 (6): 24–35.

———1988. *Molodezh' v obriadovoi zhizni russkoi obshchiny XIX–nachala XX v.* Leningrad: Nauka.

———1991. "Sovershennoletie devushki v metaforakh igrovogo fol'klora (traditsionnyi aspekt russkoi kul'tury)." In *Ètnicheskie stereotipy muzhskogo i zhenskogo povedeniia.* Ed. A. K. Baiburin and I. S. Kon. 234–257.

Bettelheim, Bruno. 1989. *The Uses of Enchantment: The Meaning and Importance of Fairy Tales.* New York: Vintage Books.

Birkhäuser-Oeri, Sibylle. 1988. *The Mother: Archetypal Image in Fairy Tales.* Trans. Michael Mitchell. Toronto: Inner City Books.

Blazhes, V. V. 1976. "Priskazka. Zakon kompozitsionnogo kontrasta." In *Fol'klor Urala. Narodnaia proza.* Ed. V. P. Krugliashova. Sverdlovsk: Ural'skii universitet. 56–63.

Blazhes, V. V., and È. A. Akhaimova. 1976. "Iz polevykh nabliudenii nad bytovaniem skazki (zametki sobiratelei)." In *Fol'klor Urala. Narodnaia proza.* Ed. V. P. Krugliashova. Sverdlovsk: Ural'skii universitet. 64–79.

Bleichsteiner, Robert. 1914. "Iranische Entsprechungen zu Frau Holle und Baba Jaga." *Mitra. Monatsschrift für vergleichende Mythenforschung* 1914 (3): 65–71.

———1953. "Perchtengestalten in Mittelasien." *Archiv für Völkerkunde* 8: 58–75. Vienna.

Bogatyrev, Petr G. 1929. *Actes magiques, rites et croyances en Russie Subcarpathique.* Paris: Librairie Ancienne Honoré Champion.

———1963. *Slovatskie èpicheskie rasskazy i liro-èpicheskie pesni ("Zboinitskii tsikl").* Moscow: AN SSSR.

———1969. "Izobrazhenie perezhivanii deistvuiushchikh lits v russkoi narodnoi volshebnoi skazke." In *Fol'klor kak iskusstvo slova. Vyp. 2. Psikhologicheskoe izobrazhenie v russkom narodnom poèticheskom tvorchestve.* Ed. N. I. Kravtsov. Moscow: Izdatel'stvo Moskovskogo universiteta. 57–67.

———1971. *Voprosy teorii narodnogo iskusstva.* Moscow: Izdatel'stvo Iskusstvo.

Bogatyrev, Petr, and Roman Jakobson. 1966. "Die Folklore als eine besondere Form des Schaffens." In *Roman Jakobson: Selected Writings.* The Hague and Paris: Mouton. Vol. IV: 1–15.

Bogoras, Waldemar. 1902. "The Folklore of Northeastern Asia, as compared with that of Northwestern America." *American Anthropologist* New Series 4 (4): 577–683.

———1918. "Tales of Yukaghir, Lamut, and Russianized Natives of Eastern Siberia." *Anthropological Papers of the American Museum of Natural History* 20, Part 1: 1–148.

Boriak, Olena. 2002. "The Midwife in Traditional Ukrainian Culture: Ritual, Folklore, and Mythology." *SEEFA Journal* 7 (2): 29–49.

Breckenfeld, Vivian G. 1917. *The Character and Technique of the Russian Folk Tale.* M. A. thesis. Berkeley: University of California.

Bremond, Claude, and Jean Verrier. 1982. "Afanassiev et Propp." *Littérature* 45: 61–78. Paris.

Bronfenbrenner, Urie. 1972. *Two Worlds of Childhood: U.S. and U.S.S.R.* New York: Simon and Schuster.

Buchan, David. 1982. "Propp's Tale Role and a Ballad Repertoire." *JAF* 95: 159–172.

Budziszewska, Wanda. 1982. "Fauna z Katalogu magii brata Rudolfa." *Poradnik językowy,* zeszyt 6: 411–414.

Burkhart, Dagmar. 1982. "Aspekte des Weiblichen im bulgarischen Tier- und Zaubermärchen." *Fabula* 23 (3–4): 207–220.

326   *Baba Yaga*

Buslaev, F. 1861. *Istoricheskie ocherki russkoi narodnoi slovesnosti i iskusstva. Tom I. Russkaia narodnaia poèziia.* St. Petersburg. Slavistic Printings and Reprintings 202/1. The Hague: Mouton, 1969.

Busygin, E. P., N. V. Zorin, and E. V. Mikhailichenko. 1973. *Obshchestvennyi i semeinyi byt russkogo sel'skogo naseleniia srednego Povolzh'ia. Istoriko-ètnograficheskoe issledovanie (seredina XIX–nachalo XX vv.).* Kazan': Izdatel'stvo Kazanskogo universiteta.

Calame-Griaule, Geneviève. 1975. "Le conte des 'Deux Filles' en Haute-Volta." *Recherche, pédagogie et culture* 20: 2–11.

———1976. "La calebasse brisée: Étude du thème initiatique dans quelques versions africaines des 'Deux Filles' (T 480)." *Cahiers de littérature orale* 1: 23–66.

———1987. *Ethnologie et langage. La parole chez les Dogon.* Paris: Institut d'Ethnologie.

———1987a. *Des Cauris au marché. Essais sur des contes africains.* [Paris?]: Société des africanistes.

———1989. "Une Cendrillon sans pantoufle (Niger)." *Cahiers de littérature orale* 25: 187–200.

———1990. "Variations stylistiques dans un conte touareg." In *D'un conte… à l'autre: la variabilité dans la littérature orale.* Ed. Veronika Görög-Karady. Paris: Centre National de la Recherche Scientifique. 83–103.

———1993. "Le goitre indiscret." *Cahiers de littérature orale* 33: 99–110.

———1996. "Les chemins de l'autre monde. Contes initiatiques africains." *Cahiers de littérature orale* 39–40: 29–59.

———2002. *Contes tendres, contes cruels du Sahel nigérien.* Paris: Gallimard.

Cardigos, Isabel. 1996. *In and out of Enchantment: Blood Symbolism and Gender in Portuguese Fairytales.* FFC 260. Helsinki: Academia Scientiarum Fennica.

Carey, Bonnie M. 1983. *Typological Models of the Heroine in the Russian Fairy Tale.* Dissertation. Chapel Hill: University of North Carolina.

Černý, Adolf. 1893, 1898. *Mythiske bytosće łužiskich Serbow.* 2 vols. Budyšin (Bautzen).

———1896. "Istoty mityczne Serbów łużyckich." *Wisła* 10: 54–97, 245–281, 531–563, 745–779.

———1898. "Mythické bytosti lužických Srbů." *Narodopisný sborník českoslovanský* 3: 26–33.

Cherepanova, Ol'ga A. 1977. "Tipologiia i genezis nazvanii likhoradok-triasavits v russkikh narodnykh zagovorakh i zaklinaniiakh." In *Iazyk zhanrov russkogo fol'klora.* Ed. Z. K. Tarlanov. Petrozavodsk: Petrozavodskii gosudarstvennyi universitet. 44–57.

————1983. *Mifologicheskaia leksika russkogo Severa*. Leningrad: Izdatel'stvo Leningradskogo universiteta.

————1996. *Mifologicheskie rasskazy i legendy Russkogo Severa*. St. Petersburg: Izdatel'stvo S.-Peterburgskogo universiteta.

Chernyshev, V. I. 1934. "Russkie skazki v izdaniiakh XVIII veka." In *Sergeiu Fedorovichu Ol'denburgu k piatidesiatiletiiu nauchno-obshchestvennoi deiatel'nosti 1882–1932. Sbornik statei*. Ed. I. Iu. Krachkovskii. Leningrad: AN SSSR. 585–609.

Chistov, K. V., and T. A. Bernshtam, eds. 1978. *Russkii narodnyi svadebnyi obriad: issledovaniia i materialy*. Leningrad: Nauka.

Chodorow, Nancy. 1978. *The Reproduction of Mothering: Psychoanalysis and the Sociology of Gender*. Berkeley: University of California Press.

Christinger, Raymond, and Willy Borgeaud. 1963, 1965. *Mythologie de la Suisse ancienne*. 2 vols. Geneva: Librairie de l'Université Georg.

Chulkov, Mikhail D. 1782. *Slovar' ruskikh sueverii*. St. Petersburg.

Clements, Barbara, Barbara Engel, and Christine Worobec, eds. 1991. *Russia's Women: Accommodation, Resistance, Transformation*. Berkeley: University of California Press.

Cooper, Brian. 1997. "Baba-Yaga, the Bony-Legged: A Short Note on the Witch and Her Name." *New Zealand Slavonic Journal* 1997: 82–88.

Cosquin, Emmanuel. 1910. "Étude de folk-lore comparé: le conte de 'la chaudière bouillante et la feinte maladresse' dans l'Inde et hors de l'Inde." *Revue des Traditions populaires* 25 (1–2): 1–18, (3): 65–86, (4–5): 126–141.

Creangă, Ion. 1931. *Contes populaires de Roumanie*. Trans. and ed. Stanciu Stoian and Ode de Chateauvieux Lebel. Paris: Maisonneuve Frères.

Čulić, Dasha D. 1982. *A Structural and Psychoanalytic Analysis of the Symbolic Ritual Process in Three Sets of Russian Folk Tales*. Dissertation. Los Angeles: University of Southern California.

Dal', Vladimir. 1957. *Poslovitsy russkogo naroda*. Moscow: Gosudarstvennoe Izdatel'stvo Khudozhestvennoi Literatury.

Daskalova-Perkovska, Liliana, Doroteia Dobreva, Iordanka Kotseva, and Evgeniia Mitseva. 1994. *Bŭlgarski folklorni prikazki: Katalog*. Sofia: Universitetsko izdatelstvo "Sv. Kliment Okhridski."

Dauenhauer, Richard. 1975. *Text and Context of Tlingit Oral Tradition*. Ann Arbor: University Microfilms. (eHRAF, Collection of Ethnography, Doc. 28).

Dégh, Linda. 1969. *Folktales and Society: Story-telling in a Hungarian Peasant Community*. Bloomington: Indiana University Press.

————1995. *Narratives in Society: A Performer-Centered Study of Narration*. FFC 255. Helsinki: Academia Scientiarum Fennica.

Dekowski, Jan Piotr. 1970. "Jabłoneczka w obrzędowości weselnej na terenie województwa łódzkiego." *Łódzkie studia etnograficzne* 11: 133–148.

Delarue, Paul. 1976. *Le Conte populaire français: Catalogue raisonné des versions de France. Tome Premier.* Paris: G.-P. Maisonneuve et Larose.

Demkova, Natal'ia S. 1997. "K interpretatsii 'Povesti o Petre i Fevronii': 'Povest' o Petre i Fevronii' Ermolaia-Erazma kak pritcha." In N. S. Demkova, *Srednevekovaia russkaia literatura. Poètika, interpretatsii, istochniki.* St. Petersburg: Izdatel'stvo S.-Peterburgskogo universiteta. 77–95.

D'iakonova, Iu. N. 1985. "Obraz Baby-iagi v olonkho i iakutskikh skazkakh." In *Fol'klor narodov RSFSR.* Ed. T. Akimova and L. Barag. Ufa: Bashkirskii gosudarstvennyi universitet. 66–71.

Divil'kovskii. 1914. "Ukhod i vospitanie detei u naroda. (Pervoe detstvo)." Ed. A. A. Charushin. *Izvestiia Arkhangel'skogo Obshchestva izucheniia Russkogo Severa (Zhurnal zhizni Severnogo Kraia)* 6, no. 18: 589–600.

Dorovskikh, L. V. 1980. "Iz nabliudenii nad naimenovaniem geroev v russkoi narodnoi skazke." In *Voprosy onomastiki. Sobstvennye imena v sisteme iazyka.* Ed. A. K. Matveev. Sverdlovsk: Ural'skii gosudarstvennyi universitet. 86–98.

Dorson, Richard. 1968. "The Eclipse of Solar Mythology." In *Myth: A Symposium.* Ed. Thomas Sebeok. Bloomington: Indiana University Press. 25–63.

Dostoevskii, Fedor M. 1972–1990. *Polnoe sobranie sochinenii v tridtsati tomakh.* 30 vols. Leningrad: Nauka.

Draitser, Emil. 1999. *Making War, Not Love: Gender and Sexuality in Russian Humor.* New York: St. Martin's Press.

Drettas, Georges. 1995. "Jamais le jeudi…à propos de sainte Paraskevi, vierge et martyre." *Revue des Études slaves* 67 (1): 167–185.

Drewermann, Eugen, and Ingritt Neuhaus. 1982. *Frau Holle.* Olten: Walter-Verlag.

Drummond, D. A., and G. Perkins. 1980. *Dictionary of Russian Obscenities.* Berkeley: Berkeley Slavic Specialties.

Dukova, Ute. 1970. "Das Bild des Drachen im bulgarischen Märchen." *Fabula* 11(3): 209–252.

———1983. "Die Bezeichnungen der Dämonen im Bulgarischen." *Balkansko ezikoznanie. Linguistique balkanique* 26 (4): 5–46.

———1984. "Die Bezeichnungen der Dämonen im Bulgarischen. II." *Balkansko ezikoznanie. Linguistique balkanique* 27 (2): 5–50.

———1985. "Die Bezeichnungen der Dämonen im Bulgarischen. III. Entlehnungen." *Balkansko ezikoznanie. Linguistique balkanique* 28 (2): 5–62.

Dunaievs'ka, Lidiia F. 1987. *Ukrains'ka narodna kazka.* Kiev: Vishcha shkola.

Dundes, Alan. 1962. "From Etic to Emic Units in the Structural Study of Folktales." *JAF* 75: 95–105.

————1962b. "The Binary Structure of 'Unsuccessful Repetition' in Lithuanian Folktales." *Western Folklore* 21: 165–174.

————1980. "The Symbolic Equivalence of Allomotifs in the Rabbit-Herd (AT 570)." *Arv* 36: 91–98.

————ed. 1982. *Cinderella: A Casebook*. Madison: University of Wisconsin Press.

————ed. 1989. *Little Red Riding Hood: A Casebook*. Madison: University of Wisconsin Press.

————1997. "The Motif-Index and the Tale Type Index: A Critique." *Journal of Folklore Research* 34(3): 195–202.

Dunn, Ethel. 1973. "Russian Use of *Amanita muscaria*: A Footnote to Wasson's *Soma*." *Current Anthropology* 14(4): 488–492.

Dunn, Stephen. 1978. "The Family as Reflected in Russian Folklore." In *The Family in Imperial Russia: New Lines of Historical Research*. Ed. David Ransel. Urbana: University of Illinois Press. 153–170.

Dunn, Stephen P., and Ethel. 1967, 1988. *The Peasants of Central Russia*. Prospect Heights, Illinois: Waveland Press.

Dynin, V. I. 1993. "Russkaia demonologiia: opyt vydeleniia lokal'nykh variantov." *Ètnograficheskoe Obozrenie* 1993 (4): 78–91.

Eleonskaia, Elena N. 1994. *Skazka, zagovor i koldovstvo v Rossii. Sb. trudov*. Moscow: Indrik.

El-Shamy, Hasan M. 1980. *Folktales of Egypt*. Chicago: University of Chicago Press.

Engel, Barbara. 1990. "Peasant Morality and Pre-marital Relations in Late 19th Century Russia." *Journal of Social History* 23 (4): 695–714.

Erdész, Sándor. 1978. "The Dragon in the Folktales of Lajos Ámi." In *Studies in East European Folk Narrative*. Ed. Linda Dégh. Bloomington: American Folklore Society and Indiana University.

Eremina, Valeriia I. 1991. *Ritual i fol'klor*. Leningrad: Nauka.

————1992. "Zagovornye kolybel'nye pesni." In *Fol'klor i ètnograficheskaia deistvitel'nost'*. Ed. A. Baiburin. St. Petersburg: Nauka. 29–34.

Farès, Nabile. 1994. *L'ogresse dans la littérature orale berbère. Littérature orale et anthropologie*. Paris: Karthala.

Farnsworth, Beatrice, and Lynne Viola, eds. 1992. *Russian Peasant Women*. Oxford: Oxford University Press.

Farrell, Dianne E. 1993. "Shamanic Elements in Some Early Eighteenth Century Russian Woodcuts." *Slavic Review* 52: 725–744.

Federowski, Michał. 1897. *Lud białoruski na Rusi litewskiej*. Vol. I. Cracow: Akademia umiejętności.

Feifalik, Julius. 1859. "Peratha bei den Slaven." *Zeitschrift für deutsche Mythologie und Sittenkunde* 4: 387–389. Göttingen.

Filin, F. P., and F. P. Sorokoletov. 1965. *Slovar' russkikh narodnykh govorov.* Leningrad: Nauka.

Filipović, Milenko S. 1954. "Folk Religion among the Orthodox Population in Eastern Yugoslavia (Some Remarks and Considerations)." *Harvard Slavic Studies* 2: 359–374.

Fischer, John L. 1963. "The Sociopsychological Analysis of Folktales." *Current Anthropology* 4: 235–295.

Franz, Marie-Louise von. 1993. *The Feminine in Fairy Tales.* Boston: Shambhala.

Freud, Sigmund. 1968. "Medusa's Head." In *The Standard Edition of the Complete Psychological Works of Sigmund Freud.* Trans. and ed.James Strachey. London: Hogarth Press. Vol. 18: 273–274.

Friedrich, Paul. 1963. "An Evolutionary Sketch of Russian Kinship." In *Symposium on Language and Culture. Proceedings of the 1962 Annual Spring Meeting of the American Ethnological Society.* Ed. Viola E. Garfield and Wallace L. Chafe. Seattle: American Ethnological Society. 1–26.

————1964. "Semantic Structure and Social Structure: An Instance from Russian." In *Explorations in Cultural Anthropology: Essays in Honor of George Peter Murdock.* Ed. Ward H. Goodenough. New York: McGraw-Hill. 131–166.

Gasparini, Evel. 1973. *Il matriarcato slavo: antropologia culturale dei Protoslavi.* Florence: Sansoni.

Gatsak, V. M, ed. 1980. *Tipologiia i vzaimosviazi fol'klora narodov SSSR.* Moscow: Nauka.

Gehrts, Heino. 1990. "Betrachtungen zum Batamärchen und zur Medeasage: Zur Datierung von AT 303 und 313." In *Wie alt sind unsere Märchen.* Ed. Charlotte Oberfeld. Regensburg: Erich Röth Verlag. 71–85.

Gennep, Arnold van. 1958. *Manuel de folklore français contemporain. Tome I: VII, première partie. Cycle des douze jours.* Paris: A. et J. Picard.

Gerasimova, N. M. 1978. "Formuly russkoi volshebnoi skazki (k probleme stereotipnosti i variativnosti traditsionnoi kul'tury)." *Sovetskaia Ètnografiia* 1978 (5): 18–28.

Gil'ferding, A. F. 1949, 1950, 1951. *Onezhskie byliny zapisannye A. F. Gil'ferdingom letom 1871 goda.* 3 vols. Moscow and Leningrad: AN SSSR.

Gin, Ia. I. 1977. "Iz nabliudenii nad grammaticheskoi kategoriei roda v russkoi narodnoi skazke." In *Iazyk zhanrov russkogo fol'klora.* Ed. Z. K. Tarlanov. Petrozavodsk: Petrozavodskii gosudarstvennyi universitet. 114–127.

Gobrecht, Barbara. 1985. "Die Frau im russischen Märchen." In *Die Frau im Märchen.* Ed. S. Früh and R. Wehse. Kassel: Erich Röth Verlag. 89–110.

Goldman, Irving. 1950. "Psychiatric Interpretation of Russian History: A Reply to Geoffrey Gorer." *American Slavic and East European Review* 9: 151–161.

Gorchakov, Dmitrii Petrovich. 1788. *Baba Iaga. Komicheskaia opera v trekh deistviiakh i s baletom.* Kaluga.

Gorer, Geoffrey. 1949. "Some Aspects of the Psychology of the People of Great Russia." *American Slavic and East European Review* 8: 155–166.

Gorer, Geoffrey, and John Rickman. 1949. *The People of Great Russia: A Psychological Study.* London: Cresset Press.

Görög, Veronika, Suzanne Platiel, Diana Rey-Hulman, Christiane Seydou, and Geneviève Calame-Griaule. 1980. *Histoires d'Enfants Terribles (Afrique noire): Études et Anthologie.* Paris: G.-P. Maisonneuve et Larose.

Gourg, Marianne. 1988. "Autour du personnage de la Boiteuse (Les Démons): quelques réflexions sur l'utilisation du folklore et du mythe dans la forme romanesque." *Revue des Études slaves* 60(1): 159–168.

Grbić, Savatije. 1909. "Srpski narodni običaji iz Sreza Boljevačkog." *Srpski etnografski zbornik* 14: 1–382.

Grechina, O. N., and M. V. Osorina. 1981. "Sovremennaia fol'klornaia proza detei." *Russkii fol'klor* 20: 96–106.

Greimas, A. J. 1965. "Le conte populaire russe (Analyse fonctionnelle)." *IJSLP* 9: 152–175.

Gromyko, Marina M. 1991. *Mir russkoi derevni.* Moscow: Molodaia Gvardiia.

Gura, Aleksandr V. 1978. "Opyt vyiavleniia struktury severnorusskogo svadebnogo obriada (po materialam vologodskoi gub.)." In *Russkii narodnyi svadebnyi obriad: issledovaniia i materialy.* Ed. K. Chistov and T. Bernshtam. Leningrad: Nauka. 72–88.

———1997. *Simvolika zhivotnykh v slavianskoi narodnoi traditsii.* Moscow: Indrik.

Guriev, T. A. 1980. "Ob odnom zhenskom obraze v osetinskom fol'klore." In *Fol'klor narodov RSFSR.* Ed. T. M. Akimova and L. G. Barag. Ufa: Bashkirskii gosudarstvennyi universitet. 12–16.

Gusev, Viktor E. 1967. *Èstetika fol'klora.* Leningrad: Nauka.

Guthrie, Matthew. 1795. *Dissertations sur les antiquités de Russie; contenant l'ancienne Mythologie, les Rites païens, les Fêtes sacrées, les Jeux ou Ludi, les Oracles, l'ancienne Musique, les Instrumens de musique villageoise, les Coutumes, les Cérémonies, l'Habillement, les Divertissements de village, les Mariages, les Funérailles, l'Hospitalité nationale, les Repas, &c. &c. des Russes; comparés avec les mêmes objets chez les Anciens, & particulièrement chez les Grecs.* St. Petersburg.

Hako, Matti. 1956. *Das Wiesel in der europäischen Volksüberlieferung mit besonderer Berücksichtigung der finnischen Tradition.* FFC 167. Helsinki: Academia Scientiarum Fennica.

Haney, Jack V. 1979. "On the 'Tale of Peter and Fevroniia, Wonderworkers of Murom'." *Canadian-American Slavic Studies* 13 (1–2): 139–162.

————1999. *An Introduction to the Russian Folktale.* Armonk, New York: M. E. Sharpe.

————ed. and trans. 2001. *Russian Wondertales. I. Tales of Heroes and Villains.* Armonk, New York: M. E. Sharpe.

Hansen, William. 2002. *Ariadne's Thread: A Guide to International Tales Found in Classical Literature.* Ithaca: Cornell University Press.

Herranen, Gun. 1990. "The Maiden without Hands (AT 706): Two tellers, two versions." In *D'un conte... à l'autre: la variabilité dans la littérature orale.* Ed. Veronika Görög-Karady. Paris: Centre National de la Recherche Scientifique. 105–116.

Hoffmann-Krayer, E., and Hanns Bächtold-Stäubli. 1934–1935. "Perhta." In *Handwörterbuch des deutschen Aberglaubens.* Berlin: Walter de Gruyter. Vol. 6: 1478–1492.

Holbek, Bengt. 1978. "The Big-Bellied Cat." In *Varia Folklorica.* Ed. A. Dundes. The Hague and Paris: Mouton. 57–70.

————1985. "The Many Abodes of Fata Morgana or The Quest for Meaning in Fairy Tales." *Journal of Folklore Research* 22 (1): 19–28.

————1987. *Interpretation of Fairy Tales. Danish Folklore in a European Perspective.* FFC 239. Helsinki: Academia Scientiarum Fennica.

————1990. "Variation and Tale Type." In *D'un conte... à l'autre: la variabilité dans la littérature orale.* Ed. Veronika Görög-Karady. Paris: Centre National de la Recherche Scientifique. 471–485.

Holuby, J. L. 1898. "Hadi, draci a šarkani v podání lidu slovenského." *Narodopisný sborník českoslovanský* 2: 58–68.

Honko, Lauri. 1964. "Memorates and the Study of Folk Beliefs." *Journal of the Folklore Institute* I (1–2): 5–19. Bloomington: Indiana University.

————1990. "Types of Comparison and Forms of Variation." In *D'un conte... à l'autre: la variabilité dans la littérature orale.* Ed. Veronika Görög-Karady. Paris: Centre National de la Recherche Scientifique. 391–402.

Horváthová, E. 1989. "Traditsionnye iunosheskie soiuzy i initsiatsionnye obriady u zapadnykh slavian." In *Slavianskii i balkanskii fol'klor. Rekonstruktsiia drevnei slavianskoi dukhovnoi kul'tury: istochniki i metody.* Ed. N. I. Tolstoi. Moscow: Nauka. 162–173.

Hovorka, Oskar. 1897. "Aus dem Volksglauben von Sabbioncello. (Beiträge zur Volkskunde Dalmatiens.)" *Zeitschrift für österreichische Volkskunde* 3: 54–60, 84–89, 299–304.

Howell, Dana Prescott. 1992. *The Development of Soviet Folkloristics.* New York: Garland.

Hubbs, Joanna. 1982. "The Worship of Mother Earth in Russian Culture." In *Mother Worship: Theme and Variations*. Ed. James Preston. Chapel Hill: University of North Carolina Press. 123–144.

———1988. *Mother Russia: The Feminine Myth in Russian Culture*. Bloomington: Indiana University Press.

Ispas, Sabina. 1985. "'The Plant Torture'—Between Fantastic Fairy Tale and Lyrical Song." In *Papers III. The 8th Congress for the International Society for Folk Narrative Research. Bergen, June 12th–17th 1984*. Ed. Reimund Kvideland and Torunn Selberg. Bergen: Etno-Folkloristisk Institutt. Vol. 3: 401–422.

Iudin, Iu. I. 1984. "Skazka i istoriia." In *Fol'klor i ètnografiia. U ètnograficheskikh istokov fol'klornykh siuzhetov i obrazov*. Ed. B. N. Putilov. Leningrad: Nauka. 93–101.

Ivanits, Linda. 1989. *Russian Folk Belief*. Armonk, New York and London: M. E. Sharpe.

Ivanitskaia, E. N. 1984. "'Tam stupa s Baboiu-Iagoi...'" *Russkaia rech'* 1984 (2): 112–115.

Ivanov, V. V., and V. N. Toporov. 1965. *Slavianskie iazykovye modeliruiushchie semioticheskie sistemy. (Drevnii period)*. Moscow: Nauka.

Ivanova, A. A. 1979. "K voprosu o proiskhozhdenii vymysla v volshebnykh skazkakh." *Sovetskaia Ètnografiia* 1979 (3): 114–122.

Jakobson, Roman. 1945. "On Russian Fairy Tales." In *Russian Fairy Tales*. Aleksandr Afanas'ev, trans. Norbert Guterman. New York: Pantheon. 631–651.

———1971. "Why 'mama' and 'papa'?" In *Roman Jakobson: Selected Writings*. The Hague and Paris: Mouton. Vol. I: 538–545.

Jason, Heda, and Aharon Kempinski. 1981. "How Old Are Folktales?" *Fabula* 22 (1–2): 1–27.

Johns, Andreas. 1998. "Baba Iaga and the Russian Mother." *Slavic and EastEuropean Journal* 42 (1): 21–36.

———2000. "The Image of Koshchei Bessmertnyi in East Slavic Folktales." *SEEFA Journal* 5 (1): 7–24.

Jones, Ernest. 1951. *On the Nightmare*. New York: Liveright.

Jones, Steven Swann. 1986. "Structural and Thematic Applications of the Comparative Method: A Case Study of 'The Kind and Unkind Girls'." *Journal of Folklore Research* 23 (2–3): 147–161.

Kabakova, G. I. 1994. "Struktura i geografiia legendy o martovskoi starukhe." In *Slavianskii i balkanskii fol'klor. Verovaniia. Tekst. Ritual*. Ed. N. I. Tolstoi. Moscow: Nauka. 209–222.

Kaindl, Raimund F. 1894. "Die Wetterzauberei bei den Rutenen und Huzulen." *Mittheilungen der kais. königl. Geographischen Gesellschaft in Wien* XXXVII Band: 624–642.

Kapełuś, Helena. 1963. "Sem' pol'skikh skazok russkogo proiskhozhdeniia." *Russkii fol'klor* 8: 67–74.

Karjalainen, K. F. 1922. *Die Religion der Jugra-Völker. II.* FFC 44. Helsinki: Academia Scientiarum Fennica.

Karnaukhova, I. 1927. "Skazochniki i skazka v Zaonezh'e." In *Krest'ianskoe iskusstvo SSSR. I. Iskusstvo Severa. Zaonezh'e.* Ed. Ia. A. Nazarenko. Leningrad: Academia. 104–120.

———1928. "Sueveriia i byval'shchiny." In *Krest'ianskoe iskusstvo SSSR. II. Iskusstvo Severa.* Ed. Ia. A. Nazarenko. Leningrad: Academia. 77–97.

———1977. "Ob izuchenii skazochnika kak artista." In *Fol'klor. Poèticheskaia sistema.* Ed. A. Balandin and V. Gatsak. Moscow: Nauka. 311–323.

Karwot, Edward. 1955. *Katalog magii Rudolfa. Źródło etnograficzne XIII wieku.* Polskie Towarzystwo Ludoznawcze, Prace Etnologiczne, tom IV. Wrocław.

Kerbelyte, Bronislava. 1979. "K voprosu o vzaimodeistvii litovskikh i vostochnoslavianskikh volshebnykh skazok." In *Otrazhenie mezhètnicheskikh protsessov v ustnoi proze.* Ed. È. Pomerantseva. Moscow: Nauka. 66–79.

———1980. "Metodika opisaniia struktur i smysla skazok i nekotorye ee vozmozhnosti." In *Tipologiia i vzaimosviazi fol'klora narodov SSSR. Poètika i stilistika.* Ed. V. M. Gatsak. Moscow: Nauka. 48–100.

———1984. "Siuzhetnyi tip volshebnoi skazki." In *Fol'klor. Obraz i poèticheskoe slovo v kontekste.* Ed. V M. Gatsak. Moscow: Nauka. 203–250.

———1994. "Mythology and Customs: Possibilities of Comparison." In *Folklore in the Identification Processes of Society.* Etnologické Štúdie 1. Ed. Gabriela Kiliánová and Eva Krekovičová. Bratislava: Ústav etnológie SAV. 27–32.

———1995. "Structural-Semantic Principles of Formation of the Types of the Folk Tale." *Estudos de Literatura Oral* 1995 (1): 125–130.

———1996. "Evaluation of Human Beings' Behaviour in Folk Tales." In *Folk Narrative and World View: Vortäge des 10. Kongresses der Internationalen Gesellschaft für Volkserzählungsforschung (ISFNR) Innsbruck 1992.* Ed. Leander Petzoldt. Frankfurt: Peter Lang. Vol. 1: 371–379.

Kerig, Patricia, Yulya Alyoshina, and Alla Volovich. 1993. "Gender-Role Socialization in Contemporary Russia: Implications for Cross-Cultural Research." *Psychology of Women Quarterly* 17: 389–408.

Kippar, Pille. 1996. "Das westliche und östliche Weltbild in den Märchen der Völker des Baltikums." In *Folk Narrative and World View: Vorträge des 10. Kongresses der Internationalen Gesellschaft für Volkserzählungsforschung (ISFNR) Innsbruck 1992.* Ed. Leander Petzoldt. Frankfurt: Peter Lang. Vol. 1: 391–394.

Klein, Melanie. 1959. *The Psycho-Analysis of Children.* London: Hogarth Press.

Kligman, Gail. 1973. *A Socio-psychological Interpretation of 'The Tale of the Kind and Unkind Girl'*. M. A. thesis. Berkeley: University of California.

Kolesov, V. V. 1979. "Finist iasnyi sokol." *Russkaia rech'* 1979 (5): 67–70.

Kolpakova, N. P. 1973. *Lirika russkoi svad'by.* Leningrad: Nauka.

Köngäs Maranda, Elli. 1976. "Individual and Tradition." *Studia Fennica* 20: 252–261.

Kononov, A. N. 1973. "Eshche raz o 'Babe-Iage'." *Russkaia rech'* 1973 (1): 118–119.

Korepova, K. E. 1978. "Volshebnye skazki s obrazom chudesnogo supruga (K probleme izucheniia istorii siuzhetov)." In *Voprosy siuzheta i kompozitsii.* Ed. G. V. Moskvicheva. Gor'kiy : Gor'kovskii universitet. 3–17.

———1982. "Russkaia skazka 'Finist iasnyi sokol' i ee siuzhetnye paralleli."In *Voprosy siuzheta i kompozitsii.* Ed. G. V. Moskvicheva. Gor'kiy: Gor'kovskii universitet. 3–12.

———1984. "Izuchenie istorii skazochnykh siuzhetov i nekotorye problemy tekstologii". In *Voprosy siuzheta i kompozitsii.* Ed. G. V. Moskvicheva. Gor'kiy: Gor'kovskii universitet. 4–14.

———1985. "Skazochnyi siuzhet 'Muzh ishchet ischeznuvshuiu zhenu' v russkoi lubochnoi knige." In *Voprosy siuzheta i kompozitsii.* Ed. G. V. Moskvicheva. Gor'kiy: Gor'kovskii universitet. 5–16.

———1987. "Lubochnye redaktsii russkikh skazok (Siuzhet 'Tsarevna liagushka')". In *Voprosy siuzheta i kompozitsii.* (ed. G. V. Moskvicheva). Gor'kiy: Gor'kovskii universitet. 5–13.

———1999. *Russkaia lubochnaia skazka.* Nizhnii Novgorod: KiTizdat.

Korinfskii, A. A. 1901. *Narodnaia Rus'. Kruglyi god skazanii, poverii, obychaev i poslovits russkogo naroda.* Moscow: M. V. Kliukin.

Kostiukhin, Evgenii A. 1988. *Prikliucheniia slavianskikh vitiazei. Iz russkoi belletristiki XVIII veka.* Moscow: Sovremennik.

Kostomarov, Nikolai I. 1992. *Ocherk domashnei zhizni i nravov velikorusskogo naroda v XVI i XVII stoletiiakh.* Moscow: Respublika. First published 1860.

Kosven, Mark O. 1963. *Semeinaia obshchina i patronimiia.* Moscow: AN SSSR.

Kowerska, Z. A. 1896. "Bajka o stelmachu, co miał skrzydła. Dwie bajki z Opatowskiego. Bajka o dwóch braciach." *Wisła* 10: 110–112, 595–596, 783–786.

Krauss, Friedrich S. 1885. *Sitte und Brauch der Südslaven.* Vienna: Alfred Hölder.

Kravchenko, Maria. 1987. *The World of the Russian Fairy Tale.* European University Studies, Series XVI, Vol. 34. Berne, Frankfurt, New York, Paris: Peter Lang.

Krivoshapkin, M. F. 1865. *Eniseiskii okrug i ego zhizn'.* St. Petersburg: IRGO.

Krohn, Kaarle. 1971. *Folklore Methodology*. Trans. Roger Welsch. Austin: University of Texas Press.

Krzyżanowski, Julian. 1947. *Polska bajka ludowa w układzie systematycznym*. 2 vols. Warsaw: Institut literatury ludowej, Towarzystwo naukowe warszawskie.

————1963. "Devushka-iunosha (k istorii motiva 'peremena pola')." *Russkii fol'klor* 8: 56–66.

Kulišić, Š., P. Z. Petrović, and N. Pantelić. 1970. *Srpski mitološki rečnik*. Belgrade: Nolit.

Kuret, Niko. 1955. "Aus der Maskenwelt der Slowenen." In *Masken in Mitteleuropa. Volkskundliche Beiträge zur europäischen Maskenforschung*. Ed. Leopold Schmidt. Vienna: Verein für Volkskunde. 201–220.

————1969. "Die Mittwinterfrau der Slowenen (Pehtra baba und Torka)." *Alpes Orientales* 5: 209–239. Ljubljana.

Kurotschkin [Kurochkin], A. V. 1991–92. "Hexengestalt in der ukrainischen Folkloretradition." *Acta Ethnographica Academiae Scientiarum Hungaricae* 37 (1–4): 191–200.

Kurtz, Stanley. 1992. *All the Mothers Are One: Hindu India and the Cultural Reshaping of Psychoanalysis*. New York: Columbia University Press.

Lacoste-Dujardin, Camille. 1970. *Le conte kabyle. Étude ethnologique*. Paris: François Maspero.

Lashuk, Lev P. 1972. *Formirovanie narodnosti komi*. Moscow: Izdatel'stvo moskovskogo universiteta.

Laushkin, K. D. 1970. "Baba-Iaga i odnonogie bogi. (K voprosu o proiskhozhdenii obraza)." In *Fol'klor i ètnografiia*. Ed. B. Putilov. Leningrad: Nauka. 181–186.

Lavrent'eva, L. S. 1991. "Sotsializatsiia devochek v russkoi derevne." In *"Mir detstva" v traditsionnoi kul'ture narodov SSSR. Sbornik nauchnykh trudov. Chast' I*. Ed. A. B. Ostrovskii et al. Leningrad: Muzei Ètnografii. 27–35.

Lavrovskii, P. A. 1866. "Razbor issledovaniia 'O mificheskom znachenii nekotorykh poverii i obriadov. Sochinenie A. Potebni. Moskva 1865.'" *Chteniia v imperatorskom obshchestve istorii i drevnostei rossiiskikh pri moskovskom universitete* 1866 (2): 1–102.

Lebarbier, Micheline. 1996. "Séductions et dangers de l'autre monde (Récits roumains)." *Cahiers de littérature orale* 39–40: 97–115.

Leonova, T. G. 1998. "Skazki o kote, petukhe i lise (61B) i o mal'chike i ved'me (327C, F) v sootnoshenii ikh struktury i semantiki." In *Traditsionnaia kul'tura i mir detstva. Traditional Culture and the World of Childhood*. Ed. M. P. Cherednikova and V. F. Shevchenko. Ul'yanovsk: Laboratoriia kul'turologii. 5–25.

Lettenbauer, Wilhelm. 1952. "Über Krankheitsdämonen im Volksglauben der Balkanslaven." In *Serta Monacensia. Franz Babinger zum 15. Januar 1951 als Festgruss dargebracht.* Ed. Hans Joachim Kissling and Alois Schmaus. Leiden: E. J. Brill. 120–135.

Lévi-Strauss, Claude. 1960. "L'analyse morphologique des contes russes." *IJSLP* 3: 122–149.

———1968. "The Structural Study of Myth." In *Myth: A Symposium.* Ed. Thomas Sebeok. Bloomington: Indiana University Press. 81–106.

———1969. *The Raw and the Cooked.* New York: Harper & Row.

———1973. *From Honey to Ashes.* New York: Harper & Row.

Lichtenberger, Sigrid. 1986. "Die Rolle der Frau im deutschen und russischen Volksmärchen." In *Festschrift für Wolfgang Gesemann. Band 2. Beiträge zur slawischen Literaturwissenschaft.* Munich: Hieronymus Verlag. 137–159.

Lilek, Emilian. 1896. "Volksglaube und volksthümlicher Cultus in Bosnien und der Hercegovina." *Wissenschaftliche Mittheilungen aus Bosnien und der Hercegovina* 4: 401–492.

Lintur, Petro. 1994. *A Survey of Ukrainian Folk Tales.* Trans. Bohdan Medwidsky. Occasional Research Report No. 56. Edmonton, Alberta: University of Alberta, Canadian Institute of Ukrainian Studies Press.

Lobkova, Galina V. 2000. *Drevnosti Pskovskoi zemli. Zhatvennaia obriadnost': Obrazy, ritualy, khudozhestvennaia sistema.* St. Petersburg: Ministerstvo kul'tury rossiiskoi federatsii, Fol'klorno-ètnograficheskii tsentr.

Loiter, Sof'ia M. 1991. *Russkii detskii fol'klor Karelii.* Petrozavodsk: Kareliia.

Lomonosov, M. V. 1950–1983. *Polnoe sobranie sochinenii.* 11 volumes. Moscow and Leningrad: AN SSSR.

Losonczy, Anne M. 1986. "Le chamane-cheval et la sage-femme ferrée." *L'Ethnographie* LXXXII (98–99): 51–70.

Löwis of Menar, August von. 1912. *Der Held im deutschen und russischen Märchen.* Jena: Eugen Diederichs.

———1923. *Die Brünhildsage in Russland.* Leipzig: Mayer & Müller.

Lüthi, Max. 1960. *Das europäische Volksmärchen: Form und Wesen.* Berne and Munich: Francke.

———1964. *Märchen.* Stuttgart: Metzler.

MacCulloch, J. A. 1911. *The Religion of the Ancient Celts.* Edinburgh: T. & T. Clark.

Máchal, Hanuš [Jan]. 1891. *Nákres slovanského bájesloví.* Prague: F. Šimáček.

Maikov, L. N. 1994. *Velikorusskie zaklinaniia.* St. Petersburg: Izdatel'stvo Evropeiskogo Doma. Originally published 1869.

Maillet, Germaine. 1980. "Sur différents types de 'Pédauques'." In *Mélanges de Mythologie française offerts au Président-Fondateur Henri Dontenville.* Ed. H. Fromage. Paris: G.-P. Maisonneuve et Larose. 183–192.

Makarov, Mikhail N. 1827. "Iz slovaria osobennykh rechenii i proch." *Vestnik Evropy* no. 10: 148–153. Moscow.

———1827a. "Krivich-khristiianin i Iagaia. Drevniaia Smolenskaia povest'." *Vestnik Evropy* no. 13: 3–20. Moscow.

Makashina, T. S. 1966. "Sovremennaia severnorusskaia skazochnitsa A. M. Melekhova." In *Sovremennyi russkii fol'klor.* Ed. È. Pomerantseva. Moscow: Nauka. 78–94.

Mansikka, V. 1909. "Predstaviteli zlogo nachala v russkikh zagovorakh." *Zhivaia Starina* 18 (4): 3–30.

———1909a. *Über russische Zauberformeln mit Berücksichtigung der Blut- und Verrenkungssegen.* Helsinki: Suomalaisen Tiedeakatemian Kustantama.

Maranda, Pierre, ed. 1974. *Soviet Structural Folkloristics.* The Hague and Paris: Mouton.

Maranda, Elli Köngäs and Pierre. 1971. *Structural Models in Folklore and Transformational Essays.* The Hague and Paris: Mouton.

Martynova, Antonina N. 1975. "Otrazhenie deistvitel'nosti v krest'ianskoi kolybel'noi pesne." *Russkii fol'klor* 15: 145–155.

———1978. "Life of the Pre-Revolutionary Village as Reflected in Popular Lullabies." In *The Family in Imperial Russia: New Lines of Historical Research.* Ed. David Ransel. Urbana: University of Illinois Press. 171–185.

———1979. "Obrashchenie v russkoi kolybel'noi." *Russkaia rech'* 1979 (1): 73–76.

———ed. 1997. *Detskii poèticheskii fol'klor. Antologiia.* Studiorum Slavicorum Monumenta, Tomus 15. St. Petersburg: RAN.

Mead, Margaret. 1954. "The Swaddling Hypothesis: Its Reception." *American Anthropologist* 56: 395–409.

Meletinskii, Eleazar M. 1958. *Geroi volshebnoi skazki. Proiskhozhdenie obraza.* Moscow: Nauka.

———1969. "Strukturno-tipologicheskoe izuchenie skazki." In *Morfologiia skazki.* V. Propp. Moscow: Nauka. 134–166.

———1970. "Mif i skazka." In *Fol'klor i ètnografiia.* Ed. B. Putilov. Leningrad: Nauka. 139–148.

———1972. "Pervobytnye istoki slovesnogo iskusstva." In *Rannie formy iskusstva. Sbornik statei.* Ed. S. Nekliudov and E. Meletinskii. Moscow. 148–189.

———1974. "Marriage: Its Function and Position in the Structure of Folktales." In *Soviet Structural Folkloristics*. Ed. Pierre Maranda. The Hague and Paris: Mouton. 61–72.

Meletinskii, E. M., S. Iu. Nekliudov, E. S. Novik, and D. M. Segal. 1969. "Problemy strukturnogo opisaniia volshebnoi skazki." *Trudy po znakovym sistemam* 4: 86–135. Tartu.

———1971. "Eshche raz o probleme strukturnogo opisaniia volshebnoi skazki." *Trudy po znakovym sistemam* 5: 63–91. Tartu.

Mesnil, Marianne, and Assia Popova. 1993. "Démone et chrétienne: sainte Vendredi." *Revue des Études slaves* 65 (4): 743–762.

Meyer zur Capellen, Renate. 1980. "Das schöne Mädchen. Psychoanalytische Betrachtungen zur 'Formwerdung der Seele' des Mädchens." In *Und wenn sie nicht gestorben sind...Perspektiven auf das Märchen*. Ed. H. Brackert. Frankfurt: Suhrkamp. 89–119.

Mikov, Lyubomir. 1994. "Bulgarian Folk *Martenitsa*—Amulet and Trinket." In *The Magical and Aesthetic in the Folklore of Balkan Slavs*. Ed. Dejan Ajdačić. Belgrade: Library Vuk Karadžić. 131–134.

Morozova, M. N. 1977. "Antroponimiia russkikh narodnykh skazok." In *Fol'klor. Poèticheskaia sistema*. Ed. A. Balandin and V. Gatsak. Moscow: Nauka. 231–241.

Motz, Lotte. 1984. "The Winter Goddess: Percht, Holda, and Related Figures." *Folklore* 95: 151–166. London.

Mouchketique, Lesia. 1991–92. "Les croyances démonologiques du folklore de la contrée limitrophe de l'Ukraine et de la Hongrie." *Acta Ethnographica Academiae Scientiarum Hungaricae* 37 (1–4): 201–213.

Mouliéras, Auguste. 1965. *Traduction des légendes et contes merveilleux de la Grande Kabylie*. 2 vols. Trans. Camille Lacoste. Paris: Paul Geuthner.

Moyle [Kononenko], Natalie K. 1987. "Mermaids (*Rusalki*) and Russian Beliefs about Women." In *New Studies in Russian Language and Literature*. Ed. Anna Crone and Catherine Chvany. Columbus: Slavica. 221–238.

Muhawi, Ibrahim, and Sharif Kanaana. 1989. *Speak, Bird, Speak Again: Palestinian Arab Folktales*. Berkeley: University of California Press.

Neëlov, Evgenii M. 1989. *Naturfilosofiia russkoi volshebnoi skazki. Uchebnoe posobie po spetskursu*. Petrozavodsk: RIO Petrozavodskogo gosudarstvennogo universiteta.

Nekrasov, Nikolai A. 1981. *Polnoe sobranie sochinenii i pisem v piatnadtsati tomakh*. Leningrad: Nauka.

Neumann, Erich. 1955. *The Great Mother: An Analysis of the Archetype*. Bollingen Series 47. New York: Pantheon.

Nevskaia, L. G. 1999. *"Pech'* v fol'klornoi modeli mira." In *Issledovaniia v oblasti balto-slavianskoi dukhovnoi kul'tury. Zagadka kak tekst. 2.* Ed. T. M. Nikolaeva. Moscow: RAN, Indrik. 101–109.

Newell, William Wells. 1890. "Game of the Child-Stealing Witch." *JAF* 3: 139–148.

Niculescu, Radu. 1991. "Une contribution roumaine à l'esthétique du conte." In R. Nicolescu, *Folclorul-Sens-Valoare.* Bucharest: Minerva. 331–342.

Nikiforov, A. I. 1928. "K voprosu o morfologicheskom izuchenii narodnoi skazki." *Sbornik otdeleniia russkogo iazyka i slovesnosti AN SSSR* 101 (3): 173–178. *Stat'i po slavianskoi filologii i russkoi slovesnosti. Sbornik statei v chest' akademika A. I. Sobolevskogo.*

————1930. "Skazka, ee bytovanie i nositeli." In *Russkie narodnye skazki.* Ed. O. Kapitsa. Moscow and Leningrad: Gosudarstvennoe izdatel'stvo. 7–62.

————1934. "Motiv, funktsiia, stil' i klassovyi refleks v skazke." In *Sbornik statei k sorokaletiiu uchenoi deiatel'nosti akademika A. S. Orlova.* Ed. V. Peretts. Leningrad: AN SSSR. 287–293.

————1934a. "Sotsial'no-èkonomicheskii oblik severno-russkoi skazki 1926–1928 godov." In *Sergeiu Fedorovichu Ol'denburgu k piatidesiatiletiiu nauchno-obshchestvennoi deiatel'nosti 1882–1932. Sbornik statei.* Ed. I. Iu. Krachkovskii. Leningrad: AN SSSR. 377–397.

————1973. "On the morphological study of folklore." Trans. and ed. Heda Jason. *Linguistica Biblica* 27–28: 25–35.

Novik, E. S. 1975. "Sistema personazhei russkoi volshebnoi skazki." In *Tipologicheskie issledovaniia po fol'kloru. Sbornik statei pamiati Vladimira Iakovlevicha Proppa (1895–1970).* Ed. E. Meletinskii and S. Nekliudov. Moscow: Nauka. 214–246.

————1993. "Struktura skazochnogo triuka." In *Ot mifa k literature.* Ed. S. Iu. Nekliudov and E. S. Novik. Moscow: Rossiiskii gosudarstvennyi gumanitarnyi universitet.

Novikov, Nikolai V. 1957. "Satira v russkoi volshebnoi skazke zapisi XIX–nachala XX veka." *Russkii fol'klor* 2: 40–61.

————1966. "O spetsifike obraza v vostochnoslavianskoi skazke (Kashchei Bessmertnyi)." *Russkii fol'klor* 10: 149–175.

————1968. "Obrazy russkoi i bolgarskoi volshebno-fantasticheskoi skazki." *Russkii fol'klor* 11: 140–158.

————1974. *Obrazy vostochnoslavianskoi volshebnoi skazki.* Leningrad: Nauka.

————1977. "Baba-Jaga." In *Enzyklopädie des Märchens.* Ed. Kurt Ranke. Berlin: de Gruyter. Vol. 1: 1121–1123.

Oinas, Felix. 1985. *Essays on Russian Folklore and Mythology.* Columbus: Slavica.

Olrik, Axel. 1999. "Epic Laws of Folk Narrative." In *International Folkloristics: Classic Contributions by the Founders of Folklore*. Ed. Alan Dundes. Lanham, Maryland: Rowman & Littlefield. 83–97.

Onchukov, N. E. 1934. "Skazki odnoi derevni." In *Sergeiu Fedorovichu Ol'denburgu k piatidesiatiletiiu nauchno-obshchestvennoi deiatel'nosti 1882–1932. Sbornik statei.* Ed. I. Iu. Krachkovskii. Leningrad: AN SSSR. 399–412.

Onegina, N. F. 1974. "Sposoby izobrazheniia daritelia v russkoi i karel'skoi volshebnoi skazke." *Russkii fol'klor* 14: 132–143.

———1980. "Russko-karel'skie fol'klornye sviazi (iz opyta izucheniia obshchnosti poètiki volshebnykh skazok)." *Fol'kloristika Karelii* 44–57.

———1983. "Vepsskie volshebnye skazki o nevinno gonimykh." *Fol'kloristika Karelii* 135–157.

Ortner, Sherry. 1974. "Is Female to Male as Nature Is to Culture?" In *Woman, Culture, and Society*. Ed. Michelle Z. Rosaldo and Louise Lamphere. Stanford: Stanford University Press. 67–87.

Paulme, Denise. 1976. *La mère dévorante. Essai sur la morphologie des contes africains.* Paris: Gallimard.

Pentikäinen, Juha, and Satu Apo. 1978. "The Structural Schemes of a Fairy-Tale Repertoire: A Structural Analysis of Marina Takalo's Fairy Tales." In *Varia Folklorica*. Ed. A. Dundes. The Hague and Paris: Mouton. 23–55.

Periañez-Chaverneff, Olga. 1983. "Analyse ethnopsychiatrique de la Baba-Jaga: apport à l'ethnogenèse des slaves." *Revue des Études slaves* 55 (1): 185–195.

Perrie, Maureen. 1989. "Folklore as Evidence of Peasant *Mentalité*: Social Attitudes and Values in Russian Popular Culture." *Russian Review* 48: 119–143.

Plekhanov, A. 1992. "Russian Folk Wisdom about Upbringing." *Russian Social Science Review* 33 (3): 79–88.

Pletneva, S. A. 1978. "Zhivotnyi mir v russkikh volshebnykh skazkakh." In *Drevniaia Rus' i slaviane*. Ed. T. V. Nikolaeva. Moscow: Nauka. 388–397.

Pócs, Éva. 1989. *Fairies and Witches at the Boundary of South-Eastern and Central Europe.* FFC 243. Helsinki: Academia Scientiarum Fennica.

———1999. *Between the Living and the Dead: A Perspective on Witches and Seers in the Early Modern Age.* Trans. Szilvia Rédey and Michael Webb. Budapest: Central European University Press.

Polák, Václav. 1977. "Etymologické příspěvky k slov. démonologii." *Slavia. Časopis pro slovanskou filologii* 46 (3): 283–291.

Polívka, Jiří. 1922. "Du surnaturel dans les contes slovaques: les êtres surnaturels; les êtres doués de pouvoirs surnaturels." *Revue des Études slaves* 2: 104–124, 256–271.

————1932. *Slovanské pohádky. I. Úvod. Východoslovanské pohádky.* Práce Slovanského Ústavu v Praze, svazek 6. Prague.

Pomerantseva, Èrna V. 1963. *Russkaia narodnaia skazka.* Moscow: Izdatel'stvo AN SSSR.

————1965. *Sud'by russkoi skazki.* Moscow: Nauka.

————ed. 1966. *Sovremennyi russkii fol'klor.* Moscow: Nauka.

————1975. *Mifologicheskie personazhi v russkom fol'klore.* Moscow: Nauka.

————1978. "Mezhètnicheskaia obshchnost' poverii i bylichek o poludnitse." In *Slavianskii i balkanskii fol'klor. Genezis, arkhaika, traditsii.* Ed. I. M. Sheptunov. Moscow: Nauka. 143–158.

————1979. "Russkaia skazka v ustnom repertuare komi." *Sovetskaia Ètnografiia* 1979 (6): 32–45.

————ed. 1979a. *Otrazhenie mezhètnicheskikh protsessov v ustnoi proze.* Moscow: Nauka.

Potebnia, Aleksandr A. 1865. "O mificheskom znachenii nekotorykh obriadov i poverii. II. Baba-Iaga." *Chteniia v imperatorskom obshchestve istorii i drevnostei rossiiskikh pri moskovskom universitete* 1865 (3): 85–232.

Preobrazhenskii, A. 1959. *Ètimologicheskii slovar' russkogo iazyka.* Moscow.

Preston, James, ed. 1982. *Mother Worship: Theme and Variations.* Chapel Hill: University of North Carolina Press.

Prishvin, Mikhail M. 1970. *V kraiu nepuganykh ptits. Osudareva doroga.* Petrozavodsk: Kareliia.

Propp, Vladimir Ia. 1941. "Motiv chudesnogo rozhdeniia." *Uchenye zapiski LGU* no. 81, *Seriia filologicheskikh nauk* vyp. 12: 67–97.

————1946. *Istoricheskie korni volshebnoi skazki.* Leningrad: LGU.

————1969. *Morfologiia skazki.* Moscow: Nauka. First edition 1928.

————1976. *Fol'lklor i deistvitel'nost'. Izbrannye stat'i.* Moscow: Nauka.

————1984. *Russkaia skazka.* Leningrad: Izdatel'stvo Leningradskogo Universiteta.

Putanec, Valentin. 1962. "Starohrvatski glagoljski uklin protiv zmija u rukopisu 14. stoljeća." *Zbornik za narodni život i običaje južnih Slavena* 40: 409–412.

Putilov, Boris N., ed. 1970. *Fol'klor i ètnografiia.* Leningrad: Nauka.

————ed. 1977. *Fol'klor i ètnografiia. Sviazi fol'klora s drevnimi predstavleniiami i obriadami.* Leningrad: Nauka.

————ed. 1984. *Fol'klor i ètnografiia. U ètnograficheskikh istokov fol'klornykh siuzhetov i obrazov.* Leningrad: Nauka.

————1988. *Geroicheskii èpos i deistvitel'nost'.* Leningrad: Nauka.

————ed. 1990. *Fol'klor i ètnografiia. Problemy rekonstruktsii faktov traditsionnoi kul'tury.* Leningrad: Nauka.

Radloff, W. 1866. *Proben der Volksliteratur der türkischen Stämme Süd-Sibiriens.* St. Petersburg: Imperatorskaia Akademiia Nauk.

Ralston, W. R. S. 1873. *Russian Folk-tales.* London: Smith, Elder, & Co.

————1970. *The Songs of the Russian People, as Illustrative of Slavonic Mythology and Russian Social Life.* New York: Haskell. First edition 1872.

Rancour-Laferriere, Daniel. 1985. *Signs of the Flesh: An Essay on the Evolution of Hominid Sexuality.* Bloomington: Indiana University Press.

————1995. *The Slave Soul of Russia: Moral Masochism and the Cult of Suffering.* New York: New York University Press.

Rank, Otto. 1909. *Der Mythus von der Geburt des Helden. Versuch einer psychologischen Mythendeutung.* Leipzig and Vienna: Franz Deuticke.

————1922. *Psychoanalytische Beiträge zur Mythenforschung.* Leipzig, Vienna, Zurich: Internationaler Psychoanalytischer Verlag.

Ranke, Kurt. 1977. *Enzyklopädie des Märchens.* Berlin: de Gruyter.

Razumova, Irina A. 1983. "Povestvovatel'naia stereotipiia v volshebnoi skazke (k postanovke voprosa)." *Fol'kloristika Karelii* 158–179.

————1991. *Stilisticheskaia obriadnost' russkoi volshebnoi skazki.* Petrozavodsk: Kareliia.

————1993. *Skazka i bylichka. (Mifologicheskii personazh v sisteme zhanra).* Petrozavodsk: Karel'skii nauchnyi tsentr RAN.

Rhys, John. 1966. *Studies in the Arthurian Legend.* New York: Russell & Russell.

Rich, Elisabeth. 1995. "Russian Literature after Perestroika." *South Central Review* 12 (3–4): 1–147.

Roberts, Warren. 1994. *The Tale of the Kind and the Unkind Girls: Aa-Th 480 and Related Tales.* Detroit: Wayne State University Press. First published 1958.

Róheim, Géza. 1946. "Saint Agatha and the Tuesday Woman." *International Journal of Psycho-Analysis* 27 (3–4): 119–126.

————1947. "The Story of the Light That Disappeared." *Samiksa* 1 (1): 51–85.

————1953. "Hansel and Gretel." *Bulletin of the Menninger Clinic* 17: 90–92.

————1992. *Fire in the Dragon and Other Psychoanalytic Essays on Folklore.* Princeton: Princeton University Press.

Röhrich, Lutz. 1991. *Folktales and Reality.* Bloomington: Indiana University Press.

Romanova, A. V., and A. N. Myreeva. 1971. *Fol'klor èvenkov Iakutii.* Leningrad: Nauka.

Roşianu, Nicolae. 1974. *Traditsionnye formuly skazki.* Moscow: Nauka.

Rumpf, Marianne. 1991. *Perchten: populäre Glaubensgestalten zwischen Mythos und Katechese.* Quellen und Forschungen zur europäischen Ethnologie Band XII. Würzburg: Königshausen & Neumann.

Rybakov, Boris A. 1953. "Iskusstvo drevnikh slavian." In *Istoriia russkogo iskusstva*. Tom I. Ed. I. È. Grabar', V. N. Lazarev, and V. S. Kemenov. Moscow: AN SSSR. 39–92.

———1981. *Iazychestvo drevnikh slavian*. Moscow: Nauka.

———1987. *Iazychestvo drevnei Rusi*. Moscow: Nauka.

Sadovnikov, D. N. 1959. *Zagadki russkogo naroda. Sbornik zagadok, voprosov, pritch i zadach*. Moscow: Izdatel'stvo Moskovskogo universiteta. First published 1876.

Sanarov, Valerii I. 1981. "On the Nature and Origin of Flying Saucers and Little Green Men." *Current Anthropology* 22 (2): 163–167.

Sannikova, O. V. 1994. "Pol'skaia mifologicheskaia leksika v structure fol'klornogo teksta." In *Slavianskii i balkanskii fol'klor. Verovaniia. Tekst. Ritual.* Ed. N. I. Tolstoi. Moscow: Nauka. 209–222.

Sartori, Paul. 1930. "Erzählen als Zauber." *Zeitschrift für Volkskunde* II: 40–45. Berlin.

Savchenko, S. V. 1914. *Russkaia narodnaia skazka (Istoriia sobiraniia i izucheniia)*. Kiev: Imperatorskii Universitet Sv. Vladimira.

Schatzman, Ruth. 1999. "Quatre contes russes." *Cahiers de littérature orale* 46: 149–180.

Schneeweis, Edmund. 1953. *Feste und Volksbräuche der Sorben vergleichend dargestellt.* Berlin: Akademie-Verlag.

Scholz, Friedrich. 1987. "Methoden der Analyse des Volksmärchens." In *Beiträge zur russischen Volksdichtung*. Ed. Klaus-Dieter Seemann. Berlin: Osteuropa Institut an der Freien Universität. 75–91.

Schulenburg, Wilibald von. 1880. *Wendische Volkssagen und Gebräuche aus dem Spreewald.* Leipzig: Brockhaus.

Scielzo, Caroline. 1983. "An Analysis of Bába-Yagá in Folklore and Fairy Tales." *American Journal of Psychoanalysis* 43 (2): 167–175.

Sedakova, Irina. 1984. "Kŭm izuchavaneto na bŭlgarskata obredna terminologiia (slovosŭchetaniia ot osnovite *bab-, ded-* i *star-* v terminologiiata na koledno-novogodishnata obrednost na bŭlgarite)." *Bŭlgarski folklor* 10 (1): 45–52.

Semenova-Tian-Shanskaia, Ol'ga. 1914. *Zhizn' "Ivana". Ocherki iz byta krest'ian odnoi iz chernozemnykh gubernii*. Zapiski IRGO 39. St. Petersburg.

———1993. *Village Life in Late Tsarist Russia*. Trans. and ed. D. Ransel and M. Levine. Bloomington: Indiana University Press.

Sen'kina, Tat'iana I. 1978. "Sotsial'nye funktsii 'durachestv' demokraticheskogo geroia russkoi volshebnoi skazki." *Fol'kloristika Karelii* 58–71.

———1980. *Sotsial'naia problematika v volshebnykh skazkakh Karel'skogo Pomor'ia.* Petrozavodsk: Kareliia.

————1980a. "Ob ispolnitel'skoi manere pudozhskogo skazochnika." *Fol'kloristika Karelii* 75–88.

————1983. "K voprosu o vzaimodeistvii russkoi, karel'skoi i finskoi skazochnykh traditsii (siuzhet 'Podmenennaia nevesta')." *Fol'kloristika Karelii* 116–135.

————1986. "Proiavlenie arkhaicheskikh èlementov v funktsiiakh russkoi skazki Karelii." *Fol'kloristika Karelii* 97–112.

————1987. "Tipy russkikh skazochnikov Karelii." *Fol'kloristika Karelii* 60–74.

————1988. *Russkaia skazka Karelii.* Petrozavodsk: Kareliia.

————1989. "O sootnoshenii skazki i bylichki v fol'klore Karelii." *Fol'kloristika Karelii* 92–108.

Shapiro, Michael. 1983. "Baba-Jaga: A Search for Mythopoeic Origins and Affinities." *IJSLP* 28: 109–135.

Shastina, E. I. 1972. "Verkhnelenskaia skazochnaia traditsiia (Po zapisiam 1966–1968 gg.)." In *Slavianskii fol'klor.* Ed. B. Putilov and V. Sokolova. Moscow: Nauka. 181–201.

————1976. "Sibirskaia shkola brodiachikh skazochnikov (K probleme sotsial'no-biograficheskikh obobshchenii v sovremennom skazitel'stve)." In *Literatura i fol'klor Zabaikal'ia. (Respublikanskii sbornik).* Ed. A. A. Tatuiko. Irkutsk: Irkutskii gosudarstvennyi pedagogicheskii institut. 167–184.

————1976a. "K voprosu o sotsial'no-biograficheskikh obobshcheniiakh v volshebnoi skazke." In *Fol'klor i literatura Sibiri. Vypusk 3.* Ed. T. G. Leonova. Omsk: Omskii pedagogicheskii institut imeni A. M. Gor'kogo. 3–22.

————1977. "Sovremennoe sostoianie volshebno-fantasticheskoi traditsii v Vostochnoi Sibiri (K metodike issledovaniia)." In *Literatura i fol'klor Vostochnoi Sibiri. (Respublikanskii sbornik).* Ed. A. A. Tatuiko. Irkutsk: Irkutskii gosudarstvennyi pedagogicheskii institut. 24–28.

————1978. "O kharakternom i nekharakternom v sovremennom skazitel'stve (Po zapisiam 1970–1973 gg. v selakh Prilen'ia)." In *Literatura i fol'klor vostochnoi Sibiri. (Respublikanskii sbornik).* Ed. A. A. Tatuiko. Irkutsk: Irkutskii gosudarstvennyi pedagogicheskii institut. 101–109.

————ed. 1986. *Problemy nravstvenno-psikhologicheskogo soderzhaniia v literature i fol'klore Sibiri.* Irkutsk: Irkutskii gosudarstvennyi pedagogicheskii institut.

Shcheglov, Yuri K. 1994. "Some Themes and Archetypes in Babel"s *Red Cavalry.*" Slavic Review 53 (3): 653–670.

Shevchenko, V. F. 1998. "Novye materialy po narodnoi pediatrii: 'sukhaia sten' i 'sobach'ia starost'." In *Traditsionnaia kul'tura i mir detstva. Traditional Culture and the World of Childhood.* Ed. M. P. Cherednikova and V. F. Shevchenko. Ul'yanovsk: Laboratoriia kul'turologii. 112–120.

Shimkin, D. B., and Pedro Sanjuan. 1953. "Culture and World View: A Method of Analysis Applied to Rural Russia." *American Anthropologist* 55: 329–348.

Silva, Francisco Vaz da. 2002. *Metamorphosis: The Dynamics of Symbolism in European Fairy Tales*. New York: Peter Lang.

Simonsen, Michèle. 1984. *Le conte populaire*. Paris: Presses Universitaires de France.

————1985. "Do Fairy Tales Make Sense?" *Journal of Folklore Research* 22 (1): 29–36.

————1990. "La variabilite dans les légendes: les récits danois sur les loups-garous." In *D'un conte... à l'autre: la variabilité dans la littérature orale*. Ed. Veronika Görög-Karady. Paris: Centre National de la Recherche Scientifique. 181–190.

————1998. "Culture and Symbols. Some Thoughts about Bengt Holbek's Interpretation of Fairy Tales." *Estudos de Literatura Oral* 1998 (4): 209–214.

Smirnov, A. 1905. "Ivanushka durachek." *Voprosy zhizni* 1905 (12): 5–73. St. Petersburg.

Sokolov, B. M. 1995. "'Baba Iaga dereviana noga edet s karkarladilom dratitisia': Slovo v lubke kak simvol 'pis'mennoi kul'tury'." *Zhivaia starina* 3 (7): 52–55.

Sokolov, Iurii M. 1938. *Russkii fol'klor*. Moscow: Uchpedgiz.

Sokolova, Vera K. 1972. "Tipy vostochnoslavianskikh toponimicheskikh predanii." In *Slavianskii fol'klor*. Ed. B. Putilov and V. Sokolova. Moscow: Nauka. 202–233.

————1976. "The Interaction of the Historical Legend with Other Folkloristic Genres." *Studia Fennica* 20: 58–66.

————1978. "Some Traditional Symbols in Slavonic Folk Poetry." In *Varia Folklorica*. Ed. A. Dundes. The Hague and Paris: Mouton. 155–163.

Solymossy, Sándor. 1927. "A 'vasorrú bába' és mítikus rokonai." *Ethnographia* 38 (4): 217–235. Budapest.

————1984. "Die Burg auf dem Entenbein." In *Die Welt im Märchen*. Ed. Jürgen Janning and Heino Gehrts. Kassel: Erich Röth Verlag. 123–139.

Somoff [Nesterenko], Victoria. 1997. "Chudo kak sobytie v slove." *Voprosy literatury* 1: 103–116.

————2002. "On the Metahistorical Roots of the Fairytale." *Western Folklore* 61 (3–4): 277–293.

Speranskii, M. 1917. *Russkaia ustnaia slovesnost'*. Moscow: A. M. Mikhailov.

Spiro, Melford. 1993. *Oedipus in the Trobriands*. New Brunswick and London: Transaction Publishers.

Spirovska, Lepa. 1971. "Kultot kon zmiite vo seloto Orman (Skopsko)." *Makedonski folklor* 4 (7–8): 141–146.

Spitz, Sheryl. 1977. "The Impact of Structure on Solzhenitsyn's 'Matryona's Home'." *Russian Review* 36 (2): 167–183.

Stankiewicz, Edward. 1958. "Slavic Kinship Terms and the Perils of the Soul." *JAF* 71: 115–122.

Stecki, Jan, and J. S. Zięba. 1896. "Poglądy ludu na przyrodę." *Wisła* 10: 135–138.

Stepanov, Iu. S. 1995. "*Baba-Iaga, Iama, Ianus, Iason* i drugie. K voprosu o 'nestrogom' sravnitel'no-istoricheskom metode." *Voprosy iazykoznaniia* 1995 (5): 3–16.

Stoliarov, Ivan. 1986. *Zapiski russkogo krest'ianina. Récit d'un paysan russe.* Paris: Institut d'études slaves.

Stoller, Robert. 1985. *Presentations of Gender.* New Haven: Yale University Press.

Sudnik, T. M., and T. V. Tsiv'ian. 1982. "O mifologii liagushki (balto-balkanskie dannye)." In *Balto-slavianskie issledovaniia 1981.* Ed. V. V. Ivanov. Moscow: Nauka. 137–154.

Surazakov, S. S. 1985. *Altaiskii geroicheskii èpos.* Moscow: Nauka.

Swahn, Jan-Öjvind. 1955. *The Tale of Cupid and Psyche (Aarne-Thompson 425 & 428).* Lund: C W K Gleerup.

———1990. "Tradierungskonstanten: Wie weit reicht unsere mündliche Tradition zurück?" In *Wie alt sind unsere Märchen.* Ed. Charlotte Oberfeld. Regensburg: Erich Röth Verlag. 36–50.

Swan, Charles, and Wynnard Hooper, trans. and ed. 1959. *Gesta Romanorum: or, Entertaining Moral Stories.* New York: Dover.

Sydow, Carl Wilhelm von. 1948. *Selected Papers on Folklore. Published on the Occasion of His 70th Birthday.* Copenhagen: Rosenkilde and Bagger.

———1999. "Geography and Folk-Tale Oicotypes." In *International Folkloristics: Classic Contributions by the Founders of Folklore.* Ed. Alan Dundes. Lanham, Maryland: Rowman & Littlefield. 140–151.

Taggart, James. 1977. "Metaphors and Symbols of Deviance in Nahuat Narratives." *Journal of Latin American Lore* 3 (2): 279–308.

———1979. "Men's Changing Image of Women in Nahuat Oral Tradition." *American Ethnologist* 6 (4): 723–741.

———1990. *Enchanted Maidens: Gender Relations in Spanish Folktales of Courtship and Marriage.* Princeton: Princeton Univesity Press.

Tempest, Snejana. 1997. "Stovelore in Russian Folklife." In *Food in Russian History and Culture.* Ed. Musya Glants and Joyce Toomre. Bloomington: Indiana University Press. 1–14.

———2001. "Acquiring an Identity: Gender Distinctions in Russian Childlore and Rituals." In *Gender and Sexuality in Russian Civilisation.* Ed. Peter I. Barta. London: Routledge. 89–104.

Tenèze, Marie-Louise. 1970. "Du conte merveilleux comme genre." *Arts et Traditions populaires* 18 (1–3): 11–65.

Tertz, Abram [Andrei Siniavskii]. 1975. *V teni Gogolia.* London: Overseas Publications Interchange, and Collins.

Thompson, Stith. 1977. *The Folktale.* Berkeley: University of California Press.

———1989. *Motif-Index of Folk-Literature.* 6 vols. Bloomington: Indiana University Press.

Tokarev, S. A. 1957. *Religioznye verovaniia vostochnoslavianskikh narodov XIX nachala XX veka.* Moscow and Leningrad: AN SSSR.

Tolstaia, S. M. 1986. "Liagushka, uzh i drugie zhivotnye v obriadakh vyzyvaniia i ostanovki dozhdia." In *Slavianskii i balkanskii fol'klor. Dukhovnaia kul'tura Poles'ia na obshcheslavianskom fone.* Ed. N. I. Tolstoi. Moscow: Nauka. 22–27.

———1997. "Dozhd' v fol'klornoi kartine mira." In *Issledovaniia po slavianskomu fol'kloru i narodnoi kul'ture. Studies in Slavic Folklore and Folk Culture.* Ed. A. Arkhipov and I. Polinskaia. Oakland: Berkeley Slavic Specialties. Vypusk 1: 105–119.

Tolstoi, Ivan I. 1941. "'Gekala' Kallimakha i russkaia skazka o babe-iage." *Uchenye zapiski LGU, Seriia filologicheskikh nauk* vyp. 7: 7–19.

———1966. *Stat'i o fol'klore.* Moscow and Leningrad: Nauka.

Tolstoi, Nikita I. 1994. "*Vita herbae et vita rei* v slavianskoi narodnoi traditsii." In *Slavianskii i balkanskii fol'klor. Verovaniia, tekst, ritual.* Ed. N. I. Tolstoi. Moscow: Nauka. 139–168, 263–266.

———1995. "Baba." In *Slavianskaia mifologiia. Èntsiklopedicheskii slovar'.* Ed. V. Ia. Petrukhin et al. Moscow: Èllis Lak. 38–39.

———1995a. "Glaza i zrenie pokoinikov." In N. I. Tolstoi, *Iazyk i narodnaia kul'tura. Ocherki po slavianskoi mifologii i ètnolingvistike.* Moscow: Indrik. 185–205.

Tolstoi, N. I., and S. M. Tolstaia. 1978. "Zametki po slavianskomu iazychestvu. 2. Vyzyvanie dozhdia v Poles'e." In *Slavianskii i balkanskii fol'klor. Genezis, arkhaika, traditsii.* Ed. I. M. Sheptunov. Moscow: Nauka. 95–130.

———1981. "Zametki po slavianskomu iazychestvu. 1. Vyzyvanie dozhdia u kolodtsa." *Russkii fol'klor* 21: 87–98.

———1981a. "Zametki po slavianskomu iazychestvu. 5. Zashchita ot grada v Dragacheve i drugikh serbskikh zonakh." In *Slavianskii i balkanskii fol'klor. Obriad. Tekst.* Ed. N. I. Tolstoi et al. Moscow: Nauka. 44–120.

———1982. "Zametki po slavianskomu iazychestvu. 3. Pervyi grom v Poles'e. 4. Zashchita ot grada v Poles'e." In *Obriady i obriadovyi fol'klor.* Ed. V. K. Sokolova. Moscow: Nauka. 49–83.

Toporkov, Andrei L. 1984. "Etnolingvistichni aspekti pri izuchavaneto na slavianite. Vŭtreshna rekonstruktsiia na frazeologizma *nosia voda v resheto.*" *Bŭlgarski folklor* 10 (1): 81–89.

———1989. "Otkuda u Baby-Iagi stupa?" *Russkaia rech'* 1989 (4): 126–130.

———1992. "'Perepekanie' detei v ritualakh i skazkakh vostochnykh slavian." In *Fol'klor i ètnograficheskaia deistvitel'nost'.* Ed. A. Baiburin. St. Petersburg: Nauka. 114–118.

———1995. "Stupa." In *Slavianskaia mifologiia. Èntsiklopedicheskii slovar'.* Ed. V. Ia. Petrukhin et al. Moscow: Èllis Lak. 369.

———1997. *Teoriia mifa v russkoi filologicheskoi nauke XIX veka.* Moscow: Indrik.

Toporov, V. N. 1963. "Khettskaia salŠU.GI i slavianskaia Baba-Iaga." *AN SSSR. Institut slavianovedeniia. Kratkie soobshcheniia* 38: 28–37.

———1986. "Indoevropeiskii ritual'nyi termin SOUH1- ETRO- (-ETLO-, -EDHLO-)." In *Balto-slavianskie issledovaniia 1984.* Ed. V. V. Ivanov. Moscow: Nauka. 80–89.

———1987. "Zametki po pokhoronnoi obriadnosti (K 150-letiiu so dnia rozhdeniia A. N. Veselovskogo)." In *Balto-slavianskie issledovaniia 1985.* Ed. V. V. Ivanov. Moscow: Nauka. 10–52.

Troiakov, P. A. 1969. "Promyslovaia i magicheskaia funktsiia skazyvaniia skazok u khakasov." *Sovetskaia Ètnografiia* 1969 (2): 24–34.

———1977. "Ot ètnograficheskikh realii k skazochnomu motivu." In *Fol'klor. Poèticheskaia sistema.* Ed. A. I. Balandin and V. M. Gatsak. Moscow: Nauka. 135–142.

Trubachev, O. N. 1959. *Istoriia slavianskikh terminov rodstva i nekotorykh drevneishikh terminov obshchestvennogo stroia.* Moscow: AN SSSR.

———1974. *Ètimologicheskii slovar' slavianskikh iazykov. Praslavianskii leksicheskii fond.* Moscow: Nauka.

Trubetskoi, Evgenii. 1922. *Inoe tsarstvo i ego iskateli v russkoi narodnoi skazke.* Moscow: G. A. Leman.

Trushkina, N. Iu. 1998. "Lechenie 'kurinoi bolezni' v traditsionnoi kul'ture: struktura i semantika (po zapisiam 1997 g. v Ul'ianovskoi oblasti)." In *Traditsionnaia kul'tura i mir detstva. Traditional Culture and the World of Childhood.* Ed. M. P. Cherednikova and V. F. Shevchenko. Ul'yanovsk: Laboratoriia kul'turologii. 120–127.

Tsar'kova, T. S. 1981. "K probleme stanovleniia poètiki N. A. Nekrasova." *Russkaia literatura* 1981 (3): 134–146.

Tucker, Elizabeth. 1981. "Danger and Control in Children's Storytelling." *Arv* 37: 141–146.

Tudorovskaia, E. A. 1960. "Nekotorye cherty doklassovogo mirovozzreniia v russkoi narodnoi volshebnoi skazke." *Russkii fol'klor* 5: 102–126.

————1974. "Poètika volshebnoi skazki." In *Prozaicheskie zhanry fol'klora narodov SSSR. Tezisy dokladov na Vsesoiuznoi nauchnoi konferentsii.* Ed. V. K. Bondarchik. Minsk: AN BSSR. 71–85.

————1975. "Klassovyi konflikt v siuzhete volshebnoi skazke." *Russkii fol'klor* 15: 93–101.

Vakarelski, Christo. 1969. *Bulgarische Volkskunde.* Berlin: Walter de Gruyter.

Valk, Ülo. 2001. *The Black Gentleman: Manifestations of the Devil in Estonian Folk Religion.* FFC 276. Helsinki: Academia Scientiarum Fennica.

Vasmer, Max. 1958. *Russisches etymologisches Wörterbuch.* 3 vols. Heidelberg: Carl Winter.

Vedernikova, Natal'ia M. 1975. *Russkaia narodnaia skazka.* Moscow: Nauka.

————1980. "Èpitet v volshebnoi skazke." In *Fol'klor kak iskusstvo slova. Vypusk 4. Èpitet v russkom narodnom tvorchestve.* Ed. V. Anikin et al. Moscow: Izdatel'stvo Moskovskogo universiteta. 120–133.

————1980a. "Obshchie i otlichitel'nye cherty v siuzhetoslozhenii i stile vostochnoslavianskikh skazok (A=A 403, 409, 450, 511)." In *Tipologiia i vzaimosviazi fol'klora narodov SSSR. Poètika i stilistika.* Ed. V. M. Gatsak. Moscow: Nauka. 248–262.

Vinogradova, L. N. 1983. "Arkhaicheskie formy polesskikh magicheskikh priemov i oberegov, sviazannykh s ukhodom za rebenkom." In *Poles'e i ètnogenez slavian. Predvaritel'nye materialy i tezisy konferentsii.* Ed. N. I. Tolstoi et al. Moscow: Nauka. 100–103.

————1992. "Obshchee i spetsificheskoe v slavianskikh poveriiakh o ved'me." In *Obraz mira v slove i rituale. Balkanskie chteniia I.* Ed. N. V. Zlydneva, V. N. Toporov, and T. V. Tsiv'ian. Moscow: Institut slavianovedeniia i balkanistiki RAN. 58–73.

————2000. *Narodnaia demonologiia i mifo-ritual'naia traditsiia slavian.* Moscow: Indrik.

Vladimirov, P. V. 1896. *Vvedenie v istoriiu russkoi slovesnosti.* Kiev: Imperatorskii Universitet Sv. Vladimira.

Volkov, Roman M. 1924. *Skazka. Razyskaniia po siuzhetoslozheniiu narodnoi skazki.* Odessa: Gosudarstvennoe Izdatel'stvo Ukrainy.

Wachtel, Andrew. 1990. *The Battle for Childhood: Creation of a Russian Myth.* Stanford: Stanford University Press.

Warner, Elizabeth. 1980. "The Russian Folk Tale after the Revolution." *Arv* 36: 133–141.

Waschnitius, Viktor. 1913. "Perht, Holda und verwandte Gestalten. Ein Beitrag zur deutschen Religionsgeschichte." *Sitzungsberichte der Kaiserlichen Akademie der Wissenschaften in Wien. Philosophisch-Historische Klasse.* 174. Band, 2. Abhandlung.

Weiss, Halina. 1999. "*Draznilkas*—Russian Children's Taunts (1)." *SEEFA Journal* 4 (1): 35–46.

Wixman, Ronald. 1984. *The Peoples of the USSR: An Ethnographic Handbook.* Armonk, New York: M. E. Sharpe.

Wolf-Knuts, Ulrika. 1992. "The Devil between Nature and Culture." *Ethnologia Europaea* 22: 109–114.

Worobec, Christine. 1991. *Peasant Russia: Family and Community in the Post-Emancipation Period.* Princeton: Princeton University Press.

————1995. "Witchcraft Beliefs and Practices in Prerevolutionary Russian and Ukrainian Villages." *Russian Review* 54 (2): 165–187.

Wosien, Maria-Gabriele. 1969. *The Russian Folk-Tale: Some Structural and Thematic Aspects.* Slavistische Beiträge 41. Munich: Otto Sagner.

Zabylin, M. 1880. *Russkii narod. Ego obychai, obriady, predaniia, sueveriia i poèziia.* Moscow: M. Berezin. Reprinted 1992.

Zaitsev, A. I. 1984. "K voprosu o proiskhozhdenii volshebnoi skazki." In *Fol'klor i ètnografiia. U ètnograficheskikh istokov fol'klornykh siuzhetov i obrazov.* Ed. B. N. Putilov. Leningrad: Nauka. 69–83.

Zaitseva, I. K. 1977. "Terminologiia rodstvennykh otnoshenii v iazyke skazok." In *Iazyk zhanrov russkogo fol'klora.* Ed. Z. K. Tarlanov. Petrozavodsk: . Petrozavodskii gosudarstvennyi universitet. 88–92.

Zavoiko, G. K. 1914. "Verovaniia, obriady i obychai velikorossov Vladimirskoi gubernii." *Ètnograficheskoe Obozrenie* 1914 (3–4): 81–178.

Zečević, Slobodan. 1981. *Mitska bića srpskih predanja.* Belgrade: Etnografski muzej.

Zelenin, Dmitrii. 1927. *Russische (Ostslavische) Volkskunde.* Berlin and Leipzig: Walter de Gruyter & Co.

————1930. "Die religiöse Funktion der Volksmärchen." *Internationales Archiv für Ethnographie* 31: 21–31. Leiden.

————1934. "Religiozno-magicheskaia funktsiia fol'klornykh skazok." In *Sergeiu Fedorovichu Ol'denburgu k piatidesiatiletiiu nauchno-obshchestvennoi deiatel'nosti 1882–1932. Sbornik statei.* Ed. I. Iu. Krachkovskii. Leningrad: AN SSSR. 215–240.

————1940. "The Genesis of the Fairy Tale." *Ethnos* 1940 (1–2): 54–58.

————1991. *Vostochnoslavianskaia ètnografiia.* Trans. K. D. Tsivina. Moscow: Nauka.

————1994. *Izbrannye trudy. Stat'i po dukhovnoi kul'ture 1901–1913.* Moscow: Indrik.

————1995. *Izbrannye trudy. Ocherki russkoi mifologii: Umershie neestestvennoiu smert'iu i rusalki.* Moscow: Indrik.

Zemtsovskii, I. I. 1970. *Poèziia krest'ianskikh prazdnikov.* Leningrad: Sovetskii pisatel'.

Zholkovsky, Alexander. 1994. "How a Russian Maupassant Was Made in Odessa and Yasnaya Polyana: Isaak Babel' and the Tolstoy Legacy." *Slavic Review* 53 (3): 671–693.

Zipes, Jack. 1979. *Breaking the Magic Spell: Radical Theories of Folk and Fairy Tales.* Austin: University of Texas Press.

Zorin, Nikolai V. 1981. *Russkaia svad'ba v Srednem Povolzh'e.* Kazan': Izdatel'stvo Kazanskogo universiteta.

Zovko, Johann. 1893. "Ursprungsgeschichten und andere Volksmeinungen." *Wissenschaftliche Mittheilungen aus Bosnien und der Hercegovina* 1: 426–444.

Index

Index of Tale Types

Alan Dundes
General Editor

This series will include theoretical studies of any genre or aspect of folklore—however, it will not include mere collections of data or bibliographies. The emphasis will be on analytic and methodological innovations in the consideration of myth, folktale, legend, superstition, riddle, folksong, festival, games, or any other form of folklore, as well as in any of the various interpretative approaches to folklore topics.

For additional information about this series or for the submission of manuscripts, please contact:

Professor Alan Dundes
Department of Anthropology
University of California, Berkeley
Berkeley, CA 94720

To order other books in this series, please contact our Customer Service Department:

(800) 770-LANG (within the U.S.)
(212) 647-7706 (outside the U.S.)
(212) 647-7707 FAX

Or browse online by series:

www.peterlangusa.com